AA

STATELY HOMES, MUSEUMS, CASTLES & GARDENS IN BRITAIN

D1637573

Editor: Patricia Kelly
Designer: Turnergraphic Ltd
Illustrations by: Paul Fry
Compiled by: Publications Research Unit
Advertising: Peter Whitworth, Tel: Basingstoke 20123

Maps produced by the Cartographic Department of the Automobile Association and based upon Ordnance Survey maps with the permission of the Controller of HM Stationery Office. Crown copyright reserved.

Castle Howard

(North Yorkshire) 18th century palace, the first creation of Sir John Vanbrugh. Unique collection of pictures, furniture, tapestries, porcelain and historic costume. 15 miles from York, off A64.

Harewood House

(West Yorkshire) 1759 Home of the Earl and Countess of Harewood. Seven miles north of Leeds on A61. Also Harewood Bird Garden and Butterfly House.

Warwick Castle

(Warwickshire) Magnificent medieval fortress. State Rooms. Armoury. Dungeon. Torture Chamber. Ghost Tower. Clock Tower and Barbican. Guy's Tower. Peacock Gardens.

Woburn Abbey

(Bedfordshire) Home of the Dukes of Bedford. Only one hour by road from London, Oxford, Cambridge, Stratford, Birmingham and Leicester.

Blenheim Palace

(Oxfordshire) Home of the 11th Duke of Marlborough, birthplace of Sir Winston Churchill. A gift from the nation to the victor of Blenheim.

Longleat House

(Wiltshire) Prime Elizabethan mansion, built 1566-1580, home of the Marquess of Bath. Longleat Safari Park. Restored Victorian Kitchens and many other summer attractions.

Beaulieu

(Hampshire) Palace House (1538) home of Lord and Lady Montagu of Beaulieu; Ruins of 13th century Beaulieu Abbey; The National Motor Museum.

The Magnificent Seven

HAREWOOD · WARWICK · CASTLE HOWARD

BLENHEIM · WOBURN · LONGLEAT · BEAULIEU

The history of Britain is written into the landscape. It is in dark woods and green fields. It is in quiet villages. And, most dramatically of all, it is in the ancient castles and great country houses that tell their own story of kings and wars and the colourful life of past centuries.

Seven of these magnificent properties are presented here. They stretch from Castle Howard in North Yorkshire via Harewood, Warwick, Woburn, Blenheim, Longleat, to Beaulieu on the South Coast. Each House is a jewel in its own right; a truly magnificent living piece of history.

The owners of the 'Magnificent Seven' invite you to visit and enjoy their homes which are a key to Britain's History.

Contents

Produced by the Publications Division of the Automobile Association, Fanum House, Basingstoke, Hants RG21 2EA.

Phototypeset by Vantage Photosetting Co Ltd, Southampton.
Printed by Fletcher & Son Ltd, Norwich, and bound by Richard Clay (The Chaucer Press) Ltd, Bungay, Suffolk.
Colour printing by Camgate Litho Ltd, London.

Photographs by courtesy of Aerofilms Ltd, Borehamwood; Martin Boddy; Morgan-Grampian (Professional Press) Ltd; Alan Rutter; Don Squibb and Chris Taylor.

The contents of the publication are believed correct at the time of printing but the current position may be checked through the AA. While every effort is made to ensure that information appearing in advertisements is correct, no responsibility can be accepted by the AA for inaccuracies.

ISBN 0 86145 010 8   55877

Country House Outlook – '1980 is a crucial year'

by Marcus Binney, Chairman, Save Britain's Heritage

In recent years when owners have wanted to hand great houses and estates over in settlement of tax (as they may do) the critical problem has been one of endowment. In such circumstances, the Treasury almost invariably wants to hand the house on to the National Trust, or the National Trust for Scotland, but the Trusts understandably will rarely accept such houses without an endowment to cover the deficit in repairs and running costs. A protection against future fiascos like the break-up of Mentmore Towers should be provided by the establishment of the new National Heritage Fund. With its inauguration, the Inland Revenue will be able to accept a house in lieu of tax, and then the National Trust will be able to seek an endowment from the National Heritage Fund.

The new Fund's initial capital will be provided by transferring to it the assets of the existing Land Fund (over £17 million in July 1979) set up by Dr Dalton with the proceeds from the sale of surplus war stores as a memorial to the nation's war dead. 'For many years', Dr Dalton wrote in *Country Life* in 1946, 'I have felt real concern at the loss to the nation which was involved in the commercial sale, often piecemeal, of famous properties following the death of their owners . . . It has always seemed to me that the State should have had the means to prevent such desecration'. In addition, the new Heritage Fund will receive an annual grant (thought to be in the region of £3 million), though this is only partial recompense for the £50 million which on the advice of the Treasury was removed from the Fund in 1957.

The National Heritage Fund, one hopes, will only be the solution of last resort. Government ministers (of both parties) have repeatedly stressed that the best way of maintaining great houses is to allow their existing owners to continue to look after them. In response to one of the largest petitions ever presented to Parliament – with some 1.5 million signatures – the last government provided exemptions from Capital Transfer Tax for outstanding houses in return for public access: considerable, but by no means insoluble problems remain over providing funds for maintenance, and over allowing many of the smaller houses to set costs of upkeep against income as the larger ones are able to do.

Another key issue is the question of contents. An owner faced with a sudden repair bill which is well beyond his income, will inevitably consider whether there is not some piece of furniture or a work of art that can be sold to provide the necessary funds. Yet such sales inevitably undermine the very purpose of preserving the house.

The answer in some cases, at least, must be for a work of art to be accepted in lieu of tax and then, providing certain safeguards concerning security, conservation and access are met, for it to be loaned back to the house for display to the public. This is a proposal strongly supported by many museum directors and by the Museums Association and the Standing Commission on Museums and Galleries.

Then, of course, there is the difficulty of houses, fine architecturally, which have lost not only their contents but their owners as well. In the past such empty and decaying shells, even when they contain handsome panelling or plasterwork, have often seemed useless white elephants. The last few years, however, have seen an extraordinary upsurge of interest in such properties not only from incurable romantics but practical-minded businessmen and sober administrators. Large country houses are now sought for conversion into holiday apartments, hotels, offices, working communities and even spiritual retreats.

Kinmel Park in Clwyd, a remarkable Victorian house inspired by Wren's Hampton Court, stood roofless for three winters after a savage fire in 1975. Last year, it was acquired as a Christian Conference Centre, and acres of mansard roof have been entirely reconstructed. Within months Kinmel was receiving its first visitors.

At Dingley in Northampton, a young architect has bought a long derelict but beautiful 16th and 17th-century house and is converting it into eleven self-contained houses and apartments: all of these have been sold before completion. Boringdon in Devon, an Elizabethan house unoccupied for half a century, has been bought by a new owner who is restoring the main house to live in and converting the stables for holiday lets.

Other long-neglected houses have recently been bought back by their original owners. Robin Brackenbury and his wife bought Holme Pierrepont in Nottingham (see page 157), eleven years ago to prevent it leaving the family and have launched an enterprising and ambitious repair scheme with help from the Manpower Services Commission. Also in Nottinghamshire a young company director has bought back Winkburn Hall, a handsome early 18th-century house his father had been forced to sell the year before he was born.

Other important houses, however, do remain empty. Barlaston Hall in Staffordshire, a Grade 1 Georgian house which is a landmark for miles around, has been left closed and forlorn despite the offer of a substantial Historic Buildings Council repairs grant to the owners, Wedgwood Ltd. Pelwall Hall, near Market Drayton in Shropshire, one of the few surviving houses by Sir John Soane, is still deteriorating.

But while a house continues to exist, however abandoned, there is always a chance that it will be saved eventually. In the last decade the national preservation societies have fought and won a series of inquiries to prevent the demolition of a number of outstanding country houses – Barlaston Hall; Hylands Hall, Essex; Revesby Abbey, Lincolnshire and Llangoed, Powys.

Yet the curious British addiction to demolition remains. The Italians and the French appear happy to leave their villas and châteaux closed and falling gently and gracefully into decay, for decades if necessary. Here, a crisis lasting a matter of years can spell destruction for a lovely house that has perhaps stood for a century and a half or more, and which, with some attention, could last for generations.

In Britain a total of at least 628 notable country houses were demolished between 1945 and 1974 – 431 in England, 175 in Scotland and 23 in Wales. Since 1974 the number has happily fallen to a trickle – maybe two or three a year. There it must stay.

Marcus Binney

Britain has countless museums with collections ranging from the all-embracing British Museum in London to tiny local museums which tell the story of a particular community or concentrate on an aspect of one specialised subject. If the profusion of wealth confuses you or if you have particular interests you would like to research, you might be interested in *Britain: What's Where in the Museums*, published by the British Tourist Authority and available from the 'Welcome to Britain' Centre at 64 St. James's Street, London SW1A 1NF, or from their offices overseas.

This guide reverses the usual principle of listing museums and enumerating their contents by working from collections and items to the museums which house them. It also contains lists of artists with galleries having important collections of their works, of famous people who have museums, houses or significant collections devoted to them, and useful lists of museums whose exhibits fall into various categories. If you are interested in jewellery, for instance, look it up in the index and you will find which museums house what kinds of collections.

British Cathedrals

Cathedrals are usually open daily at all reasonable times and will be found in the following places:

Aberdeen	Coventry	Lincoln
Arundel	Derby	Liverpool
Bangor	Dornoch	Llandaff
Birmingham	Dunblane	London
Blackburn	Dunkeld	Manchester
Bradford	Durham	Newcastle
Brechin	Edinburgh	Newport
Brecon	Elgin	Norwich
Bristol	Ely	Oxford
Bury St Edmunds	Exeter	Peel
Canterbury	Fortrose	Peterborough
Carlisle	Glasgow	Portsmouth
Chelmsford	Gloucester	Ripon
Chester	Guildford	Rochester
Chichester	Hereford	St Albans
	Iona	St Andrews
	Kirkwall	St Asaph
	Leicester	St Davids
	Lichfield	Salisbury
		Sheffield
		Southwell
		Truro
		Wakefield
		Wells
		Winchester
		Worcester
		York

Norwich Cathedral

ST JOHNS WOOD

Cricket Memorial
Gallery ●

REGENT'S PARK

MAIDA VALE

ST MARYLEBONE

MARYLEBONE
STATION

Madame
Tussaud's
● Planetarium ● ●

PADDINGTON

Wallace
Collection ●

PADDINGTON
STATION

BAYSWATER

Marble Arch

MAYFAIR

K E N S I N G T O N

H Y D E   P A R K

The S e r p e n t i n e

Hyde Park Corner

Kensington
Palace ●

G A R D E N S

Wellington
Museum ●

KENSINGTON

Science
Museum ●
Geological Museum ●

Victoria
and Albert
Museum ●

BROMPTON

Natural History Museum

BELGRAVIA

SOUTH KENSINGTON

CHELSEA

National Army
Museum ●

The AA Map of London
with detailed maps of Inner and Outer London,
is available from: The Automobile Association,
Mail Order Department, Fanum House,
Basingstoke, Hants.   Price 95p post free

III

The National Grid

The National Grid provides one system of reference for the whole country correct for a scale map. The major squares are 62½ miles across and each sub-division 6¼ miles across. In the National Grid system the letters of major squares are always given first followed by numbers into which the major squares are sub-divided (in the margins of each map page eg: **SP50**) this is the reference for **Oxford** which lies within major square **SP** and is **5** sub-divisions east (or from left to right) and **0** sub-divisions north (reading from zero upwards). Where a major or sub-division line cuts through a town, the letter or number given are based on the square containing the larger part of town eg: **Manchester SJ 89** For a fuller explanation see the Ordnance Survey maps.

Key to Atlas

16 Orkney and Shetland Islands

Thurso
Wick
Stornoway
13 Portree
14 Inverness
Banff
15 Peterhead
Aberdeen
Fort William
Pitlochry
SCALE
mls 0   30   60
kms 0   50   100

Oban
Perth
Dundee
Stirling
Largs
Glasgow
Edinburgh
Berwick
Campbeltown
Peebles
12
10 Ayr
11 Dumfries
Stranraer
Carlisle
Workington

Douglas
Kendal
Scarborough
Lancaster
York
Blackpool
Leeds
8 Hull
Grimsby
9
Manchester
6 Liverpool
7 Sheffield
Caernarfon
Chester
Stoke
Nottingham
Shrewsbury
Leicester
King's Lynn
Norwich
Peterborough
Aberystwyth
Birmingham
Coventry
Worcester
Northampton
Cambridge
Carmarthen
Hereford
Gloucester
Oxford
Chelmsford
Pembroke
Swansea
Cardiff
Bristol
4 Reading
LONDON
5
Maidstone
2
Taunton
3
Salisbury
Basingstoke
Guildford
Brighton
Exeter
Bournemouth
Truro

Maps produced by
The AA Cartographic Department
(Publications Division), Fanum House,
Basingstoke, Hampshire RG21 2EA

Scale

| 0 | 10 | 20 miles |

| 0 | 10 | 20 | 30 kilometres |

NORTH   SEA

TA

MABLETHORPE

Alford

Burgh le Marsh
SKEGNESS

THE WASH

TF

HUNSTANTON
Heacham

North Creake

Sandringham

Castle Rising

KING'S LYNN

Castle Acre

Leverington

WISBECH

Terrington St

SWAFFHAM

DOWNHAM MARKET

WELLS-NEXT-
THE-SEA
Holkham Burnham
Market
Glandford

Walsingham
Thursford Green
Mannington Hall

Houghton
Blickling

DEREHAM

NORWICH

WYMONDHAM

Kelling SHERINGHAM
CROMER
Felbrigg
Baconsthorpe Mundesley

NORTH WALSHAM
Stalham
Horsey
Norfolk Wildlife Park
Wroxham
South Walsham
Filby Caister - on - Sea

5

**GREAT
YARMOUTH**

9

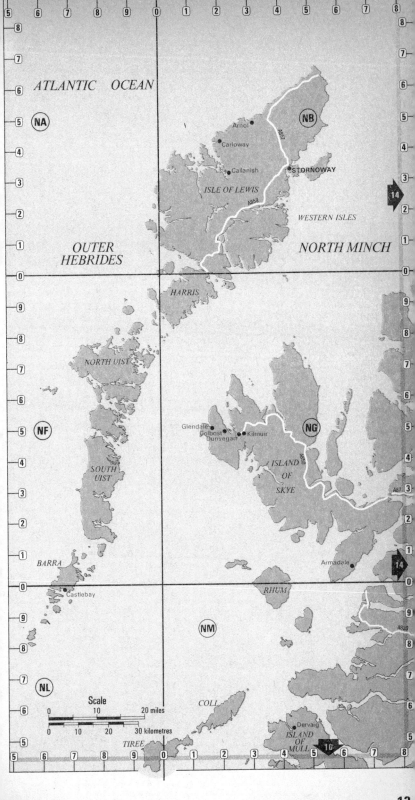

ATLANTIC OCEAN

NA

OUTER
HEBRIDES

NORTH MINCH

NB

Arnol
Carloway
Callanish
STORNOWAY

ISLE OF LEWIS

WESTERN ISLES

14

HARRIS

NORTH UIST

NF

NG

Glendale
Colbost
Dunvegan
Kilmuir

ISLAND
OF
SKYE

SOUTH
UIST

BARRA

Armadale

14

Castlebay

RHUM

NM

NL

COLL

Scale
10
20 miles
0
10   20   30 kilometres

TIREE

Dervaig
ISLAND
OF
MULL

10

13

NORTH SEA

FIRTH

ORKNEY ISLANDS

Westray • HY

Dounby • MAINLAND A967 A986 A965

Finstown KIRKWALL

STROMNESS A964 A960

HOY A961

ND

Scale
0   10   20 miles
0   10   20   30 kilometres

SHETLAND ISLANDS

HP

YELL A968

A970 MAINLAND A971

A970 HU

Scalloway • LERWICK

A970

Mousa Island

Sumburgh

Scale
0   10   20 miles
0   10   20   30 kilometres

TOURIST INFORMATION CENTRES

Look for this sign:

i Tourist information

16

Hever Castle Maze – aerial view.

The Mazes of England

by Adrian Fisher

The words 'maze' and 'labyrinth' are derived from different cultures, but both have the same meaning – complex network of paths. English mazes have a certain appeal all of their own, and can be traced back to rock carvings in Cornwall made 3,500 years ago.

There are two types of mazes. One type consists of a single path that leads in a meandering fashion to the middle of the maze and this is known as a Uni-cursal maze. The other type is a Multi-cursal maze. The uni-cursal form is much older, and was originally used to give protection from evil spirits, that reputedly weren't able to turn corners. Usually cut in turf, uni-cursal mazes have been known, for various reasons, by such names as Troy Town, Walls of Troy, Julian's Bower, Maiden's Bower, Shepherd's Race or Mizmaze. The traditional Cretan design found at Tintagel (see illustration page 30) was widely used, and in medieval times a Christan version also became popular. Many other turf mazes had unique designs.

About the author
Adrian Fisher developed his taste for uncharted three-dimensional passages while exploring caves in the Mendip Hills. He started his first hedge maze in Bournemouth in 1975. His work on the unravelling of turf maze designs enabled him to develop a new generation of maze design for the Pilgrimage Maze at St Albans Cathedral. An archaeological dig is planned for 1981, after which the site will become available for this new turf maze, the first in Britain for 200 years.

Designed in the shape of a rose, to symbolise the martyrdom of St Alban, it will take the theme of the Path of Life.

Adrian is currently participating in the Munich Labyrinth Exhibition, which continues until February 1980. At the moment he is also designing a maze as part of a Robin Hood Theme Park near Nottingham.

The author undertakes commissions to design mazes and is writing a book on British mazes. He is always pleased to hear from other maze enthusiasts.

Tintagel or Cretan design.

Medieval Christian design.

Uni-cursal mazes

You will find that most turf mazes are located in charming and quiet places that are well worth a visit. They have a fascinating history, although local legends have grown up, making it difficult to distinguish between fact and fiction. In Devon 'Maze Sunday' was a day set aside for feasting and drinking. In Nottingham, a three-day fair used a turf maze as one of its main attractions. The maze was called 'Robin Hood's Race'. Sadly it was ploughed up in 1797.

There were several examples of mazes known as 'Maiden's Bower', which probably recollected an ancient fertility rite; the young maidens were given a short start, before being chased by young men to the middle. The Minotaur legend springs to mind with its obvious similarities with the maidens fleeing along a single path, and only a closed goal to look forward to!

One Julian's Bower maze remains at Alkborough. The name could be derived either from Iulus, the son of Aeneas, or from Saint Julian. Aeneas and his son Iulus wandered for years around the Greek Islands after the fall of Troy and Aeneas is reputed to have drawn maze patterns in the sandy beaches to amuse little Iulus.

Not all mazes are made of hedges or turf. King Henry II kept his mistress, the 'Fair Rosamund', in a building called Rosamund's Bower, near his palace at Woodstock, Oxfordshire. His indignant Queen, Eleanor of Aquitaine, penetrated the maze of rooms and passages with its 150 doors, and forced Henry's mistress to drink poison. In 1870 Sir Gilbert Scott laid a pavement maze in stone at Ely Cathedral.

Since the Second World War, Greg Bright, a contemporary maze designer, spent a year in 1971 digging a trench maze at Worthy Farm, Pilton, in Somerset; Paul Edwards, another maze fan, has built a maze out of upright larch logs in a Birmingham Park; and the new maze at Ragley Hall is built of stone and concrete. Lord Eliot's new maze in Cornwall is a hedge maze with a difference. It also has a series of moveable gates, so that the maze can be arranged in billions of different ways.

Hampton Court is the earliest hedge maze in England, and the most famous. It was replanted in 1690, and possibly goes back to Cardinal Wolsey's time. The outer shape is fixed by the different paths that criss-cross the area of garden known as the Wilderness. This distinctive triangular shape, as well as the actual design, has been

Hampton Court Maze – aerial view.

copied over a dozen times, in England alone. The maze was immortalised in Jerome K Jerome's *Three Men in a Boat*, and the description still captures its spirit today.

Hedge mazes are expensive to build and to maintain, which is why they were originally found only in Royal or Baronial grounds. Formal grounds, which often included a maze, flourished until the 18th century, when Capability Brown introduced the Natural Landscape. He destroyed many of these in order to achieve his new look. Ironically, as the Royal Gardener for twenty years, Capability Brown lived alongside the maze at Hampton Court, but he was expressly ordered not to interfere with it.

The great upsurge in hedge mazes came in Victorian times. The second Earl Stanhope was an eminent mathematician, and he designed at least three mazes, including that at Chevening in Kent (see illustration, page 32). This maze, built in the 1820s, was the firs to use 'islands'. If you study the Chevening design, you will notice that the hedges have been shaded in different ways. The stippled hedges are separate 'islands', which could be removed without making much difference to the puzzle. The centre is also located within an island. The effect of islands is to prevent you from finding the centre of the maze by keeping left (or right) all the way round the edge. Chevening is now the private home of the Prince of Wales, and the maze is not open to the public, the Chevening design was highly respected and was copied in three other mazes, at Anerley, North Woolwich and Beauport.

With the growing prosperity of Victorian times, an increasing number of wealthy people built mazes for their private pleasure; for example, at Glendurgan, Somerleyton Hall, Worden Park and Hever Castle. However, the great majority of Victorian mazes were built as part of the Victorian leisure industry. Some were made in new public parks, laid out between newly-built Victorian suburbs, and many more were found in Pleasure Gardens, run for profit, whose attractions were provided within an hour's walk of Victorian cities. These mazes have mostly been covered by 20th-century suburbs, and no trace of them remains. In London an hotel occupies the site of a maze in Paddington, a council estate anonymously covers the Anerley maze, and in South Kensington, Prince Albert initiated a maze a stone's throw from the Albert Hall, financed from the profits of the

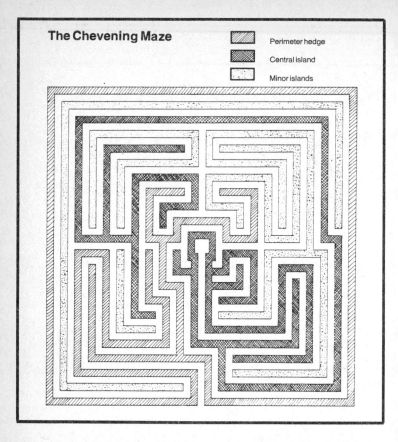

The Chevening Maze

Perimeter hedge

Central island

Minor islands

Crystal Palace Exhibition. This last maze, now covered by the Science Museum, was designed by William Nesfield, who also designed Kew Gardens and the Somerleyton Maze.

Between the two World Wars, few mazes were built. Indeed, both World Wars were a great threat to mazes; after five years of enforced neglect, mazes became overgrown beyond repair and had to be removed. The mazes at Arley Hall, Totteridge Park and Debdale Hall were all lost in this way. More dramatically, the Belton Maze was abruptly replaced by a Ministry of Defence building in 1939; the nearest parallel to this was the destruction of the Theobald's Maze by Parliamentary troops in 1643; during the English Civil War.

Since 1945 mazes have enjoyed a new lease of life. Seaside resorts have built mazes as an added attraction for their holiday visitors, in particular there is the maze at Blackgang Chine on the Isle of Wight, and there are two in Scarborough. The Stately Homes have opened their gates to ever increasing numbers of the public, offering gardens, wildlife parks, amusements and mazes, new mazes have been built at Longleat, Chatsworth and Ragley Hall.

The writer's private holly maze in Bournemouth, and Randoll Coate's work in Gloucestershire provide further diversity. The unique Maze of the Mysteries of the Gospel, at Wyck Rissington in Gloucestershire conveys the Christian gospel of Life, Death and Eternal Life to its visitors, an annual service is held each August when the church congregation processes through the maze.

There is a simple method to follow, when solving puzzle mazes. If the hedge that surrounds the goal also connects with the outside hedge, use the hand-on-wall method: simply follow the perimeter hedge in and out of each dead end until you reach the goal. The Chevening Maze defeats this method by placing the goal within a central island. Wall huggers now travel harmlessly around the perimeter and return to the entrance without finding the goal. For further confusion, the Chevening Maze also contains five minor islands, which are clearly visible.

The Longleat Maze opened in June 1978 brings us right up to date. It is the world's largest maze and Britain's first three-dimensional maze; and Greg Bright has used his latest ideas on partial values and Mutually Accessible Centres. After a few yards, the goal is seen just the other side of a hedge. Even in Chevening, by following the hedge round, you would reach the goal. Not so at Longleat: bridges and underpasses create a new pattern of logic, which is only beginning to be analysed. The end of the twentieth century promises to be a great time for mazes!

The following summary shows most of the exciting mazes open to the public: there are at least seventeen other mazes in private grounds, whose privacy must be respected.

BRITISH HEDGE MAZES

Date	Place	Material	Size	Designer	Remarks
Earlier than 1670	Hampton Court Palace East Molesey, Surrey	Yew	68×25 m	Unknown	The earliest hedge maze in Britain; receives ½ million visitors a year.
c.1670	High Rocks Hotel Nr. Tunbridge Wells, Kent	Laurel	57×21 m	Exact copy of Hampton Court Maze	Visited by James II, who used to attend the wells.
1833	Glendurgan Near Falmouth, Cornwall	Laurel	—	Alfred Fox	Only open on certain days during the summer. Owned by National Trust.
1846	Somerleyton Hall Nr. Lowestoft, Suffolk	Yew	75×49 m	William Nesfield	Central Pagoda on top of knoll.
1886	Worden Park Leyland, Lancs	Beech	—	A member of the Harington family	Worden Hall burnt down in 1943; now the maze is in a public park.
1905	Hever Castle Nr. Edenbridge, Kent	Yew	23×23 m	William Waldorf Astor	Maze used to recreate the Tudor setting where Henry VIII courted Anne Boleyn.
1935	Hazlehead Park Aberdeen	Privet	58×49 m	Sir Henry Alexander?	Given to the citizens of Aberdeen by Sir Henry Alexander.
1950	St. Laurence's Rectory Wyck Rissington, Glos.	Hawthorn and ivy	25×20 m	Canon H. S. Cheales	Maze of the Mysteries of the Gospels. More for the pilgrim than the sightseer.
1959	Victoria Park Scarborough, North Yorks	Privet	41×30 m	Scarborough Borough Council	—
1962	Chatsworth Bakewell, Derbyshire	Yew	40×35 m	D. A. Fisher	On the site of Joseph Paxton's Great Conservatory; design based on earlier maze of First Duke of Devonshire.
1962	Blackgang Chine Isle of Wight	Privet	27×25 m	John Dabell	Floodlit between June and September.
1963	Esplanade Maze Scarborough, North Yorks	Privet	32×22 m	Scarborough Borough Council	—
c.1930	Tatton Park Knutsford, Cheshire	Beech	—	4th Baron, Lord Egerton of Tatton	Maze in good condition and a great feature of the gardens.
1978	Longleat House Warminster, Wilts	Yew	116×54 m	Greg Bright	The world's largest maze. Britain's first three-dimensional maze.

BRITISH TURF MAZES

Date	Place	Material	Size	Designer	Remarks
Unknown	Breamore House Breamore, Hants	Turf paths in chalk	27 m diam	Monks?	'Mizmaze' Medieval Christian design.
1200	Alkborough Nr. Scunthorpe, Lincs	Turf paths	13 m diam	Benedictine monks	'Julian's Bower' medieval Christian design.
Unknown	Brandsby North Yorkshire	Turf paths	9 m diam	Unknown	'City of Troy' traditional Cretan design.
Earlier than 1710	St Catherine's Hill Nr. Winchester, Hants	Furrows within turf	26×26 m	A Winchester schoolboy?	'Mizmaze' built inside Roman Camp with view of city
Unknown	Village Green, Wing, Leics	Turf paths	12 m diam	Unknown	Medieval Christian design.
Earlier than 1699	The Common Saffron Walden, Essex	Brick path in turf	42 m diag	Unknown	The largest turf maze in Britain, with 4 Bastions.
1660	Village Green, Hilton, Cambs.	Turf paths	16 m diam	William Sparrow	Medieval Christian design, with unique sundial at centre.

MISCELLANEOUS BRITISH MAZES

Date	Place	Material	Size	Designer	Remarks
At least 1500 BC	Rocky Valley Tintagel, Cornwall	Rock carving	—	Unknown	The original maze design, and the earliest in Britain.
Presumed later than 1770	Church of SS Helena and Mary, Bourn, Cambs.	Red and black tiles	—	Based on Hampton Court design	Surrounds font beneath church tower.
1870	Ely Cathedral Ely, Cambs.	Black and white stone	6×6 m	Sir Gilbert Scott	Constructed during restoration to the cathedral in 1870.
1979	Ragley Hall Alcester, Warwickshire	Re-con. stone and concrete	—	Maurice Rich	—

These lists are almost certainly incomplete, any additions or corrections will be gratefully received.

Making the most of your guide

The **gazetteer section** of this book is divided into the following sections:
England; Isle of Man, Isles of Scilly, Isle of Wight and Channel Islands; Wales; Scotland and Scottish Islands.

For your convenience towns and villages are listed alphabetically by name within each section. As far as possible the places of interest situated within one mile or two of a town or village are placed under the nearest town or village heading. However, some places of interest are too far from any town or village; in this case, such places are listed under the name of the establishment.

This simple method of arranging entries allows you to make use of this book in several ways, either by:

Town   If you know the name of the town/village you want to go to, turn straight to the alphabetically-arranged gazetteer section.

or Place of interest   If you know the particular place of interest that you want to visit, refer to the index at the back of the book. This will give you the relevant page in the gazetteer.

or General area   If you are planning a day out, or a holiday in a particular area; look first at the key to atlas pages at the front of the two-colour map section. From this key you can locate the map that covers the area you require. Towns and places of interest are picked out in red on each map.

Alternatively, you can look up a known place of interest in the gazetteer section and refer to the map reference beside that entry. You will see from the relevant map page if there are any other places of interest in that area.

Telephone numbers

All exchange names are the same as the town/village heading unless shown otherwise.

Index

Please note that the index at the back of this book is an index to **establishments only**. You will not find any town or village names shown, as they are easy to find in the gazetteer which is in straight alphabetical order within each country section. Likewise, an establishment whose name begins with a town name (eg Chertsey Museum) is also omitted from the index.

Symbols   The following symbols and abbreviations are used throughout the book:

♿	Accessible to visitors in wheelchairs. All parts accessible	ex	except
		Free	Admission free
		10p	Admission 10p
♿ B	Ground floor and/or gardens only	ch 20p	Children 20p
		ch 15 20p	Children under 15 20p
(79)	Indicates 1979 information	Pen	Senior Citizens
BH	Bank Holidays	Party	Special or reduced rates for parties booked in advance
PH	Public Holidays (Scotland)		
⚠	Parking at establishment		
P.	Parking nearby	Party 30+	Special or reduced rates for parties of 30 or more booked in advance
⚠	No parking		
⊡	Refreshments and/or restaurant		

35

Zeichenerklärung: Die nachstehenden Zeichen und Abkürzungen werden in diesem Reiseführer verwendet.

♿	für Rollstuhlfahrer zugänglich. Zutritt zu allen Teiler	ch 20p	Kinder 20p
		ch 15 20p	Kinder unter 15 Jahre 20p
♿ B	Nur einige Teile zugänglich/ bzw Garten	Pen	Rentner
		Party	Sondertarife bzw. Ermässigungen für im voraus bestellte Gesellschaften
(79)	1979 Angaben		
BH	Bankfeiertage		
PH	Feiertage (Schottland)		
⚠	Parken an Ort und Stelle	Party 30+	Sondertarife bzw. Ermässigungen für im voraus bestellte Gesellschaften von wenigstens 30 Personen
P.	Parken in der Nähe		
⚠	Parkenverbot		
⚓	Erfrischungen		
ex	ausser		
Free	Freier Eintritt		
10p	Eintritt 10p		

Symboles: Les symboles et abréviatons suivants sont utilisés dans tout le manuel.

♿	Les invalides et fauteuils roulants pourront y accéder Le tout ouvert au public	Free	Entrée libre
		10p	Entrée 10p
		ch 20p	Enfants 20p
♿ B	Seulement certaines parties ouvertes et/en les jardins	ch 15 20p	Enfants de moins de 15 ans 20p
		Pen	Retraités
(79)	Indique des renseignements pour 1979	Party	Tarifs spéciaux ou réduits pour groupes réservés d'avance
BH	Jours fériés		
PH	Jours fériés en Ecosse	Party 30+	Tarifs spéciaux ou réduits pour groupes de 30 et plus réservés d'avance.
⚠	Stationnement à l'établissement		
P.	Stationnement dans le voisinage		
⚠	Stationnement interdit		
⚓	Rafraîchissements		
ex	sauf		

Verklaring der tekens: de volgende tekens en afkortingen worden in deze reisgids gebruikt.

♿	toegankelijk voor bezoekers in rolstoel Alle gedeelten toegankelijk	ch 20p	kinderen 20p
		ch 15 20p	kinderen onder 15 jaar 20p
♿ B	Gedeeltelijk en/of tuinen	Pen	Gepensioneerden
(79)	1979 informatie	Party	speciale of gereduceerde prijs voor vooraf gemaakte boekingen voor gezelschappen
BH	Nationale officiële vakantiedag		
PH	officiele vakantiedag (Schotland)		
⚠	parkeerplaats bij gebouw	Party 30+	speciale of gereduceerde prijs voor vooraf gemaakte boekingen voor gezelschappen van 30 of meer person.
P.	nabijgelegen parkeerplaats		
⚠	Parkeerverbod		
⚓	verfrissingen		
ex	uitgezonderd		
Free	toegang gratis		
10p	toegand 10p		

ENGLAND

ABBOTSBURY *Dorset* Map 3 SY58
Abbotsbury Gardens Beach Road. Stone walled garden set in wild garden in 16 acres of grounds. Peacocks, fine trees, and notable collection of flowering shrubs. Plant sales. Open mid Mar to Oct, Mon to Sat 10–5, Sun 2–5.30. 40p (ch 15 20p). Under revision for 1980. ⚠ *(Tel 387)* ⓖ
Abbotsbury Swannery New Barn Road. Famous breeding ground for swans and a home or port of call for a great many species of wild birds. Open mid May to mid Sep 10–5 daily. 40p (ch 20p). Admission prices for 1979 not yet decided. P. ⓖ **(79)**

ABINGDON *Oxfordshire* Map 4 SU49
Town Museum County Hall. Built 1678 by Christopher Kempster, one of Wren's master-masons; described as the grandest Market-House in England. Local history museum; archaeological finds, charters, two 18th-C uniforms, smocks; changing exhibitions. Open all year, daily (ex BH) 2–5p (ch 16 2p). P. *(Tel 23703)*

ACCRINGTON *Lancashire* Map 7 SD72
Haworth Art Gallery Manchester Road. Constructed in 1909 for the Haworth family, the building was given to the Corporation of Accrington in 1921 for use as an art gallery. Fine wood panelling, plaster ceilings and fireplaces, plus collection of Early English water-colours and oil paintings, also one of the world's finest collections of Tiffany Glass. Art exhibitions change monthly. Brass Rubbing Centre and Nature Trail. ⚟ Open all year (ex 4 Apr, 25/26 Dec and 1 Jan), Mon to Sat 2–5; Sun Apr to Sep 2–7, Sun Oct to Mar 2–5. Free. ⚠ *(Tel 33782)* ⓖ B

ACTON BURNELL *Salop* Map 7 SJ50
Acton Burnell Castle Ruined 13th-C fortified manor house. First English Parliament said to have met here in 1283. Open at all reasonable times. Free. *(AM)*

ACTON SCOTT *Salop* Map 7 SO48
Acton Scott Working Farm Museum 3m S of Church Stretton off A49. Important site museum sited on the centre of a 1,200-acre estate in south Shropshire used to demonstrate agricultural practice as it was at the turn of the century. The farm is stocked with rare breeds of farm animals, and the work is largely done by hand or horse. The site is unique in that visitors may actively participate in several of the jobs that need to be done throughout the farming year. Shop illustrating and selling Shropshire crafts. Demonstrations of the various crafts are given throughout the season at weekends (details on application). Shop (refreshments).

Picnic area open after 12 noon. Open Apr to Oct Mon to Sat 1 – 5, Sun & BH 10 – 6 (last admission 30 mins before closing time). Parties at other times by appointment. 25p (ch 5 – 16 10p). Guide free for school parties booked in advance. Guide for adult parties booked in advance an additional £2. Admission prices under revision for 1980. No dogs. ⚠ *(Tel Marshbrook 306/7)* ⓖ

ADLINGTON *Cheshire* Map 7 SJ98
Adlington Hall W of Adlington Sta. Tudor banqueting hall, Elizabethan 'black-and-white' portion, 18th-C south front, and 'Bernard Smith' organ, restored in 1959 and associated with Handel. Gardens include yew walk and lime avenue. ⚟ Open 4 Apr to end Sep, Sun and BH weekends 2.30 – 6 (also Wed and Sat during Jul and Aug); parties on weekdays by arrangement. 70p (ch 35p). Party 25+. ⚠ *(Tel Prestbury 829206).* (Mr C F Legh) ⓖ B

ALBURY *Surrey* Map 4 TQ04
Albury Park Former home of Duchess of Northumberland. A country mansion which was re-fashioned in 1846 by Pugin. Open May to end Sep, Wed, Thu 2 – 5. 40p (ch 25p). ⚠

ALCESTER *Warwickshire* Map 4 SP05
Pleck Gardens 2m NW on B4090. Over three acres of roses, heather, azaleas, rhododendrons, etc, with formal garden, three ponds, and budgerigars. Open 1 Apr to 1 Oct, daily 10 – 6.30. 30p (ch 14 and pen 10p). Admission prices under revision for 1980. ⚠ *(Tel 2553).* (Miss Evelyn C Chapman) ⓖ
Ragley Hall 2m SW. 17th-C home of Seymours, with splendid great hall by James Gibbs, featuring baroque plasterwork and wealth of English and French pictures, furniture and porcelain. Fine gardens. Park, including adventure wood, country trail and lakeside picnic places. ⚟ House and gardens open Easter to Sep, Tue, Wed, Thu, Sat and Sun (including BH) 1.30 – 5.30, last admission 5. See local press for opening times of park. Admission prices not yet decided. ⚠ *(Tel 2090).* (Marquess of Hertford) ⓖ

ALDBOROUGH *North Yorkshire* Map 8 SE46
Roman Town Remains of northernmost Roman town (though not northernmost military station). Portions of boundary wall, two tessellated pavements, and small museum. Open Apr to Sep, see inside front cover. Museum closed Mon and Tue. 15p (ch 16 and pen 5p). Remains free. *(AM)*

ALDEBURGH *Suffolk* Map 5 TM45
Moot Hall Restored, two-storey, early 16th-C timber-framed building. Council chamber on upper floor, reached by external staircase, contains old maps and prints, objects of local

interest. Open Easter to May, Sun 2.30–6;
Jun and Oct 2.30–5 (6 Sun); Jul to Sep 11–1
and 2.30–5 (6 Sun). 10p (ch and pen 5p).
P(limited). *(Tel 2158)*

ALDERSHOT *Hampshire* Map 4 SU85
Airborne Forces Exhibition Browning
Barracks, Queen's Avenue. One of Army's
finest museums in newly erected barracks.
On display are weapons, including briefing
models from 1939–45 War and captured
enemy arms, airborne vehicles, dioramas of
actions, many scale models, parachutes and
equipment, photographs and medals
including VC and GCs. Open daily (ex 25
Dec) Mon to Fri 9–12.30, 2–5. Sat
9.30–12.30, 2–5 Sun 10–12.30, 2–4.30.
20p (ch and pen 10p). Party 20+. P. *(Tel
24431 ext 619)* &

Royal Corps of Transport Museum Buller
Barracks. Uniforms and badges of Royal
Corps of Transport and predecessors, and
models and photographs of vehicles used
from 1795 to present day. Open all year. Mon
to Fri (ex BH) 9–12 and 2–4. Free. ⚠ *(Tel
24431 ext 2417)* &

ALFORD *Lincolnshire* Map 9 TF47
Alford Manor House *c*1540. Museum
includes period shops, school room, maid's
bedroom, dairy, agricultural and transport
galleries. ⚐ (Tue & Fri). Opening times and
dates not yet decided. 15p (ch 5p). Under
revision for 1980. ⚠ *(Tel 6247)*

Mawthorpe Collection of Bygones
'Woodlands', Mawthorpe 2m S. A collection of
things from most aspects of the Bygone Era of
both house and farm including rural crafts.
Steam engines are in steam on open days, 8
and 29 Jun, 20 Jul, 10 and 31 Aug, also 5 Oct,
27, 28 Sep steam threshing. 11–6. Vintage
farm tractors on display, also farm
implements undergoing restoration. Large
collection of farm machinery including horse-
drawn implements. Departments in large
shed depict rural crafts and farming tools,
grocer's shop, war-time dept and washday
dept. Another collection of household bygone
equipment from cooking range to clothes.
Royalty section, chemist's shops and many
more items of interest. ⚐. ⚠ *(Tel 2336)* &

ALFRISTON *East Sussex* Map 5 TQ50
Clergy House Mid 14th-C half-timbered
thatched priests' house. Open Apr to end Oct
daily 11–6 (or dusk if earlier). 1 Nov to 23 Dec
(Medieval Hall and shop only) Wed, Fri, Sat
and Sun 11–sunset. Last admission ½hr
before closing. Medieval Hall, exhibition
room, garden and shop 30p (Nov and Dec no
charge as Hall and shop only open). *(NT)*

Drusillas Zoo Park One of the best small
zoos in the south, with greatly varied
collection of breeding groups including,
capuchin and diana monkeys, racoons, coati
mundis, rare breeds of cattle and sheep, also
penguins, parrots and flamingo lagoon.
Children's adventure playground and railway,
working pottery, Sussex craft shop and
bakery, antique shop and Bennett collection
of tropical moths and butterflies. ⚐ Open Apr
to end Oct daily 11–6 (or dusk if earlier),
winter Sat and Sun 11–dusk. Grounds free,
Zoo Park 70p (ch 12 and pen 35p). ⚠ *(Tel
870234)* &

ALLINGTON *Kent* Map 5 TQ75
Allington Castle Former home of Lord
Conway of Allington, on banks of River
Medway. A 13th-C moated castle with later
alterations by the Wyatts, it retains castellated
curtain wall, gatehouse, and great hall.
Medieval market 14 Jun. ⚐ May to Sep. Open
all year, (ex 25 Dec) daily 2–4. 50p (ch 12,
25p). ⚠ *(Tel Maidstone 54080)*. *(The Order
of Carmelites)* & B

ALNWICK *Northumberland* Map 12 NU11
Alnwick Castle Norman border stronghold of
Percy family, restored by Salvin. Keep,
armoury, museum (10p, ch 5p. 1979 charge)
and main apartments containing pictures by
Titian, Canaletto, Van Dyck, and other
famous artists, Meissen china, and historic
heirlooms are shown. Open 4 May to 26 Sep,
daily (ex Sat) 1–5 (no admission after
4.30pm). 80p (ch 16 40p); Party 70p (ch 30p)
No dogs. ⚠ free *(Tel 2722 or 2207)*. *(Duke of
Northumberland)*

ALRESFORD *Hampshire* Map 4 SU53
Mid Hants Railway (Watercress Line),
Alresford Station. Steam railway runs on
three miles of the old Winchester to Alton line
between Alresford and Ropley. Beautiful
Hampshire countryside with views of hills and
watercress beds, after which the railway is
named. At Ropley a variety of steam
locomotives are in various stages of
restoration. ⚐ (Alresford Station). Open 24
Mar to 28 Oct Sat 1.05–5.55, Sun
11.30–5.55 (leaflet available giving details,
times of trains etc). Fares 1st class return £1
(ch 3–14 50p); 3rd class return 80p (ch 3–14
40p). Party 20+. All under revision for 1980.
⚠ (Alresford Station). *(Tel 3810)* & parties
welcome; special coach and toilets should be
available for 1980.

ALTHORP *Northamptonshire* Map 4 SP66
Exit 16 on M1. House redecorated 1790 by
Henry Holland. Magnificent collection of
pictures, furniture and china. Arboretum and

pleasure grounds. Home of the Spencer family since 1508. ℘ Open 15 Apr to end Sep, Tue, Thu and Sun. Daily in Aug (ex Mon) 2.30 – 5.30. Also Sun in winter and BH 11.30 – 5.30. Pleasure grounds, gift shop and tearoom open all year Sat and Sun. House £1 (ch 50p), Grounds only 30p. House not suitable for young children. ⚠ *(Tel East Haddon 209)* ᵴ

ALTON *Hampshire* Map 4 SU73
Curtis Museum Contains local collections of geology, botany, zoology, archaeology and history; also craft tools, dolls, toys and games. Annexe and Allen gallery contains exhibition of paintings by W H Allen (1863 – 1943), loan exhibitions and English pottery. Open all year (ex Sun) Mon to Sat 10 – 5. Free. Parties by arrangement. P. *(Tel 82802)*. *(Hampshire County Museum Service)* ᵴ B

ALTON *Staffordshire* Map 7 SK04
Alton Towers Ruined early 19th-C mansion, former home of Charles Earl of Shrewsbury, set in beautiful grounds. Numerous lakes and pools were created with various fountains, foremost of which is the Chinese Pagoda Fountain. Also amusements including cable cars, boating lake, amusement park, planetarium and pottery studio. Large touring caravan park. ℘ Open Easter to mid Oct, daily grounds 9.30 – dusk, towers ruins 11 – 6. Admission prices under review. ⚠ *(Tel Oakamoor 702449)* ᵴ B

ALVINGHAM *Lincolnshire* Map 8 TF39
Water Mill An 18th-C Water cornmill restored as a working museum. There has been a mill on this site since domesday and it was once worked by the monks of Alvingham Abbey. The present machinery was probably installed in 1782 and is powered by one of the few remaining breast wheels. Open Aug and Sep Mon and Thu 2 – 5, 2nd and 4th Suns 2 – 5.30, BH Sun and Mon 11 – 5.30. 25p (ch 15 15p). ⚠ *(Tel South Cockerington 544)*

AMBLESIDE *Cumbria* Map 7 NY30
Stagshaw Gardens 1m S on A591. A garden created in mature woodland on a fell side overlooking Windermere lake. A magnificent and unique collection of species and hybrid rhododendrons, azaleas, camellias and other flowering shrubs. Open daily at all reasonable hours. 30p (ch 15p) *(NGS)* *(NT)*

AMPFIELD *Hampshire* Map 4 SU42
Hillier Arboretum Jermyn's Lane. Over 115 acres of trees and shrubs from most countries of the world. Large collections of alpines and herbaceous perennials. An all year round collection containing many rarities. Open all year Mon to Fri 9 – 4.30; 6 Apr to 26 Oct Sun

and BH 10 – 5. 50p (ch 20p). No dogs or picnicing. Parties by prior arrangement. ⚠ *(Tel Braishfield 68787)* ᵴ (dry weather only)

AMPTHILL *Bedfordshire* Map 4 TL03
Houghton House N off A418. Associated with the Countess of Pembroke, sister of Sir Philip Sidney, and possibly 'House Beautiful' of Bunyan's *Pilgrim's Progress*, ruined 17th-C mansion dismantled in 1794. Open, see inside front cover. Free. ⚠ *(AM)*

ANSTY *West Sussex* Map 4 TQ22
Legh Manor 16th-C house, with interesting furnishings and attractive gardens. Open Apr to Oct, second and third Weds and second Sat in each month. 2.30 – 5.30. ⚠ (ex coaches) *(Tel Haywards Heath 413428)*. *(Sussex Archaeological Society)*

APPLEDORE *Devon* Map 2 SS43
North Devon Maritime Museum Odun House, Odun Road. Exhibitions and displays on North Devon's maritime history. Models in authentic settings together with photographs and paintings illustrate seafaring, trade, shipbuilding, fishing and coastal craft, pilotage navigation, wreck and rescue. Also full size reconstruction of an Appledore kitchen *c*1900. Open Easter to 30 Sep daily 2.30 – 5.30 also Tue to Fri 11 – 1. 30p (ch 10p). Coaches and parties welcome. ⚠ *(Tel Bideford 6042)*

ARBORFIELD *Berkshire* Map 4 SU76
Royal Electrical and Mechanical Engineers' Museum Moat House. Devoted to REME history and equipment; models, photographs, uniforms, etc. Open all year, Mon to Fri (ex BH) 9 – 5 (4.30 Fri). Free. ⚠ (limited). *(Tel Arborfield Cross 760421 ext 220)*

ARBOR LOW STONE CIRCLE *Derbyshire* Map 7 SK16
Circle of 40 stones enclosing others, forming megalithic structure within ditch and rampart. Open, see inside front cover. Free. ⚠ *(AM)*

ARBURY HALL *Warwickshire* Map 4 SP38
Unique Elizabethan and 18th-C Gothic house, seat of the Newdegates since the 16th C. 18th-C alterations were made by Sanderson Miller and Henry Keene. Fine plaster ceilings, furniture, pictures, and china. 17th-C stable block, porch designed by Wren, housing museum of veteran cycles. ℘ Open Easter Sun to 1 Oct, Sun and BH 2.30 – 6; parties by special arrangement with *Administrator, Arbury Estate Office, Windmill Hill, Astley*. 80p (ch 14 35p); gardens and park only 60p subject to possible increase for 1980. ⚠ *(Tel Fillongley 40529)*

ARDINGLY *West Sussex* Map 4 TQ32
Wakehurst Place 1½m N. A great Elizabethan mansion restored, with gardens noted for exotic plant species, rare trees, and flowering shrubs. A picturesque water course links a series of ponds and lakes. The gardens are administered by the Royal Botanical Gardens, Kew. Gardens only open daily (ex 25 Dec, 1 Jan, and 5 May), Nov to Jan 10 – 4; Feb and Oct 10 – 5; Mar 10 – 6; Apr to Sep 10 – 7. 75p (ch 35p) Party Mon to Fri 50p (ch 25p) No dogs. ⚠ Ch 10 only admitted if accompanied. *(NT)* ⅙

ARLEY HALL GARDENS *Cheshire*
Map 7 SJ68
6m W Knutsford and 5m from M6 junc 19 and 20; M56 junc 9 and 10. These 8 acres of private gardens have belonged to one family for 500 years and provide great variety of style and design. Fine herbaceous border, unusual avenue of clipped ilex trees, walled gardens, yew hedges, shrub roses, azaleas, rhododendrons, and 15th-C 'cruck' barn. In 1975 these gardens gained a premier award in the British Tourist Authority's Landscape Heritage Competition. ⚲ Open (gardens only) Easter to mid Oct daily (ex Mon but open BH) 2 – 6.30 (last admission 6pm). 55p (ch 28p). Under revision for 1980. Hall and private chapel open to organised parties by prior arrangement. ⚠ *(Tel Arley (Northwich) 353)*. *(Viscount and Viscountess Ashbrook)* ⅙

ARLINGTON *Devon* Map 2 SS64
Arlington Court 7m NE of Barnstaple, off A39. Mansion of 1822 in large wooded estate with terraced garden and lake. House contains collection of model ships, pewter, and seashells, and the stables a large collection of horse-drawn vehicles. ⚲ Open 1 Apr to 31 Oct, daily 11 – 6, (house only closed on Mon). £1.50, gardens open also Nov to Mar, during daylight hours. Grounds, garden, park and stables £1; gardens and park free (Nov to Mar). *(NT)*

ARUNDEL *West Sussex* Map 4 TQ00
Arundel Castle Entrance at Lower Lodge in Mill Road. Norman stronghold restored in 18th and 19th C in magnificent grounds. Fine portraits by Van Dyck, Gainsborough, Reynolds, etc, and furniture from 15th C. Also Fitzalan Chapel. Open Apr to Oct. Opening times, dates and admission prices for 1980 not yet known. No dogs. ⚠ cars 20p *(Tel 883136 or 882173)* ⅙
Museum of Curiosity 6 High Street. The life work of the Victorian naturalist and taxidermist, Walter Potter, formerly housed at Bramber. First opened in 1861. Has a good collection of natural history and also the famous animal tableaux – Kittens Wedding, Rabbits Village School, Death of Cock Robin, Guinea Pigs Cricket Match etc. Also curios, toys, dolls, from all over the world. Open Easter to end Oct 10.30 – 5.30. 35p (ch 4 – 16 and pen 15p). P. *(Tel 882420)*
Wildfowl Trust Mill Road. 55 acres of well landscaped pens, lakes and paddocks with more than 1,000 ducks, geese and swans from all over the world. Hides overlook ponds, reed beds and a wader scrape which are sanctuaries for numerous species of wild birds. Open all year (ex 25 Dec) daily 9.30 – 6.30 (dusk in winter). 65p (ch 16 30p, pen 50p). Party 20+. ⚠ *(Tel 883355)* ⅙ **(79)**

ASHBOURNE *Derbyshire* Map 8 SK14
Hamilton House Toy Museum 27 Church Street. Houses a wide range of dolls and associated items, toy trains and model railways covering the period 1790s to 1950s. Open Tue to Sat 11 – 5.30, Sun and BH Mon 2 – 5.30. *(Tel 5343)*

ASHBURTON *Devon* Map 3 SX77
Ashburton Museum West Street. Exhibits include local antiquities, weapons, American Indian antiques, geology specimens. Open May – Sep Tue, Thur, Fri, Sat 2.50 – 5. Free. P. *(Tel 52298)*

ASHBURY *Oxfordshire* Map 4 SU28
Ashdown House 2½m SE on B4000. 17th-C mansion in lonely downland, built of chalk blocks and rising to four storeys. Built by 1st Lord Craven for Elizabeth of Bohemia. Paintings from Craven Collection hang in hall and on staircase. Open (grounds and roof only) Apr (Wed only), and May to Sep, Wed and first and third weekend in month 2 – 6. Conducted tours to roof 2.30, 3.30, 4.30 and 5.30. 50p (grounds only 30p). *(NT)*

ASHBY-DE-LA-ZOUCH *Leicestershire*
Map 8 SK31
Ashby-de-la-Zouch Castle Mainly 14th-C, but Hastings Tower added in 1474 by Lord Hastings. Royalist strongholds in Civil War, later slighted. Open, see inside front cover, but closed Wed and Thu. 15p (ch 16 and pen 5p) ⚔ *(AM)*

ASHCHURCH *Gloucestershire* Map 3 SO93
Dowty Railway Preservation Society Northway Lane. Five sidings in which are preserved several steam locomotives and some rolling stock, including GWR restaurant car. Extensive narrow gauge system with steam and diesel locomotives plus varied rolling stock. Open all year Sat and Sun 2 – 6. 10p (ch 5p, ch 8 and pen free) ex. steam days then as advertised. ⚲ ⚠. May move during

Arley Hall Gardens,
Cheshire

In 1975 these privately-owned gardens of 8 acres gained a premier award in the British Tourist Authority's Landscape Heritage Competition. Principal features are twin herbaceous borders (among the first to be established in England), a most unusual avenue of large clipped ilex trees, an avenue of pleached lime trees, walled gardens, yew hedges, shrub roses, azaleas and rhododendrons.

1980. Please phone first to avoid a wasted journey. *R Wilcox, Publicity Manager DRPS, 27 Quail Park Drive, Heronswood Park, Kidderminster. (Tel Kidderminster 743079)* &

ASHFORD *Kent* Map 5 TR04
Godinton Park 2½m NW Gabled house, dating from 1628, with fine panelling and carving, portraits, furniture, and china, and 18th- and 19th-C garden layout, including topiary work. Open Easter Sat, Sun, Mon and 1 Jun to 30 Sep, Sun and BH 2 – 5, or by appointment. 50p (ch 16 25p). Admission prices under revision for 1980. No dogs. & *(Tel 20773). (Mr A Wyndham Green)* & B
Intelligence Corps Museum Templer Barracks. Items concerning the corps from two World Wars and other articles up to the present day. Open all year (ex BH), Mon to Fri 10 – 12 and 2 – 4. Free. & *(Tel 25251 ext 206)* & B

ASHLEWORTH *Gloucestershire* Map 3 SO82
Tithe Barn 15th-C building, 120ft long with porch bays and queen-post roof. Open daily until sunset. 10p. No dogs. *(NT)*

ASHTON *Hereford and Worcester* Map 3 SO56
Berrington Hall 3½m N Leominster. Built 1778 – 83 by Henry Holland. Fine interior decoration, including painted and plaster ceilings, much of it unaltered, and recently restored stonework. 455-acre park, laid out by 'Capability' Brown in 1780, includes 14-acre 'pool', fine trees, shrubs, and plants. Wide views towards Wales. & (teas Sat and Sun). Open Apr to end Sep, Wed, Thu, Sat, Sun, BH Mon; Oct, Sat and Sun only 2 – 6; other times by written appointment to estate office. 85p. Joint ticket with Croft Castle £1.50. No dogs. *(NT)*

ASHWELL *Hertfordshire* Map 4 TL23
Village Museum Early Tudor timber-framed house, once tithe office of abbots of Westminster. Now a scheduled ancient monument. Contains collection showing life of village from Stone Age to present day. Open all year Sun 3 – 5.30; other times by appointment in writing to the *Hon Curator*. 10p *(Tel 2176)*

ASTON MUNSLOW *Salop* Map 7 SO58
The White House Museum of Buildings and Country Life 6m NE of Craven Arms on B4368. The Stedman Homestead, four houses in one, continuously inhabited. Undercroft of the manor house to which the dovecote was granted in 1250; 14th-C Cruck Hall; 16th-C cross-wing with 18th-C addition. Another open bay dwelling-house of 16th-C. Stable of 1680, with original cobbled floor and other stone buildings of various functions and periods. Rooms and buildings equipped with domestic utensils, farming tools and implements in their functional setting. Open Easter to 30 Oct. Other details under review. Schools and parties 20+ by prior arrangement. & Picnic area. No dogs. *(Miss J C Purser)* **(79)**

ATCHAM *Salop* Map 7 SJ50
Attingham Park 3m SE Shrewsbury. House dates from 1758 and was designed by George Steuart; fine interior containing Nash pictures and furnishings. Stands in 1,159-acre Humphrey Repton Park. Open 6 Apr to end Sep, Tue to Thu, Sat, Sun and BH Mon 2 – 5.30. 80p (grounds only 20p) *(NT)*

ATHELHAMPTON *Dorset* Map 3 SY79
Athelhampton On A35 1m E of Puddletown. Family home for 500 years, one of finest medieval houses in Southern England. 15th-C Great Hall, Tudor Great Chamber, fine staircase, interesting furnishings. Ten acres of formal and landscape gardens, and 15th-C dovecote. River gardens. & teas. Open Wed before Easter to 1st Sun in Oct, Wed, Thu, Sun BH and also Tue and Fri in Aug 2 – 6. Admission prices for 1980 not yet known. Plants and antiques for sale. No dogs. & *(Tel Puddletown 363). (Sir Robert Cooke) (NGS)*

AUBOURN *Lincolnshire* Map 8 SK96
Aubourn Hall 16th-C house with fine Jacobean staircase and panelled rooms. Open 27 Apr, 25 May, Jul and Aug. Wed 2 – 6 other times by appointment. 50p. No dogs. & *(Tel Bassingham 224). (Mr H N Nevile)*

AUDLEY END *Essex* Map 5 TL53
17th-C house, only part of original, built by Thomas Howard, Earl of Suffolk, with some work by Robert Adam, and standing in fine park. Pictures and furnishings in state rooms, miniature railway in grounds. & Open Apr to early Oct, daily (ex Mon) and BH 10 – 5.30 (grounds close 6.30pm). 70p (ch 16 and pen 30p). &5p. *(AM)*

AUGHTON *Lancashire* Map 7 SD30
Cranford Unusually planned, modern ½-acre garden, with rare trees, shrubs and roses. Open Apr to mid Oct, daily 10 to dusk. *(Mr T J C Taylor). (NGS)* &

AVEBURY *Wiltshire* Map 4 SU06
Avebury Manor Fine example of Tudor Manor on edge of largest prehistoric megalithic circle in Europe. Open May and Sep, Sat and Sun and daily Jun, Jul and Aug 2.30 – 5.30. BH 10 – 6. 60p (ch 12.30p). Under revision for 1980. No dogs. P. *(Tel 203). (Marquess and Marchioness of Ailesbury)* & B
Avebury Museum Alexander Keiller Museum. Finds from late Neolithic Age site and nearby Neolithic Windmill Hill site. Near museum a circle of sarsen stones is enclosed by bank and ditches. Open*, see inside front cover. 15p (ch 16 and pen 5p). & *(AM and NT)*

AXBRIDGE *Somerset* Map 3 ST45
King John's Hunting Lodge Market Place. Restored early Tudor house with old photographs, and exhibits of local interest including coins, flint items, and animal bones. Town stocks and constables' staves also on show. Open Apr to end Sep, daily 2 – 5. Free. & *(NT)*

AYLESBURY *Buckinghamshire* Map 4 SP81
Bucks County Museum Church Street. Housed in former grammar school built in 1720 and two 15th-C houses, which were completely altered in the mid 18th-C. There is a fine plaster ceiling dating from 1760. The displays relate to the geology, natural history, archaeology and history of the county and include costume and a Rural Life Gallery. Open all year daily (ex 4 Apr; 25, 26 Dec; 1 Jan) Mon to Fri 9.30 – 5, Sat 9.30 – 12.30, 1.30 – 5. Free. *(Tel 82158 and 88849)*

AYLESFORD *Kent* Map 5 TQ75
Priory Restored 13th- to 14th-C Carmelite house with fine cloisters; now conference centre and place of pilgrimage and retreat. Sculpture and ceramics by modern artists, pottery, and rose garden. Souvenir shop, pottery shop, & open 10.30 – 12.45 and 2 – 5 daily (closed Mons Nov to Easter). Open all

year, daily 9am to dusk. Donations. (guided tours by arrangement). ⚠ *(Order of Carmelites) (Tel Maidstone 77272)* ⓑ

AYNHO *Northamptonshire* Map 4 SP53
Aynhoe Park 6m SE Banbury. 17th-C mansion. The interior was largely remodelled in the 19th-C by Sir John Soanes. Open May to Sep Wed and Thu 2 – 5. 40p (ch 25p). ⚠ *(Tel Croughton 810636)*

AYOT ST LAWRENCE *Hertfordshire* Map 4 TL11
Shaw's Corner At SW end of village. Dates from this century and was the home of George Bernard Shaw between 1906 and his death in 1950. He donated the house in 1944 and the contents are as in his lifetime. His ashes were scattered in the garden. Open Mar and Nov Sat and Sun, also Apr to Oct daily (ex Mon and Tue, but open BH Mon) 11 – 1 and 2 – 6 or sunset. 80p *(NT)*

AYSGARTH *North Yorkshire* Map 7 SE08
National Park Centre Permanent interpretation centre for the Aysgarth Falls area with display, books, maps etc. Aysgarth mini trail starts here. Open Apr to end Sep daily, mid morning to late afternoon. Free. ⚠ *(Tel 424)*
The Old Mill, The Yorkshire Museum of Carriages and Horse-Drawn Vehicles ¾m E adjacent to bridge on unclass road N off A684. In an old stone mill at Aysgarth Falls. This mill now houses approximately 50 horse-drawn vehicles including some splendid coaches, carriages and much impedimenta of the Era of Horse-Drawn Transport. Open Easter to late Oct (if closed during this period, apply at cottage next to office). 10 – 12 and 1.30 – 6. 25p (ch 10p). P. *(Tel Richmond, Yorks 3325)*

BACONSTHORPE *Norfolk* Map 9 TG13
Baconsthorpe Castle Late 15th-C moated, semi-fortified house, incorporating gatehouse and range of curtain walls with towers. Open, see inside front cover. 10p (ch 16 and pen 5p). ⚠ *(AM)*

BADMINTON *Avon* Map 3 ST88
Badminton House Off B4040. 17th- to 18th-C Palladian mansion, partly by Kent, with fine paintings and furnishings. Situated in great park where famous Badminton Horse Trials are held (17 – 21 Apr) and home of Dukes of Beaufort since 17th C. ♨ in orangery. Open each Wed from 4 Jun to 3 Sep, 2.30 – 5. 50p (ch 10p, pen 25p). Church, stables and kennels open to visitors. ⚠ *(Tel 202). (Duke of Beaufort KG PC GCVO)* ⓑ

BAKEWELL *Derbyshire* Map 8 SK26
Magpie Mine 3m W. The surface remains are the best example in Britain of a 19th-C lead

mine. Open 22 Jul to 9 Sep daily (ex Sat) from 2.30. Free. Further information can be obtained from Peak District Mining Museum, Matlock Bath *(Tel Matlock 3834)*
The Old House Museum Off Church Lane. Early Tudor house with original wattle and daub interior walls, and an open timbered chamber. Exhibition of costumes, kitchen and household utensils, tools, etc. Open Easter Sat to end Oct, daily (ex Bakewell Show Day) 2.30 – 5; 25p (ch of school age 15p). Party bookings: E T Goodwin, 32 Castle Mount Crescent, Bakewell. *(Tel 3647)*

BALSALL COMMON *Warwickshire* Map 4 SP27
Berkswell Windmill Windmill Lane. Also known as Balsall Windmill. A fine example of a Warwickshire tower mill complete in both machinery and fittings, including tools. Open 6 May to end Sep, Sun only, 11 – 1 and 2.30 – 5.30. All other days by appointment. 20p (ch and pen 10p). ⚠ limited. *(Tel Berkswell 33403)*

BAMBURGH *Northumberland* Map 12 NU13
Bamburgh Castle Restored Norman castle in splendid North Sea coast setting. Impressive hall, and armoury with large weapon collection, also loan collection of armour from HM Tower of London. Guided tours of interior when conditions permit. Open Apr to Sep, daily from 1pm. 60p (ch 30p), subject to possible review. Party rates for morning or afternoon tours. ⚠ *(Tel 208). (Lord Armstrong)*
Grace Darling Museum Pictures, documents, and various relics of the heroine, including boat in which she and her father, keeper of Longstone Lighthouse, Farne Islands, rescued nine survivors from wrecked 'SS Forfarshire' in 1838. Open 1 Apr to 1 Oct, daily 11 – 7. Free. P. ⓑ

BANBURY *Oxfordshire* Map 4 SP44
Banbury Museum and Globe Room Marlborough Road. Due to move to 8 Horsefair, Banbury summer 1980. A small museum with exhibits of local history and folk life. Permanent exhibition of the history of Banbury and the Cherwell Valley. Changing exhibitions. Bookshop. Open all year, daily (ex Sun) Mon, Wed – Fri 10 – 1, 2 – 5, Tue, Sat 10 – 1. Free. P. *(Tel 2282)*

BANHAM *Norfolk* Map 5 TM08
Banham International Motor Museum at Banham Zoo. Lord Cranworth's collection of cars, racing cars, motorcycles and children's pedal cars from the 1920s to the 1960s are on display in a new and imaginative setting. Now enlarged with over 40 vehicles, also large

collection of dolls. A vehicle adventure ground for children to climb and play on. Open daily in summer 11.30–5. 60p (ch 30p). Party 50p (ch 25p). ⚠ *(Tel Grundisburg 202)* &

P.K.F.

Banham Zoo and Monkey Sanctuary The Grove. Situated in over 20 acres of grounds, this zoo which specialises in monkeys and apes, contains a world-wide collection of animals and birds. The collection includes gibbons, chimps, bears, otters, seals, penguins, llamas, wallabies, ostriches, pelicans, cranes, flamingoes, macaws, etc. Fruit, farm and dairy produce on sale in Grove Farm Barn opposite. ☕ (licensed). Open all year, daily 10.30–6.30 or dusk if earlier. Party. ⚠ *(Tel Quidenham 476)* &

BARDON MILL *Northumberland*
Map 12 NY76
Vindolanda (Chesterholm) Remains of 3rd- and 4th-C Roman fort and frontier town. Replicas of Hadrian's turf wall and stone wall. Large museums. Also ornamental garden. Main excavations take place Apr to end Sep, annually. ☕ licensed. Open all year (ex 25 Dec) daily 10–6.30. 50p (ch 18 and pen 25p). ⚠ *(Tel 277)*. *(Vindolanda Trust)* & **(79)**

BARLASTON *Staffordshire* Map 7 SJ83
Wedgwood Museum and Visitor Centre
Traditional skills in the production of Wedgwood can be seen in the craft demonstration area, and the museum

contains a comprehensive collection of the works of Josiah Wedgwood from 1750, and includes a film show and shopping facilities are also available. Open all year Mon to Fri 9–5, last complete visit 3.30, appointment preferred. 50p (ch 25p). Ch 5 not admitted, ch 5–15 must be accompanied by an adult. P. *(Tel 3218 or 4141)* &

BARNARD CASTLE *Co Durham*
Map 12 NZ01
The Bowes Museum Splendid French-style château, built in 1869 and situated in the countryside of upper Teesdale. Houses a collection of fine and decorative arts of international importance: paintings, tapestries, furniture, porcelain, silver etc. Series of English period rooms 1570–1870, galleries of costume, textiles, Gothic art, music and other subjects. Children's Room, local history, temporary exhibitions. ☕ Open all year (closed 25–26 Dec and 1 Jan), May to Sep Mon–Sat 10–5.30, Sun 2–5. Closes 4 Nov to Feb and 5 Mar, Apr and Oct. 45p (ch and pen 10p). Admission charges under revision for 1980. ⚠ *(Tel Teesdale 37139)* &
The Castle 11th- to 13th-C ruin with circular three-storeyed keep. Open*, see inside front cover. 15p (ch 16 and pen 5p). *(AM)* &
Egglestone Abbey 1 m SW. Picturesque remains of Premonstratensian Abbey on right bank of River Tees. Open, see inside front cover. Free. *(AM)*

BARNSLEY *Gloucestershire* Map 4 SP00
Barnsley House Garden Old Garden, completely re-designed since 1962. Laburnum walk (early June), Lime walk, Knot garden, herb garden and borders with use of ground cover, kitchen garden laid out as decorative potager. Two 18th-C summerhouses, one Gothic, the other

Classical. Garden open Wed Apr to Oct 10–6, 1st Sun in May Jun, Jul and Aug 2–7 (every Wed throughout year for plant sales). House not open. 40p (pen 25p). ⚠ (coaches in village). *(Tel Bibury 281)* &

BARNSLEY *South Yorkshire* Map 8 SE30
2m E of M1 (junction 37).
Monk Bretton Priory 1½m E. An important Cluniac house with considerable remains of the church and claustral buildings. Open, see inside front cover. 10p (ch 16 5p). ⚠ *(AM)*
Worsborough Mill Museum Worsborough. 2½m S of Barnsley on A61. The corn mill is a working industrial site museum. It consists of a 17th-C water-powered mill and an adjoining 19th-C mill powered by a rare 1911 hot bulb oil engine. Both mills are built of local sandstone and are set in the wooded valley of the river Dove. The mill is a central feature of the Worsborough Country Park. The water mill works whenever the museum is open and there are frequent special exhibitions and displays relating to milling, agriculture and local history. Open all year, Wed to Sun 10–6 or dusk if earlier. Special openings and working steam engines and craft displays. 10p (ch 5p, pen free). ⚠ *(Tel 203961)* & (by arrangement with attendant staff).

BARNSTAPLE *Devon* Map 2 SS53
St Anne's Chapel Museum 14th-C former chapel, now small but interesting museum of largely local interest. Historical records of industry and social life. Open 1 Jun to 20 Sep, Mon to Sat 10–1 and 2–5. 10p (ch free). Catalogues 5p. P. *(Tel 72511 ext 272 for enquiries)*
The North Devon Athenaeum The Square. The museum contains a collection of local antiquities and North Devon earthenware, ceremonial spoons, geological and fossil collections, Roman pottery excavated at Trentishoe, butterfly collection, coin collection, maps, etc. The reference library also housed here was established by William Frederick Rock in 1888 and has a special collection of books on local history, geography, geology, biology, classical literature, topography and travel. Open all year, Mon to Sat (ex Sat pm and Sun) 10–1, 2.15–6. Free. Ch 14 must be accompanied by an adult. P. *(Tel 2174)*
Marwood Hill 8–10 acres of rare trees and shrubs, rose garden, quarry garden with alpine plants, 2 small lakes and a bog garden. Greenhouses include a Camellia house and Australian house. Plants for sale. Open all year 20p (ch 5p). ⚠ *(Tel 2528)*
Youlston Park 4½m NE on A39. Former 18th-C Chichester residence. Fine ceilings, staircase and Chinese Room. Woodland garden and lake. ⚐ Opening times 2–6 (closed Mon). Prices not available. ⚠ *(Tel Shirwell 200)* & B

BARRINGTON *Somerset* Map 3 ST42
Barrington Court 3m NE of Ilminster, on B3168. Beautiful Tudor mansion of Ham Hill stone, built 1514–20 by Lord Daubeny. Nearby is converted stable building of 1670. Open Apr to Sep, Wed 10.15–12.15 and 2–6; Oct to Easter, Wed 2–4; last guided tour 5.30. Admission to house and gardens 40p. Special charity days house 40p, gardens 40p. No dogs. No picnics. *(NT)*

BARROW-IN-FURNESS *Cumbria*
Map 7 SD26
Furness Abbey 1½m NE on unclass road. Cistercian Abbey with extensive remains of the church, sited in the 'Glen of Deadly Nightshade' near Barrow. Open, see inside front cover. 20p (ch 16 and pen 5p). ⚠ *(AM)*
The Furness Museum Ramsden Square. Museum of Furness district with finds from late Stone Age sites. Also Vickers-Armstrong ship models and Lake District bygones. Various monthly exhibitions. Open all year, Mon to Sat 10–5 (ex Thu 10–1). Closed Sun, BH and Public Hols. Free *(Tel 20650)*

BASILDON *Berkshire* Map 4 SU67
Child Beale Wildlife Trust Riverside walks, and lakes with ornamental pheasants, peacocks, wildfowl, flamingoes, cranes, Highland cattle and Soay sheep. Children's playground and paddling pool. Open Easter to mid Sep, Wed, Thu, Sun and BH 10–6. ⚠ cars 50p, minibuses £1, coaches £3; Sat free (closed Mon, Tue and Fri). Times and charges for 1980 under review. *(Tel Pangbourne 2386, Upper Basildon 325)* &
Basildon Park 2½m NW of Pangbourne on W side of A329. Classical 18th-C house by John Carr of York in a magnificent setting overlooking the Thames valley. There is some fine plasterwork and an Octagon room, also pictures and furniture. Open Apr to Oct (ex 4 Apr) Wed to Sun 2–6 (Oct 2–5.30), BH Mon 11–1, 2–6. Last admission to house 30 mins before closing. House and grounds £1.10. *(NT)*

BASING *Hampshire* Map 4 SU65
House Ruins of a great Tudor palace built in 1530's on the site of a former Norman Castle. All the Tudor Kings and Queens visited here. The house was destroyed in 1645 during the civil war by Cromwell's troops after a three-year siege. Exhibitions. Outdoor trail and tape recorded guides tell the story of the house. ⚐ Open Easter to Sep, Tue to Sat 2–5.30, Sun and BH 11–5.30. Prices for 1979 not yet available. ⚠ *(Tel Basingstoke 67294)* **(79)**

BASINGSTOKE *Hampshire* Map 4 SU65
Willis Museum and Art Gallery Contains local collections of archaeology, geology, natural history, Basingstoke Canal, horology, watch and clock makers' tools. Displays of recent accessions and temporary exhibitions in the Art Gallery, also a new Town History Gallery. Open all year (ex Sun and Mon morning) Mon 1–5, Tue to Sat 10–5. Free. Parties by arrangement. *(Tel 65902)*. *(Hampshire County Museum Service)* & B

BATH *Avon* Map 3 ST76
American Museum in Britain Claverton Manor. 2½m E. Built in 1820 by Sir Jeffrey Wyatville, overlooks Avon valley, and now museum of American decorative arts and gardens from 17th, 18th and 19th C. Winston Churchill delivered his first ever political speech in the grounds in 1897. ⚐ Open 29 Mar to 2 Nov daily (ex Mon) 2–5, BH Mon and preceding Sun 11–5. House and grounds £1.20 (ch 14 and pen £1). Grounds only 40p. Reduced rates 1st Fri in month and whole Oct. Parties of ch not admitted during normal opening hours. ⚠ *(Tel 60503)* & B
Assembly Rooms Bennett Street. Designed c 1771 by John Wood the Younger. Redecorated in 1979. Associated with novels by Charles Dickens and Jane Austen. ⚐ (Easter–Sep). Open all year (ex 25 Dec), weekdays 9.30–6, Sun 10–6, last admission ½hr before closing time. ⚠(limited) *(Tel 61111)/(NT)* also *Museum of Costume* housed in the assembly Rooms. Based on the internationally famous collections built up by Doris Langley-Moore OBE. The collections have been enriched by donations and loans from many sources and are amongst the

largest and most comprehensive in the world. Also on display are toys and dolls and an important collection of jewellery. Modern fashions include costumes from Dior and Yves St Laurent Couture Houses, also the 'Dress of the Year'. Fashions from the Regency to the 1920s are displayed in period rooms and settings, many based on well known scenes in Bath. ⚲ Open all year, Mar to Oct Mon to Sat 9.30 – 6, Sun 10 – 6; Nov to Feb Mon to Sat 10 – 5, Sun 11 – 5. 80p (ch 16 25p). P. *(Tel 61111 ext 324)* &

Bath Carriage Museum Circus Mews. Finest and most comprehensive collection of horse-drawn carriages in the country. Large exhibition of harnesses etc from the coaching era. Housed in Circus Mews, built in 1759 by John Wood the Younger. Carriage rides available daily throughout the season. Open all year (ex Dec 25) Summer (Sun 10 – 6) Summer; 10 – 5 (Sun 11 – 5) winter. Admission price not available. P. *(Tel 25175)* &

Beckford's Tower and Museum Lansdown. Built in 1827 by H E Goodridge for William Beckford of Fonthill, in a striking Neo-Classical style. Fine views from Belvedere, 156 steps. Small museum of Beckfordiana on 1st floor. Open Apr to Oct, Sat and Sun only 2 – 5. 15p (ch 14 and pen 10p). ⚲ *(Tel 858106)*

Camden Works Industrial Museum Housing the Bowler collection, the entire stock-in-trade of a Victorian Brass Founder, General Engineer and Aerated Water manufacturer, displayed in settings that capture the atmosphere of the original premises. Open all year, daily (ex Fri, 6 Apr also 24 and 25 Dec) 2 – 5. 40p (ch 16 and pen 25p). *(Tel 318348)*

Holburne of Menstrie Museum (University of Bath) Gt Pulteney Street. Outstanding collection of paintings, porcelain, silver, miniatures and furniture housed in an 18th-C building. The Crafts Study Centre shows work by 20th-C British craftsmen. ⚲ May to Sep. Open all year (ex Christmas) Mon to Sat 11 – 5, Sun 2.30 – 6. 40p (ch, students and pen 20p). ⚲ *(Tel 66669)*

No. 1 Royal Crescent Stone-built Georgian house in perhaps best known of Bath's terraces and crescents. House restored to original condition and furnished with fine examples of 18th-C furniture. Open first Tue in Mar to last Sun in Oct, Tue to Sat 11 – 5, Sun 2 – 5. 40p (ch, students and pen 20p). Street P. limited to 2 hours. Admission charges under review for 1980. *(Tel 28126)*

Prior Park College Overlooking city, Georgian mansion built c 1735 by John Wood

the Elder for Ralph Allen, now Roman Catholic public school, run by the Christian Brothers. Well-known Palladian bridge in grounds. Chapel and grounds open all year, daily 11 – 4, by kind permission of President; mansion open May to Sep, Tue, Wed; Aug Mon to Thu 2 – 6. 20p (ch 14 10p, pen free). ⚲ *(Tel Combe Down 832752)* & B

Roman Baths and Pump Room Abbey Churchyard. Remains of Roman baths of 'Aquae Sulis', with museum devoted to the Roman history of Bath and containing important archaeological finds from the City. Britain's only hot water springs and largest Roman bathing complex. Open all year, Apr to Oct daily 9 – 6, Nov to Mar, Mon to Sat 9 – 5, Sun 11 – 5. 80p (ch 16 25p). Party 20+ 65p (ch 35p). ⚲ (Apr to Nov). Under revision for 1980. P in City. *(Tel 61111)*

BATLEY *West Yorkshire* Map 8 SE22
Art Gallery Market Place. Permanent collection of British oil paintings, water colours, drawings and sculpture from mid 19th C onwards. Temporary loan and special exhibitions throughout the year. Open all year daily (ex Sun) 10 – 7 (Sat 9 – 4). Free. ⚲ *(Tel 473141)*

Bagshaw Museum Wilton Park. 19th-C building housing museum of local history, archaeology, geology, ethnography and Oriental arts, natural history, and folk life opened in 1911. Best approached from Upper Batley Lane. Open all year Apr to Oct, Tue to Sat 10 – 6 (Sun 1 – 5); Nov to Mar, Tue to Sat 10 – 5. Coal mine open weekdays by special appointment. Free ⚲ *(Tel 472514)* &

BATTLE *East Sussex* Map 5 TQ71
Battle and District Historical Society Museum Langton House. Diorama of Battle of Hastings and reproduction of Bayeux Tapestry. Exhibits show local history, including Romano-British and Sussex ironwork. Open Easter to Oct, Mon to Sat 10 – 1 and 2 – 5 (Sun only 2.30 – 5.30). 10p (ch 5p). Under revision for 1980. P. *(Tel 2722)*

BEACONSFIELD *Buckinghamshire* Map 4 SU99
Bekonscot Model Village Off A40. Well laidout rock gardens, with model village and large model railway. Model trains run frequently from 10 – 5.30 Easter to Oct (weather permitting). Gardens open all year (ex Christmas hols) daily. Easter to Oct Mon to Fri 10 – 4.45, Sat and Sun 10 – 5.30; Winter 10 – 3.45. 50p (ch 3 – 16 25p). Reduction in winter. Party 20+ (weekdays only) 40p (ch 20p). P. *(Tel 2919)* & (small wheelchairs only, narrow paths)

Holburne of Menstrie Museum

(University of Bath)

Great Pulteney Street, Bath.

Outstanding collection of paintings, porcelain, silver, miniatures and furniture housed in an 18th century building. The Crafts Study Centre showing work by 20th Century British craftsmen.

BEAMINSTER *Dorset* Map 3 ST40
Parnham House Impressive Tudor mansion set in 14 acres of traditional gardens and formal terraces. Home of the John Makepeace Furniture Workshop and the School for Craftsmen in Wood. Great Hall has exhibition of unique furniture. Riverside picnic area. Open Apr to Oct (ex Sun 15 Jun) Wed, Sun and BH 10–5. 90p (ch 16 50p). ⚠ *(Tel 862204)* ⅊.
Mapperton Gardens 2m SE off A356 and B3163. Extensive terraced and hillside gardens with formal borders and specimen shrubs and trees, 18th-C stone fish-ponds and summer-house, Orangery. ⚓. Open 10 Mar to 10 Oct, Mon to Fri 2–6. Admission prices not yet available. ⚠
BEAMISH *Co Durham* Map 12 NZ25
North of England Open-Air Museum
Beamish off A693 and A6076. England's first open-air museum. Beamish is about Northern people and their way of life. On a 200-acre site, buildings of all kinds have been rebuilt and furnished with the contents they once held. Already on the site is a railway area with station, goods shed, weighbridge house and signal box. At Home Farm can be seen exhibitions on harvests and farm animals, as well as old farm tools, implements, farm animals and a fine collection of North Eastern farm carts. A Colliery has been rebuilt with steam locos working and a full scale replica of Locomotion No. 1 is demonstrated. Also at the Colliery can be seen a row of rebuilt fully furnished pitmen's cottages. Visitors can ride behind steam locos and in trams across the site. Transport collection and demonstrations of traditional crafts. Open all year daily Apr to end Aug 10–6, Sep to Mar (closed Mon) 10–5. Last admission 1 hour before closing

time. 70p (ch and pen 35p). Subject to revision for 1980. *(Tel Stanley (0207) 31811)* ⑤

BEAULIEU *Hampshire* Map 4 SU30
Beaulieu Abbey, National Motor Museum and Palace House On B3054. 70,000 sq ft of exhibition floor space, and large library, in National Motor Museum containing over 300 veteran and vintage cars, motor cycles, and pedal cycles. Abbey was founded in 1204 and refectory now parish church. Palace House, once Abbey gatehouse, has large additions from 1870. Monorail, veteran bus rides, model railway, Transporama and other features. Special events include rallies and steam fairs. Gift shops. ⬚ (licensed). House, Motor Museum, Abbey and gardens open all year (ex Dec 25) daily summer 10 – 6 (5 winter). Inclusive admission charged, (ch and pen half price). ⚠ *(Tel 612345). (Lord Montagu of Beaulieu).* ⑤ *(ex Palace House).* See also **BUCKLER'S HARD,** *Maritime Museum.*

P.K.F.

BEDALE *North Yorkshire* Map 8 SE28
7m SW of Northallerton
Bedale Hall On A684; 1½m W of A1 at Leeming Bar. Georgian house with ballroom wing and museum room. Open May to Sep, Tue 10 – 4, other days by appointment. Free. P. *(Tel 3131)* ⑤ B

BEDFORD *Bedfordshire* Map 4 TL04
Bunyan Museum Mill Street. In Bunyan Meeting House (1850), on site of barn, where John Bunyan preached. Contains all surviving personal relics, and world-famous collection of over 400 foreign language editions of his works, including *The Pilgrim's Progress* in over 165 languages. Open Apr to Oct Tue – Sat 2 – 4 20p. P. *(Tel 58627)* ⑤
Cecil Higgins Art Gallery Castle Close. New extension contains outstanding collections of ceramics, glass, water-colours, prints. Late Victorian style room settings in adjoining house. Costume and lace by appointment only. Special arrangements for group visits, evening parties. Open Tue to Fri 12.30 – 5.00, Sat 11.00 – 5.00 Sun 2.00 – 5.00, BH. Closed Mon and Christmas. Admission charges during summer months and opening hours under revision. *(Tel Bedford 211222)* ⑤

BEER *Devon* Map 3 SY28
Beer Heights Light Railway and Peco Modelrama Situated on a hillside at the back of the village exists Modelrama featuring Beer Heights Light Railway, a steam-operated passenger carrying line which runs through the Peco Pleasure Park, with interesting scenic features and delightful views across the bay. Miniature putting green. The main building houses an exhibition of Model Railways in various small gauges displayed in typical locations around the house and garden. Souvenir and model railway shops. Snacks at Beer Victoria Station buffet. ⬚ Main meals in Orion Pullman Car. Indoor Exhibition open all year. Outdoor amenities open after Spring BH to mid Oct, Mon to Fri 10 – 5, Sat 10 – 12.30 (closed Sun and BH). Grounds and exhibition 40p (ch 5, free,

YOURS FOR THE DAY
**National Motor Museum
Palace House and Gardens
Beaulieu Abbey Buckler's Hard**

In the New Forest
between Bournemouth
and Southampton.

5–11 15p, 12–17 30p). Drive a train 5p. Rides on railway 15p (all ages). ⚠ *(Tel Seaton 21542 ext 36)*

BEESTON *Cheshire* Map 7 SJ55
Beeston Castle Off A49. 13th-C stronghold built by Earl of Chester in almost inaccessible position on steep hill. Open Mon to Fri 9.30–4.30. Free. Closed Sat and Sun. ⚠ *(AM)*

BEKESBOURNE *Kent* Map 5 TR15
Howletts Zoo Park Off A257. Famous collection of wild animals, including breeding groups of gorillas, tigers, wolves, free-running deer and antelope, also snow leopards, tapirs, and wild boar. ⚲ Open all year 10–6 (1 hour before dusk winter). Prices not yet available. ⚠ *(Tel Hythe 60618)* ⓺ B

BELTON *Lincolnshire* Map 8 SK93
Belton House Park and Gardens On A607.

Attributed to Wren, home of Lord Brownlow's family since built in 1685. Magnificent carvings by Grinling Gibbons, pictures, silver, furniture, tapestries and souvenirs of Duke of Windsor. Fine gardens and 700-acre deer park. Children's Adventureland, Museum of Horse and Nature Trails. Special events on most Sundays. ⚲ Open 29 Mar to 5 Oct daily from 11am. £1.20 (ch and pen 60p) all inclusive tickets. ⚠ *(Tel Grantham 66116). (Lord Brownlow)* ⓺ B

BELVOIR *Leicestershire* Map 8 SK83
Belvoir Castle Between A52 and A607. Home of the Duke of Rutland. Palatial early 19th-C reconstruction by James Wyatt, on hilltop overlooking Vale of Belvoir, with notable *objets d'art*, armoury and museums of 17th/21st Lancers and Grenadier Guards. Many special events on Sundays at no extra charge. ⚲ (also waitress service for booked

parties Wed, Thu and Sat only). Open 26 Mar to 28 Sep Wed, Thu, Sat and BH Tue also 4 Apr 12–6, Sun 2–7. Sun Jun, Jul and Aug 12–7. Oct, open only on Sun 2–6. BH Mon 11–7 (last admissions ½hr before Castle closes). Party 30+ (Adults and pen). Admission charges on enquiry. No dogs. *(Tel Knipton 262)* & B

BENINGBROUGH *North Yorkshire* Map 8 SE55

Beningbrough Hall Off A19. Entrance at Newton Lodge. Built about 1716, this attractive house stands in a wooded park. In the principal rooms are 100 pictures from the National Portrait Gallery. The Victorian laundry is open and exhibitions describe domestic life of the period, also gardens. Open Apr to Oct, daily 12–6. £1 *(NT)*

BENTHALL *Salop* Map 7 SJ60

Benthall Hall On B4375. 16th-C house with fine panelling, carved oak staircase, and 17th-C ceilings, on a much older site. Housed Royalist garrison during Civil War, but later taken by rebels. Garden contains shrubs and plants. Open 5 Apr to end Sep, Tue, Wed, Sat, BH Mon 2–6. 60p (garden only 20p). *(NT)*

BERKELEY *Gloucestershire* Map 3 ST69

Berkeley Castle On B4509, 1½m W of A38. Home of Berkeleys for over 800 years, splendid 12th-C and later castle, in which Edward II was murdered in 1327. Keep, dungeon, great hall, state apartments and medieval kitchens shown. Elizabethan terraced gardens include bowling alley, and nearby is an extensive deer park. ⚐ Open Apr and Sep, daily (ex Mon) 2–5, May to Aug Tue to Sat 11–5, Sun 2–5. Oct, Sun only 2–4.30, BH Mon 11–5. 80p (ch 40p). Admission prices for 1980 under review. No dogs. ⚠ *(Tel Dursley 810332). (Mr R J Berkely MFH)* & B

Jenner Museum Commemorates Edward Jenner (1749–1823), who discovered smallpox vaccine. The museum is housed in the cottage he erected for the first boy he vaccinated. Open 1 Apr to 30 Sep, daily (ex Mon) and BH 2.30–6. 10p (ch 14 5p). Parties can be booked out of hours if necessary. *(Tel 631)* &

BERKHAMSTED *Hertfordshire* Map 4 SP90

Berkhamsted Castle Remains of 11th-C motte and bailey castle with later circular keep. Former home of Black Prince and prison of King John of France. Open Mon to Fri 9–4.15. Closed weekends and BH. Free. *(AM)*

BERNEY ARMS WINDMILL Norfolk Map 5 TG40

Access by boat from Gt Yarmouth or by rail to Berney Arms station; road to mill unmade, gated, rough, and unsuitable for cars. Tall, late 19th-C marsh windmill in lonely part of Halvergate Marshes, near where River Yare is joined by River Waveney. Open Apr to Sep, daily 9.30–7. 15p (ch 16 and pen 5p). *(AM)*

BERWICK-UPON-TWEED *Northumberland* Map 12 NT95

Castle and Town Walls Remains of 12th-C stronghold incorporating three towers and west wall. Medieval town walls reconstructed during Elizabethan period. Open see inside front cover. Free. P. *(Tel 7881). (AM)*

Museum and Art Gallery Marygate. Local antiquities, ceramics and brasswork, and pictures, including representative display of French school. Open Jun to Sep, Mon to Fri 2–5. Sat 10–1. Free. P. *(Tel 7320)*

Museum of the King's Own Scottish Borderers The Barracks. Designed by Vanbrugh in 1717, said to be oldest barracks

in Britain. Open all year (ex BH and Suns) Mon to Fri 9–12 and 1–4.30, Sat 9–12; other times by prior arrangement with *Curator, Lt-Col D C R Ward*. 10p (ch 16 5p). P. *(Tel 7426/7)* & B

Town Hall Fine 18th-C building on site of three previous structures. Council chamber assembly room, and old town gaol. Open by prior arrangement with *Clerk of the Trustees*. 10p ⚠ *(Tel 6332 ext 50)* **(79)**

BEVERLEY *Humberside* Map 8 TA03

Art Gallery and Museum Champney Road. Local antiquities, Victorian bygones and china, pictures by F W Elwell of Beverley and others, and bust of Sir Winston Churchill by Bryant Baker of New York. Various solo Art Exhibitions. Open all year (ex Sun) Mon, Tue, Wed and Fri 9.30–5.30, Thu 9.30–12 noon, Sat 9.30–4. Free. P. *(Tel Hull 882255)*

Lairgate Hall Dates from 1710–80, now used as council offices. Interesting late 18th-C stucco ceiling, marble mantelpiece. Chinese room with hand-painted wallpaper. Open all year. Mon to Thu 8.45–5.30, Fri 9–4. Free. ⚠ *(Tel Hull 882255)*

The Museum of the East Yorkshire Regiment (The Prince of Wales Own Regiment of Yorkshire) 11 Butcher Row. The exhibits are arranged in six rooms which include one recalling the warmth and comfort of an Officers' Mess, one which houses the Library and another full of uniforms as well as having two dioramas. Open Tue–Fri (ex BH) 2–4 Free. Party. *(Tel Hull 882157)*

BEWDLEY *Hereford and Worcester* Map 7 SO77

Bewdley Museum The Shambles, Load Street. A folk museum, situated in a row of 18th-C shops. The crafts and industries of the Bewdley area are illustrated, including displays on charcoal burning, basket making, and coopering. Craftsmen's workshops within the museum and demonstrations of pottery throwing, glass blowing and the making of traditional straw corn-dollies can often be seen. Open 1 Mar to 30 Nov, Mon–Sat 10–5.30, Sun 2–5.30. 12p (ch and pen free). P. *(Tel 403573)*

West Midland Safari and Leisure Park On A456 to Kidderminster. 200-acre wildlife and leisure park. All-inclusive price includes animal reserves, pets corner, sea lion show, amusement park rides, splash cats, rowing boats, canoes, skate park, picnic and leisure areas and the 'Rio Grande' railway. ⚐ Open mid Mar to Oct daily 10–5. Admission prices not available. ⚠ free. *(Tel 402144)* &

BEXHILL-ON-SEA *East Sussex* Map 5 TQ70

Bexhill-on-Sea Museum Egerton Park. Local archaeological and natural history collection. Open all year, Mon–Sat (ex Fri) 10–4.30, Sun Jul to Sep 2–4.30. 10p (ch 4p). P. *(Tel 211769)*

Bexhill Manor Costume Museum Set in small gardens, the manor contains a display of costumes, 1740–1960 accessories, toys and dolls. Open Easter to 30 Sep, Tue to Fri and BH 10.30–1 and 2.30–5.30, Sat and Sun 2.30–5.30 (closed Mon, ex BH Mon). 25p (ch 5–16 15p). Admission prices under revision for 1980. ⚠ *(Tel 215361)* &

BIBURY *Gloucestershire* Map 4 SP10

Arlington Mill On A433. 17th-C corn mill on site on River Coln mentioned in 'Domesday Book'. Now a museum with working machinery, agricultural implements and bygones. Open daily Mar to Oct and winter weekends 10.30–7 (dusk in winter). 50p (ch 20p, pen 30p). ⚠ *(Tel 368)*

BICKLEIGH *Devon* Map 3 SS90
Bickleigh Castle Off A396. Take A3072 from Bickleigh Bridge, then fork left. Medieval romantic home of the heirs of the Earls of Devon. Great Hall, Armoury, Guard Room, thatched Jacobean Wing. Early Norman Chapel. Moat and Gardens. Open Easter to Sep, Wed, Sun, and BH Mon, also from Jul to 1st week Sep daily (ex Sat) 2–5. 80p (ch 40p, pen 60p). Prices subject to alteration for 1980. *(Tel 363). (Mr O N Boxall)* & B
Bickleigh Mill Craft Centre and Farm A picturesque old working watermill adapted to the production of craftwork (pottery, glass engraving, woodturning, jewellery making, corn dollies etc). One of the largest and most comprehensive working craft centres in the West Country adjacent to a heritage farm with rare breeds of animals and poultry where cows and goats are milked by hand and the

farm worked by shire horses complete with its own museum. A British Tourist Authority Award Winner. Open all year daily (ex 25 Dec to 5 Jan incl). 6 Jan to 21 Mar 2–5; 22 Mar to 24 Dec 10–6. Admission prices under review for 1980. ⚠ *(Tel 419)*

BICTON *Devon* Map 3 SY08
Railway, Countryside Museum, Hall of Transport and Gardens On A376 N of Budleigh Salterton. Large countryside museum. Narrow-guage railway. Italian garden laid out in 1735. Collection of veteran and vintage motor vehicles. Exotic greenhouses, children's adventure playground. Picnic areas. Vintage bus rides. Pinetum. ⚑ Open 1 Apr to 31 Oct daily 10–6. Admission prices for 1980 not yet decided. ⚠ *(Tel Colaton Raleigh 68465). (Clinton Devon Estates)* &

BIDDENDEN *Kent* Map 5 TQ83
Baby Carriage Collection Bettenham
Manor. A unique collection of 350 baby
carriages (prams) displays examples of the
craftsmanship of a bygone era. Exhibits
portray the history of the pram up to the
present day and include 18th-C stickwagons,
Victorian perambulators and mailcarts,
Edwardian bassinettes, Victorias and large
coachbuilt prams of twenties. The museum, in
a Kentish oast house, adjoins a 15th-C
moated manor house of historical and
architectural interest and is set in a 15-acre
garden. Collection open all year, house and
garden May to Sep, both by appointment only.
Free. *(Tel 291343). (Mr J Hampshire)* &

BIDEFORD *Devon* Map 2 SS42
Burton Art Gallery Victoria Park, Kingsley
Road. Built in 1951, to house a collection of
pictures and *objets d'art*. Other gifts and
loans have been made. Visiting exhibitions.
Open all year daily (ex Sun) Mon to Fri 10–1
and 2–5; Sat 9.45–12.45. Free. P. *(Tel 6711)*
& **(79)**

BIDFORD-ON-AVON *Warwickshire*
Map 4 SP15
Domestic Fowl Trust Dorsington Manor. 8m
W of Stratford-upon-Avon on unclass road off
B4085. Unique collection of domestic ducks,
geese, hens and turkeys, over sixty breeds in
all, covering some 4 acres. Many species to
be seen are in danger of extinction. ⚲ picnic
area and giftshop. Steam/vintage rally end of
May. Open Apr to Oct daily 10.30–6 (closed
Mon ex BH). 50p (ch 14 30p). ⚠ *(Tel 2442)* &
(79)

BIGGLESWADE *Bedfordshire* Map 4 TL14
*Shuttleworth Collection of Historic
Aeroplanes and Cars* Old Warden
Aerodrome 2m W from roundabout on (A1)
Biggleswade bypass. A highly interesting
collection of historical aircraft, cars, bicycles
and other items of transport. Open all year,
daily (except for one week at Christmas)
10–5. 75p (ch and pen 40p, ch 5 free). ⚲ and
shop. Special Flying Days (historic aircraft) on
last Sun in month, May to Sep. 2 Special
pageant days Jul and Sep; £5 per vehicle incl
occupants. Cyclists and pedestrians £1, ch
50p. Prices for flying days to be announced.
⚠ £1. *(Tel Northill 288)* &

BIGNOR *West Sussex* Map 4 SU91
Roman Villa and Museum Between A29 and
A285. Occupied in 2nd and 4th C, first
discovered in 1811; preserves some of finest
mosaic pavements in Britain, new mosaic
recently uncovered. Open 1 Mar to 31 Oct
(closed Mon ex Aug and BH) 10–5 (6.30 Apr
to Sep). Admission charges for 1980 not
available. ⚠ *(Tel Sutton 259)* &

BILLINGFORD MILL *Norfolk* Map 5 TM17
Built in 1860 as a replacement for a former
post mill destroyed in a storm. The five-
storeyed brick tower still contains most of the
original machinery and equipment. Open all
year 9–dusk, key available (see notice on
mill). Free. Parking on common. *(Tel Norwich
611122 ext 5224)*

BIRCHINGTON *Kent* Map 5 TR36
Powell-Cotton Museum Quex Park. 1m SE
of village, off B2048. Ethnography, and
natural history of Africa and Asia. Also on view
are furnished rooms in Quex house and the
gardens. Museum open Thu all year;
museum, house and gardens open 6 Apr to
28 Sep Wed, Thu, Sun and BH; 15 Jul to 5
Sep daily (ex Sat and Mon). 2.30–6. 45p (ch
25p). Party. *(Tel Thanet 42168)* & B

BIRKENHEAD *Merseyside* Map 7 SJ38
Birkenhead Priory Priory Street. Founded in
1150, the Priory provided accommodation for
a prior and 16 monks of the Benedictine
Order. Most of the buildings were neglected
after the Dissolution of the Monasteries and
only the ruins remain. Open all year May to
Sep, Tue to Fri, 10–1, 2–4; Oct to Apr, Tue to
Fri 10–1 (Sat all year 10–12). Free ⚠ *(Tel
051–6524177)* & B

Williamson Art Gallery and Museum Slatey
Road. Exhibits include: major collection of
work by English water-colourists and
Liverpool school of painters; sculpture;
decorative arts; ceramics (English,
Continental, Oriental wares); glass, silver and
furniture. Also a large collection of paintings
by P Wilson Steer, as well as approximately
25 special exhibitions throughout the year. A
local history and maritime museum
containing model ships, adjoins. Open all
year (ex 25, 26 Dec and BH) 10–5 (ex Thu
10–9, Sun 2–5). Free. ⚲ *(Tel 051–652 4177)*

BIRMINGHAM *West Midlands* Map 7 SP08
Aston Hall Aston. Jacobean mansion built by
Sir Thomas Holt, now museum. Panelled long
gallery and marble chimney pieces. ⚲ Open
daily 1 Apr to 31 Oct, Mon to Sat 10–1, 2–5,
Sun 2–5. 30p (ch and pen 15p, school parties
booked in advance free). ⚠

Birmingham Railways Museum Warwick
Road, Tyseley (SE of city, off A41); near
Tyseley station. Live steam depot with well-
known express passenger locomotives,
reproductions of historic coaches, and former
working machinery. Special opening days
featuring traction engines, vintage cars, etc.
Open all year (ex BH), Sun 2–5.30. 20p (ch
14 10p). Conducted parties by arrangement.
(Tel Northfield 3934). **(79)**

Blakesley Hall Yardley (6m SE). A timber-
framed yeoman's farmhouse, built *c*1575,

now partly furnished as a period house of the 17th C. Displays on the history of the house, local crafts and the ancient parish of Yardley. Open all year (ex 4 Apr, Christmas) Mon to Sat 1.30–5.30. 15p (ch and pen 5p). *(Tel 021–783 2193)*

Cannon Hill Nature Centre At the SW entrance to Cannon Hill Park, opposite Pebble Mill Road. The Nature Centre displays living animals of the British Isles and Europe in both outdoor and indoor enclosures. Conditions have been created to resemble natural habitats also to attract wild birds and butterflies etc, forming a miniature wildlife park. Open all year (ex Tue, 4 Apr and 25, 26 Dec) 10–6 (4 winter; also closes 5 Fri, summer). *(Tel 021–472 7775)*

Museum and Art Gallery Chamberlain Square. Important archaeological exhibits, collection of modern sculpture, and paintings (including large pre-Raphaelite section, numerous major works by Bellini, Guercino and Canaletto, English water-colour landscapes, and representatives of French and Dutch schools). ⚊ Open all year (ex 4 Apr and Christmas) Mon to Sat 10–5.30, Sun 2–5.30. Free. P. *(Tel 021–235 2834)* ⅗ See also **Sarehole Mill**

Museum of Science and Industry Newhall Street (close to Post Office Tower). Industrial, technological and scientific displays from the Industrial Revolution up to the present. Engineering hall is architecturally interesting (formerly a Victorian plating works) and contains machine tools, electrical equipment, working steam, gas and hot air engines. Locomotive hall has steam locomotives, including Pacific locomotive 'City of Birmingham', steam road locomotives, and working machinery. Transport section contains veteran cars, motorcycles, John Cobb's world speed record car, fire engine, Birmingham tramcar. Science section has working demonstrations of many aspects of science and electronics. Pen room displays writing instruments from all parts of the world. Music room with organs, musical boxes, pianola and various mechanical musical instruments. In the aircraft section is a World War II Spitfire and Hurricane, and collection of aircraft engines, including early jet, also displays of bicycles, small arms, clocks and watches. Steam weekends Mar and Oct. Traction Engine Rally May. Engines steamed 1st and 3rd Wed each month. Open all year (ex 4 Apr and Christmas) Mon to Fri 10–5 (9pm 1st Wed in month), Sat 10–5.30, Sun 2–5.30. Free. P. *(Tel 021–236 1022)*

Sarehole Mill Hall Green. Well-restored 18th-C water mill, last surviving in district. Opened as branch of Birmingham City Museum in Jul 1969, with exhibits on agricultural history and rural crafts. Milling parts on view include items from Pinto Collection. South wheel of mill operational. Open 1 Apr to 30 Nov, (ex 4 Apr) Wed to Sat 1.30–5.30. 20p (ch must be accompanied and pen 10p). ⚠ *(Tel 021–777 6612)*

Selly Manor and Minworth Greaves Sycamore Road, Bournville. Off A38. Two 13th- and early 14th-C timbered houses re-erected in Bournville. Collection of old furniture and domestic equipment. Open mid Jan to mid Dec, Tue, Wed, Fri 2–5 (ex BH). Parties by arrangement with curator. Free. P. *(Tel 021–472 0199)*

Weoley Castle Selly Oak, off A38. Remains of a fortified 13th-C manor house, with small site museum displaying finds from excavations. Open all year (ex 4 Apr,

Christmas also Mons and Tues), Wed, Thu, Fri, Sat 10–5. 10p (ch and pen 5p). P. (roadside). *(Tel 021–427 4270)*

BISHOP'S STORTFORD *Hertfordshire* Map 5 TL42

Rhodes Memorial Museum and Commonwealth Centre South Road. Early 19th-C house with exhibits illustrating life of Cecil Rhodes, also aspects of his life and work in Africa. Open all year (ex Sun & BH) Mon to Sat 10–4, Free.⚠ *(Tel 51746)* ⅗ B

BISHOP'S WALTHAM *Hampshire* Map 4 SU51

Bishop's Waltham Palace On A333. Dates from 12th C and consists of state apartments around cloister court, with great hall and four-storeyed tower. Surrendered to Parliamentary forces in 1644 during Civil War. Open, see inside front cover but closed Mon (ex BH) and Sat. 10p (ch 16 and pen 5p). ⚠ *(AM)*

BLACKBURN *Lancashire* Map 7 SD62

Lewis Museum of Textile Machinery Noted for series of period rooms portraying continuous development of textile industry from 18th C onwards. Open all year, Mon to Sat 9.30–6, closed Sun. Free. P. *(Tel 667130)*

Museum and Art Gallery Library Street. Local history, militaria, coins, ceramics, fine books and manuscripts, paintings, water-colours, and Japanese prints. Open all year, Mon to Sat 9.30–6. Closed Sun. Free. P. *(Tel 667130)*

BLACKPOOL *Lancashire* Map 7 SD33

Grundy Art Gallery Queen Street. Established 1911, this gallery exhibits a permanent collection of paintings by 19th- and 20th-C artists. Also touring exhibitions, one man shows, and group exhibitions. Open all year (ex BH) Mon to Sat 10–5. Free. ⚠ *(Tel 23977)*

Tower Buildings and Circus The tower stands 518ft high. The buildings at its base contain a spacious ballroom with bar. Ocean room cabaret lounge, children's daytime non-stop entertainment, tropical gardens and free flight aviary, aquarium, butterfly gardens, children's fun farm. ⚊ Open May to Oct Mon to Sun 9.30–11pm. Admission prices not yet known. P. *(Tel 25252)* ⅗

Zoopark East Park Drive. An interesting collection of 660 large and small mammals and birds. New house and enclosure for Lowland Gorillas. Miniature railway. Shop, picnic area. Open all year, daily (ex 25 Dec) from 10 onwards. 80p (ch 40p). ⚠ (20p). Prices subject to revision for 1980. Free ⚠ for coaches. Zoo bus service to and from Blackpool town centre, 1¼m. *(Tel 65027)* ⅗ B

BLANDFORD FORUM *Dorset* Map 3 ST80

Royal Signals Museum Blandford Camp. New museum of history of army signalling methods. Also photographs, paintings, and uniforms. Open all year (ex 4 Apr, Christmas holiday) Mon to Fri 10–1 and 2–5; Sat 10–12 by appointment. BH Sat 10–12. Free. P. *(Tel 2581 ext 248)*

BLICKLING *Norfolk* Map 9 TG12

Blickling Hall On B1354. Early 17th-C red-brick house in fine park. Dutch gables, state rooms with fine pictures and furnishings, fine Jacobean plaster ceiling in gallery. Formal gardens laid out in 1793 and re-designed in 1930, and park with crescent-shaped lake, and mausoleum of 1793 by Bonomi. Orangery and Temple designed by Ivory of

Norwich. Open Apr to 12 Oct, Tue to Thu, Sat, Sun, BH Mon Apr to 22 May and 1 to 12 Oct 2–6; 24 May to 30 Sep 11–6 (last admissions 5.30). House closed 12.30–1.30. £1.10. Gardens only Mon–Fri 24 May to 30 Sep 70p. Party 15+ 24 May to 30 Sep. No dogs. *(NT)*

BODIAM *East Sussex* Map 5 TQ72
Bodiam Castle Off A229. Picturesque moated structure, built 1386 and dismantled 1643, with gatehouse, and 37 fireplaces inside. Open Apr to end Oct, daily 10–7; Nov to end Mar, Mon to Sat 10–sunset. 60p ⚠ (fee) *(NT)*

BODMIN *Cornwall* Map 2 SX06
Military Museum The Keep, Victoria Barracks. The Duke of Cornwall's Light Infantry. Open 1 Apr–28 Feb, Mon to Fri 9–12.30 and 2–4.45 (ex BH and Mar). Free. ⚠ ⚐

BOLDRE *Hampshire* Map 4 SZ39
Spinners School Lane. Gardens entirely made and maintained by owners; azaleas, rhododendrons, camellias, magnolias etc. interplanted with primulas, blue poppies and other choice woodland and ground cover plants. Rare plants and shrubs for sale. Open 21 Apr to 14 Jul daily (ex Mon) 2–7. Other times by arrangement. 20p ⚠ No dogs. *(Mr and Mrs P G G Chappell). (Tel Lymington 73347). (NGS)* ⚐ B

BOLSOVER *Derbyshire* Map 8 SK47
Bolsover Castle On A632. Norman, but rebuilt and enlarged in 1613, partly by John Smythson. Fine fireplaces and ornate panelling, and range of buildings added after 1617, including remarkable 170ft-long Riding School and Gallery, with rows of dormer windows carrying pediments. Fine views. Open*, see inside front cover, 25p (ch 16 and pen 10p). ⚠ *(AM)*

BOLTON *Gt Manchester* Map 7 SD71
Hall I'th'Wood Museum 16th- and 17th-C house, partly half-timbered, associated with Crompton. Open all year (ex Thu, 25 & 26 Dec, 1 Jan & 13 Apr also Sun in winter) 1 Apr to 30 Sep weekdays 10–5.45, Sun 2–5.45; 1 Oct to 31 Mar 10–5. Free. P. *(Tel 51159)* (79)
Tonge Moor Textile Museum Tonge Moor Road. Includes Arkwright's waterframe (1768), Crompton's spinning mule (1779), and Hargreave's original spinning jenny. Open all year (ex Sun and BH) Mon, Tue, Thu 9.30–7.30, Wed 9.30–1, Fri 9.30–5, Sat 9.30–12.30. Free. P. (street) *(Tel 21394)* ⚐

BOOTLE *Merseyside* Map 7 SJ39
Bootle Library Stanley Road. This new library (opened Sep 1979) holds a continuous programme of exhibitions of paintings by

Merseyside and regional artists. Additionally selections from the Bootle permanent collections, notably English pottery and porcelain (particularly Liverpool pottery) are on display. Open normal Library hours Mon, Wed, Fri 10–7; Tue 10–5; Thu and Sat 10–1. P. ⚐

BOROUGHBRIDGE *North Yorkshire* Map 8 SE36
Devil's Arrows Off A1 to SW of town, famous trio of probably Bronze Age monoliths, 16–22ft high, spanning some 360ft, probably part of what may have been a double alignment.

BOROUGH GREEN *Kent* Map 5 TQ65
Great Comp Off B2016. 7-acre garden replanned and maintained by owners for many years. Shrubs, heathers herbaceous plants, and fine lawns and paths. Early 17th-C house (not open). Open 1 May to 15 Oct, Fri, Sun and BH these dates. ⚐ on Sun. 50p (ch 20p). No dogs. *(Mr and Mrs Cameron). (NGS)* ⚐

BOSCASTLE *Cornwall* Map 2 SX09
Museum of Witchcraft and Black Magic Illustrates the past and present customs of witches and their implements in the South West. Open Easter to 24 Oct, daily 10–7. 30p. Under revision for 1980. Dogs on leads only. ⚠ *(Tel Buckfastleigh 3452)*

BOSCOBEL *Salop* Map 7 SJ80
Boscobel House Off A5. House, c 1600, which preserves place where Charles II hid in 1651. Descendant of Royal oak in grounds. Open, see inside front cover (closed daily 1–2). 25p (ch 16 and pen 10p). ⚠ *(AM)*
Whiteladies Priory (St Leonard's Priory) Remains of an Augustinian nunnery, dating from 1158. Largely destroyed in the Civil War. Charles II stayed here on his way to Boscobel House. Open any reasonable time. Free. Guide book available at nearby **Boscobel House**. *(AM)*

BOSTON *Lincolnshire* Map 8 TF34
Fydell House South Square. Georgian house, dating from 1726, now Pilgrim College. Open during term time, weekdays 10–5; other times by appointment with Warden. Free. P. *(Tel 63116)*
Guildhall South Street. Borough art gallery and museum in fine 15th-C building. Cells in which first Pilgrim Fathers were held prisoner in 1607 still here. Open all year Mon to Sat 9.30–12.15 and 1.15–5 (Oct to Apr, 9.30–12 and 1.30–4.30 Mon to Fri, Sat 9.30–12 only). 10p (ch 16 free). P. *(Tel 64601)*

BOUGHTON HOUSE Northamptonshire Map 4 SP98
15th-C monastery greatly enlarged between

BODIAM CASTLE
East Sussex

This exciting castle, most advanced in design, was built in 1386 for the defence of the Rother valley. It is surrounded by a moat and inside access has recently been extended to the entrance tower. NT property.

For admission please refer to the gazetteer entry.

1530 and 1695. Celebrated collection of paintings, furniture, tapestries, carpets, porcelain and painted ceilings. State rooms. Beautiful grounds, picnic area, woodland adventure playground. Open Easter, Spring holiday weekends, and Aug, Sep and Oct afternoons. Telephone for detailed dates, times and admission prices. P. *(Tel Kettering 82248)* &

BOUGHTON MONCHELSEA *Kent*
Map 5 TQ74
Boughton Monchelsea Place Off A229. Battlemented Elizabethan and Regency manor house still inhabited, with breathtaking views of its 18th-C deer park and the Kentish Weald. Records preserved since 1570. Also collection of dresses and ancient vehicles. Open Easter to 7 Oct, Sat, Sun, BH (each Wed in Aug) 2.30 – 6. Parties by arrangement anytime. House and grounds 70p (ch 14 30p). Grounds only 35p (ch 10p). Under revision for 1980. No dogs in house. ⚠ *(Tel Maidstone 43120)*. *(Mr M B Winch)* & B (gardens)

BOURN *Cambridgeshire* Map 5 TL35
Bourn Windmill Off B1046. Old post mill dating from 1636 – probably earliest example to have survived. Open during reasonable daylight hours. Notice re local keyholders displayed at mill. Free. P. (roadside only)

BOURNEMOUTH *Dorset* Map 4 SZ09
Big Four Railway Museum Dalkeith Hall, Dalkeith Steps, rear of 81A Old Christchurch Road. Contains over 1,000 railway items, including one of the largest collections of locomotive nameplates, work plates etc, in the country. A large working model railway is in operation. Also models, book and relic shop. Open all year 10 – 5, 1 Jun to 30 Sep daily (1 Oct to 31 May, Wed and Sat only) 50p (ch 16 30p). P. *(Tel 27995)*
British Typewriter Museum Now situated in the Rothesay Museum, almost opposite Bournemouth Pier. There are over 300 typewriters on display which were collected by Mr W A Beeching, author of 'Century of the Typewriter' and donated to Bournemouth Corporation. This is the only museum in the world devoted to typewriters and it is open daily (ex Sun). P. (3 municipal). *(Tel 21009)*
Bournemouth Mobile Museum A double-decker bus built in 1960 and converted into a mobile museum in 1976 – 77. Bournemouth's Open-Air Museum illustrating 10,000 years of history. The museum is parked at different areas in the town during the week. Open all year as and when advertised. 15p (ch 5p, ch 5 free). The museum may be hired at a daily block charge of £10 plus transit charge outside Bournemouth area. Prices under revision for 1980. *(Tel 21009)*

Rothesay Museum 8 Bath Road. Lucas collection of early Italian paintings and pottery, English china and furniture, New Zealand room, armoury room and marine room including relics from Sir Cloudesley Shovell's flagship, *HMS Association*, sunk in 1707. The British Typewriter Museum (Beeching Collection) now occupies part of the first floor of this museum. Open all year (ex 4 Apr, 25 and 26 Dec and Sun) Mon to Sat 10.30 – 5. 20p (ch 5 – 14 5p) 1 Nov to 31 Mar free (ex Thu 20p). Admission charges under review for 1980. P. *(Tel 21009)*
Russell-Coates Art Gallery and Museum Built in 1894 as East Cliff Hall, contains period rooms, section on Oriental art, Henry Irving theatrical collection, freshwater aquarium. ☜ Open all year (ex 4 Apr, 25 & 26 Dec, and Sun), Mon to Sat 10.30 – 5. Free 1 Nov to 31 Mar (ex Thu 10p); 1 Apr to 31 Oct. 20p (ch 14 5p, ch 5 free). Subject to alteration in 1980. P. *(Tel 21009)*

BOURTON-ON-THE-WATER
Gloucestershire Map 4 SP12
Birdland Zoo Gardens and Wildlife Art Gallery On A429. 4-acre garden with over 600 species of foreign and exotic birds. Ponds, groves, aviaries and tropical house. Open daily (ex 25.Dec) Mar to Nov 10 – 6; Dec, Jan and Feb 10 – 4. 60p (ch 14 30p, pen 50p). Party. Dogs on lead (at owner's risk). Art gallery open daily 11 – 5. P. *(Tel 20689)* &
Model Village In garden of old New Inn, built to scale of one ninth original. Includes miniature replica of River Windrush and working model waterwheel, and churches, shops, and New Inn faithfully portrayed in Cotswold stone. ☜ in Hotel. Open all year, summer 9.30 – 6.30 (9.30 – dusk winter). 30p (ch 14 20p). Under revision for 1980. *(Tel 20467)* &
Motor Museum 30 cars and motorcycles ranging from vintage to the 1950s, also large collection of old advertising signs together with a vast number of other interesting items from yester-year. All housed in an 18th-C water mill on the River Windrush in beautiful Cotswold country. Open all year, Jun to Sep 9.30 – 7; Sep to May 10 – 6. 45p (ch 16 30p, ch 5 free). Max family price £1.50. Party. P. *(Tel 21255)* &

BOVINGTON CAMP *Dorset* Map 3 SY88
The Tank Museum (Royal Armoured Corps and Royal Tank Regiment) Off A352. Over 140 armoured fighting vehicles (wheeled and tracked) dating from 1915 onwards. Separate displays of armament, power plant, and associated equipment. ☜ Open all year (ex Christmas week), Mon to Fri 10 – 12.30 and 2 – 4.45 Sat, Sun and BH 10.30 – 12.30 and 2 – 4. Times may change for 1980. 20p ⚠ *(Tel Bindon Abbey 462721 ext 463)* &

BOWES *Co Durham* Map 12 NY91
Bowes Castle On A66. Norman keep, built
between 1171 and 1187, in angle of Roman
fort of 'Lavatrae'. Open, see inside front
cover. Free. *(AM)*

BOWNESS-ON-WINDERMERE *Cumbria*
Map 7 SD49 (see also WINDERMERE)
Belle Isle Beautiful 38-acre island situated in
the middle of Lake Windermere. The unique
house was the first completely round house
built in England and contains portraits of the
Curwen family, views of Lake Windermere by
Philip de Loutherburg and specially designed
furniture by Gillow of Lancaster. Nature trail.
Children's playground. Motor launch runs
continuously from far end of Bowness
promenade. ⚲ Open May to Sep, Sun, Mon,
Tue, Thu 10.30 – 5. 60p (ch 30p) boat trip to
island. Guided tour of house 11.15, 12.30,
2.30 and 4pm, 30p P. *(Tel 3353)*
Hill Top 2m SW. Here Beatrix Potter wrote
many of the Peter Rabbit books. The 17th-C
house contains some of her original drawings,
furniture, china and pictures. Owing to the
small size of this house it may be necessary to
restrict the numbers visiting at any one time.
Visitors are warned that considerable delays
may occur at peak visiting times and that
there is no electric light in the house. Shop.
Open Apr to end Oct daily (ex Fri) 10 – 5.30,
Sun 2 – 5.30 or dusk if earlier. 80p (ch 40p).
No indoor photography. Enquiries to the
Curator *(Tel Hawkshead 334)*

BRADFORD *West Yorkshire* Map 7 SE13
Bolling Hall Bowling Hall Road. Period
house dating from 15th-C containing local
history museum with fine furniture including
rare Chippendale bed, heraldic glass and
'ghost room'. Open all year daily (ex 25/26
Dec and 4 Apr) 10 – 5, (enquire for summer
opening times). Free. P. *(Tel 23057)*
Cartwright Hall Lister Park. Contains
permanent collections of European and
British paintings, sculpture, drawings,
modern prints and ceramics. Recent
acquisition Joshua Reynolds' painting 'The
Brown Boy'. Also temporary exhibitions of
natural history, geology and archaeology. ⚲
Open, as Bolling Hall above. Free. ⚠ *(Tel
493313)* ⚲
Industrial Museum Moorside Mills,
Eccleshill. Museum of Industrial Archaeology
featuring the growth of the worsted industry of
the area. Textile, Motive Power and Transport
galleries. Tank locomotive, veteran and
vintage cars. Trolleybus and tram shed. Mill
house furnished early 1900. ⚲ Open all year
daily (ex 25/26 Dec and 4 Apr) 10 – 5. Free. ⚠
*(Tel 631756, school visits may be booked on
this number)* ⚲

BRADFORD-ON-AVON *Wiltshire*
Map 3 ST86
Barton Tithe Barn 14th-C building, once
property of Shaftesbury Abbey, since
presented to Wiltshire Archaeological
Society. Open any reasonable time. Free.
(AM)
The Hall Grounds of Elizabethan house, *c*
1600, formerly known as Kingston Hall, used
as model for British exhibit at 1900 Paris
Exhibition. Grounds only open all year 9 – 5.
Free. ⚠ No dogs. ⚲
Great Chalfield Manor 2½ NE. Restored
stone-built 15th-C house, with moat and great
hall. Small 13th-C church adjacent. Open 16
Apr to 24 Sep, Wed 12 – 1 and 2 – 5. 70p. *(NT)*

**BRADGATE PARK and SWITHLAND
WOODS** *Leicestershire* Map 8 SK51
850-acre country park with Old John Tower
(1786), and ruins of Bradgate House, brick
mansion, completed *c* 1510 by son of 1st
Marquis of Dorset, birthplace of Lady Jane
Grey (1537 – 54). Open all year to
pedestrians; no cars, except those carrying
invalids – special arrangements can be made.
Ruins open Apr to Oct, Wed, Thu, Sat
2.30 – 5, Sun 10 – 12.30. Free. (5 car parks,
Park and Swithland woods). ⚠ 10p. *(Tel
Leicester 871313 The Ranger)* ⚲
Also *Marion's Cottage* Newtown Linford.
Contains exhibitions and information, shop,
bookstall. Open all year, Apr to Oct, Wed,
Thu, Sat, Sun 2 – 6 (Sat, Sun 2 – 5 Nov to Mar).
⚠ ⚲

BRADWELL-ON-SEA *Essex* Map 5 TL90
Bradwell Lodge Off B1021, S of town. Early
16th-C house of Tudor and Georgian periods,
with wing (1785) by Robert Adam. Bow-
windowed belvedere used by Gainsborough
in 18th C. Saxon St Peter's Church (AD654)
on sea-wall 1½m E of house. House open by
appointment only. 50p (ch 12 25p). ⚠ *Mr and
Mrs J Mann)*

BRAMBER *West Sussex* Map 4 TQ11
Bramber Castle Formerly owned by Dukes
of Norfolk, ruined Norman stronghold on
South Downs ridge with wide views. Open
always. Free. *(NT)*
House of Pipes Museum with 25,000
exhibits covering 150 countries and 1,500
years, believed to be the only 'smokiana'
exhibition in the world. It is a fascinating study
of social history in everyday life, set in a
19th-C shopping arcade. Awarded a British
Tourist Authority Commendation. Open all
year daily (ex 25 Dec) 9 – 8 (6.30 Oct to Apr).
20p (ch 4 – 14 10p). Under revision for 1980.
Party. ⚠ ⚲
BRAMHALL *Gt Manchester* Map 7 SJ88
Bramhall Hall S of Stockport off A5102. 14th

BRAMALL HALL
STOCKPORT, CHESHIRE

For over 500 years, the home of the Davenport
family, and now owned and administered by the
Metropolitan Borough of Stockport. This magpie-style
building is outstanding in its parkland setting. Some
2 miles south-east of the centre of Stockport, the Hall
is open April to Sept. Daily 10am-12 noon. Schools and
other organised parties (by appointment). 12 noon-5pm
general public. Closed Mondays. Sat & Sun & Bank
Holidays 12 noon-5pm. Oct-March. Daily 10am-12 noon.
Schools and other organised parties (by appointment).
12 noon-4pm general public. Closed Mondays and
December. Sat, Sun & appropriate Bank Holidays
12 noon-4pm.

Admission 30p Adults: 15p Children and subject to price review. Free parking.

and 15th-C house with fine timber and plaster work. Extensive restoration work is in hand. Open Apr to Sep Tue to Sun and BH 12–5, Oct to Mar, Tue to Sun and BH 12–4. 30p (ch 15p) plus VAT. Parties 10–12. ⚠ *(Tel 061–485 3708)* ⚐ B

BRAMHAM *West Yorkshire* Map 8 SE44
Bramham Park On A1 4m S of Wetherby. This Queen Anne House, containing fine furniture, pictures and porcelain, is the home of Mr and Mrs George Lane Fox, decendants of the builder, Robert Benson (Lord Bingley). The gardens, landscaped in the French style, extend to 65 acres and contain ornamental ponds and cascades, temples and beech avenues. Gift shop. ☞ Open Easter BH then 1 May to end Sep, Sun, Tue, Wed, Thu and BH Mon. Closed 27 May to 3 Jun during Bramham Horse Trials. Grounds 11–6, House 1.15–5.30. Admission price for 1980 not yet decided. ⚠ Free. Further details and party rates from *House Administrator, Estate Office, Bramham Park, Wetherby, West Yorkshire.* (Tel Boston Spa 844265)

BRAMHOPE *West Yorkshire* Map 8 SE24
Puritan Chapel On A660. In grounds of former hall, well-restored, almost unique chapel (1646–49), with many 17th-C fittings, such as box pews and a two-decker pulpit. Illustrated pamphlet and post cards available. Open 1 Apr to 31 Oct, Wed, Sat, Sun, BH, 10–12 and 1–4 (5, Jun to Sep). P. *(Tel Leeds 678791)*

BRAMPTON *Cambridgeshire* Map 4 TL27
Pepys' House On A141. Old gabled cottage where parents of Samuel Pepys once lived, and where famous diarist once buried his gold for fear of Dutch invasion. He owned house from 1664 until his death in 1703. Open all year, Mon to Sat (ex BH) by prior appointment only. ⚠ for one car only (no coaches). *(Tel Huntingdon 53431)*

BRAMPTON *Cumbria* Map 12 NY56
Lanercost Priory 2½m NE. Was a house of Augustinian Canons founded about 1166 by William de Vaux. Remains of quire and transepts. Open, see inside front cover. 15p (ch 16 and pen 5p). ⚠ *(AM)*

BRASTED *Kent* Map 5 TQ45
Emmetts 4-acre hillside shrub garden. Open Apr and Jul to Oct, Wed and Sun, May and Jun Tue to Thu and Sun, 2–6 (last admissions 5). 40p. *(NT)*

BRATTON *Wiltshire* Map 3 ST95
Bratton Camp and White Horse Off B3098. 18th-C White Horse below Iron Age Camp. Open at all reasonable times. Free. ⚠ *(AM)*

BREAMORE *Hampshire* Map 4 SU11
Breamore House, Countryside and Carriage Museums On A338. Elizabethan Manor House (1583), with fine collection of works of art, including paintings, china and tapestries. Countryside Museum displays rural arts and agricultural machinery, and Carriage Museum with old coaches. ☞ (teas). Open 1 Apr to 30 Sep, Tue to Thu, Sat, Sun and all BH 2–5.30. Admission to house £1 (ch 50p), Countryside Museum 70p (ch 35p), Carriage Museum 50p (ch 25p), combined ticket £1.30 (ch 65p). ⚠ *(Tel 270)*. *(Sir Westrow Hulse)* ⚐

BREAN *Somerset* Map 3 ST35
Brean Down Bird Garden Situated at the base of Brean Down, adjacent to the sea and 7 miles of sand. The Downs is NT property and a bird sanctuary. The garden was built in 1972 and there are 250–300 birds from all parts of the world kept in very long flights. ☞ Open Apr to Oct daily 10–6. 35p (ch 20p). P. *(Tel 209)*

BRENDON *Hereford and Worcester* Map 3 SO93
Tithe Barn 14th-C building with fine porches and outside staircase. Open all year, daily until sunset. 10p. *(NT)*

BRENZETT *Kent* Map 5 TR02
Brenzett Aeronautical Museum Ivychurch Road. Founded in 1972. Exhibits relics of many famous aircraft including: Focke-Wulf FW190, Zeppelin, Messerschmitt 109E/410, Junkers 88, Spitfire and many more. Also aero engines, aircraft armaments and other aeronautical items. Open Easter to 31 Oct, Sun and BH 11–6; Jul and Aug, Tue, Wed and Thu 2–5. 25p (ch 10p). ⚠ *(Tel Tenterden 3197)* ⚐

BRESSINGHAM *Norfolk* Map 5 TM07
Bressingham Gardens and Live Steam Museum On A1066. 6 acres of informal gardens near live steam museum. There are three steam-hauled trains: a 9½-inch gauge, a 15-inch gauge running through two miles of the wooded Waveney Valley and a 2ft-gauge through two miles of Europe's largest hardy plant nursery. Also collection of 40 road and rail engines, mostly restored to working order. Voigt street organ. Exhibition hall. Steam roundabout. ☞ Open early May to late Sep, Sun 1.30–6; late May to mid Sep also Thu 1.30–5.30; Aug also Wed 1.30–5.30; also 15 Apr and BH (ex winter) from 1.30pm. Admission prices for 1980 not yet available. ⚠ *(Tel 386)*. *(Mr Alan Bloom)* ⚐

BRIDGNORTH *Salop* Map 7 SO79
Midland Motor Museum Stanmore Hall, 1½m on A458 Stourbridge Road. A collection of

very well restored sports cars and sports and racing motor cycles, housed in the converted stable of Stanmore Hall and surrounded by beautiful grounds. 8-acre bird garden set around 1½-acre lake. ⚑ Open all year, daily (ex 25 Dec) 10 – 6, dusk if earlier. Admission prices not yet decided. (ch and pen approx half price). ⚠ *(Tel 61761)* ⓑ

Severn Valley Railway The leading Standard Gauge Steam Railway, with one of the largest collections of locomotives and rolling stock in the country. Services from Bewdley to Bridgnorth through 12½ miles of picturesque scenery along the river Severn. Intensive services of passenger trains every weekend from the beginning of Mar to end Oct and most weekdays from May to Sep, in addition to all P & BH. Special events planned for Apr, Jun and Sep. Family tickets available in addition to special party discounts. 1980 charges not yet decided. *(Tel Bewdley 403816 and Bridgnorth 4361)* ⓑ

BRIDGWATER *Somerset* Map 3 ST33
Admiral Blake Museum Blake Street. 15th-C house, birthplace in 1598 of Admiral Blake, now museum of relics of admiral's time, exhibits of local interest, and items relating to Battle of Sedgemoor. Exhibition of watercolours by John Chubb, Mayor of Bridwater 1788. Open all year (ex BH), Tue to Sat 11 – 4. Free (no ch 14 unless with adult). P. *(Tel 56127)* **(79)**

BRIDLINGTON *Humberside* Map 8 TA16
Sewerby hall, Park and Zoo Georgian House dating from 1714 – 20 and 1808, now Art Gallery and Museum of history and archaeology, Amy Johnson Trophy Room. Gardens of botanical interest, especially the Old English walled garden. Miniature Zoo and Aviary in gardens. Band concerts, Sun May to Aug. ⚑ Clock Tower Tavern. 'Sewerby Trains' operate from Limekiln Lane, Bridlington to Park Gates. Grounds open all year 9 – dusk, 25p (ch 10p) to Park from Spring BH to mid-Sep when games facilities are available to public. Prices under revision for 1980. Party. Enquiries to Director of Parks and Recreation *(Tel 73769 enquiries, 78255 for booking)* ⓑ B

BRIDPORT *Dorset* Map 3 SY49
Museum and Art Gallery South Street. Housed in a Tudor building, thought to have once been the house of the chantry priests of the oratory of St Leonards. Its exhibits concentrate on the local trade of nets, ropes and twines, and old 'Jumper' net making loom, which has been in use since 1830. There are also exhibits of archaeology, geology, natural history, former domestic and agricultural tools, Victorian costume, a dolls house and a collection of dolls in native and historical dress. The art gallery contains paintings from the collection of the donor of the building Capt A P Codd. Open all year, daily (ex Sun and Thu also Sat pm) 10.30 – 1; Jun – Sep also 2.30 – 4.30. 20p (ch 12 10p). P. *(Tel 22116)* ⓑ

BRIGHOUSE *West Yorkshire* Map 7 SE12
1m NW of M62 (junc 25)
Brighouse Art Gallery Halifax Road. Contains a permanent collection of work by mainly 19th-C English artists, but also shows temporary exhibitions throughout the year. Open all year (ex 25, 26 Dec and 1 Jan) Mon to Sat 10 – 5 Sun 2.30 – 5 (closed Sun Oct to Mar). Free. ⚠ *(Tel 719222)* ⓑ

BRIGHTON *East Sussex* Map 4 TQ30
Aquarium and Dolphinarium Marine Parade. Dolphins may be seen performing in a massive pool. Their show culminates in a

leap of 18ft. Also an aquarium of 80 large tanks containing marine life. ℒ and licensed bar. Open all year 9 – 6.30. 80p (ch 40p). P. *(Tel 604233)* & (by arrangement)

Booth Museum of Natural History Dyke Road. Contains British birds mounted in natural settings, evolution gallery and temporary exhibitions. New Gallery 'The Unnatural History of an English County'. Bookshop with extensive stock of books on Natural History, especially birds. Open all year, Mon to Fri 10 – 5, Sun 2 – 5. (Temporarily closed Thu). Free. P (in street). *(Tel 552586/603005 ext 64)* &

Museum and Art Gallery Church Street. The collections include Old Master Paintings, watercolours, Sussex archaeology and folklife, ethnography and musical instruments. Also the Willet Collection of pottery and porcelain and display of 20th-C fine and applied art, including Art Nouveau and Art Deco. Also various special exhibitions. ℒ Open all year (ex 4 Apr, 25 & 26 Dec and Mons) Tue to Sat 10 – 5.45, Sun 2 – 5 (6 in summer). Free. Parking meters outside main entrance. *(Tel 603005)* & B

Preston Manor Off A23. Georgian house with additions in 1905. Houses a notable collection of furniture, portraits, and family memorabilia. Open all year, (ex 4 Apr, 25/26 Dec, 1 Jan also Mon and Tue), Wed to Sat 10 – 5, Sun 2 – 5. 35p (ch 15p, pen 25p). Party 20 + 30p. Joint admission ticket with Royal Pavilion 90p. ⚠ in drive. *(Tel 552101)*

Royal Pavilion Marine Palace of the Prince Regent (George IV). Henry Holland's Palladian villa (1787) transformed by John Nash with an Indian-style exterior and fantastic Chinoiserie internal decorations. Now restored to former splendour. Important collection of furniture, some returned on loan by HM the Queen. Regency exhibition Jul to end Sep. ℒ Easter to early Nov. Open all year Oct to 28 Jun daily 10 – 5 (8, 1 Jul to 30 Sep). Closed 25, 26 Dec, 29, 30 Jun. Admission varies according to season. 70/90p (ch 25. 35p). Charges from Apr 1980 under review. P. *(Tel 603005)* & B

Volks Railway First electric railway in Great Britain. Opened in 1883. Runs along sea front from Aquarium to Black Rock Marina (1¼ miles, 2ft 8½in guage). Open Easter to end Sep. Daily 10 – 6.30. P. *(Tel 681061)*

BRILL *Buckinghamshire* Map 4 SP61
Boarstall Duck Decoy and Nature Reserve Exhibition hall, collection of wildfowl, woodland walk, incorporating seven numbered stops where certain features, trees and plants will be of particular interest. Many different types of birds have been recorded at the Decoy. Demonstrations Sun 4, BH 11, 12, 2 and 4. Picnic area. Open 1 Mar to 28 Aug, Tue to Sun 10 – 5, also open BH Mons. 40p (ch 20p, ch 5 free). ⚠ *(Tel 237488)*

Brill Windmill Off B4011. One of the oldest post mills in England, with parts dating back to c1680. Worked until 1916 and now owned by the Buckinghamshire County Council. Open Apr to Sep, Sun 2.30 – 5.30, and other times by appointment. 20p (ch 14 5p). *(Tel Aylesbury 22171)*

Dorton House Off B4011. 17th- to 18th-C house with later alterations, now Ashfold School. Open May to Jul, and Sep, Sat, Sun 2 – 5. 40p (ch 14 and pen 20p). ⚠. *(Tel 237)* & B

BRIMHAM *North Yorkshire* Map 8 SE26
Rocks Off B6265. Grotesquely shaped rocks on heathery moorland at height of 950ft.

Described in Victorian guide-books as 'a place wrecked with grim and hideous forms defying all description and definition'. Old shooting lodge being converted into information point and shop. Always accessible. ⚠ 50p *(NT)*

BRINKBURN *Northumberland* Map 12 NZ19
Priory Church Off B6344. Well-restored Augustinian priory church, founded 1135 in bend of River Coquet, fine example of period. Roof replaced in 1858, but remaining medieval fittings include font, double piscina and some grave slabs. Open* see inside front cover. 15p (ch 16 and pen 5p). ⚠ *(AM)*

BRISTOL *Avon* Map 3 ST57
Blaise Castle House Henbury. 4m NW of city, off B4957. 18th-C mansion, now folk museum, situated in extensive grounds. Open all year (ex 1 Jan, 4 Apr, 5 May, 26, 27 May, 25 – 27 Dec). Mon to Sat 2 – 5. Free. ⚠ *(Tel 506789)* & B

Bristol Industrial Museum Prince's Wharf, Prince Street. A converted dockside transit shed in the heart of Bristol, 400yd from SS Great Britain. Display of vehicles, horse-drawn and motorised, from the Bristol area, locally built aircraft, aero engines, railway exhibits include full size industrial locomotive Henbury steamed c. once a month. Various kinds of machinery illustrating local trade and manufacturing. Open all year Sat to Wed incl, 10 – 12 and 1 – 5 (closed Thu, Fri also 1 Jan, 4 Apr, 25 – 27 Dec). Free. P. *(Tel 299771 ext 290)*

Cabot Tower More than 100ft high and dating from 1897 – 8, commemorates quatercentenary of Cabot's discovery of North America on 24 Jun 1497. Fine viewpoint. Open all year, daily 9 – dusk. 5p. P. (meters) **(79)**

City Museum and Art Gallery Queen's Road. Fine collections of archaeological, geological, natural history, scientific, and transport exhibits, and also pictures, ceramics, sculpture, fine art, and an aquarium. There will be numerous special exhibitions. Museum shop, coffee shop. Open all year, Mon to Sat (ex 1 Jan, 4 Apr, 5, 26, 27 May, 25 – 27 Dec). 10 – 5. Free. ⚠ *(Tel 299771)* &

John Wesley's Chapel Broadmead. The oldest Methodist Chapel in the world, built 1739, rebuilt 1748, in each case by John Wesley. Living rooms added above in 1748 and both chapel and living rooms are preserved in their original form. John Wesley frequently resided in the rooms, also used as headquarters of his work in West and Midlands. Charles Wesley looked after chapel and rooms and lived nearby 1739 – 71. Wesley Day celebrations 24 May. Open all year, daily (ex Sun, Wed and BH) 10 – 4. Free. ⚠ *(Tel 24740)*

Red Lodge Park Row. 16th-C house altered in the early 18th C, with fine oak carvings and furnishings of both periods. Open all year (ex Sun and 1 Jan, 4 Apr, 5, 26, 27 May, 25 – 27 Dec). Mon to Sat 2 – 5. Free. *(Tel 299771)*

SS Great Britain In floating harbour off Cumberland Road. Designed by I K Brunel, she was the first iron, screw-propelled ocean-going ship; launched in 1843, her long career, with many vicissitudes, ended after a ship-wreck in the Falkland Islands, from where she was raised and towed back in 1970 to the dock in which she was built. ℒ and gift shop. Museum, dockside displays. Open all year (ex 24 and 25 Dec), daily 10 – 6 (5 in winter). 60p (ch and pen 30p). Prices under revision for 1980. Party. ⚠ *(Tel 20680)*

St Nicholas Church Museum St Nicholas Street. Contains the history of Bristol from its beginning until the Reformation including Bristol church art, especially silver of all periods. Also a changing display of watercolours and drawings showing topographical features of the city mainly during the 18th/19th C, and the Hogarth altar piece originally painted for St Mary Redcliffe. Brass rubbing centre. Open Mon to Sat (ex 1 Jan, 4 Apr, 5, 26, 27 May, 25 – 27 Dec). 10 – 5. Free. P. ᗷ

The Georgian House 7 Gt George Street. Georgian house with 18th-C furniture and fittings. Open all year Mon to Sat 10 – 5 (ex Sun, and 1 Jan, 4 Apr, 5, 26, 27 May, 25 – 27 Dec). Free. Street parking (meters). *(Tel 299771)*

Vine House Henbury (3m NW of city, off B4055). Planted by resident family since 1946, 2-acre garden with trees, shrubs, water and naturalised garden. Open all year by arrangement. 25p (ch 16 and pen 10p). *(Tel 503573). (Professor and Mrs T F Hewer). (NGS)* ᗷ

Westbury College Westbury-on-Trym (3m N of city, off B4055). 15th-C gatehouse of 13th-C Priest's College. Key with *Vicar, 12 Eastfield Road. (NT)*

Zoological Gardens Clifton Down. Extensive gardens, and varied collection of animals, reptiles, and fishes. ⬚ & licensed bar. Open daily (ex 25 Dec), Mon – Sat from 9am, Sun from 10am (closing times vary with season). Admission prices not yet decided. No dogs admitted. P. *(Tel 38951)*

BROADSTAIRS *Kent* Map 5 TR36
Bleak House Overlooks town, noted for associations with Charles Dickens also Coastal Maritime Section in Garden. Open Easter weekend than 14 May to 30 Sep, daily 2 – 5. 50p (ch 12 25p). Party. P. *(Tel Thanet 62224)*

Dickens House Museum Immortalised by Charles Dickens in 'David Copperfield' as the home of Betsey Trotwood. Contains Dickens' letters and former possessions, local and Dickensian prints, costumes and Victoriana. The parlour is refurbished as described in 'David Copperfield'. Open Apr to Oct, daily 2.30 – 5.30. (Tue, Wed, Thu evenings 7 – 9, Jun to Sep.) Parties by arrangement. Prices of admission under revision for 1980. P. *(Hon Curator Tel Thanet 62853)*

BROADWAY *Hereford and Worcester* Map 4 SP03
Broadway Tower Country Park 65ft tower built in 18th C by the 6th Earl of Coventry, housing an observation room, history of the tower 'period exhibitions' and a shop (selling books, souvenirs, etc). A countryside

exhibition is located in the 150-year-old Tower barn. Tower Barn Natural History Centre with live and static displays on British mammals, birds, deer, sheep etc. Nature walks and picnic areas. ⬚ Open Apr to end Sep 10 – 6. 40p (ch 20p). Party. ⚠ *(Tel 2390)* ᗷ B

BROCKHAMPTON *Hereford and Worcester* Map 3 SO65
Lower Brockhampton 3m E Bromyard. On high ground, north side of A44; entrance by Bromyard Lodge. Half-timbered 14th-C house with a rare 15th-C gatehouse. Medieval hall open all year (ex Jan and 4 Apr), Mon, Wed, Fri, Sat and BH Mon 10 – 1 and 2 – 6, Sun 10 – 1. 60p (ch 30p). *(NT)*

BROKERSWOOD *Wiltshire* Map 3 ST85
Phillips Countryside Museum and Woodland Park Off A361. 88 acres of natural woodlands, with nature walks, lake, wildfowl, etc, and a Natural History Museum opened in 1970. Forestry exhibition in museum. Guided walks. Collection of birds' eggs of the world can be inspected on prior application. ⬚ and shop. Open all year, daily 10 – dusk. 50p (ch 14 20p, accompanied, free). Special rates for parties and youth organisations. ⚠ *(Tel Westbury 822238)* ᗷ

BROMSGROVE *Hereford and Worcester* Map 7 SO90
The Norton Collection Museum Davenal House, 28 Birmingham Road, Bromsgrove. A wide selection of Victorian musical boxes, gramophones, wireless and crystal sets, organs, kitchenware, lamps and Victoriana can be seen. Crafts and Industries Room. Costume and Chemist's Shop. Local History also Boar Coffee House. Open Mon to Sat 10 – 5, Sun 12 – 6. *(Tel 77934)* ᗷ (prior notice)
Avoncroft Museum of Buildings Redditch Road, Stoke Heath. Open-air museum displaying old buildings saved from demolition and re-erected. Exhibits include 18th-C windmill operational on certain days, a granary and thatched barn; timber framed houses, medieval roofs, a cock pit theatre and nail and chainmakers' workshops. Museum shop. Picnic site. Open 1 Mar to 30 Nov, daily 10.30 – 5.30 (or dusk if earlier). Admission prices for 1980 not available. ⚠ *(Tel 31886)* ᗷ B

BROOK *Kent* Map 5 TR04
Wye College Museum of Agriculture 4m ENE of Ashford on unclass road. An exhbition of old farm implements and machinery housed in a fine old tithe barn dating from the 14th C. Display of hop cultivation in old oast house. Open May to Sep, Wed 2 – 5 and Sat in Aug. Free. Parties by arrangement. ⚠ limited. *(Tel Wye 812401 ext 239)* ᗷ B

BROOMY HILL *Hereford and Worcester*
Map 3 SO43
Herefordshire Waterworks Museum The
museum is housed in a Victorian Pumping
Station of 1856, near the banks of the River
Wye. The first phase of the museum was
opened in Apr 1975 and contains two steam
pumping engines built in 1895 and 1906.
These have now been restored to working
order. The rest of the museum is expected to
be ready within the next 2–3 years where a
number of very old pumping engines and
other waterworks equipment from
Herefordshire will be displayed. There are
also plans for a narrow-gauge waterworks
railway. Open first Sun in each month Apr to
Sep also every Sat & Sun, Jul/Aug 1–5;
Dates and times for 1980 not yet available.
Party ⚠ Enquiries to *The Secretary HR
Penhale, 87 Ledbury Road, Hereford
HR1 2TR (Tel Hereford 4101)* &

BROUGH *Cumbria* Map 12 NY71
Brough Castle On A66. Dates from 12th to
13th C, repaired in 17th C by Lady Anne
Clifford. Stands on site of Roman 'Verterae'.
Open, see inside front cover. 10p (ch 16 and
pen 5p). ⚠ *(AM)*

BROUGHAM *Cumbria* Map 12 NY52
Brougham Castle On A66. 12th- to 14th-C
castle, repaired in late 16th C by Lady Anne
Clifford. Open*, see inside front cover. 15p
(ch 16 and pen 5p). ⚠ *(AM)*

BROUGHTON *Oxfordshire* Map 4 SP43
Broughton Castle 2m W of Banbury on
B4035. Originally owned by William of
Wykeham later passing into hands of first
Lord Saye and Sele, early 14th- and mid
16th-C house with moat and gatehouse, 16th-
C ceilings and mantelpieces. Period furniture
and paintings and Civil War relics. ⚛ Open
Wed and Sun 1 Jun to 14 Sep also Thu Jul
and Aug and BH Sun and Mon 2–5. Party (all
year). Admission probably 90p (ch 10 50p). P.
(Tel Banbury 2624). (Lord Saye and Sele)

BROUGHTON POGGS *Oxfordshire*
Map 4 SP20
Filkins and Broughton Poggs Museum On
A361. Domestic articles (including cooking
utensils), village lock-up, and example of
mantrap. Usually open all year, Fri, Sat and
Sun 9–6. *(Apply Mr Foster, Filkins 365)* &

BROWNHILLS *West Midlands* Map 7 Sk00
Chasewater Light Railway Chasewater
Park. On unclassified road, off A5. Society,
founded in 1959, has preserved collection of
small relics, as well as mainly Victorian rolling
stock and several industrial locomotives.
Some 2m of track. Steam-operated trains run
second and fourth Sun in each month, Apr to
Sep. ⚛ Open all year, Sat and Sun from
2–dusk. ⚠ *(Tel 5852)*

BROWNSEA ISLAND, Poole Harbour
Dorset Map 4 SZ08
500 acres of heath and woodland, with nature
reserve, two lakes, mile of bathing beach and
fine views of Dorset coastline. First scout
camp held here under Lord Baden-Powell in
1907. ⚛ Throughout the day in Villano
cafeteria. Open Apr to 30 Sep, daily 10–7 (or
dusk), by boat from Poole Quay or
Sandbanks. 50p (ch 25p). *(NT)*

BROXBOURNE *Hertfordshire* Map 5 TL30
Broxbourne Zoo White Stubbs Lane. 2m W
of Broxbourne on unclass road. This zoo
covers some 22 acres housing over 250
animals and birds, which are continually
being added to. ⚛ Open all year (ex 25 Dec)
10–6 (5 winter). 60p (ch 2 free). ⚠
(Tel Hoddesdon 62852) & *(79)*

BRYMPTON *Somerset* Map 3 ST51
Brympton d'Evercy Mansion House Stuart
and Tudor mansion in superb setting. Also
Priest House Country Life Museum. State
rooms, Felix dress collection. Parish church
alongside. Extensive grounds. ⚛ teas. Picnic
area, vineyard, cider and wine available.
Open 1 May to 26 Sep, daily (ex Thu and Fri)
2–6. Admission prices for 1980 not yet
decided. ⚠ *(Tel West Coker 2528)* &

BUCKDEN *Cambridgeshire* Map 4 TL16
Buckden Palace Off A1. Remains of ancient
palace, once residence of Bishops of Lincoln.
Fine Tudor tower and inner gatehouse of red
brick, dating probably from *c*1490, and
modern house in grounds. Open Jul, Aug,
Sep, Sun 3–7; exterior always viewable.
Admission charges to be decided. ⚠ *(The
Claretian Missionaries)*

BUCKFAST *Devon* Map 3 SX76
The Museum of Shellcraft Off A38. Large
collection of shellcraft from all over world, and
shows art of the shellcraft workers. Open
Easter to 24 Oct, daily 10–7. Admission
charges not avilable. Dogs on lead only. P.
(Tel Buckfastleigh 3452)

BUCKFASTLEIGH *Devon* Map 3 SX76
Dart Valley Railway Steam locomotive
hauled trains run between Buckfastleigh and
Totnes Riverside. **Note** Passengers cannot
leave or join trains at Totnes. Store of ex
Great Western rolling stock, including a
number of locomotives. ⚛ Bookshop, **also
Riverside Miniature Railway** A passenger-
carrying miniature railway round the Dart
Valley station area ½m ride. Open Easter then
mid May to mid Sep, daily (ex Sat), 11–5.
Access from Dart Valley Railway. P. *(Tel
2338)*

BUCKLAND *Gloucestershire* Map 4 SP03
Buckland Rectory Off A46. England's oldest
rectory, medieval house with 15th-C great hall

with open timber roof and contemporary glass. Associated with John Wesley. Also earlier half-timbered house and spiral stone staircase. Open May, Jun, Jul, Sep, Mon 11 – 4; Aug, Mon and Fri 11 – 4. Free. ⚠ *(Tel Broadway 2479). (Rev Michael Bland MA)*

BUCKLAND ABBEY *Devon* Map 2 SX46
3m W of Yelverton, off A386. Original house altered by Grenvilles, former owners and present house sold to Sir Francis Drake in 1581. Now partly Drake Museum, including legendary Drake's Drum. Also shrub and herb gardens, and tithe barn. Refreshments in afternoon. Open Good Fri to end Sep, Mon – Sat and BH 11 – 6, Sun 2 – 6; Oct to Wed before Easter, Wed, Sat, Sun 3 – 5, last admission ½ hour before closing. 80p (ch 40p) *(NT)*

BUCKLER'S HARD *Hampshire* Map 4 SZ49
Maritime Museum Off B3054. Small museum, opened by the late Earl Mountbatten of Burma in 1963, in village where wooden warships, including vessels for Nelson's fleet were once built from New Forest oak. Village Festival in July. ⚏ Open all year (ex 25 Dec). Easter to Spring BH. 10 – 6. Spring BH to Sep 10 – 9, Oct to Easter 10 – 4.40. Admission prices not yet known. &

BUDLEIGH SALTERTON *Devon*
Map 3 SY08
Fairlynch Arts Centre and Museum Fore Street. In 18th-C house, museum with exhibits of mainly local interest. Entirely new exhibitions annually. Costume display. Local history exhibition. Smuggler's Cellar. Open Easter to end Oct 2.30 – 5; Jul to end Aug also 10.30 – 12.30 (ex Sun mornings) 20p (ch 10, pen and students 10p). Honiton Lace making demonstrations, Sat and Sun afternoons. *(Tel 2666)*

BUILDWAS *Salop* Map 7 SJ60
Buildwas Abbey A beautiful ruined Savignac Abbey founded in 1135 standing in picturesque setting. Vaulted Chapter House dates from end of 12th C or early 13th C. Open, see inside front cover. 10p (ch 16 and pen 5p). *(AM)*

BUNGAY *Suffolk* Map 5 TM38
Bungay Castle On A144. Dates from 12th C, with restored late 13th-C gatehouse and drawbridge leading to keep and curtain wall. Large outer bailey, and views across Waveney valley. Open all year; guide book and keys available 9 – 1, 2.15 – 4.30 at *Sayer's shop or Council Office both in Earsham Street.* Free. P. *(Tel 2176)*
Otter Trust Earsham. A 23-acre site bounded by the River Waveney, including three lakes. World's largest collection of otters in semi-natural conditions for captive breeding for

release and research purposes. Mobile Interpretative Centre and a fine collection of waterfowl on the lakes. The Trust's main aim is to help save the world's otters from extinction. Shop and ⚏. Open 1 Mar to 30 Nov daily 10.30 – 6 (dusk if earlier). 80p (ch 16 40p). ⚠ *(Tel 3470)* &

BURFORD *Oxfordshire* Map 4 SP21
Cotswold Wildlife Park 2m S off A361. Landscaped open plan zoological park with exotic mammals, tropical birds, etc in landscaped enclosures. Also large reptile collection, aquarium and insect house. Other attractions include woodland walks, formal gardens, adventure playground, train and pony rides. ⚏ (Parties up to 30, menus on request). Open all year daily (ex 25 Dec) 10 – 6 (or sunset Oct – Mar). £1 (ch 14 and pen 60p, ch 3 free) (subject to change). ⚠ *(Tel 3006)* & (wheelchairs available)
Tolsey Museum Local crafts museum of charters and seals of Burford dating from 16th-C, old manuscripts, Burford craftsman's model 17th-C dolls house, furnished and dressed in Regency style. Open Easter to late Oct, daily 2.30 – 5.30. 20p (ch 5p). P. *(Tel 2168, Hon Sec)*

BURFORD *Salop* Map 7 SO56
Burford House Gardens Off A456. Near River Teme, house (1720) with gardens designed by John Treasure, featuring trees, shrubs, clematis, herbaceous plants, roses and 18th-C summer house. The ground floor of Burford House is open and flower arrangements are displayed on antique furniture. Permanent exhibition by the 'Teme Painters' local artists. Garden shop. ⚏ Gardens open mid Apr to mid Oct daily 2 – 5. Admission prices not available. Reduced rates for parties. ⚠ No dogs. *(Tel Tenbury Wells 810777)*

BURGH CASTLE *Norfolk* Map 5 TG40
The Castle Off A143. Massive walls from former 3rd-C fort of the Saxon shore system, guarded by six pear-shaped bastions. Accessible any reasonable time. Free. *(AM)*

BURGHCLERE *Hampshire* Map 4 SU46
Sandham Memorial Chapel Off A34. Built 1926 – 7, and presented to NT in 1947, the walls are covered with paintings by Stanley Spencer and depict war scenes from the Salonika front in 1914 – 18 War. Open all year (ex 4 Apr, 25 Dec and 1 Jan) daily until 7 pm or sunset; key at adjacent almshouses. Free. *(NT)*

BURGH-LE-MARSH *Lincolnshire*
Map 9 TF56
Burgh-le-Marsh Windmill On A158. Five-sailed tower windmill (c 1833), in working order, with four floors for inspection. Completely overhauled. Shop. ⚏ Open all

year, daily during daylight. Free. ⚠ *(Tel Burgh 281 due to alter to Skegness 810281). (Lindsey County Council)* ♿ **(79)**
Gunby Hall 2½m NE off A158. Red-brick house built *c* 1700 by Sir William Massingberd, with oak staircase, wainscoted rooms, and Reynolds portraits. Formal gardens and herbaceous borders. House open by prior written appointment with *J Wrisdale, Gunby hall, Gunby, Grantham, Lincs.* Garden open Wed afternoons. 70p. Gardens only 50p (ch half-price). *(NT)*

BURGHLEY HOUSE *Cambridgeshire*
Map 4 TF00
England's greatest Elizabethan house. Contains painted ceilings, silver, fireplaces, largest private collection of Italian Old Masters, Verrio's masterpiece, the Heaven Room, a miracle of perspective. Burghley horse trials held in Sep. ⚐ Open 1 Apr to 5 Oct, Tue to Thu, Sat, BH 11 – 5, Sun 2 – 5. Admission prices not yet decided. No dogs. ⚠ *(Tel Stamford 52451). (Marquess of Exeter).* Nearby Barnack Church has Saxon Tower and 13th-C font. ♿ park only

BURNHAM MARKET *Norfolk* Map 9 TF84
Carmelite Friary ½m NE Burnham Market on unclass road, Gatehouse and remains of Carmelite Friary founded in 1241 with some original windows and interesting flint and stone panelling. The adjoining farmhouse incorporates a 14th-C doorway and a large buttress. Open all year. Accessible at all times. Free. P. *(Tel Norwich 611122 ext 5224)*

BURNLEY *Lancashire* Map 7 SD83
Towneley Hall Art Gallery and Museum and Museum of Local Crafts and Industries 14th-C house with later modifications. Collection of oil paintings, early English water-colours, period furniture, ivories, 18th-C glassware, archaeology and natural history. Loan exhibitions from Apr to Sep. Large park with playing fields. Nature trail. ⚐ Open all year (ex 25 & 26 Dec & 1 Jan & Sat all year), summer Mon – Fri 10 – 5.30, Sun 12 – 5; winter Mon – Fri 10 – 5.15, Sun 12 – 5. Free. ⚠ *(Tel 24213)* ♿ B

BURROW BRIDGE *Somerset* Map 3 ST32
Pumping Station Museum 10m SE of Bridgwater, off A361; approach by turning off A361 opposite King Alfred Hotel, down unclassified road to River Authority sign by river past Lyng farm. Steam pumping engines in 1864 and 1869 preserved in excellent condition in small museum on River Parrett. Also antique hand pump and other items. Open, subject to attendant being available, Mon to Fri 9 – 5. Free. ⚠ *(Tel Bridgwater 57333 or Burrow Bridge 324)*

BURTON AGNES *Humberside* Map 8 TA16
Burton Agnes Hall On A166. Built in 1598, magnificent Elizabethan house with five centuries of furniture, pictures, china, and tapestries. Old gatehouse. Woodland gardens and herbaceous borders on view. ⚐ Open 1 Apr to 31 Oct, daily (ex Sat) 1.45 – 5 (6, Sun). Hall and gardens 60p (ch 40p). Gardens and grounds only 40p. *(Tel 324).* *(Mr M Wickham Boynton)* ♿ B
Norman Manor House Dates from 1170 and preserves original Norman piers and groined roof of a lower chamber. Upper room, probably 15th-C, and old donkey wheel. Open any reasonable time. Free. ⚠ *(AM)*

BURTON COURT *Hereford and Worcester*
Map 3 SO45
14th- to 18th-C house with original 14th-C great hall, and other interesting work. Notable collection of Chinese and European costumes, and model fairground exhibition. ⚐ (teas). Open Spring BH to mid Sep, Wed, Thu, Sat, Sun, BH Mon 2.30 – 6. 40p (ch 20p, coach parites 30p per person). ⚠ *(Tel Pembridge 231). (Mrs R M Simpson)* ♿

BURTON UPON TRENT *Staffordshire*
Map 8 SK22
The Bass Museum Horninglow Street. Housed in the Company's ex joiners shop dated 1866, a permanent exhibition traces the development of brewing in Burton from earliest times up to the present. External exhibits include a steam locomotive, an experimental brewhouse and a maltings engine. Museum shop. ⚐ Open all year (ex 25, 26 Dec) Mon to Fri 10.30 – 4.30, Sat, Sun and BH 11 – 5. 35p (ch and pen 15p). Party. ⚠ *(Tel Burton 42031 during opening hours)* ♿ B
Museum and Art Gallery Guild Street. Mainly devoted to local history with exhibits on the area from prehistoric times to the present day. Also a comprehensive exhibition of British birds which has been recently redisplayed. Open all year, daily (ex Sun) 11 – 6, Sat 11 – 5. Free. P. *(Tel 63042)*

BURWASH *East Sussex* Map 5 TQ62
Bateman's 1m SW. Lovely 17th-C house, once home of Rudyard Kipling (*Puck of Pook's Hill* was written here). Study remains as it was during his time here (1902 – 36). Attractive gardens. Water-mill recently restored. ⚐ Open Mar to end May and Oct, daily (ex Fri), 2 – 6; Jun to end Sep, Mon to Thu 11 – 6, Sat and Sun 2 – 6. 80p. No dogs. Indoor photography by permission only. *(NT)*

BURY *Gt Manchester* Map 7 SD81
Bury Art Gallery and Museum Moss Street. Contains a fine collection of 19th-C British paintings including works by Turner, Constable and Landseer. The museum outlines the social history of the town and the natural history of the area. Open all year ex Sun and BH. Mon to Fri 10 – 6, Sat 10 – 5. Free. P. *(Tel 7644110)* ♿ by appointment.
Regimental Museum XX The Lancashire Fusiliers Wellington Barracks, Bolton Road. Covers the history of XX The Lancashire Fusiliers from 1688 to the present day, including: period uniforms, relics of Napoleon Bonaparte, who was guarded by the Regiment at St Helena; relics of Major-General James Wolfe of Quebec fame and of Major-General Robert Ross who captured Washington in the American Wars. There is a special VC section (this Regiment won more VCs than any other in the British Army in the 1914 – 18 war), and a collection of campaigning medals and decorations. Open all year daily (ex Thu, Sun) 9 – 5. 5p (ch 15 2p). ⚠ *(Tel 2208)* ♿ B
Transport Museum East Lancashire Railway Preservation Society. Number of railway items from the steam age on display, and it is hoped to operate a train service on the Bury – Rawtenstall line, now closed by British Rail. Road exhibits include preserved buses, fire engines and steam roller. Model railway, operating and engine in steam last Sun in each month Mar to Sep, 6/7 Apr, Spring and Summer BH. ⚐ on steam days. Open all year Sat, Sun, 7 Apr, Spring and late Summer BH 11 – 5. 20p (ch 10p). Party. ⚠ Helpers in work of preservation welcomed. *(Tel 061 – 764 7790 during open hours)* ♿ B

BURY ST EDMUNDS *Suffolk* Map 5 TL86
Angel Corner Queen Anne house containing Gershom-Parkington collection of clocks and watches. Open all year, daily (ex Christmas and New Year holidays, also 4 Apr and Sun). 10–1 and 2–5 (4 Nov to Feb inclusive). Free.
Moyse's Hall Cornhill. Rare 12th-C house, now museum of Suffolk local history, archaeology, and natural history. Open all year, Mon to Sat 10–1 and 2–5 (4, Nov to Feb). 20p (ch 15 10p; if accompanied by adult free, pen 10p, organised school parties 5p each). P. *(Tel 63233 ext 236)* **(79)**
Norton Bird Gardens A very interesting collection of foreign birds and waterfowl etc. Aviaries well designed and planted to create natural conditions for the birds. Set in 4-acre garden with flowering bulbs, roses, herbaceous beds, shrubs and trees. ⬚ Open all year daily 11–7 or dusk. Admission prices for 1980 not yet available. ⚠ *(Tel Pakenham 30957)* ⅃
BUSCOT *Oxfordshire* Map 4 SU29
Buscot Park Off A417. 18th-C house with fine collection of paintings and notable water garden layout. Apr to end Sep, Wed to Fri, second and fourth Sat and following Sun in month 2–6. (Last admission to house 5.30). 80p (grounds only 40p). No dogs; no indoor photography. *(NT)*
BUXTON *Derbyshire* Map 7 SK07
Museum and Art Gallery Terrace Road. Local history, archaeology, and extensive collections from local caves; local fossils, minerals, and ornaments of Blue John and Ashford Marble; ceramics and glass; 19th and 20th-C oil and watercolour paintings, local maps, prints and photographs. Open all year Mon to Fri 9.30–6 (5, Sat). Free. *(Tel 4658)* ⅃

BYLAND ABBEY *North Yorkshire* Map 8 SE57
Considerable remains of the church and monastic buildings dating from late 12th C and early 13th C. Well preserved glazed tiles. Open, see inside front cover. 15p (ch 16 and pen 5p). *(AM)*

CADEBY *Leicestershire* Map 4 SK40
Cadeby Light Railway In grounds of Cadeby Rectory. Probably the smallest of Britain's narrow gauge railways. Engine normally running is a 1919 steam saddle tank locomotive. Other exhibits include a 1927 Foster Traction Engine and three steam rollers from 1903 onwards. Exhibition model railway in 4mm scale representing the Great Western Railway in South Devon of about 1935. Music Festival in Nov. Catering by prior arrangement. Open all year on second Sat of each month 2–5.30. Free. P. (Roadside). *(Tel Market Bosworth 290462)* ⅃
CAISTER-ON-SEA *Norfolk* Map 9 TG51
Caister Castle, Motor Museum, Tower, and Grounds Off A1064. Purpose-built Motor Museum contains vehicles of all ages from 1896 to present day, set out in easy to view 'arena' type building. Moated castle ruins (home of Shakespeare's Sir John Falstaff and where many of the 'Paston Letters' were

The Mighty Engine . . .

Hurrah for the mighty engine:
As he bounds along his track;
Hurrah for the life that is in him,
And his breath so thick and black.
And hurrah for our fellows,
    who in their need
Could fashion a thing like him –
With a heart of fire, and a soul
    of steel
And a Samson in every limb.

      Alexander Anderson (19th-century navvy poet)

Railway preservation has come a long way since the pioneer days of the Bluebell and Festiniog lines twenty years ago. Today, it is difficult to estimate the total number of railway enthusiasts, but it is certain that interest in railways and preservation has been growing steadily. In Britain, almost every county has its own preserved railway or steam centre. The numbers of visitors can be measured in millions each year, and the value of assets in land and equipment runs into tens of millions of pounds. Even British Rail, whose elimination of steam in 1968 and total ban on movement of preserved locomotives in steam represented the nadir of preservationists' hopes, has passed through a relaxation of the ban to positive indulgence by the passing of nearly 1,000 miles of secondary lines for regular steam-hauled railtours and

Steam hauled railtour: LMS Jubilee Loco 5596 Bahamas at Ludlow Station.

even the hiring back of some of its former locos for its own steam tours.

Preservation takes many forms – standard gauge, narrow gauge and miniature; as museum exhibits, working at a steam centre or on a preserved railway, or on a BR line hauling railtours. It is not confined solely to steam, as there is considerable interest in diesel locos and a fair number are preserved with the prospect, as they are withdrawn by BR, of more to come. Nor is it confined to locos, either. Rolling stock, civil engineering and railway architecture, and signalling are equally important and all are well represented. In fact, because the enthusiast interest is there, it will (subject to continued public interest), in the years to come, be the preserved railways rather than the museums which will maintain the historic traditions and atmosphere of Britain's long, varied and pioneering railway industry.

As most people are likely to visit and travel on a preserved standard gauge railway, it is worthwhile giving an examination of the main components of such a line. Of greatest concern to the passenger will be the steam or diesel motive power, followed closely by the appearance and comfort of the rolling stock. Less obvious, but vitally important, is the signalling while also in the background will be the

Locomotive scrapyard at Barry, South Wales.

civil engineering element. Lastly, and the key to the entire operation, will be the organisation itself and its management of paid staff and volunteers.

There is a good chance that whichever standard gauge line or steam centre you visit you will see at least one loco from the now world-famous Woodham's scrapyard at Barry in South Wales. Of more than 250 ex BR steam locos preserved in Britain, over 100 have been rescued from this yard and many are now in working order.

Restoration problems of an ex Barry loco well illustrate the standard of mechanical overhaul required if it is to haul public passenger trains or pass the critical examinations of BR inspectors for operating on steam railtours. The boiler has to be lifted out of the frames for examination of the firebox, and all flue and steam tubes replaced before hydraulic pressure testing of the shell. Bogies, wheel tyres, axleboxes, brakes, cylinders and valve gear have to be checked and overhauled, and all essential parts such as missing coupling rods, gauges, safety valves, injectors etc obtained or manufactured. Sometimes this work is done in purpose-built workshops such as at Sheffield Park (Bluebell), but usually, for lack of facilities, carried out in the open. Restoration takes up to five years and can cost between ten and thirty thousand pounds.

Passenger rolling stock is of two distinct types. Firstly, there are the ex-BR Mark 1 main-line and suburban coaches of a standard design dating from the late 1950s. These are available in large numbers and require relatively little restoration. Secondly, are the historically more interesting coaches of pre-Nationalisation origin, such as the Stanier straight-sided type (LMS), Gresley varnished teak coaches of the LNER, Collett and Hawksworth coaches of the GWR in chocolate and cream, and the Maunsell and later Bulleid malachite green coaches of the Southern. Almost all were scrapped by the late 1960s, but a few still survive.

For these older coaches, restoration is a daunting task which can take skilled volunteers up to a year to complete and add several thousand pounds to the original cost. Body panels, roof, floor, bogies and all timber framing have to be examined and possibly replaced, and seats (upholstered in the correct material), compartments, wiring, plumbing and all the other fittings which go into a 40-year-old carriage have to be re-instated. Finally, there is the repetitive job of painting, lining and varnishing. Some of the finest examples of restored coaching stock in this group may be seen at Didcot (GWR) and on the Severn Valley Railway (GWR and LMS) and Bluebell Line (Southern).

Restored coach.   Severn Valley Railway.   ▶

In addition, there are many contemporary and earlier miscellaneous passenger vehicles (4- and 6-wheelers, dining and sleeping cars etc) undergoing restoration to complement the historic collection on display at the National Railway Museum, York.

The track, or permanent way, has to be maintained to a high standard and this requires regular attention to rails, chairs, sleepers, ballast and drainage. Replacement of rotten timber sleepers is a frequent task and where possible is done with second-hand concrete sleepers. The North York Moors Railway, Britain's second largest preserved line at 18 miles, has 38,000 sleepers, and a replacement programme extending over eight or nine years. The ballast must be maintained in good condition to prevent any movement of the track and it, as well as embankments and cuttings, have to be well-drained to prevent water-logging or earth slips.

The civil engineering aspect of a preserved railway will cover the stations, goods and locomotive sheds, workshops and carriage sheds, over- and underline bridges, viaducts and tunnels. Over-bridges are sometimes the responsibility of the county council, but underline structures are the owning railway's responsibility and the cost of replacing a life-expired wrought iron bridge with steel or concrete is considerable. Several lines have substantial stone or wrought iron viaducts, notable examples being the massive single-span of the Victoria Bridge across the River Severn (Severn Valley Railway) and the Swithland Reservoir viaducts on the Main Line Steam Trust, south of Loughborough.

Tunnels can be found on the Keighley and Worth Valley, North York Moors, Dart Valley Railway (Torbay Section) and Severn Valley Railway. The most spectacular of any line for engineering works is the Festiniog which has completed the 'Deviation' route from Dduallt up to Tan-y-Grisiau. Involving the construction of a spiral (a unique feature in Britain), a 300-yard tunnel (17 months' work) and a new route and bridges behind the CEGB power station, it has cost over a million pounds, (the direct cost to the Festiniog being far less as a result of compensation, grants and volunteer labour).

Stations are a most important feature and have a character of their own as each railway company had its own special style of architecture. British Rail has found this out to their cost, with several hundred station buildings listed as being of architectural or historical interest. Often preservation companies will try to maintain the pre-Nationalisation or even pre-Grouping character of their lines with locos and rolling stock in, for example, Great Western or LNER livery and will select one or more stations for restoration in a Victorian or Edwardian setting. Outstanding examples are Sheffield Park (Bluebell), Highley (Severn Valley), Rothley (Main Line Steam Trust), Ropley (Mid-Hants) and on the North York Moors Railway, which will re-create throughout an early 20th-century North Eastern setting.

Signalling and all traffic movements have to be operated under DoT regulations and so the signalling visible on a line is definitely not there as a colourful decoration. However, decoration is present because of the individuality of design of the original railway companies' signalling equipment. Signal posts can be of wood, tubular steel, steel lattice, concrete or double rail bolted together, and each can be topped off with an elaborate company finial. Signal boxes varied in design and construction from one company to another, and could be built of timber, a combination of timber and brick or stone, or entirely of brick or stone. Two of the largest so far preserved are at Loughborough (MLST) and Wansford (Nene Valley Railway).

All railways require a great number of staff to run them. Drivers, firemen, guards, ticket inspectors, station managers and car park, ticket office, refreshment and sales attendants are in the fore-front, but, in the background and not to be forgotten, are the carriage and wagon, permanent way and signalling and telegraph staff and the loco fitters and restorers as well as the general administration and publicity people. At first most of these jobs were undertaken by volunteers, but with the increasing professionalism that is needed by commercial pressures, administration and sheer volume of work, an increasing number of full-time staff is being employed. Some preserved railways started off being owned by volunteers in a society, and partly through choice have remained unaltered, resisting to this day, the commercial pressures which have transformed others. This is revealed in the difference between the Talyllyn Railway and the Festiniog. The latter, like the Severn Valley Railway, has developed into a commercial company and will carry out whatever modifications are necessary in order to handle the maximum number of passengers.

The third type of preserved railway is the one where enforced closure of a line by BR after a long fight by protesters has led to the forming of a society and company at the same time, with the intention of purchasing through public subscription the entire line and reopening it to fulfill a social need, with steam operation as a profit-making attraction at weekends. Two lines in this category are the Mid-Hants which has, so far, raised an incredible £120,000 of public money (but regrettably because of British Rail's valuation of the Alton-Winchester route at over £300,000 have had to considerably reduce their ambitions and operate a weekend steam service only) and the West Somerset Railway, who are in the relatively fortunate position of leasing the entire route from the Somerset County Council who bought the track bed. They have been more successful in providing a service for the local community with regular daily diesel multiple unit trains.

Most railway companies have in addition to their own paid staff the backing of their own railway preservation societies who cater for the railway enthusiasts and co-ordinate the volunteer labour. Membership of individual societies varies, but can be up to six or seven thousand. Drivers, firemen, guards etc have to be rostered and therefore give up a lot of time. Others will give up entire summer holidays to help out, and subject to interest and qualification, can be put under supervision, usually from current or ex-BR staff, to do any job on the line. However, that does not mean that any enthusiastic amateur can be put in charge of a locomotive. In fact, the opposite is the case. All standard gauge railways conveying the general public have to be examined by the Railway Inspectorate of the Department of Transport before a Light Railway Order is granted for them to operate passenger trains. This limits train speeds to a maximum of 25 mph and, in addition, locos, rolling stock, track, signalling and structures with public access have to be up to the required standards of safety, and the operation of passenger trains has to meet requirements very similar to those on British Rail. Drivers, firemen, guards and signalmen have to undertake the same type of training as on BR, pass the same examinations and operate with the same rule books.

The railway preservation movement as a whole is now regarded as a major tourist attraction, and therefore we will now attempt to list what there is to be seen and where it can be found. England contains too many locations to be covered geographically, so the places will be categorised, but Wales, Scotland and the Isle of Man, will be covered individually.

Starting in England with the operational ex-BR lines, there are, firstly, in the North, the Lakeside and Haverthwaite Railway (Lake District) (p 116), Keighley and Worth Valley Railway which passes through the Brontë town of Haworth (p 116), and the North Yorkshire Moors Railway from Grosmont to Pickering (p 162). In the Midlands there is perhaps the 'premier' line, the Severn Valley Railway from Bridgnorth to Bewdley (p 58), at Loughborough the Great Central Railway Ltd (Main Line Steam Trust) which operates

Welshpool and Llanfair Railway

North Yorks Moors Railway rolling stock.

from Loughborough to Rothley (p 146), and at nearby Shackerstone, the Market Bosworth Light Railway (p 149). In East Anglia there are the Nene Valley Railway from Peterborough westwards to Wansford (p 196), and at Sheringham near Cromer, the North Norfolk Railway running to Weybourne (p 177).

There are no working lines in the London area, but in the South-East are the Mid-Hants Railway (Watercress Line) from Ropley to Alresford near Winchester (p 39), the Bluebell at Sheffield Park near East Grinstead (p 176), and the Kent and East Sussex line at Tenterden (p 191). Southern and South-West England have four lines – the Isle of Wight Steam Railway (Haven Street to Wootton) (p 209), the West Somerset (Britain's longest preserved line at 23 miles) from Minehead almost into Taunton (p 151) and the two scenically magnificent sections of the Dart Valley Railway in Devon (p 61) from Buckfastleigh to Totnes, and Paignton to Kingswear.

Moving on to steam depots and preservation centres, these can be found in the North-West at Carnforth ('Steamtown' is the largest

ex-BR loco depot in private ownership, and provides motive power for British Rail and other railtours) (p 83), Southport ('Steamport' is another ex-BR depot) (p 181), Bury (East Lancs RPS) (p 63) and in the Manchester area at the Dinting Railway Centre near Glossop (another railtour depot) (p 99). In the West Midlands there are the Bulmer Railway Centre, Hereford (railtour depot) (p 118) and the Birmingham Railway Museum, Tyseley (railtour depot) (p 52).

In Central, Southern and South-East England, there are the Dowty Railway Preservation Society, Ashchurch near Tewkesbury (p 41); the Great Western Society's Didcot Railway Centre (ex GW loco-depot) (p 99), Quainton Railway Centre near Aylesbury (p 165), the Stour Valley RPS at Chappel and Wakes Colne Station near Sudbury (p 85) and the Bressingham Steam Centre at Diss in Norfolk (p 57).

The next major group are the societies and companies intending to relay track or who have not yet obtained a Light Railway Order. This includes the Yorkshire Dales Railway at Embsay near Skipton; Cambrian Railway Society at Oswestry; Peak Railway Society at Matlock; North Staffordshire Railway Society at Cheddleton, near Leek; Midland Railway Centre at Butterley near Nottingham; Dean Forest Railway at Lydney (p 147), the East Somerset Railway at Cranmore near Shepton Mallet (p 95); the Bitton Railway Centre at Bristol; the Colne Valley Railway Society at Castle Hedingham in Essex (p 85) and the Swanage Railway Society in Dorset.

Of mainly industrial interest are the Bowes and Tanfield Railways near Gateshead, the North of England Open-Air Museum at Beamish, Co Durham (p 47), the Middleton Colliery Railway in Leeds (p 129), the Foxfield Light Railway near Cheadle (p 99) and the Chasewater Light Railway near Brownhills (p 61), both in Staffs. In the South, steam is to be found at the Bristol Industrial Museum (p 59), at Quainton, which has the greatest number of industrial

Dart Valley Railway (Torbay Section) Kingswear Station loco 4588.

Midland Railway 2 – 4 – 0 loco at Butterley.

steam locos, and at the Cornish RPS depot at Bugle.

In addition to the world-famous National Railway Museum at York (p 207) which also acts as a steam centre for BR railtours, the following museums contain locos:

The Science Museum, London (p 139); Great Western Railway Museum, Swindon (p 53); Birmingham Science Museum (p 188); North Road Station Museum, Darlington (p 97) which houses Stockton and Darlington Railway relics and the Tiverton Museum, Devon (p 192).

For anyone interested in standard gauge railway relics, there are the following: Winchcombe Railway Museum, near Cheltenham; Big Four Railway Museum, Bournemouth (p 55); Monkwearmouth Station Museum, Sunderland (p 187) and the South Devon Railway Museum, Dawlish Warren Station (p 98).

Diesel motive power is to be found on the North Yorkshire Moors line which has five, the Severn Valley Railway (two), West Somerset (one), Didcot Railway Centre (one), and BR Engineering Swindon Works (on open days only) (two). They consist mainly of the famous 'Western' class. These and other lines are likely to take on

Didcot Steam Centre.

more types as they are withdrawn from British Rail. The NYMR, Keighley and Worth Valley and West Somerset also operate diesel multiple units and railbuses.

For narrow gauge enthusiasts, the following will be of interest: The Motive Power Museum, Lytham St Annes; Cadeby Light Railway, Cadeby (p 64); Whipsnade and Umfolozi (Whipsnade Zoo) (p 200) and Leighton Buzzard Narrow Gauge Railways (p 130), Lincolnshire Coast Light Railway, Cleethorpes (p 91); Sittingbourne and Kemsley Light Railway, Kent; Brockham Museum, near Dorking; Hollycombe Steam Museum, near Liphook (p 133); Bicton Woodland Railway, Bicton Gardens, near Sidmouth (p 51); Lappa Valley Railway near Newquay (p 172) and the Bressingham Steam Centre at Diss which also has narrow gauge and miniature railways.

Miniature railways (18-inch gauge down to $7\frac{1}{4}$-inch) fans should visit the following: Ravenglass and Eskdale (Lake District) (p 165) and Romney, Hythe and Dymchurch Railway, Kent (p 155), which although of only 15-inch gauge are in a class of their own and more comparable to the Welsh two-foot gauge lines; Hilton Valley Railway at Weston Park (p 199); Stapleford Park Miniature Railway (p 183), Leicestershire; Oakhill Manor Railway near Shepton Mallet (p 158); Pecorama at Beer, (p 48) and the unique Forest Railway at Dobwalls (p 99).

Restored locomotive (diesel) D1062 Western Courier (now in operation on SVR).

Finally, for devotees of trams, there are, in addition to the Blackpool line, the Crich Tramway Museum, Derbyshire (p 95); the Beamish Open-Air Museum system (p 47) and the narrow gauge tramway from Seaton to Colyton, Devon.

The eight Welsh narrow gauge lines (see *AA Touring Guide to Wales*) are as healthy and as popular as ever and are being joined by the Welsh Highland Railway at Porthmadog. The Festiniog has reached Tan-y-Grisiau and is now within $1\frac{1}{2}$ miles of its destination at Blaenau Festiniog, where, under a joint scheme with British Rail and local councils, it will run into a new station providing a unique cross-Snowdonia rail-link from Porthmadog to Llandudno Junction.

Other developments include the first standard gauge line in Wales, the Gwili Railway, north of Carmarthen (p 215), and the restoration of Llangollen Station by the Flint and Deeside group and their relaying of track westwards along the beautiful Dee Valley towards Corwen. Elsewhere, locos and railway items are to be found at the industrial museums in Cardiff and Swansea, the Corris Railway Museum, Corris (p 218), the Conwy Valley Railway Museum, Betws-y-Coed (p 214); the Caerphilly Railway Society; the Great Orme Tramway, Llandudno, and Penrhyn Castle Museum, Bangor (p 214).

Dduallt Station, Festiniog Railway.   Llanberis Lake Railway.

In Scotland the Strathspey Railway (p 233) has opened up five miles of line along the lovely Spey valley from Aviemore to Boat of Garten. Having obtained the original steam shed at Aviemore, they are now concentrating on completing the new passenger station there. Scotland's other major steam organisation, the Scottish Railway Preservation Society, now have approval for an ambitious new steam centre and passenger line at Bo'ness on the Firth of Forth which will involve withdrawal in the near future from their present headquarters at Falkirk. Also in Scotland is the smaller Lochty Railway in Fife, and of a static nature is the historic collection of Scottish railway companies' locos in the Glasgow Transport Museum (p 242).

Lastly, and in a 'world of its own' is the Isle of Man which has three separate systems: the three-foot gauge steam IoM Railway (now reduced to Douglas – Port Erin) and the two electric tramway systems the Manx Electric and Snaefell Mountain Railways.

A brochure and timetable covering the Welsh narrow gauge lines and called *The Great Little Trains of Wales* is available from the Narrow Gauge Railways of Wales Joint Marketing Panel, c/o Wharf Station, Tywyn, Gwynedd.

Further information on any of the railways mentioned may be obtained from the Association of Railway Preservation Societies (Sheringham Station, Norfolk, Tel 0263 822045), who publish a brochure entitled *The 1980 Guide to Steam Trains in the British Isles*, or you could consult the map-guide *Steam in Britain* published by the BTA.

1980 is a momentous year for railway preservation, as it will see the 150th anniversary of the opening of the Liverpool and Manchester Railway in 1830. Events planned throughout the year will include permanent exhibitions at Rainhill and Earlestown until October, tours of the original station facilities and exhibitions at Edge Hill, Liverpool and Liverpool Road, Manchester, steam-hauled railtours between Liverpool and Manchester on Sundays from June to August, and the highlight will be the re-enactment at Rainhill near St Helens of the Locomotive Trials of 1829 on each of the three days of the Spring Bank Holiday, in which newly constructed replicas of Stephenson's 'Rocket' and other early locos will take part. This will be followed by a grand cavalcade of preserved steam, diesel and electric locos.

Further details should be available from main BR stations (or direct from 'Rocket' 150, BR, Room 405, Rail House, Lord Nelson Street, Liverpool), Tourist Info Centres and the railway press.

written), 98ft-tower. 1951 Festival of Britain Tree Walk removed from Battersea Park. ♨ Museum, grounds and tea-rooms open mid May to end Sep, daily (ex Sat) 10.30–5. Admission prices not yet known for 1980. Dogs on lead only. ⚇ *(Tel Wymondham 251). (Dr P R Hill JP CC D Tech)*
Roman Town On A1064. South gateway, town wall built of flint concrete with brick bonding courses, and part of what may have been a seaman's hostel. Open, see inside front cover. Free. *(AM)*

CALNE *Wiltshire* Map 3 ST96
Bowood 2m W off A4. Georgian house of magnificent proportions dating from Henry Keene (1754), including additions by Robert Adam, C R Cockerell and Sir Charles Barry. Rooms open to visitors include the laboratory where Dr Joseph Priestley discovered oxygen (1774), Orangery/picture gallery, Chapel, Sculpture Gallery and three newly converted exhibition rooms. Pleasure grounds and gardens extend over 100 acres and include Capability Brown's lake, cascade and grottos. Adventure play area, shop ♨ and restaurant. Open 4 Apr to end Sep daily (ex Mon) but including BH 2–6, Sun and BH 12–6. £1.15 (ch and pen 60p). Rhododendron walks off A342. 50 acres open mid May to mid Jun, daily (ex Mon) but including Spring BH 2–6. 70p (ch and pen 35p). ⚇ *(Tel 812102). (The Earl of Shelburne)* ♿ B

CALSTOCK *Cornwall* Map 2 SX46
Cotehele House 2m W on W bank of Tamar. 8m SW of Tavistock, off A390. Granite house of 1485 to 1627 built around two courts, formerly home of Earls of Mount Edgcumbe. Beautiful gardens on different levels, including Victorian terraces, shrub garden,

and medieval dovecote. There is restored Morden Mill, the manorial watermill in valley below. House contains 17th- and early 18th-C armour, furniture, and tapestry. ♨ Open 1 Apr to end Oct, Tue to Sun (house only closed Mon ex BH Mon) 11–6 (last admissions 5.30); Nov to Mar garden only open during daylight hours. House, garden and mill £1.50; garden, grounds and mill 90p. *(NT)*
CAMBERLEY *Surrey* Map 4 SU86
Camberley Museum Knoll Road. Contains exhibits on local history, archaeology, costume, flora and fauna, and notable persons including Bret Harte, Ethel Smythe, Sir Arthur Sullivan and Admiral John Sturdee. Open all year Tue to Fri 2–5, Sat 10–12 and 2–4. Free. ⚇ *(Tel 64483)* ♿
National Army Museum, Sandhurst Departments RMA Sandhurst. The Indian Army Memorial Room and the Hastings Room house collections of uniforms, medals, weapons, silver and paintings connected with the army of the East India Company and the Indian Army from their early days up to 1947. A similar collection devoted to the Irish regiments disbanded in 1922 is located nearby in the Blenheim wing of Old College. Open by appointment (closed 24 to 26 Dec; 1 Jan; 4 Apr and certain ceremonial occasions) 10–5 (Sun 11–5). Free. ⚇ *(Tel 63344 ext 485)* ♿ B
CAMBO *Northumberland* Map 12 NZ08
Wallington 1m S on B6342. 17th- and 18th-C house with rococo plasterwork, and a central hall added in the 19th C, situated in a great moorland estate of over 12,000 acres rising to an altitude of over 1,000ft. Additional rooms opened up 1968/69. Magnificent fuchsias in conservatory in walled garden. ♨ Open: House Apr to end Sep daily ex Tue, 1–6; Oct, Wed, Sat and Sun 2–5. Grounds open all

year. House and grounds £1.20. Grounds Apr to Sep 50p, Oct, Sat and Sun 50p. Free remainder of year. *(NT)*

CAMBRIDGE *Cambridgeshire* Map 5 TL45
Ancient University city on the River Cam. Many of the colleges line the East bank, overlooking the Backs: sweeping lawns set with willow trees, on the opposite side of river transformed from rough marshland by Richard Bently (Master of Trinity College from 1699 to 1734). The colleges are open to the public on most days during daylight though there are some restrictions during term time.
Cambridge and County Folk Museum Castle Street. Formerly White Horse Inn, exhibits include domestic objects, toys, furniture and agricultural tools, and large collection of pictures and photographs relating to county. Open all year (ex BH), Tue to Fri 10.30 – 5, Sat 10.30 – 1 & 2 – 5, Sun 2.30 – 4.30. 25p (ch 16 and pen 10p). P street (meters). Coach car park (free) at top of Castle Street. *(Tel 355159)*
Fitzwilliam Museum Trumpington Street. Exhibits extensive art and archaeological collections including Egyptian, Greek and Roman antiquities, coins, medals, European paintings, Medieval and literary manuscripts, ceramics, textiles, Medieval and Renaissance *objets d'art*, arms and armour and a library. ⚲ Tue to Sat 10.30 – 4. Upper or lower floor open all year Tue to Sat 10 – 5, Sun 2.15 – 5. Closed Mon (ex 7 Apr, 26 May, 25 Aug) 4 Apr and 24 Dec to 1 Jan inclusive. Free. P. *(Tel 69501)* ૯ (advance notice)
Jesus College Founded in 1496 by Bishop Alcock of Ely in the former Benedictine nunnery of St Radegund, which he had suppressed and taken over. Several of the buildings retained their former uses (the chapel remaining a chapel, the refectory became the dining room) but were also improved and added to, including an extra storey on the living quarters.
King's College A complex of buildings overlooking the banks of the Cam. The magnificent chapel is the only complete medieval part of this college built in 1441 – 1515 in Perpendicular style. It retains all its original stained glass and contains Rubens' Adoration of the Magi. Subsequent buildings belong mainly to the 19th C, apart from the Gibbs Building, a fine Classical addition begun in 1723
St John's College Founded 1511 by Lady Margaret Beaufort, mother of Henry VII. It consists of three red-brick courts with a fine gate-tower, 17th-C library and chapel designed by Sir Gilbert Scott
Museum of Archaeology and Anthropology Downing Street. Covers pre-historic archaeology of the world in general, with section on Cambridge area from Stone Age to Middle Ages, and cultures of the peoples of the Americas, Africa, the Pacific and South-East Asia. Open all year (ex Christmas, Easter week and Suns), Mon to Fri 2 – 4, Sat 9.30 – 12.30. Free. P. *(Tel 59714)*
Scott Polar Research Institute Lensfield Road. Museum of Polar exploration and research. Contains relics, manuscripts, paintings, photographs, etc relating to Arctic and Antarctic expeditions, with special emphasis on the expeditions of Captain Scott. Also contains displays illustrating polar native peoples, Eskimo art, and modern scientific exploration. Open all year Mon to Sat 2.30 – 4. Free. ⚠ *(Tel 66499)*
Trinity College The early college comprised two adjacent elements, King's Hall founded

by Edward II 1317 and Michaelhouse founded 1323. They were consolidated into one unit in 1546, when Henry VIII disbanded Michaelhouse at the Dissolution. Remnants of these buildings are still visible. The various buildings of differing dates were converted into two quadrangles by further additions in 1593 – 7 by Thomas Nevile. The library, begun in 1676 to designs by Sir Christopher Wren, formed a fourth side to Nevile's Court, the smaller of the two quadrangles.
University Botanic Garden Trumpington Road. Original site of 5 acres founded in 1762, present area of 40 acres being acquired in 1831. Fine botanical collections. Open all year (except Christmas Day and Boxing Day), weekdays 8 – 7.30 (dusk in winter); Sun 10 – 6.30 (key holders) 2.30 – 6.30 (non-key holders May to Sep only); glasshouses 2 – 5 (or dusk). Free (£1 returnable deposit charged for keys on Sun; keys issued on professional reference only – particulars from Director). No dogs or bicycles. P (limited street). *(Tel 350101)* ૯

CAMELFORD *Cornwall* Map 2 SX18
North Cornwall Museum and Gallery The Clease. Museum of rural life with sections on agriculture, slate and granite quarrying, blacksmith's and wheelwright's tools, cobbling, dairy and domestic scene including a collection of bonnets. The gallery holds various exhibitions. Open 1 Apr to 30 Sep, Mon to Sat 10.30 – 5. Closed Sun. 30p (ch 16 5p). P. *(Tel 3229)*

CANFORD CLIFFS *Dorset* Map 4 SZ08
Compton Acres Gardens On B3065. Rock and water gardens, and heather, Japanese, Roman, English and Italian gardens covering 15 acres, with fine views over Poole Harbour and Purbeck Hills. ⚲ Open 1 Apr to end of Oct, daily 10.30 – 6.30 (Jun to Aug, Thu until dusk). 60p (ch 35p). No dogs or radios. Picnic area. ⚠ *(Tel 708036)* ૯

CANTERBURY *Kent* Map 5 TR15
Eastbridge (St Thomas's) Hospital 25 High Street. Dating from 12th C, one of the oldest buildings in city, used partly as almshouses since 16th C. Flint-faced façade has 14th-C windows, refectory has 13th-C mural. There are two chapels and a vaulted undercroft noted in the Norman Heritage Trail 'in the steps of the Conqueror'. Open all year (ex 4 Apr and 25 Dec), 10 – 1 and 2 – 5, Sun 11 – 1 and 2 – 5. Free.
Greyfriars Friary Off Stour Street. By River Stour. Recently restored 13th-C remains of first friary of Franciscan movement. Open in summer, Mon to Sat 12 – 1 and 2 – 5. 10p (ch and pen 5p). Parties by arrangement. *(Tel 622292)* ૯
Howe Barracks Contains exhibits of all the former county regiments of Kent, Surrey, Sussex and Middlesex from which the Queen's Regiment was formed on 31 Dec 1966. Open all year Mon to Fri (ex BH) 10 – 12 and 2 – 4, other times by appointment. Regimental shop. Free. ⚠ *(Tel 65281 ext 30)*
Roman Pavement Butchery Lane. Part of a Roman town house, with mosaic floor and hypocaust, excavated after war damage and incorporated into rebuilding. Displays of Roman finds, mainly local, of pottery, coins, jewellery and small objects. Open Apr to Sep, weekdays 10 – 1 and 2 – 5; Oct to Mar, weekdays 2 – 4. 15p (ch 10p). Under revision for 1980. *(Tel 52747)*
Royal Museum, Art Gallery and Buffs Regimental Museum High Street. The archaeology of east Kent, including the

Roman silver spoon hoard, Roman coin hoard, Anglo Saxon glass and jewellery with the silver 'Canterbury Cross'; paintings include works by local artist Sidney Cooper, engravings and photographs; collections of medals, uniforms, weapons and trophies of the Royal East Kent Regiment. Monthly changing exhibitions. Open all year, weekdays 10–5. Free. *(Tel 52747)*

St Augustine's Abbey Founded by St Augustine on land given by King Ethelbert in 598 foundations of a 7th-C church. Remains of 11th-C round church underlie extensive ruins of medieval Benedictine abbey. Open, see inside front cover, Sun all year from 9.30. 15p (ch 16 and pen 5p). *(AM)*

West Gate Museum 14th-C gateway, last of city's gates to survive: displays and material relating to the gatehouse in the city wall system, and to its use as a gaol, with cells, handcuffs, manacles, etc. Open Apr to Sep, weekdays 10–1 and 2–5; Oct to Mar, weekdays 2–4. 15p (ch 10p). Under revision for 1980. *(Tel 52747)*

CANVEY ISLAND *Essex* Map 5 TQ78
Dutch Cottage Museum A130. One of two early 17th-C thatched, octagonal cottages of Dutch design, probably erected when Vermuyden was reclaiming the island with a sea-wall. Exhibits of furnishings and models of shipping used on Thames from earliest times. Also small but fine collection of corn dollies. Open Spring BH to end Sep, Wed, Sat, and Sun 2.30–5, BH 10–1 and 2–5. Parties by arrangement. ⚠ limited. *(Tel South Benfleet 52368)* **(79)**

CAPESTHORNE *Cheshire* Map 7 SJ87
Capesthorne Hall On main London – Manchester road (A34), near Jodrell Bank radio telescope. The home of the Bromley-Davenport family, built in 1722 and altered later by Blore and Salvin, with pictures, ancient vases, furniture, silver and Americana. The adjoining chapel is believed to be by John Wood of Bath, and if this is so, it appears to be his earliest surviving work. ♐ 3–6 on open days. Open 25 Mar to Sep Suns 2–5; May to Sep Wed and Sat 2–5; 24 Jul to 13 Sep Tue & Thu 2–4. Parties at other times by arrangement. 80p (ch 40p), gardens only 40p (ch 20p). Dogs allowed in park only. ⚠ Further information from *Hall Manager, Capesthorne Hall, Macclesfield, Cheshire SK11 9JY. (Tel Chelford 221). (Lt-Col Sir Walter H Bromley-Davenport TD DL)*

CARLISLE *Cumbria* Map 11 NY45
Carlisle Castle Restored castle and dungeons built by William II in 1092, but dating mainly from 12th-C. Open*, see inside front cover. 50p winter 25p (ch 16 and pen

20p winter 10p). ⚠ *(AM)* Also **The Border Regiment and King's Own Royal Border Regiment Museum** Queen Mary's Tower. 300 years of the Regiment's history depicted in trophies, models, weapons, medals, silver, documents, pictures and prints, together with the story of Cumbria's part-time soldiers. Open as castle. No extra admission charge. ⚠ *(Tel 32774)*

The Guildhall Greenmarket. A splendid and recently renovated early 15th-C timbered building containing displays about Guild, Civic and local history. Open May to Aug Mon to Fri 10–6, Sat 10–5. Winter Mon to Sat 10–4. Free

Museum and Art Gallery Castle Street. Housed in Tullie House, a 17th-C town house, is the Regional Collection of Cumbrian Archaeology (especially Roman) and Natural History; English paintings (19th and 20th-C); English porcelain, costume, toys and dolls, musical instruments. Temporary Exhibitions. Open Apr to Sep Mon to Fri 9–7 (5 winter), Sat 9–5, Sun 2.30–5 Jun to Aug only. Free. *(Tel 34781)*

The Prior's Room Prior's Tower, Cathedral grounds. The 13th-C tower has a first-floor room domesticated by Prior Senhouse *c* 1510, with remarkable painted ceiling of 45 panels bearing devices of Cumbrian families. Also interesting bosses and inscriptions. Admission from Cathedral. Open Mon to Sat 2–5 (May to Sep 10–9) Suns by appointment. 10p (ch 14, 5p). P

CARNFORTH *Lancashire* Map 7 SD47
Steamtown Railway Museum Former British Rail motive power depot. A complete large engine shed housing 30 steam locomotives of all sizes, from Great Britain, France and Germany. Home of the famous 'Flying Scotsman'. Gift shop and ♐ Open daily (ex 25 Dec) 9–5. Steam days Sun Easter to Oct, daily Jul, Aug and BH. 50p (ch and pen 25p), rises to 70p (ch and pen 30p) when locos are in steam, for rides in vintage coaches. ⚠ *(Tel 4220)*

CARRAWBROUGH *Northumberland* Map 12 NY87
Roman Wall (Mithraic Temple) On B6318. Remains of Mithraic temple measuring only 35ft by 15ft, dating from 3rd C but with later alterations, on line of Roman Wall near fort of 'Procolitia'. Excavations in 1950 revealed three dedicatory altars to Mithras and figure of the Mother Goddess. Open any reasonable time. Free. ⚠ *(AM)*

CARTMEL *Cumbria* Map 7 SD37
Priory Gatehouse Off B5277. Only remaining fragment, apart from the church, of 14th-C Augustinian Priory, formerly a school,

now a local craft shop. Open daily. Christmas at reasonable hours. Free. *(NT)*

CASTLE ACRE *Norfolk* Map 9 TF81
Earthworks of former castle, slight remains of keep, and 13th-C Bailey from fortified borough. Admission free at any reasonable time. Remains of late 11th-C priory, including 12th-C church noted for its arcaded west front, 11th-C Prior's Lodging, and early 16th-C gatehouse. 20p (ch 16 and pen 5p). Priory open*, see inside front cover. ⚠ *(AM)*

CASTLE ASHBY *Northamptonshire*
Map 4 SP85
Castle Ashby House Off A428. In fine grounds, 16th- to 17th-C mansion with interior noted for pictures, furnishings, and 17th-C woodwork, including chimney pieces and moulded ceilings; outstanding private

collection of Greek vases. South front added by Inigo Jones. Lettered stone parapet (1624) surrounds house, and grounds and terraces date largely from 1860. Gift shop. ⚓ Open 4 to 13 Apr then 1 Jul to 31 Aug daily 2 – 5. Sun and BH 11 – 5. Admission prices not available. *(Tel Yardley Hastings 332). (The Marquess of Northampton)*

CASTLE BOLTON *West Yorkshire*
Map 7 SE09
Dates from 1379 – 97, part restored to original state this century, in pretty Wensleydale setting. Former stronghold of the Scropes, prison of Mary, Queen of Scots, 1568 – 69, and besieged and taken in 1645 by Parliament forces. Copy of original Dales kitchen. ⚓ (licensed). Open all year, daily (ex Mon) during daylight hours. 30p (ch 15p) ⚠ *(Tel Wensleydale 23408)*

CASTLE DONINGTON *Leicestershire*
Map 8 SK42
The Donington Collection Houses the
world's largest collection (over 80) of single-
seater racing cars and over 60 vehicles
covering the development of Leyland cars
and many other transport exhibits. Also
Britain's newest motor racing circuit. ⚲ Open
all year (ex Christmas week) daily 10–6.
£1.65 (ch 15 5o p, ch 7 free). ♿ *(Tel Derby
810048)* ⚲

CASTLE HEDINGHAM *Essex* Map 5 TL73
Colne Valley Railway and Museum Access
to site is on A604 between Castle Hedingham
and Great Yeldham. Stock includes six steam
locomotives and items of rolling stock.
Original Colne Valley and Halstead railway
buildings are being rebuilt on the site.
Locomotives in steam every BH (ex
Christmas) and other weekends as
advertised. Book and souvenir shop. ⚲ Open
all year Sat, Sun and BH 9–dusk. Non steam
days 20p (ch 16 and pen 10p, ch 3 free). On
steam days 45p (ch and pen 30p, ch 3 free).
All rides free. Prices under revision for 1980.
♿ *(Tel Hedingham 61174)*
The Castle Off A604. Norman keep
overlooking attractive village. Open 1 May to
end Sep, Tue, Thu, Sat 2–6, BH (ex 13 Apr)
10–6. 15p (ch 10p). P on Castle Hill. *(Tel
Hedingham 60435). (Miss M Majendie and
Dr Margery Blackie)* **(79)**

CASTLE HOWARD *North Yorkshire*
Map 8 SE76
Magnificent 18th-C house, designed by
Vanbrugh and built in 1699–1726 for Charles
Howard, 3rd Earl of Carlisle; still lived in by
Howard family. Contains famous collection of
porcelain, paintings and furniture.
Surrounding the house are extensive grounds
with lakes and fountain. Hawksmoor's great
Mausoleum and Vanbrugh's restored Temple
of the Four Winds. Costume galleries in 18th-
C stable court, house Britain's largest private
collection of 18th- to 20th-C costume. Steam
Fair Aug. ⚲ licensed). Open 4 Apr to end Oct,
daily. Grounds and restaurant from 11, House
and Costume Galleries 11.30–5. Admission
prices not yet decided for 1980. ♿ *(Tel
Coneysthorpe 333)* ⚲

CASTLE RISING *Norfolk* Map 9 TF62
Castle Rising Off A149. Fine Norman keep,
probably built by Earl of Arundel, within
impressive earthworks. Open*, see inside
front cover. 20p (ch 16 and pen 5p). ♿ 5p.
(AM)
Trinity Hospital Almshouses founded 1616
by Earl of Northampton, building with towered
gatehouse, and courtyard leading to hall, resi-
dences, and rebuilt chapel. Original fireplace
and refectory in common room. Open all
year, Tue, Thu and Sat 10–12 and 2–6 (4, Oct
to May). Free. P (roadside). *(Tel 241)* ⚲

CASTLETON *Derbyshire* Map 7 SK18
Blue-John Caverns and Mine Over two
miles long, with chambers 200ft high, the best
of the local caves. Contains rare deposits of
amethystine spar. ⚲ Open all year, daily (ex
25 Dec) 9.30–5.30 (dusk winter). 80p (ch
40p). P. *(Tel Hope Valley 20638)*
Peak Cavern On A625. One of the most
spectacular natural limestone caves in
district. Underground walk (half a mile) is
electrically lit. There is running water, and
many grotesque shapes are visible. Grand
Entrance Hall, where ropes have been made
for over 500 years, and traces of a row of
cottages can be seen. Open 4 Apr to mid Sep,
daily 10–5. 60p (ch and pen 30p). Party 20+

48p (ch 24p). P. *(Tel Hope Valley 20285)*
Peveril (or Peak) Castle Ruined keep
erected originally by Henry II. Later portion
has vanished. Open*, see inside front cover.
20p (ch 16 and pen 5p). ♿ *(AM)*
Speedwell Cavern Floodlit cavern with
illuminated canal and bottomless pit. One
mile underground boat trip. ⚲ Open all year,
daily (ex 25, 26 Dec) 10–6 90p (ch 45p). ♿
(Tel Hope Valley 20512)

CAWTHORNE *South Yorkshire* Map 8 SE20
Cannon Hall On A635. Built c 1765, mainly
by John Carr of York, the museum set in 70
acres of parkland is owned by Barnsley
Metropolitan Borough Council. Contains
furniture, paintings, and glassware. Also
Regimental Museum of the 13th/18th Royal
Hussars (Queen Mary's Own). The Harvey
Collection of Dutch and Flemish paintings
(formerly the National Loan Collection) is now
on permanent display. Open all year (ex 4
Apr, 25/26 Dec), 10.30–5, Sun 2.30–5. Free.
♿ *(Tel Barnsley 790270)*

CHADDERTON *Gt Manchester* Map 7 SD80
Foxdenton Hall Foxdenton Lane, off B6189.
Dates from 1665 and c1700, restored in 1965.
Open all year, Sun, Apr to Sep, Tue 2–dusk.
(Park daily until dusk). Free. ♿

CHALFONT ST GILES *Buckinghamshire*
Map 4 SU99
Milton's Cottage Half-timbered 16th-C
cottage and the only existing home in which
John Milton lived and worked. Whilst in the
cottage he completed 'Paradise Lost' and
commenced 'Paradise Regained'.
Mementoes of Milton on display. Cottage
garden. Open 1 Feb to 31 Oct daily (ex Sun
am and Mon) 10–1 and 2–6. Nov weekends
only. closed Dec and Jan. 40p (ch 15 10p).
Party 20+. P. *(Tel 2313)* ⚲

CHAPPEL *Essex* Map 5 TL92
Chappel Steam Centre Chappel Station. Off
A604 by Viaduct. Ten steam locomotives plus
historic rolling stock, restored railway
buildings and associated equipment.
Chappel is not just a museum but a centre
where every aspect of railway preservation
can be seen at close quarters, down to the
smallest detail. Open every weekend (ex 25
Dec) 11–dusk. Steam days 2 Mar, 5–7 Apr,
4–5 and 25–26 May, 1 Jun, 6 Jul, 3 and
24–25 Aug, 7 Sep, 5 Oct and 2 Nov. 60p (ch
and pen 30p), includes admission, parking
and unlimited steam hauled rides. ♿ ⚲

CHARD *Dorset* Map 3 ST30
Forde Abbey 12th-C Cistercian monastery,
with notable gatehouse, enlarged by Abbot
Chard, and converted to house in 17th C by
Cromwell's Attorney-General. Inhabited by
present family since 1864, contains set of five
famous Mortlake tapestries. 20 acres of
grounds, with water and rock gardens. ⚲
Open May to Sep Wed, Sun and BH 2–6. 75p
Admission charges for 1980 not yet decided.
♿ *(Tel South Chard 20231). (Mr Geoffrey D
Roper)* ⚲

CHARLECOTE *Warwickshire* Map 4 SP25
Charlecote Park On B4086. Fine restored
Elizabethan house (1558), built originally for
Lucy family, with picturesque gatehouse.
Museum on first floor of house, and in Great
Hall, Shakespeare was said to have been
brought before Sir Thomas Lucy for poaching
in 228-park deer park. ⚲ Open 14 Apr to end
Apr and Oct, Sat and Sun, May to Sep, daily
(ex Mon, but including BH) 11.15–5.45 (last
tour 5.15). £1.10, deer park and garden 75p;
school parties on Thu mornings only by prior
arrangement. *(NT)*

CHARLWOOD Surrey Map 4 TQ24
Gatwick Garden Aviaries and Garden Zoo
½m SW at Russ hill. Colourful collection of
birds varying from macaws, flamingoes,
penguins and waterfowl. Colonies of
monkeys, some totally free. Otters, wallabies
etc. In natural setting, lawns and lakes. ⌂
Open Easter to end Sep daily 10.30–6. 45p
(ch 3–14 and pen 30p, ch 3 free). ⚠ (Tel
Crawley 862312) ⓑ **(79)**

CHARTWELL Kent Map 5 TQ45
2m SE of Westerham. Former home of Sir
Winston Churchill, now Churchill memorial
Museum with many relics of the famous
statesman. House open 1 Mar to end Nov,
Tue, Wed, Thu (closed Mon and Fri) but open
BH Mon, 2–6 or sunset. Sat, Sun and BH Mon
11–6 or sunset. Garden and studio Apr to mid
Oct same times. Admission to house and
gardens £1.20, gardens only 60p (ch half
price); studio 30p extra. Entrance by
numbered ticket at times in summer to avoid
delay; waiting time can be spent in the
gardens. ⌂ licensed, 10.30–5.30 on open
days. (NT)

CHATSWORTH Derbyshire Map 8 SK27
Built largely by Talman and Wyatville, 17th-
and 19th-C palatial home of Dukes of
Devonshire in magnificent park and water
gardens. Wood carvings by Samuel Watson,
ironwork by Tijou, paintings by Verrio and
Laguerre, Old Master drawings, and fine
collection of pictures, books, and furniture.
Farming and Forestry Exhibition. ⌂ House
open late Mar to early Oct Tue, Wed, Thu and
Fri 11.30–4, Sat and Sun 1.30–5, BH Mon
and Tue 11–5. Farmyard open daily 30 Mar to
9 Oct Subject to alteration. Admission prices
for 1980 not yet decided. ⚠ (Tel Baslow 2204)
(The Trustees of the Chatsworth Settlement)

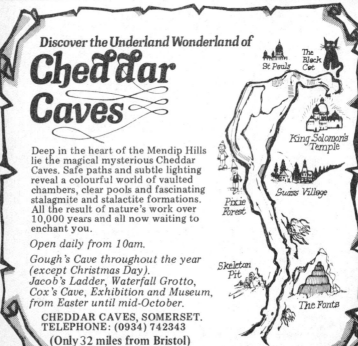

CHAWTON *Hampshire* Map 4 SU73
Jane Austen's House In the village street
now a museum. Visitors are allowed to picnic
in the garden. Open all year, daily (ex Mon
and Tue Nov to Mar and 25, 26 Dec) 11 – 4.30.
50p (ch 14 10p). Party 20+ ⚠ *(Tel Alton
83262)* 㧑 B

CHEDDAR *Somerset* Map 3 ST45
Cheddar Caves Museum The Cliffs. A
natural museum on archaeology and zoology
containing Paleolithic – Pleistocene finds. A
burial of the last phase of the Ice Age together
with flint and bone implements of this period
found in Gough's Cave are preserved in the
museum. Evidence of Iron Age and Romano-
British occupation has also been found. ⚐
Open Easter – Oct daily 10 – 5.30. 25p (ch
15p) P. *(Tel 742343)*

CHEDDLETON *Staffordshire* Map 7 SJ95
Flint Mill Beside Caldon Canal. Two mills are
preserved here with their low-breast wheels in
working order. The original 17th-C south
watermill ground corn but the 18th-C north
mill was built to grind flint for the pottery
industry. Museum collection includes
examples of motive power (100HP Robey
steam engine and model Newcomen engine)
and transport (miller's cart and restored 70ft
horse-drawn narrow boat 'Vienna' moored on
the Caldon Canal). Open all year, Sat, Sun
afternoons. Application in advance for
weekday visits to Mr Underwood, 4 Cherry Hill
Avenue, Meir, Stoke-on-Trent. Free. ⚠

CHEDWORTH *Gloucestershire* Map 4 SP01
Roman Villa Fossebridge, off A429. In
Chedworth Woods, dating from AD 350 – 350,
with mosaic pavements. One of the best-
preserved examples in England. Open Mar to
Oct, Tue to Sun and BH (closed 4 Apr), Feb
and Nov to 16 Dec, Wed to Sun 11 – 4 (or
sunset). 85p, school parties 40p. No dogs or
picnics. *(NT)*

CHELMSFORD *Essex* Map 5 TL70
Chelmsford and Essex Museum Oaklands
Park, Moulsham Street. Collections of
Prehistoric and Roman Essex, bygones,
coins, costumes, paintings, British birds and
mammals, glass, ceramics, geology and local
industries display. Also Victorian room,
Tunstill collection of glass and temporary
exhibition programme. Incorporates Essex
Regiment Museum brought here from
Warley. Open all year (ex 4 Apr; 25, 26 Dec; 1
Jan), Mon to Sat 10 – 5, Sun 2 – 5. Free. ⚠
*(Tel 353066, Essex Regiment Museum
60614)* 㧑 B

CHELTENHAM *Gloucestershire* Map 3 SO92
Art Gallery and Museum Clarence Street.
Dutch and British paintings, Cotswold
furniture, English and Chinese ceramics,
pewter, glass, furniture, modern art, art and
craft exhibitions. Local history. Temporary
exhibitions throughout the year. Open all year
(ex Suns and BH) Mon to Sat 10 – 5.30. Free.
P. *(Tel 37431)*
Gustav Holst Museum Clarence Road.
Holst personalia. Contains Regency and
Victorian room settings, also leading
Victorian kitchen and basement. Open all
year (ex BH) Tue to Sat 11 – 5.30. Free. *(Tel
24846)*
Pittville Pump Room Probably finest
building in town, and masterpiece of 19th-C
Greek revival, built between 1825 and 1830
by Forbes and Papworth, and bought by
borough in 1890. Notable colonnaded
façades, portico, and pillared and balconied
hall. Pump Room restored and spa fountain
repositioned in 1960. Now used for
receptions, concerts, dances, and other
functions. Open Mon to Sat 10 – 4 (closed
1 – 2), Sun and BH 2 – 5. Free. May be closed
when caretaker not available. ⚠ *(Tel 21621)*
㧑

CHERTSEY *Surrey* Map 4 TQ06
Chertsey Museum Windsor Street. A late
Georgian house, The Cedars, Museum
opened in 1972 contains Matthews collection
of costumes and accessories, local history
collection, and silver. Exhibitions 'Family
History' 26 Feb to 15 Mar; 'Fluid & Flow' 17
May to 7 Jun. Open all year, Tue and Thu
2 – 5, Wed, Fri and Sat 10 – 1 and 2 – 5. Free.
P. *(Tel 65764)*

CHESSINGTON *Surrey* Map 4 TQ16
Chessington Zoo On A243. Set in 65 acres
of lovely Surrey countryside. Large and varied
collection of animals and birds including
gorillas and orangutans. Children's zoo. Bird
garden. World of Mechanical Music
Exhibition. During the summer there is a
funfair, model railway and circus. ⚐
(licensed). Open daily (ex 25 Dec) 10 – 5 (7
summer hol period; 4 Oct to Mar). £1.30 (ch
60p). Under revision for 1980. ⚠ *(Tel Epsom
27227)* 㧑

CHESTER *Cheshire* Map 7 SJ46
The British Heritage Vicars Lane (opposite
Roman Amphitheatre). Home of World
Champion Town Crier. An exhibition telling
over 2,000 years of Chester history. Audio-
visual theatre, map and print room, showing
the development of Chester since Roman
days. A unique life size reconstruction of the
Rows as they might have been in early

CHEDDLETON FLINT MILL
Staffordshire

Specialises in the history of pottery raw
materials. Original buildings and equipment
restored to running order, many items
having been collected to show the related
processes. Two of the working exhibits -
Robey steam engine, model Newcomen
engine. The restored narrow boat "Vienna"
is moored permanently on the Caldon
Canal at the wharf. Cheddleton Flint Mill
Industrial Heritage Trust is a registered
Charity.

Victorian days. The Cobbled Street contains six shops which include cooper, blacksmith and pharmacy. A Brass Rubbing Centre is on the ground floor. Admission to Brass Rubbing Centre free. 25p (to rub various brasses including instruction and equipment). Craft Shop specialising in British made goods. Guided tours of City at 11 and 3 (May to Sep). Open from 9 daily. 70p (ch and pen 35p). Please telephone for winter opening hours. *(Tel 42222)*

Cheshire Military Museum Chester Castle, Castle Street. Mainly 19th C. Museum is located in 'A' block and has exhibits from Cheshire Regiment, Cheshire Yeomanry, 5th Inniskilling Dragoon Guards and 3rd Carabiniers. Open daily, Apr to Sep 9.30–6; Oct to Mar 9.30–5; Sun Apr to Sep 12–6, Oct to Mar 1–5. 10p (ch 5p). P. *(Tel 27617)* **(79)**

Chester Heritage Centre St Michael's Church, Bridge Street. Exhibition of Chester's architectural heritage, including 20-minute audio-visual shows and displays relating to the city's history and the large-scale conservation programme now in operation. Open all year 1 Oct to 31 Mar, daily (ex Wed) 1.30–4.30; 1 Apr to 30 Sep, weekdays (ex Wed) 10–5, Sun 2–5. 30p (ch 18 and pen 15p). Party 10+ 10% reduction. *(Tel 317948)*

Grosvenor Museum Grosvenor Street. Contains one of finest collections of Roman remains in Britain, including special Roman Army gallery and many inscribed and sculptured stones excavated in Chester. Natural History gallery. Temporary exhibitions. Period house closed for renovation. Open all year (ex 4 Apr; 25, 26 Dec), Mon to Sat 10–5, Sun 2–5.30. Free (Schools should book in advance). *(Tel 21616/313858)*

Stanley Palace Watergate Street. Dating from 1591, restored in 1935, half-timbered former home of the Stanleys, Earls of Derby. Now local headquarters of English-Speaking Union. Open all year Mon to Fri (ex BH) 10–4.30. Free. ⚕ *(Tel 25586)* **(79)**

Zoo and Gardens Interesting collection of animals in open-air enclosures amid fine gardens. Tropical House, aquarium, and walk-through aviary. ⚲ (licensed). Open all year daily (ex 25 Dec) 9–dusk. £1 (ch 14 50p). Party 25+. Tropical House 15p. Aquarium 5p, Waterbus trips 15p (ch 10p). Under revision for 1980. ⚕ *(Tel 20106)* ♿

CHETTLE *Dorset* Map 3 ST91

Chettle House Early 18th-C baroque house in red brick, designed by Thomas Archer, with staircase of same period. Open all year, exterior daily 10.30–sunset, interior by appointment. Admission free. Limited parking. *(Tel Tarrant Hinton 209). (Mr Bourke)* **(79)**

CHICHELEY *Buckinghamshire* Map 4 SP94

Chicheley Hall Built for Sir John Chester between 1719 and 1723. It is one of the finest and least altered 18th-C houses in the country. Fine Georgian craftsmanship: brickwork, stone and wood carving, joinery and plasterwork. ⚲ Open 4 Apr to 26 May Sat, Sun and BH 2.30–6, then Wed, Thu, Sat, Sun and BH until 28 Sep. 70p (ch 12 and pen 30p). Prices under revision for 1980. Party 20+. ⚕ *(Tel North Crawley 252)* ♿

CHICHESTER *West Sussex* Map 4 SU80

District Museum In former 18th-C corn store, with local history, archaeological, and Royal Sussex Regiment relics. Open all year, Tue to Sat 10–6 (5, Oct to Mar). Free. P. *(Tel 784683)* ♿ B

Guildhall Museum Priory Park. Branch of District Museum, containing archaeological finds from district. Open Jun to Sep, Tue to Sat 1–5. Free. P. ♿

St Mary's Hospital Refounded c1240, with interesting hall with wagon roof supported by oak posts, and a notable chapel screen. Open all year, Tue to Sat 11–12 and 2–5 (4, Oct to Mar) (closed BH and staff holidays). Admission not less than 3p per person. P (charge). *(Tel 783377)* ♿

CHIDDINGSTONE *Kent* Map 5 TQ54

Chiddingstone Castle Off B2027. In a park, mainly 17th- to 18th-C house containing pictures, furnishings, rare Oriental art treasures, including largest collection of Japanese lacquer on show outside Japan, and Royal Stuart and Jacobite, and Egyptian collections. Fishing in lake £2 per day, onlookers (one only per £2 ticket). Open 1 Apr to 26 Oct Tue to Fri 2–5. Sat, Sun and BH Mons 11.30–5. 50p (ch 12 25p). ⚕ *(Tel Penshurst 347). (Mr Denys E Bower)* ♿ B

CHILHAM *Kent* Map 5 TR05

Chilham Castle Impressive hexagonal Jacobean castle and massive Norman flintstone keep (neither open) on site of ancient Saxon fortifications and manor house overlooking the valley of the River Stour. Extensive garden, woodland and lakeside walks with wildfowl and peacocks. Free flying eagles and falconry display. Medieval Jousting Sundays. Woodwings Flying Circus (radio controlled planes) BH Suns and Mons.

Also The Kent Battle of Britain Museum A registered charity. Fine collection of relics including Spitfire and Messerschmitt engines, propellers, airframes, photographs, uniforms, badges and swords. ⚲ Garden and museum open Easter to Oct (closed Mon and Fri ex BH Mon) afterwards only. Provisionally £1 (ch 50p). ⚠ (free). *(Tel 319). (The Viscount Massereene and Ferrard)* ⓖ

CHILLINGHAM *Northumberland*
Map 12 NU02
Chillingham Wild Cattle (Castle *not* open to public). Off B6348. Park containing herd of some 50 remarkable wild white cattle. Viewable 1 Apr to 31 Oct, weekdays (ex Tue) and BH 10–12 and 2–5, Sun 2–5; Tickets 50p (ch 14 20p) from keeper's cottage. ⚠ *(Tel Chatton 213 or 250)*

CHILLINGTON HALL Staffordshire
Map 7 SJ80
Home of the Giffards since 1178, present house dates from 1724 and 1785 (when Sir John Soane was architect), and grounds are by 'Capability' Brown. Fine saloon, and association with flight of Charles II after Battle of Worcester in 1651. Open 1 May to 11 Sep, Thu 2.30–5.30; also 6 Apr, Sun before Spring and Summer BH and all Sun in Aug. Party (other days). Admission prices for 1980 not yet decided. ⚠ *(Tel Brewood 850236). (Mr P Giffard)* ⓖ

CHIPPENHAM *Wilts* Map 3 ST97
Sheldon Manor Plantagenet Manor House, 13th-C porch 15th-C detached Chapel. Beautiful terraced gardens, roses, water garden, ancient yew trees and hedges. Historic Houses Festival 'Festival of Gardens' 21 May to 8 Jul. ⚟ (teas). Open 30 Mar to 28 Sep, Thu, Sun and BH 2–6. 65p (ch 15 30p), ch 5 free). Under revision for 1980. ⚠ *(Tel 3120)*

CHIPPING CAMPDEN *Gloucestershire*
Map 4 SP13
Campden Car Collection High Street. Twenty two immaculate sports, and sports racing cars 1927 to 1963, each of distinctive history, together with a number of engines and a display of photographs of motor sport. Open Easter then May to Sep daily 2–6. 25p (ch 10p). Under review for 1980. P. (street). *(Tel Evesham 840289). (Curator)* ⓖ
Market Hall Gabled, Jacobean structure, built on open arches, and standing in main street of most beautiful of stone-built Cotswold towns. Open regularly. Free. *(NT)*
Woolstaplers Hall High Street. Building c1340, with interesting collection of bygones. Open Easter then May to Sep daily 11–6. 35p (ch 10p). Under revision for 1980. P (street). *(Tel Evesham 840289)*

CHOLMONDELEY *Cheshire* Map 7 SJ55
Cholmondeley Castle Gardens 7m W of Nantwich on A49. The gardens were originally laid out in the beginning of the 19th C and have shrub and water gardens

with walks and picnic areas by the lake, also an ancient Chapel in the park and the farm has a collection of rare breeds of farm animals. The castle is **not** open to the public. Various events, Band concerts, Morris dancing etc as advertised in local press. Gift shop. ⚟ Open 15 Apr to 7 Oct Sun and BH 1–6. 35p (ch 10p). ⚠ *(Tel 202). (Marquess of Cholmondeley)* ⓖ **(79)**

CHORLEY *Lancashire* Map 7 SD51
Astley Hall Timbered and richly plastered 16th-C and later house in some 99 acres of park and woodland. Fine furnishings, pottery, ceilings, and pictures. Special exhibitions. ⚟ Open daily afternoons only. 20p (ch 10p). ⚠ *(Tel 2166)* ⓖ B

CHRISTCHURCH *Dorset* Map 4 SZ19
Christchurch Castle and Norman House Rare example of ruined Norman house (c1160). Stands in bailey of 11th-C house, of which part of this stands. Open, see inside front cover. Free. *(AM)*
Red House Museum and Art Gallery Quay Road. Local history, archaeology, bygones, Victoriana, dolls and costumes, wildlife, and natural history contained in Georgian building. Gardens with old roses, herbs and trees. Open all year (ex Mons, 25 Dec), Tue to Sat 10–5, Sun 2–5. 10p (ch 16 and pen 5p). P. for 30 mins at roadside, 100yd, 2hrs 10p. *(Tel 2860). (Hampshire County Museum Service)* ⓖ B
Tucktonia Stour Road. Best of Britain in miniature (exhibits to 1/24th scale. Including buildings of London, Industrial Britain, Cornish fishing village plus many more. The exhibits are illuminated and animated. Also leisure complex with features for all ages. ⚟ Open Mar to Oct (details can be checked before visiting with *tel no* given below), from 10. Admission 85p (ch and pen 65p). Party. Prices may be subject to alteration. ⚠ *(Tel 485100/482710)* ⓖ

CHURCH CROOKHAM *Hampshire*
Map 4 SU85
The Gurkha Museum Queen Elizabeth's Barracks. Contains a record of the Gurkha's service to the crown from 1815. Open all year Mon to Fri (ex BH and certain Gurkha Hols) 9.30–4.45. Free. ⚠ *(Tel Fleet 3541 ext 63)* ⓖ

CHYSAUSTER ANCIENT VILLAGE
Cornwall Map 2 SW43
Eight drystone masonry houses leading off a courtyard and incorporating characteristic Cornish underground chamber, or 'fogou'. Adjoining dwellings are byres for cattle, giving foretaste of so-called later 'long-house'. Inhabited between 1st and 3rd C AD. Open*, see inside front cover. 15p (ch 16 and pen 5p). ⚠ *(AM)*

Sheldon Manor
near CHIPPENHAM

Plantagenet Manor-House dating from 1282, still a family home with a warm welcome, a delicious home-made cream tea, and many ancient and beautiful things to see. Connoisseur gardens with roses, water and very old yew trees.
Open: Sundays, Thursdays and Bank Holidays from 2-6pm, Easter to October. Also Wednesdays in August, 2-6pm.
Approach: 1½ miles west of Chippenham, signposted from A420, eastbound traffic signposted from A4. M4 (Exit 17) 4 miles.
Participating in West Country Festival of Gardens, May, June, July 1980.

CIRENCESTER *Gloucestershire*
Map 4 SP00
Corinium Museum Park Street. Contains
one of the country's most comprehensive
collections of Roman remains – mosaic floors,
Romano-British sculpture, and items of
everyday life, plus a remarkable example of a
five-letter square palindrome. Considerably
enlarged and modernised in 1974 to become
a regional museum for the Cotswolds.
Temporary exhibitions throughout the year.
Open all year May to Sep, Mon to Sat 10–6,
Sun 2–6; Oct to Apr (closed Christmas), Tue
to Sat 10–5, Sun 2–5. 25p (ch 5p, students
and pen 15p). Party (adults) 15p. P. *(Tel
5611)* &

CLANDON *Surrey* Map 4 TQ05
Clandon Park On A247, near West Clandon.
18th-C house, built by Leoni for 1st Lord
Onslow, with fine plasterwork, furniture, and
pictures. Famous collection of valuable
furniture added in 1970. ♫ Open Apr to 19
Oct, BH Mon, Tue (ex following BH), Wed,
Thu, Sat, Sun 2–6. £1 *(NT)*

CLAPHAM *North Yorkshire* Map 7 SD76
*Yorkshire Dales National Park Information
Centre* Permanent exhibition centre for
region, with photographs, maps, teaching
aids, etc. Reginald Farrer Trail commences
here. Open Apr to end Sep daily mid mornings
to late afternoon. Free. ⚠ *(Tel 419)*

CLEARWELL *Gloucestershire* Map 3 SO50
Clearwell Caves Ancient Iron Mines
Ancient iron mine with exhibits of local mining
and geological interest from Forest of Dean
area, including several vintage stationary
engines. Large picnic area. Open Easter to
end Sep, Tue to Fri, Sun and BH 10–5. 50p

(ch and pen 25p). Under revision for 1980.
Educational parties at other times by
arrangement with proprietor, *Mr Ray Wright,
The Bungalow, Heywood Road, Cinderford,
Glos.* ⚠ *(Tel Cinderwood 23700)* & B
Clearwell Castle A 'mock' Gothic castle
reputed to be the oldest in Britain with a
Regency interior. There are 8 acres of formal
gardens on five different levels which are still
being restored. Bird Park. ♫ Open 4 Apr to 1
Oct, Tue to Fri 2–6, Sun and BH 11–6
(closed Mon and Sat). Closed at certain times
for special functions. 75p (ch and pen 50p).
Party. Admission prices under revision for
1980. ⚠ *(Tel Coleford 2320)*

CLEETHORPES *Humberside* Map 8 TA30
Lincolnshire Coast Light Railway North
Sea Lane Station, Humberston. Historic
narrow-gauge passenger-carrying light
railway. Open Spring BH week, daily then Sat
and Sun until 12 Jul, then daily until 7 Sep.
Single fare 7½p (ch 3 free). ⚠ &
Zoo and Leisure Park a 27-acre site with
lions, tigers, elephants, camels, chimps,
seals, reptile house, monkey house, large
free-flight aviary, emu, deer, cattle, wolves
and a pets corner. Play areas for children and
fairground. Colussus Day 1 Apr. Picnic areas.
♫ Open all year daily (ex 25 Dec) 10–dusk.
50p (ch and pen 30p). Under revision for
1979. *(Tel 813533)* & **(79)**

CLEOBURY *Salop* Map 7 SO67
Clee Hill Bird and Animal Garden Contains
birds, poultry and waterfowl from 6
continents. Also mammals including deer,
Llamas, wallabies, sheep, etc. Gift shop. ♫
(licenced). Open all year (ex 25 Dec) Summer
10–6, winter 10–4. 45p (ch 25p, ch 3 free). ⚠
(Tel Cleo Hillstone 274) & **(79)**

CLEVEDON *Avon* Map 3 ST47
Clevedon Court Off B3130. 14th-C manor house, associated with Tennyson and Thackeray, with 14th-C chapel and 18th-C terraced garden. ⚲ Open Apr to end Sep, Wed, Thu, Sun, BH Mon 2.30 – 5.30 (last admission 5). 70p *(NT)*
Clevedon Craft Centre and Country Museum Moor Lane. Turn off B3130 opposite Clevedon Court, cross M5. Wood carving and woodturning every Sun afternoon when craftsmen are available for discussion. Ten studios, and Countryside Museum. Exhibition gallery, countryside Museum at Whitsun and Summer BH. ⚲ Open May to Dec 10 – 5.30 Tue to Sun and BH Mon. Tea room and museum closed Mon to Fri from end of Oct to Easter. Free. ⚠ *(Tel 872867)* ♿

CLIFFORD *Hereford and Worcester* Map 3 SO24
Clifford Castle Remains of 11th-C castle, traditional birthplace of 'Fair Rosamund', comprising gatehouse, hall, and round towers. Open with permission from *Mr and Mrs Parkinson*; apply at house by castle entrance. Free. P. (in lane by entrance). *(Tel 230)* **(79)**

CLITHEROE *Lancashire* Map 7 SD74
Clitheroe Castle Museum Contains important collection of carboniferous fossils and many items of local interest. It adjoins the remains of the castle, one of the oldest structures in Lancashire with the smallest Norman keep in England. The Castle grounds command magnificent views over the Ribble Valley. Open Easter to Sep, Tue, Thu, Sat and Sun 2 – 4.30, last two weeks Jul and whole Aug daily. 10p (ch free if accompanied). P. *(Tel 24635)* ♿ B
Browsholme Hall Bashall Eaves. 2½m NW. Home of Parker family, Bowbearers of the Forest of Bowland. Tudor with Elizabethan front, Queen Anne Wing and Regency additions. Portraits, furniture, antiquities. Open 5 – 13 Apr, 24 May – 1 Jun, 16 – 31 Aug daily 2 – 5. House and grounds 80p (ch 40p). Parties by written arrangement throughout the year. No dogs. ⚠ *(Tel Stoneyhurst 330/538)* ♿ B

CLIVEDEN *Buckinghamshire* Map 4 SU98
Cliveden Extensive and historic gardens overlooking Cliveden Reach of Thames. Present house, third to be constructed on the same site, is now let to Stanford University. ⚲ Gardens open all year, daily 11 – 6.30. House Apr to end Oct, Sat and Sun 2.30 – 5.30. House and grounds £1.20. Grounds only £1. No dogs in house, on lead in grounds. *(Tel Burnham 61406)*. *(NT)*

CLOUDS HILL *Dorset* Map 3 SY89
4m SW of Bere Regis. Former home of T E Lawrence (Lawrence of Arabia). Open all year, Apr to end Sep Wed – Fri, Sun and BH 2 – 5, Oct to end Mar, Sun 1 – 4. 60p. No photography. *(NT)*

CLUMBER PARK AND CHAPEL *Nottinghamshire* Map 8 SK67
2½m SE Worksop. The Chapel built (1886 – 1889) for the 7th Duke of Newcastle is open after restoration work. Described as 'a cathedral in miniature' the architect was G F Bodley RA (1827 – 1902). A superb example of the Gothic Revival based on 14th-C Decorated Style. The mansion was demolished in 1938 although the footings have recently been exposed. The remainder of this 3,800-acre park survives including the longest double lime tree avenue in Europe, stables with a tower clock dated 1763, Classical bridge over lake, lodges, pleasure gardens etc. Shops, bicycle hire, day fishing, ferry. Park open all year. ⚲ Open weekends and BH also Mon to Thu, Apr to Oct. Small vehicle charge only. *(NT)*

CLUN *Salop* Map 7 SO28
Clun Town Trust Museum In town hall, original court house to Clun Castle; court was moved to market square in 1780. Flint tools, maps of earthworks, etc, domestic and farming relics, and exhibits of local geological and mineralogical interest. Open Easter until Nov, Tue and Sat 2 – 5. Other times by request, and parties by arrangement only. School parties welcome. Free. P. *(Enquiries Mrs F Hudson, Florida Villa, Tel 247)*

COBHAM *Kent* Map 5 TQ66
Cobham Hall Off B2009. 16th-C and later mansion, with work by Inigo Jones and Wyatt, situated in large park with fine trees; now girls' public school. ⚲ Open 3 – 7 Apr then every Wed, Thu and Sun from 30 Jul to 4 Sep also 25 Aug, 2 – 6 (last tour 5.30 pm). 50p (ch and pen 25p). Party 15+. Admission prices under revision for 1980. ⚠ *(Tel Shorne 3371)* ♿ B
Luddesdown Court Norman manor house dating from the 11th C, claimed to be the oldest continuously inhabited house in Britain. Most of original structure still remains. Open by appointment with owner. Free. *(Tel Meopham 814359)*. *(Mr J A Williams)*
Owletts 17th-C house with contemporary staircase and ceiling. Open Apr to Oct, Wed and Thu 2 – 5. 40p *(NT)*

COBHAM *Surrey* Map 4 TQ16
Cedar House 15th- to 18th-C house overlooking River Mole, with open-timbered roof to hall. Open on application to tenant. Free. *(NT)*

COCKERMOUTH *Cumbria* Map 11 NY13
Wordsworth House Built 1745, birthplace in 1770 of William Wordsworth. Original staircase and fireplaces. ⚲ Open Apr to Oct, daily (ex Thu) 10.30 – 2.30 and 2 – 5. 70p (ch 30p). *(NT)*

COCKLEY CLEY *Norfolk* Map 5 TF70
Iceni Village and Museum Full-scale reconstruction on original site of Iceni encampment, showing how tribe lived 2,000 years ago. 200yd away is historical museum in cottage built 1450, with models and exhibits of local life from prehistoric times to present day. Agricultural and carriage museum. Early Saxon church (c620) in grounds. Open Easter to Sep, Sun 1.30 – 5.30. School parties by appointment. Admission charge for 1980 not yet decided. ⚠ *(Tel Swaffham 21339)*

COGGESHALL *Essex* Map 5 TL82
Paycocke's Early 16th-C house with notable panelling. Open Apr to Sep, Wed, Thu, Sun, BH Mon 2 – 5.30. 70p. No dogs. *(NT)*

COLCHESTER *Essex* Map 5 TM02
Bourne Mill Dutch-gabled fishing lodge (1591) erected from materials from St John's Abbey. Open Apr to Sep, Wed, Sat, Sun, BH Mon 2 – 6. Other times by appointment. No unaccompanied children. 40p *(NT)*
Colchester and Essex Museum North of High Street. The Castle, massive 11th-C keep built largely of Roman bricks around vaulted base of Roman temple, now houses extensive collection of Roman and other antiquities. Open all year (ex 4 Apr, 25 – 27 Dec), weekdays 10 – 1, 2 – 5 (4 Sat Oct to Mar), Sun (Apr to Sep only) 2.30 – 5.25 (ch and pen free); conducted tours of vaults and cells weekdays Jul and Aug, tours 20p (ch 10p). P. *(Tel 77475)* ♿ B

Colchester Zoo Stanway Hall, 3m W of town, off B1022. Hall, rebuilt in 16th C, and 14th- to 17th-C church in 40-acre park. Zoo, founded in 1963, includes large cats (lions, tigers, leopards etc), Nocturnal House, aquarium and birdland. Model railway. Picnic areas. ⬛ Open all year, daily 9.30 – 7.30. 70p (ch 2 – 14 30p); Party 25+. ⚠ *(Tel 330253)* ⅙ **(79)**

Hollytrees Fine Georgian house, dating from 1718, with collection of costumes and antiquities. Open all year (ex 4 Apr and 25 – 27 Dec) weekdays 10 – 1, 2 – 5. Free. *(Tel 77475)*

Museum of Social History Holy Trinity Church, Trinity Street. Historical displays of County life and crafts, with some bicycles etc. Open all year Mon to Sat 10 – 1, 2 – 5 (4 Sat, Oct to Mar). Free. P. *(Tel 77475)* ⅙

Natural History Museum High Street. Formerly 15th-C All Saints Church, with fine flint tower. Natural History of Essex with special reference to the Colchester area. Dioramas and aquarium. Open all year (ex 4 Apr, 25 – 28 Dec), weekdays 10 – 1 and 2 – 5 (4 Sat Oct – Mar). Free. P. *(Tel 76071 ext 344)*

The Minories Victor Batte-Lay Trust, 74 High Street. Georgian house, rebuilt in 1776 from original Tudor buildings. Opened as art gallery and centre for visual arts in 1958; continuous programme of exhibitions of contemporary fine and applied art, also lectures, concerts etc. ⬛ Open all year Tue to Sat 11 – 5, Sun 2 – 6. 20p (ch, students and pen 5p). P. *(Tel 77067)* ⅙ B

White Barn House 4m E on A133 at Elmstead Market. The garden, begun only 20 years ago, has a variety of contrasting plantings. The Dry garden, on gravel soil and full sun, contains plants adapted to drought. The Shade garden has plants with fine foliage, eg, hostas and ferns as well as flowering plants. A spring fed ditch has been dammed to make 5 large pools, full of fish and surrounded by exotic bog plants. The nursery adjoining contains over 1,000 different plants. Open all year (ex Sun and BH) 9 – 5. 25p, subject to review for 1980. ⚠ *(Tel Wivenhoe 2007)* ⅙

COLNE *Lancashire* Map 7 SD83
British in India Museum Sun Street. Dioramas, working model railway, coins, medals, stamps, and other items relating to British in India up to 1947. Open 1 May to 30 Sep, Sat and Sun only, 2 – 5. 25p (ch 15 and pen 10p). P. *(Tel Nelson 63129)* ⅙ B

COMPTON *Devon* Map 3 SX86
Compton Castle Off A380 near Marldon. Restored 14th- to 16th-C house with courtyard, hall, chapel, and old kitchen open to public. ⬛ Open 1 Apr to Oct, Mon, Wed, Thu 10 – 12 and 2 – 5. 70p *(NT)*

COMPTON *Surrey* Map 4 SU94
Watts Picture Gallery Memorial gallery with about 150 paintings by G F Watts, who is buried above the nearby Watts Mortuary Chapel. Gallery open all year, daily (ex Thu) 2 – 6 (2 – 4 Oct to Mar), and also 11 – 1 Wed and Sat; chapel open all year, daily. Free. ⚠ *(Tel Guildford 810235)* ⅙ B

COMPTON BEAUCHAMP *Oxfordshire* Map 4 SU28
Wayland's Smithy A gallery-grave chamber, excavated in 1920 from a large prehistoric mound, and re-excavated and restored in 1962 – 3. Lies near the ancient ridgeway at about 700ft on the northern slopes of the Berkshire Downs. Accessible any reasonable time. Free. *(AM)*

COMPTON WYNYATES *Warwickshire* Map 4 SP34
Tudor mansion built 1480 – 1520 largely by Sir William Compton, a lifelong friend of King Henry VIII who stayed several times. Interior largely unaltered. In steep hillside setting below the Cotswold Scarp with beautiful topiary garden. Picnic area. Gift shop and ⬛. Open 4 to 13 Apr then 1 to 31 Aug daily 11 – 5. Admission prices not yet decided. ⚠ *(Tel Tysoe 229)*. *(The Marquess of Northampton)*

CONISBROUGH *South Yorkshire* Map 8 SK59
Conisbrough Castle Unique example of circular six-buttressed keep, built in late 12th C. Curtain walls with solid round towers. Open*, see inside front cover. 15p (ch 16 and pen 5p). ⚠ *(AM)*

CONISTON *Cumbria* Map 7 SD39
Brantwood 2½m SE off B5285. On unclass road east side of Coniston Water. Former home of John Ruskin, with garden, one of the finest nature trails in the Lake District, also deer trails. Memorial exhibition to John Ruskin on display, including pictures, coach boat and personal possessions. Picnics permitted. Open Easter to mid Oct, Sun to Fri 11 – 5.30. House and Nature Trails 65p (ch 16, pen and disabled 30p). Family Ticket (Mother, Father and ch 16) £1.50. Nature Trail only 25p (ch 10p). ⚠ Toilets for the disabled. *(Tel 396)* ⅙

CORBRIDGE *Northumberland* Map 12 NY96
Roman Station Remains of Roman 'Corstopitum', cAD210, including granaries, portico columns, and probable site of legion headquarters. Excavated finds in museum on site. Open*, see inside front cover. 40p, winter 15p (ch 16 and pen 15p, winter 5p). ⚠ *(AM)*

Hunday National Tractor and Farm Museum West Side. 3m E off A69. The collection is housed in original stone buildings from 1806. Over 250 vintage tractors and engines, showing the development of agriculture from 1900 to the Post-War period. The collection includes small hand tools, barn equipment, joiners tools, harness, farm and dairy equipment, an 1835 Bingfield steam engine and thresher, also a 1903 Ivel which won a 1st prize at the Royal show in 1903. ⬛ Open 30 Apr to 30 Sep weekdays (ex Fri) 10 – 6, Sun 12 – 6, last admission 5 pm. 70p (ch 35p, ch 4 free, pen 25p). Party. ⚠ *(Tel Stocksfield 2553)* ⅙ B

CORBY CASTLE *Cumbria* Map 12 NY45
On unclassified road from A69 at Warwick Bridge. Ancient pele tower in 17th- and early 19th-C house. Early 18th-C grounds with forest trees by River Eden. Grounds only open 1 Apr to 31 Oct, daily 10 – 7. 20p (ch free). ⚠ *(Tel Wetheral 60246)*. *(Mr J P Howard)*

CORFE CASTLE *Dorset* Map 3 SY98
Corfe Castle 12th- to 16th-C stronghold in Purbeck Hills, besieged in 1646 during Civil War and later slighted. Open Mar to Oct, daily 10 – dusk, Nov to Feb afternoons only, weather permitting. 30p (ch 16 20p). Party 20+ by arrangement. P. *(Tel 442)*

Corfe Castle Museum Tiny rectangular building, partly rebuilt in brick after fire in 1680. Small museum with old village relics. Dinosaur footprints 130 million years old. Council chamber on first floor accessible by staircase at one end, and Ancient Order of Marblers meets here each Shrove Tuesday (open by appointment only). Museum open all year, summer 9 – 9, winter 9 – 6. (Times are approximate). Free. P. ⅙

CORSHAM *Wiltshire* Map 3 ST86

Corsham Court Elizabethan manor with additions by 'Capability' Brown and Nash. Georgian state rooms with furniture by Chippendale, Adam, Cobb, and Johnson, famous Methuen collection of Old Masters, garden with flowering shrubs, herbaceous borders, Georgian bath house, peacocks and 15th-C gazebo. Open all year, Sun, Wed and Thu; mid Jul to mid Sep, daily (ex Mon and Fri); and during Bath Festival and BH Mon 11–12.30 and 2–6 (4.30 in winter). 80p (ch 40p). Party 15+ 50p each. Under revision for 1980. ⚠ *(Tel 712214). (Lord Methuen)* &

COSFORD RAF *West Midlands* Map 7 SJ70

Aerospace Museum Extensive collection of aircraft, aircraft engines, rockets and missiles. The British, German and Japanese aircraft collection includes Spitfire, Mosquito, Javelin, Messerschmitt, Avro, Bristol, and many more. Rocket collection includes V1, V2, Messerschmitt, Henchel, Rheinmettal and others. Amateur radio station in operation. ⚟ Open Sat, Sun and BH Apr to Oct 10 – 5. 1980 charges not yet decided. ⚠ *(Tel Albrighton 4872)* &

COTON *Northamptonshire* Map 4 SP67

Coton Manor Wildlife Gardens A beautiful old garden surrounding 17th-C stone manor house. Rare wildfowl, cranes and flamingoes add greatly to the attraction of the lakes and water gardens. ⚟ Gift shop. Large variety of unusual plants for sale. Open Easter or Apr 1 to end of Oct, Sun, Thu and BH 2 – 6 also Wed Jul – Aug. 50p (ch 14 25p). Admission prices under revision for 1980. ⚠ *(Tel Northampton 740219)*

COUGHTON *Warwickshire* Map 4 SP06

Coughton Court 16th-C and later house, with imposing stone gatehouse (1509), two Elizabethan half-timbered wings, and Jacobite relics. Associated with Gunpowder Plot. ⚟ Open Apr and Oct Sat and Sun; May to end Sep Wed, Thu, Sat and Sun, BH Mon and following Tue 2 – 6 (or sunset if earlier). 70p. No dogs. (NT)

COVENTRY *West Midlands* Map 4 SP37

Coventry Cathedral 7 Priory Row. The present cathedral was designed by Sir Basil Spence and consecrated in May 1962. Contains outstanding modern works of art, including the Sutherland altar tapestry, the West Screen (a wall of glass engraved by John Hutton with saints and angels) and stained glass unequalled in modern times. Also treasury and ruins, including 14th-C tower. Open all year, daily 7 – 7.30 (summer) – 5.30 (winter) ex during services. Admission: Treasury 20p (ch 10p); Tower 20p (ch 15p). ⚟ (licensed) daily (ex Sun) 10.30 – 5. Party. P. *(Tel 27597)* &

Coventry Zoological Gardens Whitley Common. Includes lions, pumas, leopards, monkeys, apes, etc. Children's amusements and leisure park. ⚲ (licensed). Picnics. Open all year daily 10 – dusk. 20p (ch 14 10p). Family ticket 50p. Restaurant for hire. ⚠ *(Tel 301772)* ⌔

Herbert Art Gallery and Museum Jordan Well. Collections include industry and technology, social history, archaeology and folk life, natural history, visual arts. Of special interest is the Iliffe collection of Graham Sutherland's sketches for the 'Christ in Glory' tapestry in Coventry Cathedral, a social history gallery with changing displays and the natural history room. Open all year (ex 4 Apr and part of Christmas period) Mon to Sat 10 – 6, Sun 2 – 5. Free. P. *(Tel 25555 ext 2662)* ⌔

Lunt Roman Fort Baginton. On S side of city, off Stonebridge highway, A45. Reconstruction of Roman fort, which stood on this site AD60 – 80, with interpretive centre housed in reconstructed granary. Other features include gateway and gyrus. Open 24 May to 28 Sep (ex Mon and Thu) 12 – 6 (advisable to telephone). 45p (ch and pen 25p). ⚠ *(Tel 25555 ext 2662)* ⌔ B

Museum of British Road Transport The museum will open in Oct 1980 and will show the part Coventry and the West Midlands area in general, have played in the development of transport throughout the world. Displays will include motor cars, commercial vehicles, motor cycles and cycles, together with associated relevant materials. ⚲ Open Oct 1980 Tue to Fri 10.30 – 5, Sat 10 – 6, Sun 12 – 6. Admission prices not yet available. P. *(Tel 465488)* ⌔

St Mary's Guild Hall Between Bayley Lane and Earl Street. Medieval guildhall, begun in 1340 and completed in 1550, with minstrels' gallery, restored hall with portraits and Flemish tapestries, and Caesar's watchtower. Open Easter then 1 May to 31 Oct, Mon to Sat 10 – 5, Sun 12 – 5 (subject to civic requirements – enquiry advised before visiting). Free. P. *(Tel 25555 ext 2874)*

Vehicle Building and Automotive Museum 63 Holyhead Road. Following the amalgamation of the National Union of Vehicle Builders with the Transport and General workers Union 1972, it was decided to preserve the historical records of the vehicle builders in a small museum, which would also trace the progress of the vehicle from the early coach days to the modern motor car. Four rooms containing preserved documents and articles related to the union. Also displays following the production in various stages of latter day and modern vehicles. Open all year Mon to Fri 9 – 5, other times by appointment. Free. ⚠ *(Tel 29628)* ⌔ B

COXWOLD *North Yorkshire* Map 8 SE57
Shandy Hall Medieval house associated with Laurence Sterne, whose books, *Tristram Shandy and Sentimental Journey* were mostly written here, between 1760 and 1768. Now a Sterne Museum. Open Jun to Sep, Wed 2 – 6, all other times by previous appointment. 50p (ch accompanied 25p). Admission for 1979 not yet decided. ⚠ *(Tel 465)* **(79)**

CRANBORNE *Dorset* Map 4 SU01
Cranborne Manor Private Gardens and Garden Centre Private gardens, laid out in 17th C, preserved Elizabethan mount and knot gardens, herb and river gardens. Gardens only open, Apr to Oct, first Sat and Sun in month, BH and some other weeks advertised locally. Sat 9 – 5, Sun 2 – 5. Garden Centre open all year, Mon to Sat 9 – 5, Sun 2 – 5. 50p (ch 10p). Under revision for 1980. ⚠ *(Tel 248 or 289)*. *(Marquess of Salisbury)*

CRANBROOK *Kent* Map 5 TQ73
Angley House Garden 12 acres containing large collection of trees, rhododendrons and other shrubs in woodland setting with lake. Open Apr to Jul and Oct daily 11 – 7. 25p (ch 12 10p). No dogs because of peacocks. No coaches because of access and parking. *(Tel 2291)* **(79)**

CRANHAM *Gloucestershire* Map 3 SO81
Prinknash Abbey On A46 between Cheltenham and Painswick. Situated in a large park, this 14th- and early 16th-C house was the residence of Benedictines and guests of Gloucester Abbey; Henry VIII and Anne Boleyn came here in 1535. The house was in private ownership from 1539 to 1928 and became a priory (later abbey) for Benedictine monks from Caldey in 1928 who completed the new buildings in 1972. ⚲ 9.30 – 5.30. Open all year daily. Abbey Church 5 – 8.30. Pottery Mon to Fri 10 – 5 also Sat am, Sun pm (Pottery shop 9 – 6). Viewing gallery 20p (ch 14 free). Guides available. ⚠ *(Tel Painswick 812239)* ⌔ B

Prinknash Bird Park Set in nine acres of beautiful parkland with lakes and wood now leading to restored 16th-C Haunted Monks Fishpond. Views of Gloucester Cathedral, and the Welsh mountains beyond. Flock of snow geese. Demoiselle Cranes, pheasants, peacocks, White and Indian Blue, Black and Mute Swans, geese and other water fowl, most free. Pygmy goats and Jacob sheep. Open 1 Mar to 31 Oct daily 10 – 6, Nov to Feb weekends only 11 – 4 (or 1 hr before dusk). 35p (ch 25p pen 30p). Party (5p reduction of all classes). ⚠ *(Tel Painswick 812727)* **(79)**

CRANMORE *Somerset* Map 3 ST64
East Somerset Railway At Cranmore Railway Station is an exhibition of steam locomotives and rolling stock, with locomotive engine shed and workshops, engine in steam Suns and BH, Mar to Oct for brake van rides. Approx 1 m country ride due to open 1980. Signal box art gallery. Souvenir shop ⚲. Open all year daily (ex Christmas) 9 – 5.30 (4 winter). 50p (ch 15 and pen 25p), admission prices under revision for 1980. *(Tel 417)*

CREWKERNE *Somerset* Map 3 ST40
Clapton Court Gardens 3 m S on B3165. One of Somerset's most beautiful gardens with rare and unusual trees and shrubs, rhododendrons, azaleas and magnolias of botanical interest in formal and woodland gardens. Outstanding Springtime display of daffodils. Garden centre. Cream teas Sun and BH. Other meals by arrangement for booked parties (not Sun or BH). Open 23 Mar to 20 Oct daily (ex Sat) 2 – 5. 50p (ch 16 25p). ⚠ *(Tel 73220 or 72200)* ⌔

CRICH *Derbyshire* Map 8 SK35
Tramway Museum Matlock Road. Off B5035. Old tramcars from many parts of Britain, and from abroad, preserved in former quarry. Many are in working order, and visitors may ride on them along a 1 m tramway with views over Derwent Valley. Also reconstructed Georgian Assembly rooms façade from Derby, with Victorian street furniture and an exhibition also display relating to Derbyshire lead mining, at the terminus. ⚲. Admission prices and opening times not yet known. ⚠ *(Tel Ambergate 2565)* ⌔

CRICKET ST THOMAS *Somerset*
Map 3 ST30
Wild Life Park and Country Life Museum
Home of the National Heavy Horse Centre.
Historic and beautiful park, with 9 lakes and
collection of wild animals and birds. Tropical
walk-through aviary. New penguin enclosure.
Large children's fort. Picnic area. ⚲
(licensed). Garden shop and gift shop. Open
all year daily. Admission prices under
revision. ⚠ *(Tel Winsham 396)* ♿

CROFT *Hereford and Worcester* Map 7 SO46
Croft Castle Off B4362. Restored, partly
14th-C mansion, with 16th- 17th-, and 18th-C
alterations, including Georgian staircase and
ceilings. Four round towers, and original 14th-
or 15th-C walls can be seen. 1,636-acre
estate includes fine oaks, beeches, and
Spanish chestnuts lining the avenues.
Notable Iron Age fort of Croft Ambrey nearby.
Open Apr to end Sep, Wed, Thu, Sat, Sun, BH
Mon 2.15–6 (or sunset); Oct, Sat and Sun
2.15–6 (or sunset). 85p. joint ticket with
Berrington Hall £1.50. *(NT)*

CROMER *Norfolk* Map 9 TG24
Cromer Zoo Well-situated, overlooking the
sea and covering approximately 5-acres with
animals including lions, leopards, bears,
monkeys, tigers, etc. ⚲ Open all year, daily
10–7 (4 in winter). 80p (ch 40p) ⚠
(Tel 2947) ♿

Cromer Museum Tucker Street. Three 19th-
C Fishermens' Cottages. One furnished as a
cottage of *c*1900, also pictures and
collections of Victorian Cromer. Collections
illustrate the natural history and archaeology
of the area. Open all year Mon to Sat 10–5,
Sun 2–5, 15p (ch 5p, ch accompanied and
pen free). P. *(Tel 513543)*
Lifeboat Museum Situated in No. 2
boathouse at the bottom of The Gangway.
Covers both local lifeboat history and general
RNLI history. Open 1 May to 30 Sep daily
10–5. Free. P. *also Lifeboat Station* on Pier.
Open as above. School parties accepted at
Lifeboat Station. ♿

CROWLAS *Cornwall* Map 2 SW53
Age of Steam Rospeath Lane, on A30
between Penzance and Hayle. An 18-acre
steam park with over a mile of 10¼″ gauge
passenger-carrying steam railway. Also
children's boating lake with island. Self-drive
slot model steam paddle boats and trains.
Large, indoor model railway, museum and
gallery. Traction engines and steam organs
etc sometimes on view. Gift shop. Picnic and
play areas. ⚲ Open Easter to Oct daily from
10.30. Admission prices not available. ⚠ *(Tel
Cockwells 631)* ♿ (free)

CROYDE *Devon* Map 2 SS43
Croyde Gem Rock and Shell Museum A
unique museum and craft workshop of
gemstones and shells. Displays of the world's
gemstones in the natural and polished state.
Demonstrations of cutting and polishing.
Shop for jewellery, equipment and materials.
Daily 1 Mar to 31 Oct 10–5.30, Jul to Aug
10–10, restricted winter opening please
phone. 10p (ch and pen 5p). Party. P. *(Tel
890407)* **(79)**

CUSWORTH *South Yorkshire* Map 8 SE50
Cusworth Hall Museum House (1741 and
1750) with fine chimney pieces, chapel in
south-west wing. Museum of South Yorkshire
life. Sections of interest to children. Extensive
grounds open all year, with fishing in ponds,
cricket and football pitches. Children's study
base; research facilities. House open all year,
daily 11–5 (4 Nov to Feb), Sun 1–5. Free. ⚠
(Tel Doncaster 61842) ♿ B

DACRE *Cumbria* Map 12 NY42
Dalemain The oldest part of this historic
house is medieval. Originally a pele tower,
added to in Tudor times and the imposing
Georgian façade was completed in 1750.
Splendid oak panelling, Chinese wall paper,
Tudor plasterwork, fine Queen Anne and
18th-C furniture. Rooms recently opened
include the Victorian nursery and the
housekeeper's work room. The tower
contains the Westmorland and Cumberland
Yeomanry Museum. Countryside Museum in
16th-C cobbled courtyard. Historic gardens.
Gift shop. ⚲ (home-made teas). Open 5 Apr
to end Sep, daily (ex Fri) 2–5.15. House and
garden 80p (ch 14 and registered disabled
40p); gardens only 20p (ch 14 and registered
disabled 5p). Under revision for 1980. ⚠ and
picnicking free. *(Tel Pooley Bridge 450)* ♿ B

DALTON-IN-FURNESS *Cumbria*
Map 7 SD27
Castle Standing in main street, 14th-C tower
built originally by Furness Abbey monks as a
court room. Owned by Duke of Buccleuch's
family since 1660. Open at all reasonable
hours; key from *Mr I J Whitehead, 18 Market
Place.* 20p *(NT)*
Tytup Hall A small early 18th-C country
mansion in Palladian style. Wood panelling
preserved in three of first floor rooms and hall.
Father West wrote his 'Antiquities of Furness',
a study of the area, here. Open all year by
appointment only. 50p ⚠ *(Tel 62929)*. *(Dr J R
Edge)*

DALWOOD *Devon* Map 3 ST20
Loughwood Meeting House Mid 17th-C
Nonconformist place of worship, in remote

wooded setting, with plastered barrel ceiling. In almost original condition. Open all year. Free. *(NT)*

DANBY *North Yorkshire* Map 8 NZ70
Danby Lodge National Park Lodge Lane. The former shooting lodge offers full information and countryside interpretation service to visitors to the North York Moors National Park. The grounds include riverside meadow, woodland and terraced gardens. Slides and films shown daily. Exhibition about the North York Moors. Bookshop information desk. Guided walks Suns and daily Jul and Aug. ♨ Open 1 Apr to 31 Oct daily 10 – 6, Nov, Feb, Mar weekends 10 – 5. 30p (ch 18 10p, pen 20p). Under revision for 1980. ⚠ *(Tel Castleton 654)* & B

DARLINGTON *Co Durham* Map 8 NZ21
Art Gallery Crown Street. Contains a permanent collection of pictures but also has temporary loan exhibitions throughout the year. Open all year, daily (ex Sun and BH) 10 – 8 (5.30 Sat). Free. P. *(Tel 62034)* &
Darlington Museum Tubwell Row. Local social and natural history, archaeology and bygones. Observation beehive and beekeeping exhibits (approx May to Sep) each year. Open all year (ex 4 Apr, 25 and 26 Dec, 1 Jan) Mon to Sat (ex Thu afternoon) 10 – 1 and 2 – 6 (5.30 Sat). Free. P. *(Tel 63795)*
North Road Station Railway Museum Opened in 1975, this museum is housed in what is probably the oldest railway station in Britain (1841), still in use and carefully restored. It contains exhibits and models connected with the Stockton and Darlington and the North Eastern Railway Companies, including an early railway coach (*c*1845), a chaldron wagon and five 19th-C locomotives,

one of which is the original 'Locomotive No. 1' built by George Stephenson in 1825 also the Derwent built 1845. A model railway. Souvenir shop. ♨ Open all year daily Easter to end Oct, Mon to Sat 10 – 5, Suns 2 – 4; Nov to Easter, Mon to Sat 10 – 3. 20p (ch 16 and pen 10p). Party. ⚠ *(Tel 60532)* &

DARTINGTON *Devon* Map 3 SX76
Dartington Hall Only 14th-C banqueting hall of house shown. Large gardens, with trees and shrubs, courtyard, and terraces. Research, education, agriculture, and other commercial enterprises on the estate are controlled by Dartington Hall Trust. ♨ Open all year, daily. Gardens and hall occasionally closed for special events. Free. ⚠ *(Tel Totnes 862271)* & B *(NGS)*

DARTMOUTH *Devon* Map 3 SX85
Agincourt House Lower Ferry. Built 1380, and restored 1671 and 1966, partly timbered house, one of the oldest in town. Formerly rich merchant's house, now antique shop and museum with two of its four floors open to public. Open all day all year (ex week after Christmas). Free. P. *(Tel 2472)* **(79)**
Bayard's Cove Castle Low, circular ruined stronghold, built by townspeople in 1537, with gunposts as at Dartmouth Castle (see below). Accessible at all reasonable times. Free. ⚠ *(AM)*
Butterwalk Museum Half timbered 17th-C house, part of restored colonnaded arcade, with small maritime and nautical museum (over 100 ship models). Open end Oct to end Apr, Mon – Sat 2 – 4; May to Oct, Mon – Sat 11 – 5. 10p (ch 15 5p, ch 5 free). P. *(Tel 2923)*
Dartmouth Castle Tudor stronghold, dating from 1481, with some remains of earlier structure. Stands on estuary of River Dart facing Kingswear Castle on opposite shore, to

which it was attached by chain in times of war. Timber-framed opening for the chain can still be seen. Open*, see inside front cover. 25p (ch 16 and pen 10p). ⚠ *(AM)*

Newcomen Memorial Engine In Royal avenue Gardens by River Dart, this glass-fronted building commemorates the 300th anniversary of Newcomen's birth, and houses his atmospheric pressure steam pumping engine of 1725. Possibly the oldest of its type in world, it may be seen working. Open to view Easter to end Oct Mon–Sat 11–5, Sun 2–5. Special opening times in winter for pre-arranged parties. 10p (ch 15 5p, ch 5 free). P. *(Tel 2923)*. 18-page booklet is available, 25p incl postage. ⚹

DAWLISH WARREN *Devon* Map 3 SX97
South Devon Railway Museum and Model Railway Dawlish Warren Station A large collection of smaller railway relics including locomotive name/number plates, station signs, notices, tickets, documents, etc and model railway ('oo' scale). Shop stocking railway books, records, photographs, model equipment etc. Open daily Sun before Easter to Sun after Easter, Sun only until Spring BH then daily to end Sep 10–dusk. 50p (school child 25p). P. *(Tel 862131)* ⚹

DEAL *Kent* Map 5 TR35
Deal Castle Built by Henry VIII, with massive central citadel, houses exhibits of Iron Age weapons, early pottery, and relics of Deal's history. Open*, see inside front cover. 25p (ch 16 and pen 10p). ⚠ *(AM)*
Maritime and Local History Museum 22 St George's Road. Opened 1972 with exhibits including local boats, model sailing-ships, 'bygones', maps, old photographs, etc. Annexe where land and sea finds are examined, treated and classified. Local booklets, postcards etc on sale. Open Spring BH to end Sep daily 2–5. 20p (ch 5p), accompanied free). Under revision for 1980. P. *(Tel 4524)* ⚹ B
Walmer Castle 1m S, on coast. Built in 16th C, official residence of the Lord Warden of the Cinque Ports. Open*, see inside front cover, but closed always between 1 pm and 2 pm and also on Mons, ex BH. Gardens closed in winter. 40p (ch 16 and pen 15p), winter 15p (ch and pen 5p). Closed for a period, usually in Aug, when the Lord Warden is in residence. ⚠ *(Tel 01-734 6010 ext 448) (AM)*

DEDDINGTON *Oxfordshire* Map 4 SP43
Deddington Castle Mainly earthworks from outer bailey and inner ward. Excavations have revealed portions of 13th-C chapel. Piers Gaveston (favourite of Edward II) taken prisoner here before being executed in 14th-C. Open any reasonable time. Free. *(AM)*

DEDHAM *Essex* Map 5 TM03
Castle House Former home and studio of the late Sir Alfred Munnings KCVO, PRA. Contains paintings, drawings, sketches, and other works. Open 11 May to 12 Oct, Wed, Sun, BH, Thu and Sat in Aug 2–5; parties by arrangement. 40p (ch 15, 10p). Under review for 1980. ⚠ *(Tel Colchester 322127)*

DEENE *Northamptonshire* Map 4 SP99
Deene Park Mainly 16th-C house of great architectural importance and historical interest. Large lake and park. Extensive gardens with old fashioned roses, rare trees and shrubs. ⚐ Open 6, 7 Apr; 25, 26 May, Suns Jun and Jul, also 24, 25 Aug, 2–6. Admission prices not available. ⚠ *(Tel Bulwick 223 or 278)* ⚹

Kirby Hall 1½m W. Fine, partially restored house, begun in 1572, but altered in mid 17th C for Sir Christopher Hatton, Lord Chancellor, by John Thorpe, and later portion ascribed to Inigo Jones. Attractive garden layout. Open, see inside front cover. 20p (ch 16 and pen 5p). ⚠ *(Tel Corby 3230) (AM)*

DEERHURST *Gloucestershire* Map 3 SO82
Odda's Chapel Off B4213 near River Severn. Rare Saxon chapel, dating back to 1056, and erected originally by the Lord of the Manor. Attached to old half-timbered house. Open, see inside front cover. 10p (ch 16 and pen 5p). *(Tel Tewkesbury 292663) (AM)* ⚹

DELABOLE *Cornwall* Map 2 SX08
Delabole Slate Quarry and Museum Ancient slate quarry, worked continuously since 1555. Over 500ft deep and 1⅛ miles round. Featured in the Guinness Book of Records as being the largest man-made hole in England (possibly Europe). Museum and craft shop. Open 2 week Easter and May to Sep Mon–Fri 10–6. 25p (ch 15p). Under revision for 1980. ⚠ *(Tel Camelford 2242)*

DENVER MILL *Norfolk* Map 5 TF60
Large tower built in 1835, with 6 storeys and a complex of buildings formerly containing a steam mill. Steam gave way to diesel power and the engine and equipment is still in place, together with much of the wind-driven machinery. Open all year (by appointment) 9–dusk (closed Sun). Free. P. *(Tel Downham Market 2285)*

DERBY *Derbyshire* Map 8 SK33
Derby Museum and Art Gallery Antiquities, social history, natural history, militaria, Bonnie Prince Charlie room (1745 rebellion), scaled working layout of the former Midland Railway. Paintings by Joseph Wright of Derby (1734–1797), Derby porcelain, costume. Open all year, daily (closed Sun, Mon, and BH) Tue to Fri 10–6, Sat 10–5. Free. Parking in town. *(Tel 31111 ext 782)* ⚹
Industrial Museum Silk Mill, off Full Street. Housed in an early 17th-C silk mill substantially rebuilt in 1910. The Rolls-Royce aero engine occupies the ground floor gallery, alongside the history of aviation from the Wright Brothers to the present day. 'An Introduction to Derbyshire Industries' occupies the first floor gallery. Open all year (closed Sun, Mon and BH) Tue to Fri 10–5.45, Sat 10–4.45. Free. *(Tel 31111 ext 740)* ⚹

DEREHAM *Norfolk* Map 9 TF91
Bishop Bonner's Cottages Row of restored cottages, with coloured East Anglian pargeting (1502), now a museum, with local archaeological discoveries, and exhibitions of rural crafts during summer months. Open mid May to Sep, Tue, Thu, and Fri 2.30–5, Sat 3–5.30; contact *Mrs Webb, 6 Sandy Lane,* Free. P. *(Tel 2789)* **(79)**
Norfolk Rural Life Museum 2½m NW on unclass road at Gressenhall. A Museum of Norfolk rural life to show history of the County of Norfolk over past 200 years with particular emphasis on agriculture. Open daily (ex Mon) 10–5, Sun 2–5.30. 30p (ch and pen free) ⚠ *(Tel Gressenhall 563)*

DEVIZES *Wiltshire* Map 4 SU06
Devizes Museum Exhibits from prehistoric, Roman, and medieval periods in Wiltshire, including 1st-C Belgic 'Marlborough Bucket'. Open all year, Tue to Sat 11–1, 2–5. 25p (ch 16 free, students and pen 10p). Under revision for 1980. P. *(Tel 2765)* ⚹ B

DIDCOT *Oxfordshire* Map 4 SU58
Great Western Society Didcot Railway Centre Access through main entrance of Didcot station. Largest collection of ex-Great Western rolling stock assembled in GWR engine shed, including 20 steam locomotives, a diesel railcar, and large selection of passenger and freight rolling stock. ⚑ and gift shop. Open Sun also BH Mon Apr to Oct. Steam days first and last Sun of each month also BH Mon and Sun in Aug, 11 – 5. GWR steam train in operation. BH weekends and Enthusiasts' Day 80p (ch 40p) otherwise 60p (ch 30p). Special rates for family parties. Prices under revision. P. Enquiries to *Great Great Western Society, Didcot Railway Centre, Oxon*

DIDSBURY *Gt Manchester* Map 7 SJ89
Fletcher Moss Museum Wilmslow Road. New displays, due to open in 1980, of art and design in Manchester. Drawings and watercolours by the Pre-Raphaelites and 20th-C artists. Temporary exhibitions during the summer. Open Mon to Sat 10 – 6 (4 Nov to Feb); Sun 2 – 6 (4 Nov to Feb) 12 – 6 May to Aug. Free. (Tel 061-445 1109)

DILHORNE *Staffordshire* Map 7 SJ94
Foxfield Light Railway Society New museum of industrial steam locomotives, under auspices of Foxfield Light Railway Society. There are twelve steam locomotives, two or more which may be in steam on an open day. The former mineral line on which they run passes over 3½ miles of track through undulating rural scenery. ⚑ Souvenir shop. Open Apr to Sep, Sun and BH 2 – 6. Day membership of society essential 60p (ch 14 and pen 30p), subject to possible increase. ⚠ (Tel Stoke-on-Trent 313920) ♿

DINMORE *Hereford and Worcester* Map 3 SO45
Dinmore Manor 12th- to 14th-C Chapel of the Knights Hospitaller of St John of Jerusalem, with cloisters and music room. Chapel and gardens open all year 10 – 6. 40p (ch 16 and pen 20p). ⚠ (limited). Tel 061-943 2313). (Mr J S Murray) ♿

DINTING VALE *Derbyshire* Map 7 SK09
Dinting Railway Centre Off A57 in Dinting Lane. One engine is always in steam Mar to Oct, Sun and BH. Large picnic area. ⚑. Steam weekends 1 Jan, 4 – 7 Apr, 3 – 5 and 25/26 May also 23 – 25 Aug. Open all year, daily (ex 24 May and 25/26 Dec) 10.30 – 5. 30p (ch 16 15p) subject to confirmation. Party. ⚠ (Tel Glossop 5596) ♿

DISLEY *Cheshire* Map 7 SJ98
Lyme Park Of Elizabethan origin, enlarged in 1726 by Leoni and in 1817 by Lewis Wyatt, with fine Palladian façade, Jacobean rooms, and collection of pictures and furnishings. A park of more than 1,300 acres, contains herd of deer.Hall shown Mar to Oct, daily (ex Mon) Apr to Sep, Sun and BH 1 – 6, Tue to Sat 2 – 5. Mar and Oct Sun 1 – 4.30 and Tue to Sat 2 – 4. House 37p. Park and gardens open all year, daily 8 – sunset. Free. Prices subject to revision for 1980. ⚠ 30p. (NT)

DITCHLEY *Oxfordshire* Map 4 SP32
Ditchley Park 18th-C mansion by James Gibbs, now Anglo-American conference centre, in landscaped park. Interior decoration includes rooms by Flitcroft and Kent. Open 21 Jul to 1 Aug daily 2 – 5. 60p P. (Tel Enstone 346). No photography except by prior permission. ♿ B (gardens)

DOBWALLS *Cornwall* Map 2 SX26
Forest Railroad Park Very extensive miniature railway based on the era of steam on the American railroad. A mile ride modelled on the Cumbres Pass route of the Denver and Rio Grande railroad, and another spectacular mile of track based on the Sherman Hill route of the Union Pacific railroad. Forest, tunnels, embankments, canyons and the steepest gradients on a miniature railway anywhere. Large picnic areas; railway walk; indoor railway exhibition; children's play areas; radio controlled boats; ⚑ Open 4 Apr to 14 Apr then 1 May to end Sep daily 10.30 – 6. Admission prices not yet decided. ⚠ (Tel 20325)

Thorburn Museum and Gallery The unique world renowned permanent memorial exhibition of paintings, sketches, prints, books, letters, photographs etc, by Britain's greatest bird painter – Archibald Thorburn (1860 – 1935). Over 120 original paintings (many of major importance) on display in the collection which is housed in a large converted barn. Award winner in the 'Museum of the year' award 1977 also British Tourist Authority's 'Come to Britain' competition. Open Easter 10 days then 1 May to end of Sep, daily 10.30 – 6. At other times by appointment only. Admission charges not yet decided for 1980. P. (Tel 20325)

DODDINGTON *Lincolnshire* Map 8 SK87
Doddington Hall Romantic Elizabethan mansion with Tudor gatehouse, walled rose garden. Fine furniture, porcelain, textiles and pictures. Souvenir and gift shop. ⚑ (tea) Open 2 – 6, Wed May to Sep also Sun, Jun, Jul and Aug, and 7 Apr, 5 and 26 May, 25 Aug. Parties at other times by arrangement. School project. Prices for 1980 not yet decided. (Tel 227. (Mrs A Jarvis)

DODINGTON *Avon* Map 3 ST77
***Dodington House, Park and Carriage
Museum*** 200yds N of M4 junction 18. 18th-C
classic house, built by James Watt and
approached by a mile-long drive through 700
acres of parkland laid out by 'Capability'
Brown. Furniture, paintings, *objets d'art*, and
unusual fireplaces by Wyatt can be seen in
the house. **Carriage Museum** Horses and
over 30 carriages, **Family Museum** aviation
scale model collection. Children's
adventureland, children's farm, antique
agricultural implements exhibition and nature
trails. ⚏ and bar. Open Apr to Sep, daily
11 – 5. Admission prices not yet decided.
Train and carriage rides extra. Dogs on lead
only (not in house). ⚠ *(Tel Chipping Sodbury
318899)* ⅃

DONCASTER *South Yorkshire* Map 8 SE50
Museum and Art Gallery Chequer Road.
Prehistoric and Romano-British archaeology,
British natural history, local history and
costumes, British and European Art
Collection, paintings, sculpture, ceramics,
glass and silver. ⚏ Open all year (ex 25 and
26 Dec) and 1 Jan), Mon – Fri 10 – 5, Sun 2 – 5.
Free. ⚠ *(Tel 62095)* ⅃

DONINGTON-LE-HEATH *Leicestershire*
Map 8 SK41
Donington-le-Heath Manor House Near
Coalville. Medieval manor house of *c*1280
with very few alterations. 2 Apr to 1 Oct Wed
to Sun also BH Mon and Tue 2 – 6. Free. ⚠
(Tel Coalville 31259)

DONNINGTON *Berkshire* Map 4 SU46
Donnington Castle Late 14th-C gatehouse,
with earthworks from Civil War sieges of
1644 – 46. Open at any reasonable time
(exterior only). Free. ⚠ *(AM)*

DORCHESTER *Dorset* Map 3 SY69
Came House 2m SE of Dorchester, off A352
near Winterbourne Came. 18th-C house with
columned 7 bay entrance façade, and interior
with good fireplaces and plasterwork. Open
only by appointment to Major N D Martin. 50p
⚠

Dorset County Museum High West Street.
Fine County collection of prehistoric and
Roman antiquities, geology, natural history,
rural crafts, and relics of both Thomas Hardy
and William Barnes. Hardy's manuscripts for
The Mayor of Casterbridge, and his
reconstructed study can be seen. concerts,
lectures, films. Open all year (ex Sun, 4 Apr,
25/26 Dec), Mon to Fri 10 – 5, Sat 10 – 1 and
2 – 5. 30p (ch and pen 15p), ch 5 free). ⚠ *(Tel
2735)*

Dorset Military Museum The Keep. Covers
nearly 300 years of military history, with
exhibits of Dorset Regiment, Militia,
Volunteers, Queen's Own Dorset Yeomanry
and Devonshire and Dorset Regiment (from
1958). Also well-stocked reference library.
Open all year (ex Sun, 13 and 16 Apr, 25 and
26 Dec), Mon to Fri 9 – 1 and 2 – 5, Sat 9 – 12
(Jul to Sep 9 – 1 and 2 – 5). 20p (ch 10p). ⚠
(Tel 4066)

Hardy's Cottage 3m E, off A35 near Higher
Bockhampton. Thatched house, birthplace in
1840 of Thomas Hardy. Cottage open only by
appointment with tenant. *(Tel Dorchester
2366)*; exterior viewable Mar to Oct, daily
11 – 6 (or sunset). 60p. P in woods 10 min
walk from house. *(NT)*

Old Crown Court In 1834, in the Court Room
of the Old Shire Hall, the Tolpuddle Martyrs
were sentenced to transportation to Botany
Bay in Australia for demanding a wage
increase. Building is now a Tolpuddle

Memorial. Open all year, Mon to Fri 10–12 and 2.30–4 (Nov to Apr 10–12); other times only by arrangement at adjacent West Dorset District Council. Free. P. *(Tel 5211)*

Maiden Castle 1m SW. Prehistoric earthworks, the name being derived from Celtic 'Mai-Jun' (the stronghold by the plain)' Huge, oval, triple-ramparted camp, with extensive plateau on summit. Complicated defensive system of ditches and ramparts. Open at any reasonable time. Free. ⚠ *(AM)*

Wolfeton House 1½m NW on A37. A fine medieval and Elizabethan manor house with magnificent stonework, great stairs, fire places and ceilings. 17th-C furniture and pictures. Gatehouse chapel and cider house. ⛄ for parties by appointment. Open 1 May to 30 Sep Sun, Tue, Wed and BH plus daily Aug (ex Sat) 2.30–6. Parties throughout the year by appointment. 75p. ⚠ *(Tel 3500)*

DOVER *Kent* Map 5 TR34
Crabble Watermill Lower Road. A six-storey building erected in about 1812 to provide flour for the troops stationed in the area when Britain was threatened with invasion by Napoleon. The mill gradually ceased to function and finally went out of use in about 1890. The mill was restored to full working order by the Cleary Foundation in 1973. Open Easter, then Spring BH to end Sep, Wed and Sat 2–5, Sun and BH 10–1 and 2–6. When machinery working ch 14 not admitted. Ch 14 admitted Wed and Sat, if accompanied by a parent. 15p (ch 10p). Party. *(Tel Dover 201066)* ♿

Dover Castle Norman castle with keep (1181–87) containing 242ft deep well. Roman 'Pharos', or lighthouse, and restored Saxon St Mary de Castro's church nearby. Keep* grounds and underground passages, see inside front cover. ⛄ Admission to keep 50p, winter 25p (ch 16 and pen 20p, winter 10p); underground passages 25p (ch 16 and pen 10p). Grounds free. ⚠ 10p. *(AM)*

Roman Painted House New Street. Large part of an exceptionally preserved Roman town house 1,800 years old containing the best preserved and oldest Roman wall paintings north of the Alps. Also substantially complete underfloor central heating systems, part of later Roman fort wall, stone tower, extensive display panel on Roman Dover and some recent finds. Free guided tours for parties. Open Mar to Nov, Tue to Sun 10–5. 20p (ch and pen 10p). ⚠ *(Tel 203279)* ♿ B

Town Hall Includes 13th-C Hall of Maison Dieu, part of former pilgrim's hostel founded by Hubert de Burgh. Museum, founded 1836, contains exhibits of local history, archaeology, ceramics, coins, natural history,

geology. There is a monthly programme of temporary exhibitions. Open 10–4.45 (closed Wed and Sun). Free. *(Tel 201066)* ♿

DOWN AMPNEY *Gloucestershire* Map 4 SU09
Down Ampney House and Art Exhibition 6m SE of Cirencester, 3m NW of Cricklade, off A419. Tudor and later house with well restored mid 15th-C hall. Exhibition of paintings by local artists held annually. Open 28 Jul to 5 Aug. Daily 10–7. 10p. ⚠ **(79)**

DOWNE *Gt London* Map 5 TQ46
Down House Contains the Darwin Memorial. Gardens also open. Open 1 Mar to 31 Jan (ex Mon, Fri, 24–27 Dec and all Feb) 1–6 (last visitor 5.30). Open BH Mons. 50p (ch 15 20p). ⚠ *(Tel Farnborough, Kent 59119, Tue to Thu 10–6)* ♿

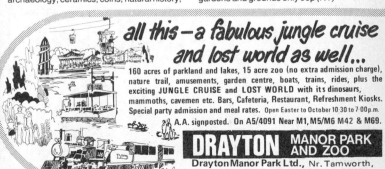

DRAYTON MANOR PARK AND ZOO
Staffordshire Map 4 SK10
On A4091 1m S of junction with A5(T). 1½m S of Tamworth. 160 acres of parkland with 15-acre zoo, including lions, pumas, tigers, monkeys, reptile house, birds, paddocks and farm section. Jungle cruise on the lower lake. Miniature railway, cable cars, amusement park, boats, garden centre, Dinosaurs in the 'Lost World'; shops. ⛄ (licensed) (party tearoom). Open Easter to Oct, daily 10.30–7. Admission prices as advertised. Reduced rates for parties. ⚠ (Parked on parkland). *(Tel Tamworth 68481)* ♿

DREWSTEIGNTON *Devon* Map 3 SX79
Castle Drogo 2m NE of Chagford, turn off A382 at Sandy Park. A granite castle built between 1910 and 1930, one of the most remarkable works of Sir Edwin Lutyens. Standing at 900ft it overlooks the wooded gorge of the River Teign. Open 1 Apr to Oct, daily 11–6 (last admission 5.30). £1.30, gardens and grounds only 90p *(NT)*

DUDLEY *West Midlands* Map 7 SO99
Black Country Museum Tipton Road
(opposite Dudley Guest Hospital). An open-
air museum of the region with buildings re-
erected to form a village representing the way
of life in this area. The village has a 19th-C
canal boat dock with a range of narrow boats
on display. A chainmaker's house with its
brewhouse has been re-erected and in the
garden, the chainshop stages regular
demonstrations of chainmaking. At weekends
trips into the famous Dudley Tunnel start from
the site. Also a coal mine, chemist's shop and
chapel are on display. Open from 1 May to 30
Sep. Admission charges not available. ⚠ *(Tel
Birmingham 557 9643)*
Central Museum and Art Galley St James's
Road. Permanent collection of fine art and a
wide variety of temporary exhibitions
throughout the year. Fine geological gallery.
Reconstructed Black Country Nail Forge, also
the Brooke Robinson Museum. The Brierley
Hill Glass collection will be on display until
amalgamation with the Stourbridge Glass
collection at Kingswinford in 1980. Open all
year, Mon to Sat 10–6. Free. P. *(Tel 55433)*
Dudley Zoo Situated in 40 acres of
attractively wooded grounds, the great variety
of animals, birds, reptiles and fish includes a
white tiger, okapis, ring-tailed lemurs and
silvery marmosets. Children's corner, a chair-
lift and part of the ruins of Dudley castle can
be explored. Picnic area. ⚲ Open daily,
weekdays from 9.30, Sun from 10. ⚠ No pets
admitted.

DUNGENESS *Kent* Map 5 TR01
Dungeness Lighthouses Old lighthouse,
standing slightly inland, was replaced in 1961
because its light had been obscured by the
nuclear power station. Ground floor of new
lighthouse open all year daily (ex Sun and
during fog) 1 pm to 1 hr before sunset (at
visitors' own risk). Free. P. *(Tel Lydd 20236)*
'A' Nuclear Power Station Building open
throughout the year for organised group tours
by pre-arrangement, and to the general public
Jun–Sep, Wed 2–4. Ticket obtainable from
the local South Eastern Electricity Board
shops. Ch 14 not admitted. Free. ⚠ *(Tel Lydd
20461) (79)*

DUNSTER *Somerset* Map 3 SS95
Dunster Castle Restored 11th-C and later
castle, with rare portraits, hall leading to
famous carved staircase; banqueting hall
containing leather hangings. Open Apr to Sep
daily (ex Fri and Sat) 11–5, Mar, Oct and Nov,
Tue, Wed and Sun 2–4. £1 (ch 14 50p). Party
15+. ⚠ *(Tel 314) (NT)*

Old Dovecote 12th-C dovecote, part of
former priory, retaining rare original potence
(revolving ladder for reaching nesting boxes).
Open Easter to mid Oct, daily 10–dusk. Free;
leaflet 5p.
DUNWICH *Suffolk* Map 5 TM47
Dunwich Museum St James Street.
Contains the history and relics of the ancient
city of Dunwich, also flora and fauna of the
area. Open all year (ex Christmas and New
Year) Sat and Sun 2–4.30, also Tue and Thu
May to Jul and Sep and Oct 2–4.30, and daily
Aug 2–4.30. Free. ⚠ *(Tel Westleton 218 or
276)*

DUPATH *Cornwall* Map 2 SX37
Holy Well Dedicated to St Sampson of
Guernsey and erected c1500, one of best
known ancient Holy Wells of Cornwall.
Viewable at any reasonable time. Free. *(AM)*

DURHAM *Co Durham* Map 12 NZ24
Durham Castle Norman structure, utilised
since 1832 by University of Durham. Open
first three weeks of Apr and 1 Jul to 30 Sep,
Mon–Sat 10–12 and 2–4.30; rest of year,
Mon, Wed, Sat 2–4; closed at times owing to
university functions. 60p (ch 14 and pen 30p).
Guides are available at no extra cost and
guide books are on sale at the Porter's Lodge.
P. *(Tel 65481)*
**Durham Light Infantry Museum and Arts
Centre** Aykley Heads. History of famous
regiment, including armaments, medals, and
uniforms, in modern setting. Also Arts centre
on first floor of building. Exhibitions, films and
family activities. Military Vehicle Rally Aug
BH. ⚲ Open all year Tue to Sat 10–5, Sun
2–5 (closed Mon ex BH). 20p (ch and pen
5p). P. Free brochure. *(Tel 67798)* ♿
Gulbenkian Museum of Oriental Art
University of Durham, Elvet Hill. Contains
Egyptian and Mesopotamian antiquities;
Chinese and Japanese pottery, porcelain,
jades, ivories, textiles and paintings; Indian
and Tibetan paintings and sculpture; and
works from the Near East. Open Mon to Fri
9.30–1, 2.15–5; Sat 9.30–12, 2.15–5, Sun
2.15–5 (closed Sat and Sun Christmas to
Easter). 30p (ch, students and pen 15p). P.
(Tel 66711)
St Aidan's College Grounds Windmill Hill.
The college was designed by Sir Basil
Spence, architect of Coventry Cathedral, and
built in the early sixties. The spacious and
well-stocked grounds were landscaped by
Professor Brian Hackett and are at their best
during July, when the shrub beds are in
flower. Features of interest include a
laburnham walk and a reflecting pool, well

DUNSTER CASTLE
Exmoor

Romantic fortified home of the Luttrells for 600 years. Terraces of sub-tropical
shrubs. Refreshments in village.
See gazetteer for details.

stocked with aquatic plants and fish. Open all year, daily from 9 – dusk. Free, but donation to NGS. ⚠ *(Tel 65011)* ㅤB

DUXFORD *Cambridgeshire* Map 5 TL44
Duxford Airfield 2m W of village on A505. This former Battle of Britain fighter station with hangars dating from the First World War now houses most of the Imperial War Museum's collections of military aircraft, armoured fighting vehicles and other large exhibits. The airfield has changed little in outward appearance since the Second World War. There are more than sixty historic aircraft on the airfield including a B-17 Flying Fortress, P-51 Mustang, Junkers 52, Lightning, Javelin, Super Sabre and Victor. Also on display is the Duxford Aviation Society's civil aircraft collection including Concorde 01. Details available from *Imperial War Museum, Lambeth Road, London SE1 6HZ*. Open 15 Mar to 2 Nov, daily 11 – 5 (or dusk). Admission/parking fee charged, telephone for details. *(Tel 01-735 8922 or Cambridge 833963)* ㅤ

DYMCHURCH *Kent* Map 5 TR02
Martello Tower (No. 24) One of a series of circular towers designed to repel expected Napoleonic invasion in early 19th C, with rooftop mounting for heavy gun. Open*, see inside front cover (Apr to Sep only). 15p (ch 16 and pen 5p). ⚠ *(AM)*

DYRHAM *Avon* Map 3 ST77
Dyrham Park 17th-C mansion, designed partly by William Talman in 1698, with contemporary Dutch-style furnishings. Garden front of 1692 by Hauduroy. ⚐ Open house and garden Apr, May and Oct daily, except Thu and Fri, 2 – 6; Jun to Sep daily, except Fri, 2 – 6. £1 *(NT)*

EAGLESCLIFF *Cleveland* Map 8 NZ41
Preston Hall Museum Museum illustrates social history of Stockton, and collections include ceramics, personalia, arms and armour, and period rooms. ⚐ Open all year Mon to Sat 10 – 6. Sun 2 – 6. Free. ⚠ *(Tel 871184)* ㅤB

EASBY *North Yorkshire* Map 7 NZ10
Easby Abbey Sited on banks of River Swale, a Premonstratensian Abbey dedicated to St Agatha, founded 1155. Considerable remains of monastic buildings. Open, see inside front cover. 15p (ch 16 and pen 5p). Free Mon and Tue, Apr to Sep only. ⚠ *(AM)*

EAST BERGHOLT *Suffolk* Map 5 TM03
Flatford Lock Similar in appearance to the lock shown in many of John Constable's paintings, the unique lock has been restored by voluntary workers of the River Stour Trust and is now used by non-powered craft. Demonstrations can be arranged for parties. Contact *F Batten, Wissington Grove, Nayland*. A restored Stour Lighter is also available for inspection on request. Open at all times. Free. ⚠ ㅤ

Flatford Mill and Willy Lott's Cottage 18th-C water mill and mill house once owned by Constable's father, subject of *The Hay Wain* and other famous pictures by the painter. 17th-C Willy Lott's Cottage stands nearby. Both in full time use by Field Studies Council. Exteriors only viewable. *(NT)*

EASTBOURNE *East Sussex* Map 5 TV69
Eastbourne Circular Redoubt Royal Parade. Extensive fortification built in 1804 during Napoleonic Wars against the threat of invasion. Now the home of the Sussex Combined Services Museum which illustrates the military history of Sussex. Access to the gun platform and aquarium. Open May to Sep, daily, Oct to Apr Mon to Fri, 10 – 6. 25p (ch 16 and pen 15p). Under review for 1980. ⚠ *(Tel 33952)*

Coastal Defence Museum Tower 73 (The Wish Tower), King Edward's Parade. One of the Martello Towers erected to combat threatened Napoleonic invasion in early 19th C now restored as museum displaying defence methods and equipment of that period. Open Easter to Nov, daily 10 – 5.30. 12p (ch 14 and pen 8p). Prices under review for 1980. ⚠ *(Tel 35809)*

Towner Art Gallery Borough Lane. Georgian manor house (1776) with later alterations, in pleasant gardens, containing collection of 19th and 20th-C British paintings, contemporary artists' prints and Georgian caricatures. Art exhibitions. Open all year (ex 4 Apr, 25 and 26 Dec) Mon to Sat 10 – 5 (closed 1 – 2), Sun 2 – 5. Free. ⚠ *(Tel 21635)* ㅤB

EAST CLANDON *Surrey* Map 4 TQ05
Hatchlands 18th-C house, with interiors of 1759, including plaster drawing room ceiling and library by Robert Adam. Open 1 Apr – 30 Sep, Wed and Sat 2 – 5.30 (last entries at 5pm). 40p (ch 12 20p). ⚠ (limited). *(Tel Guildford 222787)*. See also **Clandon Park**.

EAST GRINSTEAD *West Sussex* Map 5 TQ33
Sackville College Early Jacobean almshouse, with hall and chapel, built round a quadrangular courtyard, and founded in 1609 by 2nd Earl of Dorset. Contains fine oak furniture. Open May to Sep, daily (ex Sat) 2 – 5. 25p (ch 14 15p). P. *(Tel 21639)* ㅤ **(79)**

Standen 1½m S signposted from B2110. Designed in 1894 by Philip Webb with original William Morris textiles and wallpapers. Hillside garden. Open Apr to end Oct, Wed, Thu and Sat 2–5.30 (last admission 5pm). 80p. Garden only 30p. Dogs on lead in garden only. *(NT)*

EAST LAMBROOK *Somerset* Map 3 ST41
East Lambrook Manor, Gardens & Margery Fish Nursery 15th- and 16th-C house, with old panelling and a well-known garden with rare plants – a memorial to Margery Fish. Garden and Nursery open all the year daily 9–5, house open every Thu 2–5 1 Mar to 31 Oct. Admission to house 15p (ch 10p) garden and Nursery 15p (ch 10p). Party. ⚠ House and garden open first Sun in Jul for Gardeners Royal Benevolent Society. *(Tel South Petherton 40328). (Mr F Boyd-Carpenter)* ふ (garden)

EAST MEON *Hampshire* Map 4 SU62
Court House 14th-C ecclesiastical court hall, solar, etc, in walled gardens, in unspoilt village. Open by appointment only with Mr A D Gill. 25p (ch 10p). ⚠ *(Tel 274)*

EASTNOR *Hereford and Worcester* Map 3 SO73
Eastnor Castle Built by Sir Robert Smirke for 1st Earl Somers in early 19th C, contains fine furnishings, pictures, and armour. Grounds have specimen trees. ⚏ Open Sun, 20 May to end Sep also Wed and Thu Jul and Aug, also BH Mons. Other times by appointment for parties only. Admission prices not yet known, ch and pen half price. ⚠ *(Tel Ledbury 2304). (The Hon Mrs Hervey-Bathurst)* **(79)**

EASTON *Suffolk* Map 5 TM25
Easton Farm Park Rare breeds of farm animals, Victorian Dairy, pets paddock and adventure playpit. Visitors can watch the cows being milked each afternoon. Country bygones, picnic area, Bee keeping exhibition, coarse fishing, Craft shop. ⚏ Open 4 Apr to 5 Oct daily 10.30–6. ⚠ *(Tel Wickham Market 746475)* ふ

ECCLES *Gt Manchester* Map 7 SJ79
Monks Hall Museum Wellington Road. 16th-C building with later additions, with permanent collection of Nasmyth machinery, paintings, ceramics, and local bygones, and frequent temporary exhibitions. Small toy museum in part of building. Open all year (ex Sun, 4 Apr, 24/25 Dec and 1 Jan) Mon to Fri 10–6, Sat 10–5. Free. P. *(Tel 061-789 4372)* ふ

EDNASTON *Derbyshire* Map 8 SK24
Ednaston Manor A Lutyens house with garden of botanical interest. Large collection of shrubs, shrub roses, clematis and unusual plants; most varieties in containers for sale. ⚏ Sun. Gardens open 15 Apr to 30 Sep, Wed, Thu 1–4.30. Sun 2–6. Parties weekdays, meals by arrangement. Coach parties welcome. 40p (ch 10p). ⚠ *(Tel Brailsford 325). (Mr S D Player) (NGS)* ふ **(79)**

ELCOT PARK HOTEL *Berkshire* Map 4 SU36
5½m W Newbury off A4. 16-acre garden overlooking the Kennet Valley with extensive views. Mainly lawns and woodland laid out by Sir William Paxton in 1848. Magnificent displays of daffodils, rhododendrons and other shrubs in spring. ⚏ Open all year 10–6. Free (ex on National Gardens Scheme Suns). ⚠ *(Tel Kintbury 276 or 421). (NGS)* ふ B

ELDS WOOD, THE WILLOUGHBRIDGE GARDEN TRUST *Staffordshire* Map 7 SJ73
200-year-old gravel quarry converted into woodland garden, with daffodils, rhododendrons, and azaleas. Water and rock gardens. Gardens open Mar to Nov, 11–7.30 (or dusk). *(Tel Pipe Gate 237)* ふ

ELSHAM *Humberside* Map 8 TA01
Elsham Hall Country Park With domestic animals, bird sanctuary, carp feeding, craft shop, open-air gallery for local artists, walk round a trail and attempt a country quiz, pony-trekking and fly fishing (by appointment, *Tel Barnetby 698*). Wrawby Moor art gallery, Pottery, Blacksmith. Air museum (Preservation Society). Craftsmen at work when advertised. ⚏ all year. Parties by appointment. Hi-fi music by volunteers on Sun during summer, 3–6.30. Open all year (ex 4 Apr, 25 Dec), daily 1–8 (or dusk); Sat and Sun and BH 11–8 (or dusk). 45p (ch 30p). Prices under revision for 1980. Trails with warden Suns 2.30 (summertime). ⚠ *(Tel Barnetby 738 or Barnetby 689 Caravan Club Site)* ふ

ELSTOW *Bedfordshire* Map 4 TL04
Moot Hall 1½m SW of Bedford on A6. 15th-C market hall with 17th-C collection portraying life and times of John Bunyan. Open all year, daily (ex Mon, but incl summer BH) 10–1 and 2–5 (dusk in winter), Sun 2–5.30 (dusk in winter). 10p (ch 5p, School parties up to 40 ch £1.50). Family ticket 25p. ⚠ *(Tel Bedford 66889)* ふ B

ELVASTON *Derbyshire* Map 8 SK43
Elvaston Castle and Country Park Mansion built by Wyatt in 1817, remains of 17th-C house incorporated in the fabric, standing in attractive grounds landscaped by William Barron. Small agricultural museum in stable yard and display of restored horse-drawn caravans and wagons in courtyard. Family history, Estate and Countryside museums now being developed. Park, with lake, formal gardens and Old English garden, includes 140 acres of woodland and facilities for caravanning/camping, horse riding, field studies and nature trail. House contains information centre, shop and ⚏ (Easter to Oct). Park open all year; Castle and Old English garden 10–5. Free. ⚠ 30p weekends and BH, other times free. *(Tel Derby 71342 Park Supervisor, 73735 Caravan/camp site Warden)* ふ B

EMBLETON *Northumberland* Map 12 NU22
Dunstanburgh Castle 1½m E. Ruins of early 14th-C castle, facing North Sea, and built partly by John of Gaunt. Open*, see inside front cover (incl 13 Apr). 15p (ch 16 and pen 5p). *(AM and NT)*

EPWORTH *Humberside* Map 8 SE70
Old Rectory Birthplace and former home of John and Charles Wesley built in 1709 after a previous Rectory had been destroyed by fire, restored in 1957. Open Mar–Oct Mon–Sat 10–12 and 2–4, Sun 2–4, winter months by arrangement. Donations requested. Accommodation available, meals by arrangement. ⚠ *(Tel 872268)* ふ B

ESHER *Surrey* Map 4 TQ16
Claremont Entrance by Claremont Lane A244, designed 1772 for Clive of India by Henry Holland and 'Capability' Brown, replaced former early 18th-C house built by Vanbrugh for himself. Façade has columned portico, and there are good fireplaces and plaster ceilings. Now school for sons and daughters of Christian Scientists and others. Open Feb to Nov, first Sat and following Sun in month 2–4.30. 50p (ch and pen 25p). ⚠ *(Tel 67841)*

Claremont Landscape Garden On S edge of Esher, E of A307. The earliest surviving English landscape garden, recently restored. Lake, island with pavilion, grotto and turf amphitheatre, viewpoint and avenues. House not NT property. Open every day Apr to end Oct, 9–7 or sunset if earlier; Nov to end Mar 9–4. 20p. *(NT)*

ETON *Berkshire* Map 4 SU97
Eton College World-famous public school, founded by Henry VI in 1440, with beautiful chapel. Chapel open 2–5 (10.30–12.30 in school hols, closed Sun in school hols). School Yard and Cloisters open weekdays 2–5 (6 during summer term); 10.30–12.30 in school holidays. 30p. Guided tours pm. May to Oct, 60p. ⚠ *(Tel Windsor 66461)* ఉ B

EUSTON *Suffolk* Map 5 TL87
Euston Hall 16th-C house with fine collection of paintings, including Stubbs, Van Dyck and Lely. 'Pleasure grounds' gardens by John Evelyn. Picnic area. Also 17th-C parish church in Wren style. ☕ Open 3 May to 27 Sep. Thu 2.30–5.30. 50p (ch 15 and pen 25p). ⚠ *(Tel Thetford 3281). (Duke of Grafton)* **(79)**

EVESHAM *Hereford and Worcester* Map 4 SP04
The Almonry Vine Street. 14th-C stone and half-timbered building, associated with former Benedictine abbey, containing museum of local history covering culture and industry of Vale of Evesham since prehistoric times. Open 4 Apr to end Sep, daily (ex Mon and Wed) 2.30–6.30; open BH. 15p (accompanied ch free). P. *(Tel 6944)*

EWELL *Surrey* Map 4 TQ26
Bourne Hall Cultural Centre Spring Street. 18th-C house replaced by cultural centre, museum, art centre, library, and also theatre hall and banqueting rooms. Collections embrace the human and natural history of the Epsom and Ewell area, and include costumes, dolls, toys, early photography and some finds from Nonsuch Palace. The Art Gallery has a continuous temporary Exhibitions programme. Other services include the identification of objects brought in by visitors. Open all year (ex Sun and Mon) Wed and Thu 10–5 (8 pm Tue & Fri); Sat 9.30–5. Free. ⚠ *(Tel 01-393 9573)* ఉ

EXBURY *Hampshire* Map 4 SU40
Exbury Gardens Woodland gardens with azaleas, rhododendrons, and other flowering shrubs. ☕ Open early Apr to mid Jun, daily 2–6.30. 60p (ch 30p) coaches 50p per person. Prices under revision for 1980. ⚠ *(Tel Fawley 891203). (Mr E L de Rothschild) (NGS)* ఉ

EXETER *Devon* Map 3 SX99
Custom House The Quay. Brick building (1681), illustrates first use of brickwork in city. Contains some fine plasterwork ceilings. Visitors shown interior by arrangement with HM Customs and Excise, casual visitors usually accepted. *(Tel 74021)*
The Devonshire Regiment Museum Wyvern Barracks. The exhibits cover the history of the Devonshire Regiment from its formation in 1685 to 1958 when the Regiment amalgamated with the Dorset Regiment. Exhibits include, uniforms, weapons, medals, historical documents and military souvenirs collected by the Regiment over the years. Open all year (ex Sat, Sun and BH) Mon to Fri 9–4.30. Free. ⚠ *(Tel 76581 ext 268)*
Guildhall High Street. Dates from 1330, partially rebuilt 1446, arches and façade added 1592–5. Open all year, Mon to Sat 10–5.30 except when used for meetings. P. Free. *(Tel 77888)* ఉ B

Maritime Museum At Town Quay and Canal Basin; approach via Alphington Street and Haven Road. Over 100 old sail, rowing and steam vessels, some afloat, others under cover, including craft from Near East and South America. The museum has the biggest boat collection of its kind in the world. Included in the display if the world's oldest working steamboat, the fascinating Ellerman Collection of Portuguese craft, and the Ocean Rowers Collection, featuring boats which have been rowed across the Atlantic and Pacific Oceans. The museum's buildings and boats have featured in the TV series *The Onedin Line*. Quays and old warehouses, and the oldest pound lock canal in England. Maritime book and gift shop. Steam launch trips in summer. ☕ Easter then Jun to Sep. Open all year daily (ex 25/26 Dec) 10–6

summer (5 winter). £1 (ch 50p and pen 75p).
Under revision for 1980. Party 20+. Rowing
boats for hire. ⚠ free. *(Tel 58075)* ⅅ B
Rougemont House Museum Castle Street.
Georgian town-house, now museum of
Devon and Exeter prehistoric, Roman and
medieval archaeology. Open all year,
Tue–Sat 10–1 and 2–5.30. Free. P. *(Tel 56724)*
Royal Albert Memorial Museum Queen
Street. Founded in 1865, and extended
several times. Large permanent displays of
fine and applied art, natural history and
ethnography, local industry. Of particular
interest are collections of Devon paintings,
Exeter silver, glass, local and foreign natural
history. Museum shop and programme of
temporary exhibitions. Open all year, Tue to
Sat 10–5.30. Free. P. *(Tel 56724)*
St Nicholas' Priory Off Fore Street. Remains
of 11th- to 16th-C Benedictine priory, with
Norman undercroft, Tudor room, and 15th-C
kitchen. Only complete monastic western
range in England to have survived the
dissolution and be restored. Displays of
pewter, furniture and wood carving. Open all
year Tue to Sat 10–1 and 2–5.30. 25p (ch
10p). Under revision for 1980. P. *(Tel 56724)*
Tuckers Hall Fore Street. Old Hall of the
Weavers, Fullers, and Shearmen, occupied
since 1471 by their incorporation which was
granted Royal Charter in 1479–81. Wagon
roof and panelling of 1638. Open all year Tue,
Thu, Fri 10.30–12.30 (Oct to May, Fri only).
⚠ *(Tel 36244)*
Underground Passages Princesshay
Medieval aqueducts which once supplied
water to the city. Open all year, Tue to Sat
2–4.30. 25p (ch 10p). P. Under revision for
1980. *(Tel 56724)*
EXMOUTH *Devon* Map 3 SY08
A la Ronde Summer Lane, 2m N on A377.
Curious 16-sided (hexadecaponal) house,
dating from 1798, belonging to the
Parminters. Regency gallery and interesting
furnishings. The gallery and approaching
staircase are covered in thousands of shells,
the work of the 'Parminter Ladies'. There are
unique collages of sand and seaweed, and a
feather frieze around the drawing room. Wide
coastal views from the house. ⚓ Open Easter
to Oct, Mon–Sat 10–6, Sun 2–7. 60p (ch 14
30p). Under revision for 1980. ⚠ *(Tel 5514)*.
(Mrs Tudor-Perkins) ⅅ
The Steam and Countryside Museum
Sandy Bay, 1m SE. A museum for all the
family. One of the largest working museums
in the country. Hundreds of exhibits.
Thatched Devon cottage, Shire horses,
ponies and many other friendly animals.

Open 4 Apr to 28 Sep, from 10.30 am. 80p (ch
5–16 30p). ⚠ *(Tel 74533)* ⅅ

EYE MANOR *Hereford and Worcester*
Map 3 SO46
4m N of Leominster. Built in 1680 by
Ferdinando Gorges, and noted for its nine
magnificent plaster ceilings. Contains
exhibitions of decorative straw-work, dolls
period costumes, needlework, etc. Students
can sometimes be seen making corn dollies in
August. Picnic area. Open 25 May to 14 Sep,
Wed, Thu, Sat, Sun 2.30–5.30 also every
afternoon Aug and 26/27 May. 50p (ch 19
20p). Party. ⚠ *(Tel Yarpole 244). (Mr and Mrs
C Sandford)* ⅅ B

EYNSFORD *Kent* Map 5 TQ56
Eynsford Castle Remains of 12th-C castle,
including rectangular hall, walls, and ditch.
Open*, see inside front cover. 15p (ch 16 and
pen 5p). ⚠ *(AM)*
Lullingstone Castle 1m SW off A225. Mainly
18th-C house with fine 16th-C gate tower, the
first large scale building to be of brick
throughout with cut brick for detail. Other
notable features include; The Great Hall,
State Dining Room, Grand Staircase, State
Drawing Room, State Bedroom and the Ante
Room. Open Apr to Sep, Wed, Sat and Sun,
also public hols 2–6. 75p (ch 13 15p, pen
25p). Party 30+. ⚠ *(Tel Farningham 862114)*
ⅅ B
Lullingstone Roman Villa ½m W off A225.
Remains of Roman villa, with a fine
tessellated pavement. Now completely
roofed with additional exhibits in lighted
gallery. Open*, see inside front cover. 40p,
winter 15p (ch 16 and pen 15p, winter 5p). ⚠
Summer coaches 20p, car 10p, motor cycles
5p. *(AM)*

FALMOUTH *Cornwall* Map 2 SW83
Pendennis Castle One of coastal forts
erected c1540 by Henry VIII, with Elizabethan
and later additions. Exhibition of coastal
defences of the Tudor period. ⚓ Open*, see
inside front cover. 30p (ch 16 and pen 15p). ⚠
(AM)
Penjerrick Gardens 3m SW of Falmouth, off
B3291 near Budock. Beautiful sub-tropical
gardens, including display of flowering
shrubs. Open 1 Mar to end Sep Wed and Sun
1.30–4.30. 30p in box in garden. ⚠ *(Tel
Mawnan Smith 659). (Mrs J M K Fox)*

FARLEIGH HUNGERFORD *Somerset*
Map 3 ST85
Farleigh Castle Ruined 14th-C castle with
chapel containing monuments to the
Hungerfords. Open*, see inside front cover.
20p (ch 16 and pen 5p). ⚠ *(AM)*

FARNBOROUGH *Warwickshire* Map 4 SP44
Hall 17th- and 18th-C house with wide views across Warwickshire plain towards Edgehill. Temples in fine grounds. Open Apr to Sep, Wed and Sat 2–6. 80p, grounds only 50p. *(NT)*.

FARNDON *Cheshire* Map 7 SJ45
Stretton Mill A water-powered corn mill with two wheels dating from 16th to 19th C, recently restored by the County Museum Service. Exhibition in stables. Open Easter to end Sep, 2–6 (ex Mon). 30p (ch 15p). △ *(Tel Tilston 276)*

FARNHAM *Surrey* Map 4 SU84
Birdworld, Zoological Bird Gardens and Aquarium Holt Pound. 3½m SW of town, on A325 beyond Wrecclesham. Large variety of birds including parrots, flamingoes, hornbills, kestrels, penguins and waterfowl, also Aquarium housing tropical, fresh water and marine fish and invertebrates. ♉ Open all year (ex 25 Dec), daily 9.30–6 (or 1 hr before dusk whichever comes first). Party. Children must be accompanied. No dogs. △ *(Tel Bentley, Hants 2140)* ⅙

Farnham Castle Keep Ruined shell keep of castle originally erected 1129–71 by Bishop Henry de Blois. Open, see inside front cover (Apr to Sep only). 15p (ch 16 and pen 5p). △ *(AM)*

Willmer House Museum 38 West Street. Geology, archaeology, local history and art in Willmer House, a fine example of Georgian brickwork. Open all year (ex 25 & 26 Dec), Tue to Sat 11–1 and 2–5, Sun and BH 2.30–5 (closes ½ hr earlier in winter). Free. P. *(Tel 715094)*

FARWAY *Devon* Map 3 SY19
Farway Countryside Park 1½m S on unclass road. AA signposted on B3174. A collection of rare breeds and present day British farm animals can be seen in a beautiful farm setting with magnificent views over the Coly Valley. 130 acres of natural countryside. 'Guide Dogs for the Blind' dog show last Sun in Jun. Pony and donkey cart rides, daily Easter hols, then, Sun only until 27 May then daily to 10 Sep. Open 4 Apr to 30 Sep daily (closed Sat but open BH Sat) 10–6 (last admission 5 pm). 80p (ch 3–14 45p, pen 40p). △ *(Enquiries Mrs J M Forbes, Farway Countryside Park, Colyton, Devon. Tel 224)*

FAVERSHAM *Kent* Map 5 TR06
Chart Gunpowder Mills, Westbrook Walk. Town was once the centre of the gunpowder industry, and one of former mills dating from the late 18th C, believed to be oldest of their kind in the world, has been preserved and

restored. Also remains of others on site. Exterior on view at all times, interior open on request. Free. △ (limited). *(Tel 4542)*

Fleur de Lis Heritage Centre Preston Street. History and architecture of a thousand years vividly illustrated by displays, audio visual programme and actual bygones in former 16th-C coaching inn. Open all year Mon to Sat 9–1 and 2–5 (Thu 9–1, BH 2–5). 40p (ch 14, students and pen 20p). P. *(Tel 4542)*

Maison Dieu Ospringe, 1m SW off A2. Timber-framed 15th-C house, with collection of Roman pottery and small museum of local history. Open, see inside front cover but closed all day Mon and Tue pm. 15p (ch 16 and pen 5p). *(AM)*

FELBRIGG *Norfolk* Map 9 TG23
Felbrigg Hall Early 17th- and mid 18th-C house. Jacobean south range has tall parapet, and over three protruding bays are carved the words *Gloria Deo in excelsis*. West wing is 17th-C and drawing room has fine plaster ceiling of 1687. Park with fine trees, woodland and lakeside walks. ♉ Open (principal rooms and gardens) Apr to 12 Oct. Tue to Thu, Sat, Sun, and BH 2–6 (last admission 5.30). £1. Party 15+. No dogs. *(NT)*

FILBY *Norfolk* Map 9 TG41
Thrigby Hall Wildlife Gardens On unclass road off A1064. Selection of Asian mammals, birds and reptiles displayed in the landscaped gardens of the Hall. Features include 250-year-old summer-house, tropical house, bird house, ornamental waterfowl lake, yew walk. Stable, gift shop. ♉ Open all year, daily 9.30–dusk. 80p (ch 5 and pen 40p). △ *(Tel Fleggburgh 477)* ⅙

FINCHALE PRIORY *Durham* Map 12 NZ24
Considerable remains of the 13th-C church of the Benedictine priory in picturesque position on banks of the River Wear. Open, see inside front cover. 15p (ch 16 and pen 5p). △ *(AM)*

FINCHINGFIELD *Essex* Map 5 TL63
Finchingfield Guildhall and Museum Late 15th-C building comprising four Almhouse flats, library, meeting hall and museum. The museum exhibits items of local history from Roman times onwards. Art and Craft exhibition Spring BH week. Open Easter then 28 May to Sep, Sun and BH, 3–6. Free. △ *(Tel Great Dunmow 810412)* **(79)**

Spains Hall 1m NW on unclass road. Elizabethan Manor house with some panelled rooms, 18th- and 19th-C furniture, also works of art. There are two fine tapestries and the Chippendale chairs are embroidered with the arms of the County and 14 Districts of Essex. Flower and Kitchen gardens each with a greenhouse, and in the flower garden, a large 17th-C Cedar of Lebanon. ☕ (teas). Open 3 May to 3 Aug Sat and Sun, also 5 and 26 May, 2–5.30. House and garden £1 (ch 50p). Party. ⚠ *(Tel Great Dunmow 810266).* *(Sir J Ruggles-Brise)* ⅃ B

FIRLE *East Sussex* Map 5 TQ40
Firle Place Mainly Georgian house, with Tudor core. South Downs home of the Gage family for 500 yrs, containing connoisseurs' collection of European and English Old Masters, Sèvres porcelain and fine furniture. Shop and ☕ Open Jun to end Sep Sun, Wed and Thu, also Easter, 5, 25/26 May, and 24/25 Aug 2.15–5.30. Conducted tours 75p (ch 30p). 1st Wed in month unguided tour £1.10 (no reduction for ch). Party 30+. Admission prices under revision for 1980. ⚠ *(Tel Hailsham 843902 or Glynde 256)*

FISHBOURNE *West Sussex* Map 4 SU80
Roman Palace Salthill Road. Occupied 1st to 4th C, largest Roman Palace in Britain, with numerous mosaic pavements. Open Mar and Apr daily 10–5; May to Sep 10–6; Oct 10–5; Nov 10–4. 65p (ch 10p, students 35p). Under revision for 1980. *(Tel Chichester 785859).* *(Sussex Archaeological Society)*

FLADBURY *Hereford and Worcester* Map 3 SO94
Delamere Bird Gardens Hill Furze off B4084. A collection of birds, pet animals and model railways. Picnic area. Open all year, daily 9.30–dusk. 30p (ch 14 15p). ⚠ *(Tel Evesham 860580)* ⅃

FLIMWELL *Kent* Map 5 TQ73
Bedgebury National Pinetum 1½m N off A21. Established by Forestry Commission in 1925, 160 acres of trees, including the most comprehensive collection of conifers in Europe, planted round old hammer pond. Over 100 research plots. ☕ weekdays during summer. Open all year, daily 10–8 or dusk (whichever is earlier). 25p (schoolchildren 10p). ⚠ *(Tel Goudhurst 392)*

FOLKESTONE *Kent* Map 5 TR23
Museum and Art Gallery Grace Hill. Local history, archaeology, and natural science. Temporary art exhibitions. Open all year (ex BH), weekdays 10–1 and 2.30–5.30 (5 Sat). Free. P. *(Tel 57583)*

FORD *Northumberland* Map 12 NT93
The Lady Waterford Hall Once the village school, it is now famous for the late, 19th-C mural pictures painted by Lady Waterford depicting members of the Ford Estate characters in Bible story scenes. Open all year 10–6. 10p (ch 5p). ⚠ *(Tel Crookham 224)* ⅃ Also

Heatherslaw Mill Dating back to the 13th C, but probably largely rebuilt in the 18th C, one of the oldest water-driven flour mills, with its machinery still intact. The mill was last used in 1946. ☕ Open Apr to Oct, daily 11–6. 30p (pen 10p). ⚠ *(Tel Crookham 338, caretaker)*

FORDWICH *Kent* Map 5 TR15
Old Town Hall Timber-framed building overlooking River Stour, one of the smallest of such buildings in Britain. Contains ducking stool, reputedly used to duck malefactors in river. Open Easter and Whitsun to 30 Sep, Mon to Sat 10.30–12.30, 2.30–5.30. (Other times by arrangement.) 10p (ch 5p). ⚠

FOREST ROW *East Sussex* Map 5 TQ43
The Spring Hill Wildfowl Park Over 1,000 exotic birds including flamingos, cranes, peacocks, swans and rare species of geese and ducks, in a ten-acre Ashdown forest garden, around a 15th-C farmhouse. ☕ in Aviary Gift Shop. Open all year daily (ex 25 Dec) 10–6. Admission prices for 1980 not available. *(Tel 2783)* ⅃

FOWEY *Cornwall* Map 2 SX15
St Catherine's Castle Ruined stronghold, erected in 16th C by Henry VIII to defend coast, and restored in 1855. Open all year, daily 9–dusk. Free. *(AM)*

FRAMLINGHAM *Suffolk* Map 5 TM26
Framlingham Castle Built by Roger Bigod between 1177 and 1215. Fine curtain walls, thirteen towers, array of Tudor chimneys, and almshouses built within inside walls by Pembroke College, Cambridge, in 1639. Open*, see inside front cover. 20p (ch 16p and pen 5p). ⚠ *(AM)*

FRITTON *Norfolk* Map 5 TG40
Fritton Lake Country Park Rare plants, shrubs, and herbaceous borders, and paths through wood to lake noted for fishing. Fishing in season, fishing and row boats for hire. Children's playground. ☕ and picnic areas. Gardens and grounds open 1 Apr to 15 Jun 11–6, 16 Jun to 30 Sep 7–7. 35p Prices under revision for 1980. Dogs on lead only. ⚠ *(Tel 208)* ⅃

GAINSBOROUGH *Lincolnshire* Map 8 SK88
Old Hall Parnell Street. 15th-C and later, with great hall, period rooms, and medieval kitchen. ☕ Tue afternoons. Open all year (ex 25, 26 Dec, 1 Jan) weekdays 2–5; Easter to Oct, Sun also 2–5. Admission prices not yet decided. ⚠ *(Tel 2669 afternoons)*

GAWSWORTH *Cheshire* Map 7 SJ86
Gawsworth Hall Tudor black and white manor house associated with Mary Fitton possibly the 'Dark Lady' of Shakespeare's

sonnets, with rare tilting ground, pictures, armour and furniture. Carriage Museum. Open mid Mar to end Oct, daily 2–6. Party 20+. Dogs in grounds on lead only. Admission prices not available. ⚐ free. *(Tel North Rode 456) (Roper-Richards family)*

GEDDINGTON *Northamptonshire* Map 4 SP88
Eleanor Cross Perhaps most beautiful of the many crosses erected by Edward I in memory of his dead Queen Eleanor on the route of her last journey to Westminster Abbey. Set up in 1294, best preserved of surviving trio. Accessible at any time. Free. *(AM)*

GILLING EAST *North Yorkshire* Map 8 SE67
Gilling Castle 14th-, 16th-, and 18th-C house, now preparatory school for Ampleforth College, with Elizabethan great chamber noted for panelling, painted glass, and ceilings. Fine gardens. Great chamber and hall, open weekdays 10–12 and 2–4; gardens open Jul to Sep, Mon to Sat. Great chamber free, Gardens 10p. ⚐ *(Tel Ampleforth 238)* ⅙

GILLINGHAM *Kent* Map 5 TQ76
Royal Engineers Museum Brompton. Includes relics of General Gordon among other exhibits. Open all year, Mon to Fri (ex BH) 9.30–12.30, 2–4. Free. ⚐ *(Tel Medway 44555)* ⅙ B

GLANDFORD *Norfolk* Map 9 G04
Shell Museum Small museum with Dutch gables built 1915 to house collection of seashells and curios from all corners of the world, collected by the late Sir Alfred Jodrell of Bayfield Hall. Open May to Sep, Mon to Fri 9–1, 2–5 Sat and Sun 2–5; Oct to Apr, Mon to Fri 9–1, 2–4 Sat 2–4. 2½p. Admission prices and opening times under revision for 1980. P. *(Tel Cley 349)* ⅙

GLASTONBURY *Somerset* Map 3 ST43
Glastonbury Abbey Well-preserved 12th- and 13th-C ruins, with St Joseph's Chapel, Abbot's Kitchen, and flowering thorn tree nearby, on site of first Christian church in British Isles. West of England Pilgrimage last Sat in Jun, miracle plays twice weekly Jul and Aug. New Abbey Museum open in the ancient gatehouse with a model of the Abbey as in 1539. Open all year daily, Jun, Jul and Aug 9–7.30, rest of year 9.30–4.30 (Dec), 5 (Jan and Nov), 5.30 (Feb), 6 (Mar, Apr and Oct), 7 (May and Sep). 40p (ch 16 20p, ch 5 free) Parties. P. *(Tel 32267)* ⅙ B
Somerset Rural Life Museum Abbey Barn and Abbey Farmhouse. Late 14th-C barn of Glastonbury Abbey contains relics of farming in Somerset in the horse age, cider making, peat cutting, withy cutting, etc. The adjoining

farmhouse displays life of 19th-C Somerset peasant as shown by the things he used, and a typical farmhouse kitchen. Open all year Easter to 31 Oct, Mon to Fri 10–5 (8 Thu). Sat and Sun 2–7. 1 Nov to Easter Mon to Fri 10–5, Sat, Sun 2.30–5. 35p (ch 16 10p, pen free).
Tribunal 15th-C Court house of Abbey officials containing finds from late prehistoric Lake Village. Open, see inside front cover. 15p (ch 16 and pen 5p). ⚐ *(AM)*

GLEMHAM HALL *Suffolk* Map 5 TM36
17th-C house, in 350 acres of grounds, with panelled rooms, pictures, and Queen Anne furniture. ⚑ Open 7 Apr to 28 Sep Wed, Sun, BH 2–5.30. Admission prices for 1980 not available. ⚐ *(Tel Wickham Market 746219) (Lady Blanche Cobbold)*

GLOUCESTER *Gloucestershire* Map 3 SO81
Bishop Hooper's Lodging Folk Life Museum, Westgate Street. Group of three timber-framed buildings, traditionally associated with the martyrdom in 1555 of Bishop John Hooper, containing relics of Siege of Gloucester (1643), and collections illustrating crafts and industries of the county. Open all year, Mon to Sat 10–5. Free. *(Tel 26467)*
City Museum and Art Gallery Brunswick Road. Archaeology, natural history, and geology of county, and period furnishings, glass and silver. Temporary art exhibitions throughout year. Open all year, Mon to Sat 10–5 (ex BH). Free. *(Tel 24131)*
City Wall and Bastion Kings Walk. Roman and medieval city defences in an underground chamber. Open May to Sep, Wed, Fri and Sat 2–5. 16p (ch 5p).

GLYNDE *East Sussex* Map 5 TQ40
Glynde Place Elizabethan manor substantially altered in the mid 18th-C. ⚑ Open 15/16 Apr; then 6 May to 30 Sep, Wed, Thu and Sun 2.15–5.30. 80p (ch 12 40p). ⚐ *(Tel 337 or 224)* **(79)**

GODALMING *Surrey* Map 4 SU94
Borough Museum Old Town Hall. Dates from 1814. On site of earlier building, and now museum of local antiquities. Open all year, Tue, Fri (ex 4 Apr), Sat 3–5; other times by appointment with Kathy Callow. *(Tel 4104)*

GODOLPHIN CROSS *Cornwall* Map 2 SW63
Godolphin House Between Townshend and Godolphin Cross, on unclass road. Partly early Tudor house, former home of Earls of Godolphin, with notable granite colonnades added in 1635. Painting of the 'Godolphin Arabian' by John Wooton. ⚑ Open May and Jun, Thu 2–5, Jul, Aug and Sep, Tue and Thu 2–5. 50p (ch 20p). Admission prices under

revision for 1980. Party 20+. No dogs. ⚠ *(Tel Germoe 2409). (Mrs S E Schofield)*

GOMERSAL *West Yorkshire* Map 7 SE22
Off M62 (junc 26)
Red House Built 1660 of red brick, which because of its rarity at that time gave rise to its name. Additions by succeeding owners. Associations with the Brontës, particularly Charlotte, who often spent weekends here with here schoolfriend Mary Taylor. She immortalised it in her novel '*Shirley*', where it is described under the name of 'Briarmains'. Open Apr to Oct Tue to Sat 10 – 6, Sun 1 – 5; Nov to Mar Tue to Sat 10 – 5. Free. ⚠ *(Tel Cleckheaton 872165)* ⅃ B

GOODRICH *Hereford and Worcester* Map 3 SO51
Goodrich Castle 12th to 14th C, originally founded in 11th C, castle was slighted after Civil War. Open*, see inside front cover. 25p (ch 16 and pen 10p). ⚠ *(AM)*

GOODWOOD *West Sussex* Map 4 SU80
Goodwood House Three-sided flint faced Wyatt Mansion (1780 – 1800) with Jacobean core with notable pictures and interior furnishings. Open all year for booked parties with lunch or dinner and for commercial events. Please write for leaflet giving 1980 prices and event dates. Open May to Sep, Sun and Mon 2 – 5. ⅃

GOOSNARGH *Lancashire* Map 7 SD53
1½m E of M6 (junc 32)
Chingle Hall Standing within its own moat. Chingle Hall is a sturdy, white-walled cruciform structure built in 1260 by Adam de Singleton. It contains a chapel and four priest holes and is reputedly the most haunted house in Britain. Open Tue, Wed, Thu, Sat,

Sun and BH, 1 Jan to 24 Dec 2 – 6. 30p (ch 14 10p). Party. Admission prices under review for 1979. ⚠ *(Tel 216)* **(79)**

GOSFIELD *Essex* Map 5 TL73
Gosfield Hall Tudor and later mansion, twice visited by Queen Elizabeth I, with fine Tudor gallery. Open May to Sep, Wed, Thu 2 – 5. 40p (ch 25p). ⚠ *(Tel Halstead, Essex 2914)*

GOSPORT *Hampshire* Map 4 SZ69
Submarine Museum HMS *Dolphin* and, on shore after Spring 1980, HMS/M *Alliance*. Comprehensive display of submarine history and development with models, trophies, medals, pictures and the actual X-Craft that twice raided Bergen. Open all year Mon to Sat 9 – 4 but only by previous arrangement with Visits Office, HMS Dolphin, Gosport. Free. *(Tel Portsmouth 22351 ext 41868)*

GRANTHAM *Lincolnshire* Map 8 SK93
Grantham Museum St Peter's Hill. Housed within Public Library, the museum contains collections of local antiquities, Grantham history and items relating to Sir Isaac Newton. Changing exhibitions. Open all year (ex Sun, BH and Library holidays) Mon to Sat 9.30 – 5. Free. P. *(Tel 3926)*

GRASMERE *Cumbria* Map 11 NY30
Dove Cottage and Wordsworth Museum Former home of Wordsworth and Thomas de Quincey, with rooms furnished as in Wordsworth's time. The exhibition has been enhanced by newly discovered manuscripts of letters and poems, also by important loans, including portraits of the Wordsworth Circle from the National Portrait Gallery. Open Mar to Oct daily (ex Sun) 9.30 – 1 and 2 – 5 (4.30 Mar and Oct). Last admission half hour before closing. Admission and opening times under revision for 1980. *(Tel 464 or 418)* ⅃

GRASSINGTON *North Yorkshire*
Map 7 SE06
National Park Centre Hebden Road. Display
features conservation and the management
operations of the National Park Authority.
Open Apr to end Sep daily mid morning to late
afternoon. Free. ⚠ *(Tel 752748)*

GRAYS *Essex* Map 5 TQ67
Thurrock Museum Orsett Road. Local
history, agriculture, trade and industrial
collections. Palaeolithic to Saxon
archaeology of borough. Open all year (ex
BH), weekdays 10–8 (5, Sat). Free. P. *(Tel
76827)* ⅙

GRAYTHWAITE HALL GARDENS *Cumbria*
Map 7 SD39
4m N of Newby Bridge on W side of Lake
Windermere.
7-acre landscape garden with shrubs,
azaleas, and rhododendrons. Open 1 Apr to
30 Jun, daily 10–6. 20p (ch 15 5p). P. *(Tel
Newby Bridge 333 or 248). (Major M E M
Sandys)*

GREAT AYTON *North Yorkshire* Map 8 NZ51
Captain Cook Schoolroom Museum
Exhibits relating to the explorer, incl maps,
books, pictures, etc. Open all year, May to
Sep 10.30–12 & 2–4.30; Oct to Apr 2 to 4 or
by arrangement. 15p (ch 5p). P. *(Tel 2094)*

GREAT BARDFIELD *Essex* Map 5 TL63
Bardfield Cottage Museum Dunmow Road.
16th-C thatched cottage with exhibitions of
Essex farming history, books, and pottery,
and corn dollies for sale. Open Apr to Sep, Sat
and Sun 2–6, or by written appointment.
Free. P. **(79)**

GREAT BEDWYN *Wiltshire* Map 4 SU26
Bedwyn Stone Museum Open air museum
of the mason whose mark appears on
Stonehenge, the Kennet and Avon Canal.
The Croft Pumps, countless churches, the
Willow Pattern Plate, the secret brains behind
the great architects of the last century. There
are plaster casts, headstones and other
works set out in a humorous vein to decode
Stonehenge and other works in the manner
they control the behaviour of man. Open all
year. Free. ⚠ Information and tours of the
church, adjacent, ideal for coach parties on a
wet day (60 min). *(Tel 234 Mr Lloyd)* ⅙
Crofton Beam Engines 1½m SW. Now
unique, the 1812 Boulton and Watt, and the
1845 Harveys of Hayle Beam Engines pump
water 40ft to the top level of the Kennet and
Avon Canal. Operating in steam at Easter,
Spring and August BH and three other
weekends in summer and autumn. 50p (ch
and pen 25p), family rate £1.25. Admission
prices under revision for 1980. Public canal
trips on narrow boat, *Jubilee*, during steaming
weekends. ⚠ Open but not working every
Sun (ex Christmas) at no charge. Write to *The
Crofton Society* for further details – *273 East
Grafton, Burbage, Wilts. (Tel Burbage
810474)*

GREAT BOOKHAM *Surrey* Map 4 TQ15
Polesden Lacey 1m S. Designed by Thomas
Cubitt in 1824, houses Greville collection of
pictures, tapestries and furnishings. Beautiful
grounds. ⬛ (licensed) open from 11 am on
days when house is open. House open Mar
and Nov, Sat and Sun 2–5 (or sunset if
earlier); Apr to end Oct daily (ex Mon and Fri)
2–6; open BH Mon, closed following Tue; last
admission ½ hr before closing time; gardens
open all year, daily 11–sunset. Gardens only
50p, house 60p extra. No dogs in house and
only in garden if on lead *(NT)*

GREAT COXWELL *Oxfordshire* Map 4 SU29
Great Coxwell Barn Stone-built 14th-C barn,
possibly finest in England, with fine timber
roof. Open at all reasonable times. Free. *(NT)*

GREAT TORRINGTON *Devon* Map 2 SS41
Rosemoor Garden Charitable Trust 1m SE
of town. A garden of medium size with species
and hybrid rhododendrons, species roses
and ornamental trees and shrubs planted
since 1959. Scree and raised beds. Unusual
plants for sale. Teas for groups of 20 or more
persons by prior arrangement. Open Apr to
Oct daily, all day. 40p (ch 8 free, 8–15 20p).
Party. ⚠ *(Col J E and Lady Anne Palmer).
(NGS)* ⅙

GREAT WITCOMBE *Gloucestershire*
Map 3 SO91
Witcombe Roman Villa A large courtyard
Roman Villa in which a hypocaust and several
mosaic pavements are preserved. Open at
any reasonable times. Keys at farmhouse
adjoining. Free. *(AM)*

GREAT YARMOUTH *Norfolk* Map 5 TG50
Anna Sewell House Church Plain. This 17th-
C Tudor-fronted building, which is adjacent to
England's largest parish church, was the
birthplace of the authoress of *Black Beauty* on
30 Mar 1820. Guided tours. Souvenirs. Open
all year, Mon to Sat 10–4 (Thu 10–12 noon).
Admission charges not yet decided. ⚠ *(Tel
3372)*
Elizabethan House Museum built by a
wealthy merchant in 1596. It has a late
Georgian front, and contains panelled 16th-C
room, one with a magnificent Elizabethan
plaster ceiling. Other rooms have features
from later periods, some containing
contemporary furniture and exhibits
illustrating domestic life in the 19th-C.
Displays of Victorian children's toys,
Lowestoft porcelain and a collection of 18th-
19th-C drinking glasses. Open all year (ex 4 to
7 Apr, 25, 26 Dec and 1 Jan) Jun to Sep daily
(ex Sat) 10–1 and 2–5.30; Oct to May (Mon
to Fri) 10–1 and 2–5.30. Free. *(Tel 55746)*
The House of Wax Regent Road. A varied
and up-to-date exhibition of wax figures
contained in a fine Victorian house and
stables. Our Royal Family, past and present,
statesmen, screen and sports stars etc, a
'Murderers Gallery' depicting infamous
crimes and the basement contains macabre
'Torture Cellars'. Also a traditional Hall of
Funny Mirrors. Open Apr to Sep daily
10–dusk. 50p. Party. P. *(Tel 4851)*
Maritime Museum For East Anglia Marine
Parade. Maritime history of East Anglia
including the herring fishery, the wherry, life-
saving and the oil and gas industry. Open all
year (ex 4 to Apr, 25, 26 Dec, 1 Jan), Jun to
Sep 10–1 and 2–8; Oct to May Mon to Fri
10–1 and 2–5.30. 15p (ch 5p, free if
accompanied; pen free). Admission prices
under revision for 1980. ⚠ *(Tel 2267)*
Merrivale Model Village Near Wellington
Pier, Comprehensive village layout including
2⅜in-gauge model railway, radio-controlled
boats and many models on scale of 1:12, set
in an acre of landscaped gardens and
illuminated after dusk from Jun to mid Sep.
Also indoor 'oo' gauge model railway. ⬛
Open May to Sep, daily from 9.30am. P. *(Tel
2097)*
Museum Exhibition Galleries Central
Library. Travelling and local art exhibitions.
Open all year (ex 4 and 7 Apr, 25/26 Dec and
1 Jan) Mon to Fri 9.30–5.30, Sat 9.30–1.
Free. *(Tel 58900)*

Norfolk Pillar South Beach Parade. Monument to Nelson built in 1819. The column is 144ft high, capped by a figure of Britannia, and the summit is reached by an internal staircase of 217 steps. Open Jul and Aug daily (ex Sat) 2–6. 10p (ch 5p). P. *(Tel 55746)*

Old Merchant's House Row 117. Restored 300-year-old house with examples of 17th- to 19th-C local building craftsmanship, situated in one of the old narrow lanes, or Rows, leading from town wall to quay. Open Apr to Sep Mon to Fri by guided tour only starting from Row 111 Houses at 9.45, 11.20, 2.15 and 3.45. 15p (ch 16 and pen 5p). Ticket includes Row 111 Houses and Greyfriars Cloister. *(Tel 57900) (AM)*

Tolhouse Museum Tolhouse Street. Late 13th-C building with old dungeons and exhibits on local history. Open all year (ex 4 to 7 Apr, 25, 26 Dec, 1 Jan) Jun to Sep, daily (ex Sat) 10–1 and 2–5.30; Oct to May, Mon to Fri. Free. ⚠ *(Tel 58900)*

GRIMES GRAVES Norfolk Map 5 TL88
Neolithic flint mines worked from underground galleries. Roughly worked flints were once exported for finishing elsewhere. Re-opens 1980, see inside front cover for open times. 15p (ch and pen 5p). Torch is useful. ⚠ *(AM)*

GRIMSBY Humberside Map 8 TA20
Doughty Museum Town Hall Square. Will be transferred to Welholme Galleries, Hainton Avenue early 1980. Collection of 18th- and 19th-C ship models, pictures, and china bequeathed to town in 1941 by late Mr Wilfred Vere Doughty. Open all year, Tue to Sat 10–12.30 and 2–5.30. Free. P. *(Tel 59161)* ⚠

GRIZEDALE Cumbria Map 7 SD39
Visitor and Wild Life Centre Operated by Forestry Commission in Grizedale Forest, deer museum with large-scale photographic dioramas illustrating animal life, Forest Information office, Theatre in the Forest with various events covering classical, folk, natural history, jazz, drama, and dance, and mile-long Millwood Forest nature trail and other walks nearby. New Visitor Centre, Hotel and restaurant nearby. Open all year daily Easter to Oct 10–5; Oct to Easter 11–4. 10p (ch 14 5p). ⚠ *(Tel Satterthwaite 273, theatre bookings 291)*

GUILDFORD Surrey Map 4 SU94
Guildford Castle Castle Street. Early 12th-C, rectangular, three-storeyed keep with fine views. The castle ditch has been transformed into a flower garden, seen at its best in May. ⚕ Open daily Mon to Fri; grounds all year 7.30–dusk; keep Apr to Sep 11–6. Grounds free; keep 12p (ch 6p). P. *(Tel 71111)*
Guildford House Gallery 155 High Street. Built 1660, and acquired by Corporation in 1957, timber-framed building containing richly carved elm and oak staircase and finely decorated plaster ceilings. Frequently changing art exhibitions. Open all year, Mon to Sat 10.30–5 (ex for a few days prior to each exhibition). For details and dates of exhibitions, apply for leaflet. Free. P. *(Tel 32133)*
Guildford Museum Castle Arch, Quarry Street. Local history, archaeology, and needlework. Open all year, Mon–Sat 11–5 (ex Sun, 4 Apr, and Christmas). Free. P. *(Tel 66551)*
Loseley House 2½m SW. Elizabeth house, built of stone from Waverley Abbey, with fine

panelling, furniture, ceilings, carved chalk chimney piece, and tapestries. Farm tours. ⚕ Farm shop. Open Jun to Sep, Wed, Thu, Fri, Sat also 26 May, 25 Aug 2–5. 70p (ch 40p). Party 20+. Admission prices under revision for 1980. P. *(Tel 71881)* ⚠ B

Hospital of the Blessed Trinity (Abbot's Hospital) High Street. Tudor brick building, magnificent Doric arched gateway with four turrets and enclosed courtyard. Notable Flemish painted Chapel windows and moulded chimneys. Open May to Oct Mon, Wed and Sat; Sat only Nov to Apr; 11–12 and 3–4. Applications for conducted parties to the Master *(Mr H G Taylor)*. Free. ⚠ *(Tel 62670)* ⚠ B

Sutton Place Gardens 4m NE, off A3. A very beautiful 16th-C house in red brick and terracotta. There is a large and picturesque garden layout. Gardens only open 3, 10, 17, 24 Apr; 1, 8, 15, 22 May. 2.30–5.30. 30p (ch 14 15p), in aid of local charities. ⚠ *(Tel 32055)* ⚠ (NGS)

GUILSBOROUGH Northamptonshire Map 4 SP67
Guilsborough Grange Bird and Pet Park West Haddon Road. Collection of birds, waterfowl and animals set in beautiful natural surroundings in grounds of 19th-C country house. Also children's playground, pets corner and rides. Gift shop. Country stroll. ⚕ Picnic area. Open 1 Mar to 2 Nov daily 11–7. Admission prices not available. ⚠ Dogs admitted on leads. *(Tel 740278)* ⚠

GUISBOROUGH Cleveland Map 8 NZ61
Chapel Beck Gallery Fountain Street. A varied programme of changing exhibitions with particular emphasis on local history of Cleveland and the work of locally-based artists and craftsmen. Regular travelling exhibitions. Special events and demonstrations. Open all year (ex 4 Apr, 25 Dec, 1 Jan) Mon to Sat 10–5.30. Free. ⚠ *(Tel 35240)*
Gisborough Priory Fine remains of east end of church of 14th C. The priory, founded in first half of 12th C, was of Augustinian canons. Accessible any reasonable time. Free. ⚠ *(AM)*

GUITING POWER Gloucestershire Map 4 SP02
Cotswold Farm Park 3¾m NE on unclass road. An exhibition of the development of British livestock breeding on a typical Cotswold farm. Rare farm animals. Local handcrafts on sale. Pony-trap rides. ⚕ Open May Day to 1 Oct, daily 10.30–6. 60p (ch 14 35p, pen 45p). ⚠ and picnic area. *(Tel 307)* ⚠

GWEEK Cornwall Map 2 SW72
Seal Sanctuary Hospital caring for all sea creatures such as seals, birds, dolphins, porpoises and turtles which are washed up around the Cornish coast. There are five hospital pools situated on the banks of the beautiful Helford River, surrounded by woodlands. Magnificent views. Always plenty of seals to see. Open all year daily 9.30–sunset. 60p (ch 16 30p, pen 40p). Under review for 1979. ⚠ *(Tel Mawgan 361)* ⚠ **(79)**

HADDON HALL Derbyshire Map 8 SK26
2m SE Bakewell. 12th- to 15th-C house with notable chapel and hall, terraced rose gardens, the romantic associations with Dorothy Vernon. ⚕ Open 1 Apr to 30 Sep, Tue to Sat and BH Mon 11–6, BH Sun 2–6. 90p (ch 40p). Admission prices under revision for 1980. No dogs. ⚠ 10p. *(Tel Bakewell 2855)*. *(Duke of Rutland)*

HADLEIGH *Essex* Map 5 TQ88
Hadleigh Castle Founded in 1231 by Hubert de Burgh and rebuilt by Edward III in 14th C, walls are of Kentish rag; and castle retains two of original towers. Accessible any reasonable time. Free. *(AM)*

HADLEIGH *Suffolk* Map 5 TM04
Guildhall Partly timbered building, extended in the 14th C with superb beams and King posts. Further extended in the 18th C with assembly room. Facing church and 15th-C Deanery all make a unique collection of early building styles. Open all year, daily, 10.30 – dusk. Free. *(Tel 823576)*

HAILES *Gloucestershire* Map 4 SP02
Hailes Abbey Museum Remains of Cistercian house founded by Earl of Cornwall in 1246. Roof bosses, tiles, and other relics in Museum. Open, see inside front cover. 15p (ch 16 and pen 5p). ⚠ *(AM and NT)*

PKF

HAILSHAM *East Sussex* Map 5 TQ50
Michelham Priory 2½m W. Augustinian Priory, founded in 1229 on earlier moated site. 14th-C gatehouse and 16th-C Tudor house; 17th-C furniture, stained glass, tapestries, and Sussex ironwork. Art exhibitions in Tudor great barn. Sussex crafts shop. Folk night held 20, 21 Jun; Rural Industries exhibition 6 to 10 Aug; Archery May to Sep, last Sun in each month. ⚲ (licensed). Open 4 Apr to 19 Oct, daily 11 – 5.30 (house closed 1 – 2). 70p (ch 30p). ⚠ *(Tel 844224)*. *(Sussex Archaeological Society)*

HALIFAX *West Yorkshire* Map 7 SE02
Shibden Hall 15th-C half-timbered house with old barns and collection of horse-drawn vehicles. Now Folk Museum of West Yorkshire. ⚲ Open Apr to Sep, Mon to Sat 11 – 7, Sun 2 – 5; Oct, Nov and Mar, Mon to Sat 11 – 5, Sun 2 – 5; Feb, Sun only 2 – 5. 20p (ch 16 and pen 10p). P. *(Tel 52246)* ⚲ B

HALLAND *East Sussex* Map 5 TQ51
Bentley Wildfowl House, extensive grounds and major wildfowl collection of over 100 species of wildfowl. Also flamingoes, cranes, peacocks and ornamental pheasants. Picnic area, woodland walk. ⚲ Open daily Easter to end Sep 11 – 6; (last admission 4.30) 10.30 – 6.30 Sun (last admission 5); weekends only Oct to Easter 11 – 5.30 (last admission 4), house by appointment only during winter. 80p (ch 16 35p, pen 65p). Party. Prices under revision for 1980. No dogs in wildfowl enclosures. ⚠ free. *(Tel 573)* ⚲

HAMBLEDON *Hampshire* Map 4 SU61
9m SW of Petersfield, on B2150.
Vineyard and Winepress Mill Down. Unusual example of vineyard and press house. On slopes of Windmill Down. Wine-

making briefly explained. ℒ Open last Sun in Jul to first Sun in Oct, Sun 2.30–5.30, also 6, 9, 16 and 25 Aug, 3, 6, 13, 27 Sep and 1 Oct. Booked parties 31 Jul, 28 Aug, 9, 11, 17 and 20 Sep. 70p (ch 18 30p, pen 50p) price includes a taste of wine for persons over 18 years. Wine on sale (ex Sun). ⚠ *(Tel 475).* *(Maj Gen Sir Guy Salisbury-Jones GCVO CMG CBE MC)* ⌗

HAMBLEDON *Surrey* Map 4 SU93
Feathercombe 2m from Milford station on Hambledon road. Attractive gardens with flowering shrubs and wide views. Plants for sale. Open 20, 27 Apr; 4, 5, 11, 18, 25, 26 May; 1, 8 Jun; 24, 25 Aug; 2–6. 20p (ch free). *(Mrs Wieler and Miss Parker)* ⌗ *(NGS)*

HANBURY *Hereford and Worcester* Map 3 SO96
Hanbury Hall Pedimented, red-brick, Queen Anne period house, dating from 1701, noted for hall and staircase painted by Sir James Thornhill. Good plaster decoration in Long Room, contemporary orangery and Watney collection of porcelain. ℒ Open Apr to Sep, Wed to Sun and BH Mon and following Tue 2–6, Oct Sat and Sun 2–6. 85p *(NT)*

HANDCROSS *West Sussex* Map 4 TQ22
Nymans Garden Thirty acres of gardens featuring flowering shrubs and roses in large estate. Open Apr to Oct, Tue Wed, Thu and Sat 2–7; Sun, Bh Mon 11–7 (or sunset); last admission 1hr before closing. 70p. *(NT)*

HARDKNOTT CASTLE ROMAN FORT
Cumbria Map 7 NY20
On Hardknott Pass above Eskdale, 375ft-square fort with three double gateways enclosing walled and ramparted area of almost 3 acres. Situated above western end of steep and narrow pass (maximum gradient 1 in 3), fort was occupied in mid 2nd C. Accessible any reasonable time. Free. *(AM)*

HARDWICK HALL *Derbyshire* Map 8 SK46
2m S M1 Junc 29
Elizabethan mansion, built 1597 by Robert Smythson for famous Bess of Hardwick (Dowager Countess of Shrewsbury). Remarkable vast area of windows, fine tapestries, needlework, Cavendish portraits, High Great Chamber, and walled courtyard gardens. ℒ teas Apr to end Oct, Mon. Lunches May to Sep (on days when Hall is open). Open Apr to end Oct, Wed, Thu, Sat, Sun, BH Mon 1–5.30 (or sunset); gardens open during season, daily 12–5.30. Park open all year daily. Hall and gardens £1.20; gardens only 60p; Country Park 20p parking. *(NT) (NGS)*

HAREWOOD *West Yorkshire* Map 8 SE34
Harewood House, Bird Garden and Butterfly World The house, home of the Earl and Countess of Harewood, was designed 1759 by John Carr of York and Robert Adam, with 19th-C alterations by Sir Charles Barry. It contains splendid Chippendale furniture, English and Italian paintings and Chinese and Sèvres porcelain. The Park, landscaped by 'Capability' Brown, now includes 4-acre bird garden with species from all over the world. Adventure playground and shops. ℒ party catering. All facilities open daily 1 Apr to 31 Oct from 11 am. Limited opening Nov, Feb and Mar. House Tue, Wed and Thu only 11 am. Bird garden as house, plus Sun. Harewood closed Dec/Jan ex Bird Garden and Adventure playground special opening 10 am daily 26 Dec to 3 Jan inclusive. ⚠ *(24-hr information service, Tel 886225)* ⌗

HARROGATE *North Yorkshire* Map 8 SE35
Harlow Car Gardens Crag Lane, Otley Road. 60 acres of ornamental and woodland gardens, and the Northern Trial Grounds. Plant Bring and Buy Sat 3 May. Open all year dawn to dusk. 60p (ch 20p). Party 50p. ⌗
Rudding Park Gardens Extensive landscaped gardens, enclosing the early 19th-C Regency Country House. The gardens are especially noted for their magnificent beech and rare oak trees, vast parkland and lawns, shrubberies of rhododendrons, magnolias, and azaleas (of which the celebrated Rhododendron Walk is an outstanding example). The exterior of the house, in Grecian style is remarkable for its symmetry, lack of ornament and constant use of bow windows. Aug BH, Rudding Park Antiques Fair. ℒ Open daily Apr to Sep, 11–5.30. ⚠ 50p (occupants free). *(Tel 871350)* ⌗

HARTLEBURY *Hereford and Worcester* Map 7 SO87
Hereford and Worcester County Museum Hartlebury Castle. County crafts and industries, horse-drawn vehicles, gipsy caravans, period furnishings, costumes, toys and dolls, and forge and wheelwright's shop. ℒ Picnic area available. Open 1 Feb to 30 Nov, Mon to Thu 10–5, Sat and Sun 2–5. 25p (ch and pen 10p); students and school parties free. Under revision for 1980. ⚠ *(Tel 416)* ⌗ B

HARTLEPOOL *Cleveland* Map 8 NZ53
Gray Art Gallery and Museum Clarence Road. Permanent collection of pictures. Museum collections feature local history, archaeology, engineering, Indian idols,

porcelain, British birds, working blacksmith's shop in museum grounds. Open all year (ex 1 Jan, 4 Apr, 25 & 26 Dec) Mon – Sat 10 – 5.30, Sun 3 – 5. Free. ⚠ *(Tel 68916)* ♿

Maritime Museum Northgate. Collections feature the maritime history of the town and shipbuilding industry. Also reconstructed fisherman's cottage, a ship's bridge and an early lighthouse lantern. Open all year (ex 1 Jan, 25 & 26 Dec) Mon to Sat 10 – 5. Free. ⚠ *(Tel 72814)*

HARTLEY WINTNEY *Hampshire*
Map 4 SU75
West Green House 1½m W on unclass road. 18th-C house, with a series of busts on the outside walls. It belonged once to General Hawley, of Culloden ill-fame. Attractive garden. Open Apr to Sep: garden Wed, Thu Sun 2 – 6; house Wed 2 – 6 by appointment in writing with the tenant (minimum notice 7 days). Admission: house and garden 70p; garden only 50p. *(NT)*

HARTWELL *Buckinghamshire* Map 4 SP71
Hartwell House E-shaped Jacobean mansion with east façade of 1759 – 61 and early 17th-C staircase. Now Hartwell House Independent College of Further Education for Young Women. Louis XVIII spent part of exile here 1807 – 14. House and gardens open 14 May to 16 Jul, Wed only 2 – 5. 50p (ch 8 25p), ⚠ *(Tel Aylesbury 748355)*

HARVINGTON *Hereford and Worcester* Map 7 SO87
Harvington Hall Moated Elizabethan manor house with secret hiding places. ☕ Open 1 Feb to 30 Nov, Tue to Sat 2 – 6 (or dusk if earlier); also Easter to Sep 11.30 – 1, Sun 2 – 6 (or dusk if earlier). Other times by appointment. Last admission ½hr before closing time. 50p (ch 14 25p). ⚠ *(Tel Chaddesley Corbett 267)*

HARWICH *Essex* Map 5 TM23
The Redoubt 180ft diameter circular fort surrounded by dry moat, built 1808 to defend port against Napoleonic invasion. Walls are 8ft thick, and 18 rooms were provided to contain stores, ammunition, and quarters for 300 men. Now being restored by Harwich Society and part will be museum. Special fête, Spring BH. ☕ Open Easter to end Oct, Sun 10 – 12 and 2 – 5. Free. P.

HASCOMBE *Surrey* Map 4 SU94
Winkworth Arboretum 1m NW on B2130. A hillside of nearly 100 acres planted with shrubs and rare trees; bluebells; two lakes. Displays are best in May and end of Oct. Views towards the North Downs. Open always. Free. *(NT)*

HASTINGS *East Sussex* Map 5 TQ80
Fishermen's Museum Rock a Nore Road. Former fishermen's church, now museum of local interest, including last of Hastings luggers built for sail. Open Easter to 30 Sep, daily (ex Fri) 10 – 6. Free. P. ♿

Hastings Castle Castle Hill. Remains of Norman castle on cliffs. Excavations were made 1825 and 1968, and old dungeons were discovered 1894. Open Easter to Sep daily 10 – 5. 22p (ch 11p) (prices may be subject to increase). P. ♿

Hastings Museum and Art Gallery Cambridge Road. Collections of natural history of Hastings area, archaeology and history of Hastings and neighbouring areas, Sussex ironwork and pottery. Fine and applied art. Durbar Hall (Indian Palace). Extensive collection of pictures. Special Exhibition Gallery. Open all year (ex 4 Apr, 25 and 26 Dec) Mon to Sat 10 – 1, 2 – 5, Sun 3 – 5 including BH. Free. ⚠ ♿

Museum of Local History Old Town Hall, High Street. Archaeology of Hastings area. History of Hastings, especially Fishing Industry and the Cinque Ports. Open Easter (ex 4 Apr) to Oct 10 – 12.30 and 1.30 – 5.30 Mon to Sat. Free. *(Tel 425855)* ♿ B

St Clement's Caves West Hill. Cut into slopes of West Hill, extending over 4 acres, and associated with smugglers. Open all year daily, summer 10.30 – 5.30; winter 10.30 – 12.30 and 2 – 5. 32p (ch 16p) (prices may be subject to increase). P. *(Tel 422964)*

HATFIELD *Hertfordshire* Map 4 TL20
Hatfield House The historic home of the Marquess of Salisbury, a magnificent Jacobean house built 1607 – 11 by Robert Cecil, standing in a great park and gardens. Special exhibition of Fashion through the Ages plus the National Collection of Model Soldiers, open one hour before house. Guided tours weekdays. Dogs not admitted to house, must be on lead in gardens. ☕ in Old Palace Yard. Open 25 Mar to 12 Oct (ex 4 Apr and Mon, but open BH Mons) Tue to Sat and BH 12 – 5 (Sun 2 – 5.30) Garden open 10.30 – 6 daily. Admission: House, Park and Gardens £1 (ch 5 – 15, 55p). Exhibition extra 25p (ch 5 – 15, 20p); Park and Gardens only 45p (ch 5 – 15, 25p). Under revision for 1980. Party 20+ ⚠ *(Tel 62823, Catering 62055)*. *(Marquess of Salisbury)* ♿

The Old Palace Hatfield House. Standing within the gardens is the surviving wing of the Royal Palace in which Queen Elizabeth I spent much of her childhood. Elizabethan banquets held throughout the year. Tue, Thu, Fri, and Sat evenings, also Wed May to Sep; other evenings and luncheons for privately booked parties. ⚠ *(Tel 62055 or 62030)* ♿ B

HATHERN *Leicestershire* Map 8 SK42
Whatton House Gardens 4½m NW of
Loughborough on A6 between Hathern and
Kegworth. The 25-acre gardens display
flowering shrubs and have water, rose and
Chinese gardens. A dog cemetery and Dutch
garden, also a Bogy Hole, a curious garden
ornament, built c1885. Garden Centre and ⚑.
Open Easter Sun to end Sep Sun only, also
BH Mon 2–7. 25p (ch 10p, pen 15p). Under
revision for 1980. Party. ⚠ *(Tel
Loughborough 842225)* &

HAUGHLEY *Suffolk* Map 5 TM06
Haughley Park Newly restored house, dating
from 1620, built on E-plan with crow-stepped
gables and octagonal chimneys. Fine park
and gardens. Open May to end Sep, Tue 3–6.
50p (ch 16, 25p). ⚠ *(Tel Elmswell 40205). (Mr
A J Williams)* & B

HAUGHMOND ABBEY *Salop* Map 7 SJ51
Extensive remains of a house of Augustinian
canons founded about 1135. Chapter House
has fine Norman doorway and the abbot's
lodging is exceptionally well-preserved.
Open, see inside front cover but closes 4.30
Tue and Wed. 10p (ch 16 and pen 5p). ⚠
(AM)

HAVERTHWAITE *Cumbria* Map 7 SD38
Lakeside and Haverthwaite Railway
Preserved here are two 2–6–4 class 4
Fairburn tank engines and nine other
locomotives together with diesel locomotives
and passenger and freight rolling stock. ⚑ at
Haverthwaite station. Open 4 Apr to 8 Apr
(incl), Sun only to 27 April. Daily May to 5 Oct,
then Sun only to 26 Oct. Sun to Fri 11–5.30,
Sat 11.30–5. Standard gauge steam-hauled
passenger trains operate hourly 11–5, when
open, and most connect with the Lake
Windermere steamers at the lakeside. Fares
as published. ⚠ at Haverthwaite (20p). *(Tel
Newby Bridge 594)* &

HAWES *North Yorkshire* Map 7 SD89
National Park Centre Station Yard.
Interpretative display relating the
Wensleydale railway line to the social and
economic history of the area as part of a
National Park. Open Apr to end Sep, mid
morning to late afternoon. Free. ⚠ *(Tel 450)*
&
Upper Dales Folk Museum Museum of life in
the Upper Dales, opened in 1979. Open 1 Apr
(or Easter) to 30 Sep Mon to Sat 11–1, 2–5,
Sun 1–5; Oct Tue, Sat and Sun only. 30p (ch
and pen 15p). ⚠ *(Tel 494)* & B

HAWKSHEAD *Cumbria* Map 7 SD39
Courthouse Relic of pre-Reformation priory.

Houses Folk Museum of Rural Crafts, with
forestry, textile, and farm exhibits, a branch of
the Museum of Lakeland Life and Industry.
Open Easter, then May to Oct, daily (ex Mon)
2–5. 20p (ch 10p) *(NT)*

HAWORTH *West Yorkshire* Map 7 SE03
Brontë Parsonage The parsonage was the
home of the three gifted 19th-C novelists,
Charlotte, Emily and Anne. Contains Brontë
relics. Open daily 11–5.30 (11–4.30
Oct–Mar) Sun 2–5.30 (2–4.30 Oct–Mar).
Closed last 3 weeks in Dec. 20p (ch 16 10p).
P. *(Tel 42323)*

***Keighley and Worth Valley Railway and
Museums*** Keighley, Haworth and Oxenhope.
32 steam engines, 7 diesels. Weekend
service and daily Jul, Aug and Spring BH
week of trains from Keighley (connections
with BR) to Oxenhope via Haworth, 90p (ch
and pen 45p, ch 5 free; reduced fares for
shorter journeys). 15p (ch 16 10p) includes
entry to Haworth yards and Oxenhope
displays. ⚠ small charge at Haworth; free at
Oxenhope, Oakworth and Ingrow. (24-hour
Talking Timetable *Tel Haworth 43629;* or
enquiries *45214)* &

HAXTED *Surrey* Map 5 TQ44
Watermill Museum Late 16th-C mill on 14th-
C foundations, weather-boarded, with a
mansard roof and adjoining tile-hung mill
house, standing on Eden Water. Museum
contains mill machinery, two working water-
wheels, and picture gallery. Also exhibition by
Wealden Iron Research Group. ⚑ Open
Easter to end Sep, Sat and Sun 11–6, also
daily 2–6 (ex Mon) during summer holiday
period. 25p (ch 14 and pen 15p). ⚠ & B

HAYLE *Cornwall* Map 2 SW53
Bird Paradise A collection of colourful and
exotic birds, including some rare and
endangered species. Among these are the St
Vincent Parrot, Thick-billed Parrot from
Mexico, Hyacinthine Macaw, Great African
Wattled Crane and Toco Toucans. There are
also a Children's Zoo. Miniature steam
railway, Craft village, pub and restaurant. ⚑
Open all year, daily 10–dusk. £1.20 (ch 3–14
70p, pen 90p, ch 3 free). ⚠ *(Tel 753365)* &
The Craft Village and pub can be visited
without payment of parking or admission fees.

HAYWARDS HEATH *West Sussex*
Map 4 TQ32
Borde Hill 1½m N on Balcombe Road. A large
garden with woods and parkland. Many rare
trees and shrubs of considerable botanical
interest. ⚑ Open 15 Mar to 28 Sep, Wed, Sat
and Sun and BH 10–6. 50p (ch 20p). Party
12+40p. Dogs on lead only. ⚠ with picnic
area. *(Tel 50326)* &

HEACHAM *Norfolk* Map 9 TF63
Norfolk Lavender Caley Mill. Largest
growers and distillers of lavender in Britain.
Harvest during Jul to mid Aug. Shop for
lavender, lavender products and herb plants.
⚲ (from May). Open all year, Sep to May,
Mon to Fri 9 – 4, Jun to Aug 9 – 6. Distillery 20p
(ch and pen 10p). ⚠ Parties should be
booked in advance. Individuals call at Caley
Mill for directions. *(Tel 70384)* &

HEATHFIELD *East Sussex* Map 5 TQ52
Heathfield Wildlife Park Hailsham Road. A
variety of attractions which include wildlife,
Bird City, 200 acres of woodland. 'Fab One'
and 'Chitty-Chitty-Bang-Bang' on permanent
display, and the Figes Museum of Agricultural
Archaeology in Queen Victoria's Royal
Pavilion. Among the wildlife exhibits are deer,
vultures, monkeys, sealions, chimpanzees,
and ostriches. The Gibraltar tower was built in
1792 as a memorial to Lord Heathfield,
formerly General George Eliot, defender of
Gibraltar 1779 – 83, and is classified as a
Schedule building. Special events include
Traction Engine Rally 18/19 Aug also
monthly events. ⚲ Open all year (ex 25 & 26
Dec) daily 10 – 6 (or dusk if earlier). 80p (ch 14
and pen 60p, ch 3 free). ⚠ *(Tel 4656 and
4748)* & **(79)**

HEBDEN BRIDGE *West Yorkshire*
Map 7 SD92
Heptonstall Grammar School Museum 1 m
NW on minor road. A 17th-C village school
situated in a churchyard with the ruins of a
medieval church and a 19th-C church. The
school contains the original desks etc and folk
exhibits from the surrounding area. Open all
year (ex 1 Jan, 25 and 26 Dec) Apr to Sep, Sat
and Sun 2 – 6; Oct to Mar Sat and Sun 1 – 5.
Open BH. Free. P. *(Tel 3738)* & B

HECKINGTON *Lincolnshire* Map 8 TF14
Heckington Windmill Well-restored tower-
mill of 1830, with eight sails formerly used on
mill at Boston, and machinery still in working
order. Only one of its kind to have survived.
Open all year Mon to Fri 9 – 5, Sat 9 – 12;
enquiries to *Mr J Pocklington* at mill house
adjacent. Free. ⚠ (small fee). 14th-C village
church nearby. *(Tel 241)* **(79)**

HELMINGHAM *Suffolk* Map 5 TM15
Helmingham Hall Gardens Home of Lord
and Lady Tollemache, moated house with two
drawbridges which are raised every night.
Moated gardens in ancient deer park with
ornamental waterfowl, Highland cattle, large
herd of over 500 red and Fallow deer and
safari rides. Fresh vegetables and flowers
from garden on sale in addition to East
Anglian crafts from stable shop. Coach house
tea-rooms and picnic area. Gardens open 4
May then every Sun from 25 May to 28 Sep,
2 – 6. 80p (ch 40p, pen 50p). Party. ⚠ *(Tel
363)* &

HELMSLEY *North Yorkshire* Map 8 SE68
Helmsley Castle Ruined 12th- to 13th-C
stronghold with domestic buildings added in
14th C. Open*, see inside front cover. 20p (ch
16 and pen 5p). ⚠ *(AM)*

HELSTON *Cornwall* Map 2 SW62
Cornwall Aero Park See actual aeroplanes
used in Yorkshire Television's successful
Flambards also *Flambards* period room
settings. Wall Gallery. Sit at the controls of a
Shackleton and other historic aircraft or climb
aboard the flight deck of Concorde. Beautiful
landscaped grounds. Historic Wheels and
Wings exhibition 1980. Fun amusements.
Free crazy golf for children. Shop and ⚲.
Open Easter to early Nov, daily, 10 – 5 (6 Jul

and Aug). £1 (ch 60p). Party. ⚠ *(Tel 3404/4549)* ⓓ
Helston Museum Old Butter Market. Folk museum covering local history and articles from Lizard district. Open all year, Mon – Sat (ex Wed closed noon) 10.30 – 12.30 and 2 – 4.30. Touring Schools and visiting groups welcome by prior arrangement. Free. P. *(Hon Curator Lt Cdr A E Simmonds RN MBE Tel 2480)*

HENLEY-IN-ARDEN *Warwickshire* Map 4 SP16
Guildhall Gabled, timber-framed building of 1448, restored in 1915, with outside staircase leading from Dutch-style garden to hall with fine roof timbering. Many relics and town records on display. Open any reasonable time on application to *Caretaker, Guild Cottage*. Free. Under revision for 1980. *(Tel 2309) (Mr E W Berry)*
Henley Bird Gardens High Street. Situated in the 4-acre grounds of an Elizabethan Manor House is a fine collection of over 400 foreign birds. Open Apr to Oct. 60p (ch 16 30p) P. *(Tel 2562)* ⓓ

HENLEY-ON-THAMES *Oxfordshire* Map 4 SU78
Greys Court 2m W. Gabled Elizabethan house with fine chimney-pieces and plasterwork and interesting English and Swiss furniture. Medieval fortified courtyard with three towers and a keep, remains from former 13th-C house, and there is a 200ft-deep well with 19ft-wide wooden donkey wheel. ⚲ Sat and BH and for booked parties. Open Apr to Sep, grounds and Carlisle Collection Mon to Sat, house Mon, Wed, Fri 2.15 – 6. Gardens 60p, house 30p extra, Carlisle Collection 30p extra. *(NT)*

HEREFORD *Hereford and Worcester* Map 3 SO54
Bulmers Railway Centre Whitecross Road. On site of the former Midland Railways Goods Yard, operated by the 6000 Locomotive Association for and on behalf of H P Bulmer Ltd. Additional attractions on open days. ⚲ Open first weekend in Apr to last weekend in Sep for static display 2 – 5. Open days with engines in steam Easter and Spring BH weekends, small engine in steam one Sun per month (enquire before visit). Party. Weekend steamings of small locomotives (enquire before visit). All admission prices under review for 1980. ⚠ *(Tel 4791)* ⓓ
Churchill Gardens Museum and Brian Hatton Art Gallery 3 Venn's Lane. Branch Museum located in Regency house with fine grounds. Victorian nursery, butler's pantry and parlour. Costumes, furniture and watercolours. Also the Hatton Gallery primarily devoted to works by the local artist Brian Hatton. Open all year, daily 2 – 5. Free. ⚠ *(Tel 68121 ext 207)*
St John's and Coningsby Museum 110 Widemarsh Street. Early 13th-C hall arranged with armour and other subjects connected with the Order and Chapel of Knights of St John, with almshouses added in 1614 by Sir Thomas Coningsby of Hampton Court. Unique Friars' Preaching Cross in adjoining public gardens. Open Apr to Oct daily (ex Mon and Fri) 1 – 5. 15p (ch 5p). Party. ⚠ *(Tel 2837 mornings)* ⓓ
Hereford Museum and Art Gallery Broad Street. Roman remains (*ie* tessellated pavements), natural history, English watercolours, local geology, and county's archaeology, also folk life and folklore material. Exhibitions at City Art Gallery change every month. Open all year, Mon to Sat 10 – 6 (5, Thu); 1 Sep to 1 Apr Sat 10 – 5. Free. P. *(Tel 68121 ext 207)* ⓓ
The Old House High Town. Restored half-timbered house, dating from 1621 with Jacobean furniture. Open all year Mon to Fri 10 – 1 and 2 – 5.30, Sat 10 – 1, Sun 2 – 5 (closed Sun Oct to Mar). 15p (ch 5p). Free admission Thu. *(Tel 68121 ext 207)*

HERSTMONCEUX *East Sussex* Map 5 TQ61
Royal Greenwich Observatory (Herstmonceux Castle) Entry off Wartling Road. Public exhibition and grounds only of castle. ⚲ Open from Easter to end Sep, Mon to Fri 2 – 5.30, Sat, Sun and BH 10.30 – 5.30. 55p (ch and pen 25p). Under revision for 1980. ⚠ Castle **not** open to the public. *(Tel 3171 ext 320)* ⓓ

HERTFORD *Hertfordshire* Map 4 TL31
Hertford Castle Early 16th-C brick gatehouse, much altered *c*1800, partly by Henry Holland, with slight remains of original Norman castle. Interior now used as municipal offices. Open May to Sep, first Sat in each month 10 – 1, grounds open all year, daily until dusk. Free. P (limited). *(Tel 54977)* ⓓ B
Hertford Museum 18 Bull Plain. Local archaeology, history, geology, and natural history. Open all year (ex 4 Apr, 25/26 Dec and Suns). Mar to Oct Mon to Fri 11 – 5 (10 – 5 Sat); Nov to Feb Mon to Fri 11 – 4 (Sat 10 – 4). Free. ⚠ *(Tel 52686)* ⓓ B

HEVER *Kent* Map 5 TQ44
Hever Castle and Gardens 3m SE Edenbridge off B2026. 13th-C moated castle where Henry VIII courted Anne Boleyn. Large gardens and grounds including lake, Italian garden, fountains and topiary work. Open 30

Mar to 28 Sep (ex 4 Apr) Tue, Wed, Fri, Sun and BH. Gardens 1 – 7, castle 1.30 – 6 or 7 depending on day (last entry ½hr before closing). Tue and Fri extra rooms on show. Grounds only 80p (ch 12 30p); castle additional £1 (ch 50p), Tue and Fri £1.50. Dogs on lead in grounds only. ⚠ *(Tel Edenbridge 862205 ext 1, 865224 ext 4)* & B

HEVINGHAM *Suffolk* Map 5 TM37
Heveningham Hall 4m SW of Halesworth. Georgian house by Sir Robert Taylor and James Wyatt, with famous entrance hall, Etruscan room, library, etc; original furniture; park laid out by 'Capability' Brown; orangery by Wyatt. Gift shop, picnics, ♨ and fishing tickets. Open 2 Apr to 12 Oct, Wed, Thu, Sat, Sun, BH Mons. May to end Sep, Tue also, house 2 – 6 (last entry 5.30) park and gardens 2 – 6 (12 – 6, Sun and BH). 90p (ch 15 40p). ⚠ *(Tel Ubbeston 355)* &

HIGHDOWN *West Sussex* Map 4 TQ00
N off A259 halfway between Worthing and Littlehampton. Gardens laid out in chalk pit on Highdown Hill, with rock plants, flowering shrubs, and daffodils. Also Miller's tomb and excellent views. Open all year. Mon to Fri 9 – 4.30 (Sat and Sun Apr to Sep). Free. ⚠ *(Tel Worthing 204226)* &

HIGH WYCOMBE *Buckinghamshire* Map 4 SU89
Wycombe Chair and Local History Museum Castle Hill House, Priory Avenue. Fine house set in gardens with museum of chairs, old tools, and chair making apparatus. Open all year, Mon (ex BH), Tue, Thu, Fri, Sat 10 – 1, 2 – 5. Free. P. *(Tel 23879)* & B

HIMLEY *Staffordshire* Map 7 SO89
Himley Hall 6m S of Wolverhampton off A449, 4m N of Stourbridge off A449. Extensive parkland, trout and coarse fishing

(extra charge). ♨ Grounds only open all year, daily 8 – 8 (or ½hr before dusk). Free. Cars 20p. *(Tel Dudley 56321)* &

HINTON CHARTERHOUSE *Avon* Map 3 ST75
Hinton Priory Carthusian priory founded 1232, with remains of chapter house and refectory. 15th-C gatehouse forms part of 16th-C manor house on site. Open 1 Apr to 1 Oct, Wed, Sat, and BH 2 – 6. 20p ⚠ *(Tel Limpley Stoke 3596)*

HITCHIN *Hertfordshire* Map 4 TL12
Hitchin Museum and Art Gallery Paynes Park. Contains new displays of local history collections, natural history and tropical fish. Regimental Museum of the Hertfordshire Yeomanry, costume and Victoriana. Special temporary exhibitions changed monthly. Good reserve collection of water-colours, especially those by local Quaker artist Samuel Lucas Snr 1805 – 1870, photographs and costume, which can be seen by appointment. Open all year (ex Sun and BH) 10 – 5. Free. ⚠ *(Tel 4476)* & B

HOAR CROSS *Staffordshire* Map 7 SK12
Hoar Cross Hall Off A515 near Newborough. Elizabethan-style mansion, built 1871 and modelled in part on Elizabethan Temple Newsam in Leeds, with fine plasterwork on ceilings and private chapel. Restored gardens contain fine trees and shrubs, yew-tree walks, and ponds. Picnic/play area. ♨ Open Spring BH to Late Summer BH, Sun 2 – 6, BH Mon and Tue 12.30 – 6; other times by appointment only. Hall and gardens 50p (ch 20p). ⚠ (10p). *(Tel 427).* *(Mr W A Bickerton-Jones)* &

HODNET *Salop* Map 7 SJ62
Hodnet Hall Gardens 6m SW Market Drayton, 12m NE Shrewsbury. Re-designed Elizabethan-style Victorian house (not open

to public), with 60-acre landscape garden.
Collection of big-game trophies in 17th-C
tearooms. Gift shop, plants for sale in Garden
Centre featured on TV and radio. ℒ Sun and
BH then daily May to Aug, picnicking allowed.
Open 4 Apr to 28 Sep, Mon to Sat 2–5
(gardens cleared 6pm), Sun and BH 12–6
(gardens cleared 8pm). Party. Dogs only on
lead. ⚠ *(Tel 202). (Mr and Hon Mrs Heber-Percy)* ⚓

HOGHTON *Lancashire* Map 7 SD62
Hoghton Tower 5m SE Preston on A675.
16th-C fortified Hilltop Mansion with
magnificent Banqueting Hall where, in 1617,
the 'Loin of Beef' was knighted by James I,
also the King's Bedchamber, Audience
Chamber, Ballroom and other state rooms,
and the Tudor Well House with its horse-
drawn pump and oaken windlass and the
Stone Cells which housed malefactors and
cattle thieves of bygone days. Walled
gardens, lawns and Old English Rose
Garden. Walks and grounds with views of
sea, moors, hills of Lake District and Welsh
mountains. Permanent Dolls House and Dolls
collection and various other exhibitions. Open
5 Apr then every Sun until end Oct, also Sat
Jul and Aug and all BH. 2–5. 75p (ch 25p). ⚠
10p *(Tel 2986)* ⚓ (garden)

HOLKER *Cumbria* Map 7 SD37
Holker Hall Near Grange-over-Sands. 16th-
to 19th-C country house with beautiful
woodcarvings, home of Cavendish family. 22
acres of gardens, and deer park with fallow,
sika and red deer. Regular equestrian, dog
and airsport events during season. Horse
driving trials end Apr. Sheep dog trials 21 Jun.
Lakeland Rose show 14 & 15 Jul. Equestrian
championships 3 Sep. (These dates are
provisional.) Children's play area, newly
opened Motor Museum, exhibition centre. Art
Gallery gift shop. ℒ Licensed. Open 6 Apr to
30 Sep, daily (ex Sat) 11–6. £1 (ch 50p).
Party, Motor museum extra 70p (ch 45p).
Party. Admission prices under revision for
1980. ⚠ *(Tel Flookburgh 328). (Mr and Mrs
Hugh Cavendish) (NGS)*

HOLKHAM *Norfolk* Map 9 TF84
Holkham Hall 1½m W of Wells-next-the-Sea
off A149. Entrance by Almshouses Gate in
Holkham village. Palladian mansion, built
1734 by William Kent and former home of
Coke of Norfolk. Marble hall and state
apartments with pictures and furnishings,
terraces, Holkham Pottery, also Holkham
bygones collection of agricultural and rural
craft tools. Garden centre. Large Park. ℒ
Open 26 May and 25 Aug also 29 May; Thu
Jun to Sep also Mon Jul and Aug 11.30–5.

50p (ch 25p, pen in parties 25p). Admission
prices under revision for 1980. No dogs. ⚠
25p. *(Tel Wells 227). (Earl of Leicester)*

HOLLINGBOURNE *Kent* Map 5 TQ85
Eyehome Manor SW of village, 15th-C half-
timbered house with 17th-C additions.
Laundry museum. Also herb garden. ℒ Open
4 Apr to 30 Sep, Sat and Sun, 2–6; Tue, Wed,
Thu, Sat and Sun Aug also BH 2–6. Parties at
other times by arrangement. 70p (ch 35p). ⚠
(Tel 514) (Mr and Mrs Simmons)

HOLT *Wiltshire* Map 3 ST86
The Courts House dates from *c*1700.
Topiary gardens, with lily pond and
arboretum, open Apr to end Oct, daily (ex Sat
and Sun) 2–6. 30p *(NT)*

HONITON *Devon* Map 3 ST10
Allhallows Museum High Street (next to
church). Honiton lace on display, also lace-
making demonstrations. Historical
documents etc. Locally excavated prehistoric
animal bones and artifacts. Open May to Sep,
10–5. 20p (ch 16 5p). P. *(Tel Farway 307,
Hon Sec)*

HORNSEA *Humberside* Map 8 TA24
Hornsea Pottery Rolston Road. Factory
tours, seconds shop, gift shop, holiday shop,
country crafts centre, ℒ picnic area, mini-zoo
and 28 acres of landscaped gardens with
lake. Open all year daily from 10am. Factory
tours 35p (ch and pen 20p). Parties. 'Minidale'
model village open early May to end Sep, 30p
(ch and pen 15p). ⚠ *(Tel 2161)* ⚓

HORRINGER *Suffolk* Map 5 TL75
Ickworth 2½m SW of Bury St Edmunds.
Elliptical rotunda (1794–1830), with 18th-C
and Regency French furniture, silver, and
pictures, and formal garden with fine trees. ℒ
Open Apr to 12 Oct, Tue, Wed, Thu, Sat, Sun,
BH Mon 2–6 (last admission 5.30) park open
all year, daily. £1. Party 15+. Park free. No
dogs in house or garden, on lead in park. *(NT)*

HORSEY *Norfolk* Map 9 TG42
Drainage Windmill Erected in 1912 on
foundations of earlier mill, restored after being
struck by lightning in 1943, and ceasing to
work. Accessible during summer. Free *(NT)*

HORSHAM *West Sussex* Map 4 TQ13
Horsham Museum 9 The Causeway. 16th-C
black and white timbered house, showing
collections of local history, costume, jewellery
(The Grundy Collection), toys, early bicycles,
domestic and rural life, crafts and industries of
Sussex. Including a period Sussex kitchen,
blacksmith's forge, wheelwright's and
saddler's shops, prehistoric and geology
room. Frequent temporary exhibitions
throughout the year. Open all year (ex BH),
Tue to Fri 1–5, Sat 10–5. Free. P. *(Tel 4959)*

A day to remember
at Hornsea Pottery

Come and visit our leisure parks at Hornsea on the East Yorkshire Coast and at Lancaster on the West coast. You can browse over the award winning ranges of Hornsea Pottery and buy it at much less than suggested retail prices. But do try to find time for some of the other attractions.

Hornsea
At our Hornsea leisure park we have *Guided Factory Tours, a Children's Playground, Mini-zoo, Gift Shop, Tea Garden, Cafe, Picnic Area, Country Craft Centre and a Model Village, 'Minidale', all set in 28 acres of landscaped gardens.
Hornsea Pottery Co Ltd, Hornsea, Yorkshire HU18 1UD
Telephone : 040 12 (Hornsea) 2161

Lancaster
At our Lancaster leisure park (only 15 minutes off the M6, exits 33 or 34) we have *Guided Factory Tours, Children's Farmyard and Playground, Cafe, Tea Garden, Gift Shop and a Rare Breeds Survival Unit all set in 42 beautiful acres of parkland.
Hornsea Pottery Co Ltd, (Lancaster), Wyresdale Road, Lancaster LA1 3LA Telephone : 0524 (Lancaster) 68444

*Our Factory Tours are in such great demand that we advise you to come early and avoid disappointment. Don't forget we make no charge for parking.

HORNSEA POTTERY
Open daily from 10 am

HORTON *Avon* Map 3 ST78
Horton Court Restored Cotswold house,
altered in 19th-C, with rare Norman halt. Hall
and perpendicular ambulatory. Open Apr to
Oct, Wed and Sat 2–6; other times by written
application to tenant. 20p *(NT)*

HOUGHTON *Norfolk* Map 9 TF72
Houghton Hall 1¼m off A148 between Kings
Lynn (12m) and Fakenham (8m). One of the
finest examples of Palladian architecture in
England, Houghton Hall designed by Colen
Campbell and Thomas Ripley was built in the
18th-C for Sir Robert Walpole. State rooms
have interior decorations and furniture by
William Kent and contain paintings and china.
Stables with heavy horses and Shetland
ponies, harness room and coach house.
Beautiful parkland and pleasure grounds. ⚏
and picnic area. Opening times and
admission prices not available for 1980. Party
20+. ⚠ *(Tel East Rudham 247)* &

HOUSESTEADS *Northumberland*
Map 12 NY76
Roman Wall (Housesteads Museum) Near
Bardon Mill. Roman fort of 'Vir covicium', with
mile-castles and 3-mile stretch of wall.
Museum has finds excavated in vicinity.
Open*, see inside front cover. 40p (winter 15p
(ch 15p winter 5p). ⚠ *(AM and NT)*

HOVE *East Sussex* Map 4 TQ20
Brighton and Hove Engineerium off Nevill
Road. Beam pumping engines of 1876 and
French Corliss horizontal engine, traction
engines, railway engines, fire engines etc.
The exhibition hall contains many hundreds of
full size and model engines, machines and
hand tools, household and cooking machines
which relate the progress of steam power and
its development from the 1780s'. Periodic
special exhibitions. Boiler house and steam
driven workshops also open. Easter and 12,
13 Aug, Steam and Craft Fairs. ⚏ weekends
only. Open all year (ex 23, 24, 25 Dec) daily
10–5. 70p (ch and pen 30p) when in steam;
weekdays (not in steam) 50p (ch and pen
20p). Prices under revision for 1980. No dogs.
P. *(Tel Brighton 559583)* & B

HOWICK *Northumberland* Map 12 NU21
Howick Hall Gardens and Grounds
Entrance by East Lodge. Late 18th-C
mansion with fine gardens and grounds.
Gardens and grounds only open 1 Apr to 30
Sep, daily 2–7, 20p (ch 15 10p). ⚠ *(Howick
Trustees Ltd) (Tel Longhoughton 285)*

HUDDERSFIELD *West Yorkshire*
Map 7 SE11
Art Gallery Princess Alexandra Walk.
Contains a permanent collection of British oil
paintings, watercolours, drawings, sculpture
from mid 19th-C onwards. Temporary loan
exhibitions throughout the year. Scherer
gallery of Bamforth photographs, lantern
slides and postcards. Open all year daily (ex
Sun) 9–7.30 (4 Sat). Free. P. *(Tel 21356)* &
Colne Valley Museum Cliffe Ash, Golcar.
Restored weaver's cottage, with living room
c 1860, weaver's workshop with working
looms, and local history display. New
clogmaker's workshop. Craft weekends Apr
to Oct. ⚏ shop – books of local interest and
industrial history. Open all year, Sat, Sun and
BH 2–5. 15p (ch 16 10p, pen free). P. Golcar.
(Tel 659762) **(79)**
Museum of Hand Tools Banney Road
Teacher's Centre, Halifax Road. Collection
includes trades equipment from joiners,
coopers, blacksmiths, plumbers, clog makers
etc, and special feature of 500 joiners'

moulding planes, hand tools only, all of which
can be examined. Many of the tools used by
the custodian to demonstrate the older crafts.
Open all year first Sat of each month
1.30–5.30 or by special appointment. Free.
⚠ *(Mr D Broadbeat) (Tel 39531 school hours
only)* & B
Tolson Memorial Museum Ravensknowle
Park. Geology, natural history, archaeology,
folk life, toys, development of cloth industry,
and collection of horse-drawn vehicles. Open
all year, Mon to Sat 10.30–5, Sun 2–5
(closed 25, 26 Dec). At weekends only 5p (ch
2½p, pen free). ⚠ *(Tel 30591)* &

HUGHENDEN *Buckinghamshire*
Map 4 SU89
Hughenden Manor 1½m N High Wycombe.
Disraeli's old home, remodelled by him in
1862, in 169-acre estate, with furniture and
books of the statesman. Open Apr to Oct.
House and garden Wed to Sat 2–6; Sun and
BH Mon 12.30–6; Mar and Nov Sat and Sun
only 2–5 or sunset. 90p. *(NT)*

HULL *Humberside* Map 8 TA02
Ferens Art Gallery Queen Victoria Square.
Contains a collection of works by European
Old Masters; 19th-C marine paintings from
Humberside; 20th-C English art and a regular
programme of visiting exhibitions. ⚏ (closed
Sun) 10.45–4. Open all year (ex 4 Apr, 24, 25
and 26 Dec) Mon to Sat 10–5, Sun
2.30–4.30. P. *(Tel 223111 ext 2750)*
Maister House 160 High Street. Georgian
house (1743), with stone and wrought iron
staircase and balustrade, some ornate stucco
work, and finely carved doors. Staircase and
entrance hall only shown all year. Mon to Fri
(ex BH) 10–4. 20p (incl guide book). *(NT)*
Town Docks Museum Queen Victoria
Square. Displays include 'Whales and
Whaling', 'Fishing and Trawling', 'Hull and the
Humber', 'Ships and Shipping', plus Victorian
Court Room. Open all year (ex 4 Apr, 24, 25 &
26 Dec) Mon to Sat 10–5, Sun 2.30–4.30.
Free. P. Osbourne Street. *(Tel 22311 ext
2737)* &
Transport and Archaeological Museum 36
High Street. Development of road transport
through the ages. Archaeology of
Humberside and Roman mosaics including
the Horkslow Pavement. Open all year (ex 4
Apr 24, 25 and 26 Dec) Mon to Sat 10–5, Sun
2.30–4.30. Free. P at Wilberforce house. *(Tel
223111 ext 2737)*
Wilberforce House 23–25 High Street. Early
17th-C mansion, where William Wilberforce
was born, with Jacobean and Georgian
Rooms, Slavery collection. Secluded garden.
Open all year (ex 4 Apr, 24, 25, 26 Dec),
weekdays 10–5, Sun 2.30–4.30. Free. ⚠
(Tel 223111 ext 2737)

HUNGARTON *Leicestershire* Map 4 SK60
Quenby Hall 7m NE Leicester on unclass
road. A Jacobean mansion built about 162
and extensively restored in 1974–5.
Excellent panelling, ceilings and furniture.
Fine view of cedars from library, walled
garden with lawns and flowers. ⚏ Hall open
Sun, Jun to Sep also 6/7 Apr, 4/5 and 25/26
May, 24/25 Aug, 2–6. ⚠ *(Tel 224)*

HUNGERFORD *Berkshire* Map 4 SU36
Littlecote House 2m NW on unclass road S
of River Kennet. Tudor manor with unique
collection of Cromwellian armour. Chapel,
haunted bedroom and a fine collection of oak
furniture. Roman excavations and Orpheus
mosaic. Beautiful gardens in Kennet Valley.
Walled garden and trout stream. ⚏ Sat, Sun

plus pre-booked parties. Open 1 Apr to 1 Oct Sat, Sun and BH 2 – 6. Party (weekdays). Prices not available for 1980. *(Tel 2509). (Mr D S Wills)* ⅃ B

HUNTINGDON *Cambridgeshire* Map 4 TL27
Cromwell Museum Market Square. Restored Norman building, once a school where Oliver Cromwell and Samuel Pepys were taught, now museum of Cromwellian relics. Open all year Tue to Sat 11 – 1 and 2 – 5 (4, Sat), Sun 2 – 4, closed BH ex 4 Apr. Free. P. *(Tel 52181 or outside office hours 52861)*
Hinchingbrooke House ½m W on A141. Tudor and later mansion, incorporating medieval Benedictine Nunnery. Former home of the Cromwells and Earls of Sandwich and now restored and used as a school. ⅃ Open Mar, Apr, May, Jun, Jul. Sun 2 – 5. Also Easter, BH Mon. 40p (ch 14 20p) Party 30p. P. *(Tel 51121)* ⅃ B

HURST CASTLE *Hampshire* Map 4 SZ38
On peninsula 4m S of Lymington. Erected 1544 by Henry VIII, occupied during Civil War by Cromwell's forces and restored in 1873. Accessible on foot or by boat from Keyhaven (weather permitting). Open*, see inside front cover. 15p (ch 16 and pen 5p). Nearest car park on beach. 1½m. *(AM)*

HURSTPIERPOINT *West Sussex*
Map 4 TQ21
Danny Elizabethan E-shaped house dating from 1593. Early in the 18th C the South front was faced with a Queen Anne elevation. Open May to Sep, Wed and Thu 2 – 5. 40p (ch 25p). ⚠ *(Tel 833000)*

HUTTON-LE-HOLE *North Yorkshire*
Map 8 SE78
Ryedale Folk Museum Ryedale antiquities from prehistoric times to beginning of this century, including reconstructed cruck houses, barn, wheelshed and Elizabethan furnace in grounds. Open day (21 Jun) all crafts in operation. Open Easter to end Sep daily 2 – 5.30 (11 – 5.30, mid Jul and Aug). 30p (ch 14 15p, pen reduced) may be subject to increase. P. *(Tel Lastingham 367)* ⅃ B

HYDE *Gt Manchester* Map 7 SJ99
Newton Hall ½m N of town centre in Dukinfield Road (A627). Restored 14th-C manor hall with original cruck beams, spurs and side-walls, set in two acres of parkland. Open all year, weekdays 9 – 4.30. Free. ⚠ *(Tel 061-308 2721)* **(79)**

HYTHE *Kent* Map 5 TR13
Saltwood Castle On N edge of Saltwood. Murderers of Thomas-à-Beckett rode from here. Grounds and parts of castle, including battlement walk, undercroft, armoury and

torture chamber. Open Sun and BH from 25 May to 27 Jul. Then daily in Aug (ex Mon and Sat) 2 – 5.30 but open 25 Aug. By appointment on other days for parties of fifteen or more, when guided tours of private rooms may be arranged (extra charge). ⅃ (teas). 50p (ch 12 25p). ⚠ *(Tel 67190, Secretary)*

ILFRACOMBE *Devon* Map 2 SS54
Chambercombe Manor 1 m E off A399. One of England's oldest inhabited houses, parts of which are 800 years old. Haunted room, chapel, period furniture, armour and porcelain. Open Easter Su to end Sep, Mon to Fri 10.30 – 5, Sun 2 – 5 (closed Sat). A charge will be made for admission to the house only. ⚠ *(Tel 62624)*
Hele Mill 1 m E. This mill dates back to 1525. It has been restored to full working order and is producing wholemeal flour. There is an 18ft overshot water wheel and inside are many interesting items of mill machinery. Open Easter to end Sep, Mon to Fri 10 – 5, also Sun 2 – 5. Admission prices not available. ⚠ *(Tel 63162)*
Ilfracombe Museum Natural history, Victoriana, archaeology, geology, photographs. Open daily 10 – 5 (10 – 1 winter), other times by arrangement. 20p (ch 10p). ⚠ *(Tel 63541)*

ILKLEY *West Yorkshire* Map 7 SE14
Manor House Castle Yard, Church Street. Elizabethan Manor House built on site of Roman fort, showing exposed Roman wall and collections of Roman material. Special art exhibitions each month. Ilkley Literature Festival. Open daily (ex 4 Apr, 25, 26 Dec) 10 – 5, enquire for summer opening hours. Free. ⚠ *(Tel 600066)* ⅃ B

INGATESTONE *Essex* Map 5 TQ69
Ingatestone Hall Brick-built house (c1545), with portraits and armorial china in long gallery, and annual exhibitions of documents and pictures. An exhibition on 'Industry in Essex' will be displayed in 1980. Open 5 Apr to 4 Oct, Tue to Sat and BH Mon 10 – 12.30 and 2 – 4.30. Free. No dogs. ⚠ *(Tel 3340)*. *(Lord Petre and Essex County Council)* ⅃ B

INSTOW *Devon* Map 2 SS42
Tapeley Park House and Gardens 1½m W on A39 Bideford – Barnstaple Road. Italian-style gardens and woodland walk to lake. Pets and putting green. ⅃ Conducted tours for parties of part of the house. Open Easter to Oct, BH and daily (ex Mon) 10 – 6. Admission charges not yet decided. ⚠ *(Tel 860528)*. *(NGS)* **(79)**

IPSDEN *Oxfordshire* Map 4 SU68
Wellplace Bird Farm Over 100 varieties of birds, pet lambs, goats, monkeys, foxes,

badgers, donkeys, otters, ponies, racoons, etc. ♨ Open Fec to end Nov, Sat and Sun from 10am; Easter to Sep also Mon to Fri from 1pm. 45p (ch 20p, ch 2 free). Party. ⚠ *(Tel Checkendon 680473)* ♿

IPSWICH *Suffolk* Map 5 TM14
Ancient House Butter Market. A superb example of 16th-C English domestic architecture. The exterior is richly ornamented in pargetting and carved oak-frame windows. Inside is an 'Oak' room with panelling, beams and a Jacobean mantelpiece. Above the main doorway is the Royal Coat of Arms of Charles II, and it is claimed that he hid in a secret chapel within the house after the Battle of Worcester. It is now converted into a busy bookshop, but visitors are always welcome. Open all year, daily (ex Sun and BH) 9 – 5.30. Free. *(Tel 57761)*
Christchurch Mansion South side of Christchurch Park. 16th-C country house. Art Gallery attached. Period rooms, pictures, pottery, ship models and costume. Open all year (ex some BH) Mon to Sat 10 – 5 (or dusk), Sun 2.30 – 4.30. Free. P. Written enquiries to main museum below. *(Tel 53246). (Borough of Ipswich Dept of Recreation Amenities)*
The Museum High Street. Local geology, prehistory, Roman to medieval archaeology in eastern counties, and natural history collection. Ethnography. Art gallery with temporary exhibitions. Open all year (ex BH), Mon to Sat 10 – 5. Free. P. *(Tel 213761/2). (Borough of Ipswich Dept of Recreation & Amenities)*

IRONBRIDGE *Salop* Map 7 SJ60
Blists Hill Open Air Museum Coalport Road, Madeley, Telford. Buildings and machines illustrating industrial and social history of Ironbridge area, on 42-acre site. Part of Ironbridge Gorge Museum Trust (see below for details of opening times, etc). Also
Tar Tunnel an 18th-C tunnel under Blists Hill with access to artificial 'wells' which collect natural bitumen. Part of Ironbridge Gorge Museum Trust. Open at variable hours. ♿ B
Coalbrookdale Furnace and Museum of Iron Iron-founding museum and site of original furnace built by Abraham Darby, where first smelting of iron by coke was carried out in early 18th C. Outdoor exhibits and indoor museum open all year, daily 10 – 6 (5, Nov to Mar). Admission prices not yet known for 1980. ⚠ *(Tel 3522)*. Part of Ironbridge Gorge Museum Trust. ♿. Also
Coach House Gallery Coalbrookdale. Prints, drawings etc from Elton collection on display and special exhibitions. See above for details of opening.
Coalport China Works Museum Original buildings, workshop and social history displays about Coalport China Company, active here from c1790 to 1926. Part of Ironbridge Gorge Museum Trust (see above for details of opening times etc). ♿
Severn Warehouse Visitor Centre Dale End. Exhibits displays and slide show introducing the historic Ironbridge Gorge. *See Coalbrookdale Museum for details of opening times etc.* ♿

IXWORTH *Suffolk* Map 5 TL97
Abbey Extensive remains of monastic claustral buildings incorporated within later 17th-C house. Also remains of monastic church in grounds. Special exhibition. ♨ by prior arrangement. Open 1 May to 16 Aug, also Spring BH; Tue and Sun only 2.30 – 5; other times throughout the year by prior arrangement. 60p. ⚠ limited. *(Tel Pakenham 30374)*

Ironbridge Gorge Museum

Museum of Iron Coalbrookdale

Coalport China Works Museum

The dawn of the Industrial Revolution. Here 200 years ago the first Iron Bridge symbolised the birth of a new age. Today the Ironbridge Gorge Museum presents the story of this unique valley, its people and products.

Ironbridge is thirty minutes from junction 12 on the M6. Follow the signposts to Telford. The Museum is open daily from 10.00. Come early in the day to see it all.

Ironbridge Gorge Museum Trust
Ironbridge, Telford
Salop. TF8 7AW
Telephone: Ironbridge
(095 245) 3522

JARROW *Tyne and Wear* Map 12 NZ36
St Paul's Church, Monastery and Jarrow Hall Church Bank. Standing in a conservation area on the south bank of the River Tyne, St Paul's Church (AD685) is famous as the home of the Venerable Bede. During his lifetime the monastery of St Paul was world famous as a centre of learning and culture. The chancel of the present building is the church in which he worshipped. Excavation on south side of church has revealed plan of the monastery in which he lived and has produced important archaeological finds, now housed in Jarrow Hall. The Hall, *c*1785, has been restored as a visitor centre and contains the Bede Monastery museum, information centre, craft shop and changing exhibitions. ☕ Open Easter to Oct, Tue to Sat 10–5.30, Sun 2.30–5.30 (closed Mons ex BH). Winter: open weekdays 11–4.30. Church open as Hall but including Mons. Hall 20p (ch and pen 5p). Church free. ⚠ *(Tel 892106 or 897402)*

JODRELL BANK (Nuffield Radio Astronomy Laboratories) *Cheshire* Map 7 SJ77
Mark 1 (250ft) radio telescope is one of the largest fully steerable radio telescopes in the world, and the Mark II (125ft by 85ft) has advanced form of digital control. Display material and working models on view. Also arboretum. ☕ Open 22 Mar to 31 Oct, daily 2–6; 1 Nov to 17 Mar weekends only 2–5 (closed Christmas and New Year). Jodrell Bank Concourse building 60p (school ch 30p. ch 5 free). Planetarium shows 40p (school ch 20p, infants not admitted). Prices under revision for 1980. No dogs. ⚠ *(Tel Lower Withington, Cheshire [04777] 339)* &

KEDLESTON HALL *Derbyshire* Map 8 SK33
Adam mansion, standing in 500-acre park with lakes, home of the Curzon family since 1100. Magnificent marble hall, State rooms, collection of fine pictures. 12th-C church. Indian museum. Canada goose colony in park. Gift shop. ☕ Open Easter then Sun from 27 Apr to 28 Sep (also open BH Mons). Also open for private parties by arrangement. House and museum 2–6; park gardens and church 12.30–6. Admission charges for 1980 not yet decided. ⚠ *(Tel Derby 840396)* & (park only)

KEIGHLEY *West Yorkshire* Map 7 SE04
Cliffe Castle NW of town on A629. Mansion of *c*1878 given by Sir Bracewell Smith. Contains collections of natural and local history, dolls and ceramics. Also craft workshops. Aviary, and play area in adjacent park. Suite of furnished rooms with French furniture from Victoria and Albert Museum. ☕ Open all year daily (ex 4 Apr, 25/26 Dec) 10–5; enquire for summer opening times.

Free. ⚠ approach via Spring Gardens Lane. *(Tel 64184)*
East Riddlesden Hall 1m NE. Stone-built 17th-C house, with curious wheel windows typical of certain West Riding manors. Furniture, pictures, armour, and fine tithe barn. Open Apr to Oct, Wed to Sun and BH Mon and Tue, 2–6. Jun, Jul and Aug 10.30–6. 60p. *(NT)*

KELLING *Norfolk* Map 9 TG04
Kelling Park Aviaries Weybourne Road. Situated in 14 acres of beautiful gardens is this fine collection of European and tropical birds, including ornamental pheasants, cockatoos, macaws and flamingoes. ☕ (licensed). Picnic area, children's playground. Open all year, daily 10–dusk. 70p (ch 35p). ⚠ *(Tel Holt 2235)*

KELMSCOTT *Oxfordshire* Map 4 SU 29
Manor House Old gabled Cotswold manor house, once home of William Morris. Open Apr to Sep, first Wed in month 11–1 and 2–5; also sometimes on written application to resident giving two weeks notice. 60p. Under revision for 1980. ⚠ limited. *(Society of Antiquaries)*

KENDAL *Cumbria* Map 7 SD59
Abbot Art Gallery Fine house designed by Carr of York in 1759. Ground floor rooms restored to period decor with 18th-C pictures, furniture and *objets d'art*. Modern galleries displaying contemporary and period, fine and decorative arts. Various changing exhibitions. ☕ (Mon to Fri 10.30–4). Open all year (ex 4 Apr and 2 weeks Christmas/New Year) Mon to Fri 10.30–5.30, Sat and Sun 2–5. 35p (ch 10p, pen 20p). Art gallery and museum (see below) 55p (ch 20p). ⚠ *(Tel 22464)* &
Abbot Hall Museum of Lakeland Life and Industry Housed in stable block designed by Carr of York in 1759 with displays of Lakeland life, trade, social and economic history, Museum of the Year 1973. Various changing exhibitions. Craft shop. ☕ (Mon to Fri 10.30–4). Open all year (ex 4 Apr and 2 weeks Christmas/New Year) Mon to Fri 10.30–12.30 and 2–5. Sat and Sun 2–5. 35p (ch 10p, pen 20p). Museum and Art gallery (see above) 55p (ch 20p). ⚠ *(Tel 22464)*
Kendal Museum Station Road. Museum of natural history, local history and archaeology gallery and world-wide mammal collection. New Lake District natural history exhibition in course of construction. Open all year. Mon to Fri 10.30–4, weekends 2–4. 10p (ch 16 5p). ⚠ *(Tel 21374)*

KENILWORTH *Warwickshire* Map 4 SP27
Kenilworth Castle Keep dates from 1155–70, with later great hall by John of

Gaunt. Further additions, including gatehouse, now known as Lord Leicester's Buildings, built by the Dudleys during the 16th C. Open, see inside front cover. 30p, winter 15p (ch 16 and pen 15p, winter 5p). ⚠ *(AM)*

KESWICK *Cumbria* Map 11 NY22
Castlerigg Stone Circle 1m W on unclass rd. In picturesque mountain setting, prehistoric circle of 38 stones with oblong space containing 10 additional stones. Open any reasonable time. Free. *(AM and NT)*
Fitz Park Museum and Art Gallery
Outstanding among the exhibits are many manuscripts and various relics of Hugh Walpole and Robert Southley, two manuscripts of Wordsworth, a geological collection, and a fine scale model (1834) of the Lake District. Good park surrounding museum. Open 1 Apr to 30 Oct, Mon to Sat 10–12, 2–5 (7, Jul and Aug). 15p (ch 16 10p), subject to alteration. P. (Roadside). *(Tel 73263)*
Lingholm Turn off A66 for Portinscale and continue on the road to Grange 1m. Formal and woodland gardens with a large collection of rhododendrons, azaleas, and other interesting shrubs. Woodland walk of 1½m. Open Apr to Oct, daily (ex Sun) 10–5. 50p (ch, accompanied, free). No dogs. ⚠ *(Tel 72003). (The Viscount Rochdale)* ⅊

KETTERING *Northamptonshire* Map 4 SP87
Alfred East Art Gallery Sheep Street. Exhibitions, approximately twelve per year, visit the gallery, each lasting for about 3 weeks. Open all year, daily (ex Thu and Sun) 10–5. Free. P. *(Tel 85215)* ⅊

KIDDERMINSTER *Hereford and Worcester* Map 7 SO87
Kidderminster Art Gallery and Museum Market Street. Exhibitions include work by local artists and art schools, and a permanent collection of prints by Frank Brangwyn as well as temporary exhibitions of a more general interest. Displays of local archaeology and history are also on view. Open all year, daily (ex Wed, Sun and BH) 11–4. Free. ⚠ *(Tel 66610)* **(79)**

KILLERTON HOUSE AND GARDEN *Devon* Map 3 SS99
5m NE of Exeter on B3185 off B3181. 18th-C house containing the Paulise de Bush collection of costume, shown in a series of room settings furnished in different periods, ranging from the second half of the 18th C to the present day. 15 acres of gardens with rare trees and shrubs. The estate covers more than 5,000 acres. Shop ⅊ licensed 11–6 (last admission 5.30). House and garden £1.30 (ch

5–15 65p), garden only 90p. Party (morning). Garden open all year during daylight. ⚠ *(Tel Hele 345). (NT)* ⅊

KILVERSTONE *Norfolk* Map 5 TL98
'Latin American' Wildlife Park 50-acre wildlife park and miniature horse stud, specialising in South American animals and birds, including 7 species of South American cats, also 14 species of monkeys, grissons, maned wolves, tapirs, parrots, penguins, and semi-tropical birds. Pets corner, patting area, English walled garden, deer park, riverside walk, adventure playground and picnic areas. ⅊ Open all year, daily 10–6.30 (dusk in winter). Admission prices not available for 1980. Party. ⚠ *(Tel Thetford 5369). (Lord and Lady Fisher)* ⅊

KIMBOLTON *Cambridgeshire* Map 4 TL06
Kimbolton School 11m SW of Huntingdon, on A45. Partly Tudor and 17th-C, and partly 18th-C by Vanbrugh with fine mural paintings in chapel and on staircase by Pellegrini and gatehouse by Robert Adam. State rooms and grounds open to the public. Open 6/7 Apr, 25/26 May, and Sun 12 Jul to 31 Aug. 25p (ch 16 5p). ⚠ *(Tel 505)*

KIMMERIDGE *Dorset* Map 3 SY97
Smedmore ½m SE. Jacobean, Queen Anne and Georgian house with a collection of antique dolls and walled gardens. Fine coastal views on attractive approach from Wareham. Open Jun, Jul and Aug, Wed 2.15–5.30 also first 2 Wed Sep. 60p (ch 14 30p). Subject to revision for 1980. ⚠ *(Tel Corfe Castle 717). (Major J C Mansel)* ⅊

KINGSBRIDGE *Devon* Map 3 SX74
Cookworthy Museum Fore Street. Commemorates William Cookworthy, Quaker 'father' of English china clay industry, born in Kingsbridge. Exhibition of his history and porcelain is shown in this old former grammar school, utilising original schoolrooms of 1670. Victorian kitchen and scullery also shown. Costume room and comprehensive local history collection. New farm gallery illustrates farming history of the area. Open Easter to mid Oct, Mon–Sat 10–5 (last admission 4.30). 25p (ch 10p, pen 15p). Admission prices under revision for 1980. P. *(Tel 3235)*
Kingsbridge Miniature Railway The Quay. A 7¼ inch gauge passenger carrying miniature railway, ½m trip. Open Easter, then mid May to mid Sep daily 11–5.

KINGSDON *Somerset* Map 3 ST52
Lytes Cary Home of Lyte family for 500 years, preserving 14th-C chapel and 15th-C Great Hall. Open Mar to end Oct, Wed, and Sat 2–6 (last admission 5.30). 70p. No dogs. *(NT)*

KING'S LYNN *Norfolk* Map 9 TF62
Lynn Museum Market Street. Exhibits on local archaeology, geology and natural history. Medieval Pilgrims badges of special interest. Temporary exhibitions throughout year. Open all year (ex 4 Apr, 25, 26 Dec, 1 Jan and all BH) Mon to Sat 10–5. 10p (ch and pen free). P. *(Tel 5001)* &
Museum of Social History At 27 King Street displays costume, ceramics, glass, toys and domestic material. Open all year (ex BH) Tue to Sat 10–5. Free. *(Tel 5004)*
St George's Guildhall Kings Street. Early 15th-C, largest surviving English medieval Guildhall, now used as a theatre. Open all year, daily when not in use (ex 1 Jan, 4 Apr, 25, 26 Dec, Sat afternoon, Sun), 10–12.30 and 2.30–5. 10p. *(NT)* &

KINWARTON *Warwickshire* Map 4 SP15
Dovecote A stone-built 14th-C dovecote with ogee-shaped doorway, conical roof, and 600 nesting boxes. Open daily until sunset; key at adjacent Glebe Farm. 10p. *(NT)*

KIRBY MISPERTON *North Yorkshire* Map 8 SE77
Flamingoland At Kirby Misperton Hall. Late 18th-C house and 350 acres of Zoo and Pleasure Park. 1,000 animals, birds and reptiles. Jungle Cruise, Children's Farm, Gnomeland, Fairground. Model Railway and Caravan Village. ⚗ (licensed). Open Easter–Sep daily 10–4. £1.20 (ch 14 75p) (under review) & *(Tel 287)* &

KIRBY MUXLOE *Leicestershire* Map 4 SK50
Kirby Muxloe Castle Off B5380. Ruined moated 15th-C fortified manor house, built of brick. Open, see inside front cover but closed Tue pm and all day Wed. 15p (ch 16 and pen 5p). *(AM)*

KIRKHAM *North Yorkshire* Map 8 SE76
Kirkham Priory Beautifully situated by River Derwent, with a particularly fine sculptures 13th-C gatehouse. Open*, see inside front cover. 15p (ch 16 and pen 5p). ⚗ *(AM)*

KIRKSTALL *West Yorkshire* Map 8 SE23
Kirkstall Abbey House Museum Original Gatehouse of the ruined Cistercian Abbey, which was occupied continuously for 800 years, now an interesting museum of local archaeology and folk studies, including three streets of craft workshops, houses, shops, Victorian parlour and public house, Abbey Fold, Stephen Harding Gate, and Harewood Square. Collection of costumes and toys. ⚗ Open daily (ex 25, 26 Dec, 1 Jan) Mon to Sat 10–5, Sun 2–5. 25p (ch 16 5p, ch 5 and pen free). ⚗ *(Tel Leeds 755821)* & B

KNARESBOROUGH *North Yorkshire* Map 8 SE35
Knaresborough Castle Remains of 14th-C stronghold, including the keep, two baileys, and gatehouse. Situated high above the River Nidd. Open Easter to end Sep, daily 10–7. Guided tours on request. Parties of schoolchildren (apply to Director, Resort Services, Council Offices, Harrogate) ***Old Court House Museum*** now open in castle grounds. Admission prices not yet decided. ⚗ *(Tel Harrogate 504684)* **(79)**
Zoological Gardens Conyngham Hall grounds. Lions, tigers, pumas, black panthers, sea lions, llamas, and wallabies. The world's largest snakes in captivity, snake handling shows Easter to Sep by Nyoka who trains the animals for films and TV. ⚗ Gift shop. Open all year (ex 25 Dec), daily 10–7 (4 in winter). 60p (ch 30p). Under revision for 1980. P. *(Tel Harrogate 862793)* &

KNEBWORTH *Hertfordshire* Map 4 TL22
Knebworth House and Country Park Direct access from A1 (M) at Stevenage (South) roundabout. Home of Lytton family from 1492 to the present day, with magnificent Tudor banqueting hall, and furniture, paintings and other treasures covering 500 years of English history. In a country park with skate park, picnicking, riding, narrow-gauge railway, spectacular children's adventure playground. ⚗ (licensed). Open Apr to Sep, daily (ex Mon) BH and Sun in Oct. Park 11–6, House 11.30–5.30. Knebworth Park 75p covers unlimited access to all park facilities. Knebworth House and Park £1 includes House, gardens, exhibition and park facilities (no reduction for ch). Skate park, for details Nov to Easter please telephone. ⚗ *(Tel Stevenage 812661)* & B

KNIGHTSHAYES COURT *Devon* Map 3 SS91
19th-C house in large woodland gardens of interest at all seasons, with flowering shrubs and rhododendrons. ⚗ Open 1 Apr to Oct daily Garden 12.30–6, House 1.30–6. £1.30; garden and grounds only 90p *(NGS)*. *(NT)*

KNOWSLEY *Merseyside* Map 7 SJ49
Safari Park Lions, tigers, cheetahs, elephants, rhinos, monkeys, giraffes, zebras, buffaloes, and many other animals displayed in drive-through game reserves. Picnic areas. Open all year 10–5 summer (3.30 winter). £3.50 per Saloon car (incl all passengers). No soft-topped cars (Safari bus available). No dogs permitted in game reserves (kennels

available). Extra attractions Easter to Sep, dolphinarium, children's amusement park, pets corner. ⚓ (licensed). Souvenir shops. ⚠ *(Tel Prescott 9009)* ⅙

LACOCK *Wiltshire* Map 3 ST96
Lacock Abbey 13th-C cloisters, house dating from 1540 and later, octagonal Tudor tower, half-timbered gables in courtyard, and 17th-C 'Gothick' hall by Sanderson Miller. Fox Talbot conducted photographic experiments here in 1835 and a museum of his work is now open at the entrance gate. Shop and information room. House and grounds open Apr, May and Oct, Wed to Sun and BH Mon 2–6; Jun to Sep daily 2–6; Nov to Mar closed except to historical and other societies by previous written arrangement. £1 (ch 50p). No dogs. *(NT)*. Village is also *NT* property.

LAMBERHURST *Kent* Map 5 TQ63
Bayham Abbey 2m W in East Sussex. In wooded River Teise valley on Kent border, ruins dating back to 13th C and including parts of church, cloistral buildings, and gatehouse. Preservation work still in progress, and museum to be opened with other facilities for visitors. Accessible any reasonable time. Free. *(AM)*
Owl House Gardens 1m NE. 13 acres of romantic walks, spring flowers, azaleas, roses, rhododendrons. Rare shrubs, woodland lakes. Setting of Marchioness of Dufferin & Ava's 16th-C 'Owlers' or smugglers' haunt. Open all year daily (ex Tue, Thu and Sat, but open BH weekends), Sun 3–6, 50p (ch 20p) subject to revision. ⚠ *(Tel 01-235 1432)*. *(Marchioness of Dufferin and Ava)* ⅙
Scotney Castle 1m SE. A partly ruined 14th-C and later moated castle in a picturesque landscape garden of trees and flowering shrubs. Open Apr to Oct, Wed to Sun and BH 2–6 (5, Apr and Oct) 80p (ch 40p). No dogs. Exhibition in old castle 26 May to 31 Aug, times and days as above. Gardens and exhibition 90p (ch 40p). ⚠ *(NT)*

LAMBTON *Co Durham* Map 12 NZ25
Lambton Pleasure Park 200 acres, drive-through Safari section with lions, elephants, zebra, white rhinos, etc, and 'Walkabout Area' with fenced enclosures, cages, etc. Enlarged pets corner, adventure playground, kiddies' playground, 'The Magic Castle' and Miniature Railway. Astroglide and roundabouts in castle grounds. ⚓ and licensed. Open Mar to Oct, daily 10–5. Bus service for non-motorists £1 (ch and pen 50p). Under revision for 1980. No soft-top cars, no pets in Safari Park (free kennels at entrance). Telephone for current details. ⚠ *(Tel Fencehouses 3311)* ⅙

LAMPORT *Northamptonshire* Map 4 SP77
Lamport Hall 8m N of Northampton on A508. The house, most of which dates from the 17th and 18th Cs, is set in an attractive park, the garden contains one of the earliest Alpine rock gardens in England and has been in the Isham family home since 1560. The South-West Front is the work of John Webb, pupil and son-in-law of Inigo Jones, and was built in 1655, with wings added in 1732 and 1740. The lofty music hall contains Webb's stone chimney piece and 18th-C plaster work by John Woolston. There is a fine collection of family portraits and some of the Stuarts – supported by the Ishams – together with other 17th-C paintings, including work by Van Dyck, Guido Reni, Mierevelt, Maratti, Lely, etc and a collection of china and furniture. ⚓ Open Easter to end Sep. Sun, and BH Mon and Tue, also Thu Jun to Aug 2.15–5.30. 70p (ch 14 35p). P. *(Tel Maidwell 272)* ⅙

LANCASTER *Lancashire* Map 7 SD46
City Museum Old Town Hall, Market Square. Georgian building with local archaeology, history and museum of the King's Own Royal Lancaster Regiment. Open daily (ex Sun, 25, 26 Dec, 1 Jan) 10–5. Free. P. *(Tel 64637)*
Hornsea Pottery Co Ltd Wyresdale Road. Set in 42 acres of landscaped parkland includes new 19-acre Rare Breeds Survival Unit, picnic area, and children's playground. Self-service cafe and pottery shop. ⚓ Open all year, Jul to Sep Mon to Sat 10–5.30, Sun 10–6, Easter and BH 9–6. All other times Mon to Fri 9–5, Sat and Sun 10–5. Factory tours should be booked in advance. *(Tel 68444)* ⅙

LANHYDROCK *Cornwall* Map 2 SX06
Lanhydrock Restored 17th-C mansion in richly-wooded setting, with a fine gatehouse and picture gallery with plaster ceiling and 17th- to 20th-C family portraits. ⚓ Open 1 Apr to end Oct, daily 11–6 (last admissions ½hr before closing). £1.50. Gardens only 90p. Winter, gardens Nov to Mar during daylight hours. Shop and ⚓ Nov to 23 Dec. *(NT)*

LAUNCESTON *Cornwall* Map 2 SX38
Launceston Castle Formerly known as Dunheved, and the one-time seat of William the Conqueror's brother, fine round keep forms part of the 12th- to 13th-C remains. Open*, see inside front cover. 15p (ch 16 and pen 5p). ⚠ *(AM)*
Lawrence House Mid Georgian house part of which is now museum of local interest. Open Apr to Sep, Mon to Sat (ex BH), 2.30–4.30, also Mon, Wed and Thu 10.30–12.30, Oct, Nov, Feb, Mar, Wed only. Free. *(NT)*

Trecarrel Manor 4m S off A388, near Lezant. Restored Hall and Chapel from 1488. On view all year by appointment only. Admission prices under review for 1980. *(Tel Coads Green 286)* &

LAVENHAM *Suffolk* Map 5 TL94
Guildhall Picturesque, restored timber-framed building, built in 1529, the former hall of the Guild of Corpus Christi. Open Mar to Nov regularly, 10.30–12.30, 2–5.30 (closed Fri Mar and Nov). 60p. No dogs. *(NT)*
Little Hall 15th-C 'Hall' house is the only furnished house open to the public in Lavenham. Belonging to the Suffolk Preservation Society, it contains the Gayer-Anderson collection of antique furniture, pictures, ceramics, books, sculptures etc. Open Easter to mid Oct, Sat, Sun and BH 2–6. Parties by appointment. 30p (ch 15p). &
(Tel 247179)

LAXFIELD *Suffolk* Map 5 TM27
Laxfield and District Museum The Guildhall. Housed in 16th-C building the museum contains hundreds of items relating to village life, mostly of the last century. Displays change from year to year and include a village shop, domestic interior, odd job man's workshop, costume, agricultural implements, the archaeology of Laxfield and photographs. Open May to Sep, Sat, Sun and BH 3–5.30, also Wed Jul and Aug. Midweek school parties by prior arrangement. Free. &
(Tel Ubbeston 312 and 464)

LAYER MARNEY *Essex* Map 5 TL91
Layer Marney Tower Off B1022. Magnificent early 16th-C brick and terra-cotta tower, entrance gate-tower to Lord Marney's mansion. West wing has similar architectural detail; southside incorporates two-storeyed long gallery in black and red diapered brickwork. Long gallery, swimming pool and tennis court may be hired by written arrangement. ⚓ (by appointment). Gallery, tower and garden open 1 Apr to 30 Sep, Sun and Thu (Tue also in Jul and Aug) 2–6; BH Mons 11–6. 50p (ch 15 10p). & *(Tel Colchester 330202). (Major and Mrs Gerald Charrington)* & B

LEA *Derbyshire* Map 8 SK35
Rhododendron Gardens Attractive woodland gardens of three acres featuring rhododendrons, azaleas and rock garden. Gardens open Easter to mid July, daily 10–8. 30p (ch 10p). & *(Tel Dethick 380 or 374)*. *(Mrs Tye and Miss Colyer). (NGS)* &

LEAMINGTON SPA *Warwickshire* Map 4 SP36
Warwick District Council Art Gallery and Museum Avenue Road. The art gallery

specialises in British, Dutch and Flemish paintings and water-colours of the 16th–20th-C. The museum contains ceramics, Delft, Saltglaze, Wedgwood, Whieldon, Worcester, Derby Ware, etc, and an 18th-C glass collection. Open all year (ex 4 Apr, 25, 26 Dec, 1 Jan) Mon, Tue, Thu, Fri, Sat 10.45–12.45, 2.30–5. Thu also 6–8; Wed 10.45–12.45. Free. & limited. *(Tel 26559)*

LEEDS *Kent* Map 5 TQ85
Leeds Castle 5m ESE of Maidstone on B2163 off A20. Described by Lord Conway as 'the loveliest Castle in the world'. Named after Led, Chief Minister of Wthelbert IV, King of Kent, in AD857. Built on two islands in the middle of a lake, the Castle was originally a stronghold until converted into a Royal Palace by Henry VIII. Beautifully furnished and lovingly restored, a Royal Residence for over three centuries. Museum of Medieval Dog Collars. Water and woodland gardens, duckery and aviary. ⚓ (restaurant). Open 1 Apr to 30 Oct Tue, Wed, Thu, Sun and BH Mon and daily throughout Aug, grounds, ⚓ and bar 12 noon, Castle 1–5. Grounds 85p (ch and pen 50p); Castle extra £1 (ch and pen 50p extra). Admission prices under revision for 1980. & *(Tel Maidstone 65400)*. 9-hole golf course open every day.

LEEDS *West Yorkshire* Map 8 SE33
Middleton Colliery Railway Garnet Road. First railway authorised by Act of Parliament, in 1758, and first to succeed with steam locomotives in 1812. Number of industrial locomotives and examples of rolling stock are in use. Trains, normally steam, for visitors. ⚓ Open Easter to end Sep, Sat, Sun, and BH Mons, 2–4.30. Steam trains each weekend of season, from Tunstall Road roundabout (junct 45 on M1) to Middleton Park which includes picnic area, boating pool, swings etc and cafe. Fares, single 15p, return 30p (ch ½ price). Prices for 1980 under revision. & Enquiries to *Middleton Railway Trust Ltd, Garnet Road, Leeds LS11 5JY* &
Temple Newsam House and Park On south-east outskirts of city. Splendid Tudor and Jacobean house, standing in over 900 acres of parkland, landscaped by 'Capability' Brown. Georgian rooms and a collection of furniture, decorative arts, and paintings. Lord Darnley was born here, and later the house was owned by Lord Halifax, who, in 1922, sold it to the Corporation of Leeds. Gardens have magnificent rhododendrons and azaleas in spring. ⚓ Open all year, Tue to Sun (closed Mon but open BH Mon) 10.30–6.15 or dusk (Wed until 8.30, May to Sep). Closed 25, 26 Dec. 30p (ch and pen 10p). & *(Tel 647321)*

LEEK *Staffordshire* Map 7 SJ95
Brindley Mill Mill Street A523. Designed by James Brindley 1752, and used as a corn-mill until the late 1940s. Between 1970 and 1974 a preservation trust restored the derelict building and put the old machinery, which had remained intact, into working order. A delightful garden is at the rear of the mill. The James Brindley Museum due to open during the early season. Open 5 Apr to end Oct, Sat, Sun and BH Mon 2–5. 20p (ch 5p). P. *(Tel 384195). (Hon Sec, 5 Daintry Street)*

LEICESTER *Leicestershire* Map 4 SK50
Belgrave Hall Fine early 18th-C house, now museum with furnishings. Stables with coaches, and agricultural collection. Also gardens. Open all year (ex 4 Apr, 25/26 Dec) Mon to Sat 10–5.30, Sun 2–5.30. Free. P roadside. *(Tel 554100)* & B
Guildhall Guildhall Lane. Medieval Guildhall and later Town Hall of Leicester. Great Hall, Mayors Parlour, Library and police cells. Open all year (ex 4 Apr, 25/26 Dec), Mon to Sat 10–5.30, Sun 2–5.30. Free. P. *(Tel 554100)* & B
Jewry Wall Museum and Site St Nicholas Circle. Museum of archaeology from prehistoric times to 1500. Remains of Roman baths and Jewry Wall. Open all year (ex 14 Apr, 25/26 Dec), Mon to Sat 10–5.30, Sun 2–5.30. Jewry Wall open any reasonable time. Free. P. *(Tel 554100)* &
John Doran Museum East Midland Gas, Leicester Service Centre Aylestone Road. Housed in a historic building, a part of the Aylestone Road Gasworks, a collection of all aspects of the history of the gas industry. This includes the history of the manufacture, distribution and utilisation of gas, with documentary material as well as old appliances and equipment. Open all year Tue to Fri 12.30 to 4.30. Free. ▲ *(Tel 549414 ext 2192)*
Leicestershire Museum and Art Gallery New Walk. Collections of 18th- to 20th-C English paintings and drawings, unique collection of 20th-C German art, especially of Expressionism, ceramics, silver, Egyptology, new geology and natural history environmental galleries in preparation. Extensive reference and study collections in Art and Natural Sciences with a very active educational programme. Closed 4 Apr, 25/26 Dec. Weekdays 10–5.30, Sun 2–5.30. Free. P. *(Tel 554100)*
Leicestershire Museum of Technology Abbey Pumping Station, Corporation Road. Under development. Power gallery, new knitting gallery, transport items, steam shovel. Originally beam engines of 1891. Open all year (ex 4 Apr, 25/26 Dec) Mon to Sat 10–5.30, Sun 2–5.30. Free, except for special events. ▲ *(Tel 61330)* &
Leicestershire Record Office 57 New Walk. Extensive collection of official and private archives, both rural and urban, relating to the County of Leicestershire. Open all year Mon to Thu 9.15–5; Fri 9.15–4.45; Sat 9.15–12.15. *(Tel 554100)*
Museum of Royal Leicestershire Regiment Oxford Street. Housed in Magazine Gateway is Museum of the Leicestershire Regiment. Open all year (ex 13 Apr, 25/26 Dec) Mon to Sat 10–5.30, Sun 2–5.30. Free. P roadside. *(Tel 554100)*
Newarke Houses The Newarke. Social history of the city from 1500 to present day. 19th-C street scene, 17th-C room, local clocks, musical instruments. Open all year (ex 13 Apr, 25/26 Dec) Mon to Sat 10–5.30, Sun

2–5.30. P (roadside). *(Tel 554100)*
University Botanic Gardens Stoughton Drive South (on SE side of city). Rock gardens; pools; herbaceous, shrub and woodland borders; rose beds; systematic beds; herb garden; heather garden. Cool and warm glasshouses. Open all year Mon to Fri (ex BH) 10–5 (or dusk if earlier). Free. P. *(Tel 717725)*
Wygston's House Museum of Costume St Nicholas Circle. Displays of English costume from 1769 to 1924. Reconstruction of draper's, milliner's, and shoe shops of 1920s. Open all year (ex 4 Apr, 25/26 Dec), Mon to Sat 10–5.30, Sun 2–5. Free. P. *(Tel 554100)*

LEIGH *Kent* Map 5 TQ54
Hall Place Outstanding gardens with rhododendrons, specimen trees and shrubs (labelled), Dutch and rose gardens, and 11-acre lake. ♨ (tea pavilion). Open Suns 6, 13, 20, 27 May; 3, 10, 17 Jun 2.30–6.30. 30p (ch 14 10p). Dogs on lead only. ▲ *(Lord Hollenden)* & **(79)**

LEIGHTON BUZZARD *Bedfordshire* Map 4 SP92
Narrow Gauge Railway Pages Park. Original light railway was built to carry sand in 1919, and after its redundancy in 1967 the railway society obtained permission to operate over its 3½-mile length. 13 diesel, steam and petrol locomotives, and others from Spain and India. ♨ Open Suns 23 Mar to 28 Sep also 4, 5, 7 Apr; 3, 5, 24, 26 May; 23, 25 Aug 11–5 (ex Sat 2–5). Trains run to Vandyke Junction. Return journey time 45 mins. Fare 60p (ch 5–16 30p). Postal enquiries and further information from LBNGRS Ltd, Pages Park Station, Billington Road, Leighton Buzzard, Beds LU7 8TN. *(Tel 373888)* &

LEIGHTON HALL *Lancashire* Map 7 SD47
3m N of Carnforth off A6, through Yealand Conyers village. Neo-Gothic mansion with fine interior, including early Gillow furniture. Extensive grounds. Collection of Birds of Prey. Eagles flown each afternoon, weather permitting. ♨ Open May to Sep, Tue to Fri and Sun 2–5; Grounds and birds only Tue and Fri, or by arrangement for parties of over 25. Admission to house and grounds 60p (ch 15 40p). Grounds and tea-room only 40p (ch 15 30p). Admission prices under revision for 1980. No dogs. ▲ *(Tel Carnforth 2729). (Major and Mrs Reynolds)*

LEISTON *Suffolk* Map 5 TM46
Leiston Abbey Remains of this 14th-C abbey include choir and transepts of church, and ranges of cloisters. Georgian house built into the fabric. Accessible any reasonable time. Free. ▲ *(AM)*

LEITHHILL TOWER *Surrey* Map 4 TQ14
4½m SW of Dorking on unclass road. Leith Hill (965ft) is highest point in the south-east. View from the tower (1,029ft) includes many counties, and in clear weather, both St Paul's Cathedral and the English Channel near Shoreham can be seen. Tower approachable by foot only. ♨ Open 1 Mar to 31 Oct, on fine days 12–6. 5p (ch 3p). ▲ *(NT)*

LELANT *Cornwall* Map 2 SW53
Lelant Model Village Model village built to scale and portraying in miniature a selection of Cornwall's most interesting buildings. The delightfully landscaped grounds also include a museum, water gardens, art gallery, tin mining exhibition, junior commando assault course, playground, craft shop. Also included is an exhibition of smuggling and another special exhibition of Cornwall's colourful characters. Open Easter to end Oct, daily

10 – 5 (high season) 10 – 10). 75p (ch 16 and pen 40p, ch 5 free). Prices under revision for 1980. ⚠ *(Tel Hayle 752676)*

LEOMINSTER *Hereford and Worcester* Map 3 SO45

Leominster and District Folk Museum
Etnam Street. Contains a fine display of smocks, coins, farm implements, corn dollies, tools, and maps. Local history exhibits all given or lent to the museum by local people. The museum is housed in a building of 1855, on site of two old malt houses recently extended to provide two additional large exhibits rooms. Works of John Scarlett Davis, born in town 1804, including album of sketches and drawings. Open all year Apr to Oct, weekdays 10 – 1, 2 – 5, Sun 2 – 5; Nov to Mar, arrangements with *Hon Secretary, Norman Davis, Leominster Museum*. 10p (ch 16 5p). P. *(Tel 2567 or 2520)* �🕭

LETCHWORTH *Hertfordshire* Map 4 TL23
First Garden City Museum 296 Norton Way South. Thatched house with new extension, containing the original offices of the architects of the Garden City, Barry Parker and Raymond Unwin. Displays explain the concept and development of Letchworth as the first Garden City of 1903. Open Mon to Fri 2 – 4.30, Sat 10 – 1 and 2 – 4 (closed Sun and BH). Free. *(Tel 3149)* �🕭

Museum and Art Gallery Broadway. Museum contains archaeological material of North Hertfordshire, and natural history. Monthly art exhibitions. Open all year, weekdays (ex Suns, BH) 10 – 5. Free. P. *(Tel 5647)* �🕭

LETHERINGHAM *Suffolk* Map 5 TM25
Watermill and Gardens On River Deben and near Easton village. Domesday Book mentions a mill in this site. Mill is some 250 years old and house is Tudor. The machinery was dismantled 60 years ago. 4 acres of gardens and woodland park with stream. Visitors may picnic in gardens or by river. ⚗ (3 – 5.30). Plants and pottery for sale. Mill and gardens open Easter to end Sep, Sun Apr to mid May; Wed, Sun and BH mid May to Sep 12.30 – 6. 30p (ch 15 15p, ch 5 free). ⚠ *(Tel Wickham Market 746349)* �🕭 B

LEVENS *Cumbria* Map 7 SD48
Leave M6 from exit 36. On A6 5m S of Kendal.
Levens Hall Elizabethan mansion added to 13th-C pele tower. Fine pictures and Charles II furniture, etc. Unique steam collection in steam on house open days, traction engines in steam on Suns and BH Mon. The famous topiary garden, laid-out in 1692 still adheres to the original plan. Plant centre. Gift shop. ⚗ (licensed) open when house open. House open 6 Apr to end Sep, Tue, Wed, Thu, Sun and BH Mon 2 – 5. Garden and plant centre open daily 10 – 5. Admission charges for 1980 not yet decided. No dogs. ⚠ *(Tel Sedgwick 60321)*. *(Mr C H Bagot)* ঙ B

LEVERINGTON *Cambridgeshire* Map 9 TF41
Leverington Hall Part of this Elizabethan house was rebuilt in second half of 17th C. There have been 18th-C alterations, notably the hall fireplace*.* Open all year by written appointment only. Donation to charity. ⚠ *(Tel Wisbech 2055)*. *(Mr S Graham Thompson FRCS)* ঙ B

LEWES *Sussex* Map 5 TQ41
Anne of Cleves House Southover. Dates from 16th C, now folk museum with extensive collections of domestic bygones, Sussex ironwork and Lewes gallery. Open mid Feb to Nov 10 – 5.30 (last entries 5pm); also Sun afternoons Apr to Oct. 35p (ch 20p). P

roadside. *(Tel 4610). (Sussex Archaeological Society)*

Castle and Barbican House Museum of Sussex Archaeology High Street. Norman castle, with shell keep and 14th-C barbican. Open all year, weekdays 10–5.30, Apr to Oct, Sun also 2–5.30 (last entries 5pm). Admission to castle 30p (ch 20p, students 25p) **also** museum as above; combined ticket 45p (ch 25p). P. *(Tel 4379). (Sussex Archaeological Society)*

The Military Heritage Museum Regency House, Albion Street. Displays of military uniforms, weapons and related items covering the period 1640–1914. *Room 1* contains a brief history of the British Army, *Room 2* features the Cavalry and Artillery, including a fine cavalcade of headdress. Open all year Tue to Sat 10–5. 25p (ch 15 and pen 10p, service personnel in uniform free). P. *(Tel 3137)*

LEYBURN *North Yorks* Map 7 SE19
Constable Burton Hall Gardens 3½m E on A684. Large informal garden, extensive borders, alpines, roses, walks amongst fine trees, small lake. Open 1 Apr to 1 Aug daily 9–6. 30p (ch 10 and pen free). ⚠ *(Tel Bedale 50428)*

LICHFIELD *Staffordshire* Map 7 SK10
Johnson Birthplace Museum Breadmarket Street. Birthplace of Dr Johnson in 1709, now Johnson Museum. Open all year (ex public and BH, other than 27 Aug) Mon to Sat, and 27 Aug 10–5 (4, Oct to Apr); Sun also May to Sep. 2.30–5. 25p (ch 16 10p). Under revision for 1980. P. *(Tel 24972)*

LILFORD PARK *Northamptonshire* Map 4 TL08
On A605 between Oundle and Thrapston. 240-acre Park with interests for all the family, including birds, children's farm with pony rides, adventure playground, gift shop, crafts/museum centre, antiques centre and log cabin cafeteria. Special events include Crafts Market at Easter and East of England Motor Show at Spring BH. Lilford Hall, a 17th-C Jacobean building, stands in the Park but is not at present open to the public except for some events. 40p (ch 16 20p, ch 3 free). Sun 50p (ch 16 25p, ch 3 free) (ex BH and events). Admission prices under revision for 1980. Party 15+. P *(Tel Clopton 648 or 665)*

LILLESHALL *Salop* Map 7 SJ71
Lilleshall Abbey 1½m SW off A518 on unclass rd. An abbey of Augustinian canons established shortly before the middle of 12th C. Considerable remains of 12th-C and 13th-C church with aisleless nave. Accessible any reasonable time. Free. ⚠ *(AM)*

LIMPSFIELD *Surrey* Map 5 TQ45
Detillens 15th-C Wealden Hall House with kingpost roof. Contains collections of furniture, china, porcelain, militaria and guns. Largest collection of orders and decorations in UK. Open 1 May to 30 Jun, Sat; 1 Jul to 30 Sep, Wed and Sat also BH 2–5. Parties at other times by arrangement (including BH). 75p (ch 40p). Under revision for 1980. ⚠ *(Tel Oxted 3342)* ⅊ B

LINCOLN *Lincolnshire* Map 8 SK97
Lincoln Castle Castle Hill. 11th-C and later structure, founded by William the Conqueror and retaining Norman bailey and two motte mounds. Parapet walk on walls. Open all year (ex Christmas), Mon to Sat 10–6 (4, Oct to Apr); Apr to Oct, Sun 2–5 (7.30, May to Sep). 25p (ch 14 12½p). Prices under revision for 1980. ⚠ *(Tel 25951)* ⅊

Greyfriars City and County Museum Broadgate. Former friary, dating from 13th C, with fine barrel roof in upper room. Now museum of local antiquities and natural history. Open all year (ex 24 Mar, 25, 26 Dec), Mon to Sat 10–5.30, Sun 2–5. Free. P. *(Tel 30401)*

Museum of Lincolnshire Life Lincolnshire Museums, Burton Road. This museum has been designed to give a picture of all aspects of county's life from Elizabethan times to present day and features horse-drawn and passenger vehicles, farm implements, and industrial machinery. Open 1 Feb to 30 Nov, Mon to Sat 10–5.30; Sun 2–5 (6, Jun to Aug). 15p (ch 18 and pen 10p). Party ch 5p. Admission prices under revision for 1980. ⚠ *(Tel 28448)*

Museum of the 10th Foot Royal Lincolnshire Regiment Sobraon Barracks, Burton Road. Regimental collection of military items including weapons, uniforms and medals. Exhibits dating from late 18th C. Open all year (ex BH) Mon to Fri 9–4.30. Free. P. *(Tel 25444)* ⅊

Usher Gallery Lindum Road. Collection of water-colours by Peter de Wint, miniatures, glass, ceramics and watches. Open all year (ex 4 Apr, 25, 26 Dec), weekdays 10–5.30, Sun 2.30–5. Free. ⚠ *(Tel 27980)*

LINDISFARNE (Holy Island) *Northumberland* Map 12 NU14
Lindisfarne Castle 16th-C castle, restored in 1900 by Sir Edwin Lutyens, with gardens designed originally by Gertrude Jekyll. Open only when tidal conditions permit, Apr to end Sep, daily (ex Fri) 11–1 (last admission 12.30) and 2–5; Oct Sat/Sun 2–5 (not accessible two hours before and four hours after high tide); other times by previous arrangement with Caretaker. £1 (ch 50p). *(NT)*

Lindisfarne Priory The cradle of English Christianity in the north, situated on Holy Island which is accessible at low tide across a causeway. Tide tables are posted at ends of causeway or telephone *Custodian (Holy*

Island 200). Open*, see inside front cover. 20p (ch 16 and pen 5p). ⚘ *(AM)*

LINDSEY *Suffolk* Map 5 TL94
St James's Chapel Rose Green. Small, thatched flint and stone chapel, built in the 13th C. Open, see inside front cover. Free. *(AM)*

LINGFIELD *Surrey* Map 5 TQ34
Greathed Manor 1m SE off B2028. Spacious Victorian house, with pool in grounds. Open 1 May to 30 Sep, Wed and Thu 2–5. 40p (ch 25p). ⚘ No dogs. *(Tel 832577)* ⅃ B (Gardens)

LINTON *Cambridgeshire* Map 5 TL54
Linton Zoological Gardens Mortimer House, Hadstock Road. Established in 1972, this zoo has concentrated on breeding animals to increase the already large collection which includes big cats, bears, wolves, llamas, parrots, macaws, birds of prey, emu, snakes, spiders and insects etc. Baby animals can usually be seen. Animals and birds are housed in landscaped enclosures, covering 10 acres, as similar as possible to their natural habitats. Flower beds, shrubberies and exotic trees provide botanical interest. Children's play area. Gift or Souvenir Shop. ⚲ 1 Mar to 31 Oct. Picnic area. Open all year (ex 25 Dec) 10–7 or dusk. 70p (ch 14 35, pen 45p), subject to alteration. Party. ⚘ *(Tel Cambridge 891308)* ⅃

LIPHOOK *Hampshire* Map 4 SU83
Bohunt Manor Medium-sized woodland gardens, with lakeside walk, water garden, roses, herbaceous borders, and collection of over 100 ornamental ducks, geese and cranes. Property has been given to World Wildlife Fund. Open Apr to Sep, Mon to Sat 12–5. 25p (ch 5p). Open at weekend on application. No dogs. ⚘ *(Tel 722208). (Lady Holman)* ⅃

Hollycombe House Steam Collection Railways and Woodland Gardens In West Sussex about 1½m SE on Midhurst Road (unclass) off A3. Collection of steam-driven equipment, including 2ft-gauge railway, in woodland setting of azaleas, rhododendrons, trees planted at turn of century, and downland views. Roundabout with own steam organ, steam swing yacht 'Neptune', road loco 'Princess Mary', Cake-walk and only Razzle Dazzle and Steam Swings still in existence. Demonstrations of ploughing, threshing and steam rolling, traction engine rides, and other items. ⚲ Open Easter to early Oct, BH and Sun, garden and picnic areas 12–6 rides 2–6. 75p (ch and pen 40p) subject to alteration. Dogs in car park only. ⚘ *(Tel 723233)* ⅃

LITTLE BILLING *Northamptonshire* Map 4 SP86
Billing Aquadrome 19th-C water mill converted into a Mill Museum with a photographic gallery of all the well-known Mills of the Nene Valley in 300 acres of parklands, lawns and lakes providing facilities for camping, fishing, boating and swimming. Children's playground. ⚲ (licensed). Shop. Open 16 Mar to 7 Oct, 24hrs per day. £1 per car (including occupants). ⚘ *(Tel Northampton 890849)* ⅃ **(79)**

LITTLE GADDESDEN *Hertfordshire* Map 4 SP91
Ashridge Management College Large Gothic Revival mansion (1808–14) by James Wyatt, with porch by Wyatville and 13th-C crypt. Main hall has hammer-beam roof and there is fan-vaulting in main tower and chapel. House became residential college in 1929 and was emergency hospital during 1939–45 War. Since 1959 it has been college for management education. Park *(NT)* landscaped by 'Capability' Brown, and gardens by Humphrey Repton. Open, gardens only Apr to Oct, Sat, Sun 2–6; house and gardens 5 to 8 Apr, 2–4; 24 and 27 May 2–4, 25 and 26 May 2–6; 26 to 30 Jul 2–4. 30p (ch 7 15p); gardens only 20p (ch 10p). ⚘ *(Tel 3491)* ⅃ B

LITTLEHAMPTON *West Sussex* Map 4 TQ00
Littlehampton Museum 12A River Road. Devoted mainly to exhibitions of old marine and sailing items together with a number of paintings of local interest. Open 1 Jan to 9 Apr and 25 Oct to 31 Dec Wed only; 10 Apr to 30 Jun and 21 Sep to 24 Oct Mon, Wed and Fri; 1 Jul to 20 Sep Mon, Wed, Fri and Sat, 10.30–1 and 2.15–4.30. Opening times are under review for 1980. Free. ⚘ *(Tel 5149)*

LITTLE MORETON HALL *Cheshire* Map 7 SJ85
1m N of Kent Green. Splendid example of 16th-C half-timbering, with moat and gatehouse, chapel, great hall, long gallery, collection of oak furniture. Open Mar to 31 Oct, Mar, Sat, Sun 2–6 (or sunset); Apr to 31 Oct daily (ex Tue) 2–6 (or sunset) 80p (ch 35p) *(NT)*

LITTLE SODBURY *Avon* Map 3 ST78
Little Sodbury Manor 15th-C house with fine Great Hall and Queen Anne wing, associated with William Tyndale, translator of the New Testament. Open 1 Apr to 30 Sep, by appointment only. 80p. Under revision for 1980. ⚘ *(Tel Chipping Sodbury 312232)*

LIVERPOOL *Merseyside* Map 7 SJ39
Croxteth Country Park Formerly the family seat of the Earls of Sefton, Croxteth Hall and Park are now being developed for public use. A modern Visitor Centre with large exhibition; walled garden; woodland nature trail; picnic areas. Park open all year daily 9–dusk. Free. Visitor Centre 10–5 Mon to Sat, 12–7 Sun; 1 Oct to 31 Mar 10–5 Mon to Sat; 12–5 Sun; Walled garden, guided tours weekends only

1–5. Tours at other times on request, small charge for facilities. ⚠ *(Tel 051-228 5311)* ૯. B

Liverpool City Libraries William Brown Street. One of the oldest and largest public libraries in the country, with a bookstock of over two million, Commercial, Technical, Arts and Recreations, Philosophy and Religion Departments; the International Library; the Local History Library, Music Library; and the Hornby Library containing 8,000 fine and rare books, fine bindings, 8,000 prints, and more than 4,000 autograph letters, as well as a permanent exhibition on 'The Art of the Book, manuscript and print'. Guided tours by prior arrangement. ⚐ Mon to Fri 10.30–11.30, 4–5.30. Open all year daily (ex Sun and BH) Mon to Fri 9–9 Sat, 9–5. Free. P. (meter) *(Tel 051-207 2147)* ૯. **(79)**

Merseyside County Museums William Brown Street. Displays include, gallery of world natural history, an aquarium and vivarium, humanities gallery devoted to antiquities (Egypt, Near East, Cyprus, Greece, Celtic, Anglo-Saxon and Viking) and ethnology (Africa, Oceania, and the New World) including section on primitive art; basement gallery devoted to land transport (trains, coaches, cycles and cars) of the Merseyside area; gallery showing the development of Liverpool, particularly as a port. Displays illustrating history of time-keeping and space exploration are associated with the Planetarium (programmes twice daily, ex Mon). ⚐ Mon to Fri 10–2, 3–4.15. Open all year daily (ex 1 Jan, 4 Apr, 24–26 Dec) Mon to Sat 10–5, Sun 2–5. Free; planetarium 30p (ch and pen 15p). P. *(Tel 051-207 0001)* ૯.

Sudley Art Gallery Mossley Hill Road. Contains the Emma Holt Bequest of 18th- and 19thC British paintings including works by Reynolds, Gainsborough, Wilkie, Mulready, Holman Hunt and Turner, as well as a few French 19th-C paintings. Also displayed is some 19th-C British sculpture. Special exhibitions. Open all year daily (ex 4 Apr 24–26 Dec, 1 Jan) 10–5 (Sun 2–5). Free. ⚠ *(Tel 051-227 5324)*

Walker Art Gallery William Brown Street. Permanent collection of European paintings, sculpture and drawings dating from 1300 to the present day, including early Italian and Netherlandish paintings and 18th- and 19th-C British paintings. Loan exhibitions include John Moores' Liverpool Exhibitions and Peter Moores' Liverpool Projects. Open all year daily (ex 4 Apr, 24–26 Dec, 1 Jan) 10–5 (Sun 2–5). Free. P. *(Tel 051-227 5234 ext 2064)* ૯.

LIVERPOOL UNIVERSITY BOTANIC GARDENS *Cheshire* Map 7 SJ37 Off A540, near Ness-on-Wirral. Included in these gardens are rock gardens noted for very large collection of alpines, and the best known heather garden in country. Also herbaceous borders, roses, and rhododendrons. There is a fine herb garden, and scented plant garden for the blind. Open all year (ex 25 Dec) daily 9–sunset. Free. ⚠ 20p, coaches £1. *(Tel 051-336 2135)* ૯.

LODE *Cambridgeshire* Map 5 TL56 ***Anglesey Abbey*** 5m NW of Cambridge on B1102. Remodelled c1600, house incorporates 13th-C monastic undercroft. 100 acres of gardens, laid out this century, include long avenues of trees, flower beds and sculptures. Abbey and gardens open Apr to 12 Oct, Tue, Wed, Thu, Sat, Sun, and BH Mon 2–6; garden only open Mon and Fri 2–6 (last admission 5.30). £1, garden only 60p. Party 15+. No dogs. *(NT)*

AGNEW'S GALLERIES Map 11 2980 43 Old Bond Street, W1. Opened in 1876 as part of the Vittori Zanetti art business which originated in Manchester. Thomas Agnew, who entered the business in 1810, later became a partner. In 1932 a limited company Thomas Agnew and Sons was formed. Annual exhibitions include a water-colour exhibition devoted to English water-colours and drawings of the 18th and 19th Cs in Jan, Feb and a selling exhibition of Old Master paintings from the 14th–19th Cs. There are also exhibitions of French and English drawings from c1800 to the present day, work by English painters of this century, and loan exhibitions in aid of charity. Many oil paintings, drawings, water-colours and engravings pass through their hands, many on their way to famous art galleries and museums. Open all year Mon to Fri 9.30–5.30 (7, Thu, Oct to Jul) closed BH. Free, ex for some loan exhibitions. *(Tel 01-6296176)*

BANQUETING HOUSE Map 11 3080 Palace of Whitehall, SW1. Built in 1619, to a design by Inigo Jones, to replace the former home of Cardinal Wolsey, which had been destroyed by fire. It is in severe classical style, with a flat roof surrounded by a balustrade and the interior is enriched by Rubens' paintings. During the 17th-C London court life was centred here and many historic events took place here, including the execution of Charles 1 in 1649, restoration of Charles II, and the offer of the throne to Prince William of Orange and Princess Mary. It was converted into a royal chapel by Sir Christopher Wren for George I, and enlarged a century later by James Wyatt. In 1894 it was granted to the Royal United Service Institution as a museum but in 1964 it was restored to its original function. Open all year, daily (ex Mon, Oct to Mar and 13 Apr; open 16 Apr) Mon to Sat 10–5, Sun 2–5 (may be closed at short notice for government functions). 15p (ch 16 and pen 5p). ⚠ *(Tel 01-2124785)*. *(AM)*

BEAR GARDENS MUSEUM AND ARTS CENTRE Map 111 3280 It has recently been enlarged and is devoted to the influence and development of the Elizabethan and Jacobean theatre, and of course, Shakespeare. The Museum stands on the site of the last bear-baiting ring on Bankside, close to the site of the Hope Theatre and 100 yds from Shakespeare's Globe. The permanent exhibition takes the form of models of the Bankside theatres, together with information on the plays, players and history of each, which creates an awareness of the ambience and atmosphere of 16th C Southwark as it reflects local and national history. Open all year, daily Mon to Fri 10.30–5.30, Sat and Sun 11–5. 50p (ch, students and pen 20p). Party. Under revision for 1980. P. *(Tel 01-928 6342)* ૯. B

HMS BELFAST Map 111 3380 Symons Wharf, Vine Lane, SE1. This 11,000-ton cruiser, which is now part of the Imperial War Museum, is permanently moored in the Pool of London as a floating naval museum. ⚐ (summer only). Open all year, daily (ex 1 Jan, 4 Apr, 5 May, 24–26 Dec) from 11 am. £1.40 (ch 16 and pen 70p). P in Potter's Fields, 100yds. *(Tel 01-407 6434)*

BRITISH CRAFTS CENTRE Map II 3081
43 Earlham Street, WC2. The British Crafts
Centre's object is to promote and sell work by
British craftsmen. Exhibits change rapidly and
cover a wide variety of crafts, including fine
examples of silver and jewellery, metalwork,
glass, ceramics, furniture and woodwork,
textiles, bookbinding, embroidery and
calligraphy. Open all year, (ex Sun) 10–5.30
Mon to Fri; 10–4 Sat. Free. ⚠ *(Tel 01-
836 6993)* ⅏ B

BRITISH MUSEUM Map II 3081
Great Russell Street, WC1. Founded 1753,
based on the collection of Sir Robert Cotton,
antiquary and book collector, who died in
1631, and on the collection of scientific books
and manuscripts bequeathed to the nation by
Sir Hans Sloane, 18th-C physician. Today it
contains vast archaeological collections,
many thousands of prints and drawings
illustrating the history of graphic art from the
15th C onwards, as well as many other
exhibits. Not all the collections are exhibited
at once. Each year, special exhibitions focus
more detailed attention on certain aspects of
the collections. Programmes on request.
Reserve collections are available for study by
scholars. ⚏ Open all year, daily (ex 1 Jan, 4
Apr, 5 May, 24–26 Dec) 10–5, Sun 2.30–6.
Free. ⚠ *(Tel 01-636 1555 ext 525)* ⅏

COURTAULD INSTITUTE GALLERIES
Map II 2982
Woburn Square, WC1. The galleries of
London University contain the most important
collection of Impressionist paintings in Britain,
including work by Manet, Renoir, Degas,
Cezanne, Van Gogh, Gaugin and Toulouse-
Lautrec. Also Old Master paintings, especially
Italian primitives. Exhibitions of British
landscape water-colours in Spring, and in the
summer an exhibition of Impressionist
drawings and water-colours. Open all year
(ex Christmas and most BH) Mon to Sat
10–5, Sun 2–5. Free. Meter P. *(Tel 01-
580 1015)* ⅏

CRICKET MEMORIAL GALLERY
Map I 2682
Lord's Ground, NW8. Founded about 1865,
with collections of cricket bygones and 18th-C
paintings of cricket. Collection of pictures and
other exhibits and a library of cricket literature,
enriched by the notable book collections of A
L Ford and Sir Julien Cahn. In 1953, the
present gallery and museum was opened as a
memorial to cricketers of all nations, who
gave their lives in the two World Wars. Open
on match days Mon to Sat 10.30–5, other
times by appointment. 30p (ch and pen 15p).
Library open free of charge to students by
appointment with the Curator. ⚠ (limited).
(Tel 01-289 1611) ⅏ B

CUMING MUSEUM Map III 3278
155/157 Walworth Road, SE17. Contains
Roman and medieval finds from the nearly
2,000-year-old suburb of Southwark, south of
London Bridge. Examples from the local
'Delft' pottery industry, items associated with
Dickens, personal relics of Michael Faraday
(born locally in 1791), the equipment of a
family dairy firm which served the
neighbourhood for over 150 years, and a
collection of London superstitions. Open all
year Mon to Fri 10–5.30 (7, Thu), Sat 10–5.
Free. Limited street P. *(Tel 01-703 6514)*.
(London Borough of Southwark)

DICKENS' HOUSE Map II 3082
48 Doughty Street, WC1. Dickens lived here
during his twenties and here completed
Pickwick Papers and wrote *Oliver Twist* and
Nicholas Nickleby. Pages of the original
manuscripts of his early books and others are
on view, together with valuable first editions in
the original paper parts of his works, his
special marriage licence; his family Bible
which contains a personal record of his sons
and daughters, and many other personal
relics. Entrance includes the Suzannet
Rooms. Open all year, daily (ex Sun, BH,
Christmas week and 13 Apr) 10–5. 60p (ch
15 25p, students 50p). Party. Under revision
for 1980. *(Tel 01-405 2127)*

**EMBANKMENT GALLERY, PADDLE
STEAMER TATTERSHALL CASTLE**
Map II 3080
Victoria Embankment, SW1. Gallery and arts
centre contained within a restored paddle
steamer, first commissioned in 1934.
Changing exhibitions are shown including:
established artists, public interest topics, and
facilities for aspiring and unknown artists.
Bookshop and functions facilities. Open all
year, Tue to Sun 10–6. 20p (ch 14 and pen
10p). P (charge) also across the river. *(Tel
01-839 6548/9)*

GEOLOGICAL MUSEUM Map I 2679
Exhibition Road, South Kensington.
Established 1935, its exhibitions include a
piece of the Moon and the largest exhibition
on basic earth science in the world – The
Story of the Earth. This is split into four main
sections: The Earth in Space which includes
an exhibit showing that an observer 150
million light years away, looking through an
immensely powerful telescope, would see
dinosaurs roaming around in a Jurassic
landscape; The Earth's Interior and Crust;
Geological Processes; and Geological
Time. There is also a famous collection of fine gem
stones, showing them in their parent rock, in

natural crystal form and in their final cut state. The regional geology of Great Britain and the ore deposits of the world are also displayed. A new permanent exhibition 'Britain Before Man' provides much fascinating information about 3,000 million years of pre-history. Open all year (ex 4 Apr, 5 May, 24 – 26 Dec and 1 Jan) Mon to Sat 10 – 6, Sun 2.30 – 6. Free. *(Tel 01-589 3444)* &

GUILDHALL Map III 3281
EC2. Rebuilt in 1411 but only the walls of the great hall porch and crypt survive from the medieval building. It was severely damaged in the Great Fire and the Blitz. Restoration work, completed in 1954 was carried out to designs by Sir Giles Scott. Here the Court of Common Council, which administers the city, meets and entertains. Open all year Mon to Sat 10 – 5 (Sun, May to Sep and Bh 2 – 5). The **Guildhall Library** contains an unrivalled collection of books, manuscripts, and illustrations on all aspects of London. Open all year, daily (ex Sun, BH) 9.30 – 5. The **Guildhall Clock Museum** with 700 exhibits illustrating 500 years of time keeping. Open Mon to Fri 9.30 – 5 (ex BH). Free. ⚖ *(Tel 01-606 3030)* &

HOUSES OF PARLIAMENT Map II 3079
SW1. A mid 19th-C building in Gothic style, based on a design by Sir Charles Barry, with additional detail by Augusta Pugin. It replaced the previously mainly medieval structure, destroyed by fire in 1834. The two chambers are set either side of a central hall and corridor, the House of Lords to the south and the House of Commons to the north, with identical projecting pavilions at either end of the river façade. The clock tower, 320ft high, contains Big Ben, the hour bell weighing 13½ tons, and the Victoria tower stands 340ft high. The House of Commons Chamber was burnt out in 1941 by incendiary bombs, and a new chamber was constructed to the design of Sir Giles Gilbert Scott and opened in 1950. During sessions, admission to the Stranger's Gallery, House of Commons Mon to Thu from 4.15 pm, Fri from 11.30 am by joining queue at St Stephen's Hall entrance; alternatively on application in advance to an MP Mon to Thu from 2.30, Fri from 11 am. Admission to Stranger's Gallery, House of Lords Mon to Wed from 2.30 pm, Thu from 3 pm, Fri from 11 am by joining queue at St Stephen's entrance (Old Palace yard side) or alternatively applying in advance to a Peer. Palace of Westminster open to a limited number of the public every Sat (ex one immediately preceding State opening) and 7 & 8 Apr, 5 & 26/27 May, 25/26 Aug; Mon, Tue and Thu in Aug; Thu in Sep providing neither house is sitting. 10 – 4.30. Free, although Guides require payment if employed. ⚖ *(Tel 01-219 3000)* & also
Westminster Hall Built 1097 – 99 by William Rufus, it is the oldest remaining part of Westminster. The glory of the hall is the cantilever or hammerbeam roof, the earliest and largest roof of its kind in existence, built between 1394 and 1401. Open during Session: Mon to Thu 10 – 1.30, providing neither House is sitting at the time. Sun 10 – 5. During Recess: Mon to Fri 10 – 4, Sat 10 – 5. Free. ⚖ & (by arrangement)

IMPERIAL WAR MUSEUM Map III 3179
Lambeth Road, SE1. Founded 1917 and established 1920 by Act of Parliament, this museum illustrates and records all aspects of the two World Wars and other military operations involving Britain and the

Commonwealth since 1914. A wide range of weapons and equipment is on display, including aircraft, armoured vehicles, field guns and small arms, together with models, decorations, uniforms, posters, photographs and paintings. Also various reference departments, open by appointment only. ⚍ Open all year, daily (ex 1 Jan, 4 Apr, 5 May, 24 to 26 Dec) Mon to Sat 10 – 5.50, Sun 2 – 5.50. Free (except special exhibitions which have a small entrance fee). P meters only. *(Tel 01-735 8922)* & *(by appointment)* **(79)**

DR JOHNSON'S HOUSE Map III 3181
17 Gough Square, EC4. Gough Square was built c1700 and the timber used in the construction of the building is American white and yellow pine. Dr Johnson lived here 1749 – 1759 and here he compiled his famous English dictionary (a first edition is on display and wrote *The Rambler* and *The Idler*. The house was opened as a museum in 1914 and contains a fine collection of prints as well as letters and other relics. Open all year, daily (ex Sun, BH) May to Sep 11 – 5.30; Oct to Apr 11 – 5. 40p (ch, students and pen 20p). ⚖ *(Tel 01-353 3745)*

KENSINGTON PALACE, STATE APARTMENTS Map I 2579
W8. Kensington Palace was acquired by King William III in 1689 and remodelled and enlarged by Sir Christopher Wren, and is today still a Royal residence. Queen Victoria was born here, and a suite of rooms is devoted to her memory. Contained within the state apartments are picture and furniture from the royal collection. The redecorated Victorian rooms and the room devoted to the Great Exhibition are now open. Open all year (ex 1 Jan, 3 & 4 Apr, 24/25 & 26 Dec). Mar to Sep, Mon to Sat 10 – 6, Sun 2 – 6; Oct and Feb, Mon to Sat 10 – 5, Sun 2 – 5; Nov to Jan, Mon to Sat 10 – 4, Sun 2 – 4. 30p (ch 16 and pen 15p). Party 11+ 10% discount on arrival. *(Tel 01-937 9561 ext 2)*. Nearest car park in Bayswater Road. *(AM)*

LANCASTER HOUSE Map II 2979
Stable Yard, SW1. Built in the 19th C by the 'Grand Old Duke of York' and originally called 'York House'. It is now used as a centre for government hospitality. Open Easter Eve to mid Dec (ex during government functions) Sat, Sun and BH 2 – 6. 25p (ch 16 and pen 10p). ⚖ *(AM)*

THE LONDON DUNGEON Map III 3280
28/34 Tooley Street, SE1. A fantasy Medieval History exhibition/experience. Vast dark vaults house strange and horrifying scenes of Man's Inhumanity to Man in Britain's dark past. Awarded the British Tourist Authority award for Outstanding Tourist Enterprise. Open all year Apr to Sep 10 – 6, Oct to Mar 10 – 4.30. £1.25 (ch and pen 75p). Under revision for 1980. ⚖ *(Tel 01-403 0606)*

LONDON TRANSPORT MUSEUM Map II 3080
Housed in the former Flower Market in Covent Garden. Due to open Spring 1980. The museum aims to tell the story of the development of London's transport from its earliest beginnings right up to the present day. Vehicles include steam locomotives, trams, trolleybuses, railway coaches and horse buses, there are also extensive displays using working and static models, posters, and audio-visual material. A reference library is also available by appointment. Souvenir shop. ⚍ Open daily (ex 25/26 Dec) 10 – 6.

Entrance off the Piazza, clearly signposted. For further information contact the Head of Administration. Admission prices not available. *(Tel 01-935 6688 ext 48)* & B

MADAME TUSSAUD'S Map I2882
Marylebone Road, NW1. Founded in Paris in 1770, Madame Tussaud's Wax Exhibition came to England in 1802, and settled in London in 1835. Exhibits include the Chamber of Horrors; historical figures, including kings and queens of the French and English royal families; 'Heroes'; The Battle of Trafalgar; and the Conservatory. ⚓ Open all year daily (ex 25 Dec) Oct to Mar 10–5.30; Apr to Sep 10–6. Please telephone for admission prices. P. *(Tel 01-935 6861)* & (Oct to Mar preferred)

MALL GALLERIES Map II 2980
The Mall, SW1. The exhibition galleries of the Federation of British Artists, where most of the Art Societies administered by this organisation hold their annual exhibitions. Open all year, daily (ex Sun, BH) 10–5 (1pm, Sat). 20p (ch and pen 10p). P. *(Tel 01-930 6844)*

MARLBOROUGH HOUSE Map II 2980
Pall Mall, SW1. Built 1709–11 by Wren for Sarah, Duchess of Marlborough, and renowned for the series of murals by Laguerre depicting Marlborough's battles. In 1817 it became a royal palace, of which the last occupant was Queen Mary. It is now used as a Commonwealth conference centre. Open by appointment only. 5p ⚓ *(Tel 01-930 9249)*. The **Queen's Chapel** designed by Inigo Jones for Charles I, stands in the grounds. Open Mon, Wed and Thu by prior arrangement only. **(79)**

MIDDLE TEMPLE HALL Map II 3180
The Temple, EC4. A fine example of Tudor architecture built during the reign of Queen Elizabeth I and completed about 1570. Hall features fine double hammer beam roof (only 2 or 3 other examples believed to exist in England). Also stained glass showing shields of past treasurers. The most treasured possession is the 29ft-long high table, made from a single oak tree of Windsor Forest. Another table was made from timbers of the Golden Hind, in which Sir Francis Drake, a member of the Middle Temple, sailed around the world. Portraits of George I, Elizabeth I, Anne, Charles I, Charles II, James, Duke of York and William III line the walls behind the high table. Open all year (ex Sun, BH) 10–12, 3–4.30. Free. ⚓ *(Tel 01-353 4355)*

THE MONUMENT Map III 3280
Monument Street, EC4. Erected by Wren and Hooke 1671–77 to commemorate the Great Fire of 1666, which is reputed to have started in nearby Pudding Lane. It stands 202ft-high and from the railed-in summit, a climb of 311 steps, there is an extensive view over London. Open all year, daily (ex Sun 1 Oct to 30 Mar, 13 Apr, 25, 26 Dec) Mon to Sat 9–4 (5.40, 1 Apr to 30 Sep) Sun 1 Apr to 30 Sep 2–5.40. 30p (ch 15p). *(Tel 01-626 2717)*. These times and prices are provisional for 1979. **(79)**

MUSEUM OF LONDON Map III 3281
London Wall. The museum was formed by amalgamating the former London Museum and the Guildhall Museum. The present purpose-built building was opened in 1976 and the museum is devoted entirely to London and its people. Everything on show contributes to the story of London during the past 2,000 years. Included are Royal relics and treasures from the City, a barber's shop from Islington, sculptures from the Temple of Mithras, a 1930 Ford, Selfridge's lift, medieval hen's egg together with a Roman Bikini and the experience of the Great Fire. Awarded the title 'Museum of the Year 1978'. ⚓ Open all year Tue to Sat 10–6, Sun 2–6. (Closed Mon incl BH Mon also 25/26 Dec). Parties by arrangement. Free. P. (NCP opposite in Aldersgate Street). *(Tel 01-600 3699)* & Please telephone ext 265 for information. **(79)**

MUSEUM OF MANKIND Map II 2980
6, Burlington Gardens, W1. Houses the exhibitions, library and offices of the ethnography department of the British Museum. Its collections embrace the art and material culture of tribal, village and other pre-industrial societies, from most areas of the world excluding Western Europe. Also archaeological collections from the Americas and Africa. A few important pieces are on permanent exhibition, but the museum's policy is to mount a number of temporary exhibitions lasting for at least a year. A separate store in Shoreditch contains the reserve collection which can be made available for serious study by arrangement. Open all year (ex 4 Apr, 24, 25 and 26 Dec and 1 Jan) Mon to Sat 10–5, Sun 2.30–6. Free. *(Tel 01-437 2224)*

NATIONAL ARMY MUSEUM Map I2777
Royal Hospital Road, SW3. Contains a permanent chronological display of the history of the British, Indian and Colonial forces from 1485. Among the exhibits are uniforms, weapons, prints and photographs,

silver, glass and china, manuscripts and letters, relics of British commanders and mementos of Britain's soldiers. There is a special display of the orders and decorations of the Duke of Windsor and also those of five great field marshals – Lords Roberts, Gough, Kitchener and Wolseley and Sir George White VC. The picture gallery includes portraits by Reynolds, Gainsborough, Romney and Lawrence, battle scenes and pictures of Indian regiments. The reading room is open to holders of readers' tickets, obtainable by written application to the Director. Open all year, daily (ex 1 Jan, 4 Apr, 5 May, 24 to 26 Dec) 10 – 5.30, Sun 2 – 5.30. Free. ⚠ *(Tel 01-730 0717)* ♿ (prior arrangement)

NATIONAL GALLERY Map II 2980
Trafalgar Square, WC2. Founded by vote of Parliament in 1824, but was first opened in the present building in 1838. Collection includes van Eyck's *Arnolfini Marriage*, Velazquez's *The Toilet of Venus*, Leonardo da Vinci's *Cartoon: The Virgin and the Child with SS Anne and John the Baptist*, Rembrandt's *Belshazzar's Feast*, Titian's *Bacchus and Ariadne*, and many more. ⚐ Open daily (ex 1 Jan, 13 Apr, 7 May, 24 – 26 Dec) Mon to Sat 10 – 6, Sun 2 – 6. Free. Accessible to wheelchairs by Orange Street entrance. For information about exhibitions during 1980 contact the Press Office *ex 252. (Tel 01-839 3321)* ♿ (Orange Street entrance).

NATIONAL PORTRAIT GALLERY
Map II 3080
2 St Martin's Place, WC2. Contains national collection of portraits of the famous and infamous in British history, including paintings, sculpture, miniatures, engravings, photographs, and cartoons. Special exhibitions several times a year. Gallery shop. Exhibitions are also held at the new exhibition rooms at 15 Carlton House Terrace, London SW1. Open all year, daily (ex 1 Jan, 4 Apr, 5 May, 24 – 26 Dec) 10 – 5, Sat 10 – 6, Sun 2 – 6. Free (ex special exhibitions). ⚠ *(Tel 01-930 1552)* ♿

NATIONAL POSTAL MUSEUM Map III 3181
King Edward Street, EC1. Contains probably the finest and most comprehensive collection of postage stamps in the world. Included are: the R M Philips collection of 19th-C Great Britain (with special emphasis on the One Penny Black and its creation); the Post Office Collection; a world-wide collection including practically every stamp issued since 1878; and the philatelic correspondence archives of Thomas de la Rue and Co who furnished stamps to over 150 countries between 1855 and 1965. Within these collections are thousands of original drawings and unique proof sheets of every British stamp since 1840. Special exhibitions. Visits for parties up to 40 may be arranged with a guide and film show. Open all year, daily (ex Sat, Sun, BH) Mon to Fri (10 – 4.30. Free. Meter parking in adjacent streets. *(Tel 01-432 3851)*

NATURAL HISTORY MUSEUM Map I 2679
Cromwell Road, South Kensington SW7. Three new exhibitions are now open: *Dinosaurs and their living relatives* features a spectacular display of fossil skeletons and a series of special exhibits producing a new way of looking at dinosaurs. In the *Hall of Human Biology* visitors can learn more about the way their bodies work, while *Introducing Ecology* uses an oak woodland and a rocky seashore to introduce a new way of looking at our natural surroundings. A new exhibition,

opening in the summer of 1980, takes a fresh look at man's place in evolution. In other parts of the Museum there are many traditional displays of living and fossil plants and animals, minerals, rocks and meteorites from the national collections. Exhibits of special interest include a lifesize model of a blue whale, the Cranbourne meteorite, a specimen of a coelacanth (a fish known as a living fossil) and the British bird pavillion where visitors can hear recordings of many different bird songs. As the museum is currently reorganising its public displays, some of the galleries may be temporarily closed. The museum's educational services provide some public lectures. Childrens centre open Sat afternoons and Tue to Sat during school hols. ⚐ (open 10 – 5.30). Open everyday (ex 4 Apr, 5 May, 24 – 26 Dec and 1 Jan) Mon to Sat 10 – 6, Sun 2.30 – 6. Free. Meter P. Access for wheelchair-bound visitors by rear entrance. *(Tel 01-589 6323)* ♿

PERCIVAL DAVID FOUNDATION OF CHINESE ART Map II 2982
53 Gordon Square, WC1. Houses collection of Chinese ceramics from Sung Dynasty (960 – 1279) to 18th C including many inscribed and documented pieces important to the study of Chinese art history. The collection is famous for a pair of blue and white temple vases known as 'David vases', dated 1351, which are the earliest dated pieces of this ware in existence. Open all year (ex Sun, BH, including 1pm 3 Apr until Tue following) Mon 2 – 5, Tue to Fri 10.30 – 5, Sat 10.30 – 1. Free. P. (meters). *(Tel 01-387 3909)*

PLANETARIUM Map I 2882
Marylebone Road, NW1. Here the night skies are projected in all their beauty onto the inside of the dome from the two-ton Zeiss instrument, to an accompanying commentary. The skies are seen not only from Britain, but from Africa and Australia and even from outer space or the future. ⚐ Open all year, daily (ex 25 Dec), presentations Apr to Sep 11 – 6; Oct to Mar 11 – 4.30. Please telephone for admission prices. P. *(Tel 01-486 1121)*

PUBLIC RECORD OFFICE MUSEUM
Map II 3181
Chancery Lane, WC2. The Public Record Office contains records of central government dating from the Norman conquest to the present day. The museum contains a small selection of the several million separate documents kept in the Office including the Domesday Book, Shakespeare's will, various royal letters and other documents of wide historical interest. Open Mon to Fri 1 – 4 (ex official holidays, first two weeks Oct). Parties at other times by arrangement. Free. ⚠ *(Tel 01-405 0741)* ♿ (prior arrangement only)

QUEEN'S GALLERY Map II 2979
Buckingham Palace, SW1. Items from the Royal collection are housed in a building of 1831, originally designed as a conservatory by John Nash and later converted by Blore into a chapel in 1843. After suffering severe bomb damage in 1940, the building was eventually reconstructed in 1962, partly as the Private Chapel of Buckingham Palace and partly as an art gallery. Exhibits display various aspects of the Royal Collection. Open all year, daily (ex Mon, and for short periods between exhibitions) Tue to Sat, BH 11 – 5, Sun 2 – 5. 40p (ch 16 and pen 20p, also students on production of valid student card). ⚠ *(Tel 01-930 3007)*

ROYAL ACADEMY OF ARTS Map II 2980
Piccadilly, W1. Founded in 1768 by George
III. The summer exhibition, from May to Aug,
shows works by living artists, and loan
exhibitions are held throughout the rest of the
year. Treasures of the academy include the
Michelangelo *Tondo*. ⚒ Licensed (10.30 – 5
Mon to Sat, 12.30 – 5 Sun). Open daily 10 – 6
(incl Sun). Admission prices vary but
generally are 60p – £1 (ch, students, pen and
group visitors half price). ⚐ *(Tel 01-734 9052)*
⅋

ROYAL MEWS Map II 2879
Buckingham Palace, SW1. Designed by John
Nash and completed in 1825, the Royal Mews
contain the state coaches including the Gold
State Coach made in 1762, with panels
painted by the Florentine artist Cipriani, which
has been used for every coronation since that
of George IV, the Irish State Coach, the
Scottish State Coach, together with private
driving carriages and royal sleighs. In the
stables are kept the Windsor Greys and
Cleveland Bay carriage horses. Open Wed,
Thu 2 – 4 every week (ex certain times) and at
other times when published. 25p (ch and pen
10p). *(Tel 01-930 4832)* ⅋

ST KATHARINE by the TOWER Map III
3380
Maritime Trust's Historic Ship Collection
comprises a number of British sailing and
steam-powered vessels of the 19th and early
20th C. Individual display in each ship. Open
all year Spring and Autumn 10.30 – 6; summer
10 – 7; winter 11 – 4.30. £1 (ch and pen 50p).
⅌

SCIENCE MUSEUM Map I 2679
Exhibition Road, South Kensington, SW7.
Extensive collections, including aero engines;
agriculture, astronomy; atomic and nuclear
physics; rail; road; sea and air transport; civil,
electrical, marine and mechanical
engineering; telecommunications, domestic
appliances, 'Gas Industry' gallery, etc. New
galleries on Printing, Paper making and
Lighting. Also a children's gallery with many
working demonstrations. Exhibition
'Exploration' continued during 1980. ⚒ Open
all year, daily (ex 4 Apr, 5 May, 24 – 26 Dec
and 1 Jan) 10 – 6, Sun 2.30 – 6. Meter P. *(Tel
01-589 3456)* ⅋

SIR JOHN SLOANE'S MUSEUM Map II 3081
13 Lincoln's Inn Fields, WC2. The home of Sir
John Sloane (1753 – 1837), the architect, built
in 1812 and containing his collections of
antiquities, sculpture, paintings, drawings
and books. The most famous are the
Sarcophagus of Seti I (1292 BC), *Rake's
Progress* and the *Election* series by William
Hogarth. Open all year (ex BH) Tue to Sat
10 – 5. Free. *(Tel 01-405 2107)*

STOCK EXCHANGE Map III 3281
EC2. The centre of industrial finance, where
stocks and shares in individual companies
are bought and sold. The scene on the trading
floor may be viewed from the gallery and a
guide is present to describe the scene. A
colour film may be seen. Open every working
day (ex 24 Dec) 9.45 – 3.15 (last guided tour
2.30). Party. Free. P. (meters). *(Tel 01-
588 2355)* ⅋

TATE GALLERY Map II 3078
Millbank, SW1. Opened in 1897 the gallery
houses two national art collections of British
works from the 16th C to c1900, and modern
works by British artists born after 1850
together with foreign works from the
Impressionists onwards. Hogarth, Blake,

Turner, Constable and the pre-Raphaelites
are particularly well-represented in the British
Collection and the Modern Collection has
recently been enhanced by Henry Moore's
magnificent gift of 36 of his sculptures, a
selection of which will always be on view. The
development of art is traced from
Impressionism to postwar European and
American art including Abstract
Impressionism and Pop. A major extension
increasing the size of the Tate by 50%,
opened in May 1979. The new galleries are
fully airconditioned. Free lectures are
provided every day and free films and Guided
Tours Mon to Fri. ⚒ Licensed. Restaurant
Mon to Sat 12 – 3; Coffee shop Mon to Sat
10.30 – 5.30, Sun 2 – 5.30. Open all year daily
(ex 1 Jan, 4 Apr, 5 May, 24 – 26 Dec) 10 – 6,
Sun 2 – 6. Free, ex for special exhibitions.
Meter P. *(Tel 01-821 1313, 01-821 7182
recorded information)* ⅋ *(Atterbury
entrance)*

TOWER OF LONDON Map III 3380
EC3. Begun by William the Conqueror in the
11th C in the south-east angle of the wall of
Roman Londinium. The keep or White Tower,
which was built soon after the conquest, now
contains the **Royal Armouries**. These
consist of the national collection of arms and
armour based on the great arsenal of Henry
VIII. Four of Henry VIII's personal armours
may be seen together with the finest products
of the Greenwich School of Armourers. There
are also displays of tournament and sporting
arms, arms and armour from the Middle Ages
to the 17th C, oriental armour (including an
elephant armour) and cannon. ⚒ and picnic
area. Open all year, daily (ex 1 Jan, 4 Apr,
24 – 26 Dec) Mar to Oct 9.30 – 5 Mon – Sat,
Sun 2 – 5, Nov to Feb 9.30 – 4 Mon – Sat
(closed Sun). Admission: Mar to Oct (ex Jul,
Aug) £1 (ch 16 and pen 50p); Nov to Feb 50p
(ch 16 and pen 30p), Jul and Aug £1.50 (ch 16
and pen 50p). Also the **Jewel House** where
the crown jewels are displayed. Open as for
the Tower. Admission: 50p (ch 16 and pen
20p). Also the **Royal Fusiliers Museum**,
containing uniforms, including those worn by
George V as colonel-in-chief, regimental
silver and china, four dioramas of famous
battles and campaign medals, among them
10 Victoria Crosses, including the prototype
approved by Queen Victoria. Opening times
as for Tower. 10p. All admission prices for
1980 are under revision. *(Tel 01-709 0765)* ⅋ B

VICTORIA AND ALBERT MUSEUM Map I
2679
Cromwell Road, South Kensington SW7.
Queen Victoria laid the foundation stone for
the present building in 1899 and the building
designed by Sir Aston Webb was opened in
1909 by Edward VII. In it were placed the art
treasures from the South Kensington
Museum, which had been built under the
direction of Prince Albert from money derived
from the Great Exhibition of 1851. It now
contains one of the world's outstanding
collections of fine and applied arts. Special
exhibitions include Constable paintings, the
Raphael Cartoons and the Great Bed of
Ware. Open all year, daily (ex 1 Jan, 4 Apr, 5
May and 24 – 26 Dec and **Fridays**) 10 – 5.50,
Sun 2.30 – 5.50. Free. ⚒ licensed weekdays
10.30 – 2.30, 3 – 5.30 Sun 2.30 – 5.30. ⚐ *(Tel
01-589 6371)* ⅋ B (Tel in advance)

WALLACE COLLECTION Map I 2881
Hertford House, Manchester Square, W1. An
outstanding collection of works of art
bequeathed to the nation by Lady Wallace in

1897, displayed in the house of its founders. Includes pictures by Titian, Rubens, Gainsborough and Delacroix together with an unrivalled representation of 18th-C French art including paintings, especially by Watteau, Boucher and Fragonard, sculpture, furniture, goldsmiths work and Sèvres porcelain. Also valuable collections of maiolica, European and oriental arms and armour. Open all year (ex 24 – 26 Dec, 1 Jan, 4 Apr and 5 May) Mon to Sat 10 – 5, Sun 2 – 5. Free. P meters. *(Tel 01-935 0687)* ⚅ During 1980 only half no. of rooms on show due to building works.

WELLINGTON MUSEUM Map I 2879
Apsley House, 149 Piccadilly, W1. Apsley House was designed by Robert Adam, built 1771 – 8 and extended by Benjamin Wyatt in 1828 – 1830, under the direction of the Duke of Wellington who purchased it in 1817. It was presented to the nation by the 7th Duke of Wellington in 1947, and opened to the public in 1952. Exhibits include famous paintings, silver, porcelain, orders and decorations and personal relics of the first duke (1769 – 1852); also Canova's great marble figure of Napoleon Bonaparte. An amusing collection of political caricatures on display. Open all year, daily (ex Mon and Fri also 4 Apr, 5 May, 24 – 26 Dec and 1 Jan) 10 – 6, Sun 2.30 – 6. Free. Opening hours under review for 1980. Free. Underground P 400yds in Hyde Park. *(Tel 01-499 5676)*

WESLEY'S HOUSE AND MUSEUM Map III 3282
47 City Road, EC1. The house in which John Wesley lived and died is now a museum, containing a large collection of his personal possessions, etc. Open all year (ex Sun and BH) Mon to Sat 10 – 1, 2 – 4 and by arrangement. 20p. *(Tel 01-253 2262).* Also **Wesley's Chapel** built 1778, completely restored 1978. Open daily. Main service 11am Sun. ⚅ B

LONDON—GREATER
Maps I – V precede main atlas.

BECONTREE *Gt London* Map V TQ48
Valence House Museum Becontree Avenue. Off A112. Partly moated 16th- to 17th-C house, with Fanshawe portraits and museum of local history. Open all year by appointment only. Free. ⚙ *(01-592 2211)*

BETHNAL GREEN *Gt London* Map V TQ38
Bethnal Green Museum Cambridge Heath Road. A branch of the Victoria and Albert Museum. Its chief exhibits are toys, dolls and dolls' houses; model soldiers, Rodin bronzes; 19th-C Continental decorative arts, and costume from the mid 18th C with a special emphasis on the wedding dress, children's costume and Spitalfield Silks. Open all year, daily (ex 24 to 26 Dec, 1 Jan and 4 Apr and Fridays) 10 – 6, Sun 2.30 – 6. Free. ⚙ *(Tel 01-980 2415/4315)* ⚅ (Please telephone first) ⚅ (by appointment)

BEXLEY *Gt London* Map V TQ47
Hall Place Near junction of A2 and A223. 16th- to 17th-C house with contrasting elevations of chequered flint and brick. Ornamental gardens, with topiary in form of 'Queen's Beasts', roses, rock, water, herb, and peat gardens, and conservatory. House open all year, Mon to Sat 10 – 5, Sun 2 – 6; gardens open all year Mon to Fri 7.30 – dusk, Sat and Sun 9 – dusk. Free. ⚙ **(79)**

BLACKHEATH *Gt London* Map V TQ37
Rangers House Chesterfield Walk. Suffolk collection of Jacobean and Stuart portraits

housed in 18th-C villa, former home of Philip Stanhope, 14th Earl of Chesterfield. Collection contains a set of portraits by William Larkin, one of the finest to survive from this period, and a small collection of Old masters including *The Falconer* by Ferdinand Bol, *The Holy Family in the Carpenters Shop* by Carracci, a portrait of *The Grand Duchess of Tuscany* by Justus Sustermans, and royal portraits from Charles I to William and Mary, including a Van Dyck studio portrait. *The Three Eldest Children of Charles I*. Chamber concerts during 1979. Open all year daily (ex 4 Apr & 25 Dec). 10 – 5 (4 Nov – Feb). Free. ⚙ *(Tel 01-853 0035)*

BRENTFORD *Gt London* Map IV TQ17
Kew Bridge Pumping Station Kew Bridge Road entrance in Green Dragon Lane. London's living steam museum containing four beam engines working in steam plus three others. Model engines and other steam engines all working in steam, plus traction engines and a museum for London's water supply. Step back into the 19th C and see a site which worked from 1820 – 1945; old workshop, forges etc. ⚓ Souvenirs. Open all year Sat and Sun from 11, last admission 5pm, Fri by arrangement. 60p (ch 16 and pen 30p), family rate *ie* 2 adults and up to 3 children £1.50. Under review for 1980. ⚙ *(Tel 01-568 4757)* ⚅ B

Musical Museum High Street. 7m W of London, off A315. A musical menagerie of pianos, organs, violins, orchestrations, dulcimers, phonographs, musical boxes and the only self-playing Wurlitzer in Europe. Instruments played during tours well over 1 hour during which time silence must be maintained. Open Apr to Oct, Sat and Sun 2 – 5. 70p (ch 14 50p). Under revision for 1980. Nearest P in North Road, first turning to N on W side of museum. *(Tel 01-560 8108)*

CAMBERWELL *Gt London* Map V TQ37
South London Art Gallery Peckham Road. Presents ten exhibitions a year. Exhibits include Victorian paintings and drawings; a small collection of contemporary British Art; 20th-C original prints; and a comprehensive collection of topographical paintings and drawings of local subjects. Open only when exhibitions are in progress, daily 10 – 6, Sun 3 – 6. Free. P. *(Tel 01-703 6120).* *(London Borough of Southwark)*

CHEAM *Gt London* Map IV TQ26
Whitehall 1 Malden Road. Built *c*1500 as a farmhouse. In the 17th-C Cheam school was started here and permanent displays feature the school, the building of timber framed houses, medieval Cheam pottery, and Nonsuch Palace. ⚓ Open all year (ex 24 Dec to 2 Jan), Apr to Sep, Tue to Fri and Sun 2 – 5.30, Sat 10 – 5.30; Oct to Mar, Wed, Thu and Sun 2 – 5.30, Sat 10 – 5.30; BH as Sat. 25p (ch 10p). P. *(Tel 01-643 1236)*

CHELSEA *Gt London* Map V TQ27
Carlyle's House Cheyne Row, SW3. Built in 1708, it is a fine example of an 18th-C town house now owned by the National Trust. Here Thomas Carlyle and his wife Jane lived from 1834 to 1865 and entertained among others Dickens, Thackeray, Browning and Tennyson. Many of Carlyle's letters, personal possessions and furniture are preserved, including an early piano which Chopin played and the desk where Carlyle wrote his books. Open Apr – Oct daily (ex Mon and Tue, open BH). 70p. No parties over 20 persons. Meter P only. *(Tel 01-352 7087).* *(NT)*

CHINGFORD *Gt London* Map V TQ39
Queen Elizabeth's Hunting Lodge Rangers Road, Epping Forest. Picturesque old-timbered house, dating from c1510 now museum relating the life of animals, birds and plants in Epping Forest, and Man's association with them. Open all year Wed to Sun and BH Mon 2–6 (or dusk). 10p (accompanied ch free). ⚠ *(Tel 01-529 6681)* ⅃ B

CHISWICK *Gt London* Map IV TQ27
Chiswick House Domed mansion, considered to be the finest example of Palladian architecture of Great Britain. Built 1725–30 for the 3rd Earl of Burlington, Robert Boyle with interior decoration by William Kent. Well restored by the Department of the Environment. ⚲ Open Mar, Apr and Oct 9.30–5.30, May to Sep 9.30–7, Nov to Feb 9.30–4. (Closed Mon and Tue Oct to Mar). Closed 1–2 daily for lunch. 20p (ch and pen 5p). ⚠ *(AM)*
Gunnersby Park Museum Popes Lane. Early 19th-C former Rothschild mansion, in fine park, now museum of local interest, including Rothschild coaches. ⚲ summer only. Open all year, daily (ex 4 Apr, 24–26 Dec) Apr to Sep Mon to Fri 2–5, Sat and Sun 2–6; Oct to Mar daily 2–4. Free. ⚠ *(Tel 01-992 1612)* ⅃
Hogarth's House Hogarth Lane, Great West Road. 17th-C house where Hogarth lived for 15 years, with paintings, drawings, and other relics. Open all year (ex 1 Jan, 4 Apr, 25 and 26 Dec) Mon to Sat (ex Tue Oct to Mar) 11–6 (4, Oct to Mar), Sun 2–6 (4, Oct to Mar). 10p (ch 5p). ⚠ *(Tel 01-994 6757)*

CRYSTAL PALACE *Gt London* Map V TQ37
Crystal Palace Zoo Crystal Palace Park. A children's zoo with monkeys, birds (including foreign species), otters, sheep, pygmy goats, penguins, deer and Welsh Mountain and Shetland ponies. Pony rides, pony-trap rides. Open School Easter hol to Sep, weather permitting, Mon to Fri 1–6. Sat, Sun and school hols, BH 11–6. Free. ⚠ *(Tel 01-778 4487)* ⅃

DULWICH *Gt London* Map V TQ37
Dulwich Picture Gallery College Road. Housed in building designed in 1814 by Sir John Soane, restored and re-opened after severe damage during 1939–45 War. Notable collection of European Old Masters, particularly of the Dutch school. Open 16 Mar to 15 Oct Tue to Sat 10–5 (6, May to Aug) (4, 16 Oct to 15 Mar) Sun Apr to Sep 2–5 (6, May to Aug). 25p. P in College Road and Gallery Road. *(Tel 01-693 5254)* ⅃

ELTHAM *Gt London* Map V TQ47
Eltham Palace Noted for great hall with 15th-C hammer-beam roof. Old bridge spans moat. Open Nov to Mar, Thu and Sun 10.30–4; Apr to Oct, Mon, Thu, Fri, Sat and Sun 10.30–6. Opening arrangements subject to possible alteration, advisable to contact Admin Officer. *Tel 01-859 2112 ext 255* before visit. Free. *(AM)*
Winter Gardens Avery Hill Park. About 750 species of tropical and temperate plants in cold, temperate and tropical houses, a collection second only to Royal Botanical Gardens at Kew. ⚲ (Mar to Sep). Open all year Mon to Fri 11–4 Sat, Sun and BH 11–4 (6 summer). Closed 1st Mon each month and 25 Dec. Free. P. *(Tel 01-850 2666)* ⅃

ENFIELD *Gt London* Map V TQ39
Forty Hall Built 1629 for Sir Nicholas Raynton, Lord Mayor of London, and altered 1700 and later. Contemporary plaster ceilings and screen, 17th- and 18th-C furniture, and pictures, ceramics, and glass. Temporary exhibitions. (Apr to Oct). Open daily (ex 4 Apr, 24–26 Dec) Tue to Fri 10–8 (5, Oct to Easter), Sat and Sun 10–6 (5, Oct to Easter). Free. P. *(Tel 01-363 8196)* ⅃ B

FOREST HILL *Gt London* Map V TQ37
Horniman Museum London Road. Ethnographical and zoological exhibits, with large natural history collections including vivaria and aquaria. Exhibition of musical instruments from all parts of the world. Special exhibitions. Also extensive library and lectures and concerts in spring and autumn. Education Centre programmes for ch and adults. ⚲ (open daily 2.30–5.30, Sat from 11 am). Open all year (ex 24, 25 and morning 26 Dec – special arrangements Boxing Day afternoon) Mon to Sat 10.30–6, Sun 2–6. Free. P in Sydenham Rise opposite. *(Tel 01-699 1872/2339/4911)* ⅃

GREENWICH *Gt London* Map V TQ37
Cutty Sark Clipper Ship Greenwich Pier. The Cutty Sark is a famous Tea and Wool Clipper built in 1869 and preserved in dry dock since 1957. Open daily (ex 24 and 25 Dec, 1 Jan), 11–5 (2.30 Sun and 26 Dec) (6 during summer). 50p (ch 14 25p). Party 12+ (ex Sat and Sun). P. *(Tel 01-858 3445)* **(79)**
Gipsy Moth IV Greenwich Pier. The yacht in which Sir Francis Chichester sailed single-handed round the world 1966–67, starting the fashion for 'Round the World' sailing races. Open daily (ex 24, 25 Dec and 1 Jan) Oct to Mar 11–5; Apr to Sep 11–6, Sun and 26 Dec 2.30–6. 20p (ch 14 10p). P. *(Tel 01-858 3445)* **(79)**

National Maritime Museum Romney Road. Fine collection of items relating to British seafaring. Navigation Room is outstanding. Queen's House designed by Inigo Jones 1616–35, first English house in Palladian style. ☞ Open all year, daily (ex 4 Apr, 24–26 Dec and 1 Jan) Mon to Fri 10–5 (6 in summer), Sat 10–6, Sun 2.30–6. Free. P. *(Tel 01-858 4422)* ⅙ B

Old Royal Observatory In Greenwich Park, which was laid out by Le Nôtre, famous French gardener of time of Louis XIV, and part of National Maritime Museum, with exhibits of astronomical, horological and navigational interest. Actual work of observatory now carried out at Herstmonceux Castle. Open all year, daily (ex 4 Apr, 5 May, 24–26 Dec and 1 Jan) Mon to Fri 10–5 (6 in summer), Sat 10–6, Sun 2.30–6. Free. Planetarium gives viewing during school holidays, Mon, Tue, Thu, Fri 2.30 and 3.30; special educational programmes on Sat (information from Education section). 15p (ch 5p). P. *(Tel 01-858 4422)*

Royal Naval College Group of buildings designed by Webb (late 17th C) and Wren (early 18th C), with additions by Hawksmoor, Vanbrugh, and Ripley. Formerly Naval Hospital, becoming College in 1873. Chapel rebuilt 18th C, and Painted Hall has ceiling by Sir James Thornhill. Souvenir shop. Painted Hall and Chapel only open all year, daily (ex Thu) 2.30–5. Free. ⅍ within college grounds. *(Tel 01-858 2154)*

HACKNEY *Gt London* Map V TQ38
Geffrye Museum Kingsland Road. A collection of period furniture and woodwork from the Elizabethan period to 1939, including panelling and staircases from demolished London houses, contained in the former almshouses built c1713 with a bequest from Sir Robert Geffrye (Lord Mayor of London 1685–6). Also temporary exhibitions. Open all year Tue to Sat, BH (ex 4 Apr, 25 and 26 Dec) 10–5, Sun 2–5. Free. P in nearby streets. *(Tel 01-739 8368)* ⅙ B

HAM *Gt London* Map IV TQ17
Ham House Historic Jacobean mansion (1610 and later), facing River Thames, now annexe of Victoria and Albert Museum with collection of late Stuart furniture. Shop. Open daily (ex Mon but open most BH Mon) Apr to Sep 2–6, Oct to Mar 12–4. Closed 4 Apr, 5 May and 24, 25, 26 Dec. 50p (ch and pen 20p). Children under 12 must be accompanied by an adult. Grounds free. No dogs. *(NT and Victoria and Albert Museum)*

HAMPSTEAD *Gt London* Map V TQ28
Fenton House Hampstead Grove. A William and Mary house, built c1693, set in walled garden. Collections include notable Oriental, Continental and English china, needlework, furniture and the Benton Fletcher Collection of early keyboard instruments. Some concerts in summer. Open Feb, Mar and Nov, Sat and Sun; Apr to Oct daily (ex Mon and Tue, but open BH Mon) 11–5, Sun 2–5 or sunset. £1.20 (ch 15 60p). *(Tel 01-435 3471).* *(NT)*

Keats House Keats Grove. Regency house, former home of the poet; *Ode to the Nightingale* was written in garden. Manuscripts and relics preserved. Open all year (ex 4/5 Apr, 5 May, 25 & 26 Dec and 1 Jan) Mon to Sat 10–6, Sun 2–5, other BH 2–5. Free. P on Heath. *(Tel 01-435 2062)* ⅙ B

Kenwood House Iveagh Bequest Hampstead Lane, Mansion built c1765 by Robert Adam, and fine grounds, bequeathed to nation in 1927 by Lord Iveagh. Notable library, furniture, and works of art including paintings by Rembrandt, Hals, Vermeer, Reynolds and Gainsborough. Summer Exhibition. Orangery and lakeside concerts. ☞ Old Kitchen and Coach house. Open all year (ex 4 Apr and 24/25 Dec) daily 10–7 (dusk in winter). Free. ⅍ P. *(Tel 01-348 1286)* ⅙ B

HAMPTON COURT *Gt London* Map IV TQ16
Hampton Court Palace Built by Cardinal Wolsey in early 16th C, with notable gatehouse, clock court, and great hall, and large additions by Sir Christopher Wren, including Fountain Court (c1689). Fine state apartments and banqueting houses, orangery housing Mantegna Cartoons, and Great Vine, kitchen, and maze of special interest. Fine gardens with banqueting house and park near Fountain Court. State apartments open all year May to Sep, Mon to Sat 9.30–6, Sun 11–6; Mar, Apr and Oct Mon to Sat 9.30–5, Sun 2–5; Nov to Feb Mon to Sat 9.30–4. Sun 2–4. £1, winter 50p (ch 16 and pen 40p, winter 20p). Cars 25p (m/cycles 10p). *(AM)*

HARMONDSWORTH *Gt London* Map IV TQ07
Manor Farm Tithe Barn 14th to 15th-C tithe barn, 190ft long and 36ft wide, situated by farm adjacent to parish church. Accessible at all reasonable times. Free. ⅍

HARROW *Gt London* Map IV TQ18
Kodak Museum Wealdstone. Covers 150 years of photography, including largest collection of historical photographic equipment in country. Closed at present, re-opens early 1980, Mon to Fri, Sat and Sun afternoons. Times and further information on application. ⅍ free, but limited weekdays. *(Tel 01-427 4380 ext 76 enquiries)*

HENDON *Gt London* Map IV TQ28
Church Farm House Museum Greyhound Hill. Old gabled house, dating from 1688, now museum of local interest. Open all year (ex 4 Apr, 25 and 26 Dec, 1 Jan) Mon to Sat 10–12.30 and 1.30–5.30 (Tue 10–1 only), Sun 2.30–6. Free. ⅍ *(Tel 01-203 0130)*
Royal Air Force Museum Entrance via M1, A41 (Aerodrome Road, off Watford Way) or A5 (Colindale Avenue off Edgware Road). The Museum, on the former Hendon airfield, covers all aspects of the history of the RAF and its predecessors. Over forty aircraft are on display from the *Bleriot XI* to the *'Lightning'*. Twelve galleries depict over 100 years of military aviation history and include displays of photographs, documents, bombs, guns, and uniform equipment. The Battle of Britain Museum has been built on a site adjacent to the main Museum. It contains a unique collection of British, German and Italian aircraft which were engaged in the great air battle of 1940. ☞ licensed, shop and cinema. Open all year (ex 4 Apr, 5 May, 24–26 Dec and 1 Jan) Mon to Sat 10–6, Sun 2–6. RAF Museum Free. Battle of Britain Museum 60p (ch and pen 30p). ⅍ *(Tel 01-205 2266)* ⅙

ISLEWORTH *Gt London* Map IV TQ17
Syon House Founded in 1415 as a monastery and remodelled in the 18th-C with splendid interiors by Robert Adam, in particular the superbly coloured ante-room and the gallery-library. Fine portraits and furniture. Exterior refaced c1825. 'Northumberland' lion on east front. Notable

garden layout by 'Capability' Brown. House looks across River Thames. Open Easter then Sun to Thu until 30 Sep (closed Fri and Sat) 12–5 (1 Sun, 11 BH). Last tickets 4.15. ⚠ Approach via Park Road off Twickenham Road. No dogs. 🍽 licensed bar. *(Tel 01-560 0884 during opening hours only)*. The house is separate from the **Syon Park Gardens** (see below)and a combined ticket is available. *(The Duke of Northumberland KG)*
Syon Park Follow A315 of A310 to Busch Corner, and enter via Park Road, Isleworth entrance. In grounds of Syon House, 55 acres of gardens on bank of River Thames opposite Kew Gardens, only 9 miles from Central London. Laid out in mid 16th C, it is said to be the first place in which trees were planted purely for ornament, and it owes much of its present beauty to 'Capability' Brown, who laid out most of the present gardens around the lake. The Great Conservatory, built 1820 by Fowler, was the first large glass and metal construction of its kind in the world, and was the inspiration for the Crystal Palace at the Great Exhibition of 1851. It now houses a magnificent display of house plants, as well as a walk-through aviary, and an aquarium. The 6-acre rose garden has over 12,000 roses. Syon Park has one of the largest gardening centres in England, and this itself is worth a visit. Gardens Apr to Sep, daily 10–6; Oct to Mar (ex Christmas week) 10–5 or dusk (whichever is earlier). Admission prices not yet decided. 🍽 and children's play area. ⚠ *(Tel 01-560 0882)* ৬
(Please also see page 207 for advertisement)
KENSINGTON *Gt London* Map IV TQ27
Commonwealth Institute and Art Gallery
Kensington High Street. Contains exhibitions depicting life in the countries of the Commonwealth. Films are shown daily, and art exhibitions, featuring the finest works of Commonwealth painters and sculptors are held frequently. The institute has its own library. 🍽 Open all year (ex 4 Apr, 5 May, 24–26 Dec and 1 Jan) Mon to Sat 10–5.30, Sun 2.30–6. Free. ⚠ *(Tel 01-602 3252)* ৬
Leighton House Art gallery and museum, Holland Park Road. An essentially Victorian-styled house built in 1866, to a symmetrical design by George Aitchison, which now forms the central part of the building. The Arab Hall on the western side is decorated with applied tiles, fine examples of the oriental tile makers' work of the 13th, 16th and 17th Cs, originating from Rhodes, Damascus, Cairo and elsewhere, and a mosaic frieze by Walter Crane in the Persian style. Within the house is a permanent exhibition of Victorian art, including works by Lord Frederick Leighton as well as paintings, drawings, sculpture, pottery and furniture by other artists and craftsmen of this period. Temporary exhibitions are also held throughout the year in the Winter Studio and Upper Perrin Gallery of the house, Open all year, daily (ex Sun, BH) 11–5 (6, during temporary exhibitions). Garden open Apr to Dec 11–5. Free. Meter P 30yds. *(Tel 01-602 3316)* ৬ B
KEW *Gt London* Map IV TQ17
Kew Gardens Royal Botanical Gardens of 300 acres, with plants, trees, and flowers. Museums and glasshouses, with rare orchids, ferns, and cacti. Exotic Pagoda was work of Sir William Chambers in 1761. Open all year, daily (ex 25 Dec and 1 Jan and May Day); gardens from 10am to between 4pm and 8pm (depending on season); museums from 10am; glasshouses from 11am. Closing times vary according to season, but not later

than 4.50pm Mon to Sat, 5.50pm Sun. May Day closing under revision, also admission prices for 1980. ৬
Kew Palace Dutch-gabled 17th- to 18th-C house, with souvenirs of George III. Queen Charlotte died here in 1818. Stands in the Royal Botanical Gardens of Kew. Open Apr to mid Oct daily 11–5.30. 20p (ch 16 and pen 5p). Free. ⚠ *(AM)* and **Queen Charlotte's Cottage** Built in 1772 for the Queen, wife of George III. The interior remains as it was in the 18th-C when royalty were in residence. Open Apr to mid Oct 11–5.30 Sat, Sun and BH. 15p (ch 16 and pen 5p) ch5 free. *(AM)*

NEASDEN *Gt London* Map IV TQ28
The Grange Museum Neasden Lane NW10 (centre of roundabout). The building dating from around 1700 originally formed part of the outbuildings of a large farm and was later converted into a Gothic cottage. Permanent collections tell the story of the area that is now the London Borough of Brent. Changing temporary exhibitions, local history library, display on the British Empire Exhibition for which Wembley Stadium was built. Two period rooms of late 19th C and the 1930s. Open all year (ex BH) Mon to Sat 10–5 (8 Mon and Wed). Free. ⚠ *(Tel 01-452 8311)* ৬ B

NORTH PECKHAM *Gt London* Map V TQ37
Livesey Museum 682 Old Kent Road. Museum displays two exhibitions every year, dealing mainly with Southwark's past and present. Permanent exhibition of Southwark's street furniture in the courtyard. Open when exhibition in progress. Mon to Sat 10–5. Free. Limited street P. *(Tel 01-639 5604)* ৬ B

OSTERLEY *Gt London* Map IV TQ17
Osterley Park House Off B454 (Syon Lane). Originally dates back to c1575, with alterations of 1711. Splendid decoration by Robert Adam (1763 and 1767), and hall, staircase, Etruscan room, and tapestry room outstanding. Contemporary furniture bought by Victoria and Albert Museum. 🍽 Open Apr to Sep Tue to Sun and BH 2–6 (closed Mon); Oct to Mar Tue to Sun 12–4 (closed 4 Apr, 5 May, 24–26 Dec, 1 Jan). 40p (ch and pen 15p). Under review for 1980. *(Tel 01-560 3918)*. (NT and V and A Museum)

REGENT'S PARK *Gt London* Map V TQ28
London Zoo Part of the world-famous Zoological Society of London which was founded in 1826 by Sir Stamford Raffles with the aim of 'the advancement of Zoology and Animal Physiology and the introduction of new and curious subjects of the Animal Kingdom'. The zoo was opened in 1828. In 1865 London Zoo received its first African elephant called 'Jumbo' whose name has become immortalised as a name for giant things. Two of the more interesting acquisitions are a pair of giant pandas, Ching-Ching and Chia-Chia presented to the zoo after Edward Heath's visit to China during 1974. Among the world firsts that the zoo can claim are a reptile house in 1849, aquarium 1853, and insect house in 1889. The zoo contains today over 6,000 creatures, many of which were born at the zoo, covering 1,450 species, including breeding colonies of the rare orang-utans, chimpanzees and many other rare or endangered species. In recent years new pavilions have been built for apes, lions, tigers and monkeys, elephants and rhinos, small mammals (the largest collection under one roof in the world) and a giant walk-through aviary designed by Lord Snowdon.

The London and Whipsnade Zoos are supported by the most professionally complete veterinary and research services to maintain animal management standards at the Society's uniquely high level. ⚑ Licensed. Open all year, daily (ex 25 Dec) 9 (10 Nov to Feb) – 6 (7 Sun and BH) or dusk whichever is earlier. £2 (ch 90p). Under revision for 1980. P. outer circle of Park after 11 and in car park 600yds from main gate after 10. *(Tel 01-722 3333)* ৬

SOUTHGATE *Gt London* Map V TQ39
Broomfield Museum Broomfield Lane. This is located at Broomfield House, a timbered 17th-C house, with wall-paintings and a ceiling by Gerard Lanscroon. It stands in a small park. Special exhibitions of local interest throughout the year. Natural history room. Fresh painting exhibitions every month. ⚑ summer. Open all year, daily (ex Mon) Easter to Sep 10 – 8 (6, Sat and Sun); Oct to Easter 10 – 5. Free. ⚑ *(Tel 01-882 1354)* ৬ B

TOTTENHAM *Gt London* Map V TQ39
Bruce Castle Museum Lordship Lane. An E-shaped Elizabethan, Jacobean and Georgian building, with an adjacent circular 16th-C tower, which stands in a small park. The museum contains three distinct collections on: Local History; Postal History – a private school was run by the family of Rowland Hill in this building during the 19th C; and the Middlesex Regiment, known also as the 'die-hards'. Open all year, Mon (ex BH), Tue, Thu, Fri, 10 – 5, Sat 10 – 12.30, 1.30 – 5. Free. ⚑ *(Tel 01-808 8772)* ৬

TWICKENHAM *Gt London* Map IV TQ17
Marble Hill House Marble Hill Park. Home of Countess of Suffolk, mistress of George II, and begun in 1724 to a design by Roger Morris. Standing in a public park near the River Thames and containing a notable hall and great room, with Georgian paintings and furniture. Special summer exhibitions. ⚑ in stable block. Open all year (ex 24 and 25 Dec and Fri) daily 10 – 5 (4, Nov to Jan). Free. P. 200yds. *(Tel 01-348 1286)* ৬
Orleans House Gallery Riverside. Original Orleans House, in which Louis Philippe, Duc d'Orleans, King of the French 1830 – 48, lived in early 19th C. It was originally built for Queen Anne's Secretary of State for Scotland, and was demolished in 1927. Surviving octagonal room, designed by James Gibbs in 1720, has exquisite plasterwork by Artari and Bagutti. Open all year, Tue to Sat 1 – 5.30 (4.30 Oct to Mar), Sun 2 – 5.30 (4.30 Oct to Mar); BH (ex 4 Apr, 25/26 Dec) 2 – 5.30, 1 Jan 2 – 4.30. Free. Woodland gardens open all year, daily 9 – dusk. ⚑ *(Tel 01-940 0031)* ৬ B

WALTHAMSTOW *Gt London* Map V TQ38
Vestry House Museum of Local History Vestry Road, near Hoe Street. A small museum located in a former 18th-C workhouse standing in the conservation area 'Walthamstow Village', the historic centre of the parish. Historical items of local interest from the Stone Age onwards are displayed, including a reconstructed Victorian parlour and a Gallery of Costume. Also displayed is a porcelain hand-painted topographical tea service with scenes of area. Local archives are also available for consultation. The Bremer, Britain's first internal combustion engined car, built 1892 – 1894, can be seen. Lectures on various historical themes Oct to Mar 1st Wed in each month at 8.15 pm. Open all year Mon to Sat 10 – 5 (8, Mon and Wed). Free. ⚑ *(Tel 01-527 5544 ext 391)*

William Morris Gallery Lloyd Park, Forest Road. William Morris lived in this house, known as 'Water House' from 1848 – 56. There are exhibits of his fabrics, wallpapers and furniture. The Century Guild Collection and the Brangwyn Gift. Open all year Mon to Sat 10 – 5 (10 – 8 Tue and Thu, Apr to Sep); first Sun in each month 10 – 12 and 2 – 5. Closed 1 Jan, Easter weekend, 25 Dec, and all BH. Free. ⚑ *(Tel 01-527 5544 ext 390)* ৬ B

WEMBLEY *Gt London* Map IV TQ18
Wembley Stadium The world's number one stadium built in 1923, it holds 100,000. Home of the England football team – venue for annual Cup Final and World events. Tour comprises 10-minute audio-visual slide show, visit to dressing rooms, Royal Box and retiring rooms, a walk up Player's tunnel to pitch complete with sound effects. Admission includes free tea, coffee or soft drink. Open all year (ex 25 and 26 Dec, Thu and days before and after a match) tours on the hour 10 – 4 (ex 1 pm). £1 (ch 15 and pen 70p). Under revision for 1980. Party 20+. ⚑ *(Tel 01-902 8833 ask for Guided Tours)* ৬

WEST HAM *Gt London* Map V TQ38
Passmore Edwards Museum Romford Road. Collections of Greater London and Essex archaeology, biology, geology and history. Open all year, daily (ex Sun and BH) Mon, Tue, Wed, Fri 10 – 6, Thu 10 – 8, Sat 10 – 1, 2 – 5. Free. P in streets. *(Tel 01-534 4545 ext 376 and 01-519 4296)*

WHITECHAPEL *Gt London* Map V TQ38
National Museum of Labour History Limehouse Town Hall, Commercial Road. The visual history from late 18th C to 1945 is portrayed in two sections from autocracy to democracy, and the turn to socialism 1881 to 1945. Its prime concern (through its large and rare collection) is to portray the development of democracy over the last 200 years. Open all year (closed 20 – 30 Dec, BH) Tue to Fri 9.30 – 5. Free. *(Tel 01-515 3229)* ৬

WIMBLEDON *Gt London* Map IV TQ27
Lawn Tennis Museum The museum, within the grounds of the All England Tennis Club, is the only one of its kind in the world and shows something of the games which preceded and helped in the conception of lawn tennis. Traces the development of the game over the last century. Also includes Library, the archives of which comprise collections of photographs, film, documents, postcards, autographs and other ephemera. Museum shop (gifts and souvenirs). Open all year (ex Mon, BH and Sat and Sun prior to the Championships) Tue to Sat 11 – 5, Sun 2 – 5. During Championships open daily 12 – 1, 1.30 – 2.30, 3 – 4, 4.30 – 5.30, 6 – 7.75p (ch and pen 35p). ⚑ *(Tel 01-946 2244)*

WOOLWICH *Gt London* Map V TQ47
Museum of Artillery in the Rotunda Replica of circular structure designed by John Nash, which stood at one time in St James's Park. It contains a very interesting collection of artillery recently re-displayed. Open all year, Apr to Oct, Mon to Fri 12 – 5, Sat and Sun 1 – 5; Nov to Mar, Mon to Fri 12 – 4, Sat and Sun 1 – 4. Free. Closed 4 Apr, 25 and 26 Dec and 1 Jan. ⚑ *(Tel 01-856 5533 ext 3385)* ৬

London section ends

LONDON COLNEY *Hertfordshire*
Map 4 TL20
*Salisbury Hall and de Havilland Mosquito
Aircraft Museum* 5m S of St Albans on A6.
Moated hall, dating from Charles II's reign.
Interesting fireplaces and famous early
English medallions of Roman emperors. ⬚
from Whitsun. Hall and garden open Easter to
end Sep, Sun 2–6; BH Mon 10.30–12.30 and
2–5.30, also Jul to end of Sep, Thu 2–6. 50p
(ch 15 25p, ch 5 free). De Havilland Mosquito
Mk B35, Vampire and Venom aircraft on
show. 25p (ch 10p). Under revision for 1980.
Party Tue to Fri. Dogs in grounds on leads. ⚠
*(Tel Bowmans Green 23274). (Mr W J
Goldsmith)* ⓰ B

LONG CRENDON *Buckinghamshire*
Map 4 SP60
Court House 2m N of Thame. Partly half-
timbered 14th-C building, probably at one
time a wool store. Upper storey open Wed
2–6, Sat & Sun 11–6. 20p. *(NT)*

LONGLEAT HOUSE *Wiltshire* Map 3 ST84
Entrance on Warminster–Frome road, A362.
Built for Sir John Thynne in 1580 and
decorated in the Italian Renaissance fashion
in the 19th C, with fine library, state rooms,
ceilings, pictures and furniture. Europe's first
Safari Park with hundreds of wild animals.
Shearwater lake and viewpoint from
Heaven's Gate are all outstanding. Victorian
kitchens, Maze, Garden Centre, BBC 'Dr
Who' exhibition and new Paddington Bear
exhibition open Easter to Oct. ⬚, picnic
areas. Open all year daily (ex 25 Dec). House
£1.10 (ch and pen 50p) extra for Victorian
kitchens, 19th-C dolls houses, family bygones, exhibitions, railway and maze, also
road toll inclusive of grounds, picnic area and
gardens 50p (not applicable to coaches).
Safari Park (hard topped cars only) £3.50 per
car, extra for safari boats and pets corner.
Toilet for disabled in the stable yard. Prices
and times under revision for 1980. *(Tel
Maiden Bradley 55). (Marquess of Bath)*

LONG MELFORD *Suffolk* Map 5 TL84
Kentwell Hall A mellow redbrick Elizabethan
manor with almost perfect original E-plan
exterior elevations, completely surrounded by
a broad moat in a tranquil setting. Restoration
work can be seen in progress. ⬚ on open
days, full catering for parties by arrangement.
Open Mar to Oct Sun, also Wed and Thu May
to Sep, Fri and Sat 18 Jul to 20 Sep, 4–10 Apr
incl, BH weekends Sat to Mon, 2–6. 85p
(accompanied ch 14 45p; pen 45p on Thu
only). Admission prices under revision for
1980. Party 20+. ⚠ *(Tel 207)* ⓰
Melford Hall Tudor and 18th-C mansion
home of Hyde Parkers since 1781. Fine
porcelain, furniture, and paintings. Open Apr
to 30 Sep, Wed, Thu, Sun, and BH Mon 2–6
(last admission 5.30). 90p. Party 15+. No
dogs. *(NT)*

LONG WITTENHAM *Oxfordshire*
Map 4 SU59
Pendon Museum 3½m N of Didcot on unclass
road off B4016. A small but expanding
museum depicting, in miniature, rural scenes
of the 1930s. Also the late John Ahern's
famous Madder Valley layout, and railway
relics from 1812 onwards. ⬚. Open Mar to
Oct, Sat, Sun and BH 2–6. Nov to Feb Sat
and Sun 2–5 (closed Christmas). 50p (ch 15
and pen 30p, ch 4 free). ⚠ (limited). *(Tel
Clifton Hampden 7365, weekends only)*

LOOE *Cornwall* Map 2 SX25
Cornish Museum Lower Street, East Looe.
Folklore, fishing, mining, early fire fighting and
many other local exhibits of historical interest.
Open Spring BH to 30 Sep, daily 10–1,
2–5.30. 15p (ch 10p). P. ⓰ **(79)**
Looe Aquarium Local marine aquarium
containing specimens which can be caught
within a mile of Banjo pier. Shark museum
with exhibits of blue, porbeagle and mako
sharks. Open 1 Jun to 30 Sep daily 10–6 (9
mid Jun to mid Sep). 20p (ch 10p). Under
revision for 1980. P. *(Tel 2423)* ⓰
The Monkey Sanctuary Murrayton. 3m ENE,
off B3253. Sanctuary for rare Amazon woolly
monkey species which are bred here. They
can be watched in the trees and in the
grounds. Talks given morning and afternoon.
Indoor meeting in rainy weather. Visitors
advised to bring children under 4 on dry days
only. ⬚. Open daily 30 Mar to 13 Apr then 11
May to 5 Oct 10.30–5.30. Monkeys actually
meet the visitors. Admission charges not yet
decided. ⚠ *(Tel 2532)* ⓰ (individuals only)

LOTHERTON HALL North Yorkshire
Map 8 SE43
10m E of Leeds, off B1217, near Aberford.
Built around earlier 18th-C house. Now a
country house museum, with furniture,
pictures, silver and ceramics from Gascoigne
collection, and works of art from Leeds
collections. Gallery of Oriental art. Fashion
galleries. ⚑. Open all year, daily (ex 25, 26
Dec) Tue to Sun 10.30 – 6.15 or dusk
(10.30 – 8.30, Thu, May to Sep). 25p (ch 5p,
pen and students free). ⚠ (Tel Aberford 259)
(79)

LOUGHBOROUGH Leicestershire
Map 8 SK51
Great Central Railway Great Central Road.
Operational private steam railway running
over five miles from Loughborough Central to
Rothley, all trains calling at Quorn and
Woodhouse. Museum and locomotive depot
at Loughborough Central. Buffet car on trains,
restaurant as advertised. ⚑ at Loughborough
Central and Rothley. Open all year Sat, Sun
and BH Mon and Tue, also Wed and Thu
during Jul and Aug (closed 4 Apr and 25 Dec).
Return fare from any station £1.20 (ch and
pen 60p). ⚠ at Quorn (Leisurerail Centre –
picnic area, children's railway, adventure
area, crazyrail golf etc). (Tel 30726 or
216433)

LOUND HALL MINING MUSEUM
Nottinghamshire Map 8 SK77
5½m S of East Retford on B6387. Exhibits
include locomotives, underground canal
barge, coal face machinery, headgear, hand
tools, lamps and electrical equipment. The
modern Bevercotes Colliery is adjacent to
museum. Open first Sun in each month, May
to Oct 2 – 5.30, Nov to Mar 2 – 4 (Mon to Fri
1.30 – 4 by prior arrangement for parties). 10p
(accompanied ch 16 free). ⚠

LOWER BEEDING West Sussex
Map 4 TQ22
Leonardslee Gardens 1m S off A281.
Renowned spring garden, camellias, azaleas
and rhododendrons in valley, and 15th-C
hammer ponds. Tea weekdays. Open 20 Apr
the 27 Apr to 8 Jun, Wed, Thu, Sat and Sun
also Mon 5 and 26 May. Autumn tints all Sat
and Sun Oct. 10 – 6. 80p (ch 40p). No dogs. ⚠
10p. (Tel 212 or 305). (Sir Giles Loder) ♿

LOWESTOFT Suffolk Map 5 TM59
East Anglia Transport Museum Chapel
Road, Carlton Colville. The Museum
premises are situated on a 3-acre site and
contain a range of historic cars, commercial
vehicles, trams, buses and trolleybuses, in
addition to various items of transport interest.
A tram service operates during opening hours
also a narrow-gauge railway. ⚑. Open
Easter, weekends and BH from May to end
Sep, Sat 2 – 4, Sun and BH 11 – 5, also Aug
Tue to Fri 2 – 4. 35p (ch 15p). Party. ⚠ (Tel
Ubberston 398)

LOWTHER Cumbria Map 12 NY52
Wild Life Country Park 5m S of Penrith off
A6. Deer, cranes, and rare breeds of cattle
and sheep can be viewed in a wild and natural
setting. Many European species housed in
special enclosures including otters, badgers,
wild pigs, etc. Picnic areas. ⚑. Open Apr to
Sep 10 – 5 (6, Jul and Aug). Admission not yet
decided for 1979. Gift shop and garden
centre. Dog kennels. ⚠ (Tel Hacklethorpe
392) ♿ (79)

LUCTON Hereford and Worcester
Map 3 SO46
Mortimer's Cross Water Mill 18th-C

undershot-type watermill which was working
until 1940. Open May to Sep, Thu 12 – 6; Mar,
Apr and Oct, Thu 12 – 4.30; Nov to Feb, Thu
12 – 3.30. 15p (ch 16 and pen 5p). (AM)

LUDGERSHALL Wiltshire Map 4 SU25
Ludgershall Castle 7m NW of Andover on
A342. Norman motte and bailey castle,
retaining large earthworks and flint walling of
later royal castle. Open all reasonable times.
Free. (AM)

LUDLOW Salop Map 7 SO57
Ludlow Museum Butter Cross. This
museum, housed in the Butter Cross of 1744,
has prehistoric, Roman and medieval
exhibits, examples of arms and armour,
Georgian and Victorian domestic items, local
history, biology and geology. Open Easter to
30 Sep, Mon to Sat 10.30 – 12.30 and 2 – 5,
Sun (Jun, Jul and Aug only) 10 – 1, 2 – 5. 30p
(ch 10p). P. County Museum Service reserve
collections open by appointment only. (Tel
3857)

LUNDY ISLAND Devon Map 2 SS14
In Bristol Channel. Tiny granite island, NT
property since 1969, and leased to Landmark
Trust. Puffins and other seabirds breed in
large numbers on cliffs around coastline.
Near quay are slight remains of Marisco
Castle, stronghold of early piratical ruling
family. Shutter Rock figures in Charles
Kingsley's Westward Ho! Open always,
landing fee 75p. Steamers from Ilfracombe
Quay (Tel 62687) from May to end Sep. No
cars. (NT)

LUTON Bedfordshire Map 4 TL02
Museum and Art Gallery Wardown Park.
Museum has collections illustrating natural
history, culture, and industries of Luton and
Bedfordshire with particular reference to
straw hat and pillow lace trade. 'Luton Life'
gallery includes a reconstructed 'street'
display. Also temporary exhibitions. Open all
year daily (ex 25, 26 Dec, 1 Jan and Sun in
Dec and Jan) Mon to Sat 10 – 6 (5 winter) Sun
2 – 6 (5 winter). Free. ⚠ (Tel 36941) ♿ B
Luton Hoo Entrance at Park Street gates, on
A6129. Magnificent Wernher Collection of art
treasures including tapestries and pictures;
also Russian Fabergé jewellery, in a country
mansion designed originally by Robert Adam.
Large park by 'Capability' Brown. ⚑. Open 4
Apr to 28 Sep, Mon, Wed, Thu and Sat (also 4
Apr) 11 – 6; Sun 2 – 6. House and gardens £1
(ch 40p). Gardens only 35p (ch 15p). Under
revision for 1980. No dogs. ⚠ (Tel 22955).
(NGS) ♿

LYDDINGTON Leicestershire Map 4 SP89
Bede House Former home of Bishops of
Lincoln, converted into hospital, or bede
house, by Lord Burghley in 1602. Open, see
inside front cover, Apr to Sep only. 15p (ch 16
and pen 5p). (AM)

LYDFORD Devon Map 2 SX58
Lydford Castle Midway Okehampton –
Tavistock off A386. Remains of mid 12th-C
stone keep altered a century later. Lower floor
was once a prison and the upper floor became
Stannary Court to administer local tin mines.
Open all reasonable times. Free. ⚠ (AM)
Lydford Gorge 8m N of Tavistock on unclass
road. Scooped into succession of potholes by
River Lyd the gorge emerges into steep, oak-
wooded valley and is joined by a stream at
90ft-high White Lady waterfall. Open Apr to
Oct, daily 9 – 1hr before sunset. 70p. (NT)

LYDIARD PARK Wiltshire Map 4 SU18
1m N of M4 (Junc 16) on unclass road. Fine
Georgian mansion set in pleasant park,

together with the adjoining parish church of St Mary, which contains fascinating memorials to the St John family. Small agricultural museum in the Stable block, as mansion, free. Open all year (ex 4 Apr, 25/26 Dec). Weekdays 10–1, 2–5.30, Sun 2–5.30. 22p (ch and pen 11p). Party 20+. Grounds free. ⚠ *(Tel Swindon 26161 ext 522 or Purton 770401)* ⅙ also **Agricultural Museum** 1¾m NE on unclass road at Shaw. Houses larger items of farming equipment, wagons, carts, ploughs, drills etc. Open Easter to Oct Sun 2–5. Free. ⚠ free.

LYDNEY *Gloucestershire* Map 3 SO60
Dean Forest Railway Society Ltd 1m N at New Mills on B4234. A number of locomotives, coaches, wagons and railway equipment on show at Norchard just outside Lydney on B4234. Steam days BH Sun and Mon, every Sun Aug. ⚓. Open Sat and Sun 11–5 (closed Christmas). 10p–50p depending on activities also subject to alteration. P. *(Tel 3423)* ⅙

LYME REGIS *Dorset* Map 3 SY39
Philpot Museum Bridge Street. Small museum preserving old fire engine of 1706, prints, documents, old lace exhibition, an extensive collection of geological specimens and local history exhibits. Also fossils from the Blue Lias rock nearby where, in 1811, 12-year-old Mary Anning discovered the remains of an ichthyosaurus, of which a specimen is in the museum. Open Easter to 30 Sep, daily 10.30–1, 2.30–5; Oct to Apr, Tue 10.30–12.30, Thu 2.30–4.30, Sat and Sun 10.30–12.30 and 2.30–4.30. 15p (ch 16 5p). Under revision for 1980. P (charge). ⅙ B

LYMPNE *Kent* Map 5 TR13
Lympne Castle Restored Norman to 15th-C structure, modernised in 1905, once owned by Archdeacons of Canterbury. Gardens have extensive views over Romney Marsh and across Channel to French coast. ⚓ BH only, or for parties by arrangement. Open Easter to Oct Sun 2.30–6, other times by arrangement. 1 Jul to 30 Sep and all BH daily 10.30–6. 50p (ch 14 15p). ⚠ *(Tel Hythe 67571)*. *(Mr H Margary)*
Port Lympne Zoo Park and Gardens Many different animals including, Indian elephants, wolves, rhinos, African leopards, Siberian and Indian tigers, monkeys etc. The mansion was built by Sir Herbert Baker, famous architect of his time. Many of the original internal features have survived, the most notable being the recently-restored 'Rex Whistler Tent Room', Moroccan patio, hexagonal library (where the Treaty of Paris

was signed after the First World War), and the long hall with concentric patterned marble, mosaic floor. 15 acres of spectacular gardens with elaborate terracing. ⚓. Open all year (ex 25 Dec) daily 10–6 (or sunset). Admission charges for 1980 not yet decided. ⚠ *(Tel Hythe 60618/9)*

LYNTON *Devon* Map 3 SS74
Lyn and Exmoor Museum History of life of Exmoor, housed in St Vincent Cottage, one of oldest in resort, with unique slab roof, 16th-C building now completely restored. Special exhibition of scale models and photographs of old Lynton – Barnstaple railway 1895–1935, donated to museum. Open Apr to Sep, Mon to Fri 10–12.30, 2–5, Sun 2–5. 20p (ch 14 10p). P.

LYVEDEN NEW BIELD Northamptonshire Map 4 SP98
4m SW Oundle. Shell of unfinished two-storeyed Greek-Cross house, designed c1600 by Sir Thomas Tresham to symbolise the Passion. Open daily. Party (arrangement with custodian). *(NT)*

MACCLESFIELD *Cheshire* Map 7 SJ79
Macclesfield Museum and Art Gallery West Park, Prestbury Road. Contains a notable collection of Egyptian antiquities, oil paintings, and sketches including work by C F Tunnicliffe ARA and Landseer, and drawings and prints of a topographical nature. Also a small silk exhibition and a stuffed Giant Panda. Open all year (ex Easter, BH and day following, 25 Dec and Mons) Tue to Sat 10–12 & 1–5, Sun 2–5. Free. P. *(Tel 24067)*

MADRON *Cornwall* Map 2 SW43
Trengwainton Garden 2m W of Penzance, on B3312. Gardens displaying a magnificent collection of shrubs, including magnolias and rhododendrons. Walled garden containing tender and sub-tropical plants not grown elsewhere in England. Open Mar to Oct, also BH, Wed, Thu, Fri, and Sat 11–6. 70p *(NT)*

MAIDENHEAD *Berkshire* Map 4 SU88
The Courage Shire Horse Centre Set in attractive Berkshire countryside. Up to twelve Shire horses, each weighing around a ton, can be seen in the timber-built stables. Comprehensive display room giving history of the Shire horse and showing prizes won by the horses. Farrier's shop, pets corner, playground and picnic area. ⚓. Open 1 Mar to 31 Oct daily (ex Mon unless BH) 11–5 (last admission 4). ⚠ Licensed PH adjacent with restaurant. For admission charges telephone Littlewick Green 3917, and restaurant reservations 5335. ⅙

Henry Reitlinger Bequest Oldfield, Riverside. Collection of pottery, sculpture, paintings, drawings, ceramics, and glass. Open Apr to 30 Sep, Tue and Thu 10 – 12.30 and 2.15 – 4.30, first Sun in each month 2.30 – 4.30. Other times by prior arrangement in writing. Free. ⚠

MAIDSTONE *Kent* Map 5 TQ75
Museum and Art Gallery Chillington Manor, St Faith's Street. Rebuilt in 1562, with medieval wing brought from East Farleigh. Now museum and art gallery, containing Japanese room. Museum contains Anglo-Saxon jewellery, glass and volume II of the Lambeth Byelaw (c1170). Exhibitions by local and national artists. Open all year, Mon (ex BH) to Sat 10 – 6 (5, Oct to Mar). Free. P. *(Tel 54497)*
Tyrwhitt Drake Museum of Carriages The Archbishop's Stables, Mill Street. Late medieval tithe barn or stables, containing interesting museum of horse-drawn carriages and vehicles. Near Archbishop's Palace. Open all year, weekdays (ex BH) 10 – 1 and 2 – 5. 20p (ch 10p). Party (by appointment). P. *(Tel 54497)* ⅃ B

MALHAM *North Yorkshire* Map 7 SD86
Yorkshire Dales National Park Centre Permanent interpretation centre for the Malham area with displays, books, maps, teaching aids, etc. Open Apr to end Sep daily mid morning to late afternoon. Free. ⚠ *(Tel Airton 363)* ⅃

MALTON *North Yorkshire* Map 8 SE77
Roman Museum Adjoining Milton Rooms, Market Place. Contains extensive Romano-British collections from the Roman Fort of Derventio and the settlements and villas in the

vicinity. In addition there are displays of prehistoric and medieval material from Malton and district. Open all year Spring BH to 30 Sep, Mon to Sat 11 – 5, Sun 2 – 5; 1 Oct to 28 May, Mon to Sat 2 – 4.30, Sun 2 – 5. 10p (ch and students 5p). Questionnaires available for children. P. *(Tel 4941 ext 67)*

MANCHESTER *Gt Manchester* Map 7 SJ89
The City Art Gallery Mosley Street. British and Continental paintings before 1900 including Old Masters, Gainsborough, Stubbs, Turner, The Pre-Raphaelites and Impressionists. Sculpture, English and Continental silver, pottery and porcelain. Information about exhibitions, identifications, photographs etc, please write or telephone. Open Mon to Sat 10 – 6, Sun 2.30 – 6. Free. P. *(Tel 061-236 9422)*
The Gallery of Modern Art Athenaeum, Princess Street (next door to City Art Gallery). From Sickert to Hockney. European painting, sculpture, drawings, prints and decorative arts since 1900. Opening times and telephone no. as for City Art Gallery. Free.
The John Rylands University Library of Manchester Famous library, dating from 1851, containing over 3,000,000 books, 17,000 manuscripts, extensive archival collections and c 600,000 titles in microform. Rare books division in the architecturally distinguished Rylands memorial building in Deansgate, holds regular exhibitions and lectures. Open all year (ex BH and Christmas to 1 Jan), Mon to Fri 9.30 – 5.30, Sat 9.30 – 1. Free. ⚠
The Gallery of English Costume Platt Fields, Rusholme. The famous costume collection displaying the changing styles of everyday clothes and accessories of the last

350 years, including contemporary fashion. The costume library is available to students on request. Open all year. May to Aug Mon to Sat 10–6, Sun 12–6; Mar, Apr, Sep and Oct Mon to Sat 10–6, Sun 2–6; Nov to Feb Mon to Sat 10–4, Sun 2–4. Free. *(Tel 061-224 5217)* & B

Manchester Museum The University, Oxford Road. Contains exhibits of archaeology and natural history including an extensive collection from Ancient Egypt, rocks, minerals, fossils, coins and native craftsmanship and huge study collections of over 8 million specimens. Popular lectures are given on winter Sats. Open all year daily (ex Sun, 4 Apr, 25, 26 Dec) 10–5 (9, Wed). Free but charge for P in University grounds. *(Tel 061-273 3333)*

North Western Museum of Science and Industry Grosvenor Street. Steam and internal-combustion engines, machine tools, electrical exhibits, railway photographs, paper-making, printing and textile machinery, and optical equipment among other exhibits. Working days are held on last Sat of most months (ex Jul, Aug, Dec) when the machines are demonstrated. Museum book shop. ⚏ Open all year (ex Sun, 4 Apr and several days at Christmas) 10–5. Free. Ch 11 admitted only if accompanied by an adult. P. *(Tel 061-273 6636 for Museum, 061-273 1955 for Museum Education Service)* & B

Queen's Park Art Gallery Harpurhey. Victorian and Edwardian paintings, including Millais, Watts and Brangwyn. Paintings by War Artists. Displays of the Manchester Regiment and the 14th/20th King's Hussars. Open Mon to Sat 10–6 (4 Nov to Feb); Sun 2–6 (4 Nov to Feb) 12–6 May to Aug. Free. ⚠ *(Tel 061-205 2121)*

Whitworth Art Gallery University of Manchester, Whitworth Park. Founded 1889 by Royal Charter. The principal collections are British water-colours including work by Blake, Turner, the Pre-Raphaelites and 1939–45 War Artists; Continental water-colours including works by Cézanne, Van Gogh and Picasso; drawings and prints, including examples by leading Renaissance masters such as Pollaiuolo, Mantegna and Dürer, and fine collection of Japanese prints; textiles, including the Whitworth Tapestry, designed by Paolozzi 1968; historic wall papers; and contemporary works of art. Special exhibitions for 1980 include, 100 Master Prints in the Whitworth Art collection, 19 Jan to 26 Apr; Contemporary Swiss Tapestries, 1 Mar to 8 Apr; Treasures of the University of Manchester, late Apr to 28 Jun; Outdoor Sculpture at the Whitworth, Summer 1980; Mondriaan and Hague School Drawings, 17 May to 12 Jul; Treasures from the State Jewish Museum, Prague, 4 Oct to 20 Dec. Open all year daily (ex Sun, 4 Apr, 5 May and 25/26 Dec) 10–5 (Thu 10–9). Free. ⚠ *(Tel 061-273 4865)* &

MANNINGTON HALL *Norfolk* Map 9 TG13
Built in 1460 in flint. A moated manor house, still a family home. ⚏ (teas). Gardens open May to Sep, Thu and Fri 2–5, house by written appointment only, Thu (enclose sae). Gardens 30p, House 50p. ⚠ *(The Hon Robin Walpole)* & B (gardens)

MAPLEDURHAM *Berkshire* Map 4 SU67
Mapledurham House Elizabethan mansion set in unspoilt village beside River Thames. Built by Blount family in the 16th C, and restored by their descendant. Within the house are great oak staircases, well-

proportioned rooms and moulded ceilings in white plasterwork, of the late Elizabethan period. Collection of pictures and family portraits. River launches from Caversham Bridge, Reading (4m), when house is open, (charter bookings arranged for parties). Riverside picnic park open same days as house, noon to sunset. Open 6 Apr to 28 Sep Sat, Sun, BH 2.30–5.30. Admission prices under review. Party 20+ by arrangement weekends, Tue, Wed and Thu. Enquiries: Estate Office, Mapledurham House, Reading RG4 7TR. *(tel Kidmore End 3350)*. *(Mr J J Eyston)* & B

Mapledurham Watermill Last working corn and grist mill on the Thames. Wheel, gearing and stones restored and used for grinding wholemeal flour which can be purchased. Open 6 Apr to 28 Sep Sat, Sun and BH 2.30–5.30 also Tue, Wed and Thu 2–4.30. Party 20+ as Mapledurham House. Visit the Mill by river launch from Caversham Bridge, details from the Estate Office as above.

MARAZION *Cornwall* Map 2 SW52
St Michael's Mount Offshore in Mount's Bay, reached on foot over causeway, or by ferry during summer only. Well-situated island-castle, with 14th-C chapel and collection of armour, pictures, and furniture. Open Nov to 31 Mar Mon, Wed and Fri, guided tours at 11, 12, 2, 3 and 4; 1 Apr to end May Mon, Wed and Fri 10.30–5.45 (last admission 4.45); Jun to Oct, Mon to Wed and Fri, guided tours from 10.30–4.45; £1 (ch 50p) Mar to May special educational visits by prior arrangements, Tue only. *(Tel 710507)*. *(NT)*. *(NGS)*

MARGATE *Kent* Map 5 TR37
Salmestone Grange Nash Road. A restored Medieval Monastic Grange 14th-C with Monk's Kitchen and Crypt-cellar also 'Jewel' Chapel (1326) with stained-glass windows by the Australian John Trinick between 1949–59. Open Easter weekend and thereafter 1 May to 1 Sep Sat 2–5. 10p. Other times by appointment with the Warden. ⚠ *(Tel Thanet 21136)* &

Tudor House King Street. The oldest domestic building in Margate dating from early 16th C, displaying heavily moulded beams, and an enriched plaster ceiling in an excellent state of preservation. Housed here is a small local history museum including a fine collection of foreign sea shells. Open mid May to mid Sep, daily (ex Sun) 10–12.30, 2–4.30. Free. ⚠ *(Tel Thanet 25511 ext 333)*

MARKET BOSWORTH *Leicestershire* Map 4 SK40
Market Bosworth Light Railway 5m NW on unclass road at Shackerstone Station. Regular train service from Shackerstone to Market Bosworth, mainly steam operated. Extensive railway museum of small relics and collection of rolling stock on view. ⚏. Easter to Nov, Sun and BH, ⚠ Enquiries and bookings *(Tel Atherstone 3966)* &

MARKET DEEPING *Lincolnshire* Map 8 TF11
Rectory Dates from 13th to 14th C and is said to be oldest inhabited parsonage in country. Retains original hall, carved beams, and monks' dormitory. Possibly refectory of former Abbey. Open any day after 11am when residents are at home. 25p. ⚠ *(Tel 342237)*. *(Mrs Kathleen Davies)* & B

MARKET HARBOROUGH *Leicestershire* Map 4 SP79
Langton Hall 4½m NW at West Langton off B6047. Small English country house dating

from 15th and 16th C. Contains fine collection of Chinese furniture and ornaments, also interesting French and English pieces. Garden laid-out in French style. ⚏. Open Easter to Oct, Sat, Sun and BH 2–5. 75p (ch 14 and pen 40p), subject to review for 1980. ⚠ *(Tel East Langton 240 or 435)* & B

MARSTON *Lincolnshire* Map 8 SK94
Marston Hall Tudor manor house with early 18th-C interior containing pictures and furniture. Thorold family have held the estate since 14th C and church contains Thorold tombs. Garden with fine trees and gazebo decorated by Barbara Jones. Open on certain Sun in aid of local causes (times to be announced in local press) and at other times by appointment. ⚠ *(Tel Hannington 225).* (The Rev H Thorold) &

MARTIN MERE *Lancashire* Map 7 SD41
Wildfowl Trust W of A59 at Burscough Bridge station towards Mere Brow. Comprises a waterfowl garden, wild marsh and mere. The waterfowl garden covers some 40 acres, with pens, lakes and paddocks in which can be seen a large number of tame and flying wildfowl from all parts of the world. The wild marsh consists of 262 acres of wet land on which the habitat has been improved. Here many species of indigenous birds can be seen in their completely natural state, and here also 10–15,000 pink footed geese may settle during the winter months. The mere is a large man-made lake of about 20 acres. Both the wild marsh and the mere are viewable from hides. Also of interest is the main entrance building, the largest log cabin in Britain, constructed of Norwegian log with a grass roof, where the geese are free to graze. ⚏. Open all year, daily (ex 24, 25 Dec) 9.30–6.30, or 15 min after dusk (whichever is earlier). Last admission 1 hour before closing. 80p (ch 40p, pen 65p) Party 20+. ⚠ & *(Tel Burscough 895181)*

MARWELL *Hampshire* Map 4 SU52
Marwell Zoological Park Colden Common. Opened in May 1972, it is now established as one of Britain's major wild animal collections. In 100 acres of spacious enclosures, groups of rare animals thrive and breed. These include Siberian Tigers, leopards, snow-leopards, jaguars, lynx, cheetah, Asian lions and many species of deer, antelope, zebra, Przewalski wild horses, camels, giraffes, monkeys and many other species of mammals and birds. More than 1,000 animals from over 100 species. New exhibits constantly being added. Free children's zoo. ⚏. Picnic areas. Open all year daily 10–5.30 (or dusk). £1 (ch and pen 60p). Cars £1 extra if brought into park. ⚠ outside park. Party. Prices under revision for 1979. *(Tel Owslebury 206)* **(79)**

MARYPORT *Cumbria* Map 11 NY03
Maritime Museum Shipping Brow, 1 Senhouse Street. Maritime models and artifacts of all kinds. Photographic display illustrating Maryport's history. Open all year, 1 Jun to 30 Sep Mon to Sat 10–5 (closed 1–2 Tue and Thu), Sun 2–5; 1 Oct to 31 May Tue to Sat 10–12, 2–4, (closed Sun and Mon). Free. P. *(Tel 3738)*

MATLOCK *Derbyshire* Map 8 SK36
Riber Castle Fauna Reserve Castle dates from 1862, and fauna reserve of more than 20 acres on 853ft-high Riber Hill contains comprehensive collection of European birds and animals in near-natural surroundings. Breeding colonies of European Lynx. Kittens

can be seen Jun to Sep. Large collection of domestic poultry and rare breeds of bulls, sheep, pigs, cattle and goats. Models of prehistoric animals, model railway, vintage cars, children's playground. Butterfly exhibition. ⚏ (licensed) in season, picnic area. Open all year, daily (ex 25 Dec) 10–7 (4, in winter). 70p (ch and pen 35p, ch 5 free). Admission prices under revision for 1980. No dogs except in car park. ⚠ *(Tel 2073)* &

MATLOCK BATH *Derbyshire* Map 8 SK25
Peak District Mining Museum The Pavillion. The history of the Derbyshire lead industry. The museum illustrates the many facets of the industry including geology, lead mining and miners, lead smelting, mining and quarrying today, by means of static and moving display and an audio-visual programme. Also a unique early 19th-C water pressure pumping engine – the only one of its kind in the British Isles. Open all year (ex 25 Dec) 11–4 (longer in season). 60p (ch 16, pen and students 30p). P. *(Tel Matlock 3834)*

MAWNAN SMITH *Cornwall* Map 2 SW72
Glendurgan Beautifully situated gardens near Helford River inlet on road to Helford Passage. Walled garden and also maze. Open Mar to end Sep Mon and Wed (also Fri Apr to May) 10.30–4.30. 60p *(NT)*

MELBOURNE *Derbyshire* Map 8 SK32
Melbourne Hall 8m S of Derby. The Derbyshire home of the Marquess of Lothian. Lord Melbourne, the great Prime Minister lived here, and Lady Palmerston inherited it. The contents include an important collection of pictures and antique furniture. One of the most famous formal gardens in Britain. Garden produce on sale. Shop. ⚏. Open 5 Apr to 28 Sep, Apr, May, Jun and Sep, Wed, Thu and Sun 2–6. BH weekends Sat to Tue also 5 May and BH Mon 11–6. Jul and Aug, daily (ex Mon and Fri). Last admission 5pm. Party 30+. ⚠. For further information contact the Secretary, Tue, Thu and Fri mornings. *(Tel 2502)* & B

MELTON MOWBRAY *Leicestershire* Map 8 SK71
Melton Carnegie Museum Thorpe End. New museum illustrating past and present life of the area. Open all year (ex 4 Apr, 25, 26 Dec) Mon to Sat 10–5, Sun 2–5. *(Tel 69946)* &

MERSHAM *Kent* Map 5 TR03
Swanton Mill The restored mill won the 1975 European Architectural Heritage Year Award. Mill can be seen working, with flour on sale. Exhibition on top floor. Also water garden. ⚏. Open Apr to Oct, Sat and Sun 3–6. 30p (ch 14 20p). Under revision for 1980. *(Tel Aldington 223 or 01-937 0931)*

MEVAGISSEY *Cornwall* Map 2 SX04
Folk Museum East Quay. Occupying old boatbuilders' workshop dating from 1745, specialises in local crafts, seafaring, agricultural and mining items. Monthly exhibitions on loan from Plymouth Art Gallery. Open Easter to end of May from 1 Jun to end Sep from 10.30am. Admission prices not yet decided for 1980. P (limited) on quay. *(Tel 3568)*
Model Railway British, Continental and American models run through a realistic layout which features urban and rural areas, an Alpine ski resort with cablecars and a Cornish china clay pit with refining plant. Other models are on display together with information about the china clay industry. Model shop. Open end May to end Sep 11–5

(9pm during High Season); Oct to May, Sun only 2–5. 50p (ch 35p). Admission charges for 1980 not yet decided. P. *(Tel 2457)* &

MICKLETON *Gloucestershire* Map 4 SP14
Hidcote Manor ½m SE. 17th-C Cotswold house with fine formal gardens within various species of hedges. ♨ until end Sep. Gardens only open Apr to end Oct, daily (ex Tue and Fri) 11–8 (no entry after 7pm, or 1 hour before sunset). £1.10. No dogs. *(NT)*
Kiftsgate Court Garden ½m S off A46, adjacent Hidcote NT garden. Magnificently situated house with fine views and trees. The garden has many unusal plants and shrubs, and an exceptional collection of old fashioned and specie roses including R Filipes Kiftsgate, the largest rose in England. Open 1 Apr to 30 Sep Wed, Thu and Sun including BH 2–6. 70p (ch 20p) ⚠ *(Tel 202)* *(Mrs D H Binny)*

MIDDLE CLAYDON *Buckinghamshire* Map 4 SP72
Claydon House Off A413. Entrance by North Drive only. Fine mid 18th-C west façade by Sir Thomas Robinson, notable rococo and Chinese interior decoration, state rooms with Lightfoot carvings, Joseph Rose ceiling in saloon, notable staircase, and Florence Nightingale bedroom, and museum. Concerts given there at times. Open Apr to end Oct, daily 2–6 (ex Mon, Fri and Tue following BH, but open BH Mon) 12.30–6. 90p *(Tel Steeple Claydon 349)*. *(NT)*

MIDDLEHAM *North Yorkshire* Map 7 SE18
Middleham Castle 12th-C former seat of the Nevilles, with two-storeyed keep standing within 13th-C curtain walls. Open, see inside front cover. 15p (ch 16 and pen 5p). ⚠ *(AM)*

MIDDLESBROUGH *Cleveland* Map 8 NZ42
Captain Cook Birthplace Museum 3m S on A172 at Stewart Park, Marton. Open Oct 1978 to mark the 250th anniversary of Cook's birth at Marton in 1728. Situated in spacious rolling parkland. Other attractions include an aviary of colourful parakeets including many rare breeds, a conservatory of tropical plants, and assorted animals and fowl in small paddocks. ♨. Open summer 10–6, winter 9–4. Free. *(Tel 311211)*

MIDHURST *West Sussex* Map 4 SU82
Cowdray Ruins Ruined mansion, built 1520 and burnt 1793, in which Queen Elizabeth I stayed in 1591. Three-storeyed gatehouse, hall and chapel are notable. Open most days. 10–dusk. 20p *(Tel 2215)* &

MILDENHALL *Suffolk* Map 5 TL77
Mildenhall Museum Market Place. The museum illustrates local archaeology, agricultural implements, local and natural history. Open all year, Wed, Sat and Sun 2.30–4.30. Free. P. *(Tel 712162)*

MILTON *Oxfordshire* Map 4 SU49
Milton Manor House 17th-C house with 18th-C wings and a walled garden. ♨ by arrangement. Open Easter then Sat, Sun and BH till 12 Oct, 2–6. 70p (ch 14 30p). Party. ⚠ *(Tel Abingdon 831287)*. *(Surgeon Capt and Mrs E J Mockler)* & B

MILTON ABBAS *Dorset* Map 3 ST80
Brewery Farm Museum A country museum housed in the building of the Old Brewery of Milton Abbas. Contains agricultural implements of the past, bygones and a collection of old photographs. Open all year daily dawn–dusk. 10p (ch 14 5p). ⚠ *(Tel 880221)* *(79)*

MILTON LILBOURNE *Wiltshire* Map 4 SU15
Milton Manor Gardens Gardens only open May to end Oct Wed 2–6. Free. ⚠ Antique business. *(Tel Pewsey 3344)*. *(Mrs Rupert Gentle)* &

MINEHEAD *Somerset* Map 3 SS94
West Somerset Railway Steam and railcar trains run to various points Minehead, Watchet and Bishops Lydeard. Souvenir shops at many stations. ♨ at Minehead. Services all year. Steam trains in summer months. Return tickets range from 90p to £2.50 (reductions for families, parties, ch and pen). Special coach link between Taunton (town centre or railway station) and Bishops Lydeard provided on Sats. ⚠ *(Tel 4996)* & (24hr min notice)

MINIONS *Cornwall* Map 2 SX27
Hurlers Stone Circle Off B3254. Line of three prehistoric stone circles with large round barrow nearby. Accessible at any reasonable time. Free. *(AM)*

MINSTEAD *Hampshire* Map 4 SU21
Furzey Gardens Eight acres peaceful glades with winter and summer heathers, flowering trees and shrubs, many of which are rare, spring bulbs. Of botanical interest throughout the year. Also ancient cottage (1560) now restored, with art and craft gallery, where the crafts of 50 artists and 100 local craftsmen are displayed. Open all year daily 10–7 (dusk in winter). Gardens, cottage and gallery 50p (ch 5–14 20p), Mar to Oct; 30p (ch 5–14 10p), Nov to Feb. Admission prices for 1980 not yet decided. Party 30+. ⚠ *(Tel Cadnam 2464)*. *(Mr H J Cole)*. *(NGS)* & B

MINSTER-IN-THANET *Kent* Map 5 TR36
Minster Abbey One of the oldest inhabited
houses in Kent with some 11th-C work. Now
home of religious order. Gift shop. Open all
year daily (ex Sun) 11 – 12, also 1 May to 1
Oct, Mon to Fri 2 – 4.30, Sat 3.30 – 5. ⚠ ⚲

MINSTER LOVELL *Oxfordshire* Map 4 SP31
Minster Lovell Hall Ruined 15th-C structure
associated with two strange legends
including the Mistletoe Bough Chest.
Accessible any reasonable time. Free. ⚠
(AM)

MINTERNE MAGNA *Dorset* Map 3 ST60
Minterne House 10m N of Dorchester. Large
shrub garden set in a beautiful valley. Many
varieties of Himalayan and Chinese
rhododendrons, magnolias, azaleas and rare
trees. Open Sun and BH in Apr, May and Jun,
also by appointment for parties on weekdays.
2 – 7. 40p. ⚠ *(Tel Cerne Abbas 370). (Lord
Digby)*

MISTLEY *Essex* Map 5 TM13
Mistley Towers Twin, square porticoed
towers, remaining features of church erected
originally by Robert Adam *c* 1776. Of hall,
built about the same time, only Adam lodges
of 1782 still stand. Towers accessible all
reasonable times. Free. *(AM)*

MONTACUTE *Somerset* Map 3 ST41
Montacute House Elizabethan house, built
1588 – 1601, from Ham Hill stone by Edward
Phelips. Fine old glass, and panelling.
Permanent collection of Tudor and Jacobean
portraits from the National Portrait Gallery, on
view in Long Gallery. Shop, information
rooms. ⚲ Apr to Sep. Open Apr to Oct, daily
(ex Tue) 12.30 – 6, last admission to house
5.30. Party by written appointment with the
Administrator. £1.20 (ch 60p). Dogs in car
park only. *(Tel Martock 3289). (NT)*

MORDIFORD *Hereford & Worcester*
Map 3 SO53
Sufton Court Small Paladian mansion
designed by James Wyatt. Completed *c* 1780.
Exquisite mouldings, fireplaces and doors.
Antique china, lace, embroideries and water-
colours. Park and grounds by Humphrey
Repton. ⚲ (home-made teas usually
available, advisable to book 75p). Open 1
May to 30 Sep Sun only and BH Mon
2.30 – 5.30. 50p (ch half price). ⚠ *(Tel Holme
Lacy 268)* ⚲ B

MORECAMBE *Lancashire* Map 7 SD46
Marineland Oceanarium and Aquarium
Stone Jetty, Promenade. During the summer
season there are several dolphin and sea lion
shows daily. On show a unique display of
mink, also penguins, turtles, aligators.

Tropical, fresh and marine fish, cold water,
fresh and marine fish. Open summer daily
10.30 am. Winter months; Europe's No. 1
Aquarium only, open weekends only 11 – 4.
Admission prices for 1979 not yet decided.
(Tel 414727) **(79)**

MORETON CORBET *Salop* Map 7 SJ52
Castle Triangular group comprising keep of
c 1200, gatehouse altered in 1579, and
notable Elizabethan range of the same date,
the work of Sir Andrew Corbet, all damaged
by Parliamentary forces in 1644. Open, see
inside front cover. Free. ⚠ *(AM)*

MORVAH *Cornwall* Map 2 SW43
Lanyon Quoit 4m NW of Penzance, off
B3306. In field to right of unclassified road
beyond Madron. Famous Neolithic sepulchral
monument, comprising large granite
capstone balanced on three upright stones.
Re-erected during the 19th C. Accessible
regularly. Free. *(NT)*

MORWELLHAM *Devon* Map 2 SX46
Morwellham Open-air Museum Off A390
between Tavistock and Gunnislake. A
riverside tramway going underground into an
ancient copper mine is only one of the many
attractions of Morwellham, once the 'Greatest
Copper Port in Queen Victoria's Empire'.
Unspoilt country, riverside and woodland
trails, slide shows and other exhibits will help
you to discover 1,000 years of history. A truly
fascinating experience. Open all year, daily
10 – 6 (dusk in winter). £1.10 (ch 55p). Party.
Under revision for 1980. ⚠ *(Tel Gunnislake
832766)*

MOSELEY *Staffordshire* Map 7 SJ90
Moseley Old Hall Built in Elizabethan times
as half-timbered house, now encased in 19th-
C brick, with interesting panelled rooms. Was
the refuge (hiding hole and bed) of Charles II
after Battle of Worcester in 1651. Open Mar to
Oct, Wed, Thu, Sat, Sun, BH Mon and Tue
2 – 5.30 (or sunset), Nov, Wed and Sun
2 – 5.30. 70p. No dogs. *(NT)*

MOTTISFONT *Hampshire* Map 4 SU32
Mottisfont Abbey Mainly 18th-C mansion with portions of former 12th-C priory. Fine Rex Whistler paintings in drawing room. Walled rose garden. Open Apr to end Sep, grounds daily (ex Sun and Mon) 2.30–6. House (Whistler Room and Cellarium) Wed and Sat 2.30–6. 80p; grounds only 60p. *(NT)*

MOULTON *North Yorkshire* Map 8 NZ20
Moulton hall Manor house rebuilt c1650. Fine example of carved wood staircase. Open only by appointment in writing from tenant, Hon J D Eccles. Free. *(NT)*

MUCHELNEY *Somerset* Map 3 ST42
Muchelney Abbey 15th- to 16th-C remains of Benedictine Abbey. Open, see inside front cover. 15p (ch 16 and pen 5p). ⚠ *(AM)*

MUCH WENLOCK *Salop* Map 7 SO69
Guildhall Striking half-timbered building dating from 1577, with beautiful oak panelling and furnishings. Open 1 Apr to 30 Sep, Mon, Tue and Thu to Sat 11–12.30 and 2.30–5, Wed 3–5, Sun 2–6, BH 10.30–12.30, 2.30–4.30, and 6–8. 20p (ch 16 10p). Party. P. *(Tel 727509)*
Much Wenlock Museum An interpretation of the history of the town and priory, including displays of geology, local natural history, costume and local trades, housed in the old Market hall. Regular special exhibitions and demonstrations. Comprehensive book stand. Open 20 Mar to 1 Oct, Mon to Sat, 11–12.30 and 2–5, Sun 2–6. 15p (ch 5p). Under revision for 1980. P. *(Tel 727773)* &
Wenlock Priory Remains of 13th-C abbey adjacent to chapter house, lavabo, and transepts. Only abbey ruins are open, see inside front cover. 20p (ch 16 and pen 5p). ⚠ *(AM)*

MULLION *Cornwall* Map 2 SW61
Marconi Memorial Erected in 1937 by Marconi Company to commemorate first morse signal sent across Atlantic in 1901 and received by Marconi himself in Newfoundland. Short-wave beam system was successfully tested here for first time in 1923. Accessible regularly. *(NT)*

MUNCASTER *Cumbria* Map 6 SD19
Muncaster Castle and Bird Garden Seat of Pennington since 13th C. Famous collection of rhododendrons, azaleas, etc, ornamental and tropical birds, bear garden with Himalayan bears, flamingo pool, garden centre. Collection of 16th- and 17th-C furniture, pictures, and embroideries. 𝒯 gift shop. Nature Trail. Open from Easter weekend for 1980 season. Grounds daily (ex Fri) 12–5, Castle Tue, Wed, Thu and Sun 2–5, Castle Tue, Wed, Thu and Sun 2–5. Admission prices not yet known. ⚠ *(Tel Ravenglass 614)*. *(Sir W Pennington-Ramsden)* &
Muncaster Mill 1m NW on A595 by railway bridge. The mill race brings water from the River Mite ½m to the 13ft overshot water wheel. Milling Room contains three pairs of mill stones, two elevators, flour separators, and sackhoist, all water driven. Newly opened Fish Farm. Flour milled on premises for sale. Open Easter to end Sep, daily (ex Sat) 11–6. 20p (ch 10p). Under revision for 1980.

MUNDESLEY *Norfolk* Map 9 TG33
Stow Mill Built in 1780 and in use for grinding corn until about 1920. At one time converted to residential use, but eventually restored in 1961. Open May to Sep. Free. P. *(Tel 720298)*

NANTWICH *Cheshire* Map 7 SJ65
Dorfold Hall 1m W, off A51. Attractive gabled house, dating from 1616, with fine panelling, plaster ceilings, and furniture. Open Apr to Oct Tue only, also BH Mon, at other times by appointment. 2–5. 50p (ch 16 25p). ⚠ *(Tel 65245)*
Churche's Mansion Hospital Street. An H-plan half-timbered mansion built in 1577 for Rychard and Margerye Churche. Restoration commenced in 1930 and continues to reveal the original fabric. 𝒯 Licensed. Open Apr to Oct 10–5.30. 25p (ch 16 20p). ⚠ *(Tel 65933)*

NASEBY *Northamptonshire* Map 4 SP67
Naseby Battle and Farm Museum Purlieu Farm. Contains miniature layout of Battlefield with commentary and relics from the field, village history, farm hand tools and machinery. Vintage Tractors. Open Easter to Sep, Sat and Sun 2–6. 35p (ch 16 20p) ⚠ *(Tel Northampton 740241)*

NETHER ALDERLEY *Cheshire* Map 7 SJ87
Alderley Old Mill 15th-C mill, last worked in 1939. Preserves wooden waterwheels and machinery. Open Apr, May, Jun and Oct, Wed, Sun 2–5.30. Jul–Sep, daily ex Mon but open BH Mon 2–5.30. 50p *(NT)*

NETHER STOWEY *Somerset* Map 3 ST13
Coleridge Cottage Home of Samuel Taylor Coleridge from 1897 to 1800. *The Ancient Mariner* was written here. Open Apr to end Sep, Sun to Thu 2–5. 30p. Parties by arrangement with caretaker, Mrs MacDermaid *(Tel 662)*. *(NT)*

NETHER WINCHENDON *Buckinghamshire* Map 4 SP71
Nether Winchendon House Medieval house with Elizabethan and Georgian additions, containing portraits and maps belonging to Sir Francis Bernard, Governor of Massachusetts. Open Thu 2–6; Spring and Summer BH 2–5.30. Parties 10+ by written appointment May to Aug. £1 (ch 12 and pen 50p). P. *(Tel Hadenham 290101)*. *(Mrs J G C Spencer Bernard)* & B

NETLEY *Hampshire* Map 4 SU40
Netley Abbey Extensive and beautiful remains of a Cistercian abbey founded in 1239. Open, see inside front cover. 15p (ch 16 and pen 5p). ⚠ *(AM)*

NETTLECOMBE COURT *Somerset* Map 3 ST03
Elizabethan and Georgian house, the ancestral home of the Raleigh and Trevelyan families. Two Adam-type drawing rooms. Open for viewing Mar to Oct Thu, by appointment. 25p to 50p. ⚠ *(Tel Washford 320)*. Houses the Leonard Wills Field Centre operated by the Field Studies Council open Feb to Nov. One week residential courses on various topics connected with the countryside are available. Programme of courses available (free) from warden.

NEWARK-ON-TRENT *Nottinghamshire* Map 8 SK85
Newark District Council Museum Local history, archaeology, natural history, and art. Open all year Mon to Sat 10–1 and 2–5 (closed Thu afternoons). Sun 2–5 (Apr to Sep only). Free. P *(Tel 702358)*

NEWBURGH PRIORY *North Yorkshire* Map 8 SE57
Originally an Augustinian Priory with 17th- and 18th-C additions. Wild water garden. 𝒯 Open 10 May to 13 Sep, Wed 2–5.30, other days for parties by arrangement. 40p (ch 20p), grounds only 15p (ch 5p). ⚠ No coaches up 200yd drive.

NEWBURY *Berkshire* Map 4 SU46
The Museum (Old Cloth Hall) Wharf St.
Restored timbered and plastered building,
with fine Jacobean woodwork. Now
interesting museum with prehistoric finds and
Civil War relics. Natural history section.
Camera collection, temporary exhibitions.
Open all year, weekdays (ex Wed afternoon
and BH) 10–12.30 and 1.30–5 (4, Oct to
Mar). Free. No dogs. ⚠ *(Tel 30511)* ⓑ B

NEWBY HALL AND GARDENS *North
Yorkshire* Map 8 SE36
Late 17th-C house with additions and interior
by Robert Adam. Contains important
collection of classical sculpture and Gobelin
tapestries. Gardens cover 25 acres and
includes a miniature railway. ⚏ Opening
dates, times and admission charges for 1979
not yet decided. ⚠ *(Tel Boroughbridge
2583)*. *(R E J Compton Esq)* ⓑ **(79)**

NEWCASTLE-UNDER-LYME *Staffordshire*
Map 7 SJ84
Borough Museum Brampton Park. Local
history, including Royal Charters, ceramics,
natural history, dolls and display of firearms.
Open all year Mon to Sat 9.30–1 and 2–6
(5.30 Sat), May to Sep, Sun also 2–5.30.
Free. ⚠ *(Tel 619705)*
Hobbergate Art Gallery The Brampton
Permanent collection of 18th- and 19th-C
English water-colours. Travelling exhibitions
and picture loan scheme. Open all year Tue to
Sat 9.30–1, 2–6. ⚠ *(Tel 611962)*

NEWCASTLE UPON TYNE *Tyne and Wear*
Map 12 NZ26
Bagpipe Museum Black Gate, St Nicholas
Street. Presented by Mr William Cocks of
Ryton, Co Durham, to city's Society of
Antiquaries. Among over 100 sets are
English, Scottish, Irish, European, and
Egyptian pipes, and an English Shepherd's
pipe (♮690) which may be unique. Other
exhibits include old recordings, music and
transcripts. Open all year Wed to Sat 12–4.
15p (ch 5p). P (meters). *(Tel 27938)*
Hancock Museum Barras Bridge. One of
finest natural history museums in England.
Other collections include geological
specimens, insects, birds and Bewick
drawings. Open all year (ex 4 Apr, 25, 26 Dec,
1 Jan) Mon to Sat 10–5, Sun (from 2 Apr to 24
Sep) 2–5. 20p (ch 10p). P. *(Tel 22359)*
Museum of Antiquities University
Quadrangle. The collection has been in
course of assembly since 1813, and was
opened in its present form in 1960. Valuable
collection of Roman and other antiquities,
with models, reconstructions, etc. Open all

year (ex 4 Apr, 24–26 Dec, and 1 Jan),
weekdays 10–5. Free. P (consult University
police). *(Tel 28511 ext 3844/3849)* ⓑ
Science Museum Exhibition Park.
Develoment of mining, shipbuilding,
engineering in the North East. Models of
locally built ships, collieries and their
equipment, etc. Extensive electrical
engineering collections. One of Stephenson's
earliest locomotives is preserved, and also
steam yacht 'Turbinia' (1894), pioneer turbine
propelled ship. ⚏ in park open during
summer months. Open all year (ex 13 Apr, 25,
26 Dec, 1 Jan) 1 Apr to 30 Sep Mon to Sat
10–6, Sun 2–5, 1 Oct–31 Mar Mon–Sat
10–4.30, Sun 1.30–4.30. Free. P. *(Tel
815129)* (79)

NEWCHAPEL *Surrey* Map 5 TQ34
*Mormon Temple Visitors Centre and
Gardens* Pictures, films, genealogy
assistance. Beautiful gardens. Open all year,
daily 10–dusk. Free. ⚠ *(Tel Lingfield
833842)* ⓑ

NEWENT *Gloucestershire* Map 3 SO72
*The Birds of Prey Conservation and
Falconry Centre* Leave Newent by Cliffords
Mesne Road. At foot of May Hill, has wide
variety of trained birds and an interesting
museum. Of special interest are Hawk Walk,
aviaries, and falcon flying ground. Courses in
falconry are held. Also displays and flying
demonstrations. ⚏ Open Feb to end Nov,
daily (ex Tue) 10.30–5.30 (or dusk); Guided
tours and reduced fees for parties of 25 or
more. Schools especially welcome. 80p (ch
14 35p), prices subject to alteration and VAT.
⚠ *(Tel 820286)* ⓑ

NEWPORT *Essex* Map 5 TL53
Mole Hall Wildlife Park Widdington. Partly
Elizabethan, with moat crossed by four
bridges. Wildlife Park dates from 1948 and
was opened to the public 16 years later. Large
collection of animals and birds in pools and
enclosures can be seen. Picnic area. Open all
year (ex 25 Dec) daily 10.30–6. Admission
charges for 1980 not yet decided. Party. ⚠
(Tel Saffron Walden 40400) ⓑ

NEWQUAY *Cornwall* Map 2 SW86
Newquay Zoo Trenance Park, on A3075. In
over 8 acres of landscape grounds, laid out in
1969, is a fine selection of wild animals,
tropical birds in a walk-through aviary, wild
fowl, large walking birds, reptiles, seals and
pengiun pools, pets' corner and pony rides.
Gift shop and ⚏. Open all year. 65p (ch and
pen 32p, ch 4 free). Opening times and prices
under revision for 1980. ⚠ *(Tel 3342)* ⓑ

NEW ROMNEY *Kent* Map 5 TR02
Romney, Hythe and Dymchurch Railway
Depot of 13½-mile long Romney, Hythe and
Dymchurch railway, the world's smallest
public railway from Hythe through New
Romney to Dungeness. ℒ at new Romney
and Dungeness stations. Open daily Easter to
end Sep, also weekends in Mar, Oct and Nov.
For times apply for timetable to *The Manager,
Romney, Hythe and Dymchurch Light
Railway Co, New Romney Station, New
Romney, Kent*. Also engine shed and very
large model railway exhibition. Open
whenever train service operates. Admission
prices dependent on journey (ch half price).
⚠ 12p. *(Tel 2353)* ⅄ B

NEWSTEAD *Nottinghamshire* Map 8 SK55
Newstead Abbey Former Priory, founded in
12th C, rebuilt as a house in the 16th and 17th
C, famous for its associations with Lord
Byron, who lived here, including pictures and
furniture. ℒ (summer only). Open 13 Apr to
30 Sep 2–6 (6.30 Sun and BH), conducted
tours on weekdays at 2, 3, 4, and 5, garden
open daily, all year (ex 25 Dec) 10–dusk.
Admission to grounds and garden 35p (ch
12p and pen 5p), coach parties 12p per person.
Additional charge for abbey tour 20p (ch and
pen 5p), coach parties 12p per person. ⚠ *(Tel
Blidworth 2822)* **(79)**

NEWTIMBER *West Sussex* Map 4 TQ21
Newtimber Place Moated 17th- to 18th-C
house with Etruscan-style decorations.
House and gardens open May, Jun, Jul, and
Aug, Thu 2–5. 50p (ch 25p). ⚠ *(Tel
Hurstpierpoint 833104). (His Honour Judge
and Mrs John Clay)*

NEWTON ABBOT *Devon* Map 3 SX87
Bradley Manor In deep valley of River
Lemon, 15th-C house with a fine hall and
chapel. Open 9 Apr to Sep, Wed 2 – 5. 60p. *(NT)*
*New Devon Pottery and Devon
Leathercrafts* Forde Road. Interesting tour to
see pottery and leather manufacture can be
made with guides. Picnic area available. ⚲
Open Easter to Oct, Mon to Fri 9.30 – 12 and
1.30 – 5 (last tours 12 and 4.30). Frequent
tours. 40p, joint ticket to visit both factories
50p (accompanied ch 14 free). Party 25+ 35p
single, 45p joint ticket. Reduction for pen to
end of May and all Oct. ⚠ *(Tel 4262)* ⅙ *(79)*
NORFOLK WILDLIFE PARK Norfolk
Map 9 TG11
Zoological park of 50 acres, with
comprehensive collection of British and
European mammals in natural surroundings.
Great variety of birds in specially built
aviaries. Rare ornamental pheasant Trust.
The world's largest European collection. ⚲
(licensed). Open all year, daily 10.30 – 6. £1
(ch 18 50p). Subject to alteration. ⚠ *(Tel
Great Witchingham 274)*. *(Mr Philip Wayre,
Naturalist)* ⅙
NORHAM *Northumberland* Map 12 NT94
Castle Mid 12th-C keep, built by Bishop Hugh
Puiset, with later alterations, and overlooking
River Tweed. Open, see inside front cover.
15p (ch 16 and pen 5p). *(AM)*
NORTHAMPTON *Northamptonshire*
Map 4 SP76
Abington Park Landscaped park,
ornamental gardens and collection of
ornamental and game birds. Seasonal games
facilities including bowls and pitch-and-putt.
Venue of Northampton Show third weekend
in Jul. Within park stands 15th- to 18th-C
house, now a museum. ⚲ (Apr to Oct). Open
all year (ex Sun, Oct to Mar; 24 – 26 Dec),
weekdays 10 – 12.30, and 2 – 6, Sun 2.30 – 5.
Free. P (street). *(Tel 31454)* ⅙ B
Central Museum and Art Gallery Guildhall
Road. Archaeological and geological
exhibits, as well as collections of footwear and
ceramics. Iron age discoveries from nearby
Hunsbury Hill camp are also on display. Open
weekdays 10 – 6 (closed Sun, 4 Apr, 24, 25,
26 Dec). Free. P. *(Tel 34881 ext 391)* ⅙ B
Delapre Abbey 16th- to 19th-C house, with
fine porch, built on site of Cluniac nunnery.
Contains Northamptonshire Record Office
and HQ of Northamptonshire Record Society.
Abbey grounds open all year Oct to Apr,
2.30 – 4.30; May to Sep 2.30 – 6. Wall garden,
open May to Sep only during daylight. Certain
parts of the interior shown Thu afternoon
2.30 – 4.30, Oct to Apr; 2.30 – 5, May to Sep.
Free. ⚠ ⅙

Eleanor Cross Hardingstone (on southern
outskirts of the city). One of the crosses
erected by Edward I in memory of his dead
Queen Eleanor on her last journey to
Westminster Abbey. Commenced in 1291,
this cross is octagonal in design. Located on
side of road, easily accessible at all times.
NORTHBOROUGH *Cambridgeshire*
Map 4 TF10
Northborough Castle One of the finest
medieval houses in England, built in 1330 by
William de Eyton. Great Hall with original
timbered roof, beautiful windows and stone
carved doorways, also Lady Claypole's
Room, the Solar and Cromwell's Room.
James Claypole was a friend of William Penn
and a signatory of the first Charter of Liberties
to Pennsylvania. David Claypole, of the firm
Dunlap and Claypole, printed the Declaration
of Independence, 1776. Open 1 May to 1 Oct,
Sun 2 – 6. 20p (ch 5p). ⚠
NORTH CREAKE *Norfolk* Map 9 TF83
Creake Abbey 1 m N off B1355. Ruins of the
crossing and eastern arm of the church of a
house of Augustinian canons founded in
1206. Accessible any reasonable time. Free.
(AM)
NORTHIAM *East Sussex* Map 5 TQ82
Brickwall ½ m S. Three-gabled, half-timbered
Jacobean house, now a school, dating from
1617 and 1632 with Victorian alterations and
additions. 17th-C stucco ceiling to be seen in
drawing room (only part of house open to
public). Open 30 Apr to 21 May and 4 Jun to 9
Jul, inclusive, Wed and Sat only 2 – 4. 30p. ⚠
Great Dixter 15th-C half-timbered house with
notable great hall, and fine gardens. Picnics.
Open 1 Apr to 12 Oct also 18/19 and 25/16
Oct. Tue to Sun and BH Mon 2 – 5; other times
by appointment. £1 (ch 14 30p). Gardens only
50p (ch 15p). Prices are provisional for 1980.
No dogs. ⚠ *(Tel 3160)*. *(Mr Quentin Lloyd)* ⅙
B

NORTH LEIGH *Oxfordshire* Map 4 SP31
North Leigh Roman Villa Excavations of
Roman villa occupied between 2nd and 4th C
and reconstructed late in period. Tessellated
pavement and 2 – 3ft high wall span. Open,
see inside front cover. Free. ⚠ *(AM)*
NORTH LEVERTON *Nottinghamshire*
Map 8 SK78
Windmill ½ m W of village in minor road. In
1813 the local farming community set up a
committee to build the four-sailed tower mill
which has been in use ever since. Steam
threshing tackle. Open Sun and BH 2 – 5,
other times by appointment. 10p (ch 5p, ch 5
free). ⚠ *(Tel Sturton le Steeple 200)* ⅙ *(79)*

GREAT DIXTER
Northiam, East Sussex (A28)

This fascinating timber hall house, built
in 1450, contains important antiques and
18th-20th century needlework.
Restorations, in 1912, were by Sir Edwin
Lutyens who designed the surrounding
gardens containing a wide variety of
unusual plants.

For admission please refer to the
gazetteer entry.

NORTHWICH *Cheshire* Map 7 SJ67
Vale Royal Abbey constructed around the
Monastery of 1277, which survives the Abbey
of the same date. Now under restoration and
partly in use as a Special Education Centre.
Beautiful beech-lined drive approach from the
south. Gardens available for picnics on
request. Open Apr to Sep, Sun 2 – 5. 50p (ch
16 20p). ⚠ 25p. *(Tel Sandiway 882777)*
Weaver Hall London Road. A permanent
exhibition on salt in Cheshire is on show at the
Headquarters of the County Museum
Service, together with a programme of
temporary exhibitions. Open all year (ex
Easter and all Mon also Tue following a BH,
25/26 Dec and 1 Jan) Tue to Sat 10 – 12, 1 – 5.
Sun 2 – 5. Free. Under revision for 1980. ⚠
(Tel 41331/2)

NORTH WOOTTON *Somerset* Map 3 ST54
Wootton Vines North Town House. A
vineyard, set in the foothills of the Mendips,
3m from Wells, with 8,500 vines specially
imported from the Rhine and Alsace. The old
farm buildings house a winery where fresh dry
white wine is made. Visitors can walk in the
vineyards and wines may be purchased direct
from the cellar. Open all year, 2 – 5 (closed
Tue). ⚠ *(Tel Pilton 359)*

NORWICH *Norfolk* Map 5 TG20
Bridewell Bridewell Alley. Flint-faced late
14th-C merchant house, used as a prison
from 1583 to 1828. Now interesting museum
of local crafts and industries. Open all year (ex
4 Apr, 25, 26 Dec, 1 Jan) weekdays 10 – 5.
Free.
Norwich Castle Castle Meadow. Restored
12th-C keep with walls refaced 1834 to 1839,
now museum. ⚤ (licensed). Conducted tours
of dungeons and battlements (fee payable).
Open all year (ex 4 Apr, 25, 26 Dec, 1 Jan)
weekdays 10 – 5, Sun 2 – 5. 45p (28 May to
Sep) other times 20p (ch and pen always
free). ⚠ &
City Hall St Peter Street. Opened 1938. On
display are the Civic Plate and Insignia dating
from 1549 and the Council Chamber. Open all
year Mon to Fri 10 – 4, parties by arrangement
with the *Director of Administration*. Free. P.
(Tel 22233 ext 743) &
Royal Norfolk Regiment Museum Brittania
Barracks, Brittannia Road. Contains a fine
collection of medals, uniforms and weapons,
paintings, silver and trophies amassed by the
Regiment from 1685 – 1959. There is also an
excellent library containing books on many
military subjects. Open all year (ex Sat, Sun
and BH) 9 – 12.30, 2 – 4.30. Free. ⚠ *(Tel
28455)*
Sainsbury Centre for Visual Arts University
of East Anglia. Now houses Sir Robert and
Lady Sainsbury's private art collection which
was given to the University in 1973. The
collection is indexed under the following
headings: European Art 19th and 20th C;
African Tribal Sculpture; Oceanic Traditional
Sculpture; North American Indian and Eskimo
Art; Middle and South American
Precolumbian Art; Oriental Antiquities;
Egyptian and Western Asiatic Antiquities;
European Antiquities Medieval and later.
Varying other exhibitions during the year. ⚤
(restaurant). Open all year Tue to Sun 12 – 5
(closed Mon). 25p ⚠ *(Tel 56060)* &
St Peter Hungate Church Museum Princes
Street, near Elm Hill. Fine church (1460), with
hammer-beam roof and good Norwich
painted glass, now museum of church art and
antiquities. Open all year (ex 4 Apr, 25, 26
Dec, 1 Jan) weekdays 10 – 5, Free.
Strangers' Hall Charing Cross. Late

medieval merchants' house dating from 1320
and later, with furnished period rooms from
early Tudor to late Victorian. Open all year (ex
4 Apr, 25, 26 Dec, 1 Jan) weekdays only
10 – 5. 20p, 26 May to Sep (ch free), other
times free. *(Tel 22233 ext 645)*

NOSTELL *West Yorkshire* Map 8 SE41
Nostell Priory Mid 18th-C mansion, built by
Paine in 1733, with Adam wing of 1766,
pictures and Chippendale furnishings,
notable saloon and tapestry room, collection
of old motor cycles. Lake in grounds. ⚤ Open
Apr and Oct Wed, Sat, Sun 2 – 6, May to Sep
daily (ex Fri) 2 – 6, BH Sun, Mon and Tue
11 – 6. House, garden and grounds £1;
gardens and grounds only 50p. ⚠ *(NT)*

NOTTINGHAM *Nottinghamshire* Map 8 SK53
Brewhouse Yard Museum Castle
Boulevard. Housed in 17th-C buildings on a
historic site. The museum depicts daily life in
the City, with period rooms and thematic
displays on aspects of post medieval life in the
City. Unusual rock-cut cellars open showing
their uses in the past and recent history. This
museum contains material which can be
touched or operated by the public. Extensions
are planned for 1980. Open all year (ex
Christmas) 10 – 12 and 1 – 5. Free. *(Tel
411881 ext 67,48)* & B
Holme Pierrepont Hall 4m E of Nottingham
off A52 1m beyond the National Water Sports
Centre. Early brick Tudor manor house of
medieval design built around 1500 and
contains fine old timbering. Contents are
mostly 17th-C English oak furniture of
regional design. Victorian formal courtyard
garden. Jacob and Soay sheep. ⚤ for parties
by appointment. Open Apr and Sep Sun 2 – 6,
Jun, Jul and Aug Thu and Sun 2 – 6. Also 6 – 8
Apr, 26, 27 May, 25, 26 Aug 2 – 6. Parties
throughout the year by appointment. 50p (ch
25p). Admission prices under revision. ⚠ *(Tel
Radcliffe on Trent 2371)* &
Industrial Museum Courtyard Buildings,
Wollaton Park. Housed in 18th-C stable block
are displays illustrating Nottingham's
industrial history and in particular the lace and
hosiery industries, together with exhibits on
the pharmaceutical industry, engineering,
tobacco industry and printing. New
extensions house a mid 19th-C beam
pumping engine in steam last Sun in each
month and BH Mons, and heavy agricultural
machinery. Outside yards display a horse gin
from a local coalmine, Victorian street
furniture, etc. ⚤ in park (Apr to Sep). Open all
year Apr to Sep, Mon to Sat 10 – 7, Sun 2 – 5;
Oct to Mar, Thu and Sat 10 – 4.30; Sun
1.30 – 4.30. Free. P. *(Tel 284602)*
Museum of Costume and Textiles 43 – 51
Castlegate. Displays include costume from
1730 – 1885 in furnished room settings of *c*
1790, *c* 1830, and *c* 1855; other rooms of
17th-C costume and embroidery (the Lord
Middleton Collection), map tapestries of
Nottinghamshire, dress accessories from
18th-C to *c* 1960, English, European and
Asian embroidery, hand and machine made
lace; other rooms in preparation. Open all
year (ex 25 Dec) daily 10 – 5. Free. P. *(Tel
411881)* & B
Castle Museum Mainly 17th C, with much
restored late 13th-C gateway. New museum
and art gallery. Conducted tours through
underground passages. Open all year (ex 25
Dec) summer 10 – 5.45, winter 4.45. Grounds
open all year (ex 25 Dec) Mon to Fri 8 – dusk,
Sat, Sun, BH Mon 9 – dusk. Free, ex Sun, BH
10p. ⚤ Apr to Sep. P. *(Tel 411881)* & B

Natural History Museum Wollaton Hall. Housed in imposing Elizabethan mansion by Robert Smythson, dating from 1580–88, and situated in large park with deer. ⚏ Open all year (ex 25 Dec), weekdays 10–7 (5.30 Oct and Mar; 4.30 Nov to Feb); Sun, Mar to Oct 2–5; Nov to Feb 1.30–4.30. Free. ⚠ *(Tel 281333)*

NUNEATON *Warwickshire* Map 4 SP39
Nuneaton Museum and Art Gallery
Riversley Park. A purpose-built structure, situated in a pleasant public park. It houses a permanent collection of ethnography, archaeology, the George Eliot Collection, and a display of fine miniatures painted by May B Lee (Lady Stott). Changing art exhibitions. From Apr to Jun the Nuneaton Festival of Art is held here. Open all year (ex 4 Apr, 25 Dec), summer Mon to Fri 12–7, Sat Sun 10–7 (closes 5 in winter). Times may be subject to alteration. Free. P. *(Tel 382683)*

NUNEHAM COURTENAY *Oxfordshire*
Map 4 SU59
Nuneham House Thames-side Palladian villa (with additions by Brown and Smirke) in a picturesque setting created by 'Capability' Brown with a temple-church by 'Athenian' Stuart. State rooms unfurnished. Open 19, 20, 26–28 Aug, 2, 3 Sep 2–5.30. 40p (ch 20) Admission prices under review for 1979. ⚠ *(Tel Woodstock 811624)* & **(79)**

NUNNEY *Somerset* Map 3 ST74
Nunney Castle Moated structure modelled on French 'Bastille', built by Sir John de la Mere in 1373. Held for king during civil war and surrendered after siege in 1645. Surrounded by one of the deepest moats in England. Open, see inside front cover. Free. *(AM)*

NUNNINGTON *North Yorkshire* Map 8 SE67
Nunnington Hall 16th- to 17th-C house with panelled hall and staircase. Open Apr to end Sep, (ex 4 Apr) Wed to Sun and BH Mon 2–6. 60p *(NT)*

OAKHAM *Leicestershire* Map 4 SK80
Oakham Castle Off Market Place. Preserves splendid Norman hall, with unique collection of presentation horseshoes. Open all year (ex 4 Apr, 25, 26 Dec) Apr to Oct, grounds daily 10–5.30; great hall, Sun and Mon 2–5.30, Tue to Sat and BH 10–1, 2–5.30; Nov to Mar as above but closes 4pm. Magistrates Court in session normally on Mondays. Free. P. *(Tel 3654)* &
Rutland County Museum Catmos Street. Local archaeology, especially Roman and Anglo-Saxon, craft tools, local history,

Victorian shop. Court yard contains farm wagons and agricultural implements. Open all year (ex 4 Apr and 25, 26 Dec) Apr to Oct, Tue to Sat 10–1 and 2–5, Sun 2–5; Nov to Mar, Tue to Sat 10–1 and 2–5. Mon all year by arrangement. Free. P. *(Tel 3654)* & B

OAKHILL *Somerset* Map 3 ST64
The World of Models at Oakhill Manor
Entrance by 'Mendip Inn' on A37 A country estate of 45 acres situated high in the Mendip Hills. The mansion is a fine example of one of England's smaller country houses set in eight acres of delightful gardens. Features one of the world's finest collections of models relating to transport, displayed in a furnished setting. Visitors are transported from the car park on a miniature railway which covers ¾ mile with views of the surrounding hills. ⚏ Open 12 Apr to 31 Oct, 12–6. Admission charges for 1980 not yet decided. ⚠ *(Tel 840210)* & B

OAKWELL HALL *West Yorkshire*
Map 8 SE22
In Nova Lane, near Birstall Smithies. Elizabethan moated manor house (1583), with Civil War and Brontë connections. It was 'Fieldhead' of Charlotte Brontë's novel *Shirley*. Open Apr to Oct, Tue to Sat 10–6, Sun 1–5; Nov to Mar, Tue to Sat 10–5. Free. ⚠

OKEHAMPTON *Devon* Map 2 SX59
Okehampton Castle ½m S in Castle Lane. Chapel, keep, and hall dating from 11th to 14th C on northern fringe of Dartmoor National Park. Open*, see inside front cover. 15p (ch and pen 5p). ⚠ *(AM)*

OLD WHITTINGTON *Derbyshire*
Map 8 SK37
Revolution House Old house, once known as Cock and Pynot (or Magpie) Inn, with 17th-C furnishings. Associated with 1688 revolution. Open 13 Apr to 30 Sep, daily 11–12.30, 2–5 and 6–dusk. Opening times under revision for 1980. Free. ⚠ *(Tel Chesterfield 32088)* &

OLNEY *Buckinghamshire* Map 4 SP85
Cowper and Newton Museum House where William Cowper lived from 1768 to 1786, now containing manuscripts of letters and poems, together with many personal possessions. Two small gardens open to visitors to the museum. Open Easter to Oct, Tue to Sat 10–12 and 2–5; Nov to Easter, 2.30–4.30; other times by prior arrangement with Curator. 35p (ch and pen 25p, ch 5 free). Party 10+ *(Tel Bedford 711516)*

ORFORD *Suffolk* Map 5 TM44
Orford Castle On B1084. Castle with three towers, incorporating remarkable 18-sided keep, built by Henry II, c1165. Open, see inside front cover. 20p (ch and pen 5p). ⚑ *(AM)*

ORMESBY *Cleveland* Map 8 NZ51
Ormesby Hall 18th-C mansion, with stables attributed to John Carr of York. Plasterwork, furniture, and 18th-C pictures. Open Apr to end Oct, Wed, Sun and BH Mon 2–6. 60p *(NT)*

ORPINGTON *Gt London* Map 5 TQ46
Priory Museum Church Hill. 13th- to 14th-C clergy house with addition of 15th-C manor house. Now small museum of local interest, and special exhibitions are held during year: Open all year weekdays (ex Thu and Sun) 9–5.30, Sat 9–5. Free. ⚑ *(Tel 31551)* ბ

OSMOTHERLEY *North Yorkshire* Map 8 SE49
Mount Grace Priory 1m NW. Ruined 14th-C Carthusian Priory, neighboured by 17th-C house. Priory open, see inside front cover. 20p (ch 5p). ⚑ *(AM and NT)*

OSWESTRY *Salop* Map 7 SJ23
Old Oswestry ½m N. Iron age hill-fort, covering 68 acres, with five ramparts and elaborate western portal. Abutted by part of prehistoric Wat's Dyke. Accessible any reasonable time. Free. *(AM)*

OTTERTON *Devon* Map 3 SY08
Otterton Mill A Devon cornmill, mentioned in the Domesday Book, making wholemeal flour by water power. Gallery with a series of exhibitions through the summer. Furniture making, wood turning, pottery, glass engraving, leatherwork and lace-making in our workshops. Shop and ⏲ Open Easter to end Sep, daily, 2–5.30. Workshops and flour shop all the year. Party. ⚑ *(Tel Colaton Raleigh 68521)*

OTTERY ST MARY *Devon* Map 3 SY19
Cadhay ½m from Fairmile, near junction of A30 and B3167. Beautiful and historic house, built 1550. Open 25 and 26 May, then 16 Jul to 28 Aug, Wed and Thu, also 24 and 25 Aug, 2–6. 50p (ch 14 25p). Party. ⚑ *(Tel Ottery St Mary 2432). (Lady William-Powlett)* ბ B

OUTWOOD *Surrey* Map 4 TQ34
Old Mill Fine example of post-mill dating from 1665, oldest working mill in England, one of best-preserved in existence. The former smock mill nearby collapsed in 1960. Open 2 Apr to 29 Oct, Sun only 2–6; other days and evening tours by arrangement. 35p (ch 14 15p). P. ბ

OXBOROUGH *Norfolk* Map 5 TF70
Oxburgh Hall Moated 15th-C and later. Home of Bedingfelds with turreted 80ft gatehouse, and French design parterre garden. Gatehouse, principal rooms and gardens open Apr to 12 Oct, Tue, Wed, Thu, Sat, Sun and BH Mon 2–6 (last admission 5.30). £1. Party 15+. No dogs. *(NT)*

OXFORD *Oxfordshire* Map 4 SP50
Ancient and picturesque University city on rivers Cherwell and Thames, dating back to the 8th C AD. **The University**, the oldest in Britain, probably dates from c1167 and consists of a large complex of colleges built over a period of several centuries, many of which are among the finest buildings of their age. Access to some colleges is restricted to certain times, and details may be obtained from the *Official Information Bureau, Carfax Tower*

Christ Church College Founded in 1525 by Cardinal Wolsey, it has a notable gateway, surmounted by a great octagonal bell tower of 1682, designed by Sir Christopher Wren. The College Art Gallery contains many Old Master paintings, and in the dining-hall are portraits of distinguished former members of the college.

Magdalen College Largely built in the 15th C around the 13th-C St John's Hospital. New building is a fine Georgian addition of 1733.

Merton College Founded in 1264 with parts dating from the 13th to the present century. The library, which is open to the public, dates from the 14th C.

New College A fine complex of Gothic buildings dating from 1380, the work of William Wykeham, Bishop of Winchester 1367–1404. Most of his original work survives, although much has been remodelled and added to. A stretch of the Medieval city wall marks part of the boundary of the gardens.

Trinity College Founded in 1555, and incorporating parts of the old Durham College (established 1380), which previously occupied this site. Features are Kettell Hall, a row of gabled buildings, The Garden Quadrangle, designed by Wren in 1668, and the chapel built by Bathhurst in 1691, which contains lavishly carved wooden reredos, stalls and screen.

The Sheldon Theatre Designed by Sir Christopher Wren, at the request of Sir Gilbert Sheldon, Archbishop of Canterbury, who financed the project, as a theatre for the public ceremonies of the University and a place to house the University Press. Completed in 1664–9, it is based on a Roman theatre and is roughly semicircular in plan.

Ashmolean Museum of Art and Archaeology Beaumont Street. The oldest (1683) museum in the country, housed in C R Cockerell's building of 1845 (with later extensions). Its main exhibits are of an archaeological nature of British, European, Mediterranean, Egyptian and Near Eastern origins. Also exhibited are coins and medals of all countries and periods, located in the Heberden Coin Room; Italian, Dutch, Flemish, French, and English oil paintings; Old Master and modern drawings, water-colours, prints and miniatures; the Hope collection of engraved portraits; European ceramics; English silver; Chinese and Japanese porcelain; painting and lacquer; Tibetan art; Indian sculpture and paintings; Islamic pottery and metalwork; Chinese bronzes; casts from the antique and objects of applied art. Temporary exhibits throughout year. Open all year (ex 24–26 Dec, 1 Jan, 4–6 Apr and during St Giles Fair in early Sep) Mon to Sat 10–4, Sun 2–4. Free. P. *(Tel 57522)* ✤ (by previous arrangement)
Museum of the History of Science Broad Street. Contains the finest collection of early astronomical, mathematical and optical instruments in the world, which are housed in the Old Ashmolean Building, a fine example of 17th-C architecture, originally built to hold the collection of Elias Ashmole. One of the most distinguished parts of the present display is the series of Islamic and European astrolabes, once used for astronomical calculations. Many of the exhibits are artistic as well as scientific, including sun-dials, and three fine orreries which represent the motions of heavenly bodies. Other exhibits include early microscopes, other optical instruments, photographic apparatus, clocks and watches, air-pumps, etc. Of special interest are the penicillin material, H G J Moseley's X-ray spectrometer, and a prototype of Dr C R Burch's ultra-violet reflecting microscope made in 1946. Open all year Mon to Fri (ex Christmas week and week after Easter) 10.30–1, 2.30–4. Free. ⚠ (limited). *(Tel 43997)*
Museum of Modern Art 30 Pembroke Street. Changing exhibitions of 20th-C art by British and international artists. Evening films, lectures, seminars, performances. Book stall. ⬛ Open all year, daily (ex Mon) Tue to Sat 10–5, Sun 2–5. Free. *(Tel 722733)*
Museum of Oxford St Aldates. Permanent displays of the archaeology and history of this famous University City from the earliest times to the present day. Temporary exhibitions. Facilities for parties. Bookshop. Museum assistant available for enquiries on Wed. Open all year (ex 13 Apr, 25–26 Dec) Tue to Sat 10–5. 20p (ch, students and pen 10p). P. *(Tel 815539)* **(79)**
Rotunda Museum of Antique Doll's Houses Grove House, 44 Iffley Turn, next to school. 2m from centre of Oxford, off A423. A collection of over fifty dolls' houses dating from c1700–1886 together with their furnishings, kitchen implements, china, silver, food and dolls' house dolls, which reflect the changes in social life and attitudes throughout the aforementioned period. Open 1 May to mid Sep (Sun only) 2.15–5.15. (At other times for parties of 12+ appointment only). Ch 16 not admitted. 25p. ⚠ ✤ B
University Private Botanic Garden High Street, by Magdalen Bridge. Gardens of great botanical interest, founded in 1621, and oldest in country. Open all year round (ex 4 Apr, 25 Dec), weekdays 8.30–5, Sun 10–12

and 2–6 (4.30 Oct to Apr); greenhouses open daily 2–4. Free. No dogs. P (St Clements car park). *(Tel 42737)* ✤
The *University Arboretum* is at Nuneham Courteney. On A423 just S of the village. 50 acres of Conifers and broad leaf trees. Open May to Oct Mon to Sat 8.30–5. Free. ⚠ limited. No dogs. ✤

PACKWOOD HOUSE Warwickshire
Map 7 SP17
13m SE Birmingham on unclass road off A34. Timber-framed 16th- to 17th-C house containing tapestry, needlework, and furniture. Famous for remarkable mid 17th-C yew garden representing Sermon on the Mount. Open Apr to Sep, Wed to Sun, BH Mon 2–7; Oct to Mar (ex 25 Dec), Wed, Sat, Sun, BH Mon 2–5. 85p; garden only 50p. No dogs. *(NT)*

PADIHAM Lancashire Map 7 SD73
Gawthorpe Hall Early 17th-C house built around pele tower, with contemporary ceilings, woodwork, and a minstrel's gallery. Some 19th-C alterations by Sir Charles Barry. In house is the Kay Shuttleworth collection of lace and embroidery. Open 15 Mar to 31 Oct, BH Mon, Wed, Sat, Sun also Tue Jul and Aug, 2–6. 50p (ch 25p). ⚠ *(NT)*

PADSTOW Cornwall Map 2 SW97
Tropical Bird and Butterfly Gardens Fentonluna Lane. Established for years and continues to successfully breed many birds from all corners of the world. Gardens with tropical and sub-tropical plants, many of which are labelled. Heated walk-in Tropical House with free flying birds. Butterfly Exhibition with live flight operating during summer months on sunny days. Open all year (ex 25 Dec) daily 10.30–8 or 1hr before dusk. 80p (ch 3–14 40p, pen 60p). Prices under revision for 1980. ⬛ spring and summer. Dogs allowed on leads. P on B3276. *(Tel 532262)* ✤

PAIGNTON Devon Map 3 SX86
Kirkham House Restored 15th-C house, known as the Priest's House. Open Apr to Sep, weekdays 9.30–7 (5.30, Apr), Sun 2–7 (5.30, Apr). 15p (ch 16 and pen 5p). *(AM)*
Oldway 19th-C house containing replicas of rooms at Palace of Versaille. Picturesque gardens. ⬛ summer. House open May to Sep. Mon to Sat 10–1 and 2.15–5.15, Sun 2.30–5.30; winter Mon to Fri 10–1 and 2.15–5.15 (closed Sat and Sun); closed occasionally for Council purposes. Free. ⚠ *(Tel Torquay 26244 ext 286 for bookings. Paignton 550711 enquiries)*
Torbay Aircraft Museum Higher Blagdon. Off Totnes Road, A385, near Berry Pomeroy. About 2 miles from Paignton Zoo. Features over 18 complete aircraft dating from 1924 to 1954. Comprehensive indoor exhibition of aeronautics. Special exhibition 'The Red Baron and Fighter Aces of World War 1'. Aviation shop and ⬛ licensed (summer only). Open all year (ex 25 and 26 Dec) 10–6 (4 winter). 85p (ch 45p, pen 50p, ch 5 free). Under revision for 1980. ⚠ (75% under cover) *(Tel 553540)* ✤
Torbay and Dartmouth Railway Steam trains run on former Great Western line from Paignton to Kingswear for ferry across to Dartmouth. Model railway exhibition at Paignton station. Gift shop. Open Easter then mid May to end Sep daily. Tel for other dates in season. P in Victoria Park. *(Tel 555872)* ✤
Zoological and Botanical Gardens Totnes Road. In approximately 100 acres of grounds, enhanced with tropical plants and shrubs are

extensive collection of animals and birds from all over the world. Among the main attractions are a breeding colony of Lar Gibbons on a large island in a lake, the baboon rock, monkey house, large tropical house, sub-tropical house, aquarium and reptile house. A large collection of peafowl roam the grounds. ℒ Licensed bar. Children's playground. Miniature railway. Open all year, daily (ex 25 Dec) 10 – 7.30 (5.30 winter). £1.20 (ch 3 – 14 60p). Party. Admission prices under revision for 1980. ⚠ *(Tel 557479)*

PAINSWICK *Gloucestershire* Map 3 SO80
Painswick House A Georgian Palladian house situated ½m outside the picturesque village. It has some splendid reception rooms and a special feature is the 18th-C Chinese wall paper in the drawing room. ℒ (teas for parties 20+ by appointment). Open Sun Jul, Aug, and Sep 2 – 6. 50p (ch 14 30p, pen 20p). Parties 20+ can be booked all year. ⚠ limited. *(Tel 813646)* **(79)**

PARCEVALL (PERCIVAL) HALL GARDENS *North Yorkshire* Map 7 SE06
Beautiful gardens of Elizabethan house, in hillside setting east of main Wharfedale valley. ℒ. Open Easter to end Sep. 20p. ⚠ (5p). *(Tel Burnsall 214)*

PATELEY BRIDGE *North Yorkshire* Map 7 SE16
Niderdale Museum Many rooms depicting historical Dales life. Displays include the Cobbler's shop, Victorian room, also costume, domestic, industrial, farming, geology, apothecaries, medical, religious and photographic sections. Open all year, Easter to Spring BH, Sat and Sun, summer, daily, Oct to Easter Sun only. 2 – 5. 10p (ch and pen 5p). ⚠ Party. *(Tel Harrogate 711225)*

PEAKIRK *Cambridgeshire* Map 4 TF10
Wildfowl Trust Over 600 ducks, geese and swans of 100 different species in an attractive water garden. Magnificent flock of Chilean flamingos, trumpeter, black-necked and coscoroba swans, Andean geese and many other rare and unusual waterfowl. Visitor centre, Gift shop, ℒ and picnic facilities. Open daily (ex 24/25 Dec) from 9.30. Party 20+ (evening) ⚠ free. *(Tel Peterborough 252271)* ⅓

PENSHURST *Kent* Map 5 TQ54
Penshurst Place On B2176. One of the outstanding stately homes in Britain, and birthplace of Sir Philip Sidney in 1554. The world-famous chestnut-beamed Great Hall is the oldest and finest in England. The state rooms are splendidly furnished and the toy museum is much loved by children. Extensive

Tudor gardens, leisure area includes a venture playground, Countryside Exhibition and nature trail. Open 1 Apr to 5 Oct, daily (ex Mon and Fri), House 2 – 6; all other facilities – 1 Apr to 30 Jun 12 – 6, 1 Jul to 5 Oct 11.30 – 6, BH, all facilities including house, 11.30 – 6. Grounds £1 (ch 50p), House 50p (ch 25p), Toy museum 10p, Victoria Regina Exhibition 10p; Inclusive ticket for House, Grounds and Exhibitions £1.50 (ch 75p ex BH). ⚠ *(Tel 870307)*. *(Viscount De L'Isle VC KG)*

PENZANCE *Cornwall* Map 2 SW43
Museum of Nautical Art and Man-O-War Display 19 Chapel Street, opposite the Admiral Benbow. Museum has on exhibition the hundreds of 'nautifacts' brought up by the diving teams of Roland Morris from the sunken wrecks of Anson Association Romney Eagle and Colussus. The display of the latter wreck depicting recovery of Lord Hamilton's 2,500-year-old pottery. Man-o'-war display shows full scale section of 1730 warship with four decks including gun-decks and great cabin with guns and men of the period. Open May to Sep 10 – 1 and 2 – 4 (also 7 – 9 in season). 20p (ch 15p). **(79)**

Penlee House, Penzance and District Museum Penlee Park. The Museum takes a look at the history and development of Penzance and Penwith District from earliest man to the 1950s. Open all year, Mon to Sat 12.30 – 4.30 (ex BH). Free. P. *(Tel 3625)* **(79)**

PETERBOROUGH *Cambridgeshire* Map 4 TL19
Longthorpe Tower Fortified 13th- to 14th-C house, which belonged formerly to the de Thorpe family. Contains some rare wall-paintings of religious and didactic subjects on first floor. Open, see inside front cover. 15p (ch 16 and pen 5p). *(AM)*

Lowlands Farm and Bygone Centre Fenbridge Road, Werrington. 3m NW. 40 acres of farmland with rare breeds of British farm animals. A museum of vintage and veteran cars, and working demonstrations of vintage agricultural machinery and farm work are held. ¾m river frontage for fishing. Country Festival and Game Fair 16 Sep. Open all year daily from 10am. 50p (ch 15 and pen 35p). ⚠ *(Tel 74477)* **(79)**

City of Peterborough Museum and Art Gallery Priestgate. Local geology and archaeology, natural history, Victorian rooms, and articles from former French prisoners' jail at Norman Cross. Paintings mainly of local topographical interest and small collection of ceramics and glass. Temporary exhibitions. Open all year (closed 25, 26 Dec and 4 Apr) Sep to May Tue to Sat, BH 12 – 5. Jun to Aug Tue to Sat 10 – 5. Free. P. *(Tel 43329)*

PETWORTH *West Sussex* Map 4 SU92
Petworth House Large, late 17th- to 19th-C
mansion, partly by Salvin, in great park.
Notable picture gallery, 13th-C chapel,
Grinling Gibbons carvings, and grand
staircase probably painted by Laguerre.
Open Apr to end Oct Tue, Wed, Thu, Sat, Sun
and BH Mon 2–6. £1.10 Connoisseurs' day
on Tue, extra rooms shown. £1.35. No dogs in
the house. Deer park open all year 9 till
sunset. ⚲ 2.30–5.30. *(NT)*

PEVENSEY *East Sussex* Map 5 TQ60
Old Minthouse High Street. Built in 1342 on a
site which is reputed to have been used as a
Norman mint as long ago as 1076. The
interior was considerably altered in 1542 by
Dr Andrew Borde, then court physician to
Henry VIII. It contains 18 rooms, open to the
public, carvings, frescoes, etc. Small
museum. Open all year Mon to Fri 10–5, Sat
10–1, mid Jul to Sep Sun also BH 11–5. 20p
(ch 14 10p). P. *(Tel Eastbourne 762337)* **(79)**
Pevensey Castle 3rd-C Roman fort of Saxon
Shore, with Norman and 13th-C additions,
including keep, curtain wall, and gatehouse.
Open*, see inside front cover. 20p (ch 16 and
pen 5p). ⚲ *(AM)*

PICKERING *North Yorkshire* Map 8 SE78
Beck Isle Museum of Rural Life Georgian
house, once the home of William Marshall, an
authority on agriculture. Museum contains
folk exhibits relating to Pickering and
surrounding area. Open Easter to mid Oct
daily, 10.30–12.30, 2–5.30, Aug 10.30–7.
Open evenings or in winter for parties, by
appointment only. 20p (ch 16 10p). ⚲ *(Tel
73359)* & B
North Yorkshire Moors Railway 'Moorsrail'
Operates through the heart of the North York
Moors National Park between Pickering and
Grosmont, a distance of 18 miles. Services
operate a week prior to Easter until early Nov.
Loco shed, viewing gallery, gift shop and ⚲ at
Grosmont. Audi-visual Unit, bookshop,
information centre and ⚲ at Pickering
Station. Further details available from
Moorsrail, Pickering Station, North Yorkshire.
⚲ at Grosmont Station and Pickering town.
(Tel (0751) 72508/73535) &
Pickering Castle Large shell keep on mound
between two baileys, the inner of which,
together with keep, is 12th C. Open*, see
inside front cover. 15p (ch 16 and pen 5p). ⚲
(AM)

PITSTONE *Buckinghamshire* Map 4 SP91
Pitstone Windmill Off B488. One of
England's oldest postmills, some of it part of
original structure of 1627. Recently well-
restored and is again fully operative. Open
May to Sep, Suns and BH Mon 2.30–6. 15p
(ch 7p). *(NT)*

PLAXTOL *Kent* Map 5 TQ65
Old Soar Manor Part of late 13th-C house
joined to 18th-C farmhouse. Open, see inside
front cover. 15p (ch 16 and
pen 5p). *(NT and AM)*

PLYMOUTH *Devon* Map 2 SX45
City Museum and Art Gallery Drake Circus.
Collections of paintings and drawings,
ceramics (especially Plymouth porcelain),
silver; archaeology and local history; natural
history. Cottonian collection of Old Master
drawings, engravings and early printed
books. Open all year (ex 4 Apr, 25/26 Dec)
weekdays 10–6 (8 Fri), Sun 3–5. Free. P.
(Tel 68000 ext 4378) &

Elizabethan House 32 New Street. A 16th-C
merchant's house furnished according to
period in Plymouth's historic precinct. Open
all year, weekdays 10–1 and 2.15–6 (dusk,
Oct to Mar); Apr to Sep, Sun also 3–5. Free.
P. *(Tel 68000 ext 2006)* **(79)**
The Merchant's House 33 St Andrews
Street. Large town house of 16th- and early
17th-C, with many period features. Converted
to Museum of Plymouth history up to 1670.
Open all year (ex 4 Apr, 25, 26 Dec)
weekdays 10–6, Sun 3–5. Free. P. *(Tel
68000 ext 4378)*
Prysten House Off Royal Parade (Main
Street). Old house in city, built 1490, former
Priest's house of St Andrew's Church.
Mayflower Story Room and model of
Plymouth 1620. Herb display. Open Mon to
Sat (ex 4 Apr, 25/26 Dec and 1 Jan also Sun)
10–4. 30p (ch 16 15p). ⚲ *(Tel 61414 Mon to
Fri 9.30–1)*

Royal Citadel Magnificent entrance
gateway, dated 1670, and designed probably
by Sir Thomas Fitz for stronghold
commenced by Charles II in 1666. The
remaining buildings from the fort include the
Guard House, Governor's House, and
Chapel, the two last-named rebuilt. Open any
reasonable time at the discretion of the
military. Free. *(AM)*
Smeaton Tower The Promenade, Plymouth
Hoe. A former Eddystone Lighthouse now
rebuilt on The Hoe. Open 26 Apr to 4 Oct daily
10.30–one hour before dusk. 10p. Party. *(Tel
264840)*

PLYMPTON *Devon* Map 2 SX55
Dartmoor Wild Life Park 3m NE at
Sparkwell, north of A38. 25-acre park with
birds and animals of many species. Six deer
species in separate paddocks, and free-flying
waterfowl. Donkeys for children. New monkey
pen. ⚲ and souvenir shop. Open all year,
daily 10–dusk. Admission prices not
available. ⚲ *(Tel Cornwood 209)*
Saltram House (S of bypass). Tudor house,
refronted in 18th-C, with saloon and dining
room (1768) by Robert Adam;
furniture, carpets and Reynolds portraits.
Shrub garden with 18th-C summer house and
orangery (1773) by Stockman. Open 1 Apr to
Oct, daily 11–6, house 12.30–6 (last
admission 5.30, house only closed on Mon);
Nov to Mar garden only open, daily during
daylight hours. £1.50. Garden only 90p.
Candlelit evenings 26 Apr, 30 Aug, 27 Sep
and 25 Oct, 8–10.30 pm. £2. *(NT and NGS)*

POCKLINGTON *Humberside* Map 8 SE84
*Burnby Hall Gardens and Stewart
Collection* Museum of sporting trophies,
objects of interest from world-wide travels,
and gardens with fine lily ponds. ⚲. Gardens
open all year Mon to Fri 10–7, Sat and Sun
2–7; museum and café open Easter to late
May, Sat and Sun 2–5; end of May to mid Sep
daily then Sat and Sun to end of Sep. 30p (ch
14 5p, pen 20p). Under revision for 1980. ⚲
Free. *(Tel 2068 and 2114)* & B

POLEGATE *East Sussex* Map 5 TQ50
Polegate Windmill Off A22. A complete tower-mill dating from 1817 and in use until some 20 years ago. Tower is 45ft high, and original applewood machinery and milling museum are of interest. Open Easter to Oct, Sun and BH Mon, also Wed in Aug 2.30–5.30. Other times by arrangement. 20p (ch 14 10p). P (roads round mill). *(Tel Eastbourne 54845)*

POLPERRO *Cornwall* Map 2 SX25
Museum of Smuggling Talland Street. Interesting museum of past- and present-day smuggling activities. Open Easter to 24 Oct, daily 10–7. 30p. Under revision for 1980. Dogs on lead only. P.

PONTEFRACT *West Yorkshire* Map 8 SE42
Pontefract Museum Salter Row. Opened April 1978. Museum of Pontefract history also temporary exhibitions. Open all year Mon to Sat 10.30–12.30 and 1.30–5.30. Closed Sun and BH. Free. *(Tel 77289)*

POOL *Cornwall* Map 2 SW64
Cornish Engines Five original Cornish beam engines were given to the National Trust in 1967 by Cornish Engine Preservation Society. Two of these, East Pool and Agar Mine (on either side of A30), are open 1 Apr to end Oct, daily 11–1 and 2–4 (last tour 5.30). 50p. There are others for which suitable arrangements must be made in advance for visiting: Levant Mine, St Just *(The Manager, Geevor Mine, Tel St Just 662)*, and South Crofty Mine, Camborne *(The Manager, Tel Camborne 3150)*. (NT)

POOLE *Dorset* Map 4 SZ09
Guildhall Museum Market Street. The Civic and social life of Poole during the 18th and 19th C is portrayed in the displays in this fine example of a two-storey Georgian Market House. Open all year (ex 1 Jan, 4 Apr, 25/26 Dec) Mon to Sat 10–5, Sun 2–5. 1 Apr to 30 Sep. 15p (ch 5p) combined ticket for all three museums 35p (ch 10p); 1 Oct to 31 Mar 10p (ch 5p). P. *(Tel 5323)*
Maritime Museum Paradise Street, Poole Quay. The displays in the late 15th-C Town Cellars illustrate Poole's association with the sea from prehistoric times until the early 20th C. Admission charges and opening times as Guildhall Museum. P. *(Tel 5323)*
Poole Park Zoo A small but well-equipped zoo within the limits of beautiful Poole Park. Animals at present include wild cat, pumas, leopards, bears, porcupine and otters. There is also a monkey house, tropical house, children's corner and a fine collection of flamingoes, penguins, parrots and tropical birds. Gift shop. Open Mar to Oct, 10–6 or sunset whichever is earlier; Nov to Feb Sat, Sun, PH and every day during local school holidays 10–sunset. 45p (ch 15 25p). Party. All charges subject to alteration for 1980. ⚠ *(Tel Parkstone 745296)* ⅃
Poole Pottery The Quay. Well-known pottery, founded in 1873, which has been producing 'Poole Pottery' since 1921. Craft section on several floors where making of the pottery can be seen. Open all year (ex Christmas week and BH) Tours Mon to Fri 10–12.30 and 1.50–4.15. 35p (ch 15p). Under revision for 1980. Shop Mon to Sat 9–5 (later in summer also Sun in Aug). P. *(Tel 2866)*
Scaplen's Court High Street. One of the finest examples of a 15th-C town house to be seen on the South Coast. The displays illustrate the development of Poole from

prehistoric times until the 19th C with an emphasis on archaeological material. Admission charges and opening times as Guildhall Museum. P. *(Tel 5323)*

PORCHESTER *Hampshire* Map 4 SU60
Porchester Castle Off A27. 4th-C Saxon shore fort, with 12th-C keep in one corner and Assheton's Tower (1367) in another corner. Parish church (1133) in south-west corner was church of Augustinian foundation moved later to Southwick. Open*, see inside front cover. 25p (ch 16 and pen 10p). ⚠ *(AM)*

PORTLAND *Dorset* Map 3 SY67
Portland Castle Erected originally by Henry VIII and added to in 17th and 18th C. Open Apr to Sep, weekdays 9.30–7 (5.30, Apr) Sun 2–7 (5.30, Apr). 15p (ch and pen 5p). ⚠ *(AM)*
Portland Museum 217 Wakeham. Associated with Thomas Hardy's *The Well-Beloved* (Avice's Cottage). Now a museum of local and historical interest. Open May to Sep, Mon, Wed, Thu, Fri 10–8; Tue and Sat 10–5; Sun 11–1 and 2–5. Oct to Apr, Tue to Sat 10–1 and 2–5. 10p (ch, students and pen free). *(Tel Portland 821804)*

PORTSMOUTH *Hampshire* Map 4 SZ69
City Museum and Art Gallery Museum Museum Road. Formerly military barracks, now partially art gallery and museum with furniture, pottery, glass, sculpture, and paintings. Also local history galleries, and monthly temporary exhibitions. ⚓ (licensed). Open all year, daily (ex 25, 26 Dec) 10.30–5.30. 11p (ch and pen 6p). ⚠ ⅃ B
Cumberland House Museum Eastern Parade. Local natural history and an aquarium. Open all year daily (ex 25, 26 Dec) 10.30–5.30. 11p (ch and pen 6p).
Dickens' Birthplace Museum Old Commercial Road. Georgian house where Charles Dickens was born in 1812, now restored and furnished to illustrate the style of the period. Prints and portraits are exhibited, and couch on which Dickens died is displayed in separate room. Open Mar to Oct daily 10.30–5.30. 21p (ch and pen 11p).
Eastney Pumping Station and Gas Engine House Henderson Road. A fine building containing Boulton and Watt reciprocal steam pumps installed in 1887. One operating under steam at weekends. Adjacent buildings of 1904 houses Crossley gas engines. Open Apr to Sep, daily 2–6. Weekends 27p (ch and pen 11p), weekdays 16p (ch and pen 6p). ⚠
Fort Widley Portsdown Hill Road. Fort built in the 1860s by Lord Palmerston against the threat of French invasion. Contains a labyrinth of underground passages, magazines and gun emplacements. Commands superb panoramic views. Open Apr to Sep daily 2–6. Guided tours. 27p (ch and pen 11p). P.
Point Battery and Round Tower Three-storeyed building dating back originally to 1485, with later alterations. Once part of 18-gun battery defending harbour. Good views. P.
Royal Naval Museum Museum boasts many fine exhibits connected with Nelson, his officers, and men, huge panorama of Trafalgar being outstanding, as are also ship's figureheads. Displays include exhibitions on Victorian navy and the history of Warships and Boats. The McCarthy collection of Nelson commemorative material. ⚓ 20p (ch 10p). ⚠ in dockyard. *(Tel 22351 ext 23868)* ⅃ B
HMS Victory The Hard. Entry via main dockyard gate. Nelson's famous flagship,

moored in the harbour until 1922, has since been restored and fitted out to show conditions as at Battle of Trafalgar in 1805. Open 1 Mar to 31 Oct Mon to Sat 10.30–5.30, Sun 1–5; 1 Nov to end Feb Mon to Sat 10.30–4.30, Sun 1–4.30. Free. *(Tel 22351 ext 23111)* & B (by prior arrangement)

PORT SUNLIGHT *Merseyside* Map 7 SJ38
Lady Lever Art Gallery Situated near Mersey estuary in well-known model village, this art gallery displays pictures by famous English Masters in addition to collections of English period furniture, Chinese porcelain, and Wedgwood. Open all year (ex 1 Jan, 4 Apr, 24, 25 and 26 Dec) Mon to Sat 10–5, Sun 2–5 (subject to revision). Voluntary contribution. & *(Tel 051-645 3623)* & B

POWDERHAM *Devon* Map 3 SX98
Powderham Castle Entrance off A379 Exeter/Dawlish road. Seat of Earls of Devon, built between 1390 and 1420, damaged in Civil War and restored and altered in 18th C and 19th Cs. Fine furnishings and portraits. Lovely deer park. ⚏ (teas). Open Easter then Sun until mid May, after which, daily (ex Fri and Sat) until end Sep, 2–6. £1 (ch 16 and pen 50p). Party 20+. Subject to alteration. *(Tel Starcross 243)* & B

PRESTON *Lancashire* Map 7 SD52
Harris Museum and Art Gallery The specialist collections cover the fields of fine art, decorative art, archaeology, natural history, and include works by the Devis family, the Newsham Bequest of the 19th C, paintings and sculpture, and the Cedric Houghton Bequest of ceramics. Annual Lancashire Art Exhibition Mar/Apr. Free guided tours by arrangement. ⚏ (Mon, Wed and Fri mornings). Open all year Mon to Sat (ex BH) 10–5. Free. P. *(Tel 58248)* &

PRESTWICH *Gt Manchester* Map 7 SD80
Heaton Hall Heaton Park on A665. The finest house of its period in Lancashire and one of the finest in the country. Designed for the Earl of Wilton by James Wyatt in 1772, the house has magnificent decorated interior and commands panoramic views of Manchester. Open all year Mon to Sat 10–6 (4 Nov to Feb); Sun 2–6 (4 Nov to Feb), 12–6 May to Aug. Free. & *(Tel 061-773 1231)*

PRINCES RISBOROUGH *Buckinghamshire* Map 4 SP80
Princes Risborough Manor 17th-C house with 17th- and 18th-C woodwork. Open Apr to Oct, Wed 2–6 (two room only shown). 20p *(NT)*

PRISTON *Avon* Map 3 ST66
Priston Mill Priston Farm. Historic water powered corn mill, driven by a large waterwheel. Dates from Anglo Saxon period. Records in Domesday Book indicate that flour has been milled in this area for over a thousand years. Flour is still ground in the mill today, and is used to make 'Priston Mill Whole Wheat Bread'. Farm shop. Visitors may picnic by mill in fine weather. Open 24 Mar to 31 Oct, Mon to Fri 2.15–5, Sat, Sun and BH 11–12.45 and 2.15–6. Free. Conducted tours with parties 25p per head, (by appointment only.). & *(Tel Bath 23894)*

PROBUS *Cornwall* Map 2 SW94
County Demonstration Garden and Arboretum Permanent displays of the many aspects of garden layout, plant selection, and effect of weather conditions. Plant, tree and flower propagation. Exhibits of fruit, herbs and vegetables. Emphasis on choosing right foliage, flowers, etc, to suit individual requirements and environment. For special

events see local press. Open May to Sep, Mon, Tue, Wed & Fri 2–5, Thu 2–8, Sun 2–6, Oct–Apr, Thu 2–5. 10p (ch 5 free). ⚠ *(Tel Truro 74282 ext 349)* ⅙

Trewithen Gardens Grampound Road. Internationally renowned landscaped garden of camellias, magnolias, rhododendrons and many rare plants of distinction. Open Mar to Sep, daily (ex Sun) incl BH 2–4.30. Mar to Jun, 60p (ch 30p, pen 40p); Jul to Sep, 40p (ch 20p, pen 30p). Nurseries open all year. ⚠ *(Tel St Austell 882418)* ⅙ P also *Trewithen House* An 18th-C Cornish country house built in 1720 and lived in continuously by descendants of the same family. Open Apr to Jul inclusive, Mon and Tue only 2–4.30. £1

PRUDHOE *Northumberland* Map 12 NZ06
Prudhoe Castle On River Tyne, 12th- to 14th-C former stronghold of d'Umfravelles and Percys. Keep stands in inner bailey, and notable example of gatehouse guards outside bailey. Access to Pele Tard only. Open, see inside front cover. Closed Wed and Fri. Free (ch 16 not admitted unless accompanied by an adult). *(AM)*

PUDSEY *West Yorkshire* Map 8 SE23
Fulneck Moravian Museum This museum of Moravian exhibits and Victoriana dates from 1969 and includes photographs, furniture, 150-year-old fire engine, working hand loom and spinning wheel. Open 1 Mar to 31 Oct, Wed and Sat 2–5, other times by appointment only. 10p (ch 3p). ⚠ *(Tel Pudsey 564862)*

PULBOROUGH *West Sussex* Map 4 TQ01
Parham Park 3m SE off A283. Dates from 1577, and great hall, long gallery, and principal rooms contain fine portraits, furniture, and needlework. Walled garden, pleasure grounds, and glasshouses. Beautiful downland setting. ♨ 3–5.15. Open 6 Apr to 5 Oct 2–5.30, Wed, Thu, Sun and BH. £1 (ch 17 and pen 60p). Gardens open 1–6. 25p. Connoisseurs Days 2nd and 4th Sun in each open month, visitors not guided. £1.20 (ch and pen 60p). ⚠ *(Tel Storrington 2021). (Mr and Mrs P A Tritton)*

PURSE CAUNDLE *Dorset* Map 3 ST61
Purse Caundle Manor Excellent example of medieval manor house, with great hall and chamber. Open 5 Mar to 31 Oct, Wed, Thu, Sun and BH 2–5. 75p (ch 13 20p). ⚠ *(Tel Milborne Port 250400)*

PUSEY *Oxfordshire* Map 4 SU39
Pusey House Gardens Designed 1748 with new garden terraces added 1935 by Geoffrey Jellicoe. 20 acres of garden and lake, with herbaceous borders. Plants for sale. ♨.

Gardens only open 2 Apr to 29 Jun, Wed, Thu and Sun 2–6; 2 Jul to 19 Oct, daily (ex Mon and Fri) 2–6 also BH weekends. 50p (ch 10 free). Prices for 1980 under revision. ⚠ *(Tel Buckland 222)* ⅙

QUAINTON *Buckinghamshire* Map 4 SP71
Quainton Railway Centre Quainton Station. Off A41. The largest collection of standard gauge locomotives in the country including examples built by Hunslet, Hudswell Clarke and British Rail (Metropolitan, LNER, LMS, GWR). Also items of rolling stock including many built before 1900. ♨ Steam Railway Galas 5–7 and 27 Apr, 24–26 May, 29 Jun, 27 Jul, 23–25 Aug, 28 Sep and 26 Oct, 10–6. 70p (ch and pen 35p), family ticket £1.75. Not expected to change for 1980. ⚠ ⅙

RADCLIFFE *Gt Manchester* Map 7 SD70
Radcliffe Tower Sandford Street. Remains of medieval tower once part of a larger hall occupied by the Radcliffe family. Adjacent to medieval Parish Church. Open at all times. Free. P. Enquiries to Bury Museum. *(Tel Bury 4021)* ⅙

RAINTHORPE HALL *Norfolk* Map 5 TM29
Fine medium-sized Elizabethan manor house of brick and timber. Open by appointment only. ♨. £1 (ch 50p). ⚠ *(Tel Swainsthorpe 470618). (G F Hastings)* ⅙ B

RAMPTON *Nottinghamshire* Map 8 SK77
Sundown Pets Garden Treswell Road. Caters specially for young children. The animal and bird enclosures are set amidst attractive gardens, and there is also a Play Village, modern playground and a unique life size 'Toy Jungle'. Tea garden. Open all year 10–7 or dusk (closed 25, 26 Dec). 25p (ch 2 free). Admission prices for 1980 not yet decided. ⚠ *(Tel 274)* ⅙

RAMSEY *Cambridgeshire* Map 4 TL28
Abbey Gatehouse 15th-C Benedictine relic. open Apr to 12 Oct, daily 10–5 (or sunset). Free. *(NT)*

RAVENGLASS *Cumbria* Map 6 SD09
Ravenglass and Eskdale Railway Narrow gauge (15in) steam railway established in 1875 to carry iron ore. Now passenger line with steam and diesel locomotives, open and saloon coaches. Runs 7 miles from Ravenglass to Eskdale through beautiful scenery. Railway Museum at Ravenglass. Shops and cafés at each end of line. Open 30 Mar to 2 Nov (reduced services at other times, one train a day during winter, except Christmas), 7.45–6.40 (summer). Return fare £2 (ch 15 and pen £1.30), subject to possible increase. ⚠ at each station. *(Tel 226)*

PARHAM Pulborough, West Sussex.

House open Wednesdays, Thursdays, Sundays and Bank Holidays from Easter Sunday to first Sunday in October. 2pm–5.30pm. Second and fourth Sundays in the month unguided. Gardens open same days 1pm–6pm. Free Car Park. Church. Teas in the Big Kitchen. Shop. All enquiries to the Secretary. Tel: Storrington 2021.

See gazetteer for details.

READING *Berkshire* Map 4 SU77
Museum and Art Gallery Blagrave Street.
noted especially for exceptional collection of
exhibits from Roman Silchester, but there are
also finds from River Thames area, including
splendid Bronze Age torc from Moulsford.
Displays of local natural history. Monthly
changing exhibitions. Open all year Mon to Fri
10–5.30, Sat 10–5 (closed Sun and BH).
Admission free. Station and municipal car
parks within 5 mins. *(Tel 55911 ext 2242)* See
also **SILCHESTER, Calleva Museum**
Museum of English Rural Life The
University. Whiteknights Park, Shinfield Road
entrance. Collection of highly interesting
agricultural, domestic, and crafts exhibits.
Open all year (ex BH) Tue to Fri 10–4.30; Sat
10–1 and 2–4.30. Free. ⚠ *(Tel 85123 ext
475)* & B

RECULVER *Kent* Map 5 TR26
Roman Fort Remains of 3rd-C Roman fort of
the Saxon Shore, on an even older site.
Within its walls stand the towers of a Norman
church, the body of which was destroyed in
1809, the towers being left as a mariners'
landmark. Accessible any reasonable time.
Free. P. *(AM)*

REDCAR *Cleveland* Map 8 NZ62
The Zetland Museum Exhibits include the
oldest lifeboat in the world, pictures, relics,
models, etc, relating to sea rescue on the
North-East coast and to the fishing
communities of North Yorkshire. A marine
aquarium and displays about local marine life.
Open all year Mon to Sat 10–5.30. Closed 4
Apr, 25 Dec and 1 Jan. Free. P. Esplanade
and King Street. *(Tel 71921)*

REDDITCH *Hereford and Worcester*
Map 7 SP06
Forge Mill 2m N of town, off A441. On the site
of the original mill serving Cistercian Abbey at
Bordesley. Present mill converted to needle
scouring between 1728 and 1730. Some
machinery in west wing is original. Open by
appointment only with *Mr J Luty*. ⚠ *(Tel
64412)*

REDRUTH *Cornwall* Map 2 SW64
Tolgus Tin Company Portreath Road. 2m N.
Only remaining Cornish tin steaming works
dating from 1800, retaining original water-
wheels and only surviving set of 12 headed
Cornish stamps still in commercial use.
Objects made of tin sold in Mineral House.
Guided tours around mill. Madame Tussaud's
animals tea party. ⚁ Picnic and children's
play area. Open all year daily 10–6 (later in
season). 85p (ch and pen 55p). Opening
times and admission prices under revision for
1980. Dogs not allowed around tin mill. *(Tel
215171)*

REEDHAM *Norfolk* Map 5 TG40
Pettitts Rural Industries Peacocks,
ornamental pheasants, game birds and
waterfowl on show in garden surroundings
with picnic area. Art of feather craft and
taxidermy usually being demonstrated and
products are on sale, also oven-ready game
and recipes. Conservation literature.
Museum of Reedham. ⚁ spring and summer
Mon to Fri only. Open all year Mon to Fri 9–5.
Charges for 1980 not yet known, may also open
Sat and Sun pm. ⚠ *(Tel Freethorpe 243)* &

REIGATE *Surrey* Map 4 TQ25
Priory Museum Bell Street. Founded
originally in 1235, house was converted into
Tudor mansion, of which hall fireplace is finest
surviving relic. Palladian stucco of 1779
changed face of building, and painted
staircase by Verrio *c*1710 is notable example.
House now used as school and part is a small
museum of local history, Victorian toys and
costumes. Special exhibitions for 1980 Spring
term – History of Reigate Priory. Summer
term – Costume exhibition. Autumn term –
Globe-trotters souvenirs. ⚁ Open Wed in
term-time 2–4.30. Free. P. *(Tel 45065)* &

REIGATE HEATH *Surrey* Map 4 TQ25
Old Windmill 400-year-old mill, converted for
holding of church services at 3 pm on third
Sun of each month between May and Oct.
Restored in 1964. Accessible all the year,
daily 9–dusk. Free. P. & B

RESTORMEL *Cornwall* Map 2 SX16
Restormel Castle 1m N of Lostwithiel, off
A390. Comprises circular mound and
gateway *c*1100, with notable round keep built
*c*1200. Rectangular 13th-C chapel *(AM)*
situated nearby. Castle open*, see inside
front cover. 15p (ch 16 and pen 5p). Party
11+. ⚠ *(AM)*

RIBCHESTER *Lancashire* Map 7 SD63
Roman Museum and Fort 5½m NE Preston.

On B6245. Site museum of the Roman Fort of
'Bremetennacum' in an attractive village.
Contains cavalryman's tombstone, coins,
pottery, jewellery, inscriptions and replica of
famous Parade Helmet, the original of which
is in the British Museum. Unique collection of
Celtic heads. Exposed remains of Roman
granary open to view. Open all year, May to
Aug Mon to Sat (ex Fri) 2–5.30; Sep to Nov
and Feb to Apr, Mon to Sat (ex Fri) 2–5; Dec
and Jan Sat only 2–5. 20p (ch 10p). *(Tel 261)*

RICHBOROUGH *Kent* Map 5 TR 36
Fort and Museum Roman 'Rutupiae' and
original fort of the Saxon Shore. Accessible
any reasonable time. Free. ⚲ *(AM)*

RICHMOND *North Yorkshire* Map 7 NZ 10
Richmond Castle Dates from 11th and 12th
C, one of the earliest in England, with massive
curtain walls and splendid rectangular keep
overlooking River Swale. Open*, see inside
front cover. 20p (ch 16 and pen 5p). P. *(AM)*
The Green Howards Museum Trinity
Square, Market Place. Covers history of
famous regiment, including many uniforms
dating from 1688, weapons and special VC
exhibition. Runner-up in National Heritage
Museum of the Year Award 1975. Open all
year ex Dec and Jan, 1 Apr to 31 Oct
weekdays 10–4.30, Sun 2–4.30; Nov, Feb
and Mar Mon to Sat 10–4.30, closed Sun.
20p (ch 10p). Disc P in Market Place. *(Tel
2133)*

RICKMANSWORTH *Hertfordshire*
Map 4 TQ 09
Moor Park Mansion Fine Palladian mansion
by Leoni, reconstructed in 1727, with Amigoni
and Thornhill frescoes. Now a golf club
house. Open (ex BH) Mon, all year, 10–4.30;
and 1st Sat in month May to Sep for guided
tours 10–12 and 3–4. Free. ⚲

RIEVAULX *North Yorkshire* Map 8 SE 58
Rievaulx Abbey Magnificent Cistercian
abbey begun about 1132, surrounded by
wooded hills. Earliest large Cistercian nave in
Britain. Extensive, well-preserved, monastic
buildings. Open*, see inside front cover. 40p,
winter 15p (ch 16 and pen 15p, winter 5p). ⚭
(AM)
Rievaulx Terrace The layout includes a fine
terrace providing views towards Ryedale and
the Hambleton Hills. There are two 18th-C
garden temples and some remarkable fresco
paintings by Burnici. Open Apr to Oct (ex 4
Apr) daily 10.30–6 (last admission 5.30). 60p.
⚲ *(NT)*

RIPLEY *North Yorkshire* Map 8 SE 26
Ripley Castle 16th- and late 18th-C home of
Ingilby family since 1350, with gatehouse
c1450, Cromwellian associations Royalist
armour and weaponry and priest's hiding hole
discovered in 1964. Fine gardens and
grounds. ⚲ Sun and BH 2–6, catering for
parties by arrangement. Castle and gardens
open Easter, May to Sep, Sun and BH (also
Wed and Thu Jul and Aug only) 2–6, gardens
only Sat 2–6. Parties during week by
arrangement. Charges for 1980 not yet
known. ⚲ *(Tel Harrogate 770186)* ♿ B

RIPON *North Yorkshire* Map 8 SE 37
*Fountains Abbey and Studley Royal
Country Park* 3m SW off B6265. Extensive
Deer Park in which to spend several pleasant
hours, deer, specimen trees and lake. Walk
through ornamental gardens with views of
ponds, monuments and temples before
reaching Fountains Abbey, a magnificent
ruined Cistercian Abbey and the 17th-C hall
(hall may be closed during 1980). ⚲ Deer
Park open all year during daylight hours.
Free. Abbey and gardens open all year (ex 25

Dec) from 9.30 to 4.30 Nov to Mar, 5.30 Apr and Oct, 7.30 May and Sep, 9.30 Jun, Jul, Aug. Admission, including floodlighting, Easter to Oct 50p (ch and pen 20p), Nov to Mar 25p (ch and pen 10p). Floodlighting (not on Mon) Aug 8.30 – 11, Sep 8 – 10.30. 35p (ch 5 – 16 and pen 10p). ⚠ cars 25, coaches 50. Opening hours and admission prices under revision for 1980.

Wakeman's House, Museum and Tourist Information Centre House dates back to 14th C, now a combined tourist information centre and museum of local and historical interest. Open Spring BH to late Sep daily 10 – 6, Sun 12 – 4. Sat only during winter 10 – 4. Free.

RIVERFORD FARM Devon Map 3 SX76
2½m SE of Buckfastleigh on A384. A 500-acre mixed Devonshire farm, which is open to the public on organised visits. An adapted farm trailer transports visitors around the farm to see the various farm operations, including machine milking in the afternoons, and the livestock. Every afternoon, tour starts at 2.30. Displays show the three stages of farming from Tudor to the present day. There are local crafts and produce on display and for sale. ⚏ (inclusive of price) are served in the Barn at the end of the tour £1 (ch 75p). Open Apr – Sep. Party (evening tours), which includes barn dance and barbecue. ⚠ (Tel Staverton 636) ♿ (79)

ROCHE ABBEY South Yorkshire
Map 8 SK59
1½m SE Maltby. Cistercian abbey founded in 1147 with walls of north and south transepts still standing to their full height. Firm gatehouse lies to north-west of church. Open, see inside front cover but closed 4.30 Mon and Tue. 15p (ch 16 and pen 5p). ⚠ (AM)

ROCHESTER Kent Map 5 TQ76
Rochester Castle Commenced 1087 and retaining remarkable storeyed keep dating from 1126 to 1139. Keep open, see inside front cover but closed all day Tue and Fri pm. 20p (ch and pen 5p). ⚠ (AM)
Eastgate House High Street. Elizabethan house described in Charles Dicken's Edwin Drood and Pickwick Papers, now museum of local history, including Dickens' relics. Also extensive general collections of arms and armour and ship models (principally sailing barges), furniture, Victoriana, toys and dolls etc. Dickens' Swiss Chalet from Gadshill stands in grounds. Open all year, daily (ex Sun) 10 – 12.30 and 2 – 5.30. Free. P. (Tel Medway 44176) (79)

ROCKBOURNE Hampshire Map 4 SU11
Roman Villa Excavation is still in progress on this site. Museum has unique items of pottery and jewellery and hoard of 7,717 coins. So far 73 rooms have been uncovered. Open 1 Apr to 1 Oct, Mon to Fri 2 – 6, Sat, Sun and BH 10.30 – 6. Jul and Aug every day 10.30 – 6. 25p (ch 16 15p). ⚠ (Tel 445) ♿

ROCKINGHAM Northamptonshire
Map 4 SP89
Rockingham Castle Elizabethan family home within walls of Norman royal castle. Panoramic views of four counties. Fine paintings, gardens and close associations with Charles Dickens – a frequent visitor. ⚏ Open Easter to 30 Sep, Thu, Sun, BH Mon and following Tue 2 – 6; other days, for parties by previous appointment. 90p (ch 50p) subject to alteration. ⚠ (Tel 770240). (Cmdr Michael Saunders Watson)

RODE Somerset Map 3 ST85
The Tropical Bird Gardens 17 acres of grounds planted with trees and shrubs and dotted with lakes, surround aviaries where more than 180 species of colourful birds are kept. During summer months rabbits, guinea-pigs, goats, and donkeys can be seen. Pets corner of domestic animals with donkey rides. ⚏ Easter to mid Oct. Gardens open all year (ex 25 Dec) summer 10.30 – 7 (no entry after 6.30) winter 10.30 – sunset. 85p (ch 14 45p). Party 25+. Admission prices for 1980 under revision. Ch 14 must be accompanied by adults. Wheelchairs for hire. No dogs. ⚠ (ample). (Tel Beckington 326, Catering Beckington 585) ♿

ROLVENDEN Kent Map 5 TQ83
C M Booth Collection of Historic Vehicles Falstaff Antiques, 63 High Street. Contains historic vehicles and other items of transport interest. The main feature is the unique collection of Morgan 3-wheel cars dating from 1913, plus the only known Humber tri-car of 1904, a 1929 Morris van, motorcycles, bicycles, etc. New extension opened 1979. Open all year (ex 25 Dec and BH) weekdays 10 – 6 (10 – 1 Wed), open some Sun. 25p (ch 15 10p). P. (Tel 234) ♿
Great Maythan Hall Large brick mansion, built by Sir Edwin Lutyens in 1910, and with fine grounds. Open May to Sep, Wed and Thu 2 – 5. 40p (ch 25p) ⚠ ♿ B

ROMSEY Hampshire Map 4 SU32
Broadlands Main entrance on A31 Romsey by-pass. The home of the late Lord Mountbatten. Previously the home of the Victorian Prime Minister, Lord Palmerston, and long famous as a centre of hospitality for Royal and distinguished visitors. Classic Palladian architecture and landscape by 'Capability' Brown. Richly decorated interiors and fine artworks. Special exhibition 'Mountbatten of Burma' traces Lord Mountbatten's distinguished career in War and Peace. Also an audio-visual show which illustrates events in his life. Picnic area, Gift shop and ⚏. Open 1 Apr to 28 Sep 10.30 – 6 (last admission 45 min before closing time). Closed Mon except Aug, Sep and BH. £1 (ch 5 – 13 and pen 50p, also disabled). Admission prices under revision for 1980. Party 15+. ⚠ (Tel 516878) ♿ B

ROTHBURY Northumberland Map 12 NU00
Cragside Victorian house designed for the first Lord Armstrong by Richard Norman Shaw – the first house in the world to be lit by electricity generated by water power. Contains much of its original furniture. 900 acres Country Park. Open: grounds Apr to Sep daily 10.30 – 6, Oct , Wed, Sat and Sun 2 – 5; house Apr to Sep daily ex Mon, but open BH Mon (closed following Tue) 1 – 6, Oct, Wed, Sat and Sun 2 – 5. Country Park only 50p, Country Park and House £1.20. (Tel 20333) (NT)

ROTHERHAM South Yorkshire Map 8 SK49
Art Gallery Brian O'Malley Library and Arts Centre, Walker Place. Continuous programme of temporary exhibitions including, at times, 19th and 20th-C paintings from the Museum collections and Rockingham pottery. ⚏ (licensed). Open all year daily (ex Sun and BH), Mon to Fri 10 – 6, Sat 10 – 5. Free. ⚠ (Tel 65481) ♿
Museum Clifton Park. Late 18th-C mansion, reputed by John Carr of York. Contains 18th-C furnished rooms, family portraits, period kitchen. Displays of Victoriana, local history,

local Roman antiquities, numismatics, glass and glassmaking, church silver, 19th- and 20th-C paintings; British ceramics, including Rockingham, local geology and natural history. Temporary exhibitions. Open Apr to Sep weekdays (ex Fri) 10–6. Sun 2.30–5. Nov to Mar; weekdays (ex Fri) 10–5. Sun 2.30–4.30. P. *(Tel 65481)* ⅏

ROTTINGDEAN *East Sussex* Map 5 TQ30
The Grange Museum and Art Gallery Early Georgian house, remodelled by Lutyens, now library, art gallery and museum including Kipling exhibits and part of the National Toy Museum. Frequent temporary exhibitions. Open Mon, Tue, Thu, Fri and Sat 10–5, Sun 2–5. Closed Weds and 4 Apr, 25/26 Dec. Free. ⚠ *(Tel Brighton 31004)*

ROUSHAM *Oxfordshire* Map 4 SP42
Rousham House Off A423. Attractive 17th- and 18th-C house near River Cherwell, with Civil War associations, fine pictures, furniture, and notable garden layout by William Kent. Open Wed, Sun and BH Apr to Sep, 2–5.30; gardens only daily, all year, 10–6. Garden 50p, House 75p. These prices are provisional for 1980. Party. ⚠ *(Tel Steeple Ashton 47110)* ⅏ B

ROWLANDS GILL *Tyne and Wear* Map 12 NZ15
Gibside Chapel and Avenue Repaired and rededicated in Jul 1966, originally built by James Paine in 1760, one of remaining buildings of 18th-C landscape layout. Open Apr to Sep, daily (ex Tue); Oct and Mar, Wed, Sat, Sun 2–6. Car Park, grounds and chapel 20p. ⚠ *(NT)*

ROYSTON *Hertfordshire* Map 5 TL34
Royston Museum Old Town Hall contains displays and collections of old photographs, paintings and other historical material from the town. Open all year, Sat only 10–4. Free. ⚠ *(Tel Hitchin 4476)* ⅏

RUDDINGTON *Nottinghamshire* Map 8 SK53
Ruddington Framework Knitters Museum Chapel Street. A unique early 19th-C complex of Frame shops and knitters cottages showing the working and domestic conditions of the workers. Illustrates the transition stage between domestic and factory working. Stockingers shop has eleven hand frames and allied equipment. Cottages are part tenanted and part in the process of restoration as Stockingers back-to-back cottage (1850) and hosier's cottage (1900). Open all year by appointment only. 20p. Special openings with machinery working by arrangement. P. *(Tel Nottingham 213287 or 212116)*
Ruddington Village Museum The Hermitage, Wilford Road. The Headquarters of the Ruddington local History and Amenity Society, this museum is housed in the village's oldest buildings with evidence of medieval occupation on the site. Permanent displays of local archaeological and folk material. Changing exhibitions throughout the year. ⚐ as ordered. Open all year (ex BH) Tue 10.30–12. Fri 7.30–9pm. At other times by appointment. 10p P in village *(Tel Nottingham 212116 or 213964)*

RUFFORD *Lancashire* Map 7 SD41
Rufford Old Hall Tudor and later (1662 and 1821), with a fine Great Hall and remarkable woodwork, including a rare example of a movable screen. The Philip Ashcroft museum is contained in a wing. Open Mar to Dec, Tue to Sun and BH Mon (closed Wed in Mar, Oct, Nov and Dec) 1–6 (or sunset). Hall and gardens 80p (ch 40p). *(NT)*

RUNCORN *Cheshire* Map 7 SJ58
Norton Priory Museum Warrington Road, nr Astmoor. Subject of largest excavation carried out by modern methods of any monastic site in Britain. Landscaped remains, standing 12th-C undercroft with beautifully carved passage, an exhibition of objects found by the excavators, surrounded by seven acres of Georgian woodlands. Winner of the 1978 National Archaeological Award. Archaeological excavation in progress Aug. Reconstruction model of Priory, wildlife display in restored summerhouse. Viewing gallery. ⚐ picnic area. Open Apr to Sep Mon, Tue and Wed 1–5, Sat, Sun and BH 1–6. Winter, Sun only 1–4. Special arrangements for parties booked in advance, including guided tour. 30p (ch 16 and pen 15p). *(Tel 69895 or 76531)*

RUSHTON *Northamptonshire* Map 4 SP88
Triangular Lodge Curious three-sided lodge, built 1593–96 by recusant Sir Thomas Tresham in the form of mystical and heraldic symbolism of the figure three. A Latin-inscribed frieze encircles the building. Open, see inside front cover. 15p (ch 16 and pen 5p). *(AM)*

RUSLAND *Cumbria* Map 7 SD38
Rusland Hall The house was built in 1720, and enlarged 1845. it contains many unusual mechanical instruments including a grand piano and a mechanical organ. Varied collection of antiques. Early cinema projectors and photographic equipment. Four acres of landscaped grounds of 18th-C style with peacocks, including rare whites. Demonstrations of mechanical music every afternoon. Open 1 Apr to 30 Sep daily 11–6. 60p (ch 14 40p). ⚠ *(Tel Satterthwaite 276)* ⅏

RYCOTE *Oxfordshire* Map 4 SP60
Rycote Chapel Off B4013. Small well-restored 15th-C chapel, consecrated in 1449 and visited by Princess Elizabeth in the reign of her sister, Mary I, and also by Charles I. Interior contains notable 15th-C benches and 17th-C pews. Barrel roof is noted for gilded star decor cut originally from rare Continental playing cards. Open, see inside front cover. 15p (ch 16 and pen 5p). ⚠ *(AM)*

RYDAL *Cumbria* Map 11 NY30
Rydal Mount Family home of William Wordsworth from 1813 until his death in 1850. Incorporates a pre-1574 farmer's cottage. Now owned by a descendant and containing an important group of family portraits, possessions and books. Lovely setting overlooking Windermere and Rydal Water. The 4½-acre fell garden was landscaped by the poet. ⚐ Open daily Mar to Oct, 10–5.30, Nov to mid Jan, 10–12.30 and 2–4, 40p (pen and students 30p, ch 14 20p). Party. ⚠ *(Tel Ambleside 3002)* **(79)**

RYE *East Sussex* Map 5 TQ92
Lamb House West Street. 18th-C house, home of Henry James from 1898 until his death in 1916. Attractive garden. Three rooms only open 2 Apr to Oct, Wed and Sat 2–6 (last admission 5.30) 40p *(NT)*
Rye Museum Ypres Tower. A 13th-C three-storey fortification. Contains collections of Cinque Port material, medieval and other pottery from the Rye kilns, militaria, shipbuilding, dolls, toys and local history archives. Open Easter–mid Oct daily Mon–Sat 10.30–1, 2.15–5.30, Sun 11.30–1, 2.15–5.30 (last admission half-an-hour prior to closing times). Admission charge. ⚠ *(Tel 3254)*

RYHOPE (Nr Sunderland) *Tyne and Wear* Map 12 NZ45

Ryhope Engines Museum Twin beam Engines (1868), restored by Ryhope Engines Trust. ⚓ when steaming. Bookstall. Open weekends Easter to end of year – Sat, Sun 2 – 5. Run under steam power 11 – 5, 4 to 7 Apr; 3 to 5 and 24 to 26 May; 23 to 25 Aug; 25/26 Oct. Information about midweek visits and current charges *(Tel Sunderland 210235)* ⚠

SAFFRON WALDEN *Essex* Map 5 TL53

Saffron Walden Museum Museum built 1834 for display of collections relating to anthropology, archaeology, natural history and applied arts. Special exhibition 7 Jun to 6 Jul 'The Furniture Maker's Workshop'. Open all year (ex 24, 25 Dec and 4 Apr), weekdays 11 – 5 (4 Oct to Mar), Sun and BH 2.30 – 5. Free. ⚠ *(Tel 22494)*

ST AGNES *Cornwall* Map 2 SW75

Wheal Coates Engine House The engine house lies on the cliff between St Agnes and Chapel Porth, and once housed an engine which provided the essential services of winding, pumping and ventilation for the mine. An important relic of the country's industrial past. *(NT)*

ST ALBANS *Hertfordshire* Map 4 TL10

City Museum Displays collections relating to natural history and geology of south-west Hertfordshire. Salaman colllection of tools and crafts has reconstruction of craftsmen's shops. Open all year Mon to Sat 10 – 5. Free. *(Tel 64511)*. *(Tourist Information Centre)* ⚙

Clock Tower Market Place. Example of early 15th-C curfew tower, which provides fine views over the city. Open 29 May to mid Sep, Sat 10 – 5.30, Sun 11 – 5.30. 10p (ch 5p). *(Tel 64511)*. *(Tourist Information Centre)*

Gorhambury House Entry via lodge gates at St Michael's Church, or at the Pré, on A5. Late Georgian mansion designed 1777 – 84 in modified classical style by Sir Robert Taylor. Chippendale furniture, Grimston portraits, 16th-C enamelled glass, and Francis Bacon associations. Open May to Sep Thu 2 – 5. 75p (ch and pen 35p). Party. Admission prices for 1980 under revision. ⚠ *(Tel 54051)*. *(Earl of Verulam)*

St Albans Organ Museum 326 Camp Road. Contains a unique collection of automatically operated organs and other musical instruments. Records of some of the organs and other instruments, also books on mechanical musical instruments can be purchased. Recitals Sun 2 – 4.15. 40p. Parties at other times by appointment. *(Tel 52875)*. *(Mr E Cockayne)* ⚙

The Royal National Rose Society's Gardens Chiswell Green Lane. Rose garden and trial ground for new varieties. Over 30,000 plants in 1,650 varieties. Species roses, old fashioned roses, modern roses and roses of the future. ⚓ Open 15 Jun to 30 Sep (ex BH Mon) Mon to Sat 9 – 5, Sun 2 – 6. 60p (ch 15 free). Party. Opening hours and admission charges for 1980 under revision. ⚠ *(Tel 50461)* ⚙

Verulamium Theatre, Museum and Hypocaust St Michael's. Roman theatre, built AD 140 – 150, used for presentation of plays and other functions. Superb museum of Roman finds, including tessellated pavements near by. Hypocaust, across parkland, also to be seen. Theatre open Mar to end Oct, daily 10 – 5; Nov to end Feb 10 – 2. 20p (ch 5p students 10p). Museum open Mar to end Oct, weekdays 10 – 5.30, Sun 2 – 5.30. Nov to end Feb, weekdays 10 – 4, Sun 2 – 4. 25p (ch 10p). *(Tel 54051 Theatre; 54659 Museum and Hypocaust)*

ST AUSTELL *Cornwall* Map 2 SX05

Wheal Martyn Museum 2m N on A391. Open-air site museum of the china clay industry. Complete clay works of the last century have been restored; huge granite-walled settling tanks, working water-wheels and wooden slurry pump, 220ft pan kiln or 'dry', horse-drawn wagons, two steam locomotives from the industry and the story of clay in Cornwall over two centuries shown in indoor displays. Also short slide and sound programme for visitors. Working Pottery. Open 1 Apr to 30 Oct 10 – 6 (last admission 5), open during winter for Party 12+ by prior arrangement. Admission prices for 1980 not yet decided. ⚠ *(Tel Stenalees 850362)*

ST CLEER *Cornwall* Map 2 SX26

Trethevy Quoit Famous example of a Neolithic tomb, with large slanting capstone. Accessible any reasonable time. Free. *(AM)*

ST HELENS *Mersyside* Map 7 SJ59

Pilkington Glass Museum On Prescot Road, A58, 1m from town centre. History of glass-making from Egyptians to present day, with some of the finest examples of glass in world. Various temporary exhibitions throughout the year. ⚓ Open all year (ex Christmas and New Year), Mon to Fri 10 – 5 (10 – 9 on Wed Mar to Oct), Sat, Sun and BH 2 – 4.30. Free; parties must book in advance. P. *(Tel 28882 ext 2499)* ⚙ B

ST IVES *Cambridgeshire* Map 4 TL37

Norris Museum The Broadway. Established 1933 using some 18th-C bricks from a former granary, containing a comprehensive

collection of Huntingdonshire books,
manuscripts, and local artefacts bequeathed
to the town. Agricultural tools and bygones in
new display area, water-colours of local
features, work in bone and straw by French
prisoners at Norman Cross. Ice skates – an
unusual and comprehensive selection of
fenland runners etc. Huntingdonshire
lacemaking. Open all year (ex BH and Mon).
May to Sep Tue to Fri 10 – 1 and 2 – 5, Sat
10 – 12 and 2 – 5, Sun 2 – 5, Oct to Apr Tue to
Fri 10 – 1 and 2 – 4, Sat 10 – 12 only, closed
Sun. Free. P. *(Tel 65101)*

ST IVES *Cornwall* Map 2 SW54
Park your car at Lelant Station and take
advantage of the park and ride service. The
fee includes parking and journeys on the train
between Lelant and St Ives during the day.

Barnes Museum of Cinematography
Comprehensive collection of items relating to
history of cinematography and photography.
Open Jun to Sep Mon – Sat 11 – 1 and
2.30 – 5. 20p (ch 10p). P in town.
***The Barbara Hepworth Museum and
Sculpture Garden*** Barnoon Hill. The
museum is in the house lived in by Dame
Barbara Hepworth from 1949 to her death in
1975. Sculpture by Dame Barbara from 1929
to 1974 is on display in the house and garden.
Also to be seen are many photographs, letters
and other documents showing the
background of the artist's career. Open all
year, Mon to Sat (closed Sun, 25, 26 Dec, 1
Jan and 4 Apr), Oct – Mar 10 – 4.30; Apr – Jun
and Sep 10 – 5.30; Jul and Aug Mon to Sat
10 – 6.30 also Sun 2 – 6. £1 (ch, students, and
pen 50p). P 200 yds. *(Tel 6226)* &

ST KEYNE *Cornwall* Map 2 SX26
Paul Corin Musical Collection Old Mill (St
Keyne Station). One of the finest collections in
Europe, of automatic musical intruments
which includes a rare 1929 German theatre
organ by Hupfeld, also organs from fairs,
cafés and streets of Holland. Reproducing
Player pianos with performances of famous
pianists. Orchestrions played in the cafés of
Europe and the Americas. Playing daily,
Easter week then May to Sep, 10.30 – 1,
2.30 – 5; Oct, Mar and Apr, Sun only, 2.30 – 5.
80p (ch 40p). Party. Admission prices under
revision for 1980. ⚠ free. *(Tel Liskeard
43108)* &

ST MAWES *Cornwall* Map 2 SW83
St Mawes Castle Coastal blockhouse
erected in 16th C by Henry VIII. Faces
Falmouth across Carrick Roads. Open*, see
inside front cover. 20p (ch 16 and pen 5p). ⚠
(AM)

ST NEOT *Cornwall* Map 2 SX16
Carnglaze Slate Caverns Old slate mine
unique in South West England, situated in the
beautiful valley of the River Loveny. Half a
million tons of slate were mined from these
huge caverns. Guided tours of great interest
take approx 45 minutes. Temperature
underground is 52° F all year round – jacket or
cardigan is advisable on hot summer days.
Open Easter and BH 10.30 – 5, Sun 2 – 5, May
and Jun 2 – 5, 1 Jul to 7 Sep Mon – Fri
10.30 – 5, Sun 2 – 5, 8 Sep to 30 Sep 2 – 5
(closed Sats). 70p (ch 35p, pen 50p). Parties
by appointment. Admission prices under
revision for 1980. ⚠ *(Tel Dobwalls 20251)*

ST NEWLYN EAST *Cornwall* Map 2 SW85
Lappa Valley Railway The 15in-gauge
steam railway runs along part of the old
Newquay – Chacewater GWR line. The train
makes a round trip of over two miles through
scenic countryside, and stops at East Wheal
Rose Halt where you can explore the site of a
famous old silver and lead mine. Five-acre
pleasure park (accessible by the train only),
boating lake, play area, book shop and ⚞.
Parties catered for. Open Easter week then
Weds and Suns only 2 – 6 until 23 May; 23
May to 30 Jun 11 – 5, 1 Jul to 7 Sep 10 – 5.30, 8
Sep to 4 Oct 11 – 5. 80p (ch and pen 50p, ch 3
free). *(Tel Mitchell 317)*

ST OLAVES *Norfolk* Map 5 TG49
St Olaves Priory Near Fritton Decoy.
Remains of small Augustinian priory.
Exceptional early example of brickwork
dating from late 13th C or early 14th C. Open
Apr to Sep at any reasonable time. Free. *(AM)*

ST OSYTH *Essex* Map 5 TM11
St Clere's Hall 1 m SSE on unclass road.
Moated on three sides, this Medieval manor
house has 16th-C additions and renovations.
It is one of the least altered examples of an
aisled hall with separately roofed coss-blocks
(wings) at either end. Open all year by
appointment only. ⚠ *(Tel 243)* & B

SALCOMBE *Devon* Map 3 SX73
Sharpitor ½m SW on unclass road. A modern
house with a museum and 6 acres of gardens
providing fine views. Museum of local
interest. Open 1 Apr to Oct, daily 11 – 1, 2 – 6.
Museum and gardens 70p, gardens only 50p.
(NT) (NGS)

SALFORD *Gt Manchester* Map 7 SJ89
Ordsall Hall Museum Taylorson Street.
Partly half-timbered manor house with later
brick-built wing (1639), includes Tudor Great
Hall, Star Chamber with 14th-C features and
Victorian farmhouse kitchen. On upper floor
are social history displays and temporary
exhibitions. Open all year Mon to Sat 10 – 5,
Sun 2 – 5 (ex 4 Apr, 24 – 26 Dec, 1 Jan). Free.
P (street). *(Tel 061-872 0251)*
Salford Museum and Art Gallery The
Crescent, Peel Park. The ground floor
displays a period street scene typical of a
northern industrial town at the turn of the
century. The first floor art galleries house a
large collection of works by L S Lowry, as well
as a regular series of temporary art
exhibitions and displays of decorative arts.
Open all year daily (ex 4 Apr, 24, 25, 26 Dec
and 1 Jan) 10 – 6 (Oct – Mar, 10 – 5) Sun 2 – 5.
Free. ⚠ *(Tel 061-736 2649 and 061-
737 7692)*

SALISBURY *Wiltshire* Map 4 SU12
Salisbury and South Wilts Museum St Ann
Street. Comprehensive displays of exhibits
relating to the history of the city and south
Wiltshire. Important prehistoric and medieval
collections. Display of ceramics and
costumes, and models of Old Sarum and
Stonehenge. Open daily (ex Sun) Oct to Apr
10 – 4; May to Sep 10 – 5; Sun also in Jul and
Aug 2 – 5 (closed 25, 26 Dec and 13 Apr). 40p
(ch 16 and members free, pen and students
20p). Shop on premises for replicas and
publications. P. *(Tel Mr P R Saunders, 4465)*
& B
Mompesson House Standing in the
Cathedral Close, surrounded by gracious
period houses, dates from 1701, with
splendid panelling and woodwork. Open Apr
to end Oct, daily ex Thu and Fri 12.30 – 6
(sunset if earlier). Closed Nov to end Feb.
70p. *(NT)*

Old Sarum 2m N on A345. First probably an Iron Age camp, later Roman 'Sorbiodunum' and finally site of Norman castle and cathedral town. Foundations of castle and cathedral can be seen, together with small museum. Open*, see inside front cover. 15p (ch 16 and pen 5p). ⚠ *(AM)*

SAMLESBURY *Lancashire* Map 7 SD63
Samlesbury Hall Restored half-timbered house, administered and preserved by the Samlesbury Hall Trust and the Lancashire Branch of the Council for the Protection of Rural England. Various exhibitions. ♨ Open 24 Jan – 18 Dec daily (ex Mon) 11.30 – 5. 35p (ch 15 20p). P. *(Tel Mellor 2229 and 2010)*

SANCREED *Cornwall* Map 2 SW42
Carn Euny Ancient Village 1m SW. Iron Age village site with characteristic Cornish 'fogous' (subterranean hiding hole) preserved some 66ft in length, with circular chamber. Open, see inside front cover. 15p (ch 16 and pen 15p) ⚠ *(AM)*

SANDRINGHAM *Norfolk* Map 9 TF62
Sandringham House, Grounds and Museum Bought by Queen Victoria for the Prince of Wales in 1862, this modern royal mansion contains paintings of the Royal Family from 1845, also of members of European Royal Families. Sculpture, china, ornaments and furniture. ♨ Open 6 Apr to 25 Sep (ex 21 Jul to 9 Aug). Apr Tue, Wed, and Thu. May to Sep daily (ex Fri and Sat) also open 6/7 Apr. Admission prices not available. ⚠ *(Tel King's Lynn 2675)* ♿
Wolferton Station (down side). On the Sandringham Estate, former Royal Retiring Rooms built in 1898 specifically for, and solely used by Kings and Queens and their guests en route for Sandringham, can be seen. Fine oak panelling, original fittings (some gold plated). Period railway posters, important small railway relics and Edwardian curios including some from Royal train journeys, Queen Victoria's Travelling Bed (1828). Open Apr to Sep (plus BH), Daily (ex Sat 11 – 1, 2 – 6, Sun 2 – 6. 35p (ch 14 20p). ⚠ *(Tel Dersingham 40674)* ♿

SANDTOFT *Yorkshire* Map 8 SE70
Sandtoft Transport Centre 15m E of Doncaster off A18. Developing National Transport Museum, primarily for the preservation and operation of trolleybuses, but also includes motorbuses and other items of transport interest, boasting a collection of over 50 vehicles from many parts of Britain and the Continent. Several trolleybuses are restored and operate on the centre's own overhead wiring circuit on 15, 16 Apr; 27, 28 May; 26, 27 Aug; also last weekend in Jun and Sep. 15p (ch 14 and pen 10p). Special open day 29 Jun when many interesting vehicles and items from other collections are on show. Admission prices under review for 1979. ⚠ ♿ **(79)**

SANDWICH *Kent* Map 5 TR35
Guildhall Dates from 1578, since restored. Contains a collection of local documents, paintings, and interesting relics. Open all year, Mon to Fri 10.30 – 12.30 and 2 – 4 (5, Jun to Oct), subject to Courts being held Tue, Wed, and Fri each week. 10p (ch 14 with parents, free; unaccompanied children not admitted). ⚠ *(Tel 3060 or 2200 or 3044)* ♿

SAXTEAD GREEN *Suffolk* Map 5 TM26
Windmill Off B1115. Fine 18th-C postmill, twice altered, the present superstructure dating from 1854. Open, see inside front cover, but closed on Sun. 20p (ch and pen 5p). ⚠ *(AM)*

SCARBOROUGH *North Yorkshire* Map 8 TA08
Scarborough Castle Fortified c1140 by the Earl of Albemarle and rebuilt with a four-storeyed keep in 1155 by Henry II. Damaged in the Civil War and the 1914 – 18 War. Open*, see inside front cover. 25p (ch 16 and pen 10p). ⚠ *(AM)*
Scarborough Zoo and Marineland Performing dolphins, penguins, monkeys, bears and parrots are among the attractions. Children are provided with free fish to feed the sealions, and bottles of milk for the young lambs and goats. ♨ Open Easter to 31 Oct, daily 10 – dusk. Admission prices not yet known. P. *(Tel 64401)* ♿ **(79)**

SCUNTHORPE *Humberside* Map 8 SE81
Borough Museum and Art Gallery This regional museum for South Humberside contains important prehistoric exhibits. Roman and later archaeology, geology, natural history and local industry, bygones, period rooms and Ironstone workers' cottage. New local history galleries. Continuous programme of temporary exhibitions. Open all year, Mon to Sat 10 – 5, Sun 2 – 5. Free on weekdays; 5p (ch 2½p) on Sat and Sun afternoon and BH. P. *(Tel 3533)*
Normanby Hall Normanby Park. 5m N on B1430. A Regency mansion built in 1825 by Sir Robert Smirke for the Sheffield family. Displays of costume and Regency furniture. The house is set in 350 acres of parkland, lawns and gardens. The stable complex includes a Countryside Interpretation Centre. Nature trail. Blacksmith and potter. ♨ Open all year, Apr to Oct Mon, Wed, Thu, Fri, Sat

10–12.30, 2–5.30, Sun 2–5.30; Nov to Mar weekdays (closed Sat) 10–12.30, 2–5, Sun 2–5. 20p (ch 10p). ⚠ *(Tel 720215)* ⟁ B
SEATON DELAVAL *Northumberland* Map 12 NZ37
Seaton Delaval Hall 1½m NE on A190. Baroque-style 18th-C masterpiece of Vanbrugh, with tall Doric façade flanked by twin wings, one built to house the stables. Paintings and furnishings in the west wing, historical documents and statuary in the restored centre block. Open 1 May to 30 Sep, Wed, Sun, and BH 2–6. 30p (ch and pen 20p). ⚠ *(Tel 481 493). (Lord Hastings)*
SEDBERGH *Cumbria* Map 7 SD69
National Park Centre 72 Main Street. Permanent interpretation centre for the Sedbergh area with displays, books, maps, etc. Open Apr to end Sep, daily mid morning to late afternoon. Free. ⚠ *(Tel 20125)* ⟁ B
SEDLESCOMBE *East Sussex* Map 5 TQ71
Nortons Farm Museum and Farm Trail 4½m NW of Hastings on A21. Depicts the 'cart horse era' with a fine display of carts, ploughs and hand tools. The Farm Trail takes visitors round the fruit and arable farm, where cart horses are still used. Picnic area. Open Jun to Sep 9–5. ⚠ *(Tel 471)* **(79)**
SELBORNE *Hampshire* Map 4 SU73
Oates Memorial Library and Museum and the Gilbert White Museum The Wakes. Home of the Rev Gilbert White, pioneer naturalist whose 'Natural History of Selborne' was written here. Galleries concerning the history and natural history of Selborne; galleries devoted to Captain Oates of Antarctica fame and to Frank Oates, explorer of Central Africa. Extensive gardens. Open Mar to Oct, Tue to Sun, BH 12–5.30 (last admission 5, parties outside these dates by arrangement). 45p (ch 16 20p, pen 35p). P. *(Tel 275)* ⟁
SELBY *North Yorkshire* Map 8 SE63
Carlton Towers 6m S (A1041). The Duke of Norfolk's Yorkshire home, Carlton Towers was built in 1614 on property owned by the Duke's ancestors since the Norman Conquest. It was remodelled in the 18th and 19th C and now presents a mainly Victorian appearance. The elaborate state rooms are by John Francis Bentley, architect of Westminster Cathedral. Interesting paintings, furniture, silver and heraldry. Exhibitions of family uniforms and coronation robes. Viewing of the Priest's hiding hole. Shop. Picnic area and ⚏. Open 5 to 8 Apr incl., 4/5 also 24 to 28 May incl. Thereafter Sat, Sun, Mon and Wed 31 May to end Sep also 26 Aug 1–5 (last admission 4.30).
Conducted tours by appointment only

Thu evenings. Also 5–8 Apr, 4/5 May. Admission prices not available. ⚠ *(Tel Goole 860243)*

SEVENOAKS *Kent* Map 5 TQ55
Black Charles 2½m SE at Underriver. A Hall House, built about 1400. It has fine panelling and fire-places and other interesting features. The original structure can be easily seen. Open 1 May to 10 Sep for parties by arrangement. 40p (ch 14 25p). ⚠ *(Tel Hildenborough 833036)*
Knole Famous mansion of Sackvilles, one of the largest in England, begun in 1456 by Thomas Bourchier, Archbishop of Canterbury, with many early 17th-C additions. Notable state-rooms with pictures and 17th- and 18th-C furnishings. Cartoon and Brown galleries and vast park. Open Apr to Sep, Wed to Sat and BH Mons 11–5, Sun 2–5; Oct and Nov Wed to Sat 11–4, Sun 2–4. £1.20 (ch 60p). Connoisseurs' day Fri (ex 4 Apr), £1.60, no reduction for children. Last admission one hour before closing. House closed Dec to end Mar. Gardens open 1st Wed in month, May to Sep 50p Park open free to pedestrians. ⚠ £1. *(Tel 53006 for special concessions for cars). (NT)*
Long Barn 2m S at south end of Weald village. 14th-C house, reputed birthplace of William Caxton. Restored by Edwin Lutyens and enlarged by addition of 16th-C barn in 1915 for Sir Harold Nicolson and his wife, Vita Sackville-West, who lived here for 15 years prior to Sissinghurst Castle. Fine beams, fireplaces, old brick paving, small galleried hall with ornamental panelling. Home of the late Charles Lindbergh from 1936–1938. Medium-sized garden, created by Vita Sackville-West; terraced lawns, yew trees and raised herbaceous borders. Open Apr to Sep Wed 2–6. Parties by prior arrangement. 60p (ch 25p). Under revision for 1980. No dogs. *(Tel Weald 282)*

SHAFTESBURY *Dorset* Map 3 ST82
Local History Museum Gold Hill. Small museum of needlework toys, agricultural and domestic items, fans, pottery and finds from local excavations. Fire engine of 1744. Award winner in 'Museum of the Year' award scheme for 1976. Open Easter to end Sep daily 11–5, Sun 2.30–5. 10p (ch 5p). Admission prices under revision for 1980. P. *(Tel 2157)* ⟁ B

SHALFORD *Surrey* Map 4 TQ04
Shalford Mill An 18th-C watermill with a small garden, on the River Tillingbourne. Part open on application to 45 The Street. *(NT)*

The Famous Five
of Yorkshire

FIVE HOUSES OVER FOUR CENTURIES

Bramham Park
Burton Constable
Carlton Towers
Sledmere House
Sutton Park

The Famous Five of Yorkshire are a group of Stately Homes within about 40 miles of York, which are still lived in and cared for by their owners.

Each house is fascinating in its own right, but seen as a group they show the changing styles of houses built by wealthy country families over four centuries, from the grace of the sixteenth century to the grandeur of Victorian Gothic.

The Houses stand in grounds varying from the French formal design, to the natural landscaping of Capability Brown. In addition there are lakes, lily ponds, fountains, cascades, rose gardens and nature walks. We hope you will come and share the pleasures of these lovely places with us;

Our voucher scheme allows a substantial saving.

There is a Free Car Park, a Cafeteria and a gift shop at each House and between us we are open every day during the Summer.

BRAMHAM PARK
Wetherby

BURTON CONSTABLE
Sproatley

SUTTON PARK
Sutton on the Forest

CARLTON TOWERS
Selby

SLEDMERE HOUSE
Driffield

See each gazetteer entry for details, and send for the free leaflet and vouchers giving details of opening times, special attractions and booked party rates.

WE LOOK FORWARD TO SEEING YOU!

SHALLOWFORD *Staffordshire* Map 7 SJ82
Izaak Walton's Cottage A restored cottage
where Izaak Walton, the famous angler,
stayed at times during his retirement. There is
a small museum. Open all year, Thu to Sun
10 – 1, 2 – 5, also Mons 29 May and 28 Aug. 5p
(ch 3p). ⚠ (in lane). *(Tel Yarnfield 278)*

SHAP *Cumbria* Map 12 NY51
Shap Abbey An abbey of the
Premonstratensian order, dedicated to St
Mary Magdalene, with buildings dating from
1201 – Jan 1540, when abbey was dissolved.
Open, see inside front cover. Free. P. *(Tel
670). (AM)* &
Keld Chapel 1 m SW off A6, close to River
Lowther. Small, pre-Reformation building, in
which occasional services are still held. Key
available at cottage in village, see notice on
chapel door. Free. *(NT)*

SHARPTHORNE *West Sussex* Map 5 TQ33
Tanyard A medieval tannery and manor with
16th- and 17th-C additions, set in attractive
walled gardens. Formerly reputed to have
been a royal household where Queen Victoria
once stayed. The main rooms with oak beams
and timbering are on view, displaying large
open fireplaces, furniture, *objets d'art* and
early Victorian photographs typical of the
period. Open 1 May to 30 Sep, Mon and Wed
2 – 5 (other times by prior appointment). 75p
(ch and pen, no reduction). ⚠ *(Tel 01-
643 5448). (Mr M R Lewinsohn)*

SHEBBEAR *Devon* Map 2 SS40
Alscott Farm Agricultural Museum A
remarkable collection of vintage farm tractors,
ploughs, dairy and household implements,
photographs and information on North
Devon's agricultural past. Special exhibition
of unique scale model of an Edwardian
travelling fair and contemporary photographs
and original circus posters. Open Easter to 30
Sep, daily, 12 – dusk. 40p (ch 10p). Party &
coaches welcome. ⚠ *(Tel 206)* &

SHEFFIELD *South Yorkshire* Map 8 SK38
Abbeydale Industrial Hamlet Abbeydale
Road South. One of the first examples of
industrial archaeology to be preserved and
made accessible to the public. The late 18th-
and early 19th-C steel and scythe works, with
their machinery, show production from the
raw material stage to the finished production.
⚐. Children's Working Days 7 Mar, 3 Oct, 7
Nov. Working Days 8/9 Mar, 4 Oct, 8 Nov.
Craftsman's Fair 14 – 22 Jun. Open daily (ex
24 – 26 Dec), Mon to Sat 10 – 5, Sun 11 – 5;
open until 8, 26 May to 27 Aug. 30p (ch 15p,
pen free). ⚠ 10p car, 5p m/c, 40p coach. *(Tel
367731)*
Bishops' House Meersbrook Park. A 15th- to
16th-C Yeoman's house, restored as a
museum of local and social history. Open all
year, Wed to Sat 10 – 5, Sun 11 – 5, closed
24 – 26 Dec. 10p (ch 5p). ⚠ *(Tel 57701)* &
City Museum Weston Park. A regional
museum of geology, natural sciences,
archaeology, and Sheffield area trades,
including cutlery, plate and ceramics. North
Derbyshire antiquities and changing
exhibitions are also featured. Open daily (ex
24 – 26 Dec), weekdays 10 – 5, Sun 11 – 5; 26
May to 25 Aug, weekdays 10 – 8, Sun 11 – 8.
Free. *(Tel 27226)*
Shepherd Wheel Whiteley Woods. An early
water-powered cutler's grinding
establishment. Open Wed to Sat (ex 24 – 26
Dec) 10 – 12.30 and 1.30 – 5, Sun 11 – 12.30
and 1.30 – 5. Free. *(Tel 367731)* &

SHEFFIELD PARK *East Sussex* Map 5 TQ42
On A275. Belonged to King Harold's father
and later was mentioned in Domesday Book.
Basically Tudor, it was remodelled by James
Wyatt 1775 – 8 for 1st Lord Sheffield. In last
century was famous for the inter-Australian
cricket matches, started by 3rd Lord Sheffield,
whose own team included W G Grace.
Guests to house included Henry VIII, Edward
Gibbon, King Edward VII. Present owners, Mr
and Mrs P J Radford, purchased property in
1972 and are engaged in restoring and
redecorating over a long period. It is one of the
most beautiful houses in Sussex and the
situation is unrivalled. Open Easter to end
Oct, Wed, Thu, Sun and BH Mons 2 – 5. 50p
Party 40+. ⚠ *(Tel Danehill 790531)* & *(79)*

SHEFFIELD PARK GARDEN *East Sussex*
Map 5 TQ42
On A275. Magnificent gardens and a lake-
watered park of nearly 150 acres, laid out
from the 18th to the 20th C; they surround a
house by James Wyatt (see previous entry).
Rhododendrons, azaleas (May to Jun), and
notable trees and shrubs (autumn). ⚐ (not
under NT management). Gardens open Apr
to Sep, Tue to Sat 11 – 7, Sun 2 – 7; Oct to 15
Nov, Tue to Sat 11 – 5, Sun 2 – 5; BH Mon
11 – 7. £1. No dogs. *(NT)*

**SHEFFIELD PARK STATION, BLUEBELL
RAILWAY MUSEUM** *East Sussex*
Map 5 TQ42
Off A275. A station of the revived Bluebell
Railway, a former London, Brighton and
South Coast line. Parade Day 11 May, 20th
Anniversary celebrations 3 Aug, Vintage
Sunday 14 Sep. Vintage steam trains run as
follows: weekends throughout the year (Sun
only in Dec, Jan, and Feb); weekends and
Wed in May and Oct, daily Jun to end Sep,
and daily during Easter week. Fares 90p (ch
45p). Party. Under revision for 1980. Part of
the station is a small museum of old railways
relics and records. Open from 10.30am on
days when trains run, on other days open for
limited viewing. ⚠ 20p. ⚐ *(Tel Newick 2370)*
&

SHERBORNE *Dorset* Map 3 ST61
Sherborne Castle A 16th-C house built by Sir
Walter Raleigh, home of the Digby family
(17th-C Earls of Bristol) since 1617, with fine
furniture, paintings, porcelain, and items of
historical interest in their natural settings.
Twenty acres of 'Capability' Brown planned
lakeside lawns and pleasure grounds with
cascade and orangery. Old Castle ruins and
Abbey. Varied programme of special events
on most Sundays during summer. Teas and
refreshments in the Gothic Dairy by the lake.
Picnic grounds. Open 5 Apr to end Sep, Thu,
Sat, Sun, and BH Mon 2 – 6. Admission prices
under review. ⚠ *Tel 3182). (Mr S Wingfield
Digby)* & B
Sherborne Museum, Abbey Gate House
Church Lane. Opened in 1968 and extended
to the second floor in 1970. On show are a
model of the Norman castle, a fine Victorian
dolls' house, local geological and Roman
material, coloured photographs of the
Sherborne missal of 1400, local photographs
from 1850 and other items. Natural history
section. Open 1 Apr to 31 Oct daily (ex Mon)
10.30 – 12.30 and 3 – 4.30, Sun 3 – 5. 1 Nov to
31 Mar, Tue, Sat and Sun afternoon only. 10p
(ch 19 5p). P. *(Tel 2252)*
Sherborne Old Castle This ruined castle
about half a mile east of the town was built by
Roger, Bishop of Salisbury between 1107 and

1135. The keep, curtain walls, towers and gates date from the period. Minor alterations were carried out by Sir Walter Raleigh in 1592. Open*, see inside front cover. 15p (ch 16 and pen 5p). ⚖ *(AM)*

Worldwide Butterflies Ltd and Lullingstone Silk Farm Compton House. Entrance on A30 2½m W. Unique example of butterfly farm in stately home and grounds. Collections from across the world. Natural jungle with living exotic butterflies and tropical palm-house. Also the home of the Lullingstone Silk Farm which produced unique English reared silk for the last two Coronations and the Queen's wedding dress. Open 1 Apr to 31 Oct, 10–5. £1.10 (ch 16 55p) under revision for 1980. ⚖ *(Tel Yeovil 4608/9)* ⅃

SHERBORNE ST JOHN *Hampshire* Map 4 SU65

The Vyne ½m NE. A notable early 16th-C house, showing diaper brickwork, built for the Sandys family, with additions of 1654 by John Webb, including the earliest classical portico. Chapel contains Renaissance glass. Fine linenfold panelling in long gallery. Open Apr to end Oct, Tue, Wed, Thu, Sat and Sun 2–6 (5.30 Oct). BH Mon 11–1 and 2–6. £1 (ch 50p), gardens only 40p (ch 20p). ⍑ in the Old Brewhouse 3–5.30. *(NT)*

SHERIFF HUTTON *North Yorkshire* Map 8 SE66

Sheriff Hutton Castle The ruins of a 12th-C castle, originally five storeys high with massive square towers and an extensive gallery. Strong Royal connections existed from the 14th century onwards, but from the time of James I the castle was greatly neglected. Still an impressive structure, the highest remaining part is the south west tower, 100ft high, beneath which there is a dungeon. Open all year during daylight hours. ⚖ *(Tel 341)* ⅃

SHERINGHAM *Norfolk* Map 9 TG14

Sheringham Hall ½m W of town, off A149. Regency mansion and park, work of Humphrey Repton in 1812. Magnificent rhododendron woods (one mile drive) planted in the 19th C. Hall open on Fri 2–6, from May to Sep, only by previous written application to the Secretary. 25p in aid of charity. Gardens generally open on five Suns during the year. 25p. Park open all weekdays. 25p per person. Rhododendron Woods open 1 May to 30 Jun. 25p. ⚖ *(Tel 822074)*. *(Mr T Upcher)* ⅃ B

North Norfolk Railway Sheringham Station. A collection of steam locomotives and rolling stock, some undergoing or awaiting restoration. Among the former are several industrial tank engines and two examples of

ex-Great Eastern Railway main line engines. Rolling stock includes suburban coaches, Brighton Belle, Pullmans and directors private saloons. Model railway. Souvenirs and bookshop. Museums of railwayana. Steam-hauled trains to operate weekends, Easter, Spring Bank Hol, the every Sun and certain weekdays throughout summer, until Oct. ⍑ Open Easter to mid Oct, daily from 10–5 (or later). Admission prices under revision for 1980. Party. P. *(Tel 822045)* ⅃

SHILDON *Co Durham* Map 8 NZ22

Timothy Hackworth Museum Soho House, Hackworth Cottage. A sixteen-room house, fully renovated, originally the home of Timothy Hackworth, famous locomotive engineer and first manager of the Stockton-Darlington railway. Four of the rooms contain furniture from the 1830s and the other rooms hold displays of Hackworth's papers and personal trivia, Stockton and Darlington railway items, etc. Timothy Hackworth original engine shed. Copies of the booklet 'Shildon Urban Rail Trails' available from museum. Open 1 Apr to 30 Sep 10–6, Wed to Sun. 15p (ch 15 and pen 10p). ⚖ *(Tel Spennymoor 816166 ext 385)*

SHIPLEY *West Sussex* Map 4 TQ12

Belloc's Mill King's Mill. A fine example of a smock mill (1879, restored 1957) in full working order. Hilaire Belloc, the writer, lived here from 1906–53. Small exhibition of his work in mill. Open for conducted tours May to Oct, first weekend in month 2.30–5.30. 30p (ch 5–16 15p). Parties at other times by written appointment to *Mr P J Crowther, West Sussex RH13 8PJ.* P. *(Tel Coolham 310)*

SHIPTON *Salop* Map 7 SO59

Shipton Hall 6½m SW of Much Wenlock on B4378. A beautiful Elizabethan Manor house in picturesque Corvedale setting. Notable interior plasterwork of 1762 also fine Georgian stable block. There is an attractive walled garden, medieval dovecote and old parish church. ⍑ for parties by arrangement. Open May to Sep Thu 2.30–5.30; Sun 2.30–5.30 during Aug, also 4, 5, 25, 26 May, 24, 25 Aug. 70p (ch 14 40p). Party. ⚖ *(Tel Brockton 225)*. *(C R N Bishop Ltd)* ⅃ B (gardens)

SHOREHAM-BY-SEA *West Sussex* Map 4 TQ20

Marlipins A Norman-and-later flint building possibly a warehouse, now a maritime and local history museum. Open May to Sep Mon to Sat 10–12.30 and 2–5, Sun 2.30–5. ⚖ *(Tel 62994)*. *(Sussex Archaeological Society)*

Sherborne Castle

Built by Sir Walter Raleigh 1594

Home of the Digby family (17th-century Earls of Bristol) since 1617. A fascinating fully-furnished historic home in a beautiful setting of lake, woods and parkland with ruins of the old castle in the background. Described by Alexander Pope in 1722 as a 'phantasy castle — so peculiar and of so uncommon kind that it merits a more particular description'. Situated 1 mile to the east of the attractive town of Sherborne, with its ancient abbey, Almshouses and 2 castles. For details of the opening times see the gazetteer entry.

SHOTTERY *Warwickshire* Map 4 SP 15
Anne Hathaway's Cottage The thatched and timbered Elizabethan cottage, where Anne Hathaway, who became Shakespeare's wife, was born. Open all year (ex 4 Apr, morning, 24–26 Dec) Jun, Jul, Aug, Sep, weekdays 9–7, Sun 10–6; Apr, May, Oct, Thu and Sat 9–7, Mon to Wed and Fri 9–6, Sun 10–6; Nov to Mar, weekdays 9–4.30 Sun 1.30–4.30. 50p (ch school age 20p). Admission prices under revision for 1980. ⚠ P. *(Tel Stratford-upon-Avon 292100)* ⅃ B

SHREWSBURY *Salop* Map 7 SJ 41
Bear Steps St Alkmund's Square. Recently restored, timber-framed, 14th-C cottage with shops and meeting hall. Hall has mid 14th-C crown-post roof, and buildings are of considerable antiquarian interest. A winner of European Architectural Heritage Year Award. Open all year Mon to Sat 10–5. Free. P. *(Tel 52019)* ⅃ B

Shrewsbury Castle Castle Gates. A 12th-C-and-later building, with historic associations, altered by Thomas Telford after 1780. Open Easter Sat to Oct, daily 10–5; Oct to Easter, Mon to Sat 10–4. 22p (ch and pen 11p). P. *(Tel 52019)*

Clive House Museum An 18th-C town house occupied by the 1st Lord Clive during his period as Mayor of Shrewsbury in 1762. Now houses a collection of Caughley and Coalport China, maw tiles, costume, church silver, Georgian room and the Museum of the 1st The Queen's Dragoon Guards. Open all year (ex Sun and BH) Mon 12–1 and 2–6 (4.30 in winter), Tue to Sat 10–1 and 2–6 (4.30 winter). Free. P in streets. *(Tel 54811)*

Longden Coleham Pumping Station Two compound beam engines installed in 1900 and worked until 1970, restored to working order. Open all year Wed to Fri 2–5; other times by arrangement with Curator. Free. P. *(Tel 54811)*

Rowley's House Barker Street. A fine restored half-timbered house, containing Roman remains from Wroxeter, and Shropshire bygones. Geology and prehistory can be seen by arrangement. Open all year Mon to Sat (ex Sun and BH) 10–1, 2–5. Free. P. *(Tel 61196)*

SHUGBOROUGH *Staffordshire* Map 7 SJ 92
Shugborough Hall and Staffordshire County Museum 5m E of Stafford off A513. Mansion (NT) built 1693–1810, including work by Samuel Wyatt. Plasterwork, pictures, fine collection of French furniture, mementoes of Admiral George Anson (1697–1762). Notable landscape includes Chinese House in neo-Grecian style by James 'Athenian' Stuart. Riverside gardens. Museum exhibits include social history, agriculture, crafts, natural history and geology in Staffordshire. ⚐ Open Mar to Oct Tue to Fri, 10.30–5.30, Sat, Sun and BH 2–6. Entrance to site weekends and BH only 40p (ch 15p). School parties booked in advance free. Party 20+. House 60p (ch 25p). Parties as above. Park Farm 20p (ch 15p), school parties booked in advance 10p per person. ⚠ free. All details subject to alteration. *(Tel Little Haywood 881388)* ⅃ *(NT)*

SIDMOUTH *Devon* Map 3 SY 18
Sidmouth Museum An elegant Georgian House adjacent parish church. Open 10 days Easter and from Spring BH to end Sep. 10.30–12.30 and 2.30–4.30 Mon to Sat, and Sun 2.30–4.30. When closed can be visited by appointment. 15p (ch school 5p). *(Tel 2946 or 2357)* **(79)**

SILCHESTER *Hampshire* Map 4 SU66
Calleva Museum A small museum dealing
with the Roman town of Calleva Atrebatum,
which was recently rearranged and updated
to include panels of photographs, maps and
other illustrative materials as well as actual
objects excavated here, in order to present a
brief account of life in this Roman town.
Accessible daily from 9 – sunset. Free. P in
road. *(Tel 700362)* &

SILSOE *Bedfordshire* Map 4 TL03
Wrest Park Gardens Notable 18th-C garden
layout with formal canals and alterations by
'Capability' Brown. Baroque early 18th-C
banqueting house by Thomas Archer, and
Bowling Green House by Batty Langley. ⚏.
Grounds only open Sat, Sun and BH Mon
10 – 5.30 in Apr; 10 – 7 from May to Sep. 25p
(ch 16 and pen 10p). ⚠ *(AM)*

SINGLETON *West Sussex* Map 4 SU81
Weald and Downland Open-Air Museum A
museum of historic buildings from the Weald
and Downland area in Kent, Sussex, Surrey
and Hampshire which have been re-erected
here together with displays of traditional crafts
and rural industries. Exhibits include a 14th-C
house, a 15th-C farmhouse from Kent, an
18th-C granary from Littlehampton, 19th-C
Southwater forge, a 19th-C Sussex toll
cottage, the Titchfield market hall, and the
Hambrook barn which houses an exhibition of
building techniques and materials since
medieval times. Woodland nature trail
(including special trail for wheelchairs which
are pushed) and picnic area. Open 1 Apr to 30
Sep daily (ex Mon but incl BH and Mon in Aug)
11 – 5; Oct Wed, Sat, Sun 11 – 5; Nov to Mar
1980 Sun 11 – 4. Last admission 1 hr before
closing. 60p (school ch, students and pen
35p). Under revision for 1980. Party. ⚠ *(Tel
348)*

SISSINGHURST *Kent* Map 5 TQ73
Sissinghurst Castle Garden 1½m NE of
town. Tudor, with a fine gate tower and moat,
and beautiful gardens, created by the late V
Sackville-West, famous for roses in Jun and
Jul. ⚏ May to Sep. Part of castle and the
gardens are open Apr to 15 Oct. Mon to Fri
12 – 6.30; Sat, Sun, 4 Apr and BH Mon
10 – 6.30. £1.10 (ch 50p). Party 70p. Shop. No
dogs. *(Tel 250)*. *(NT)*

SITTINGBOURNE *Kent* Map 5 TQ96
Dolphin Yard Sailing Barge Museum
Crown Quay Lane. Original sail loft, forge,
shipwrights, also sailmakers and riggers
tools. Models, plans, prints, etc. ⚏. Open
Easter to end Oct, Sun also BH Mon 11 – 5.
30p (ch 16 and pen 15p). P.

SIZERGH *Cumbria* Map 7 SD48
Sizergh Castle 14th-C pele tower
incorporated in a house dating from the 15th
to 18th C. Tudor great hall, Jacobite relics.
Fine ceilings and panelling. Open Apr to end
Sep; house open Wed and Sun, Thu, 29 May
and all Thu in Jul and Aug 2 – 5.45. Closed BH
Mons. 70p Gardens only 30p. *(NT)*

SKEGNESS *Lincolnshire* Map 9 TF56
Church Farm Museum Farmhouse and
outbuildings restored to show the way of life of
a Lincolnshire farmer at the end of 19th C. The
Bernard Best collection of farm implements
and machinery together with veterinary
equipment are on display. Craftsmen at work
during summer weekends. ⚏ (teas
weekends). Open Apr to Oct daily
10.30 – 5.30. 25p (ch 16 and pen 15p). ⚠ *(Tel
66658)*
Skegness Natureland Marine Zoo North
Parade, The Promenade. A modern marine
zoo, specialising in keeping sea lions, seals
and penguins. There is also a tropical house,
aquarium, including a large Fresh Water Fish
Exhibit, and a Floral Palace full of exotic
plants, with tropical birds in free flight. The zoo
also cares for orphan baby seals, that have
been washed up on nearby beaches. Pets
Corner and a Wild Fowl Pool provide
amusement for the children. ⚏. Open all year
(ex 25 Dec), daily 29 May to Oct 10 – 7.30
(10 – 4, Oct to 28 May). Admission charges
not yet decided. P. *(Tel 4345)* &

SKELTON *Cumbria* Map 12 NY43
Hutton-in-the-Forest 17th-C house built
around a 14th-C pele tower, alterations in
18th and 19th Cs by Webster and Salvin. The
house contains contemporary pictures and
furnishings. Gardens include fine specimen
trees and an ornamental lake. ⚏ House open
during summer months, details from local
Tourist Information centres. Party. Opening
times and prices under revision for 1980. ⚠
(Tel 207). *(Lord Inglewood)* & B

SKIDBY *Humberside* Map 8 TA03
Skidby Windmill On A164. Only surviving
example of intact windmill north of Humber
and east of Pennines, this is a well-preserved
mill of 1821 which is being established as an
agricultural museum. Black-tarred tower and
white cap form prominent local landmark.
Open first Sat in May to last Sun in Sep, Sat
10 – 4, Sun 1 – 4.30 also Wed, Thu and Fri in
Aug 1 – 4.30. Parties at other times by
arrangement. 15p (ch 10p). P. *(Tel Beverley
882255)*

SKIPTON *North Yorkshire* Map 7 SD95
Craven Museum Town Hall, High Street.
Contains collection dealing especially with
the Craven district. There are important
exhibits of folk life, lead mining and prehistoric
and Roman remains. Open all year, Apr to
Sep Mon, Wed, Thu, Fri 11–5, Sat 10–12
and 1–5, Sun 2–5; Oct to Mar, Mon, Wed,
Thu, Fri 2–5, Sat 10–12 and 1.30–4.30.
Free. P. *(Tel 4079)*
George Leatt Industrial and Folk Museum
High Corn Mill, Chapel Hill. Old mill, four
storeys high to which Victorian machinery is
being added and where milling has been
carried out since the 12th C. Two
waterwheels, a turbine of 1912, and a
winnower which took a prize in 1884, are all
operational. Collection of horse traps, carts,
etc. The mill is open most Suns and BH at
visitors own risk 12–5; parties at other times
by arrangement only. Free, but possibility of
charge being made. P. *(Tel 2883)* ⅙ B
Skipton Castle High Street. Fully-roofed
12th-C and later castle, with picturesque
interior courtyard. Massive gateway and six
14th-C round towers. Besieged for three
years in Civil War. Open all day (ex Sun
mornings, 4 Apr, 25 Dec) 10–7 (Sun from 2).
Last admission, 6 or earlier sunset. Tours on
the hour, 10, 11, 12, 2, 3, 4. Admission
between tours with illustrated tour sheets in
English, French or German. 45p (ch 18 25p,
ch 5 free). Party. (school) 25p per person. P.
behind nearby Town Hall. *(Tel 2442)*

SLEDMERE *Humberside* Map 8 SE96
Sledmere House Georgian house built in
1751, and enlarged by Sir Christopher Sykes
in 1787. Decorative plasterwork by Joseph
Rose in Adam style. Contents include
Chippendale, Sheraton, and French
furnishings, paintings, porcelain, and antique
statuary. Also unique room decorated with
Turkish tiles. Park and gardens by 'Capability'
Brown include greatly extended lawns with
large water basin and Italian fountain. ⚑.
Open 6, 7 Apr then Suns only until mid May;
mid May to 1 Oct daily (ex Mon and Fri)
1.30–5.30 (last admission 5) also open BH
Mons. A children's playground is available
free of charge. Opening hours and times also
prices under revision for 1980. ⚠ *(Tel Driffield
86208). (Sir Tatton Sykes)*

SLIMBRIDGE *Gloucestershire* Map 3 SO70
Wildfowl Trust Off A38 and M5, junction 13.
This well-known wildfowl refuge, founded by
and under the direction of Peter Scott, is
famous for its large variety of ducks, geese,
and swans, which can be studied at close
quarters. The collection is the largest in the
world; in the wild area in the winter months

thousands of geese, swans, and ducks are to
be seen. First-class viewing facilities are
available and there are permanent exhibitions
and a tropical house. ⚑ licensed. Gift shop.
Exhibition Hall. Picnic area. Open daily (ex
24, 25 Dec) from 9.30–5.30 or dusk
whichever is earlier. £1.10 (ch 55p, ch 4 free,
pen 85p). Party 20+. ⚠ No dogs. *(Tel
Cambridge, Gloucestershire 333)* ⅙

SMALLHYTHE *Kent* Map 5 TQ82
Smallhythe Place Dame Ellen Terry's former
half-timbered 15th-C home with a museum
and barn theatre. Open Mar to Oct, daily (ex
Tue and Fri) 2–6, or dusk. 60p. No dogs. *(NT)*

SOMERLEYTON *Suffolk* Map 5 TM49
Somerleyton Hall Off B1074. Magnificent
Tudor to Jacobean mansion rebuilt in Anglo-
Italian style in 1846. House contains superb
antique furniture, tapestries, pictures.
Heritage Display and Grinling Gibbons
carvings. There are 12 acres of grounds with
famous maze, nature trail and miniature
railway. ⚑ Open Easter to end Sep, Thu, Sun
and BH 2–6; Tue and Wed also in Jul and
Aug. Admission prices not yet decided. No
dogs. ⚠ *(Tel Lowestoft 730224). (Lord and
Lady Somerleyton)* ⅙

SOUTHAMPTON *Hampshire* Map 4 SU41
Art Gallery Civic Centre, Commercial Road.
Collections include 18th to 20th-C English
paintings, Continental Old Masters of 14th to
18th C. Modern French paintings, including
the impressionists and a small collection of
sculpture and ceramics. Of special interest
are paintings and drawings of the 'Camden
Town Group'. There is also a regular
programme of temporary exhibitions. Open
all year (ex Mon, 4 Apr, 25 Dec), Tue to Sat
11–5.45, Sun 2–5. Free. *(Tel 23855 ext 769)*
⅙ (by arrangement)
Bargate Guildhall Museum High Street. The
medieval North gate of the city. Its upper floor,
once a guildhall, contains a museum of local
interest and also other exhibits. Open all year
(ex Mon, 4 Apr, 25, 26 Dec) Tue to Sat 11–12
and 1–5, Sun 2–5. Free. *(Tel 22544)*
Southampton Zoo The Common. An
attractively laid-out zoo, with a
comprehensive collection of animals and
birds. ⚑. Open daily 10–6. 50p (ch 25p)
subject to alteration. P in Cemetery Road.
(Tel 556603) ⅙
Spitfire Museum Kingsbridge Lane.
Contains the Spitfire Mk 24 and the Seaplane
S6A which made world speed record in 1929.
Other exhibits, models and photographs of
the famous aircraft designer R J Mitchell.
Aviation history covering the era 1914 to

1954. Winner of 1976 Tourist Award. Open all year Tue to Sat 10–4.30, Sun 2–5. 30p (ch 14 10p). ⚠ *(Tel 35830)* &

Tudor House Museum St Michael's Square. A restored, half-timbered, 16th-C house, containing a museum of antiquarian and historical interest. Open all year (ex Mon) Tue to Sat 11–5, Sun 2–5. Free. ⚠ *(Tel 24216)*

Wool House Maritime Museum Bugle Street, this 600-year-old building, once wool warehouse, has buttressed stone walls and old roof timbering. Houses an interesting maritime museum. Open all year (ex Mon) Tue to Sat 11–1 and 2–5, Sun 2–5. Free. ⚠ *(Tel 23941)*

SOUTHEND-ON-SEA *Essex* Map 5 TQ88
Historic Aircraft Museum Aviation Way, ½m off A127, on western boundary of Southend Airport. Aircraft on view include Flying Flea to Blackburn Beverley, and there are also aircraft engines, and miscellaneous equipment. ⚑ Open 1 Jun to 30 Sep, daily 10–6; Oct to May, Sat and Sun 11–6. 50p (ch 14 25p, ch 5 free, pen 10p). Under revision for 1980. ⚠ *(Tel 545881)* &

Prittlewell Priory Museum Priory Park (north side of town). A restored 12th-C Cluniac Priory, preserving the refectory, Prior's chamber, cellars, and cloister garth. The nave, south transept with side chapels, and lines of the chapter house are now laid out in a new garden. The 19th-C wing contains a museum of antiquities and also natural history exhibits appertaining to south-east Essex. ⚑ during summer. Open all year (ex 4 Apr, 25, 26 Dec) 1 Apr to 30 Sep weekdays 10.30–5.30 (closed 1–2), Sun 2–5.30; 1 Oct to 31 Mar weekdays only 10.30–4.30. 10p (ch 5p). Party (school parties weekdays). P. *(Tel 42878)* & B

Southchurch Hall Southchurch Hall Close. Early 14th-C timber-framed manor house, central hall open to roof. Restored, equipped and furnished as a medieval manor house with a small Tudor wing and an exhibition room. Open all year, weekdays 2–5.30, Sat 11–5.30, Sun (Apr to Sep only) 2.30–5.30 (closed 4 Apr, 25, 26 Dec). Organised parties by appointment weekdays 10–12.30. 10p (ch 5p). P (limited) in adjacent streets. *(Tel 67671)* &

SOUTH HARTING *West Sussex* Map 4 SU71
Uppark 1m S on B2146. A notable pedimented, red brick mansion, designed by Talman c1690 with interior decoration of 1750, including original wallpapers and curtains. Beautiful downland setting and views. Open Apr to Sep, Wed, Thu, Sun, and BH Mon 2–6. All visitors guided on Wed. £1. *(NT)*

SOUTH MOLTON *Devon* Map 3 SS72
Castle Hill 3½m W on A361. A seat of the Fortescue family. Paladian mansion built c1729–1740. Fine 18th-C furniture, tapestries, porcelain and pictures. Ornamental garden, large shrub and woodland garden and arboretum. Open Apr to Oct by appointment for conducted tours by the owner for parties of 12 or more. £1 per head. Garden only, 30p, can be seen any time by telephoning Estate Office. ⚠ *(Tel Filleigh 336)* &

South Molton Museum A part of the Guildhall, a stone-fronted building c1743, with an open, arcaded ground floor, and a pilastered upper floor. Open all year Mon to Sat 11–12.30 and 2.30–4.30 summer (Sat morning only in winter). Free. P. *(Tel 2501)* & B

SOUTHPORT *Merseyside* Map 7 SD31
Atkinson Art Gallery Lord Street. Exhibits include mainly 20th-C oil paintings and sculpture; 19th-, 20th-C water-colours, drawings and prints. Also an active visiting exhibition programme. The Art Gallery and Southport Arts Centre form a complex where the visual arts, theatre, film, music and other media are available to visitors. ⚑. Open all year daily (ex Sun) Mon, Tue, Wed, Fri 10–5, Thu and Sat 10–1. Free. P. *(Tel 33133 ext 129)*

Botanic Gardens Museum Churchtown. Situated in public park. Exhibits include collections of local history; natural history; 18th-, 19th-C collection of china; a display of the local shrimping industry; and a rare example of an early dug-out canoe from the nearby Martin Mere. Also Ainsdale National Nature Reserve display reconstructed Victorian parlour and Cecily Bate collection of dolls. Temporary exhibitions of local or topical interest. ⚑. Open all year Tue to Sat and BH Mon (closed Mon and 4 Apr, 25 Dec, 1 Jan also Fri following BH Mon) May to Sep 10–6 (5 Oct to Apr), Sun 2–5. Free. ⚠ *(Tel 27547)*

Model Village and Model Railway The Promenade. Set amidst a variety of trees, shrubs and plants, this model village opened in 1957, comprises some 250 models, hundreds of figures, and over 1,000ft of model railway, all constructed on a scale of 1:12. The residential buildings display a wide range of architectural styles from Tudor to Contemporary. Other features include a country residence, football stadium, Norman castle, stone gorge with rock climbs and lake with waterfalls spanned by a 30ft suspension bridge. ⚑ and covered area overlooking grounds. Open 1 Mar to 31 Oct, 9 until 1 hour before dusk. 50p (ch and pen 25p). Party. Subject to alteration. P. *(Tel 42133)* &

Steamport Transport Museum Derby Road. Now houses ex-British Rail locomotives, as well as several industrial locomotives. 1000ft of standard guage track, laid by museum members, connects the museum to the British rail system. Also on display are local buses, Southport tramcars, traction engines and commercial vehicles in what is planned to become the largest preservation centre of its type in North West England. Steam locomotives 'Steam-ups' summer Suns and BH. ⚑ Open Jun to mid Sep inclusive 1–5 weekdays (11–5 Jul and Aug also weekends May to Sep); Oct to Apr weekends only 2–5. Party 20+. 40p (ch 20p). Special events and BH 50p (ch 25p). Rides Brake Van (steamdays) 10p. Prices under revision for 1980. ⚠ *(Tel 30693, enquiries)* &

Southport Zoo Princes Park. A varied collection, within an area of 2½ acres, surrounded by flowers. Several of the animals breed in captivity, including a rare breeding group of Mandrills. Other attractions include leopards, bears, large Indian otters, wallabies, giant Seychelle tortoise, duck and flamingo pools, and assorted aviaries. New aquarium, reptile house, alligator beach and mandrill house. ⚑ Open all year (ex 25 Dec). 10–dusk. 50p (ch 15 25p). Party. Subject to revision. P. *(Tel 38102)* &

SOUTHSEA *Hampshire* Map 4 SZ69
Castle Clarence Esplanade. Military and naval museum within a castle by Henry VIII in 1539 which recalls fortifications of port and history of regiments of the garrison. Contains permanent exhibition of the *Mary Rose* which sank in 1545 and displays of local archaeology. Lighthouse dates from 1828.

Open 10.30–5.30 daily (ex 25 and 26 Dec).
16p (ch and pen 6p . ⚠ (weekend charge). &
B

Royal Marines Museum Eastney. A
chronological history of the Royal Marines
from 1664 to the present day. Specialist
displays of uniforms, badges, Royal Marines'
bands and medals, including the complete
collection of 10 Royal Marines' VCs. Museum
is established in the original Royal Marine
Artillery Officers' Mess, a superb example of
Victorian architecture, and retaining original
mouldings and fireplaces. Souvenir shop.
Open all year (ex 1–15 Jan, 25 and 26 Dec)
Mon to Fri 10–4.30 Sat and Sun 10–12.30.
Free. ⚠ (Tel Portsmouth 22351 ext 6132) &
(with assistance of Warder staff)

SOUTH WALSHAM *Norfolk* Map 9 TG31
The Fairhaven Garden Trust The gardens,
developed over the past 30 years, contain a
beech walk with spring flowers,
rhododendrons, a water garden and fish
pond. The King Oak is said to be 900 years
old. The Bird Sanctuary may be visited at
certain times by arrangement with the
Warden. Open 2nd Sun in Apr to last Sun in
Sep, Thu, Sat, Sun and BH 2–6. 40p (ch 12
and pen 20p). ⚠ Gates close, all cars must be
out of the car park by 6 pm. (Tel 449) &

SOUTHWOLD *Suffolk* Map 5 TM57
Southwold Museum Bartholomew Green.
Formerly known as Dutch Cottage Museum,
contains relics of Southwold light railway and
also illustrations of local history, including
archaeology, fossils, prints, and bygones.
Open 29 May to end of Sep, Tue, Wed, Fri
2.30–4.30, also Sun in Aug and spring and
summer BH other times by appointment.
Free. P.

SPALDING *Lincolnshire* Map 8 TF22
Ayscoughfee Hall and Gardens Restored
15th-C house, now museum of ornithology. ⚤
during summer. Open all year, weekdays 8 to
½hr after sunset (5 in winter), Sun from 10 am.
Free. P. (Tel 5468) &
Springfields Gardens Unique 25-acre
spring flower spectacle on eastern outskirts of
the town (A151). More than a million bulbs,
with lawns, lake and glasshouses. Recently
opened Summer Rose Gardens with over
12,500 rose bushes in 100 varieties. ⚤
Flower parade 10 May. Exhibition of floats
10–14 May. Spring gardens open Apr to mid
May, Summer gardens open mid Jun to end
Sep daily 10–6 both seasons. Spring 80p (ex
10/11 May £1). Summer 50p (ch free). ⚠ (Tel
4843) &

SPEKE *Merseyside* Map 7 SJ48
Speke Hall Grand example of 16th-C half-

timbering, with interior courtyard, Great hall,
16th- and 17th-C plasterwork, and Mortlake
tapestries. ⚤ (parties only). Open Apr to end
of Sep Mon to Sat 10–5, Sun 2–7 and BH
10–7; Oct to Mar (ex 1 Jan, 4 Apr, 24–27
Dec) Mon to Sat 10–5, Suns 2–5 (last visitor
½hr before closing). 40p (ch 20p). Party. All
details subject to alteration. ⚠ (NT and
Merseyside County Museums) & B

SPETCHLEY *Hereford and Worcester*
Map 3 SO85
Spetchley Park Fine gardens and park,
surrounding early 19th-C mansion.
Worcestershire's only deer park, with red and
fallow deer, lake with wildfowl. Gardens cover
30 acres and include many unusual trees and
shrubs. ⚤ Sun only. Gardens only shown 1
Apr to 31 Oct, Mon to Fri 11–5, Sun 2–6; BH
Mons 11–6. Other days by appointment.
Garden Centre within gardens open same
hours, also weekdays in winter. Admission
prices not yet decided. Party 25+. (Tel 213).
(Major R J G Berkley TD MFH)

SPROATLEY *Humberside* Map 8 TA13
Burton Constable Hall 1½m N. Elizabethan
house, built 1570 with 18th-C state rooms and
200 acres of parkland landscaped by
'Capability' Brown including 4 acres of lawns
and gardens and 22 acres of lakes. ⚤ picnic
grounds by lake. Caravan and camping park.
Seasonal fishing. Open 5 to 7 Apr incl, then
Sat and Sun, then daily (ex Mon and Thu) but
open BH Mon, to 24 May to 28 Sep 12–5.
Admission prices not yet decided. ⚠ (Tel
Skirlaugh 62400). (Mr & Mrs J Chichester
Constable)

STAFFORD *Staffordshire* Map 7 SJ92
Museum and Art Gallery The Green.
Display of local history and changing
temporary art exhibitions. Open all year Tue
to Sat 10–5. Free

STAGSDEN *Bedfordshire* Map 4 SP94
Stagsden Bird Gardens A breeding centre
of rare pheasants, waterfowl and old breeds
of poultry and other birds. Also a fine
collection of shrub roses. Picnics allowed. ⚤
Open all year daily (ex 25 Dec) 11–7 or dusk.
60p (ch 15 30p). ⚠ (Tel Oakley 2745) &

STAINDROP *Co Durham* Map 12 NZ12
Raby Castle Principally 14th-C, work of the
Nevilles, with 18th- and 19th-C alterations.
Fine pictures from English, Dutch and
Spanish schools, also gardens of about 10
acres. ⚤ Open Easter to end Sep; Easter
weekend including Tue; Wed and Sun Apr to
Jun also 5–8 May and Spring BH weekend'

SHUGBOROUGH
Staffordshire County Museum

18th Century House six miles
east of Stafford on the A513.

Museum containing exhibits
of Staffordshire life.

Shugborough Park Farm.

Landscaped Park and Gardens.

Museum open all year round.
House & Farm open summer only.
For further details tel. Little Haywood 881 388.

including Tue; daily (ex Sat) Jul to end Sep.
2–5. £1 (ch and pen 60p). Under revision for
1980. ⚠ *(Tel 60202). (The Lord Barnard TD)*

STALHAM *Norfolk* Map 9 TG32
Sutton Wind Mill 2m SE on unclass road.
The tallest wind mill in the country with nine
floors plus the cap floor. Built in 1789 the
milling machinery is complete and there is
access to all floors including the top outside
stage. A working fantail and many other
interesting items are on display. Open 6 Apr to
30 Sep daily 9.30–6. 30p (ch 15 15p). ⚠ *(Tel 81195)*

STAMFORD *Lincolnshire* Map 4 TF00
Brewery Museum A 19th-C brewery in
attractive stone buildings and with equipment
made from four tons of copper and brass.
Production ceased in 1974 and the museum
opened in 1978. Antique beer engine still in
use in the refreshment room. ⚏ (also
licensed). Opening times not yet decided. 55p
(ch 18 and pen 40p). P. *(Tel 52186)* ⚹ B
Browne's Hospital Broad Street. Ancient
almshouses, founded *c*1483 by William
Browne, wool merchant. Fine medieval
stained glass in Chapel and Audit room. Open
all year, daily 10–5. Free. P (in North Street
and Broad Street). *(Tel 3746)*
Stamford Museum A new museum, opening
Spring 1980, of the history of Stamford. The
display includes the clothes of Daniel
Lambert. Temporary exhibitions are also
housed here. Open Tue to Sat (closed Sun
and Mon). Admission times and prices not yet
decided. *(Tel 55611)* ⚹ B

STANSTED MOUNTFITCHET *Essex*
Map 5 TL52
Windmill Red-brick tower-mill of 1787
(restored 1966), with machinery and
furnishings intact. 65ft high and has been
used as Scouts Headquarters. Open 2.30–7
on first Sun in month from Apr to Oct, every
Sun in Aug. Also on Easter, May, Spring and
late Summer BH (Sun and Mon). 15p (ch 14
5p). Other times by telephone application to
committee secretary. ⚠ *(Tel Bishop's
Stortford 813159)*

STANTON LEES *Derbyshire* Map 8 SK26
Nine Ladies Stone Circle Off B5057
approached via Birchover village. Stone circle
on Stanton Moor. Dates back probably to late
Bronze Age and incorporates nine stones.
Accessible all reasonable times. Free. *(AM)*

STAPLEFORD *Leicestershire* Map 8 SK81
Stapleford Park Off B676. Old wing dating
from 1500 and restored in 1633 has exterior
decoration of exceptional interest. The
mansion, extended in 1670, contains
interesting furnishings, tapestries and
pictures. Miniature steam passenger railway
and liners SS Northern Star and Southern
Cross. Children's amusements. Picnic area.
Garden centre. ⚏ (licensed). Teas at Hall.
Open 6 Apr to 28 Sep BH Mon and Tue
following; Sun only Apr; Sun and Wed only
May and Sep; Sun, Tue, Wed and Thu in Jun,
Jul, Aug. 1.30–6.30. £1.05 (ch 55p). ⚠ *(Tel
Wymondham 229 or 245)* ⚹ B

STEETON *North Yorkshire* Map 8 SE43
Steeton Hall Gatehouse 14th-C fortified
gatehouse from medieval manor house,
displaying remarkable series of 53 grotesque
and heraldic carved corbels supporting
parapets and chimneys. Open any
reasonable time (exterior only). Free. *(AM)*

STEVENAGE *Hertfordshire* Map 4 TL22
Stevenage Museum St George's Way. This
Museum, in the undercroft of the parish
church of St George, tells the Story of
Stevenage from the present day back to
earliest times. Also geology, natural history,
and live exhibits. Open all year 10–5. Free. P.
(Tel 54292) ⚹

STEVENTON *Oxfordshire* Map 4 SU49
Priory Cottages Former monastic buildings
converted into attractive timbered cottages,
one of which contained the Great Hall. South
cottage open Wed Apr to Sep 2–6; Oct to Mar
2–5. Free. *(NT)*

STICKLEPATH *Devon* Map 2 SX69
***Sticklepath Museum of Rural Industry and
Finch Foundation Trust*** Once corn mill and
cloth mill known as Manor Mills, later
converted to edge-tool factory and grinding
house. Among the exhibits are two water-
powered 'tilt' hammers, unique in West
Country, and other machinery driven by three
separate water-wheels. Demonstrations of
machinery and water-wheels in motion on Sat
and Sun, or by appointment: apply to
Secretary. Many examples of hand-made
agricultural tools and equipment. Open all
year, daily 11–6. 40p (ch 16 15p). ⚠ *(Tel 352
or 286)* ⚹ B

STOKE BRUERNE *Northamptonshire*
Map 4 SP74
Stoke Park Pavilion Twin 17th-C pavilions,
attributed to Inigo Jones, remains of Stoke
Park, burnt in 1884 and subsequently rebuilt.
Exteriors of pavilions and gardens shown Jun
to Aug, Sat and Sun 2–6. 30p (ch 8 20p). ⚠
(Tel Roade 862172). (Mr R D Chancellor) ⚹
(79)
Waterways Museum Former corn mill,
situated near a flight of locks on the Grand
Union Canal, now converted into a museum
of items recording the fascinating canal story
of over two centuries. There is an old narrow
boat on show. Canal-side inn and hump-back
bridge near by. Open all year, incl BH. In
winter from second Mon in Oct to Mon before
24 Mar 10–4 (closed Mon also 25, 26 Dec); in
summer, daily (10–6. Enquiries to Curator.
40p (ch 25p). Admission prices under revision
for 1980. ⚠ *(Tel Northampton 862229)*

STOKE-ON-TRENT *Staffordshire*
Map 7 SJ84
Chatterley Whitfield Mining Museum Nr
Tunstall. Guided tours of the underground
workings showing the development of mining
technology from earliest times. Colliery
lamphouse, exhibitions and steam winding
engines also open. Museum shop and ⚏.
Open Tue to Fri 9.30–4.30. Weekends and
BH 10–5. Closed Mon. Admission prices for
1980 not yet decided but approx
£1.25–£1.50. ⚠
Ford Green Hall Ford Green Road,
Smallthorne. A black and white timber-framed
yeoman farmer's house with brick-built
additions. originally built for the Ford family
during the 16th-C and contains 16th-, 17th-
and 18th-C English furniture. Guided tours by
resident custodian (approx 1–1½hrs). Open
all year (ex Tue and Fri) 1 Apr to 30 Sep Mon,
Wed, Thu and Sat 10–12.30 and 2–5.30 (5, 1
Oct to 31 Mar), Sun all year 2–5. Closed Tue
and Fri. ⚠ limited. *(Tel 534771)*
Gladstone Pottery Museum Uttoxeter
Road, Longton, 2m SE of Stoke-on-Trent, on
A50. A Victorian pottery, still complete with
old warehouses, workshops and four bottle
ovens. Old traditional skills may be seen in

action in this living and working museum of British pottery. Historical, Tile and Colour galleries. Winner of the 1976 Museum of the Year Award. Visitors may buy wares produced here, also new quality china shop and large teapots display. Open all year weekdays (ex Mon, Oct to Mar and 25 Dec) 10.30–5.30 (9pm Wed, Apr to Sep, for booked parties). 90p (ch 16, students and pen 45p). ⚠ *(Tel 319232 or 311378)*

The Mitchell Spitfire Museum Bethesda Street, Hanley. Modern glass-domed building houses museum, which includes a Spitfire, to commemorate R J Mitchell, the famous aircraft designer who came from this area. Open all year (ex Sun). Mon to Sat 9–12.30, 1–5.30. ♿

Spode Museum and Factory Church Street. Works museum contains examples of 18th- to 20th-C Spode pottery. Visitors's shop. Tours of factory arranged Mon to Fri by appointment at 10.15 and 2.15. 50p. Admission to museum free, but strictly by prior appointment only. Ch 12 not admitted. ⚠ *(Tel 46011)* **(79)**

Trentham Gardens On SW edge of town, on A34. 700 acres of gardens and woodland include rose and Italian gardens, rock and peat block gardens, shrubs, and demonstration blocks. Many acres converted to spring shrub and bulb gardens. Tree and shrub nursery. Garden centres. Swimming pool, boats, and miniature railway. 🍴 Open all year daily (ex 25 Dec) dawn to dusk. Individual, family and group rates. Fishing. Full catering facilities. Admission charges for 1980 not yet decided. ⚠ *(Tel 657341 or 657225)* ♿

STOKESAY *Salop* Map 7 SO48
On A49 near Craven Arms.
Stokesay Castle Oldest fortified manor house in England with additions in 13th C. Open 7 Apr to 28 Sep 10–6 (last admission 5.30); Mar and Oct 10–5 (last admission 4.30). Closed Tue also Nov, Dec, Jan, Feb. All enquiries to the Custodian. 50p (ch 15 25p). ⚠ *(Sir Philip and Lady Magnus-Allcroft)*

STOKE-SUB-HAMDON *Somerset*
Map 3 ST41
Stoke-sub-Hamdon Priory 15th-C Ham-Hill stone house, once a chantry, retaining original screens and part of Great Hall. Open all year, daily 10–6. Free. *(NT)*

STONEHENGE *Wiltshire* Map 4 SU14
Prehistoric monument dating from two periods. The encircling ditch, bank, and Aubrey holes are late Neolithic. The stone circles, consisting of sarsen stones around horseshoe of trilithons encompassing the

blue stones, with an altar stone, are probably of early Bronze Age date. Two of the fallen stones were re-erected in 1958. 🍴 Open daily Mar, Apr, Oct 9.30–5.30; May to Sep 9.30–7; Nov to Feb 9.30–4.30p (ch 16 and pen 15p). *(AM)*

STONOR *Oxfordshire* Map 4 SU78
Stonor House and Park 4m NW of Henley-on-Thames on B480. The house is the home of Lord and Lady Camoys and the Stonor family and has been occupied by descendants for the past eight hundred years. Built over many centuries from c1190, the house contains examples of some of the earliest domestic architecture in Oxfordshire. It has rooms with beautiful stained and painted glass windows with interesting heraldic designs, family pictures, good furniture and tapestries, and important Italian sculpture and drawings. The beautiful gardens on the hillside behind the house have commanding views of the Park. Open 6 Apr to 30 Sep Wed, Thu, Sun and BH 2–5.30. £1 (ch 12 60p, pen 80p). ⚠ *(Tel Turville Heath 587)*

STOURBRIDGE *West Midlands* Map 7 SO98
Glass Collection Council House, Mary Stevens Park. A collection of local products, and glass from all parts of the world, from 1630 to the present day. Lectures given by arrangement with Curator. Open all year Mon to Fri 10–5. Free. P. *(Tel Dudley 55433)* ♿ B
Hagley Hall SSE at Hagley. 18th-C Palladian house, the family home of the Lyttletons, completed by George, 1st Baron Lyttleton in 1760. Renowned for the fine Rococo plasterwork by Francesco Vassali. Family portraits, 18th-C furniture and Lyttleton papers are also on view. The park, in existence since the reign of Edward III, was re-landscaped in the 18th C. Lunch and teas daily (in house). House and Park open daily 17 May to 31 Aug, 12–5. £1.10 (ch 13 50p, pen 80p). ⚠ *(Tel Hagley 882408)* ♿ B

STOURHEAD *Wiltshire* Map 3 ST73
Stourhead House and Pleasure Gardens At Stourton (B3092). 18th-C house by Colin Campbell, with paintings and Chippendale furniture. There are notable mid 18th-C lake-watered grounds laid out by Henry Hoare, which show contemporary garden temples, forming one of Europe's most famous layouts. The trees and shrubs are magnificent, many being rare varieties. The estate covers more than 2,500 acres. Shop and information room. House open Apr, Sep and Oct, Mon, Wed, Sat and Sun 2–6 or sunset if earlier; May to end Aug daily (ex Fri) 2–6; gardens open all year, daily 8–7 (or sunset). Last admissions ½hr

before stated closing time. House £1, gardens 80p; Nov to Mar 40p(ch, reduced rates). Party 15+ (should be booked two days in advance). *(Tel Bourton [Dorset] 348)*. No dogs. *(NT)*

STOWE *Buckinghamshire* Map 4 SP63
Stowe House Landscape Gardens Fine 18th-C mansion, now a public school. The splendid grounds, with statuary and garden temples by William Kent and James Gibbs. ⚲ Open 24 Mar to 22 Apr and 15 Jul to 9 Sep, daily 1 – 6. 45p (ch and pen 25p). Opening times and prices under revision for 1980. ⚠ *(Tel Buckingham 3164)* &

STOWMARKET *Suffolk* Map 5 TM05
Museum of East Anglian Life Medieval barn, collections of horse-drawn vehicles, agricultural tools and implements, craft tools and domestic items. 14th-C aisled hall, 18th-C smithy, watermill and mill house. Country walk down the centuries-old Crowe Lane and along the river bank to mill. Open 1 Apr to 31 Oct, Mon to Sat 11 – 5, Sun 2 – 5. 50p (ch 30p, pen 40p). Admission prices under revision for 1980. ⚲ Sun and BH, Jun, Jul, Aug 3 – 5. Party. ⚠ *(Tel 2229)* &

STRACEY ARMS WINDPUMP *Norfolk* Map 5 TG40
Given to the County Council by Lady Stracey. It is a drainage mill and was restored in 1960. Further major repairs were completed by the Norfolk Windmills Trust in 1974, and a special exhibition of the Trust's work is a permanent feature. Open May to Sep (other times by appointment) 9 – dusk (or as displayed). 10p (ch 14 and pen 5p). P. (limited). *(Tel Norwich 611122 ext 5224)*

STRATFIELD SAYE *Hampshire* Map 4 SU66
Stratfield Saye House Built in the reign of Charles I and presented to the Great Duke in 1817, since when it has been the family home of the Dukes of Wellington. Contains a unique collection of paintings, prints, furniture and relics of the first Duke. In the grounds are the American, Rose and Walled gardens, also the grave of Copenhagen, the Duke's favourite charger. Open daily (ex Fri) from 30 Mar to 28 Sep, 11.30 – 5. Party. ⚠ *(Tel Turgis Green 602)* &

STRATFORD-UPON-AVON *Warwickshire* Map 4 SP15
Hall's Croft Old Town. Tudor house with walled garden, former home of Shakespeare's daughter, Susanna. Exhibition: 'Dr John Hall and the medicine of his time'. Open all year (ex 4 Apr, am, 24 – 26 Dec) Apr to Oct, weekdays 9 – 6, Sun 2 – 6; Nov to Mar weekdays only 9 – 4. 30p (ch school age 15p). Admission prices under revision for 1980. P. *(Tel 292107)* & B
Harvard House High Street. An ornate half-timbered house, dating from 1596, the former home of the mother of John Harvard, who founded Harvard University in the USA. Open Apr to Sep, weekdays 9 – 1 and 2 – 6, Sun 2 – 6; Oct to Mar, weekdays 10 – 1 and 2 – 4. 40p (ch 17 20p). ⚠ *(Tel 4507)*
Louis Tussaud's Waxworks 60 Henley Street. Open all year daily. 1 May to end Aug 9.30 – 6.30 (5.30 winter). 50p (ch and pen 25p). *(Tel 5880)*
Model Car Museum Ely Street. International collection of 19,000 miniatures from 40 countries representing all forms of transport, especially motor vehicles, displayed in

historical settings. Includes interesting collection of tram cars and unique collections of model cars from Japan, Israel, and South America. Open all year daily 9–5.30. 50p (ch 5 free). ⚠ (limited). P. *(Tel 2233)* &

New Place Chapel Street. Foundations of the house (destroyed in 1759), where Shakespeare spent the last five years of his retirement and died in 1616. Picturesque Knot garden, an Elizabethan replica. Ancient mulberry tree in the Great Garden of new Place. Furniture and local history exhibits in adjacent Nash's House. Open all year (ex 4 Apr, am, 24–26 Dec) Apr to Oct, weekdays 9–6, Sun 2–6; Nov to Mar, weekdays only 9–4. 30p (ch school age 15p). Admission prices under revision for 1980. P (street). *(Tel 292325)*

Royal Shakespeare Theatre Picture Gallery and Museum Waterside. The gallery contains portraits of Shakespeare, and famous Shakespearian actors and actresses, in addition to numerous other theatrical relics. Open, daily Apr to Oct, weekdays 10–1, 2–6, Sun 2–6; Nov, weekdays 10–1, 2–4, Sun 2–4, Dec to Mar, Sat 10–4, Sun 2–4. 25p (ch 10p) subject to alteration. P. *(Tel 3693)* **(79)**

Shakespeare's Birthplace Henley Street. A half-timbered house, the birthplace of the poet in 1564. Contains numerous exhibits. Open all year (ex 4 Apr, am, 24–26 Dec) Apr to Oct weekdays 9–7 (6, Mon, Tue, Wed and Fri in Apr, May and Oct), Sun 10–6; Nov to Mar weekdays 9–4.30, Sun 1.30–4.30. 50p (ch school age 20p). Admission prices under revision for 1980. *(Tel 4016-8)*

Stratford-upon-Avon Motor Museum 1 Shakespeare Street. Housed in a former church and school, 100 yards from Shakespeare's birthplace, a charming Victorian building in which the vintage cars and motorcycles are displayed in a unique setting of the Roaring Twenties – the Golden Age of Motoring. The museum specialises in exotic sports and grand touring cars, many of which have been rescued from India and magnificently restored. In addition to the cars you will also find the fashions, music and décor of the Twenties. Displays include a fascinating collection of period enamel signs, road signs, motor clubs badges from throughout the world and numerous early motoring items of historic and nostalgic interest; typical Twenties roadside garage, picture gallery, picnic garden and speciality shop. Open all year daily (ex 25 Dec), Mar to Sep 10–6.30, Oct to Feb 10–5.30. 75p (ch accompanied by parents, free, teenagers and pen 50p). Opening times and admission prices under revision for 1980. *(Tel 69413)* & B

STREET *Somerset* Map 3 ST43

Street Shoe Museum C & J Clark Ltd, High Street. The museum is housed in the oldest part of the factory of C & J Clark Ltd. The museum contains shoes from Roman times until 1950, Georgian shoe buckles, caricatures and engravings of shoemakers, costume illustrations and fashion plates, shoe machinery from 1860s until 1920, shoes and showcards from 1850 to 1950 produced by C & J Clark, and 19th-C documents and photographs illustrating the early history of the firm from the founding in 1825 by Cyrus Clark. Open May to Oct inclusive Mon to Sat 10–1 and 2–4.45; winter months by appointment only. Free. ⚠ limited. P. *(Tel 43131)*

STROUD *Gloucestershire* Map 3 SO80

Stroud and District Museum Lansdown. The exhibits cover geology, archaeology, local crafts, industrial archaeology, including local mills and houses, and farmhouse household equipment. A full-length model of the dinosaur Megalosaurus is on display. Open all year (ex Sun, 1 Jan, 4 Apr and 3 days at Christmas) Mon to Fri 10.30–5, Sat 10.30–1 and 2–5. Free. P (roadside). *(Tel 3394)* &

STUDLEY *Oxfordshire* Map 4 SP51

Studley Priory Hotel Off B4027. Original Priory founded 12th C and sold after Dissolution to John Croke, whose descendants owned it for over 300 years. West range was altered to form Elizabethan manor, which received 17th- and 19th-C additions. Fine stone doorways and early panelling. Used to portray home of Sir Thomas More in film, *A Man for all Seasons*. Studley priory is now a hotel, open all year, but visitors most welcome.

SUDBURY *Derbyshire* Map 7 SK13

Sudbury Hall A very fine brick-built 17th-C house, the former home of the Lords Vernon, with plasterwork ceilings, murals by Laguerre, and some Grinling Gibbons' carving, Museum of Childhood. Open Apr to Oct, Wed, Thu, Fri, Sat, Sun, and BH Mons 1–5.30 or sunset. £1.10. *(NT)*

SUDBURY *Suffolk* Map 5 TL84

Gainsborough's House Half-timbered house with Georgian façade, birthplace of Thomas Gainsborough, now an art gallery and museum. Open all year (ex 25, 26 Dec) Tue to Sat 10–12.30, 2–5, Sun 2–5. 30p (students and pen 15p). P. *(Tel 72958)*

SUFFOLK WILDLIFE PARK *Suffolk* Map 5 TM58

A world-wide selection of animals, birds, ⚏

Shop. Wheelchairs available for disabled. Open Mar to Oct, daily 10–6. Admission charges not yet decided. Picnic areas; ⚠ separate park for cars bringing dogs. *(Tel Lowestoft 740291)* ♿ **(79)**

SULGRAVE *Northamptonshire* Map 4 SP54
Sulgrave Manor Off B4525. 16th-C manor house and garden, famous for its Washington associations. There are portraits, contemporary furniture, and the Washington arms carved in the main doorway. Open all year, ex Jan. 1 Apr to 30 Sep, daily (ex Wed) 10.30–1, 2–5.30 (4, after 30 Sep). 50p (ch in school parties 25p). ⚠ *(Tel 205)*

SUNDERLAND *Tyne and Wear*
Map 12 NZ35
Grindon Close Museum Grindon Lane. Edwardian period rooms, including chemist's shop and dentist's surgery. Open all year (ex Christmas, 1 Jan, and 4 Apr), Mon, Wed and Fri 9.30–12, 1–7.30; Tue and Thu closes 5; Sat 9.30–4. Summer Sun 2–5. Free. ⚠ *(Tel 284042)*

Museum and Art Gallery Borough Road. On display are examples of local lustre-ware pottery, a collection of 15th- to 19th-C silver, models of Sunderland-built ships, archaeology, natural history, local history, period rooms and 19th- and 20th-C paintings. ⚐ Open all year daily (ex Christmas, 1 Jan and 4 Apr). Mon to Fri 9.30–6, Sat 9.30–4, Sun 2–5; BH Mon 10–5. Free. P. *(Tel 41235)* ♿

Monkwearmouth Station Museum North Bridge Street. Land transport museum in classical station of 1848 designed by Thomas Moore of Sunderland. The booking office,

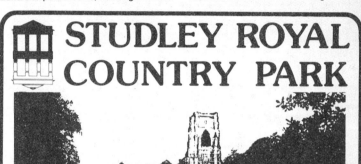

STUDLEY ROYAL COUNTRY PARK

Step back two centuries into 650 acres of historic beauty,

landscaped parkland, magnificent woodland, herds

of deer, waterfowl, ornamental gardens.

See also Fountains Hall and Fountains Abbey.

OPEN DAILY

Entrance 2 miles west of Ripon on the Pateley Bridge Road.

platform area and footbridge have all been
restored and there is an outdoor area with
rolling stock. Displays inside the museum
deal with transport in North East England.
Open all year (ex Christmas, 1 Jan and 4 Apr),
Mon to Sat 10 – 6, Sun 2 – 5. Free. ⚠ *(Tel
77075)* &

SUTTON-AT-HONE *Kent* Map 5 TQ57
St John's Jerusalem Garden A fine 13th-,
16th-, and 18th-C house, once the home of
the Kentish historian, Edward Hasted. Only
the walls and former chapel of the original
buildings remain. The River Darenth borders
the garden. Gardens and former chapel
shown Apr to Oct, Wed 2 – 6. 20p. *(NT)*

SUTTON CHENEY *Warwickshire*
Map 4 SP39
Battlefield of Bosworth Centre 7m NE of
Nuneaton on unclass road. Historic site of
battle in 1485. The Centre includes an
exhibition, model room, replica flags, shields
and figures also film theatre. There is also a
Battle Trail which guides visitors around the
area where the battle actually took place.
Picnic areas. Open Easter to Oct, Mon to Sat
2 – 5, Sun and BH 1 – 6. 40p (ch 25p). Party (all
year). ⚠ cars 20p, mini-coaches 50p,
coaches £1. Opening hours, dates and
admission prices not available for 1980. *(Tel
Market Bosworth 290429)*

SUTTON-ON-THE-FOREST *North Yorkshire*
Map 8 SE56
8m N of York, on B1363 or Helmsley Road.
Sutton Park A medium-sized garden, with a
temple and woodland walks, terraces, border
and rose gardens, a lily pond, and Georgian
ice house. The house dates from 1730 and
contains a collection of antique furniture and
pictures. ⚤ (open 2 – 5.30). Souvenir shop
with some antiques. Open 4, 6/7, 13, 20 Apr
then 27 Apr to 28 Sep Sun, Tue, Wed, Thu
and all BH Mon 2 – 6. Special openings by
arrangement, apply to Administrator. House
and Gardens 80p (ch 25p), Coach parties 65p
per person. Gardens only 40p (ch 20p).
Prices under revision for 1980. *(Tel
Easingwold 810249)* & B *(NGS)*

SWAINSHILL *Hereford and Worcester*
Map 3 SO44
The Weir Dates from 1784, with fine views of
the River Wye and the Welsh hills. Spring
gardens only open 25 Mar to 15 May, daily (ex
Sat;) 16 May to Oct, Wed and BH Mon 2 – 6.
20p. *(NT)*

SWALLOWFIELD *Berkshire* Map 4 SU76
Swallowfield Park 18th-C remodelling of
house built in 1689 designed by William
Talman. Special features include Baroque
door case or gateway, oval stucco decorated
vestibule containing the Arms of the
Clarendon family (c1700) and bold and cove
ceiling mouldings in the Main Hall and
Drawing Room. Gardens including a Walled
Garden of about 4 acres containing a variety
of flowering shrubs and roses and many fine
specimens of interesting trees. Open May to
Sep Wed and Thu 2 – 5 40p (ch 25p) ⚠ *(Tel
Reading 883815)* & B *(gardens)*

SWARTHMOOR *Cumbria* Map 7 SD27
Swarthmoor Hall Elizabethan and later, the
former home of George Fox, founder of the
Quakers. The house is now administered by
the Society of Friends. Open mid Mar to mid
Oct, Mon, Tue, Wed and Sat 10 – 12 and 2 – 5;
Thu and Sun by arrangement only (closed
Fri); mid Oct to mid Mar by appointment only.
Free. ⚠ *(Tel Ulverston 53204)* & B

SWINDON *Wiltshire* Map 4 SU18
Great Western Railway Museum Faringdon
Road. Interesting collection of locomotives
and other exhibits pertaining to the Great
Western Railway. Locomotives include the
historic 'City of Truro', and there is also a
Brunel room. Recent additions include a
model, made 1847 – 48, of the broad gauge
locomotive 'Iron Duke'. Open all year (ex 4
Apr 25, 26 Dec), weekdays 10 – 5, Sun 2 – 5.
27p (ch and pen 13p). Under revision for
1980. Party 20+ P. *(Tel 26161 ex 562)* also
Railway Village House Adjacent GWR
museum. Refurbished as it was at turn of
century. Hours as museum above. 11p (ch
and pen 5p). Party.
Jefferies Museum Coate Farm, off A345.
Birthplace in 1848 of Richard Jefferies, the
nature writer, and is now museum exhibiting
literature relating to local wildlife written by
Jefferies and Alfred Owen Williams. Open all
year, Wed Sat and Sun, 2 – 5. Free. ⚠ *(Tel
26161 ex 563)*
Town Museum Bath Road. Contains small
collections of items of local interest and an art
gallery, where visiting exhibitions alternate
with pictures by 20th-C artists including
Moore, Piper, Sutherland, Grant, Bevan and
Lowry, from the permanent collections. Open
all year (ex 4 Apr, 25, 26 Dec) weekdays
10 – 6, Sun 2 – 5. Free. P. *(Tel 26161 ext 560)*

SWINFORD *Leicestershire* Map 4 SP57
Stanford Hall 1m E. William and Mary house,
on River Avon, built 1690, with antique
furniture and paintings, and replica of Percy
Pilcher's flying machine of 1898. Old forge
and walled rose garden; motor cycle and car
museum; working crafts centre weekends;
nature trail. ⚤ Fishing. Open Easter to end of
Sep, Thu, Sat, Sun 2.30 – 6; Easter, Spring
and Late Summer BH Mons and Tue 12 – 6.
Conducted tours. Admission prices under
review for 1980. ⚠ *(Tel 250)*. *(Lord and Lady
Braye)*

TADCASTER *North Yorkshire* Map 8 SE44
The Ark Museum Kirkgate. Old restored
timbered house, now museum of pubs and
brewing. Open all year, Tue, Wed, and Thu
2 – 4. Free. P. *(Tel 833085)*. *(Mrs Brewster)* &
(79)

TAMWORTH *Staffordshire* Map 4 SK20
Tamworth Castle Museum Norman keep
and tower, 15th-C banqueting hall, and 17th-
C apartments with fine woodwork, period
furniture and painted heraldic frieze. The
building houses a small local history museum.
Restoration is in progress and sections of
building may be closed. Pleasure grounds,
swimming pools. Open all year (ex 25 Dec
and Fri Oct to Mar) Mon to Sat 10 – 6 (5 winter)
Sun 2 – 6 (5 winter). Admission prices under
revision for 1980 and will depend upon how
much is open. ⚠ (free on Sun) adjoining
castle entrance. *(Tel 3561 ext 294)*

TARLETON *Lancashire* Map 7 SD42
Leisure Lakes Boating lakes set in 90 acres
of picturesque woodland and heath setting
with picnic areas and pleasant walks. The
sandy beaches are ideal for children. ⚤.
Open Apr to end of Sep 8 – 8. 25p (ch 20p).
Sun and BH £1 per car, including all
passengers. Caravans welcome for the day.
⚠ *(Tel Hesketh Bank 3446)* &

TATTERSHALL *Lincolnshire* Map 8 TF25
Tattershall Castle The mid 15th-C, 100ft-
high brick keep of a fortified house, well-
restored. The Marquess of Curzon recovered
the stone Gothic fireplaces in 1911. Open all

year Mon to Sat (ex 13 Apr, 25/26 Dec) 11–6.30 (11–1 and 2–6.30, Oct to Mar) or sunset, Sun 1–6.30 (or sunset). 60p *(NT)*

Dogdyke Steam Pumping Station Bridge Farm. The only known land drainage beam engine with scoop wheel worked by steam in its original setting. The low pressure 16hp double acting separate condenser beam engine (1855) is capable of moving 25 tons of water per minute. Also 1940 diesel engined centrifugal pump still in use. Open 6 Apr and first Sun in month May to Oct, 2–5. 50p (ch and pen 25p) or £1 per car including passengers. ⚠ *(Tel Coningsby 42495)*

TATTON *Cheshire* Map 7 SJ78

Tatton Park 3½m from M6, junction 19; entrance by Rostherne Lodge on Ashley Road; 1½m NE of junction of A5034 with A50. Late 18th-C mansion by Samuel and Lewis Wyatt. Fine collection of paintings, furniture, china, and silver. Tenants' Hall museum contains State Coach, veteran cars, sporting trophies, and curiosities. 50 acres of ornamental gardens; 1,000 acres of parkland, including lake or mere, one mile long. Historical trails. ⬚ Open daily (ex Mon but open BH Mon). 18 May to 1 Sep: House 1–5 (Sun and BH 12–5), gardens 11–5.30 (Sun and BH 11–6). 1 Apr to 17 May and 3 Sep to 12 Oct: House 1–4 (5 Sun and BH), garden 12–4.30 (11–5 Sun and BH). 14 Oct to 12 Apr 1981 House closed ex Sun to 16 Nov and from 2 Mar 1–4. Gardens 1–4 (12–4 Sun and BH). House 60p (accompanied ch 30p); garden only 30p (accompanied ch 15p); Parkland 60p incl ⚠ (incl NT members). Winter, parkland open daily (ex Mon and 25 Dec) times variable. Entrance by Knutsford Lodge, ⚠ 25p (incl NT members). Opening times and prices are provisional and subject to revision for 1980. An additional charge may be made at times of special events. Dogs in park on leads only. ♿ B *(NT)*

TAUNTON *Somerset* Map 3 ST22

Taunton Castle containing Somerset County Museum. Partly 12th-C structure, associated with Judge Jeffreys' 'Bloody Assize' of 1685. ***Somerset County Museum*** which contains exhibits of local archaeology, natural history, geology, glass, ceramics, bygones, costume and dolls, also houses the ***Somerset Military Museum*** containing relics of the Somerset Light Infantry from 1685–1959 when the regiment was amalgamated with the Duke of Cornwall's Light Infantry. Exhibits include Jellalabad campaign of 1842, and a large collection of uniforms, medals, etc; the Yeomanry and Militia also being well represented. Open all year (ex BH), 1 Apr to 30 Sep, Mon to Sat (closed Sun) 10–5; 1 Oct to 31 Mar, Tue to Sat 10–5 (closed Sun and Mon). 35p (ch 10p) ⚠ *(Tel 3451 ext 286)* ♿ B

Hestercombe Gardens 3m N of Taunton, off A361 near Cheddon Fitzpaine. Late 19th-C house, now the headquarters of the Somerset Fire Brigade. The gardens, originally planned in 1905 by Sir Edwin Lutyens and Gertrude Jekyll, are at present being restored to their original planting. Pools and borders and terraces with fine views. Gardens open 25 May, 29 Jun and 27 Jul 2–6 and every Thu, May to Sep 12–5. Free. ⚠ *(Tel 87222/3)*

Post Office Telecommunications Museum 38 North St. Exhibits include manual exchange (1900), an automatic exchange (1929), and many smaller items. Oldest telephone is dated 1877, and section of first transatlantic telegraph cable (1857) is displayed. Open Sats, 1.30–5, other times by arrangement, special service for schools. Free. P. *(Tel 3391)*

Not just a stately home...

.... but a thousand acres
of beautiful parkland and meres perfect for walks and picnics,
swimming and sailing, fishing and horse riding.
Magnificent gardens with a Japanese temple.
A family museum with veteran cars and a fire engine.
Carriage rides, exciting trails, wild deer
and lots, lots more besides.
Just off the M6 and M56 at Knutsford, Cheshire.
Park and gardens open all the year. House, April to October.
All closed Mondays except during August and on Bank Holidays.
Telephone Knutsford (0565) 3155 — 52748
for information and opening hours.

Tatton Park
so many things to so many people

Cheshire County Council

TEIGNMOUTH *Devon* Map 3 SX97
Aqualand The Den. Specialises in Tropical
Marine Fish, but also has Tropical Freshwater
Fish and a fine exhibition of Local Marine Life.
Shell shop. Open daily Easter to Oct 10 – 6.
30p (ch 15 20p, ch 5 accompanied free, pen
15p). P. *(Tel 3383)*. Also Model Railway
exhibition 'N' gauge. Situated below
Aqualand. Open as above. 30p (ch 15 20p, ch
5 accompaned, free, pen 15p). **(79)**

TEMPLE SOWERBY *Cumbria* Map 12 NY62
Acorn Bank Garden Walled and herb
gardens, with spring bulbs and herbaceous
plants are open Apr to end of Oct, daily (ex
Mon) 10 – 5.30. 30p. No dogs. *(NT)*

TENTERDEN *Kent* Map 5 TQ83
Town Station Principal station of Britain's
first Light Railway, the Kent and East Sussex
Railway, constructed by Col H F Stephens at
turn of the century and reopened with steam
trains in 1974. Some 18 steam locomotives
(earliest built 1872, others from USA and
Norway) are in various stages of restoration.
Train services run to Wittersham Road.
Wealden Pullman specials, using Pullman
Bar Car 'Barbara' (built 1926) operate on Sat
evenings May to Oct. The station, shop,
carriage and wagon yards open all year. ⚏
(when trains operate). Trains operate every
weekend and BH, Easter to end Oct, also
Wed Jun and Jul, daily 12 Jul to 31 Aug Sun
only Nov and Dec. Fares: Day return 90p (ch
15 45p) Rover ticket £1.25 (ch 15 65p) Under
revision for 1980. ⚠ *(Tel 2943)* ♿

TETBURY *Gloucestershire* Map 3 ST89
Chavenage 2m NW. Elizabethan house
(1576) with later additions, containing some
17th-C stained glass, furniture and tapestries.
Open May to Sep, Thu, Sun and BH 2 – 6. £1
(ch 50p). ⚠ *(Tel 52329)*. *(Mr D Lowsley
Williams)*

THETFORD *Norfolk* Map 5 TL88
Ancient House Museum White Hart Street.
An early Tudor timbered house with
collections illustrating Thetford and Breckland
life, history and natural history. Open all year
(ex 4 Apr, 25, 26 Dec, 1 Jan) Mon to Sat 10 – 5
(closed Mon 1 – 2), Sun 2 – 5. Free. P. *(Tel
2599)*
Thetford Castle One of the original motte
and bailey castles, at 80ft, perhaps the largest
still in existence. This represents the earliest
form of castle, before masonry was added.
Accessible any time. Free.
Thetford Priory Extensive remains of
Cluniac monastery founded at beginning of
12th C. The 14th-C gatehouse of priory
stands to its full height. Open*, see inside
front cover. 10p (ch 16 and pen 5p). ⚠ *(AM)*

Warren Lodge 2m NW of town, on B1107.
There are remains of a two-storey hunting
lodge in 15th-C flint with stone dressings.
Open Mon to Fri only 9 – 4.15 (closed
weekends and BH). Free. *(AM)*

THORESBY *Nottinghamshire* Map 8 SK67
Thoresby Hall A great Dukeries mansion, in
the heart of Sherwood Forest, dating from
1864 – 75, the architect being Salvin. This is
the only Dukeries mansion still occupied by
descendants of the original owners open to
the public. Fine state apartments and
terraces. Adventure woodland and paddling
pool. ⚏ House open 2 – 5. Telephone for
details of opening dates and admission
prices. ⚠ *(Tel Mansfield 823210)*. *(Countess
Manvers)*

THORNBURY *Devon* Map 2 SS30
Devon Museum of Mechanical Music Mill
Leat. On unclassified road 5m NE of
Holsworthy. A fascinating collection of old
mechanical musical instruments from a tiny
music box to an eight-ton fairground organ.
The variety between these two extremes is
bewildering. All instruments are played for the
visitor and the curator demonstrates how they
work and shows the various mechanisms that
operate them. Continuous demonstrations.
Special concerts on the fairground organ to
be announced. ⚏ in the farm house. Open
Easter to Oct, daily 2 – 5. Admission prices for
1980 not yet decided. ⚠ *(Tel Milton Damerel
378 and Shebbear 483)* ♿

THORNTON *Humberside* Map 8 TA11
Thornton Abbey Displays a magnificent
example of a 14th-C gateway approached
across a dry moat spanned by a long bridge,
with arcaded walls and circular towers. Open,
see inside front cover but closes 4.30 Mon
and Tue. 15p (ch 16 and pen 5p). ⚠ *(AM)*

THURNHAM *Lancashire* Map 7 SD45
Thurnham Hall 5m S Lancaster on A588.
Dating from 13th C, the major part being
16th-C. The Great Hall contains fine
Elizabethan plaster work, Jacobean panelling
and fine Jacobean staircase, Priest Room
and Priest Hide. 19th-C private chapel. The
tour includes slide lecture on restoration, also
at the Hall the Turin Shroud exhibition. Shop
and ⚏. Open Easter to 31 Oct daily (ex Sat)
2 – 5.30. Admission charges not available at
time of going to press. Party. ⚠ *(Tel
Lancaster 751766)*

THURSFORD GREEN *Norfolk* Map 9 TF93
The Thursford Collection 6m NE
Fakenham. The collection includes
Showman's engines, traction engines,
ploughing engines, steam wagons, steam
rollers, 2ft gauge steam railway. Wurlitzer

cinema organ, fairground organs, dance and cafe organs, street and barrel organs and barrel pianos, also farm machinery. Midsummer musical evenings Tue at 8pm through summer on Wurlitzer cinema organ by the country's leading Organists. Sauages Venetian Gondola switchback ride. Picnic area and children's play area. ♨ Open all year 1 May to 31 Oct daily 2 – 5.30, 1 Nov to 30 Apr Sun only 2 – 5.30. Admission prices for 1980 not yet decided. ⚠ *(Tel Fakenham 3836 or Thursford 238)* &

TILBURY *Essex* Map 5 TQ67
Thurrock Riverside Museum Civic Square. Illustrates the history of the River Thames and the people of its riverside in the Borough of Thurrock. Ship and barge models, photographs, etc. Open daily (ex Sun and Mon) Tue, Sat 10 – 5, Wed, Fri 10 – 8, Thu 10 – 12 (closed 1 – 2 each day). Free. *(Tel 79216)* &
Tilbury Fort Dates from the reign of Henry VIII and was the scene of the review by Queen Elizabeth I of the army raised to resist the Spanish Armada. Later altered and restored. Open, see inside front cover. 25p (ch 16 and pen 10p). ⚠ *(AM)*

TILFORD *Surrey* Map 4 SU84
Old Kiln Agricultural Museum Reeds Road. Collection of farm implements and machinery of the past, and examples of the crafts and trades allied to farming. Larger exhibits are displayed in the pleasant garden and woodland surroundings, covering some ten acres. Smithy, wheel-wright's shop, hand tools, etc, are housed in the old farm buildings. Arboretum. Picnic area. Open 1 Apr to 30 Sep, Wed, Sat and Sun 12 – 6. 50p (ch 14 25p). ⚠ *(Tel Frensham 2300)* &

TINTAGEL *Cornwall* Map 2 SX08
Tintagel Castle Remains of a mid 13th-C castle, later abandoned and divided by subsequent erosion into two portions. There are also some remains of a Celtic monastery dating from the 5th C to the 9th C. Open*, see inside front cover 30p. Winter 15p (ch 16 and pen 15p, winter 5p). *(AM)*
Old Post Office A former 14th-C manor house, with a hall and an ancient slate roof. Open 1 Apr to end Oct, weekdays 11 – 1, 2 – 6 (or sunset), Sun 2 – 6; Dec, Jan, Feb. Key from caretaker (closed Nov). 50p (incl guide book) (ch 15p). P. *(NT)*

TINTINHULL *Somerset* Map 3 ST51
Tintinhull House Modern formal garden surrounding an attractive 17th-C house, with fine pedimented façade. Open Apr to Sep, Wed, Thu, Sat and BH Mons 2 – 6. 70p *(NT)*

TISBURY *Wiltshire* Map 3 SS92
Pythouse A late Palladian mansion, with family portraits. Shown May to end of Sep. Wed and Thu 2 – 5. 40p. P. *(Tel 0210)*

TITCHFIELD *Hampshire* Map 4 SU50
Titchfield Abbey Also known as 'Place House'. The surviving picturesque gatehouse of a 13th-C abbey converted into a mansion by the Earl of Southampton, Lord Chancellor of England, during the 16th C and showing fine Tudor chimneys. Open, see inside front cover. 15p (ch 16 and pen 5p). ⚠ *(AM)*

TIVERTON *Devon* Map 3 SS91
Tiverton Castle Historic fortress of Henry I founded 1106. Notable medieval gatehouse, clock museum, Joan of Arc gallery and Chapel of St Francis. Open Easter then end May to mid Sep, daily (ex Fri and Sat) 2.30 – 5.30. 70p (ch and pen 40p). Party 15+. Prices are under revision for 1980. Private visits by arrangement. ⚠ *(Tel 3200)*
Tiverton Museum St Andrew Street, near Town Hall. Here is a comprehensive folk museum housed in a restored 19th-C school and comprising numerous local exhibits, a Victorian laundry, two water-wheels, costume gallery and an industrial gallery covering the Grand Western Canal, natural history and wartime rooms. Agricultural section includes a collection of farm wagons and a complete smithy. Now one of the outstanding West Country folk museums. Loan exhibitions are changed monthly. A large railway gallery houses the GWR locomotive No. 1442 and other railway relics. Entrance from public car park. Open all year Mon to Sat 10.30 – 1 and 2 – 4.30 (ex BH). Free. P. *(Tel 56295 and 2446)* &

TOLLAND *Somerset* Map 3 ST13
Gaulden Manor 1m E of Tolland Church. Small historic manor originating from the 12th C. Unique plaster ceiling in Great Hall with oak screen leading to former chapel. Past home of the Turberville family, immortalised by Thomas Hardy, and of the Wolcotts of the USA. Herb garden, bog garden, gift shop. Plants for sale. ♨ (teas) in old stables. Open 6/7 Apr then 4 May to 7 Sep, Thu, Sun and BH 2 – 6. Admission to house and garden probably 70p (ch 13 30p). Garden only 30p. ⚠ *(Tel Lydeard St Lawrence 213)* & B

TONBRIDGE *Kent* Map 5 TQ54
Tonbridge Castle Late 12th-C curtain walls, with a ruined shell keep and a round-towered early 14th-C gatehouse. Nature trail through Castle grounds 10p. Grounds open daily 7.30 – dusk; castle open weekends only May, Jun and Jul, daily Aug, 10.30 – 4.30. Grounds

free; castle 30p (ch and pen 20p). Ch 12 must be accompanied. Opening times and admission prices under revision for 1980. P. *(Tel 353241)* & B

TONG *West Yorkshire* Map 8 SE23
Tong Hall This 18th-C house built by Sir George Tempest is an early example of 'Queen Anne' domestic architecture. Open from Easter to Oct, Sat, Sun and BH 2 – 6. Free. Educational services. ⚠ *(Tel Leeds 852356)*

TOPSHAM *Devon* Map 3 SX98
Topsham Museum 25 The Strand. This small museum, which is located in the sail-loft of one of the beautiful old Dutch-gabled 17th-C houses that are a feature of this little port, depicts its history and trade through the centuries. Open all year, Mon, Wed, Sat 2 – 5. Free. ⚠ *(Tel 3244)*

TORPOINT *Cornwall* Map 2 SX45
Antony House 2m NW off A38. Fine, largely unaltered mansion of 1711 – 21 in brick and stone, with early 19th-C porte-cochère by Sir William Carew and panelled rooms with portraits and old furniture. House open 1 Apr to Oct, Tue, Wed, Thu and BH 2 – 6. £1. *(NT)*

TORQUAY *Devon* Map 3 SX96
Aqualand Beacon Quay. The largest Aquarium in the West Country which specialises in tropical marine fish. There is also a splendid exhibition of local marine life, as well as tropical freshwater fish and a pair of Otters from Asia. Open Apr, May, Sep and Oct daily 10 to dusk; Jun to Aug daily 10 – 10. 40p (ch 14 and pen 20p). Party. ⚠ *(Tel 24439)* &
Babbacombe Model Village Situated in four acres of beautiful, miniature landscaped gardens, this attractive example of a model village contains over 400 models and 1,200ft of model railways. Open all year, daily (ex 25 Dec); Easter to Oct 9 – 10; Nov to Mar 9 – 5. 80p (ch 40p, pen 60p). Under revision for 1980. Party. ⚠ *(Tel 38669)* &
Natural History Society Museum 529 Babbacombe Road. Founded in 1844. Exhibits include finds from Kent's Cavern and other caves in South Devon; local archaeological material. Open all year daily (ex Sun, 4 Apr and Christmas period) 10 – 4.45. 25p (ch and pen 10p, ch 5 free). ⚠ *(Tel 23975)*
Torre Abbey Mansion The Kings Drive. An 18th-C house with interesting pictures and furniture. Abbey ruins and Tythe Barn (Spanish Barn) nearby. House open Apr to Oct daily 10 – 1 and 2 – 5.30, winter parties by appointment. 15p P (pen free). *(Tel 23593)*

TOTNES *Devon* Map 3 SX86
Totnes Castle A ruined 13th- and 14th-C castle with a shell keep and curtain walls. Open*, see inside front cover. 15p (ch 16 and pen 5p). ⚠ *(AM)*
Elizabethan House 70 Fore Street. Four-storey, restored, partly half-timbered, gabled house, dating from c1575, with notable interior features and a cobbled courtyard. Now a museum of furniture, domestic objects, toys, dolls, costumes and archaeology. Computer exhibition. Open Mar to Oct, Mon to Sat only 10.30 – 1 and 2 – 5.30. (Reduced hours in winter.) 15p (ch 16 10p). Under revision for 1980. ⚠ *(Tel 863821, winter 862147)*
Guildhall Off High Street. Gabled and colonnaded 16th-C building, now housing council chamber (in use since 1624). Relics on show include Saxon coins minted locally. Open Easter to Sep, Mon to Fri 9.30 – 1 and 2 – 5, Oct to Mar, by appointment. 10p (ch 5p, school parties £1). P. *(Tel 862147)*
Totnes Motor Museum The Quay. Private collection of vintage, sports and racing cars, most of which are currently raced and cover a 50-year span of motoring. Engines, motorbikes and motormania are also displayed. Souvenir shop. Open Easter to Oct, daily 10 – 6. 75p (ch 30p). Prices for 1980 under review. ⚠ *(Tel 862777)*

TRELISSICK GARDEN *Cornwall* Map 2 SW83
4m S of Truro, on B3289. A beautiful woodland park at the head of Falmouth Harbour, growing rhododendrons and sub-tropical plants. Large shrub garden. Plants available at shop. 🍴 in Trelissick Garden Barn 11 – 6. Gardens shown Mar to end of Oct Mon to Sat 11 – 6; Sun 2 – 6. £1 *(NT) (NGS)*

TRERICE *Cornwall* Map 2 SW85
Off A3058. A picturesque Elizabethan House, displaying unusual curly gables, rebuilt in 1571. There are contemporary fireplaces and plaster ceilings. 🍴 2 – 5.30. Open 1 Apr to end Oct daily 11 – 6 (last admission 5.30) £1 *(NT) (NGS)*

TREWINT *Cornwall* Map 2 SX28
Wesley's Cottage near Altarnun. Small 18th-C Methodist shrine, well-restored in 1950. John Wesley came here six times between 1744 and 1762. Annual Wesley Day service is held. Also Sun services in summer. Interesting testaments and period furnishings are on display. Wesley Day celebrations 24 May. Open all year, daily 9 – dusk. Free. ⚠ Caution necessary when leaving owing to restricted visibility on road. *(Tel Pipers Pool 561)* **(79)**

TRING *Hertfordshire* Map 4 SP91
The Zoological Museum A branch of the British Museum (Natural History) specialising in mounted specimens of animals, shells, birds, eggs, and butterflies. Open all year (ex 1 Jan, 4 Apr, 5 May, 24–26 Dec), Mon to Sat 10–5, Sun 2–5. Free. P. *(Tel 4181)* � B

TROUTBECK *Cumbria* Map 7 NY40
Townend Fine 17th-C yeoman's house, containing carved woodwork and furnishings of the Browne family. Open Wed only Mar then Apr to Oct daily (ex Mon and Sat but open BH Mon) 2–6 (or sunset). 60p (ch 30p). *(NT)*

TRURO *Cornwall* Map 2 SW84
County Museum and Art Gallery River Street. An exceptionally interesting display illustrating the history of the county. The mineral collection is world-famous. Unusually fine collections of pottery and porcelain, pewter, old-master drawings, Japanese ivories and lacquer-work. Open all year, (ex BH) 9–1, 2–5. Free. P. *(Tel 2205)*

TUNBRIDGE WELLS *Kent* Map 5 TQ53
Tunbridge Wells Museum and Art Gallery Civic Centre. Old prints, local bygones, natural history, geology, Wealden prehistory, and Tunbridge ware. Collections of Victorian paintings; toys and dolls. Temporary exhibitions in art gallery. Open Mon to Sat 10–5.30. Closed Suns, BH and Tue after Spring and Summer BH also 5 April. Free. P. *(Tel 26121 ex 171)*

TUTBURY *Staffordshire* Map 8 SK22
Tutbury Castle Ruined 14th-C stronghold. Mary Queen of Scots was twice imprisoned here for a total of seven years. Picnic grounds, putting green. Fêtes in May, Jun and Jul. Café and banquet hall. Open all year (ex 25 and 26 Dec) 10–6. 20p (ch 5p). Coach parties welcome. ⬚ ⚠ *(Tel Burton on Trent 812129)* � **(79)**

PKF

TWYCROSS ZOO PARK *Leicestershire* Map 4 SK30
Collection of all kinds of animals, especially noted for the range of primates, including gorillas, orang-utans and chimpanzees. Modern reptile house. Wild animals include giraffes, elephants, camels, lions, and tigers. Numerous exotic birds. ⬚ and picnic areas, only Tea Bar open during winter months. Open all the year (ex 25 Dec) daily 10–4 (6 in summer). £1 (ch 50p subject to alteration). Party. ⚠ (10p). *(Tel Tamworth 880250)* �

TYNEMOUTH *Tyne and Wear* Map 12 NZ36
Tynemouth Priory and Castle A 16th-C ruin, with the towers, gatehouse, and keep erected to defend the nearby 11th- to 13th-C Priory. Open*, see inside front cover. 15p (ch 16 and pen 5p). ⚠ *(AM)*

UCKFIELD *East Sussex* Map 5 TQ41
Beeches Farm 1½m W of town on Isfield road. 16th-C farmhouse with gardens, lawns, sunken garden, borders, and yew trees. Wide views. Gardens open all year, daily 10–5; house open by appointment only, conducted

tour 50p. Admission to gardens 15p (ch 12 7p). ⚠ *(Tel 2391). (Mrs V Thomas)* �&. B
Horsted Place Gardens The gardens were redesigned and landscaped in the 1960s by Geoffrey Jellicoe around the Victorian Gothic mansion, surrounded by undulating countryside and woodland. Victorian garden, rose borders, rhododendrons, shaded walks, pleached limes and laburnum tunnel. Fragrant flowers and herbs are given special emphasis. Open Apr to 29 Sep, Wed, Thu and Sun 2–6, (house not open to the public except by special arrangement). 40p (ch 14 20p, party). Under review for 1980. ⚠ *(Tel Isfield 315)* ⅐

UFFINGTON *Oxfordshire* Map 4 SU38
Castle and White Horse Situated on the ancient Ridgeway at a height of more than 700ft on the Berkshire Downs. The castle is a defensive Iron Age hill fort and below is a cut in the chalk the famous White Horse, believed to be contemporary. Both accessible any reasonable time. Free. ⚠ *(AM)*

ULEY *Gloucestershire* Map 3 ST79
Uley Tumulus 1m N. Known also as Hetty Pegler's Tump, this long barrow 120ft by 85ft, has a chamber approached by means of a deep forecourt. The chamber forms part of a gallery grave and was excavated in 1821 and 1854. Accessible any reasonable time. 10p (ch 16 and pen 5p). *(AM)*

ULVERSTON *Cumbria* Map 7 SD27
Cumbria Crystal Lightburn Road. using a fine full-lead crystal, the factory specialises in glassware based on 18th-C design. Goblets, decanters, candlesticks, tankards and many other items are made by traditional hand-blown and hand cutting techniques. Visitors welcome in factory, but large parties by appointment. Open all year, factory Mon to Fri 8–12, 12.30–4, Sat 8–11, closed Sun; shop and showroom Mon to Fri 9–12, 12.30–5.30, Sat and Sun 9–12. Free. P. *(Tel 54400)* ⅐

UPMINSTER *Gt London* Map 5 TQ58
Tithe Barn Agricultural and Folk Museum Hall Lane. 15th-C thatched timber building contains large selection of old agricultural implements, craft and farm tools, domestic bygones and items of local interest, over 1,200 exhibits in all. Open first full weekend of each month. Apr to Oct 11–1 and 2.15–5.30. Free. ⚠ *(Tel 29614)* ⅐

UPNOR *Kent* Map 5 TQ77
Upnor Castle A restored castle of 1561, designed originally as a River Medway blockhouse. A number of interesting relics have been preserved. Queen Elizabeth I reviewed the fleet here in 1581. Open, see inside front cover but closed all day Wed and Fri pm. 20p (ch 16 and pen 5p). ⚠ *(AM)*

UPPERMILL *Lancashire* Map 7 SD90
Saddleworth Museum High Street. Part of an old wooden mill converted into a museum with exhibits of local historical interest. Fine model of the Roman fort at Castleshaw and two working hand looms which show the history of weaving. Extension under construction will house new art gallery and provide full facilities for ⅐. Open all year Sat, Sun and Wed 2.30–5. Free (charge for admission under review). ⚠ *(Tel Saddleworth 2273 day, 3884 evening)*. ⅐

UPPER SLAUGHTER *Gloucestershire* Map 5 SP12
Manor House One of the finest Elizabethan houses in Gloucestershire. Grade I listed building, restored in 1973. Mainly

Elizabethan, it has a remarkable 15th-C vaulted chamber surviving from an earlier religious foundation, plus an ornamental entrance porch of the Jacobean period. Home of the Slaughter family for 500 years. Open May to Sep inclusive, Fri 2–6. 40p. *(Tel Bourton-on-the-Water 20927)*

UPTON CRESCENT *Salop* Map 7 SP69
Upton Cressett Hall Elizabethan manor house, gatehouse and gardens in beautiful countryside. Fine plasterwork, brickwork and panelling. 14th-C Great Hall. Open May to end Oct, Thu 2.30–5.30 and 25 Aug. Parties at other times by appointment. 50p ⚠ *(Tel Morville 307)*

UPTON HOUSE *Warwickshire* Map 4 SP34
7m NW of Banbury on A422. 17th-C house with fine collection of paintings, porcelain, tapestries and furniture. Terraced garden. Open Apr to Sep, Mon to Thu 2–6 (last admission to house 5.30) and some weekends in May and Aug. £1.10, garden only 60p. *(NT)*

WADDESDON *Buckinghamshire* Map 4 SP71
Waddesdon Manor 6m NW Aylesbury, gates on A41. French Renaissance-style château built in 1874–1889 for Baron Ferdinand de Rothschild by Destailleur. Rich in French decorative art of 17th and 18th Cs, Royal furniture, Sèvres and Meissen porcelain, Savonnerie carpets, fine paintings and personal mementoes of the family. New exhibition room in 1980. ⚷ Open 26 Mar to 26 Apr, Oct, Wed to Sun 2–6; 4 Apr and BH Mons 11–6 (closed Wed after BH). Sun, grounds open from 11.30am. House and grounds incl 4 Apr £1.30, other Fri £1.50 (extra rooms shown). Grounds and Aviary only 60p (ch 25p). Play area for young ch. Ch 12 not admitted to house. ⚠ *(NT)*

WAKEFIELD *West Yorkshire* Map 8 SE32
Wakefield Art Gallery Wentworth Terrace. Good collection of modern paintings and sculpture including works by Henry Moore, Barbara Hepworth, Jacob Epstein, Graham Sutherland, Ben Nicholson etc. Regular programme of temporary exhibitions. Open all year, Mon to Sat 12.30–5.30, Sun 2.30–5.30 (closed BH). Free. P. *(Tel 75402)*
Wakefield Museum Wood Street. Specialises in collections of local interest, including archaeology, costume, period rooms. Waterton Collection of natural history specimens. Temporary exhibitions. Open all year weekdays, 12.30–5.30, Sun 2.30–5.30 (closed BH). Free. P. *(Tel 61767)*

WALL *Staffordshire* Map 7 SK10
Roman Remains Remains of baths and posting stations (most complete in Britain), and a museum of excavated finds from the Roman station of 'Letocetum' at the junction of Watling Street and Ricknield Street. Open, see inside front cover but closed Mon and Tue. 15p (ch 16 and pen 5p). ⚠ *(NT and AM)*

WALSINGHAM *Norfolk* Map 9 TF93
Walsingham Abbey Grounds Contain site of the Shrine of Our Lady and the remains of an Augustinian Priory including the gatehouse, crypt, refectory and East Window Arch. The Abbey Grounds are open Apr to Sep. Wed Apr; Wed, Sat & Sun May to Jul and Sep also Mon, Wed, Fri, Sat and Sun Aug and BH Easter to Sep. 20p (ch 10p). P. *(Tel 259)* ⅐

Shirehall Museum Almost perfect 18th-C courtroom with its original fittings, including prisoner's lock-up. The museum contains items illustrating the history of Walsingham, including a new display on the History of Pilgrimage. Open daily May to Sep 10–12 and 2–4, Oct Sat and Sun only. 10p (ch and pen free). P. *(Tel 510)*

WALTHAM ABBEY *Essex* Map 5 TL30
Waltham Abbey Gatehouse, Bridge and entrance to Cloisters This example of a gatehouse is 14th-C and has separate carriage and pedestrian entrances. Harold's Bridge is attributed to the 14th C. Cloister entrance dates from 12th C. Open at any reasonable time. Free. In the historic Norman and later Abbey Church nearby is an undercroft museum. ⚖ *(AM)*

WALWICK *Northumberland* Map 12 NY97
Chesters Roman Fort and Museum ½m E. Roman Fort designed for a garrison of 500 cavalry. Extensive ruins of bath house. Museum houses Clayton collection of items excavated from local forts such as 'Cilurnum'. Open*, see inside front cover. 40p, winter 15p (ch 16 and pen 15p, winter 5p). ⚖ *(AM)*

WANDLEBURY RING *Cambridgeshire* Map 5 TL45
On the summit of the low Gog Magog Hills, this hill fort comprises a double rampart and ditch, 1,000ft in diameter; about 110 acres of the hills have been protected by the Cambridge Preservation Society. Open daily without charge but donations are welcome. Parking.

WANSFORD *Cambridgeshire* Map 4 TL09
Nene Valley Railway Standard-gauge steam railway running over five miles through Nene Park, between Wansford and Orton Mere, Peterborough. Having many steam locomotives, it offers a unique spectacle of British, French, Danish, German, Swedish and Norwegian locomotives and stock on the same railway. ⚑ Greene King bar car also lunch (reservations advisable) and tea every Sun in Wagons-Lit restaurant car. Open Apr to Sep, Sat, Sun also mid week during Jun, Jul and Aug. Also open for Christmas Specials every Sat and Sun during Dec. ⚖ For further information and reservation contact the General Manager. *(Tel Stamford 782854)*

WANTAGE *Oxfordshire* Map 4 SU48
Wantage Museum Civic Hall, Portway. A small museum with displays on the landscape history of the Vale of the White Horse and the growth of the town of Wantage. Museum Keeper available for enquiries on Wed. Open all year 2–5, Sat 10–12.30 and 2–5 (closes 4.30 Oct to Mar). Free. P. *(Tel 66838)* ⚐

Kingstone Lisle Park 4½m W off B4507. The home of Captain and Mrs Leopold Lonsdale. The central part of the mansion was built in 1677 and the wings were added in the 19th C. It has a magnificent flying staircase and an interesting collection of 17th- and 18th-C glass. Also on display are letters which belonged to Field Marshal Lord Raglan, Commander-in-Chief of the Crimea. ⚑ (by arrangement). Open Apr to Sep by appointment only, market garden also open. £1 (less than 5 min £5). Party 15+ 80p per person. ⚖ Further information write to: The Secretary, Kingstone Lisle Park, Wantage. *(Tel Uffington 223)*

WARDOUR *Wiltshire* Map 3 ST92
Wardour Castle Built by James Paine in 1768, and restored in 1960 for Cranborne Chase School. Contains a notable stairway with two semi-circular flights. Open Jul to Sep

Mon, Wed, Fri, Sat 2.30–6.35p (ch 14 20p). Party 12+. Under revision for 1980. ⚖ *(Tel Tisbury 870464)*
Wardour Old Castle Built in 1392 by John Lord Lovel, with additions by Robert Smythson after 1570. Damaged after the Civil War. Open*, see inside front cover. 15p (ch 16 and pen 5p). ⚖ *(AM)*

WARKWORTH *Northumberland* Map 12 NU20
Warkworth Castle Built between 11th- and 14th-C with a gatehouse and a great keep, probably built by the 1st Earl of Northumberland. Old bridge over River Coquet and rare bridge tower. Open Apr to Sep only, see inside front cover. 20p (ch 16 and pen 5p). ⚖ *(AM)*
Warkworth Hermitage Interesting 14th-C hermitage with a small chapel cut in solid rock. Access by rowing boat from nearby Castle. Open, see inside front cover, Apr to Sep only. 15p (ch 16 and pen 5p). P (at Castle). *(AM)*

WARNHAM *West Sussex* Map 4 TQ13
The Warnham War Museum 1m NE on east of A24. Private collection of World War II vehicles, uniforms, badges, medals, equipment, tracked and amphibious vehicles, set in ten acres of countryside. ⚑ (licensed). Open all year (ex 25 Dec) daily 1 Oct to Easter 10–4; Easter to 30 Sep 10–6. 50p (ch 5–14 25p). Party. ⚖ *(Tel Horsham 65607)* ⚐ **(79)**

WARRINGTON *Cheshire* Map 7 SJ68
South Lancashire Regiment (PWV) Regimental Museum Peninsula Barracks, Orford. Military museum of South Lancashire Regiment from 1717 onwards, containing historical records, uniforms and accoutrements, arms, badges, and medals. Open all year Mon to Fri 9–12.30, 2–4.30. Free. ⚖ limited. *(Tel 33563)*

WARWICK *Warwickshire* Map 4 SP26
Warwick Castle Off Castle Hill. Famous 14th-C and later castle, overlooking the River Avon. Guy's Tower (1394) and Caesar's Tower (1356) between which is an imposing gatehouse. Exhibition areas include the Great Hall, State rooms, Dungeon and Torture display, Armoury, Clocktower and Barbican, Guy's Tower and Ghost Tower. Peacocks and peacock gardens. Special events on Sunday afternoons (April to October). Children's adventure area. Picnic areas. Souvenir shops. Licensed restaurant (all year). ⚑ (Mar to Sep). Medieval Banquets throughout the year. Open all year (ex 25 Dec) 10–5.30 (4.30 Nov to Feb). Admission prices not yet decided. ⚖ *(Tel 45421)* ⚐ ⚖
Lord Leycester's Hospital West Gate. Lovely, half-timbered building, built in 1383, and adapted for its present use by the Earl of Leycester in 1571. It is still an almshouse for ex-servicemen and their wives. Guildhall Chapel, Regimental Museum of Queen's Own Hussars. ⚑ Easter to Sep. Open all year 10–5.30, summer; in winter 10–4 (closed Suns, 4 Apr and 25 Dec). Last admission ½hr before closing. 40p (ch 14 20p). Party 20+. ⚖ *(Tel 42797)*
Warwick Doll Museum Oken's House, Castle Street. Half-timbered Elizabethan house, the 16th-C birthplace of Thomas Oken, a benefactor of the town. Now a doll museum containing the Joy Robinson Collection of antique and period dolls, and toys. Open daily 10–6. Sun 11–5. 30p (ch 15p). Admission prices under revision for 1980. P. *(Tel 42843)*

St John's House Junction of A429 and A445 east of town. Fine 17th-C house, with gardens and notable wrought-iron gates, rebuilt by the Stoughton family on the site of an old hospital. It is now a branch of the County Museum (crafts, costume, and musical instruments), and includes the museum of the Royal Warwickshire Regiment on the first floor. Open weekdays (ex Tue) 10–12.30 and 1.30–5.30, Sun (May to Sep only) 2.30–5. Regimental museum open weekdays (ex Tue) 10–12.30, 2–4.30 (4 Fri), Sat 1.30–5, Sun 2.30–5 (May to Sep only). Free. P in St Nicholas Park. *(Tel 43431 ext 2132; for Regimental Museum, 41653)*

WASHAWAY *Cornwall* Map 2 SX07
Pencarrow House 1m N on unclass road. Georgian mansion c1770. The interior contains interesting architectural features, including an impressive Inner Hall with marbled pillars and a cantilever staircase; a music room with a Rococo ceiling; and many fine 18th-C paintings by Reynolds, Devis, Scott, Raeburn, Wilson etc, together with English, French and Oriental furniture and china. There are 35 acres of woodland gardens with arrowed trails. Plant shop. Picnic area, ☕. Open Easter to end Sep, Tue, Wed, Thu, Fri, Sun 1.45–5.30, BH Mon and 1 Jul to 10 Sep 11.30–5.30, (last tour of house 5). Gardens and plant shop open 15 Mar to end Sep daily. Admission charges not yet decided. ⚠ *(Tel St Mabyn 369)* ㅎ B

WASHFORD *Somerset* Map 3 ST04
Bardon Manor 2m SW of Watchet, off B3190. Unspoilt and reputedly haunted 14th-C manor house with Saxon fireplace in main hall, and cockpit. Historical associations with famous Bardon Papers connected with Mary, Queen of Scots. Exhibition of paintings and handicrafts by West Country artists. ☕. Open Jun to Sep, daily 10.30–5.30. 20p (ch 14 and pen 10p). ⚠ *(Tel 217)*
Cleeve Abbey Ruined 13th-C Cistercian house noted for gatehouse, dormitory, and refectory with traceried windows, timber roof, and wall paintings. Open*, see inside front cover. 15p (ch 16 and pen 5p). ⚠ *(AM)*

WASHINGTON *Tyne and Wear* Map 12 NZ35
Washington Old Hall Mainly early 17th-C, the seat of the Washington family, now restored as a museum. Open, Mar to Oct, daily (ex Tue) 1–6 (or sunset). Nov to Feb, Sat and Sun 2–5. 50p (ch 25p). *(NT)*
The Wildfowl Trust A waterfowl park on the N bank of the River Wear. 103 acres with a comprehensive collection of the world's waterfowl in attractive landscaped surroundings, including a refuge of 70 acres for wild birds, which can be viewed from a number of public hides. Attractive log cabin visitor centre, souvenir and natural history bookshop, inside viewing gallery giving excellent view over part of main collection area. Lecture theatre where free natural history films shown most days. ☕ weekends and daily Jul and Aug. Open all year (ex 24/25 Dec) daily 9.30–6.30 (9 Jun, Jul and Aug). Last admission 1 hour before closing. 65p (ch 4–15 30p, ch 4 free, pen 50p). Party 20+ (educational tours may be arranged). P. *(Tel 465454)* ㅎ

WEDNESBURY *West Midlands* Map 7 SO99
Sandwell Art Gallery and Museum
Holyhead Road. Collection of English and Continental 19th-C oil paintings and water-colours and also a collection of various applied arts. Frequent temporary exhibitions.

Open all year (ex BH) Mon, Tue, Wed, Fri 10–5. Thu, Sat, 10–1. Free. P. *(Tel 021-556 0683)*

WEETING *Norfolk* Map 5 TL78
Weeting Castle A ruined 11th-C fortified manor house, situated in a rectangular enclosure, and preserving slight remains of a three-storeyed cross-wing. Open any reasonable time. Free. ⚠ *(AM)*

WELLAND *Hereford and Worcester* Map 3 SO74
Little Malvern Court c 1380, on foundations dating from 1171. Originally part of monastic buildings, probably reconstructed by Bishop Alcock in 1480 when extensive repairs to the Priory Church were carried out. North wing built about 1500. Adjacent Priory Church has 14th-century stained glass, carved rood-screen, misericords and hatchments. Prior's Hall and associated rooms only open Easter to end Sep, Wed 2.30–5.30. 30p. P. *(Tel Hanley Swan 257)*

WELLING *Gt London* Map 5 TQ47
Danson Park Lake watered park, designed originally by 'Capability' Brown, with rock and water gardens, and recreational facilities. ☕. Gardens open all year, daily Mon to Fri 7.30–dusk (4.30 winter) Sat and Sun 9–dusk (4.30 winter). Free. P. 10p weekends and BH Apr to Sep. Free weekdays and Oct to Mar. **(79)**

WELLS *Somerset* Map 3 ST54
Bishop's Palace The early part of the Palace, the Bishop's Chapel and the ruins of the banqueting hall date from the 13th C. The Undercroft remains virtually unchanged from this date. The first floor has former State Rooms with Long Gallery containing portraits of former Bishops. Ringed with fortifications and a moat, access is gained through a 14th-C Gatehouse. The moat is fed by St Andrew's Well from which the City derives its name. ☕ (Aug only). Open Easter and then May to Oct Suns (Thu, Grounds only), Aug daily 2–6. 35p (ch 14 20p); Grounds only 25p (ch 14 15p); special rate Aug only 40p (ch 14 25p). ⚠ *(Tel 78691)* ㅎ B
Wells Museum This museum illustrates the history and natural history of the caves in the Central Mendip area. Open all year. Apr to Sep 10–6, Oct to Mar 2–4.30, Sun Jun to Sep 2.30–5.30. Closed 24–26 Dec. 10p (ch 16 5p). P. (limited in street). *(Tel 73477)* **(79)**

WELNEY *Norfolk* Map 5 TL59
The Wildfowl Trust 800-acre popular wildfowl refuge on the Ouse Washes. Winter home of vast numbers of migratory swans, geese and ducks; in spring, alive with nesting mallard, redshank, snipe, ruff, black-tailed godwit etc. Spacious observatory, a series of hides and, in winter, a floodlit lagoon containing hundreds of Bewick's swans. Open all year daily (ex 24, 25 Dec) 10–5. 50p (ch 16 25p, pen 40p). Escorted visits at 10 and 2 (weekends only) 60p (ch 16 30p, pen 50p). Party 20+. Evening visits for parties only 1 Nov to 1 Mar commencing 7pm. 60p (ch 30p, pen 50p). Overnight accommodation available. ⚠ *(Tel Ely 860711)* ㅎ **(79)**

WEMBWORTHY *Devon* Map 2 SS60
Ashley Countryside Collection Ashley House. 1½m NW on unclass rd. Signposted on A377 at Eggesford Station and on B3220 at Winkleigh. A unique collection of 45 breeds of British sheep including all the rare breeds. Fleeces exhibition, and 1,000 items of the Ox, Horse and open fireplace era. Wheelwrights',

Coopers, Blacksmiths' and Country
Craftsmen's tools and workshops. Mainly
under cover. Picnic area. Open Easter to Oct
Mon, Wed, Sat and Sun also BH and daily (ex
Thu) in Aug 10–6. 50p (ch 12 25p). Under
revision for 1980. ⚠ *(Tel Ashreigney 226)* &

WENDRON *Cornwall* Map 2 SW63
Poldark Mining and Wendron Forge
Stretching over three acres is a major
collection of antique machines around the
only underground tin mine workings in
Cornwall open to the public. A forty-foot high
beam engine runs daily in the summer, and
the licensed restaurant contains a five-ton
working waterwheel. Open Easter to 1 Nov
daily 10–6 (sunset in Jul and Aug). £1 (ch 10
50p and pen 70p). ⚠ *(Tel Helston 3531 or
3173)* & B

WEST BROMWICH *West Midlands*
Map 7 SP09
Oak House Oak Road. Half-timbered 16th-C
house, displaying furniture, and furnishings in
the Jacobean style. Open all year, May to
Sep, weekdays 10–5 (1, Thu), Sun 2.30–5;
Oct to Apr weekdays 10–1. Free. P. *(Tel
021-553 0759)*

WESTBURY-ON-SEVERN *Gloucestershire*
Map 3 SO71
Westbury Court Garden A unique example
of a 17th-C water garden layout, with angle
pavillions, the earliest survivor of its kind in
England. They have for many years lain
derelict, but were given a government grant
for repairs and have been taken over by the
National Trust. Open May to Sep, daily (ex
Mon and Tue but open BH) 11–6; Apr and
Oct, Sat and Sun only. 60p (ch 30p). No dogs.
(NT)

WESTCLIFF-ON-SEA *Essex* Map 5 TQ88
Beecroft Art Gallery Station Road.
Specialises in traditional and contemporary
British art, but also has works from the
Continental schools. A special gallery
devoted to the development of Southend and
scenes of the Thames Estuary. Temporary
exhibitions every month. Open all year, daily,
weekdays 10.30–5.30. Sun 2–5.30. Free. P.
(limited). *(Tel Southend-on-Sea 47418)*

WESTERHAM *Kent* Map 5 TQ45
Quebec House A 16th- to 17th-C house,
once the home of General Wolfe. Open 2–30
Mar, Sun only 2–6. Apr to Oct daily (ex Thu
and Sat) 2–6. 60p (ch 30p). *(NT)*
Squerryes Court Dates from 1681,
associated with General Wolfe, to whom
cenotaph stands. Much of interior shown, with
fine pictures, china, tapestries, and period
furniture. Very attractive grounds with lake,
spring bulbs, azaleas and rhododendrons.
Open 1 Mar to 29 Oct, Wed, Sat, Sun, BH Mon
2–6 (last entry to house 5.30). House and
grounds 80p (ch 14 40p); Grounds only 40p
(ch 14 20p). Party (ex Sun). ⚠ *(Tel 62345)*. *(J
St A Warde)* & B

WEST HOATHLY *West Sussex* Map 5 TQ33
West Hoathly Priest's House 15th-C house,
now a small interesting folk museum. Open
weekdays (ex Fri) 11–5.30, Sun 2–5; Easter
to end of Sep. 20p (ch 10p). ⚠ *(Tel
Sharpthorne 810479)*. *(Sussex
Archaeological Society)*

WEST MALLING *Kent* Map 5 TQ65
St Leonard's Tower The surviving part of the
former castle or fortified manor house
belonging to Bishop Gundulph. Open any
reasonable time. Free. *(AM)*

WESTONBIRT *Gloucestershire* Map 3 ST88
Westonbirt Arboretum Includes splendid examples of rare specimen trees, and was founded originally by Robert Stayner Halford in 1829. Now incorporated in a 600-acre Forestry Commission estate. ⚰ Apr to Oct. Accessible daily 10−8 or sunset (whichever is earlier) all the year. Free. ⚰ 80p. Under revision for 1980. (Tel 220). *(The Forestry Commission)* &

WESTON PARK *Staffordshire* Map 7 SJ81
A fine mansion of 1671, built by Lady Wilbraham. Notable collection of pictures, furniture, and tapestries. Disraeli letters on show. The home of the Earls of Bradford for 300 years. Fine gardens and vast parklands by 'Capability' Brown. Three lakes, pets corner, and woodland adventure playground and aquarium. Garden centre, studio pottery. Special exhibitions and events. ⚰. Open Easter to end Sep daily (ex Mon and Fri) but open BH, House 2−6 (last admission 5.30). Park 11−7.30 (last admission 5.30). School parties 1 May to 31 Jul weekdays from 10am. Admission prices not available. Party. ⚰ *(Tel Weston-under-Lizard 207 or 385). (The Earl of Bradford)* &

Hilton Valley Railway On A5 near village of Weston-under-Lizard. Narrow-gauge railway which operates five steam and three diesel locomotives. Moving from Hilton and opening early 1980. Information from Hilton Valley Railway Ltd, Hem Manor, Shifnal, Salop TF11 9PT.

WESTON RHYN *Salop* Map 7 SJ23
Tyn-y-Rhos Hall 2m W near Bron-y-Garth on unclass road. Small manor house, seat of the Phillips family for over three hundred years. Fully furnished in the style of the late 19th-C.

Many interesting items including a painting of Charles I, believed to be of Van Dyke school, also worthy of note is the family chapel within the house. Open 1 May to 15 Sep Wed, Thu, Sat and Sun 2.30−6. 60p (ch and pen 30p). ⚰ *(Tel Chirk 7898)*

WESTON-SUPER-MARE *Avon* Map 3 ST36
Woodspring Museum Burlington Street. The museum is housed in the old workshops of the Edwardian Gaslight Company. Around a central courtyard are displays of the Victorian Seaside Holiday, an old chemist's shop, a dairy and a gallery of wildlife in the district. Other exhibits include Mendip minerals and mining, archaeology, costume jewellery, toys, dolls, transport from penny farthing to Weston Autogyro, cameras, the Dentist in 1900, and a Steep Holm display. Changing exhibitions are held in the Art Gallery. ⚰. Open all year (ex 4 Apr, 25 Dec, 1 Jan) Mon to Sat 10−5. Free. ⚰ roadside (1hr). *(Tel 21028)*

WESTON UNDERWOOD *Buckinghamshire* Map 4 SP85
Flamingo Gardens and Zoological Park 1,000 birds of 200 different species, including flamingos, cranes, pelicans, penguins, Scarlet Ibis, owls, waterfowl, and birds of prey, emanating from many countries. Mammals include Llamas, Wallabies, Black Buck, Big Horn sheep, dwarf Zebu. ⚰. Open Wed, Thu, Sat, Sun and BH 2−8, from 4 Apr to end Sep. £1 (ch 14 50p, pen 60p). Party 15+. Prices under rivision for 1980. ⚰ *(Tel Bedford 711451)* &

WEST TARRING *West Sussex* Map 4 TQ10
Parsonage Row Cottages High Street (at West Worthing). A group of three late 15th-C houses, fine examples of medieval close-

WESTON PARK

The 17th-century home of the Earl and Countess of Bradford contains a treasury of beautiful objects including an exceptional art collection. **Located in 1,000 acres of picturesque wooded parkland on the Shropshire/Staffordshire border.**
Woodland adventure playground — aquarium — studio pottery — garden centre — Collection of British Wildlife — pony rides — nature and architectural trails.
Catering Facilities. Picnic in peaceful surroundings.
Open Easter till the end of September (see entry for specific dates and times).
For further information write or telephone: The Old Stables, Weston Park, Shifnel, Shropshire. Tel: Weston-under-Lizard 207 or 385.
Access is easy — head for Weston-under-Lizard on the A5, 6 miles west of Junction 12 on the M6.

timbering construction, which are known as the Thomas-à-Becket cottages. They now house a small folk museum of bygones. Open 1 Apr to 31 Oct, Tue to Sat 2.15–5; other times by appointment with the Custodian. 15p (ch 10p). P. *(Tel Worthing 36385)*

WESTWOOD *Wiltshire* Map 3 ST85
Westwood Manor A beautiful 15th- to 17th-C house showing fine Jacobean plasterwork. Modern topiary garden. Open Apr to Sep, Wed 2.30–6. 70p *(NT)*

WEST WYCOMBE *Buckinghamshire*
Map 4 SU89
West Wycombe Park Rebuilt for Sir Francis Dashwood, c1765, probably built by Robert Adam, and situated in a fine park containing garden temples by 'Capability' Brown and Humphrey Repton. Notable furnishings and painted ceilings. House and grounds open Jun, Mon to Fri; Jul and Aug, every day (ex Sat) 2.15–6. £1.40. Grounds only 60p *(NT)*. *(NGS)*
West Wycombe Caves Built between 1748 and 1752. The caves are said to have been used as a meeting place for the Hell Fire Club. The entrance to the caves is half way up West Wycombe Hill, and consists of a large forecourt with flint walls, from which a brick tunnel leads into the caves. The many halls and chambers include the Labyrinth, Hall of Statues, Treasure Chamber and the Inner Temple. ♨ Open daily 1 Mar to 28 May and 9 to 29 Sep, 1–6pm, 29 May to 8 Sep daily 11–6. Sat and Sun 30 Sep to 25 Feb 12–4. £1 (ch and pen 50p). Party. ⚠ *(Tel High Wycombe 24411)*

WEYHILL *Hampshire* Map 4 SU34
The Hawk Conservancy Weyhill Wildlife Park A specialist collection of hawks, falcons, eagles, owls, vultures etc. Open daily, including Sun, from 10.30. 1 Mar to 9 Nov. 90p (ch 14 40p) ch must be accompanied by an adult. 1979 prices under revision for 1980. No dogs or pets. *(Tel 2252)*

WEYMOUTH *Dorset* Map 3 SY67
Museum of Local History Westham Road. An illustrated survey of the history of Weymouth and Portland, including local transport, and links with visits of King George III (1789–1805). Collections include special section of 'Household bygones', with occasional temporary exhibitions. Open all year. Summer: Mon, Wed, Thu, Fri 10–8, Tue and Sat 10–5; Winter: Tue to Sat 10–1 and 2–5. Closed Sun and Mon in winter. 10p (ch, students and pen free). P. *(Tel 74246)* &

WHALLEY *Lancashire* Map 7 SD73
Whalley Abbey The Abbey ruins are in delightful surroundings reaching down to the river. Open all year daily 10–dusk. 20p (ch 13 10p). Party 30+ (school ch only). ⚠ *(Tel 2268)*

WHIPSNADE *Bedfordshire* Map 4 TL01
Whipsnade Park Zoo Open-air zoo situated on edge of Chilterns. Over 2,000 animals and birds can be seen in near natural surroundings in the 500-acre park. Children's zoo, water mammals exhibit displaying dolphins. ♨ Open daily (ex 25 Dec) 10–7 or sunset if earlier. Admission not yet know for 1980. ⚠ Cars may drive round the zoo at an extra charge. A Zoo Train operates in the park according to demand. Steam Railway runs through White Rhino enclosure, Apr to Oct. *(Tel 872171)* &

WHITBY *North Yorkshire* Map 8 BN81
Whitby Abbey Considerable remains of fine church dating from 13th C. Damaged by shell fire during the 1914–18 War. Open*, see inside front cover. 20p (ch 16 and pen 5p). ⚠ *(AM)*
Whitby Museum Pannett Park. Museum portrays the history of the town. Next door is the Pannett Art Gallery; both are open 1 May to 30 Sep daily, Mon to Sat 9.30–5.30, Sun 2–5; 1 Oct to 30 Apr Mon, Tue, Thu and Fri 10.30–1, Wed and Sat 10.30–4, Sun 2–4; Easter weekend: Fri, Sat and Mon 10.30–4, Sun 2–4; BH: normal opening times. Closed 25, 26 Dec and 1 Jan. 20p (ch 16 15p) subject to review for 1980. P. (St Hilda's Terrace). *(Tel 2908)* &

WHITEHAVEN *Cumbria* Map 11 NX91
Whitehaven Museum and Art Gallery Market Place. Lower gallery devoted to changing exhibitions, approximately 20 per year, very diverse subjects. The upper gallery features local history including geology, coal and iron mining, archaeology, ship building, Whitehaven made pottery. Slide/tape shows usually featured in lower gallery. Open Mon to Sat 10–5 (closed Sun and BH). Free. P (street; multi-storey 5p). *(Tel [0946] 3111 ext 289)*

WHITNEY-ON-WYE *Hereford and Worcester* Map 3 SO24
Brilley: Cwmmau Farmhouse Early 17th-C timber-framed and stone-tiled farmhouse. Picnics only by previous arrangement. Open 5, 6, 7 Apr; 24, 25, 26 May; 23, 24, 25 Aug 2–6; other times by previous written appointment with *Mr S M Joyce*. 20p *(NT)*

WHITTINGHAM *Northumberland* Map 12 NU00
Callaly Castle, Gardens and Grounds 2m W. Entrance by west lodge only. 17th-C

mansion incorporating 13th-C tower, with later (notably 18th-C) alterations and additions. Interesting pictures and furnishings and fine saloon with 18th-C plasterwork. ⚏ Sun and BH. Open 23 May to 28 Sep, Sat and Sun also BH 2.15–5.30; other days on application to the Estate Office, Callaly, Alnwick. 50p (ch 15 25p). Subject to alteration. Party 20+. No dogs. ⚠ *(Tel 663).* *(Major A S C Browne DL)* ⚹ B

WHTTINGTON *Staffordshire* Map 7 SK10
Whittington Barracks, Staffordshire Regiment Museum An interesting museum displaying details of the Regiment's battle honours; captured trophies, weapons old and new, uniforms past and present, and a special display of medals. Open Mon to Fri 9.30–4.30. *(Tel the Curator, Major M K Beedle MBE, Tel 433333 ext 240 or 229).* Free. ⚠ (limited.) ⚹

WICHENFORD *Hereford and Worcester* Map 3 SO76
Dovecote 17th-C half-timbered, black and white dovecote. Open daily until sunset. 10p *(NT)*

WILDERHOPE *Salop* Map 7 SO59
Wilderhope Manor Off B4371. A fine 16th-C house, with 17th-C plaster ceilings. Views of Corvedale. Leased to Youth Hostels Association. Open Apr to end of Sep, Wed and Sat, Oct to Mar Sat only, 2–4.30. 50p *(NT)*

WILDFOWL TRUST
see **Arundel, Caerlaverock** (Scotland), **Martin Mere, Peakirk, Slimbridge Washington** and **Welney.**

WILMCOTE *Warwickshire* Map 4 SP15
Mary Arden's House The picturesque, half-timbered, Tudor birthplace of Shakespeare's mother. Farming museum in barns. Open all year (ex 24–26 Dec, 4 Apr, am, and Sun Nov to Mar) Apr to Oct, weekdays 9–6, Sun 2–6; Nov to Mar, weekdays only 9–4. 30p (ch 15p). Admission prices under revision for 1980. ⚠ *(Tel Stratford-upon-Avon 293455)*

WILMINGTON *East Sussex* Map 5 TQ50
Priory Remains of a 13th-C Benedictine foundation now housing an agricultural museum. Open mid Mar to mid Oct, weekdays (ex Tue) 11–5, Sun 2–5. 25p (ch 15p). ⚠ *(Tel Alfriston 870537). (Sussex Archaeological Society)*

WILTON *Wiltshire* Map 4 SU03
Wilton House A magnificent 16th- to 19th-C house by Inigo Jones, Holbein, and James Wyatt, of great historical and architectural interest. It contains a world-famous collection

of paintings, furniture, and sculpture, in state apartments, including the great double and single 'cube' rooms. Exhibition of 7,000 miniature model soldiers. Unparalleled settings of lawns and Cedars of Lebanon. 21/22 Jun 'The Wonderful World of Wood'. ⚏ (and licensed). Open 10 Apr to 7 Oct, Tue to Sat and BH 11–6, Sun 2–6 (last admission always 5.30) (closed Mon). £1 (ch 15 and pen 50p). Party. Garden centre open. ⚠ *(Tel 3115). (Earl of Pembroke)* ⚹ B

WIMBORNE MINSTER *Dorset* Map 4 SZ09
Merley Bird Gardens 1½m S off A349. Large outdoor aviaries in three acres of lawns and gardens enclosed by wall dating from 1750. Colouring of the birds can be studied while they are in full flight. Children's pets corner, mini-golf, and children's rides. ⚏ Open all year daily 10.30–6.30, tea-room closes 5.30. Admission prices not yet decided. Children must be accompanied by adults. No dogs or radios. ⚠ *(Tel 3790)* ⚹ **(79)**
Model Town Superb 1/10th scale model of town built from genuine materials. Beautiful garden stocked with miniature trees and fish. Rare 10¼in gauge 'Beyer Garret' locomotive, 20ft length, weight 3 tons, on display. Open daily 1 Mar to 31 Nov 9–6, high season 9–9. 30p (ch 14 15p, ch 3 free). P. *(Tel 886950)* ⚹
Priest's House Museum It contains a number of exhibits of local interest including Roman objects also section devoted to rural implements. Open 7 Apr to Sep weekdays only 10.30–12.30 and 2.30–4.30. Other dates as announced locally. Special exhibition at Christmas. Museum and garden 10p (ch 3p). ⚠ *(Tel 882533)* ⚹

WIMPOLE HALL *Cambridgeshire* Map 4 TL35
8m SW of Cambridge at junction of A14 and A603. Large 18th-C country mansion. The interior has the Lord Harley's library, long gallery, Soane's yellow drawing room and Chapel painted by Thornhill. The Park was landscaped by such eminent gardeners as 'Capability' Brown, Repton and Sanderson Miller. ⚏ Open 1 Apr to 12 Oct, Tue, Wed, Thu, Sat and Sun also BH Mon 2–6 (last admission 5.30). £1. Party 15+. Wheelchairs available. *(NT)*

WINCHCOMBE *Gloucestershire* Map 4 SP02
Belas Knap 2m S. Well-known long barrow, 170ft by 60ft, with pair of side chambers in centre of mound and two others at south end. Dates probably from c2000 BC, and was excavated in 1863 and 1929–30. Accessible at all reasonable times. Free. *(AM)*
Sudeley Castle and Gardens Mainly 15th-C building with part 12th-C and 19th-C restoration. Magnificent art collection, fine

furniture and costume exhibitions. Tomb of Queen Katherine Parr in Chapel. Extensive grounds with large collection of waterfowl. Large children's playground with 3-storey replica Castle. Picnic area. ⟁ (licensed). Open 1 Mar to 31 Oct daily. Grounds from 11 am. Castle and exhibitions 12 – 5.30, BH Sun and Mon from 11 am. £1.25 (ch 50p, pen £1.05). Party 20+. Admission prices under revision for 1980. Enquiries to the Secretary. ⚠ *(Tel 602308)*. *(The Dent-Brocklehurst Family Trust)* ⅋ B

WINCHELSEA *East Sussex* Map 5 TQ91
Winchelsea Museum Located in the restored 14th-C court hall, it contains collection illustrating the history of the Cinque Ports. In addition there are maps, documents and archaeological specimens. Open May to Sep, weekdays 10.30 – 12.30 and 2.30 – 5.30, Sun 2.30 – 5.30. 50p (ch 14 10p) subject to alteration. ⚠

WINCHESTER *Hampshire* Map 4 SU42
Avington Park 3m E. 17th-C mansion built largely of red brick with state rooms and fine ballroom. In wooded park in attractive Itchen valley. ⟁ Sun and BH. Open May to end Sep, Sat, Sun and BH 2.30 – 5.30 (parties at other times by arrangement). 40p (ch 10 20p) (prices may be subject to increase). ⚠ *(Tel Itchen Abbas 202)*. *(Major J B Hickson)* ⅋ B
Winchester Castle Castle Avenue, off High Street. The surviving portion of the castle, a notable great hall of 1235, with Purbeck marble colums. At the west end is the legendary Round Table of King Arthur and his knights, their names painted in 1522. Henry III was born in the castle in 1207. Open all year (ex 4 Apr and 25 Dec) Mon to Fri 10 – 5, also Apr to Sep Sat and BH 10 – 6 and Sun 2 – 6, Oct to Mar Sat and Sun 2 – 5, BH 10 – 5. Free (contributions). No dogs. P (multi-storey). *(Tel 4411 ext 569)* ⅋
Winchester City Museum The Square. Contains a well-laid out display relating to the archaeology and history of the city and also of central Hampshire. Open Mon to Sat 10 – 5, Sun 2 – 5 (4 winter). Closed 4 Apr, 25, 26 Dec, 1 Jan. Free. ⚠ *(Tel 68166 ext 269)*
Winchester College College Street. One of England's oldest public schools, founded by William of Wykeham in 1382. Of special interest is the chapel, and during school terms, Fromond's chantry and the cloisters, which are accessible weekdays 10 – 6 (Sun 2 – 6) in summer; 10 – 4 (Sun 2 – 4) in winter. Free. Guided tours (ex Sun mornings) 11, 2 and 3 (also 4.30 May to Aug), subject to alteration. 40p (ch 16 20p). Under revision for 1980. *(Tel 64242)* ⅋
Guildhall Picture Gallery High Street. On show are local topographical views. Temporary exhibitions are held during the year. Open during exhibitions, Tue to Sat 11 – 5, Sun and Mon 2 – 5, all year. Free. P (charge) in Central car park. *(Tel 68166 ext 269)* ⅋
Hospital of St Cross S of city, off St Cross Road. Founded originally in 1136, and extended by Cardinal Beaufort in 1446. This is the oldest charitable institution in Britain still functioning. The Wayfarer's dole of bread and ale is given at the Porter's lodge, between 9.30 and 5; 10 – 12 and 2 – 3.30 in the winter. Brother's hall, old kitchen, and 12th-C church. Open Apr to Sep 9 – 12.30 and 2 – 5; Oct to Mar 10 – 12.30 and 2 – 3.30. 25p (ch and pen 10p). Party. (A guide is always available). ⚠ *(Tel 2888)*

Serle's House Southgate Street. A fine Baroque-style 18th-C house, now incorporating the Royal Hampshire Regiment museum and memorial garden. Open Mon to Fri 10 – 12.30 and 2 – 4. Closed BH. Free. *(Tel 61781 ext 261)*
Westgate Museum High Street. The medieval west gate of the city, containing exhibition of arms and armour. Open (ex 4 Apr, 25/26 Dec and 1 Jan) Mon to Sat 10 – 5, Sun 2 – 5 (4 winter). 10p (ch 5p). Party (school). ⚠ *(Tel 68166 ext 269)*
Wolvesey Castle College Street. Remains of a 12th-C bishop's castle, incorporating parts of the great hall, keep, and gatehouse. Adjacent stands the fine Palace (1684) of Bishop Morley. The interior of the castle has been closed since 1967 owing to archaeological excavation, which has now revealed a 12th-C hall larger than any in England after Westminster Hall (London). *(AM)*

WINDERMERE *Cumbria* Map 7 SD49
(see also BOWNESS ON WINDERMERE)
Lake District National Park Centre On A591. 19th-C house in 32 acres of garden and woodland on the eastern shore of Lake Windermere. National Park Visitor Centre with audio-visual displays, films and information room. Special family events during school hols. ⟁ Picnic areas. Open 18 Mar to 12 Nov daily from 10 (closing time varies with season). 50p (ch 18 25p). ⚠ *(Tel 2231)* ⅋
Steamboat Museum Bayrigg Road. Unique collection of Victorian and Edwardian vessels, typical of the steam era on the lakes, housed in covered dock and kept in working order. Other boats and exhibits illustrate the development of navigation on the lake. Museum shop. Picnic area. ⟁. Open Easter to Oct, Mon to Sat 10 – 5, Sun from 2 pm. Admission prices for 1980 not available. ⚠ (Coaches by appointment). *(Tel 5565)*

WINDSOR *Berkshire* Map 4 SU 97
Savill Garden (Windsor Great Park) (Reached via Wick Lane, Englefield Green, near Egham). Very beautiful woodland gardens with flowering shrubs and rare flowers. ⟁ (licensed). Open from 1 Mar to 31 Oct daily 10 – 6. 60p (ch and pen 40p). Party 20+, subject to alteration. ⚠ *(Tel 60222)* ⅋
Windsor Guildhall High Street. Built in 1689 and attributed to Wren. It contains an interesting exhibition of local historical and archaeological items, a collection of royal portraits and also old charters and documents. Generally open 4 Apr to mid/end Sep, daily 1.30 – 4.30. 15p (ch 10p) subject to alteration. *(Tel Maidenhead 33155)*
Windsor Castle A restored Norman royal castle with 19th-C additions for George IV by Wyatville. Precincts open daily (ex 16 Jun) 1 Jan to 15 Mar and 26 Oct to 31 Dec 10 – 4.15; 16 Mar to 30 Apr and 1 Sep to 25 Oct 10 – 5.15; 1 May to 31 Aug 10 – 7.15. Free. St George's Chapel all enquiries to Chapter Clerk *(Tel 65538)*
State Apartments Open daily 1 Jan to 15 Mar and 26 Oct to 31 Dec (ex 1 Jan, 7 – 31 Dec and Sun) 10.30 – 3; 1 May to 31 Aug and 1 Sep to 25 Oct (ex 1/2 May and 2 – 27 Jun) Mon to Sat 10.30 – 5, Sun 1.30 – 5; closed 16 Mar to 30 Apr. Opening times cannot be guaranteed as Castle is always subject to closure, sometimes at very short notice. 45p (ch 5 – 15 and pen 30p) until 15 Mar. From 3 May 60p (ch 5 – 15 and pen 30p). Some rooms closed.

Queen Mary's Dolls House Open daily 1 Jan to 15 Mar and 26 Oct to 31 Dec (ex 1 Jan, 25–27 Dec and Sun) 10.30–5; 16 Mar to 30 Apr (ex 4 Apr and Sun) 10.30–5; 1 May to 31 Aug and 1 Sep to 25 Oct (ex 16 Jun) Mon to Sat 10.30–5, Sun 1.30–5. 20p (ch 5–15 and pen 10p) until 2 May. From 3 May 30p (ch and pen 10p).

Exhibitions of Drawings Open daily. Times and prices as above. ⚠

Household Cavalry Museum Combermere Barracks. One of the finest military museums in Britain. Uniforms, weapons, horse furniture, and armour of the Household Cavalry from the Monmouth Rebellion (1685) to the present day. A series of terrain models depicts the Life Guards and Royal Horse campaigns. Open all year Mon to Fri (ex BH) 10–1 and 2–5 also Sun Apr to end Aug 10–1 and 2–4. Free. (Tel 68222 ext 203)

Windsor Safari Park and Seaworld (SW of town on B3022). Drive-in zoo where wild animals including giraffes, lions, tigers, baboons and cheetahs can be seen. Dolphin and killer whale shows in the Seaworld complex. Children's farmyard. Picnic area. ⚲. Open from 31 Mar daily 10–7 (or dusk if earlier). Last admission 5 pm. Inclusive charge £2 (ch and pen £1). party. Under revision for 1980. (Tel 69841) ♿

Valley Gardens (Windsor Great Park) Near Virginia Water. An area of some 300 acres noted especially for its outstanding range of rhododendrons, camellias, magnolias and other woodland trees and shrubs. Peak period is Apr, May and Jun but something to be seen all year. Open all year but adjoining car park open only for 6 to 8 weeks in spring when a charge is made. 60p per car.

WING Buckinghamshire Map 4 SP82
Ascott 19th-C mansion housing notable works of art – including French and Chippendale furniture and Oriental porcelain. Fine gardens. Open Apr to Sep, Wed, Sat, and BH Mon 2–6; Suns Jul and Aug 2–6. House and garden £1.40. Garden only 80p (ch 40p). (NT) (NGS)

WINSLOW Buckinghamshire Map 4 SP72
Winslow Hall Built in 1700 by Sir William Lowndes the Hall was almost certainly designed by Wren. It retains most of its original features and has recently been restored and redecorated. 18th-C English furniture, Chinese art and some fine clocks and pictures. Gardens. Open Jul to Sep daily (ex Mon) 2.30–5.30. 60p (pen 30p, ch 16 free). P. (Tel 2323) ♿ B

WINSTER Derbyshire Map 8 SK26
Market House Stone-built 17th- or 18th-C market house in main street of village. Open Apr to 30 Sep, Wed, Sat, Sun, BH Mon 2–6 (or sunset). Free. (NT)

WISBECH Cambridgeshire Map 5 TF40
Wisbech and Fenland Museum Situated near the site of the former castle and containing fine collection of ceramics and objets d'art, coins, glass, and pottery from Celtic, Roman, and Saxon England, in addition to Fenland life and birds, and objects associated with Thomas Clarkson, famous for his work in abolishing the slave trade. Open all year. Tue to Sat 10–1, 2–5 (4, winter). Free. ⚠ (Tel 3817)

Peckover House On the north bank of the River Nene, and dating from 1722. Interior Rococo decoration in plaster and wood. The garden is a delightful and colourful example of Victorian planting. Open Apr to 12 Oct, Tue, Wed, Thu, Sat, Sun, and BH Mons 2–5; Nov to Mar, prior arrangement must be made with Custodian. No dogs. 70p. (NT) (NGS)

WISLEY Surrey Map 4 TQ05
Wisley Gardens The famous and extensive garden of the Royal Horticultural Society. Information centre. Plant sales centre. Shop. ⚲ Mar to Oct. Open all year (ex 25 Dec), Feb to Oct weekdays 10–7 or sunset (whichever is earlier), Sun 2–7 or sunset; Jan, Nov and Dec weekdays 10–4.30, Sun 2–4.30 or sunset. 90p (ch 14 45p). ⚠ (Tel Ripley 2234 or 2235) ♿

WOBURN Bedfordshire Map 4 SP93
Woburn Abbey and Wild Animal Kingdom Junction B528 and A418. A palatial 18th-C mansion, designed by Holland and Flitcroft, with State apartments and pictures. Private apartments shown BH and when the family are not in residence. Stands in a 3,000–acre park famous for its rare collection of wild life. Souvenir shops, pottery, art galleries. Open all year. 1 Nov to 3 Apr, Abbey 11.30–5.15 (last entry 4); Park 11–3. 4 Apr to 31 Oct, Abbey Mon to Sat, 11.30–5.30 (last entry 4.45), Sun 11.30–6 (last entry 5.15); Park Mon to Sat 10.30–4.30, Sun 10–5. Angling in season. The Wild Animal Kingdom is a game reserve with lions, tigers, monkeys, giraffe, elephants, dolphinarium, pets corner, Sky ride, and Safari Boat trips. ⚲ Open daily throughout the year 10–dusk (fog and other weather permitting). ♿

WOLVERHAMPTON West Midlands Map 7 SO99
Bantock House Museum Bantock Park, Merridale Road. This 19th-C house contains important collections of English enamels japanned tin and papier-mâché products of the Midlands. Also shown are early Worcester

porcelain pottery, local history, and English and foreign dolls. Open all year Mon to Fri 10–7; Sat 10–6, Sun 2–5 (ex 1 Jan, 4 and 6 Apr, and 25, 26 Dec). Free. ⚠ *(Tel 24548)* & B

Bilston Museum and Art Gallery Mount Pleasant, Bilston. Houses a large collection of fine English painted and transfer print enamels from 18th and 19th C. Also iron and steel artifacts (traps, jewellery, plated ware) relating to the industrial history of the area. Collection of local and Staffordshire pottery. Permanent collection of Victorian oil paintings and periodic travelling exhibitions. Open all year, Mon to Sat 10–5. Free. P (roadside). *(Tel 42097)*

Central Art Gallery Lichfield Street. 18th- and 19th-C English water-colours and oil paintings including works by Bonington, Fuseli, Gainsborough, Zoffany and Wilson. Modern prints and drawings, including works by Warhol, Hamilton, John Salt, Caulfield, Rosenquist, Lichtenstein etc. Fine Oriental collections and full programme of temporary exhibitions. Open all year, Mon to Sat 10–6. Free. P. *(Tel 24549)*

Wightwick Manor 19th-C house with a collection of pre-Raphaelite works of art, including Morris fabric and de Morgan ware. Terraced gardens. Open all year (ex 25, 26 Dec and 1 Jan also Feb). Thu, Sat, and BH Sun and Mon 2.30–5.30. Also each Wed 2.30–5.30 from May to Sep. House 70p (ch 15p). Sat (extra rooms) 80p, students 30p; gardens only 20p. No children under 12. *(NT)*

WOODHENGE *Wiltshire* Map 4 SU14 Consisted formerly of six concentric rings of timber posts within a ditch. Positions of the posts are marked by concrete pillars. Discovered accidentally by aerial reconaissance in 1925. Accessible at all reasonable times. Free. ⚲ *(AM)*

WOODSTOCK *Oxfordshire* Map 4 SP41
Oxfordshire County Museum Located in the 16th- to 18th-C Fletcher's House. Newly completed exhibitions tell the story of Oxfordshire from the earliest times to the present day. ⚲ Bookshop and gardens. Open all year (ex 13 Apr, 25, 26 Dec) May to Sep Mon to Fri 10–5, Sat 10–6, Sun 2–6; Oct to Apr Tue to Fri 10–4, Sat 10–5, Sun 2–5. 20p (ch students and pen 10p). *(Tel 811456)* **(79)**
Blenheim Palace Started 1705 by Vanbrugh for first Duke of Marlborough, palatial baroque-style mansion in Henry Wise and 'Capability' Brown lake-watered park. Fine furnishings, china, and pictures and terraced water gardens below Long Library. Sir Winston Churchill born here in 1874, and buried in 1965 in village churchyard of Bladon on southern fringe of park. Launch trips on Lake. Narrow-gauge steam railway in grounds normally operates daily throughout the season. Garden centre. ⚲ (licensed). Charity cricket 25 May, Horse Show 26 May, opening times likely to alter for the events. Palace open 17 Mar to 31 Oct 11.30–5. Admission prices on application. Garden centre open daily, 9–5. *(Tel 811325)*. *(The Duke of Marlborough)* ⚇

WOOKEY HOLE *Somerset* Map 3 ST54
Wookey Hole Caves and Mill The great cave of Wookey Hole through which the river Axe flows was inhabited for 650 years from 250BC to AD400 – 'an outpost of the Celtic territories during the Roman occupation'. Tunnel through to new caverns containing steel bridges high above waters of River Axe. A small museum includes coins, pottery, tools of late Celtic and Roman British periods. Madame Tussaud's store room and the unique Lady Bangor's Fairground Collection are housed in the mill. The old machinery used for making paper by hand, the original purpose of the mill, has now been restored to provide a working exhibition about hand-made paper. ⚲ Picnic area. Open daily (ex 25 Dec) Apr to Sep 10–6, Oct to Mar 10–4.30. £1.60 (ch 16 and pen 90p). Party 20+. ⚲ *(Tel Wells 72243)* ⚇ B (Mill)

WOOLSTHORPE *Lincolnshire* Map 8 SK92
Woolsthorpe Manor A fine stone-built 17th-C house, the birthplace in 1642 of Sir Isaac Newton (shown). Open Apr to end Oct, Mon, Wed, Fri, Sat and BH 11–12.30 and 2–6. 70p (ch 35p). *(NT)*

WORCESTER *Hereford and Worcester* Map 3 SO85
The Commandery Sidbury. A large late 15th-C timber framed building with later additions. Fine Great Hall with hammerbeam roof. Displays of furniture, civil war material, local history from Roman times to the 20th C. Crafts, tools and industry. One small room with religious wall paintings of c1500. ⚲. Open Tue to Sat 10.30–5, Sun (1 Apr to 30 Sep) 2.30–5. Open BH Mons. 30p (ch 16 and pen 10p). P. *(Tel 355071)*
City Museum and Art Gallery Foregate Street. Contains items of archaeology, geology and natural history. Also collections of the Worcestershire Yeomanry Cavalry, Worcestershire Regiment and Stewards Chemist's Shop. Open all year Mon, Tue, Wed, Fri 9.30–6, Thu, Sat 9.30–5. Free. P. *(Tel 25371)*

Elgar's Birthplace Museum Crown East Lane, Lower Broadheath. 3m W of Worcester off A44 (to Leominster). Cottage where Sir Edward Elgar was born in 1857, now a museum displaying scores, photographs, letters and personalia. Open all year, daily (ex Wed) 1.30–6.30 (4.30 winter). 40p (ch 14 15p) subject to alteration. Parties by arrangement with Curator. *(Tel Cotheridge 224)*
Guildhall High Street. A notable, restored 18th-C building (1723–31) built by Thomas White, a local architect, with wings added later. Paintings and armour on show. Open all the year Mon to Fri 9–5. Free. *(Tel 23471)*
Dyson Perrins Museum of Worcester Porcelain Severn Street. The Dyson Perrins Museum has the finest collection of Worcester china in the world, comprising examples from the foundation of the factory by Dr John Wall, in 1751, to the present day. ⚲. Open all year Mon to Fri 10–1 and 2–5 also Sat Apr to Sep (closed BH). Free. Tours of works Mon to Fri by prior arrangement. Connoisseurs' tours twice daily. ⚲ *(Tel 20272 and 23221)* ⚇
Hawford Dovecote 3m N on A449. 16th-C half-timbered dovecot. Open daily until sunset. 10p. *(NT)*
Tudor House Friar Street. 500-year-old timber-framed house, once an inn, with a squint, and an ornate plaster ceiling. Opened 1971 as museum of local life. Features period room settings and open displays. Large exhibits displayed in yard at rear. Open all year, Mon to Sat (ex Thu and Sun) 10.30–5. Free. P. *(Tel 25371)*

WORKINGTON *Cumbria* Map 11 NY02
Helena Thompson Museum Park End Road. Museum containing collection of costumes, glass, ceramics, and other interesting exhibits. Museum and grounds open all year Tue to Sat 10–12 and 2–4. Free. *(Tel 62598)*

WORKSOP *Nottinghamshire* Map 8 SK57
Worksop Museum Memorial Avenue. Historical displays, bygones, Victoriana, birds and butterflies, and items of local archaeological interest. Open daily Mon to Sat (ex Thu) 10–4. Free. ⚲ *(Tel 5531)* ⚇
Worksop Priory Church and Gatehouse Remarkable 14th-C double archway with large upper room which from 1623 housed earliest elementary school in county. Elaborate façade with statues, and 15th-C wayside shrine and chapel. Church has unique 12th-C Transitional nave, with 20th-C additions of east end and central tower. Contains 14th-C scroll iron-work on doors in South porch. 13th-C Lady Chapel. Church open every day (ex Mon) 10–12, 2–5. Gatehouse open by application to church verger. Free. P. *(Tel 2180)*

WORTHING *West Sussex* Map 4 TQ10
Worthing Museum and Art Gallery Chapel Road. Archaeology, geology, history of Worthing. Large costume collection. Open all year Mon to Sat 10–7 (summer), 10–5 (winter). Free. P. *(Tel 204226)* ⚇

WOTTON UNDERWOOD *Buckinghamshire* Map 4 SP61
Wotton House and Pavilions Dating from 1690–1714 and the only house almost identical to Buckingham House prior to its becoming Buckingham Palace. Landscaped by 'Capability' Brown 1757–1760. Restored by Sir John Soane, 1820. Notable Tijou and Robinson wrought iron. Open Jun to end Sep

Wed 2–6 (last tour 5). 50p (ch 12 not admitted). Parties by arrangement. Guided tours by Curator *Mrs P Brunner.* ⚠ *(Tel Brill 363). (Mrs D Gladstone)* **(79)**

WRAWBY *Humberside* Map 8 TA00
Wrawby Postmill The last surviving example of its type in Lincolnshire, built c1780 and restored to working order in the 1960s. Wide views. Descriptive illustrated booklet 35p. Open 5 and 26 May, 29 Jun, 27 Jul and 25 Aug, 1–6. 20p (ch and students 10p ch 5 free). Under revision for 1980. ⚠ *(Tel Brigg 53699)* ⬥ B

WROXETER *Salop* Map 7 SJ50
Roman Town Remains of the Roman town of 'Viroconium' dating probably from AD 140–150, including public baths and a colonade. Open*, see inside front cover (closed, however, between 1–2). 20p (ch 16 and pen 5p). ⚠ *(AM)*

WROXHAM *Norfolk* Map 9 TG31
Beeston Hall 3m NE off A1151. 18th-C mansion in Gothic style with Neo-Classical interiors. Descendants of the Preston family have resided here since 1640. ⚏ (teas). Open, 6 Apr to 14 Sep Fri, Sun and BH Mon, 2–5.30. 70p (ch 30p, pen 50p). ⚠ *(Tel Horning 630771)*

YEALMPTON *Devon* Map 2 SX55
Kitley Caves Floodlit caves and lime kilns situated on the banks of the picturesque River Yealm. ⚏. Open Easter, then 28 May to 30 Sep daily 10–5. 20p (ch 16 15p). ⚠ 30p. *(Tel 202)* **(79)**

YELVERTON *Devon* Map 2 SX56
Paperweight Centre Buckland Terrace, Leg-O'Mutton. Exhibition of over 800 paperweights. Beautiful antique and modern glass, Millefiori, faceted, diamond-cut dated and signed 'investment' paperweights, many for sale (from £1 to £500). Open week before Easter to end Oct, Mon to Sat 10–5. Free. ⚠ *(Tel 4250)* ⬥

YEOVIL *Somerset* Map 3 ST51
Yeovil Museum Hendford Manor Hall. Local history and archaeology, and specialised collections of costumes and firearms. Open all year Mon to Sat (ex Thu) 9.30–1 and 2–5. Free. P. *(Tel 5171, Sat only 24774)*

YEOVILTON *Somerset* Map 3 ST52
Fleet Air Arm Museum and Concorde 002
A collection of more than 40 historic aircraft, ship and aircraft models, paintings and photographs with many other memorabilia of the Royal Naval Air Service and the Fleet Air Arm tell the story of the development of aviation at sea from 1903. The museum premises have been extended and a new display is being created. Concorde 002 is in a new exhibition hall where the development of

passenger supersonic flight is to be graphically portrayed. ⚏. Open daily (ex 24/25 Dec) Mon to Sat 10–5.30, Sun 12.30–5.30 (dusk in winter). Picnic area, flying viewing area and ⚠ are free. Coaches and caravans welcome. *(Tel Ilchester 840551 ext 521)* ⬥ B

YORK *North Yorkshire* Map 8 SE65
Borthwick Institute of Historical Research St Anthony's Hall, Peasholme Green. Originally a late 15th-C Guildhall, it has served in turn as poor-house, hospital, armoury, and Blue-Coat school. Now the Borthwick Institute of Historical Research, with a collection of ecclesiastical archives. It is part of York University. Exhibition of documents throughout the year. Hall open Mon to Fri 9.30–1 and 2–5. Closed Christmas, Easter, week before late Summer BH and first full week in Oct. Free. P. *(Tel 59861 ext 274)*

City Art Gallery Exhibition Square. An outstanding collection of European and British paintings. Particularly known for the Lycett Green collection of Old Masters, but also includes paintings and drawings by York Artists, notably William Etty, R A, and modern stoneware pottery. Provisional, for 1980, Festival Exhibition June 'Turner in Yorkshire'. Open all year (ex 1 Jan, 4 Apr, 25/26 Dec) Mon to Sat 10–5, Sun 2.30–5. Free. P. *(Tel 23839)* ⬥ B

Guildhall by River Ouse, off Coney Street. A 15th-C building, restored after severe damage during the 1939–45 war. Hall with notable timbered roof. Underground passage leading to the River. Open May to Oct Mon to Thu 9–5, Fri 9–4.30, Sat 10–5, Sun 2–5; Nov to Apr Mon to Thu 9–5, Fri 9–4.30, closed Sat and Sun, also closed 1 Jan, 4 Apr, 25/26 Dec. Free. ⚠ *(Tel 59881)* ⬥ B

King's Manor Exhibition Square. Former home of Abbot of St Mary's Abbey, later stopping place of James VI of Scotland on way to become James I of England, and of Charles I at time of Civil War. Much altered in early 17th C, and finally restored to become part of University in 1964. Open all year, daily (ex 25 Dec) 9–5 Free. ⚠ *(Tel 59861)* **(79)**

Merchant Adventurer's Hall Fossgate. A medieval guildhall, dating from 1357–68 to Tudor times, with the major part dating from the 15th C. Belonged to the wealthy and influential Company of the Merchant Adventurers. Open (ex when Hall is being used for functions) weekdays Apr to Oct 10–4.30 (4 Nov to Mar). Closed 1 Jan, 4 Apr, 25/26 Dec and Suns. Open all other BH. 30p (ch 16 and pen 15p). P in Piccadilly. *(Tel 54818)*⬥ ⬥

National Railway Museum Leeman Road. The museum, which is part of the Science Museum, illustrates the history and development of British railway engineering, including the social and economic aspects. Collection contains some 25 locomotives from the Agenoria of 1829 including Mallard and a fully sectioned rebuilt Merchant Navy class 4-6-2. Some twenty items of rolling stock as well as signalling equipment and permanent way items. Small exhibits feature models of locomotives (many working) and rolling stock. Also variety of railway equipment and material, including uniforms, station furniture, nameplates, bridge models and other categories of relics associated with the past 150 yrs of railways in the UK. Also displays and reference collections of paintings, posters, drawings and films. Reference library service provided by appointment. Lecture theatre seating eighty, is incorporated in the building and an Education programme of lecture/demonstrations is available. Please apply for details. Shop with railway books, postcards, slides, etc. ♨ Open all year except 1 Jan, 4 Apr, May Day, 24 – 26 Dec and some other public holidays (contact Museum for details). Mon to Sat 10 – 6; Sun 2.30 – 6. Free. ♿ *(Tel 21261)* も

Treasurer's House Chapter House Street. Mainly 17th- and 18th-C with fine paintings, furniture, and a sunken garden. Open Apr to 31 Oct, daily (ex 4 Apr) 10.30 – 6. 70p *(NT)*

York Castle Off Tower Street, Clifford's Tower, a two-storeyed 13th-C keep, built on an 11th-C motte raised by William the Conqueror. Open*, see inside front cover. 25p (ch 16 and pen 10p). ♿ *(AM)*

York Castle Museum Tower Street. An outstanding folk museum of Yorkshire life based on the Kirk collection of bygones and including period rooms, a cobbled street, domestic and agricultural equipment, early crafts, costumes, toys, Yorkshire militaria, an Edwardian street and a water-driven corn mill. Open all year (ex 25/26 Dec and 1 Jan) Apr to Sep, Mon to Sat 9.30 – 6, Sun 10 – 6; Oct to Mar, Mon to Sat 9.30 – 4.30, Sun 10 – 4.30. 70p (ch 30p). *(Tel (0904) 53611)* も B

The York Story The Heritage Centre, Castlegate. Britain's finest Heritage Centre, set up in 1975 to interpret the social and architectural history of the City of York. The exhibition, which includes many notable pieces by modern artists and craftsmen, is equipped with audio-visual units and a film theatre showing life in the historic core of the city today. A Heritage 'Walk Around York' is available, guiding visitors to the major buildings in the city. Open all year (ex 1 Jan, 25/26 Dec) Mon to Sat 10 – 5. 30p (ch 15p). *(Tel (0904) 28632)* も B

Yorkshire Museum and Gardens Museum Street. The museum contains Roman, medieval, geological and natural history collections. In the gardens are the ruins of St Mary's Abbey. Near by stands the Roman Wall, multangular tower, and St Leonard's Hospital. Museum open Mon – Sat 10 – 5, Sun 1 – 5. Hospitium open Mon – Sat 10 – 5 in summer only. Gardens open daily. 30p (ch 15p). Under revision for 1980. Closed 25/26 Dec. P. *(Tel 29745)* も

ZENNOR *Cornwall* Map 2 SW43

Wayside Cottage Folk Museum A small wayside museum illustrating Cornish life and archaeology, including household, farming, and mining equipment. Cottage kitchen and open hearth on show. Open daily, May to Oct 9.30 – dusk. Free. P. *(Tel St Ives 6945)* も B

ISLE OF MAN

BALLAUGH *Isle of Man* Map 6 SC39
Curraghs Wild Life Park Variety of British and foreign wild life. Otter exhibit. ℒ Open Easter then 1 May to 28 Sep, daily 10 – 6. 50p (ch 15 25p). Party 25+. Admission prices under revision for 1980. ⚠ *(Tel Sulby 323)* ♿

CASTLETOWN *Isle of Man* Map 6 SC26
Castle Rushen 14th-C stronghold with remains of earlier structure. State apartments, Norman keep flanked by 14th-C towers. Clock given by Queen Elizabeth I in 1597. ℒ Open all year, 1 May to 30 Sep Mon to Sat 10 – 7, Spring BH to 2nd Sun Sep also Sun 10 – 1; 1 Oct to 30 Apr Mon to Fri 10 – 5, Sat 10 – 12 noon. 25p (ch 16 and pen 10p). Admission prices under revision for 1980. P. *(Tel 3326)*

Nautical Museum Includes 18th-C Manx yacht 'Peggy'. Quayle Room and Cabin Room are interesting. Open mid May to late Sep, Mon to Sat 10 – 1 and 2 – 5, Sun 2 – 5. Small admission charge. Under revision for 1980. P. *(Tel Douglas 5522)*

CREGNEASH *Isle of Man* Map 6 SC16
Manx Open-Air Folk Museum Comprises group of traditional Manx cottages (some thatched), including crofter-fisherman's home, farmstead, loom-shed with hand loom, lathe shed with treadle lathe, and smithy. Open mid May to late Sep, Mon to Sat 10 – 1 and 2 – 5, Sun 2 – 5. Small admission charge. Under revision for 1980. ⚠ *(Tel Douglas 5522)* ♿ B

DOUGLAS *Isle of Man* Map 6 SC37
Manx Museum Items illustrate island's archaeology, history, natural history, folk life, and art. Also National Reference Library. Open all year (ex 25/26 Dec and 1 Jan, 4 Apr and am 5 Jul), Mon to Sat 10 – 5. Free. ⚠ *(Tel 5522)*

LAXEY *Isle of Man* Map 6 SC48
Laxey Wheel The Big Wheel 'Lady Isabella', 72½ft in diameter, was constructed in order to keep the lead mines free from water. Open Easter weekend then 1 May to 30 Sep. 20p (ch and pen 10p). Under revision for 1980. P. *(Tel Douglas 26262)*

PEEL *Isle of Man* Map 6 SC28
Peel Castle On St Patrick's Isle, facing Peel Bay. The Curtain wall and buildings range from the 10th to 19th-C. The Gatehouse featured prominently as a location for Sir Walter Scott's novel *Peveril of the Peak*. Open Easter weekends then 1 May to 30 Sep. 20p (ch and pen 10p). Opening times and admission prices under revision for 1980. P. *(Tel Douglas 26262)*

RAMSEY *Isle of Man* Map 6 SC49
'The Grove' Rural Life Museum On west side of Andreas Road. A Victorian House with a display of early agricultural equipment in the outbuildings. Open mid May to late Sep Mon to Fri 10 – 5, Sun 2 – 5 (closed Sat). Small admission charge. Under revision for 1980. ⚠

SNAEFELL MOUNTAIN *Isle of Man* Map 6 SC38
Murray's Museum The Bungalow. Junction A14 and A18. Contains an interesting collection of veteran and vintage motor cycles dating from 1902 to 1950, in addition to ancient arms and musical instruments and hundreds of bygones of yesteryear. ℒ Open May to end Sep, daily 10 – 6. 40p (ch 15 15p). Under revision for 1980. ⚠ *(Tel Laxey 719)*

ISLES OF SCILLY

TRESCO *Isles of Scilly*
Cromwell's Castle Round-towered stronghold of 1651, altered after Civil War, and again in 18th-C. Open at all reasonable times; access is by motor boat from St Mary's. Free. *(AM)*

King's Charles's Castle Coastal defence fortress built during reign of Henry VIII and added to in Civil War times. Accessible at any reasonable time by motor boat from St Mary's. Free. *(AM)*

Tresco Abbey Gardens and Museum The modern abbey stands on the site of the former 10th-C abbey. Remarkable terraced gardens with sub-tropical plants. ℒ (Apr to Oct). Gardens open all year. Mon to Sat from 10 – 4; Abbey open Apr to Oct. The Valhalla museum of ships' figureheads is open as gardens. £1.30 (Apr to Sep) 30p (Oct to Mar). Under review for 1980. Access is by motor boat from St Mary's. *(Tel Scillonia 22849)*. *(R A Dorrien-Smith)*

ISLE OF WIGHT

ARRETON *Isle of Wight* Map 4 SZ58
Arreton Manor Early 17th-C manor house, situated to S of ridge of Arreton Down. Some fine panelled rooms with contemporary furniture. A collection of old toys, including dolls and doll's houses, and a folk museum. ℒ (10 – 5.45). Open one week before Easter to last week Oct, Mon to Sat 10 – 6, Sun 2 – 6; 60p (ch 5 to 14 25p, pen party 25+ 40p each). Admission prices under revision for 1980. P (car and coach). *(Tel Arreton 255)*. Also *Pomeroy Museum and the National Wireless Museum* where the Pomeroy Regency Dolls' House together with modern dolls, baby gowns, etc, are exhibited. *(Count Slade de Pomeroy)* ♿ B

Robin Hill Country Park and Zoological Park Robin Hill, Downend. Over 100 interesting species of mammals, birds, reptiles and insects, in over 80 acres of down and woodland. Also large tropical Jungle House, 10-acre walk-through enclosure, breeding colony of monkeys. Pony, donkey and Argocat rides in high season. Nature trail, commando-styled assault course, also Continental 'TRIMM' course and playground. Mini dodgems. Radio-controlled model boats and armoured tanks. Several rooms of excavated Roman villa exposed to view. Water gardens and picnic areas. Gift shop. ℒ (licensed). Barbecue lunches daily in high season, evening barbecues five nights a week 10 Jul to 1 Sep (licensed). Open Mar to Nov 10 – 6 (high summer 10 – dusk). 70p (ch 40p). Under review for 1980. ⚠ *(Tel 430)* ♿

BEMBRIDGE *Isle of Wight* Map 4 SZ68
Bembridge Windmill Off B3390. Built c1700, in use until 1913, last windmill on island. Stone-built tower mill with wooden cap and machinery. Open Apr to end Sep. Mon to Sat 10 – 6, Sun 11 – 6. 25p (ch 15p). *(NT)*

Maritime Museum Sherborne Street. Situated in the centre of the village close to the harbour and sandy beaches. Six galleries devoted to our nautical past, designed to interest the whole family. Included is a unique collection of ship models, also early diving equipment. Gift shop. Open Easter to Oct daily 10 – 5.30; Oct to Christmas weekends only. 40p (ch 15 20p, pen 30p). School parties and groups welcome. ⚠ *(Tel 2223/2576)*

BLACKGANG *Isle of Wight* Map 4 SZ47
Blackgang Chine Opened as scenic
gardens in 1843, covering some 20 acres,
including much natural cliff scenery. The
grounds are floodlit by approximately 5,000
lamps, until 10 pm on summer evenings.
Attractions include a museum of local and
nautical interest, water gardens, model
village, nursery land, smuggler's cave,
smuggler's Galleon, Jungleland, crooked
house, maze, hall of mirrors and other
amusements. ☖ (licensed). Open Jun to Sep
daily 10–10; Apr, May and Oct 10–5. 60p (ch
35p). Under revision for 1980. ⚠ *(Tel Niton
730330)* ⅏

BRADING *Isle of Wight* Map 4 SZ68
Lilliput Museum High Street. Cottage
Museum contains a comprehensive private
collection of over 600 old dolls, with some
houses and toys. Dolls shop. Open mid Mar to
mid Oct daily 10–5 (10 pm during high
season). Admission charges not yet known.
Party. P. *(Tel 231)*
Morton Manor Built in 1680 and furnished
with period furniture. Beautiful terraced
landscaped gardens with ornamental duck
pond. ☖ (in old-world thatched cottage).
Open from Whitsun, Mon to Fri 11–6, Sun
2–6 (closed Sat). 50p (ch 20p, pen 30p). ⚠
(Tel Sandown 406168)
Osborn-Smith's Wax Museum On A3055.
Cameos of Island history, with authentic
costume, wax figures, period furniture and
harmonious settings cleverly brought to life
with the added realism of sound, light and
motion. Displayed in the oldest house on the
island dated c1228. Gift shop. Open all year
daily 10–10 (5 Oct to Apr). Party. ⚠ *(Tel 286)*
⅏ B
Roman Villa Includes mosaic pavements
and hypocaust. ☖ Open Easter to end Sep,
Mon to Sat 10–5.30, Sun 10.30–5.30. 25p
(ch 18 15p, pen 20p) ⚠ *(Tel during season
Sandown 406223)*

CALBOURNE *Isle of Wight* Map 4 SZ48
Watermill and Rural Museum On B3401.
17th-C mill. Water wheel and Mill stones still
in use. Open Apr to Oct, daily 10–6. 40p (ch
15 20p, ch 5 free, pen 30p). Under review for
1980. *(Tel 227)* ⅏ B

CARISBROOKE *Isle of Wight* Map 4 SZ48
Carisbrooke Castle On B3401. 12th-C and
later building, once the prison of Charles I. It
houses the Isle of Wight Museum. ☖ Open,
see inside front cover, museum closes Oct to
Easter. Open Sun am Apr to Sep. 70p, winter
25p (ch 16 and pen 30p, winter 10p). ⚠ 5p
(m/cycles 2½p). *(AM)*

COWES *Isle of Wight* Map 4 SZ49
Maritime Museum and Public Library
Beckford Road. Ship models, photographs,
paintings, books, etc, showing the island's
maritime past. Open all year, Mon to Fri
9.30–6, Sat 9.30–5 Free. P. *(Tel 293341)* ⅏
Curds and Whey Dottens Farm, Baring
Road. A cheese farm which gives talks on
cheese making twice daily during the
summer. Shop selling own cheese also other
English and Continental cheeses. Talks
11.30 and 2.30 weekdays Easter to Sep. 10p.
⚠ (limited), P. *(Tel 292466)*

EAST COWES *Isle of Wight* Map 4 SZ59
Barton Manor Gardens and Vineyard 20-
acre gardens, grounds and lake with 5-acre
vineyard. Winery, wine tasting, ☖ and home
produce shop. Open Sun and BH Mon from
Easter to end May, then daily (ex Fri and Sat)
to end Sep 2–6. 50p (ch 15p, pen 35p). Prices
include guide leaflet. ⚠ *(Tel Cowes 292835)*
Norris Castle 18th-C castle designed by

James Wyatt and built for Lord Henry
Seymour. Great Georgian castle containing
furniture and curiosities, weapons, armour,
sculpture, pictures and tapestries collected
from around the world over four centuries.
Queen Victoria's bedroom and the German
Emperor's Bath can be seen. Superb views of
the Solent yachting scene from the park. ☖
Open 4–7 Apr, then Sat, Sun and Mon 17
May to 5 Sep also daily during Cowes Week,
11–5. These dates may be altered without
notice. ⚠ *(Tel Cowes 293434)* ⅏ B

GODSHILL *Isle of Wight* Map 4 SZ58
Model Village Old Vicarage Gardens. Well
laid out interesting model village, many
establishments with thatched roofs. Under
construction is a model of the model part of
which is on show. Open Apr to Sep Mon to Sat
10–5.30, Sun 2–5.30. P. *(Tel 270)* ⅏
Natural History Collection Coral View.
British and tropical butterflies, some 30,000
tropical sea shells, a marine and tropical
aquarium and exhibitions of precious and
semi-precious stones. Replicas of the Crown
Jewels on display. Open daily 1 Apr to
Whitsun 10–6. Whitsun to end Sep, Sun to Fri
10–9.30, Sat 10–6. 15p (ch 9 free, 10–14
and pen 10p). P. *(Tel 333)* ⅏

HAVEN STREET *Isle of Wight* Map 4 SZ58
Isle of Wight Steam Railway Former LSWR
tank engine (1891), also IWCR loco No. 11 of
1878 which worked on island, and two other
tank engines on show. Also rolling stock,
including ex-LBSC and SEC coaches, and
19th-C goods wagons. Steam train rides
through 2 miles of unspoilt countryside.
Refreshments available. Trains run Sun May
to Sep and Easter, also Thu Jul and Aug
11–5.30. Admission prices not yet available.
⚠ *(Tel Wooton Bridge 882204)* ⅏

NEWPORT *Isle of Wight* Map 4 SZ48
Roman Villa Avondale Road. Villa built
towards end of 2nd C AD and discovered in
1926. Baths in good state of preservation and
several mosaic floors. Open Apr to Sep, Sun
to Fri 10.30–5.30 15p (ch 5p). P. (streets
only) *(Tel 522324/524541)*

NEWTOWN *Isle of Wight* Map 4 SZ49
Old Town Hall Restored 18th-C building.
Open Apr to end May, Wed, Sun and BH Mon,
Jun, Jul and Sep Wed, Thu, Sat and Sun also
daily Aug 2.30–5.30. 20p (ch 10p). *(NT)*
OSBORNE HOUSE *Isle of Wight* Map 4 SZ59
19th-C house, once Queen Victoria's home,
and where she died. State apartments, Swiss
Cottage and museum open 11–5, Mon to Sat
from 7 Apr to beginning of Oct (open at 10am
in Jul and Aug). Opening times subject to
extension. 70p (ch 16 and pen 30p). ⚠ 10p.
(AM)

ST CATHERINE'S LIGHTHOUSE *Isle of
Wight* Map 4 SZ47
Situated at St Catherine's Point, 136ft above
the sea. Open all year. Mon to Sat only from
1pm to one hour before dusk, weather and
other conditions permitting at visitors own
risk. Free. Cars not allowed within ½m except
on business. *(Tel Niton 730284)*

ST LAWRENCE *Isle of Wight* Map 4 SZ57
Tropical Bird Park Old Park. Over 400 exotic
birds in unique walk-through aviaries and
around the ornamental lake. ☖ (tea garden).
Open all year, daily, Easter to Oct 10–6 and
Oct to Easter 12–4. Prices are approximate.
50p (ch 14 30p and pen 40p). ⚠ *(Tel Ventnor
852583)*

SANDOWN *Isle of Wight* Map 4 SZ58
Museum of Isle of Wight Geology This
museum, situated in the local library, houses

a collection of fossils and exhibits of the island's geology. Open all year Mon to Sat 10–5 (ex BH). Free. ⚠ *(Tel 4344)*
SEAVIEW *Isle of Wight* Map 4 SZ69
Flamingo Park Bird Sanctuary Oakhill Road, Springvale. Island's largest bird sanctuary, set in lovely countryside overlooking the Solent, with hundreds of waterfowl which feed from the hand; geese, swans, flamingoes, peacocks, cranes and pheasants. British and foreign bird house and pets corner. Suitable for both young and old. Gifts and ⚏. Open Easter to end May 2–6; Jun to Sep 10.30–6 Mon to Sat, Sun only 2–6. 70p (ch and pen 50p). Under revision for 1980. ⚠ *(Tel 2153)* ⚂ (reduced rate).
SHANKLIN *Isle of Wight* Map 4 SZ58
Shanklin Chine A natural gorge of great scenic beauty, with a main waterfall of over 40ft. Although it now contains, amongst other attractions, an aviary, kiddy rides and a Victorian sea water bath, it differs very little from its original state. Open Easter to Sep from 9.30; 1 to 16 Oct 10.30–3.30. Floodlit at night end May to Sep. 30p (ch 14 10p, pen 20p). P (200yds). *(Tel Framfield Sussex 279)*
SHORWELL *Isle of Wight* Map 4 SZ48
Yafford Water Mill Farm Park Situated in attractive surroundings with a large mill pond, meandering stream and collection of waterfowl. The 19th-C water-mill contains much of the original machinery – still in use until a few years ago – there is also a collection of farm implements, wagons and tractors. Rare breeds survival centre. Children's playground. ⚏ Open Easter to Oct, 10–6, Sun 2–6. 50p (ch and pen 30p). Under revision for 1980. Parties by arrangement. ⚠ *(Tel Brighstone 740610)* ⚂
VENTNOR *Isle of Wight* Map 4 SZ57
Museum to the History of Smuggling
Botanic Gardens. Said to be the only museum in the world showing methods of smuggling over a 700-year period to the present day. ⚏ (licensed). Open daily Easter to end Sep 10–5; Jun to Aug also 7.30–9 in the evening. 30p (ch 7–14 and pen 10p, accompanied ch 7 free). Admission to gardens free. ⚠ *(Tel 853677)* ⚂ B
WROXALL *Isle of Wight* Map 4 SZ57
Appuldurcombe House Erected in 1710 on site of earlier house, roofless shell of mansion designed in classical style standing in ornamental grounds. Unoccupied since 1904. Open*, see inside front cover. 15p (ch 16 and pen 5p). *(AM)*
YARMOUTH *Isle of Wight* Map 4 SZ38
Fort Victoria Country Park Sconce Point. ½m W. Remains of Fort built in 1853 to protect the western approach to Portsmouth. Now being developed as a Country Park with picnic and barbecue facilities and nature trail. Spectacular views of the Solent. ⚏ Jun to Sep. Park open all year daily. *(Tel Newport 524031 ext 162)*.
Yarmouth Castle A Tudor castle, built by order of Henry VIII. Repaired in 1609 and 1632. Open, see inside front cover but closed Fri and Sat. 20p (ch 16 and pen 5p). *(AM)*

CHANNEL ISLANDS

GUERNSEY

FOREST
Occupation Museum Contains the largest exhibition of authentic Occupation relics to be found in the Channel Islands, including a

tableau of an 'Occupation Kitchen', 'Bunker rooms' and a new section on horse transport. Special tours arranged to explore the underground fortifications. ⚏. Open Apr, Sun and Thu 2–5.30 May to Oct daily 10–12.30, 2–6. 30p (ch 14 25p). ⚠ *(Tel Guernsey 38205)*
ST ANDREW
The German Military Underground Hospital and Ammunition Store La Vassalerie. The largest structural reminder of the German occupation of the Channel Islands. A concrete maze of about 75,000 sq ft, which took slave workers 3½ years to construct, at the cost of many lives. It was designed to accommodate 500 patients but could in emergency have housed three or four times that number. The hospital was only used for about 6 weeks for German wounded brought over from France soon after D-Day, but the ammunition store, which was larger than the hospital, was packed tight with thousands of tons of ammunition during its nine months of use. Most of the equipment has been removed, but there are still some signs of previous use such as the central heating plant, some hospital beds and cooking facilities. Open 1 Apr to 8 May, Thu and Sun 2–5; 9 May to 30 Sep, daily 10–12, 2–5; Oct Thu and Sun 2–5. 30p (ch 15 10p). Under revision for 1980. ⚠ *(Tel Guernsey 39100)* ⚂
ST PETER PORT
Castle Cornet An ancient castle with buildings dating from the 13th to 20th C and scene of many battles. During the Civil War it was garrisoned by the Royalist governor of the island, Sir Peter Osborne, and although the island's people sympathised with Cromwell it was not until 15 Dec 1651 that this last Royalist stronghold surrendered to Parliamentarian forces. In 1940 it was taken over by German troops and adapted to the needs of modern warfare. Today it is maintained as an ancient monument and houses the Spencer collection of uniforms and badges the Museum of Guernsey's own 201 Squadron Royal Air Force, the Royal Guernsey Miltia Museum, a Maritime Museum, Art Gallery and Armoury. Open Apr to Oct, daily 10.30–6. Guided tours 10.45. 40p (ch 5 10, pen 15p). Joint ticket with Candie Museum and Fort Grey 90p. P. *(Tel Guernsey 21657)*
Fort Grey Built as part of the Island's defences against Napoleon on the site of an ancient castle. It has recently been restored and opened as a maritime museum, featuring the wrecks on the treacherous Hanois Reef nearby. Open May to Sep daily 10–12.30, 2–6. 25p (ch 10p, pen 15p). P. *(Tel Guernsey 65036)*
Guernsey Museum and Art Gallery Candie Gardens. Opened in 1978, it is the Island's first purpose-built museum. The exhibition depicts the story of the Island and its people. It includes an audio-visual programme in the museums own theatre and paintings in the Art Gallery. Special exhibitions are featured during the winter. Museum shop. Museum tea room with excellent views. Open all year daily 10.30–5.30 (winter hours may be shorter). 40p (ch 10p, pen 15p). Joint ticket with Castle Cornet and Fort Grey 90p. *(Tel Guernsey 26518)* ⚂
Hauteville House Maison de Victor Hugo, 38 Hauteville. Built c1800 and brought by Victor Hugo, the great French writer, in 1856 who lived there until 1870 and returned in 1872, 1875 and 1878, the house contains a fine

collection of china, paintings and tapestries and the decoration and furniture is much as it was. Open 1 Apr to 30 Sep, daily (ex Thu afternoons, Sun and BH) 10 – 12, 2 – 4.30. Open once a day at 10.30 for 1 guided tour during closed season or by appointment. 30p (ch 10p, students and Party 10+, 20p per person, school parties free). P. *(Tel Guernsey 21911)*

SAUMAREZ PARK

Folk Museum Centred on a courtyard of buildings, depicting a traditional kitchen, bedroom and cartroom. One room contains a costume display, together with a range of sewing machines, prams, pushchairs, and samplers. A dairy has been laid out with a large toolroom overhead, and another building exhibits carts and ploughs, including 'la grande charrue' and other farm implements. A recent addition is a cider barn with apple crusher and press. The museum is entirely voluntary and is organised by the National Trust of Guernsey. Open Easter to mid Oct daily 10 – 12.30, 2 – 5.30. 30p (ch 15p, free if accompanied). Under revision for 1979. P. *(Tel Guernsey 55384)* ⅃ **(79)**

JERSEY

GERMAN MILITARY UNDERGROUND HOSPITAL

Tunnelled out of solid rock by Russian slave labour, during the German, occupation of 1940 – 1945. It was only ever half completed, but over a period of $2\frac{1}{2}$ years 14,000 tons of rock were removed and 4,000 tons of concrete were used to line the massive galleries and walls. Light and sound effects tell the story of Jersey during the invasion, occupation and liberation, and photographs of war personalities, events, newspaper articles and German leaflets line the walls. The Museum and Exhibition of Occupation Relics includes an excellent collection of authentic German firearms, daggers, officers' badges and awards. Open 12 Mar to 5 Nov, daily 10 – 6, winter season Thu and Sun only, 2.30 – 5. 60p (ch 15 20p). Prices under revision for 1980. ⚠ *(Tel Jersey Central 32963)* ⅃

GOREY

Mont Orgueil Castle Situated on a rocky headland, on a site of fortification dating back to the Iron Age and possibly Neolithic times. The Castle, one of the best preserved examples in Europe of the medieval concentric castle, dates from the 12th to 13th C. A series of tableaux with commentary tells the history of the building. ⅃ and souvenir shop. Open Mar to Oct, daily 9.30 – 6. 30p (ch 16 10p). Under revision for 1979. P. *(Tel Jersey Central 53292)* **(79)**

LA HOUGIE BIE

The Jersey Museum Prehistoric burial mound containing Neolithic tomb, surmounted by Medieval chapels. Underground shelter containing German Occupation Museum. Agricultural museum. Railway exhibition in original guard's van of Jersey Eastern Railway. Archaeology and geology museum. Pleasant grounds. Open Mar to Oct, Tue to Sun 10 – 5 (other times by appointment). 40p (ch and pen 20p). Party. ⚠ *(Tel Jersey 53823 or 22133)* ⅃

ST AUBIN'S

Elizabeth Castle Built off L'Islet rock about a mile from shore in St Aubin's Bay. This old fortress is steeped in history dating back to the Elizabethan period when it was named Fort Isabella Bellissima by Sir Walter Raleigh. ⅃ and souvenir shop. Open Mar to Oct daily 9.30 – 6. 30p (ch 10p) which includes entry to the tableaux with commentary, Militia museum and German bunkers. These prices do not include fares on the service to the castle. Opening times and prices under revision for 1979. *(Tel Central 23971)* **(79)**

ST HELIER

The Jersey Museum and Barreau Art Gallery Pier Road. Local collections relating to history, maritime biology, natural history, coins and medals, silver, postal service, law and order, photography, shipping and sport. Lillie Langtry displays. Victorian pharmacy and four period rooms. Art gallery. All in large Georgian house. Open Feb to Dec Mon to Sat 10 – 5. 40p (ch and pen 20p). P 200yds. *(Tel Jersey 22133)*. ⅃ B

ST MARY'S

Fantastic Gardens Tropical gardens, where natural systems of growth and flowering are presented in miniature, around replicas of shrines and other architectural structures. Past beliefs, customs, and myths of Islam, India, China, Japan and Mexico are explained on plaques, also the many ways man has used the plants for drugs, fibres, dyes, flavourings, cosmetics, etc. ⅃ Open 1 May to 6 Oct Mon to Fri 10 – 6. 50p (ch 20p, must be accompanied and remain with adult). Admission prices under revision for 1980. Party. ⚠ *(Tel Central 81585, enquiries may be made during the closed season)* ⅃

ST OUEN

Battle of the Flowers Museum La Robeline, Mont des Corvées. Contains exhibits which have appeared in the Jersey Battle of Flowers over the last 13 years. The tableaux executed in Harestails and Marram grass, represent scenes of wild and tame animals from all over the world. Open Easter to 30 Nov. daily 10 – 5. 40p (ch 20p). ⚠ *(Tel Jersey West 82408)* ⅃

ST PETER

Jersey Motor Museum Contains fascinating collection of motor vehicles from the early 1900s, together with Allied and German Military vehicles of World War Two, a Jersey Steam Railway Section and Aero Engines etc. Also pre-war Jersey AA Box and collection of AA badges of all periods. ⅃ (licensed). Open Mar to Oct daily 10 – 5. 40p. Under revision for 1980. ⚠ *(Tel Jersey 82966)* ⅃

St Peter's Bunker At junction of A12 and B41. An exhibition of Nazi German equipment and Occupation relics, housed in an actual German bunker, including uniforms, motor cycles, equipment, weapons, documents, photographs, various newspaper cuttings, badges, awards and insignia. This six-roomed bunker accommodated thirty-three men, and could be air and gas sealed in case of attack. One of the rooms contains an actual reconstruction with original bunk beds, other furniture, a store and rifle rack as well as figures of soldiers asleep and on duty. ⅃ Open 20 Mar to 31 Oct, daily 10 – 5. 40p (ch 10p). Under revision for 1980. ⚠ *(Tel Jersey 81048)*

TRINITY

Zoological Park Founded in 1959 by Gerald Durrell it became the headquarters of the Jersey Wildlife Preservation Trust in 1963. Its purpose is to breed animals critically endangered in the wild. Families include gorilla, orang-utan, spectacled bear, giant tortoise, serval cat, white-eared pheasant and numerous others. Open all year, daily (ex 25 Dec) May to Sep 10 – 6 (5 winter). £1 (ch and pen 50p) ⚠ *(Tel Central 61949)* ⅃ (wheelchairs available).

The National Trust

in Wales invites you to visit

ABERCONWY HOUSE

PLAS NEWYDD

ERDDIG

BODNANT GARDEN

PENRHYN

CHIRK CASTLE

POWIS CASTLE

FURTHER INFORMATION FROM
THE REGIONAL INFORMATION OFFICER, THE NATIONAL TRUST,
DINAS, BETWS-Y-COED, GWYNEDD TEL: 069-02-636

WALES

P.K.Fry.

ABERCRAVE *Powys* Map 3 SN81
Dan-yr-Ogof and Cathedral Showcaves
3m N on A4107. The longest and largest
showcaves in Britain contain some of the
largest stalactites and stalagmites in the
country. Guided tours of passages. ℤ
(licensed). Shops. Caravan and tent park.
Children's model Dinosaur Park (additional
charge). Open Easter to 31 Oct daily from 10;
for winter opening please telephone.
Admission prices not yet decided. ⚠ *(Tel 284
or 693 or 648)*

ABERGAVENNY *Gwent* Map 3 SO21
Abergavenny Museum The Castle.
Antiquities, rural craft tools, Welsh kitchen,
saddler's shop, costumes and exhibits of local
history Open all year, Mar to Oct, Mon to Sat
11 – 1, 2 – 5, Sun 2.30 – 5; Nov to Feb Mon to
Sat only 11 – 1, 2 – 4. 12p (ch and pen 7p). P
(in Castle Street). *(Tel 4282)*
Abergavenny Castle Remains of 12th-C
stronghold; walls, towers, and gateway. Open
daily 11 – dusk. Free. Car park as above.

ABERGWILI *Dyfed* Map 2 SN42
Carmarthen Museum Old Bishop's Palace.
Local prehistoric, Roman and medieval
displays also folk material, military history and
costume. Cheese and butter making, local
pottery and temporary exhibitions. Open all
year Mon to Sat 10 – 4.30. Free. ⚠ *(Tel
Carmarthen 31691)*

ABERYSTWYTH *Dyfed* Map 6 SN58
Aberystwyth Castle Remains of 12th- to
13th-C castle on promontory which forms
good viewpoint. Open at all times. Free.
National Library of Wales Penglais Hill.
Granted Royal Charter of Incorporation in
1907, and one of Britain's six copyright
libraries, it is housed in imposing building of
1911 – 16, added to in 1931, 1937, 1955, and
1971. Large number of books in all
languages, musical publications, prints,
drawings, and old deeds; specialises in
Welsh and Celtic literature. Exhibitions of
pictures from certain collections; Central Hall.
Special exhibitions between May and Oct.
Library open all year (ex Christmas and
Easter), reading rooms Mon to Fri 9.30 – 6,
Sat until 5 pm. Free. ⚠ *(Tel 3816/9)* ᛗ
Vale of Rheidol Light Railway Only steam
railway operated by British Rail with 3 engines
and 16 passenger coaches (1ft 11½in-gauge).
Opened in 1902. Runs between Aberystwyth
and Devil's Bridge (11¾m) passing through
some of the finest scenery in Wales. Operates
Easter to Oct. Journey time (each direction)
one hour. Reduced fares for children and
morning trains, for details telephone
Aberystwyth station. ⚠ *(Tel 612377)*

ARTHOG *Gwynedd* Map 6 SH61
Ty'n-y-Coed Peaceful woodland grounds,
with triple waterfall and peacocks. Champion
Welsh Farm ponies bred here. Welsh
craftshop. Woodland shrubs at their best mid
May to mid Jun. ℤ in ancient Welsh kitchen.
Open (grounds only) 15 Apr to 15 Oct,
weekdays 10.30 – 5.30, Sun 12.30 – 5.30, last
tickets 5.30p (ch 12 15p) subject to alteration.
⚠ No dogs during peacock breeding season,
otherwise on lead only. *(Tel Fairbourne 208)*.
(Dowager Viscountess Chetwynd)

BANGOR *Gwynedd* Map 6 SH57
Bangor Museum and Art Gallery
(University College of North Wales) Ffordd,
Gwynedd. The museum portrays history of
North Wales, collections of furniture, crafts,
costumes, maps, ceramics, and both Roman
and prehistoric antiquities. Exhibitions

illustrating history of the Menai Bridge and
Tubular Bridge and smaller items on Conwy
Bridge. Open all year (ex Sun and BH)
10.30 – 4.30. Free. P. Attendant always on
duty to deal with enquiries. *(Tel 51151 ext
437)*. The Gallery stages exhibitions of
sculpture and paintings each year changing
at approximately monthly intervals. Open
weekdays (ex BH) 10.30 – 5. Free. *(Tel 3368)*
Penrhyn Castle 1m E, at junction A5 & A55.
The 19th-C furnished castle is an
outstanding, well preserved example of neo-
Norman architecture situated with superb
views in lovely grounds, walled garden.
Industrial railway museum, exhibition of dolls
and a natural history display. Shop. ℤ Open 1
Apr to 26 Oct daily. Apr, May and Oct 2 – 5,
Jun to Sep and all BH weekends 11 – 5. £1.20
(ch 60p). Party 20+. *(NT)*

BEAUMARIS *Gwynedd* Map 6 SH67
Beaumaris Castle Moated castle begun
1295 by Edward I and completed in 1323,
perhaps finest concentrically planned
stronghold in Britain. Retains original small
dock for shipping. Open*, see inside front
cover. 35p, winter 20p (ch 16 and pen 17p,
winter 10p). ⚠ *(AM)*
The Tudor Rose 32 Castle Street. One of the
few ancient monuments in Wales of the 15th
C. A half-timbered building with a fine
example of a hall of that period at the rear.
Upstairs has a minstrel gallery which offers a
view of the barrel braced ceiling and the hall
below. Hendrik Lec bought and restored the
property in 1945 and there is a continually
changing exhibition of both his and his sons'
paintings, drawings and prints. Open 1 Jul to
15 Sep, daily, 10.30 – 1, 2 – 5.30 (out of
season by request). 10p (ch 14 and pen 5p).
P. *(Tel 810203)*

BETWS-Y-COED *Gwynedd* Map 6 SH75
Conwy Valley Railway Museum Old Goods
Yard. Houses displays covering the whole
railway scene with special reference to
standard and narrow-gauge lines in North
Wales. The smaller exhibits are in a purpose-
built museum and there is a collection of
standard-gauge vehicles and large exhibits
on the site. ℤ Open daily, Easter to 28 Sep
and weekends in Oct. BH weeks and summer
months 10.30 – 5.30. Spring and Autumn
2 – 5. 40p (ch 16 and pen 25p). Prices under
review for 1980. ⚠ Access and toilets for
wheelchair-bound visitors. *(Tel 568)* ᛗ

BLAENAU FFESTINIOG *Gwynedd*
Map 6 SH64
Gloddfa Ganol Ffestiniog Mountain Tourist
Centre. The centre is situated on the site of the
'world's largest slate mine' where the old mine
workings, massive machinery and the skill of
the slate craftsmen is displayed. A museum
and gallery tell the story of the slate industry
while a fairy grotto and play area provide
amusement for the children. Also panoramic
walks. ℤ (licensed). Land Rover conducted
tours. Craft shop. Open Easter to Oct
daily 10 – 5.30. 75p (ch 14 35p). Prices for
1980 under review. ⚠ *(Tel 664)* ᛗ
Llechwedd Slate Caverns Slate mine in
which rock formations, open quarries, and
slate chambers can be seen. Slate splitting
demonstrated in reconstructed mill.
Accessible by means of specially designed
cars hauled by battery-operated locomotives.
Exhibitions of Victorian mining, photographs,
quarry tramway and 'Slate Heritage'. Audio-
visual presentation of the history of slate over
the last 1700 years. Temperature in caverns
about 55°F. ℤ gift shop. Open Mar to Oct,

daily 10–6 (last trains 5.15 pm); 80p (ch 16 45p and pen 60p). Party 20+ (ex Aug). Prices for 1980 under review. ⚠ *(Tel 306)* ♿

BRECON *Powys* Map 3 SO02
Brecknock Museum Captain's Walk. Archaeological and local historical exhibits, folk life and decorative arts; natural history; geology. Open all year Mon to Sat 10–5. Free. ⚠ *(Tel 4121/2)* ♿
24th Regiment Museum The Barracks. Museum of South Wales Borderers and Monmouthshire Regiment, granted Freedom of the Borough in 1948. Regiment was raised in 1689 and has been awarded 23 VCs, of which 15 are displayed. Three rooms devoted to relics, photographs and medals. Special Zulu War display. Open all year (ex 25, 26 Dec) daily 9–1 and 2–5; Oct to 31 Mar closed Sat and Sun. 10p. P (limited). *(Tel 3111 ext 310)* ♿ B

BRIDGEND *Mid Glamorgan* Map 3 SS97
Newcastle Small ruined, 12th-C and later stronghold, with rectangular tower, richly carved Norman gateway to S side, and massive curtain walls enclosing polygonal courtyard. Open Apr to Sep, weekdays 10–7, Sun 2–7; Oct to Mar, weekdays 10–dusk, Sun 2–dusk. Free. *(AM)*

BRONWYDD ARMS *Dyfed* Map 2 SN42
Gwili Railway ½m along B4301 from junction with A 484. Only standard-gauge steam passenger railway in South Wales. Welsh craft centre, riverside picnic area at end of line (Cwmdwyfran – no road access). ⚟ bookshop and ⚠ at Bronwydd Arms. Usually open Sat and Sun from 28 Jun to 21 Sep also BH Sun and Mon 6/7 Apr, 4/5 and 25/26 May, 25 Aug, with special enthusiasts

weekend 27/28 Sep. Return fare 50p (ch 14 and pen 30p). Provisional dates and prices for 1980. Time tables are available from Great Western Chambers, Angel Street, Neath, West Glamorgan. *(Tel Neant 2191)* ♿ B

BRYN-CELLI-DDU *Gwynedd* Map 6 SH57
Excavated in 1865, and again 1925–29, prehistoric circular cairn covering passage grave with polygonal chamber. Open, see inside front cover. Free. *(AM)*

CAERLEON *Gwent* Map 3 ST39
Amphitheatre On A449. Roman amphitheatre, with accommodation for 6,000 people from legionary fortress dated AD 80–100. Excavated from 1849 onwards. Open*, see inside front cover. 15p (ch 16 and pen 7p). ⚠ *(AM)*
Legionary Museum A branch of the National Museum of Wales containing the principal objects from the fortress of the Second Augustan Legion. Open all year (ex 24 to 26 Dec, 1 Jan and May Day) weekdays 9.30–5.30 (6, May to Sep; 4, Nov to Feb). Sun 2–5 (6, May to Sep; 4 Nov to Feb). Free. P (by entrance to Roman amphitheatre) *(Tel 462)* ♿

CAERNARFON *Gwynedd* Map 6 SH46
Caernarfon Castle Begun by Edward I in 1283, and completed in 1323, includes polygonal angle towers, notable Eagle Tower, and extensive town walls. Birthplace of Edward II, first Prince of Wales, and site of investiture in 1969 of present Prince of Wales. Open*, see inside front cover. 55p, Oct to Mar 25p (ch 16 and pen 20p, Oct to Mar 12p). ⚠ *(AM)*
Segontium Roman Fort and Museum Branch archaeological gallery of the National Museum of Wales. Remains of Roman fort of

'Segontium', and museum of excavated relics. Open Mon to Sat from 9.30, Sun from 2pm. Closes 4 Nov to Feb, 5.30 Mar, Apr and Oct, 6 May to Sep. Closed 1 Jan, 4 Apr, 5 May and 24–26 Dec. Free. *(AM)*

CAERPHILLY *Mid Glamorgan* Map 3 ST18
Caerphilly Castle On A469. A concentrically planned castle, begun in 1268 by Gilbert de Clare and completed 1326. One of the largest in Wales with extensive land and water defences. Open*, see inside front cover. 20p (ch 16 and pen 10p). ⚠ *(AM)*

CALDICOT *Gwent* Map 3 ST48
Caldicot Castle, Museum and Countryside Park On B4245. Norman castle, started in 1100 by Fitzwalter and completed in 1396 by Thomas Woodstock, with many interesting features including a local history museum exhibiting rural crafts, costume etc. The Woodstock Tower now houses an art

exhibition. Open 1 Mar to 31 Oct, Mon to Fri 11–12.30, 1.30–5, (6 Sat and BH), Sun 1.30–6. 18p (ch and pen 7p) Park open all year. ⚠ *(Tel 420241)*

CAPEL GARMONG *Gwynedd* Map 6 SH85
Burial Chamber Off A496. Long barrow with covering mound and false portal. Excavated in 1926 revealing examples of neolithic pottery. Accessible at all reasonable times. Free. *(AM)*

CARDIFF *South Glamorgan* Map 3 ST17
Cardiff Castle Castle Street. Roman and Norman, with 12th-C keep, and 1861 additions including state apartments and curtain walls built on visible remains of Roman Wall. Conducted tours Mar, Apr and Oct, weekdays 10–12.30 and 2–4 (castle closes 5), Sun 10–12, 2–4; May to Sep daily 10–12.40 and 2–5, Sun 10–12.30, 2–5 (castle closes 6); Nov to Feb 11–3 (castle

---

Amgueddfa Genedlaethol Cymru: Caerdydd
National Museum of Wales: Cardiff

An impressive building of Portland stone, the Museum is conveniently situated in the centre of Cardiff. Although the emphasis of its permanent collections is on themes relating to Wales from earliest times, it does not restrict itself to these interests alone. It includes, for example, an exceptional collection of modern European painting and sculpture which has helped the Museum to earn its international status. Within a few miles of Cardiff, the National Museum also has branch galleries — the art gallery at Turner House, Penarth and the archaeological gallery at the Legionary Museum, Caerleon. The Welsh Folk Museum is situated at nearby St Fagans, and the new Welsh Industrial and Maritime Museum is now open in Cardiff's dockland. Other branch museums include the North Wales Quarrying Museum, Llanberis and the Segontium Roman Fort Museum, Caernarfon in Gwynedd, the Museum of the Woollen Industry, Dre-fach Felindre, the Graham Sutherland Gallery, Picton Castle, Haverfordwest and Amgueddfa'r Hen Gapel, Tre'r Ddôl in Dyfed.

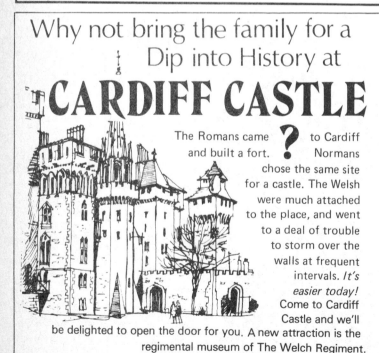

closes 4). The castle is closed occasionally for special functions. P (in Sophia Gardens and city centre). Further information from *Technical Services Dept, Hodge House, St Mary Street. (Tel 31033 ext 716)*
National Museum of Wales Cathays Park. Collections and exhibitions in archaeology, geology, botany, zoology industry and art, ♨. Open all year, daily (ex 24 to 26 Dec, 1 Jan and 4 Apr and May Day) weekdays 10–5 (6, Apr to Sep), Sun 2.30–5. Free. *(Tel 397951)* ♿

Welsh Industrial and Maritime Museum Bute Street. A branch museum of the National Museum of Wales. Working exhibits tell the story of motive power and the roles played by a variety of machines over two centuries of intense industrial production and progress in Wales. Open all year, daily (ex 24–26 Dec, 1 Jan, 4 Apr and May Day) weekdays 10–5 (6, Apr to Sep), Sun 2.30–5. Free. *(Tel 371805)* ♿

CARDIGAN *Dyfed* Map 2 SN14
Wildlife Park Coedmore Estate. Entrance S of River Teify near Cilgerran Village. The park specialises in European animals, especially of Wales past and present, incorporated in an unusually diverse area of 250-acres of natural habitats. Animal enclosures, nature trails, wildlife sanctuary also slate and lime industrial archaelogy. Craft shop and ♨. Coracle fishing demonstrations on most PH and every weekend Jul and Aug. Open all year, daily 10–6. 75p (ch 14 and pen 35p). ⚠ *(Tel Llechryd 662)* ♿ (most parts ex trails)

CARREG CENNEN CASTLE *Dyfed*
Map 3 SN61
Spectacularly sited hill-side ruin, originally native Welsh stronghold, rebuilt in late 13th C. Remarkable passage lit by loopholes cut into side of cliff. Open*, see inside front cover. 15p (ch 16 and pen 7p) ⚠ *(AM)*

CHEPSTOW *Gwent* Map 3 ST59
Chepstow Castle Earliest documented masonry castle, begun 1067–71 by William Fitz-Osborn. Fortified Port Wall. Royalist stronghold during Civil War, later garrisoned by Parliamentarians and dismantled in 1690. Open*' see inside front cover. 25p (ch 16 and pen 12p). ⚠ *(AM)*
Chepstow Museum Board School, Bridge Street. Exhibitions of all aspects of Chepstow, the lower Wye Valley and surrounding area. The wine trade and salmon fisheries exhibition is of special note. Free children's worksheet available. Open 1 Mar to 31 Oct Mon to Sat 11–1, 2–5, Sun 2–5. 12p (ch and pen 7p). P (at castle). *(Tel 5981)*

CHIRK *Clwyd* Map 7 SJ23
Chirk Castle off the A5, ½m from Chirk Village. (1½m driveway) Unique example of Marcher fortress, completed in 1310, with State rooms providing examples of 16th, 17th, 18th and early 19th-C decorations. ♨. Open 5 Apr to 26 Oct Wed, Thu, Sat and Sun 2–5; Jun to Sep Wed and Thu 11–5. All BH weekends 11–5. £1 (ch 50p). Party 20+. *(managed by NT on behalf of Secretary of State for Wales).*

CILGERRAN *Dyfed* Map 2 SN24
Cilgerran Castle Off A484. In picturesque setting above River Teifi, Norman to 13th-C castle reduced to ruins during Civil War, and subject of well-known paintings by Peter de Wint and Richard Wilson. Open, see inside front cover. 15p (ch 16 and pen 7p). Under revision for 1980. *(AM)*

COITY *Mid Glamorgan* Map 3 SS98
Coity Castle 12th- to 16th-C stronghold with hall chapel and three-storeyed round tower. Open, see inside front cover. 15 (ch 16 and pen 7p). *(AM)*

COLWYN BAY *Clwyd* Map 6 SH87
Welsh Mountain Zoo and Botanic Gardens Animals and flora of all types in area of great beauty. Daily displays of Falconry (free-flying birds of prey). Penguin pool with underwater observation. ♨ Open all year Apr to Oct 9.30–7; Oct to Mar 10–4. £1 (ch 3–14 50p, ch 3 free) Party. ⚠ Special toilets for wheelchair visitors. *(Tel 2938 catering 30891)* ♿

CONWY *Gwynedd* Map 6 SH77
Aberconwy At junction of Castle Street and High Street. Medieval house that dates from the 14th-C, now houses the Conwy Exhibition, depicting the life of the borough from Roman times to the present day. Shop. Open 1 Apr to 30 Sep, 10–5.30 daily (ex Wed in Apr, May). Oct to Mar by appointment. 30p (ch 12p). Party. *(Tel 2246) (NT)*
Conwy Castle A magnificent linear plan fortress built 1283–89 by Edward I. Also extensive town walls, originally with 27 towers, and old and new road bridges. Open*, see inside front cover. Castle 35p, winter 20p (ch 16 and pen 20p, winter 10p). Walls (open, see inside front cover, May to Sep only) 17p (ch 16 and pen 10p). ⚠ *(AM)*
Conwy Visitor Centre Off Lancaster Square. For the whole family, a fascinating journey through Conwy's colourful past, illustrated on film and in displays. Welsh craft and bookshop. Open, Jun to Sep, daily 10–9.30 (5.30 Sun); Oct to Dec and Mar to May

10 – 5.30 (closed Sun also Jan and Feb). 50p (ch and pen 30p). P.

Plas Mawr High Street. Finest example in Great Britain of an Elizabethan town house. It is in practically the same condition as when it was built (1570 – 1580), by Robert Wynne. Art exhibitions all year (closed mid Dec to mid Jan), ☕ (2 – 5). Open daily 10 – 5.30 (4.30 Oct to Mar). 25p (ch 10p, pen 15p). Party ⚠ *(Tel 3413)*

'Smallest House' So-called 'Smallest House in Great Britain', on quay, with mid Victorian Welsh cottage interior. Open Easter to Oct 10 – 6 (10 – 9 in Aug). 5p. Under revision for 1980.

CORRIS *Gwynedd* Map 6 SH70
Railway Museum In village, 300 yds from A487. Museum in century-old railway building with photographs of operation of Corris narrow-gauge railway from 1890 – 1948. Items connected with railway are constantly added, and some old wagons are on show on short length of track. Children's playground nearby. Open BH weekends and Tue to Fri Jul and Aug 1 – 5.30, and as advertised on local posters during the holiday season. Free. ⚠ &

CRICCIETH *Gwynedd* Map 6 SH43
Criccieth Castle 13th-C fortress, rebuilt with two baileys and notable gatehouse. Remains of keep, and wide views over Snowdonia. Open*, see inside front cover. 20p (ch 16 and pen 10p). *(AM)*

CWMCARN *Gwent* Map 3 ST29
Scenic Forest Drive Operated by Forestry Commission in Ebbw Forest. A 7-mile drive through mountain forest with spectacular views of the surrounding countryside and the Bristol Channel; picnic places; adventure play areas; forest and mountain walks. Open daily, Easter to Aug 11 – 8; Sep to Oct 11 – 6. 50p. Coaches by appointment. ⚠ *(Tel Newbridge 244223)* &

CYMMER *West Glamorgan* Map 3 SS89
Welsh Miners Museum and Afan Argoed Country Park Set in the wooded, picturesque Afan Valley 2½m W on A4107. The museum is housed in the Countryside Centre. By entering simulated coal faces, viewing pit gear, examining miners' equipment, the visitor will experience the harsh realities of 'coal getting' and understand the effects it had on the communities of South Wales. The Countryside Park has forest walks and trails also picnic areas. ☕ and Countryside Centre adjoin the parking area. Open Easter to end Sep 10.30 – 6; 12 – 5 winter weekends. Park open daily during daylight hours. Free. ⚠ *(Tel 7175)* &

CYMMER ABBEY *Gwynedd* Map 6 SH71
Remains of the church of a small early 13th-C Cistercian monastery. Open 9 – sunset. 10p (ch 16 and pen 5p). ⚠ *(AM)*

DENBIGH *Clwyd* Map 6 SJ06
Denbigh Castle Built 1282 – 1333, with gatehouse preserved, and fine viewpoint. Open*, see inside front cover. 20p (ch 16 and pen 10p). ⚠ *(AM)*
Town Walls and Leicester's Church Remains of walls include one of the gateways, and ruined church, 'Leicester's Folly', which was planned to become cathedral of the diocese, in place of St Asaph, after the Reformation. Open, see inside front cover. 10p (ch 16 and pen 5p). *(AM)*

DOLWYDDELAN *Gwynedd* Map 6 SH75
Dolwyddelan Castle Restored rectangular 12th-C keep, with 13th-C curtain walls, the supposed birthplace of Llewelyn the Great. Open all year, weekdays 9.30 – 7 (5.30, Mar, Apr, Oct; 4, Nov to Feb), Sun 9.30 – 4. 15p (ch 16 and pen 7p). ⚠ *(AM)*

DRE-FACH FELINDRE *Dyfed* Map 2 SN33
Museum of the Woollen Industry A branch of the National Museum of Wales administered by the Welsh Folk Museum. It occupies part of a working mill, the Cambrian Mills. Its collection of textile machinery dates back to the 18th C and the exhibition traces the development of the industry from the Middle Ages to the present day. Open 1 Apr to 30 Sep, Mon to Sat 10 – 5 (ex May Day). Free. P. &

DRYSLWYN *Dyfed* Map 2 SN52
Dryslwyn Castle Ruined, 13th-C, native Welsh stronghold on a lofty mound, important for its part in the struggles between the Welsh and English in the 13th C. Accessible at any time. Free. ⚠ *(AM)*

EWLOE *Clwyd* Map 7 SJ26
Ewloe Castle Remains of native Welsh castle in Ewloe woods, near where Henry II was defeated in 1157. Open Oct to Feb any reasonable time without charge; Mar to Apr 9.30 – 5.30, Sun 2 – 5.30; May to Sep 9.30 – 7, Sun 2 – 7. 10p (ch 16 and pen 5p). *(AM)*

FLINT *Clwyd* Map 7 SJ27
Flint Castle Ruined late 13th-C castle, erected by Edward I, with circular detached keep surrounded by moat. Open, see inside front cover. 10p (ch 16 and pen 5p). ⚠ *(AM)*

FORT BELAN *Gwynedd* Map 6 SH46
Napoleonic fort and private dock built around 1775. Featuring maritime museum, old forge, pleasure flights and sea cruises also miniature steam railway. Pottery, Gift shop, ☕

and cannon firing. Open May to Sep daily 10–5. 65p (ch 30p, and pen 55p). ⚠ *(Tel Llanwnda 830220)* &

GROSMONT *Gwent* Map 3 SO42
Grosmont Castle Ruined Marcher stronghold, rebuilt in 13th C by Hubert de Burgh, on hill above Monnow Valley. One of three 'tri-lateral' castles of Gwent. Open at all reasonable times. Free. *(AM)*

HARLECH *Gwynedd* Map 6 SH35
Harlech Castle Built 1283–90 by Edward I, and captured by Owain Glyndwr in 1404, rectangular fortress on concentric plan, with notable gatehouse. Wide views of Snowdonia and Lleyn peninsula across Tremadoc Bay. Open*, see inside front cover. 35p, winter 20p (ch 16 and pen 20p, winter 10p). ⚠ *(AM)*
Old Llanfair Slate Quarries Man-made caverns, previously blasted out of the hills in the search for slate, through which guided tours are given today. For the safety of visitors authentic quarrymen's helmets are provided. The mine, although underground, is for the first part lit by daylight, while further on it is illuminated, where the varying thicknesses of the layers of slate may be seen. On emerging from the mine, there is a splendid view of Cardigan Bay. 🍴 Slate souvenir shop. Open Easter to mid Oct, daily 10–5.30 (parties by arrangement throughout the year). 50p (ch 15 20p, pen 35p). P. *(Tel 247)* **(79)**

HAVERFORDWEST *Dyfed* Map 2 SM91
Haverfordwest Castle, Museum, Art Gallery, and Record Office Ruined 12th-C stronghold, slighted after Civil War, converted in 18th and early 19th C, used as a jail until 1820, when new county jail was built, later became police HQ and recently converted to museum and art gallery. Museum open all year Mon to Sat (ex 13 Apr 25, 26 Dec, 1 Jan) summer 10–5.30, winter 11–4. Record Office open all year Mon to Thu 9–4.45, Fri 9–4.15. Castle ruins open all times during daylight, at visitors' own risk. Free. P. *(Tel 3708, Records Office 3707)*

HAWARDEN *Clwyd* Map 7 SJ36
Hawarden Old Castle Remains of 14th-C castle twice besieged during civil wars of 17th C, and visited by Henry VII. Castle and ornamental gardens open Easter to mid Sep Sat, Sun, BH 2–5.30. Admission to castle and ornamental gardens 20p (ch 16, 10p). Full garden openings for charities, 2–6 on one Sun in Apr, May and Jun. Use garden centre park on A55.

KIDWELLY *Dyfed* Map 2 SN40
Kidwelly Castle 12th-C fortress with additions of following two centuries, and curious circular ovens of great size. Chapel dating from c1400. Open*, see inside front cover. 20p (ch 16 and pen 10p). ⚠ *(AM)*

LAMPHEY *Dyfed* Map 2 SN00
Lamphey Palace Ruined 13th-C Palace of the Archbishops of St David's Later portion added by Bishop Gower. Open, see inside front cover. 15p (ch 16 and pen 7p). ⚠ *(AM)*

LLANALLGO *Gwynedd* Map 6 SH48
Din Lligwy Ancient Village 1m NW off A5205. Remains of 4th-C village, with two circular and seven rectangular buildings encircled by pentagonal stone wall. Open all reasonable times. Free. *(AM)*

LLANBERIS *Gwynedd* Map 6 SH56
Dolbadarn Castle Native Welsh stronghold, with a three-storeyed 13th-C round tower *(AM)*. Open Mar, Apr, Oct 9.30–5.30, Sun 2–5.30; May to Jun 9.30–7, Sun 2–7; Jul to Sep 9.30–7, Sun 11–7; Nov to Feb 9.30–4. Sun 2–4. 10p (ch and pen 5p). ⚠ (limited). *(AM)*
Lake Railway Llyn Padarn. Narrow-gauge railway operated by steam trains. Four-mile journey commencing from and returning to Gilfach Ddu, adjacent to the North Wales Quarrying Museum and the centre of the Padarn County Park. Railway line was formerly used to carry slate from the Dinorwic Quarries to Port Dinorwic. The steam locomotives date from 1889 to 1948; coaches built specially for railway. Souvenir shop. 🍴 Trains run frequently, every day, from Easter to end Sep (10.30–6 in peak season). Return fare 80p (ch 40p) subject to alteration. Party–apply to Commercial Manager. ⚠ 20p, coaches free. Toilet facilities for disabled persons. *(Tel 549)* &
North Wales Quarrying Museum ½m off A4086. Contains original workshop machinery for servicing quarries and to maintain machinery and rolling stock. Foundry mill with machinery and famous Dinorwic 54ft water wheel. Also machinery from other redundant Welsh quarries. Open daily Easter to Sep (ex May Day) 9.30–7. 25p (ch 16 and pen 12p). *(AM)* &
Snowdon Mountain Railway First opened in 1896, the only rack and pinion steam railway in Britain (2ft 7½in gauge). Locomotives built by Swiss Locomotive Works at Winterthur. Climbs 4⅞ miles to summit of Snowdon providing views of North Wales, Anglesey and Cardigan Bay. Shops and 🍴 at Base station (including Welsh Craft Shops). 🍴 and shop at summit. Open early Apr to early Oct, daily from 9. Fares not yet available, details available from General Manager. ⚠ *(Tel 223)* & (not at summit)

LLANDRINDOD WELLS *Powys* Map 3 SO06
Llandrindod Wells Museum Archaeological
exhibits, and objects excavated from Roman
Camp at Castell Collen to north of town.
Paterson Doll Collection is on show. Victorian
Spa gallery with period costume and 19th-C
chemist's equipment. Temporary exhibitions
are displayed. Open all year, Mon to Fri (ex
BH) 10–12.30 and 2–5. Sat 10–12.30 (May
to Sep only) Free. P. *(Tel 2212)*

LLANELLI *Dyfed* Map 2 SN50
*British Steel Corporation, Trostre Works
Museum* Troste works cover 270 acres and
are Britains largest tinplate works. Exhibits
include model of handmill for producing
tinplate, actual handmill equipment, and
documents relating to industry. Parties of
limited numbers catered for on application.
Free. ⚠ (Limited) *(Tel 2260)* ⅋ B
Parc Howard Art Gallery and Museum
Situated in a pleasant park, and containing a
permanent collection of paintings. Llanelli
pottery and museum exhibits. From Mar to
Oct, a programme of exhibitions of paintings,
porcelain, sculpture, etc, is in operation. ⚑
May to Oct. Open all year Nov to Mar 10–4;
Apr to Oct 10–7. Free. *(Tel 3538)*

LLANFAIR CAEREINION *Powys*
Map 6 SJ10
*Welshpool & Llanfair Light (Steam)
Railway* (2ft 6in gauge). Open between
Llanfair Caereinion and Sylfaen (5½ miles).
Includes Austrian and Colonial locomotives.
⚑ at Llanfair Stn. Open at weekends from
Easter to Oct and daily from early Jun to early
Sep. Trains from Llanfair at 2.15 and 4.15,
also at 11.15 during daily running period.
Fares for 1980 not yet decided. ⚠ at Llanfair
and Castle Caereinion Stations. *(Tel 441)* ⅋

LLANGOLLEN *Clwyd* Map 7 SJ24
Llangollen Station Situated alongside the
river Dee in the centre of the town. Great
Western Railway Station restored, with steam
locomotives and rolling stock on display.
International Eisteddfod week 2–6 Jul and
most BH. ⚑ and railway shop. Open all year
Sat and Sun 10–5 also weekdays in tourist
season. Passenger service may operate
during 1980, please check. Steam days 10p,
non steam days Free. P. *(Tel 860951)* ⅋
Plas Newydd Butler Hill. Former home of
well-known 'Ladies of Llangollen' in 18th C.
Oak carvings, panelling, and leather-work.
Exhibition room, attractive grounds. Open 1
May to 30 Sep, Mon to Sat 10–7.30, Sun
11–4. 15p (ch 14 10p) subject to alteration. ⚠
(limited). *(Tel 860234)*
Valle Crucis Abbey Abbey founded in 1201
for Cistercian monks by Madog ap Gruffydd
Prince of Powys. The remaining buildings
date mainly from 13th C. Open*, see inside
front cover. 15p (ch 16 and pen 7). ⚠ *(AM)*

LLANGYBI *Gwynedd* Map 6 SH44
St Cybi's Well Rectangular structure, known
also as Ffynnon Gybi, with dry-stone structure
covering adjacent pool. Interior has wall
niches, and the corbelled beehive vaulting of
Irish type is unique in Wales. Open all
reasonable times. Free. *(AM)*

LLANIDLOES *Powys* Map 6 SN98
Old Market Hall Half-timbered building,
standing on open arches, with museum on
upper floor. Open Easter, and Spring BH to 30
Sep, daily 11–1 and 2–5. Free. P.

LLANRHIDIAN *West Glamorgan*
Map 2 SS49
Weobley Castle 12th- to 14th-C fortified

manor house above Gower marshland. Open
Apr to Sep, weekdays 10–7, Sun 1–7; Oct to
Mar 10–4, Sun 1–4. 15p (ch 16 and pen 7p).
⚠ *(AM)*

LLANRUG *Gwynedd* Map 6 SH56
Bryn Bras Castle and Grounds 1½m SE on
A4086. Early Victorian Romanesque castle
which is a delightful lived-in home with
extensive grounds of natural beauty,
including stream, waterfalls, pools,
hydrangeas, rhododendrons, woodland
walks, and panoramic, ½m-mountain walk. ⚑
Open Spring BH to end Sep, daily (ex Sat),
1–5 (10.30–5 mid Jul to end Aug). 70p (ch 15
35p). Party. ⚠ *(Tel Llanberis 210)*. *(Mr R D
Gray-Williams and Mrs M Gray-Parry)*

LLANRWST *Gwynedd* Map 6 SH86
Forest Information Centre Operated by
Forestry Commission in Gwydyr Forest to
interpret the forest as part of the landscape,
as a form of land use, as a traditional industry,
as a habitat for wildlife and as a place for
recreation and relaxation. 12 forest trails in
the vicinity, one starting from the centre. Open
daily, Easter to 30 Sep 10–4.30. Free. ⚠ 20p.
(Tel 640578)
Gwydyr Castle Historical royal residence,
magnificently furnished, from the Tudor
period. Beautiful grounds with more than 50
peacocks and many tropical birds. ⚑ Open
Easter to second week in Oct, daily (ex Sat)
10.30–5.30. 75p (ch 12 35p). Under revision
for 1980. ⚠ *(Tel 640261)* ⅋ B
Gwydyr Uchaf Chapel Former private
chapel of Gwydyr Castle (see above), and
dating from 1673, noted for rare Welsh
painted roof of the period. Open all year, any
reasonable time. 15p (ch 16 and pen 7p).
(AM)
Tu Hwnt I'r Bont Stone cottage, formerly
courthouse and restored partly by local
subscription, now let as tea-room. Open
Easter to end of touring season, daily (ex
Mon). Regret no parties. Free. *(NT)*
*Llanrwst Transport Group Museum and
Transport Workshop* Goods Warehouse,
Station Yard. Exhibition of items of transport
interest including two railway wagons, diesel
shunting locomotives, scammel three-
wheeler lorries, single-decker bus and
smaller railway exhibits. Open 1st Sun of
each month 10–4.30. Free. ⚠ (limited)
additional P nearby. *(Tel Deganwy 82394)*
(79)

LLANSTEPHAN *Dyfed* Map 2 SN31
Llanstephan Castle Remains of 11th- to
13th-C stronghold on west side of Towy
estuary. Accessible all reasonable times.
Free. *(AM)*

LLANTHONY *Gwent* Map 3 SO22
Llanthony Priory Augustinian foundation, *c*
1108, most of present structure being 12th- or
13th-C and including western towers, north
nave arcade, and south transept. Former
chapter house and western range have been
converted to secular use, and former Priest's
House is now hotel. The Honddu valley
scenery in Black Mountains is very
picturesque but roads are narrow, especially
continuing northwards towards lofty Gospel
Pass leading to Hay-on-Wye. Open all
reasonable times. Free. ⚠ *(AM)*

LLANTILIO CROSSENNY *Gwent*
Map 3 SO31
Hen Gwrt Rectangular enclosure of medieval
house which is still surrounded by wet moat.
Open any reasonable time. Free. *(AM)*

LLANTWIT MAJOR *South Glamorgan*
Map 3 SS96
Town Hall Originally 12th- and largely 17th-C
medieval courthouse and market, known
once as the 'Church loft'. Retains original plan
and comprises two storeys. Curfew bell
(1320) now in church. Drama weeks May and
Nov. Local art exhibition Jul. Horticultural
Show Aug. Open all year Mon to Fri 9 – 4. Sat
and Sun by appointment. Free. ⚠ *(Tel 3707)*

LLANUWCHLLYN *Gwynedd* Map 6 SH82
Bala Lake Railway Narrow-gauge railway
running 4½ miles from Llanuwchllyn station,
alongside Bala Lake to Bala. 3 ex-Dinorwic
quarry steam engines built between 1889 and
1903 also diesel locomotives. Llanuwchllyn
Station buildings date from 1867 and the
original GWR signal box with 21 lever double
twist frame installed in 1896 may be seen
there. Also large selection of slate wagons
and a gunpowder van. There are also early
and later pattern Lancashire and Yorkshire
railway signals in use. ⛊ Shop. Open Easter
to 23 Oct daily 9 – 6 (weekends only after 30
Sep). 90p return (ch 45p return). 2 adults and
2 ch £2.30. Under revision for 1980. ⚠ *(Tel
666 or Bala 520226)* &

LLANVAPLEY *Gwent* Map 3 SO31
Rural Crafts Museum Exhibitions of 500
items of farm and rural craft tools and
implements and other domestic and rural
bygones. Open Feb to Nov Sun 3 – 6 (or
dusk). Large or small parties wishing to view
on other days *Tel Llantilio 210*. 20p (ch and
pen 5p). ⚠ (very limited) otherwise on verge.

LLANVIHANGEL CRUCORNEY *Gwent*
Map 3 SO32
Llanvihangel Court Tudor house, with
interior remodelled in 1560. Interesting
furnishings, yew staircase, and portraits.
Attractive gardens. ⛊ Open every BH Sun
and Mon (ex winter) and first, third and fifth
Sun in Jun and every Sun in Jul and Aug
2.30 – 6. 50p (ch 15 10p). ⚠ *(Tel Crucorney
217). (Col and Mrs Somerset Hopkinson)*

LLANYSTUMDWY *Gwynedd* Map 6 SH43
Lloyd George Museum David Lloyd George,
famous Liberal Prime Minister, was educated
in the village and died at the house of Ty
Newydd in 1945. Museum has relics and
mementos of his life. Open end May to 30
Sep, Mon to Fri 10 – 5. 20p (ch 15 and pen
10p) may be subject to increase. ⚠ *(Tel
Criccieth 2654)* &

LLAWHADEN *Dyfed* Map 2 SN01
Llawhaden Castle Ruined 13th-C fortified
residence of Bishops of St David's. Open, see
inside front cover. 15p (ch 16 and pen 7p).
(AM)

LOUGHOR *West Glamorgan* Map 2 SS59
Loughor Castle Slight remains of castle,
originally Norman, but several times rebuilt by
the Welsh to defend a river ford. Accessible all
reasonable times. Free. *(AM)*

MACHYNLLETH *Powys* Map 6 SH70
Centre for Alternative Technology An old
slate quarry overlooking Snowdonia National
Park, a working demonstration independent
of mains services, showing the possibilities of
living with only a small share of the earth's
dwindling resources, and creating a minimum
of pollution and waste. Research, low energy
studies, monitoring of equipment, housing,
horticulture. Demonstrations of windpower,
solar energy and vegetable growing. Salad
lunches in summer. Open daily (ex
Christmas), 10 – 5 (or dusk in winter). 80p (ch
and pen 40p, students 60p). ⚠ *(Tel 2400)* &

MAESGWM *Gwynedd* Map 6 SH72
Forest Information Centre Operated by
Forestry Commission in Coed-y-Brenin to
interpret the forest as part of the landscape,
as a form of land use, as a traditional industry,
as a part of the local community, as a habitat
for wild life, and as a place for recreation and
relaxation. Includes a display of machinery
from local gold mines. Open Easter to Oct,
daily 10 – 5 (7, Jul and Aug). Admission and ⚠
20p. Under revision for 1980. *(Tel Ganilwyd
210)* &

MANORBIER *Dyfed* Map 2 SS09
Manorbier Castle Mainly 13th-C, including
chapel, hall and gatehouse, with 16th-C
additions. Birthplace of 12th-C historian,
Giraldus Cambrensis. Life-size wax figures in
various parts of the castle. Open for a week at
Easter then Whitsun to 30 Sep, daily 11 – 6.
25p (ch 10p). P. *(Tel 394) (79)*

MARGAM *West Glamorgan* Map 3 SS88
Margam Country Park E of junc 38 M4. 840
acres with large herd of fallow deer,
rhododendron gardens, romantic buildings
and remains, Margam Orangery (the largest
building of its kind in Britain). Gymkhana,
horse trials, pony and carriage events, band
concerts, archery competitions. Waymarked
walks. Adventure playground. Boating, riding,
putting and fishing. ⛊ Open all year 1 Apr to
30 Sep Tue to Sun 10.30 – 8 (no entry after
6.30); 1 Oct to 31 Oct Tue to Sun 10.30 – one
hour before dusk; 1 Nov to 31 Mar Wed to Sun
10.30 – one hour before dusk. 30p (ch and
pen 15p, ch 5 and reg disabled free). ⚠ free.
(Tel Port Talbot 87626) & B
Stones Museum Small collection of Early
Christian and pre-Norman carved stones and
crosses. Adjacent to Margam churchyard.
Open all year, Wed, Sat and Sun 2 – 5 (4, Nov
to Feb). 15p (ch 16 and pen 7p). ⚠ *(AM)*

MENAI BRIDGE *Gwynedd* Map 6 SH57
Museum of Childhood Water Street. The
exhibits, many of which are rare and valuable
illustrate the habits and interests of children
and families spanning 150 years. They
include children's saving boxes; dolls;
educational toys and games; pottery and
glassware depicting and used by children;
early clockwork toys, including trains, cars
and aeroplanes; music boxes; polyphons;
magic lanterns and an art gallery full of
paintings and prints of children, as well as
early samplers and needlework pictures
worked by children. Open Easter to end of
Oct, daily 10–6, Sun 1–5; Nov to Apr consult
curator. 50p (ch 35p pen 40p ch 6 free). P.
(Tel 712498)
Tegfryn Art Gallery Cadnant Road. A private
gallery, standing in its own pleasant grounds
near to shores of the Menai Straits, exhibits
paintings by contemporary, prominent artists
including many from North Wales. Pictures
may be purchased. Open all year daily 10–1,
2–6. Free. ⚠ *(Tel 712437)*. ♿

MERTHYR TYDFIL *Mid Glamorgan*
Map 3 SO00
Cyfarthfa Castle Museum and Art Gallery
Built by William Crawshay in 1825 the
collections cover paintings, ceramics, coins
and medals, silver and other *objets d'art*,
natural history and local history, also a small
Welsh kitchen. Open weekdays 10–1 and
2–6 (5 Oct to Mar) Sun 2–5. Free ex Sun and
BH 5p. Closed 4 Apr, 5 May, 25/26 Dec and 1
Jan. *(Tel 3112)*
Garwnant Forest Centre 5m N of Merthyr
Tydfil off A470. The centre provides
information about, and has an exhibition
featuring, the forests in the Brecon Beacons.
Parking and picnic places close by with
associated forest walks. Open Easter to 30
Sep weekdays 10.30–4 (also 4–6pm Wed
and Thu in Jul and Aug), BH 12–6. Open Sat
and Sun Apr and Sep 2–4; May 2–5; Jun, Jul
and Aug 2–6. Other times, phone for opening
details. Free ⚠ *(Tel 3060)* ♿

MONMOUTH *Gwent* Map 3 SO51
Monmouth Castle and Great Castle House
12th-C castle keep, birthplace of Henry V.
Great Castle House built by 1st Duke of
Beaufort in 1673. Exterior only freely
accessible any reasonable time. ⚠ *(AM)*
Monmouth Museum (Nelson Collection and
Local History Centre). Collections of Nelson
relics and mementoes. Local history centre of
Monmouth. Open all year weekdays,
10.30–1 and 2.15–5.15. Sun 2.15–5.15; Jul
and Aug, weekdays 10–6, Sun, 2.15–5.15.
Admission to local collection free; Nelson
collection 20p (ch and pen 7p). P. (Glendower
Street) 5p. *(Tel 3519)*

MUMBLES *West Glamorgan* Map 2 SS68
Oystermouth Castle Ruined gatehouse,
chapel, and great hall of 13th- to 14th-C date.
Former stronghold of Braose family. Small
park, open Jun, Jul and Aug 11–5.30, other
months Mon to Fri 11–3.30. 11p (ch 16 5p).
Under revision for 1980. P. *(Tel Swansea
50821 ext 2815)*

NEATH *West Glamorgan* Map 3 SS79
Neath Abbey Ruins of Cistercian (originally
Savignac) abbey founded by Richard de
Grainville in 1130. Open, see inside front
cover. 15p (ch 16 and pen 5p). ⚠ *(AM)*
Penscynor Wild Life Park Interesting bird
garden. New extension into forestry land. Gift
shops. Open all year (ex 25 Dec). Daily 10–6.
Admission prices not yet decided. ⚲ No dogs.
⚠ *(Tel 2189)* ♿

NEWCASTLE EMLYN *Dyfed* Map 2 SN34
Felin Geri Mill 2m N on unclass road off
B4333 at Cwmcoy. The last watermill in
Wales using the original means of production
to grind stone ground wholemeal flour on a
regular commercial basis. Built in the 16th C.
Visitors are shown all stages of production.
There is also a mill museum and a water
powered saw mill. Shop and bakery. ⚲. Open
Easter to end Oct, Mon to Fri, 10–5.30, Sat
and Sun 10–4. 40p (ch 16 20p). ⚠ *(Tel
710810)*

-P.K.F-

NEWPORT *Dyfed* Map 2 SN04
Pentre Ifan Burial Chamber 3m SE.
Remains of this chamber comprise capstone
and three uprights with semi-circular
forecourt at one end. Excavated 1936–37
when found to be part of vanished long
barrow. Open all reasonable times. Free.
(AM)

NEWPORT *Gwent* Map 3 ST38
Museum and Art Gallery John Frost Square.
Archaeology and history of Gwent including
Roman finds from Caerwent and Pontypool
Japanned ware, section on Chartist
movement of 1838–40. Natural history and
geology. Open all year (ex BH) Mon to Fri
10–5.30. Sat 9.30–4. Free. ⚠ *(Tel 840064)*
⚐

Tredegar House Former home of the Morgan
family. Finest Restoration house in Wales,
with part of the early 16th-C hall block
surviving. Extensive grounds, farm, boating
lake. ⚑ (licensed). Grounds open daily
8–sunset. House and farm open 2 Apr to 25
Sep Wed to Sun and BH 2–6. Grounds free;
House 25p (ch 15p). Under revision for 1980.
(Tel 62275).
Whitson Zoological Park Whitson Court.
Set in the grounds of an 18th-C house
designed by John Nash. Among the exhibits
are bears, monkeys, baboons, lions,
macaws, and pheasants. There is also an
aquarium set in the cellars of the house. ⚑
Open Apr to Sep daily 10–6. 30p (ch 16 and
pen 20p). Party 20+. Guided tours for school
parties. Under revision for 1979. ⚠ *(Tel
72515)*. ⚐ **(79)**

PKF

OGMORE *Mid Glamorgan* Map 3 SS87
Ogmore Castle On River Ogmore, with inner
and outer wards, and early 12th-C three-
storeyed stone keep preserving hooded
fireplace. West wall 40ft high, and dry moat
around inner ward. Open, see inside front
cover. Free. *(AM)*

PEMBROKE *Dyfed* Map 2 SM90
Pembroke Castle Impressive 12th- to 13th-C
fortress by river bank, with 80ft-high round
keep, work of Earl of Pembroke. Open all year
Easter to 30 Sep, Mon to Fri 10–7, Sat 10–6,
Sun 11–7; Oct to Easter, Mon to Sat 10.30–5
(closed Sun and 25 Dec). Castle gates close
½hr before stated closing times. 20p (ch 10p).
P. *(Tel 4585)*. ⚐

PEMBROKE DOCK *Dyfed* Map 2 SM90
Pembrokeshire Motor Museum A number
of vintage and veteran cars and motorcycles
in Garrison Theatre. Several early bicycles
can also be seen. Costumes of early motoring
period on display. Early children's toys and
replica of garage of the Twenties. Items of
local historical interest. Open 29 May to 30
Sep, Sun to Fri 10–6. 50p (ch 17 25p). ⚠ *(Tel
Pembroke 3279)* ⚐

PENARTH *South Glamorgan* Map 3 ST17
Turner House Small art gallery holding
temporary exhibitions of pictures and *objets
d'art* from the National Museum of Wales and
other sources. Open all year, weekdays (ex
Mon, 1 Jan, 4 Apr, May Day and 24–26 Dec
but open BH Mon 11–12.45 and 2–5, Sun
2–5. Free. P. *(Tel 708870)*

PENARTH FAWR *Gwynedd* Map 6 SH43
Off A497. Part of house, built probably in early
15th-C, preserving hall, buttery, and screen.
Open any reasonable time. Free. *(AM)*

PENHOW *Gwent* Map 3 ST49
Penhow Castle The oldest inhabited castle in
Wales was originally a small border fortress.
The first home in Britain of the famous
Seymour family, one of whom was living in the
Castle in 1129. The building presents a
fascinating picture of life from the 12th to
19th-C, 12th-C ramparts (with view of three
counties), 15th-C Great Hall with
reconstructed screen and minstrels' gallery,
17th-C kitchen, also Victorian house-keeper's
room. Gift and publication shop. ⚑ by
arrangement. Open Easter to Sep, Wed to
Sun (closed Mon and Tue) 10–6. 65p (ch 14
and pen 35p). Guided tours, party, evening
visits by arrangement. Educational facilities.
⚠ *(Tel 400800)* ⚐ B

PENMACHNO *Gwynedd* Map 6 SH75
Tŷ Mawr 2m NW at head of Gwybernant
Valley. The birthplace of Bishop William
Morgan c1541 – 1604, the first translator of
the Bible into Welsh. ♨ Open 4 Apr to 26 Oct
daily (ex Sat) 10 – 6. 10p. Party by
appointment *(Mrs Roberts, Ty Mawr,
Gwybernant, Dolwyddelan, Gwynedd)*.
Approach roads unsuitable for large coaches.
(Tel 213). (NT)

PENMON *Gwynedd* Map 6 SH68
Dovecote Off B5109. Dovecote dates from
c1600 and is square with domed vault and
hexagonal cupola. Open all reasonable
times. Free. *(AM)*

PICTON *Dyfed* Map 2 SN01
***Picton Castle Grounds and Graham
Sutherland Gallery*** Castle **NOT** open. The
gallery is in a building in a courtyard close to
the castle, 300yds from car park. On display,
oil paintings, water-colours, works in mixed
media, lithographs, etchings and aquatints.
The extensive grounds provide walks through
shrub gardens and woodland. Grounds open
1 Apr to 30 Sep (ex Mon & Fri) 10.30 – 6. 50p
(ch 10p). ⚠ *(Tel Rhos 201)* ♿ Graham
Sutherland Gallery Easter to end Sep (ex May
Day) daily (ex Mon & Fri, but open BH Mon)
10.30 – 12.30, 1.30 – 5.30. Oct to Easter Sat
and Sun 2 – 5. Free. ⚠ 50p. *(Tel Rhos 296)* ♿

PLAS NEWYDD *Gwynedd* Map 6 SH56
On A4080 1m SW Llanfairpwll. 18th-C house
by James Wyatt in unspoilt position adjacent
to Menai Strait; magnificent views to
Snowdonia; fine spring garden. Rex
Whistler's largest wall painting. Military
museum. Shop. ♨ Open 4 Apr to 26 Oct, daily
(ex Sat, but open BH Sat) 12.30 – 5.30 (last
admission 5 pm). £1 (ch 50p). Gardens only
50p (ch 25p). Party 20+. No dogs. *(Tel
Llanfairpwll 714795)*. (NT)

PLAS-YN-RHIW *Gwynedd* Map 6 SH22
Off B4413. 16th-C house with Georgian
features and attractive woodlands, on lower
slopes of Mynydd Rhiw with views across
Porth Neigwl. Gardens with flowering shrubs
and trees, stream, and waterfall. Open strictly
by appointment only. No room for coaches.
(Tel Rhiw 219). (NT)

PLWMP *Dyfed* Map 2 SN35
***West Wales Farm Park (Parc Fferm Gorlle
win Cymru)*** Blaenbed Isaf 1m S. 60 acres of
farmland devoted to the display or breeding
groups of old British breeds of farm animals
and poultry. Many rare species are displayed.
Beautiful views of Welsh coastline from the
top of the Park. Tractor and trailer rides

operate around the Park in peak season.
Picnic sites, children's play area, pets corner,
nature trail. ♨ Open 15 May to 30 Sep daily
10 – 6. 75p (ch 14 40p). Party. ⚠ *(Tel
Rhydlewis 317)*

PONTERWYD *Dyfed* Map 6 SN78
Bwlch Nant-Yr-Arian Forest Visitor Centre
3m W
Operated by the Forestry Commission in
Rheidol to interpret the forest as a part of the
landscape, form of land use, traditional
industry, part of local community, habitat for
wildlife, and as a place for recreation and
relaxation. Picnic areas and forest walks in
the vicinity. Open Easter to Oct 10 – 5 (7, Jul
and Aug). 10p. ⚠ ♿
Llywernog Silver-Lead Mine A mid 19th-C
water-powered silver-lead mine located in the
midst of the Welsh mountains. Restored to
provide interpretive facilities for the bygone
mining industry of the region. Way-marked
trail system (the miner's trail), museum,
audio-visual unit, underground drift mine and
working machinery. Collections include the
last Cornish Roll Crusher in Wales, jiggers,
buddles and many water-wheels and other
items. Regular working days at the Smithy,
Horse-gin and Ore Jigger. ♨ Open Easter to
Sep; Easter to 30 Jun 11 – 4.30; Jul and Aug
10 – 6; Sep 11 – 4. 65p (ch 15 35p, pen 55p).
⚠ *(Tel 620)*. Stout footwear recommended.

PORTHMADOG *Gwynedd* Map 6 SH53
Festiniog Railway Historic narrow-gauge
railway which originally carried slate from
mines at Blaenau Ffestiniog to the sea at
Porthmadog, with trucks running down from
the quarries by gravity. Steam locomotives
were introduced in 1863 and passengers
were carried soon afterwards. Line closed in
1946 but re-opened by enthusiasts to operate
between Porthmadog and Tanygrisiau with
bus connection to Blaenau Ffestiniog. Steam
locomotives including unique Fairlie type
articulated locomotive. Observation and
licensed Buffet cars on trains. Daily service
Mar to Nov. Also 26 Dec to 1 Jan and
weekends Feb and Mar. ⚠ Timetable and
fares on request. *(Tel 2384)* ♿ (Special
arrangements on trains if notified in advance).
Ffestiniog Railway Museum Located in
Harbour Station, includes old four-wheeled
hearse converted from Quarryman's coach,
historic slate waggon, model steam engine
(1869), and maps and diagrams illustrating
history of the well-known narrow-gauge
railway. ♨ Open Feb to Dec all weekends and
Mar to Nov when train service is operating.
See entry above. Free. ⚠ *(Tel 2384)* ♿

PORTMEIRION *Gwynedd* Map 6 SH53
Gwylt Gardens Wild gardens with some 20
miles of woodland paths, famous for
rhododendrons, azaleas and a variety of sub-
tropical flora. Open Apr to Oct daily
9.30 – 5.30. 75 – 95p (ch 14 20p). Under
revision for 1980. Party 20+. ⚠ *(Tel
Penrhyndeudraeth 228)* & B

RAGLAN *Gwent* Map 3 SO40
Raglan Castle Mainly 15th-C, and noted for
'Yellow Tower of Gwent'. Built by Sir William
ap Thomas, and destroyed during the Civil
War. Long Gallery, added by Lord Worcester,
was 126ft long. Castle has own bowling
green. Open*, see inside front cover. 20p (ch
16 and pen 10p). ⚠ *(AM)*

RHOOSE *South Glamorgan* Map 3 ST06
Wales Aircraft Museum Cardiff (Wales)
Airport. Opened in 1977, the privately-
operated museum is situated adjacent to the
airport. At least 18 aircraft, including a
Viscount air liner, can be inspected. Aircraft
engines and aviation related items,
photographs, models and historical items.
Children can sit in the airport Fire Engine
which is on display. ⚟ (licensed) at airport
terminal. Open all year Sun 10.30 – 7 or dusk if
earlier, or by arrangement. 30p (ch 14 and
pen 15p, ch 6 free). Under revision for 1980.
P. *(Tel Cardiff 29880 or 562780)*
RHUDDLAN *Clwyd* Map 6 SJ07
Bodrhyddan Hall 1½m E on A5151. 17th-C
house (part earlier), with armour, furniture,
and notable pictures, and in fine grounds. ⚟
Open Jun to end Sep, Tue, Thu 2 – 5.30. 50p
(ch 14 25p). ⚠ *(Tel 590414)*. *(Col the Lord
Langford)* & B

Rhuddlan Castle Begun 1277 by Edward I, to a 'diamond' plan and showing round towers, gatehouses, and 9ft-thick curtain walls. Open*, see inside front cover. 15p (ch 16 and pen 7p). ⚠ *(AM)*

ST DAVID'S *Dyfed* Map 2 SM72
Bishop's Palace Extensive remains of the principal residence of the Bishops of St David's. Dates from 13th C, with fine architectural detail. Open*, see inside front cover. 20p (ch 16 and pen 10p). *(AM)*

ST FAGAN'S *South Glamorgan* Map 3 ST17
Welsh Folk Museum Open-air branch museum of the National Museum of Wales, exhibits including 16th-C St Fagan's Castle and gardens, woollen mill complete with machinery, old Welsh farmhouses, tannery and tollgate from mid Wales, chapel from Vale of Teifi, and North Wales quarryman's cottage. ⚐ Open all year (ex 24–26 Dec, 1 Jan and May Day). Apr to Sep Mon to Sat 10–6, Sun 2.30–6 Oct to Mar 10–5, Sun 2.30–5. 10p (ch 16 5p, pen free). Sun from 2.30, admission free for pre-arranged school parties. ⚠ *(Tel Cardiff 569441)* ♿

ST FLORENCE *Dyfed* Map 2 SN10
Manor House Wildlife and Leisure Park Set in 12 acres of delightful wooded grounds and gardens. Collections of birds, tropical and freshwater fish; animal collection includes apes, monkeys, otters, deer, in a picturesque setting of flowers, plants and trees. Pets corner, adventure playground. Children's amusements and rides. Model railway exhibition. Radio-controlled models. Free flight exhibitions of birds of prey. Open from Easter to Sep daily, 10–6. Admission prices for 1980 not yet decided. No dogs. ⚠ *(Tel Carew 201)* ♿

ST HILARY *South Glamorgan* Map 3 ST07
Old Beaupré Castle 1 m SW. Ruined manor house, rebuilt in 16th C, with notable Italianate gatehouse and porch. Porch is three storeyed and displays Basset arms. Open any reasonable time (ex Sun). Free. *(AM)*

ST NICHOLAS *South Glamorgan* Map 3 ST07
Dyffryn Gardens 72 acres of gardens including rare trees and shrubs. ⚐. Open daily 31 Mar to 20 May and Sep, also weekends Oct; 21 May to 31 Aug 10–7. Plant houses close 1 hour earlier. Closed occasionally for special occasions. 30p (ch and pen 15p). Party 12+. ⚠ *(Tel Cardiff 593328)* ♿
St Lythan's Burial Chamber Isolated burial chamber which comprises three upright blocks and a capstone. It dates from *c*2000 BC. Open all reasonable times. Free. *(AM)*
Tinkinswood Burial Chamber A notable example of a long cairn, with a forecourt leading to a massively roofed chamber, rectangular in shape, with revetted walls. When excavated (1914–15) remains of human skeletons, animal bones, and pottery of *c*2000 BC were found. Accessible all reasonable times. Free. *(AM)*

SCOLTON *Dyfed* Map 2 SM92
Scolton Manor Museum and Country Park Late Georgian country mansion set in 40 acres of grounds, specially rich in fine trees and ornamental shrubs. A 'tree trail' and a nature trail are provided. The mansion, stable block and large exhibition hall provide for a comprehensive display of the history and natural history of Pembrokeshire. Picnic sites. Free ⚠ *(Tel Haverfordwest 3708)*.

SKENFRITH *Gwent* Map 3 SO42
Skenfrith Castle 7m NW of Monmouth, on
B4521. 13th-C Marcher keep within a towered
curtain wall, the work of Hubert de Burgh. One
of three 'trilaterial' castles of Gwent. Open at
all reasonable times. Free. *(AM and NT)*

STRATA FLORIDA ABBEY *Dyfed*
Map 3 SN76
Remains of church and cloister of Cistercian
abbey founded in 1164. Open, see inside
front cover. 15p (ch and pen 7p). ⚠ *(AM)*

SWANSEA *West Glamorgan* Map 3 SS69
Glynn Vivian Art Gallery and Museum
Alexandra Road. Contains works of British
and French masters, and contemporary
British artists; also collections of Continental
and Swansea porcelain and pottery. Various
exhibitions to be held through the year. Open
all year (ex 25, 26 Dec and 1 Jan), weekdays
10.30–5.30. Free. &
Maritime and Industrial Museum South
Dock. Contains complete working woollen
mill in continuous production. Displays
relating to the industry and the Port of
Swansea and its environs. Transport exhibits,
steam locomotives which run on some Sats
throughout season. Open all year (ex 25, 26
Dec, 1 Jan) weekdays 10.30–5.30. Free. P.
(Tel 55006 and 53051) &
*University College of Swansea and Royal
Institution of South Wales Museum*
Victoria Road. Founded in 1835, the museum
contains finds of local interest including
Roman and other archaeological remains,
birds, Swansea of Nantgarw china, and a
reproduction of a 19th-C Gower kitchen.
Exhibits include display of Lower Swansea
Valley. Open all year (ex 4 Apr and
Christmas/New Year week). Mon to Sat
10–5. 15p (ch 16 and students 10p, if
accompanied by adult, ch 5 free, pen 10p). ⚠
(Tel 53763)

TALLEY *Dyfed* Map 2 SN63
Talley Abbey The abbey was founded
towards the end of the 12th C probably by
Rhys ap Gruffydd, for Premonstratensian
canons. Open, see inside front cover. 15p (ch
16 and pen 7p). ⚠ *(AM)*

TAL-Y-CAFN *Gwynedd* Map 6 SH77
Bodnant Garden 8m S of Llandudno on
A470. Entrance ½m along Eglwysbach road.
Among the finest gardens in the country, with
magnificent collections of shrubs and trees.
Fine views of Snowdonia. ⚲ Apr to Sep.
Open 15 Mar to 31 Oct daily 10–5. 80p (ch
40p). Party 20+. No dogs, prams or
pushchairs. (ex guide dogs and invalid
wheelchairs). *(NT)*

TENBY *Dyfed* Map 3 SN10
St Catherine's Island Situated on a small
island fortress off Tenby beach which is only
accessible on foot for about six hours a day at
low tide. Open Whit to 30 Sep daily 10–dusk
(depending on tide). Admission prices not
available for 1980.
Tenby Castle 13th-C ruins comprising keep
and walls. Also extensive remains of 14th-C
town walls, with later alterations including
partly rebuilt gateway known as the 'Five
Arches'. Open all times. Free.
Tenby Museum Notable collections of
geological specimens, seashells, and cave
deposits, illustrative of Tenby district and the
country generally. Picture gallery, topography
and other works of art. Open Jun to Oct, daily
10–6, Nov to May, daily 10–4. 15p (ch 5p). P.
(Tel 2809)
Tudor Merchant's House Quay Hill. Good
example of gabled 15th-C architecture,
ground floor of which is now National Trust
Information Centre, with exhibition of Tudor
period. Open 14 Apr to Sep, Mon to Fri 10–1
and 2.30–6, Sun 2–6. 20p (ch 10p). No dogs.
P. *(NT)*

TINTERN *Gwent* Map 3 SO50
Tintern Abbey Extensive remains of a fine
13th-C church founded for monks of the
Cistercian Order in 1131. Open*, see inside
front cover. 20p (ch 16 and pen 5p). ⚠ *(AM)*

TONGWYNLAIS *South Glamorgan*
Map 3 ST18
Castell Coch Restored 13th-C castle,
triangular in plan, with round towers at angles,
in Taff-side setting. Open*, see inside front
cover. 35p (ch and pen 17p); winter 20p (10p).
⚠ *(AM)*

TRE'R DDOL *Dyfed* Map 6 SN69
Yr Hen Gapel Off A487. A branch museum of
the National Museum of Wales, administered
by the Welsh Folk Museum. The museum
portrays 19th-C religious life in Wales. Open
Apr to Sep, Mon to Sat 10–5 (ex 4 Apr and
May Day). &

TRETOWER *Powys* Map 3 SO12
Tretower Court and Castle Remains of a
14th- to 15th-C Welsh fortified manor house,
with nearby ruined Norman and 13th-C
castle, noted for its cylindrical keep. Open,
see inside front cover. 15p (ch 16 and pen 7p).
⚠ *(AM)*

TYWYN *Gwynedd* Map 6 SH50
Narrow-Gauge Railway Museum This
interesting small museum is located in the
Talyllyn Railway Wharf station yard, Neptune
Road. A number of locomotives and wagons
are on display. ⚲ Open Easter to Oct, Mon to

Fri 10–5, Sat and Sun, 11–5. Closes at 6 Jul
and Aug. Nov to Mar by arrangement. 15p (ch
14 5p) subject to revision. P. *(Tel 710472)* ⅋
Talyllyn Railway The oldest 2ft 3in gauge
railway in the world. Steam operated. Built
1865 and became first railway to be saved by
a voluntary preservation society. Runs 7¼
miles, from Tywyn to Nant Gwernol. ⚏
Regular daily (ex Oct) services Easter to Oct.
Timetables available. Fares for return journey
£1.40 (ch 15 70p, pen £1), subject to revision.
P. *(Tel 710472)* ⅋ (limited)

WELSHPOOL *Powys* Map 7 SJ20
Powis Castle On S edge of Welshpool,
pedestrians' access from High Street (A490),
cars 1m along main road to Newton A483 take
signposted route to Waterloo. Medieval castle
with late 16th-C plasterwork and panelling,
contents include paintings, tapestries, early
Georgian furniture and relics of Clive of India,
early 18th-C terraced garden and woodland
garden. Shop. ⚏ Open 5 to 7 Apr then 1 May
to 28 Sep, Wed to Sun, Castle 2–6, garden
1–6. Castle and garden open each BH Mon
11.30–6 (last admission 5.30). Castle and
garden £1.10 (ch 60p). Castle only 70p (ch
30p), garden only 70p (ch 30p). Children not
admitted unless accompanied by an adult. ⚠
(Tel Welshpool 2554). *(NT)*
Powysland Museum Opened in 1874, the
museum illustrates the social history of the
Powysland region through archaeological,
domestic, agricultural and craft material. It
contains many notable items such as Iron Age
shield, a model of a guillotine and a fine
collection of hatchments. Open all year,
Easter week, then Jun to Sep Mon to Fri
11–1, 2–5, Sat 2–4.30; other times as
summer opening but closed Wed. Free. P.
(Tel 3001) ⅋ *(please ring)*

WHITE CASTLE *Gwent* Map 3 SO41
An impressive 12th- to 13th-C Marcher
stronghold situated on a hill, with a gatehouse
and towers, erected by Hubert de Burgh.
Open, see inside front cover. 15p (ch 16 and
pen 7p). ⚠ The finest of the trio of 'trilateral'
castles in Gwent. See **Grosmont** and
Skenfrith Castles. *(AM)*

WOLVESNEWTON *Gwent* Map 3 ST49
*Wolvesnewton Folk Museum and Craft
Centre* 1½m off B4235 at Llangwm. Late 18th-
C cruciform barn housing a collection of
unusual and entertaining items used in
everyday life from the reign of Queen Victoria
onwards. Also agricultural implements, a
Victorian bedroom, Doulton pottery, a
medical section, Victorian lithographs and
photographs, children's toys and games.
Mementos of two world wars. Craft
workshops, gift shop, antiques showroom, ⚏
(licensed). Entertainment evenings, one-day
craft courses, exhibitions, work sheets for
children. Open Easter to 30 Sep daily 11–6, 1
Oct to Easter Sun 2–5.30. 40p (ch 20p).
Under revision for 1980. Special
arrangements for parties. ⚠ ⅋

WONASTOW *Gwent* Map 3 SO41
Tre-Owen Four-storeyed manor house
dating from mid 16th-C, now farm. Contains a
notable staircase. Open May to Aug, by
appointment only. 40p (ch 15 30p, open 20p).
⚠ Apply to the owner, *Mr R H Wheelock. (Tel
Dingestow 224)*

WREXHAM *Clwyd* Map 7 SJ35
The Doll and Toy Museum Ruabon Road.
Housed in detached residence, built in 1830,
is a large collection of Georgian, Victorian and
Edwardian dolls, miniature furniture including
beds and cradles. All in lovely settings.
Mechanical toys, rocking horses, money
boxes, birds' eggs, over 3,500 items. A
display of Victorian suits, dresses, furs, fans
and lace. Garden. Play and picnic area. Open
daily (ex Nov) 10.30–6. 35p (ch 25p). ⚠ *(Tel
52623)* ⅋
Erddig 1m S. Late 17th-C house with 18th-C
additions and containing much of its original
furniture. Garden restored to its 18th-C formal
design. The range of domestic out-buildings
include laundry, bakehouse, sawmill and
smithy, all in working order. ⚏ Open 4 Apr to
26 Oct, Agricultural museum 5 Jul to 26 Oct.
Daily (ex Mon but open BH Mon). 12–5.30
(last admission to house 4.30, Oct 3.30).
£1.20 (ch 60p). Outbuildings and garden only
60p (ch 30p). Agricultural museum 50p (ch
25p). *(NT)*

SCOTLAND

P.K.Fry

Ancient Monuments
For monuments in the care of the Secretary of State for Scotland, opening times and entry fees are under review and changes may be made during the current year.

ABERDEEN Grampian *Aberdeenshire* Map 15 NJ90

Aberdeen Art Gallery and Museums Schoolhill. Scottish art from 16th C to present day, with outstanding collection of 20th-C painting. Water-colours, print-room, and art library; contemporary sculpture and decorative arts; special exhibitions and events throughout the year. 🎨 Open all year (ex 25, 26 Dec and 1, 2 Jan) Mon to Sat 10 – 5 (8 Thu) Sun 2 – 5. Free. P. *(Tel 53517).* &

Cruickshank Botanic Gardens University of Aberdeen. First developed at the end of the 19th C, the 7 acres of mature garden include rock and water gardens, a heather garden, collections of spring bulbs, gentians and alpine plants and, under glass, succulent plants. There are also extensive collections of trees and shrubs, of both horticultural and botanical interest. Open all year Mon to Fri 9 – 5; also Sat and Sun May to Sep 2 – 5. Free. *(Tel 40241 ext 340 or 348)* &

James Dun's House 61 Schoolhill. 18th-C house used as a museum for children with a programme of changing exhibitions. Open all year (ex 25, 26 Dec and 1, 2 Jan) Mon to Sat 10 – 5. Free. P. *(Tel 22234)*

Provost Ross's House Shiprow. Due to open in 1980 as a maritime museum. Contact Aberdeen District Council for details.

Provost Skene's House Guestrow. A 17th-C house restored as a museum of local history and social life. Furnishings, panelling, and plaster ceilings of 17th and 18th C. Local bygones. 🎨 Open all year (ex 25, 26 Dec and 1, 2 Jan) Mon to Sat 10 – 5. 10p (ch 12 and pen 2p). P. *(Tel 50086).*

ABERDOUR Fife *Fife* Map 11 NT18
Aberdour Castle A 14th- to 17th-C stronghold, still partly roofed. Fine circular dovecote and gardens. Open Apr to Sep, weekdays 9.30 – 7, Sun 2 – 7; Oct to Mar, weekdays 9.30 – 4, Sun 2 – 4. 15p (ch 7p). ⚠ *(AM)*

Inchcolm Abbey Remains of an Augustinian Abbey, founded c1123 by Alexander I which are situated on a green island in the Firth of Forth, S of Aberdour. The monastic buildings thought to be the best preserved in Scotland, include a fine 13th-C octagonal Chapter House. In the original choir a fine example of a 13th-C wall painting was discovered, depicting a funeral procession of clerics. Open, see inside front cover. 15p (ch 7p). No boat service at present. *(Tel Dalgety Bay 823332) (AM)*

ABERLADY Lothian *East Lothian* Map 12 NT47
Myreton Motor Museum A collection of historic motor cars and motorcycles from 1896, cycles from 1863 and commercial vehicles. Many famous and obscure makes, latest addition is a rapidly expanding collection of historic British military vehicles. Largest motor museum in Scotland. Open Easter to Oct, daily 10 – 6; Oct to Easter, Sat and Sun 10 – 5. 50p (ch 16 10p) (subject to review). ⚠ *(Tel 288)* &
See also under **Dunbar**.

ABERNETHY Tayside *Perthshire* Map 11 NO11
Abernethy Round Tower 11th- or 12th-C

Round Tower, 74ft high, one of only two examples on Scottish mainland, the other being at Brechin (Angus). Pictish symbol stone stands near by. Open, see inside front cover. Apply to Custodian. Free. *(AM)*

ALFORD Grampian *Aberdeenshire* Map 15 NJ51
Alford Valley Railway Narrow gauge passenger railway located in Haughton Park. 1½ miles of track through nature trails and historic battlefield. Diesel traction with possible addition of steam-hauled trains. Open 1 May to 9 Sep, Sat, Sun, BH and PH 1 – 7. 70p return fare (ch and pen 35p, ch 3 free). ⚠ *(Tel Cruden Bay 410 and Alford 2045)* &

ALLOWAY Strathclyde *Ayrshire* Map 10 NS31
Burns Cottage Thatched cottage, built in 1757, now museum, birthplace in 1759 of Robert Burns. 🎨 Open all year, Apr to mid Oct Mon to Sat 9 – 7, Sun, Mar, Apr, May, Sep, Oct 2 – 7, Jun, Jul and Aug 11 – 7. Closing time 7 or dusk if earlier. P. (100 yds) Also **Burns Monument**. Built in 1823 to a design by Thomas Hamilton Junior with fine examples of sculptures of characters in Burns' poems by a self-taught artist, James Thorn. Open as cottage. Admission to both properties 30p (ch and pen 15p). Admission prices under revision for 1980. P. *(Tel 41215 for cottage or 41321 for monument).* &

ANNAN Dumfries and Galloway *Dumfries-shire* Map 11 NY16
Kinmount Gardens Gardens and signed woodland walks of ½hr, 1 hr and 2hr duration. Rhododendrons and azaleas in May and Jun. Picnic area. Open 1 Apr to 1 Oct 9 – 5. 25p (ch 10, 10p). ⚠ *(Tel Cummertrees 207)*

ANSTRUTHER Fife *Fife* Map 12 NO50
The Scottish Fisheries Museum St Ayles. A 14th- to 18th-C group of buildings around a cobbled courtyard. Contains fishing boats and gear, fisherman's house c1900, a marine aquarium and a Lecture Hall for special displays. Awarded Architectural Heritage Year Award in 1975. 🎨 Open Apr to Oct, Mon to Sat 10 – 12.30 and 2 – 6, Sun 2 – 5; Nov to Mar, daily (ex Tue) 2 – 5. 40p (ch and pen 20p). ⚠ *(Tel 310628)*

ARBROATH Tayside *Angus* Map 12 NO64
Arbroath Abbey Remains of a Tironensian Monastery founded in 1176 by William the Lion, King of Scotland. Considerable portions of the cruciform abbey remain, and the Abbot's house has been restored as a museum. Open, see inside front cover. 20p (ch 10p). *(AM)*

Art Gallery Hill Terrace. General art collection with emphasis on local artists. Also collection of pastels and watercolours by J W Herald. Occasional travelling exhibitions. Open all year (ex Public and Local Hols) Mon to Fri 9.30 – 6, Sat 9.30 – 5. Free. P. *(Tel 72248)*

Signal Tower Museum Ladyloan. Collection of local history and natural history. Open all year Mon to Sat 9.30 – 1 and 2 – 5. Free. ⚠ *(Tel 75598).*

ARDCLACH Highland *Nairnshire* Map 14 NH94
Ardclach Bell Tower Two-storeyed 14ft-square tower, with upper floor containing fireplace and shot hole. Belfry on side gable built to house the bell formerly used as a warning, or for church services. Built probably in 17th C. Accessible on application to key keeper. Free. *(AM)*

ARDFERN Strathclyde *Argyll* Map 10 NM80
Argyll Wildlife Park Lunga Reserve.
Presented in a natural setting on a small hill
with an area of old Caledonian Oak woodland
and marshland. Visitors will find birds,
mammals, trees, plants etc, formerly or
currently native to Scotland. Education and
Conservation are primary objectives with
guided tours provided whenever possible.
Open Easter to Sep daily, 11–5. 80p (ch 40p).
Party
ARDWELL Dumfries and Galloway
Wigtownshire Map 10 NX14
Ardwell House Gardens Country house
gardens and grounds with flowering shrubs
and woodland walks. House not open to
public. Gardens open March to Oct 10–6.
Voluntary donations. ⚠
AUCHINDRAIN Strathclyde *Argyll*
Map 10 NN00
Open-Air Museum A folk life museum on
ancient Communal-tenancy farm. Original
18th and 19th-C buildings being restored and
furnished. Traditional crops and livestock,
also a display centre. Picnic area and craft
shop. ☭ (Egon Roney listed). Open Easter to
30 Sep (other times by appointment), Mon to
Sat 10–6, Sun 2–6. 45p (ch 20p). Admission
prices under review for 1980. ⚠
AUCHINLECK Strathclyde *Ayrshire*
Map 11 NS52
*Auchinleck Boswell Museum and
Mausoleum* Church Hill off A76. The Boswell
Museum was the family seat of the Boswells
whose most famous member was James
Boswell 1740–1795. The Biographer of Dr
Johnson, author of the *'Tour of the Hebrides'*
etc. The old parish church, of which a portion
dates back to c 900AD, is where the family
worshipped and is now the museum
containing books, manuscripts, portraits,
china and etc of Boswelliana. Attached to the
north wall is the Mausoleum where five known
generations of Boswells are buried. 10th
Annual Boswell dinner 22 Aug. Open Aug and
Sep 10–12, 2–4, (evenings by appointment)
Sun 2–4. Free. ⚠ P (coaches). Curator at
131 Main Street. *(Tel Cumnock 20757)* & B
AUCHTERARDER Tayside *Perthshire*
Map 11 NN91
Strathallan Aircraft Collection The
collection includes various vintage aircraft
including, Hurricane, Harvard, Hudson, Tiger
Moth, Anson, Mosquito and Lancaster,
collected from all over the world. Air display
proposed 12/13 Jul. Open daily 10–5 (or
dusk during winter months). 80p (ch 30p).
Party. ⚠ *(Tel 2545)* ⚠
AULDEARN Highland *Nairnshire*
Map 14 NH95
Boath Doocot A circular 17th-C doocot or
dovecot. The standard of Charles I was raised
here, in the battle of Auldearn in 1645. Doocot
itself closed. 10p. Battle plan on display
outside. *(NTS)*

AYR Strathclyde *Ayrshire* Map 10 NS32
Tam O'Shanter Museum This is considered
to be the point where Tam O'Shanter's
memorable ride commenced. The house now
contains relics belonging to Robert Burns.
Open Apr to Sep Mon to Sat 9.30–5.30; Oct
to Mar Mon to Sat 12–4, also Sun Jun, Jul and
Aug 2.30–5. 21p (ch 10p).

BALERNO Lothian *Midlothian* Map 11 NT16
Malleny Garden Off Bavelaw Road. A
delightfully personal garden, with shrub roses
and shaped yews. Open 1 May to 30 Sep daily
10–dusk. 30p (ch 15p). ⚠ & *(NTS)*

BALLATER Grampian *Aberdeenshire*
Map 15 NO39
McEwan Gallery 1 m NW on A939. Built by
the Swiss artist Rudolf Christian in 1902. All
paintings in the main gallery are for sale.
Open all year, Mon to Sat 10–6, Sun 2.30–5.
Free. ⚠ *(Tel 429)* ⚠

P.K.F.

BALLOCH Strathclyde *Dunbartonshire*
Map 10 NS38
Balloch Castle Park Situated on the shore of
the loch, with large area of grassland, suitable
for picnics and surrounded by extensive
woodlands. Views of the Loch from the Castle
terrace (c1800). Walled garden. Nature trail.
Open all year daily. Park 8 to dusk; garden
10–9 (4.30 winter). Free. ⚠
Cameron Loch Lomond 1 m NW. Drive in
your car amongst different species of bears,
bison, yak and deer which roam freely in the
acres of parkland. Other attractions include
the children's zoo, waterfowl sanctuary,
landscaped gardens, adventure playground,
children's assault course, giant slide, paddle
boats, canoes, trampolines etc. Lochside
picnic and play areas, ☭ and shops. Also
Cameron House, home of the Smolletts of
Bonhill. Contains artifacts and documents
collected by the family for over 300 years,
including 'Whisky Galore' room, Staffordshire
pottery collection, fine porcelain, pictures,
furniture, armour, Oriental curios, nursery
with children's toys and books. Tobias
Smollett Museum. Open Easter to Sep, daily,
10.30–6. Entrance off unclass road on
lochside. £2.50 per car and occupants.
Cameron House extra. 50p (ch 25p).
Kennels. ⚠ *(Tel Alexandria 57211)*

BALMACARA Highland *Ross and Cromarty*
Map 14 NG82
Visitor Centre Situated in magnificent stretch
of West Highland mountainous scenery,
including Five Sisters of Kintail and Beinn
Fhada. Self-guided and guided walks from
Balmacara on the Kyle to Plockton Peninsula.
Ranger Naturalist Service. Woodland Garden
open all year, daily. Kiosk open 1 Jun to 30
Sep, Mon to Sat 10 – 1 and 2 – 6. Woodlands
20p (ch 10p). *(Tel 207)*. (NTS)

BALMORAL Grampian *Aberdeenshire*
Map 15 NO29
Balmoral Castle Grounds The Highland
residence of Her Majesty the Queen.
Beautiful Deeside forest setting. In the
absence of the Royal Family, the grounds
only are open from 1 May to 31 Jul, daily (ex
Sun) 10 – 5. ☕ 35p (ch 10p). Donations to
charities from charges. P (400 yds). *(Tel
Crathie 334)* ♿ (cars for ♿ allowed to enter by
separate entrance)

BANCHORY Grampian *Kincardineshire*
Map 15 NO69
Banchory Museum Council Chamber.
Exhibition of local history and bygones. Open
Jun to end Sep daily (ex Thu) 2 – 5, Sat
10 – 12. *(Tel Peterhead 2554)* ♿

BANFF Grampian *Banffshire* Map 15 NJ66
Duff House ½m S, access from bypass south
of the town. Designed by William Adam for
William Duff (later Earl of Fife). The main
block was roofed in 1739, but proposed wings
were never built. Although incomplete it ranks
among the finest works of Georgian Baroque
architecture in Britain. An exhibition,
illustrating the history of the house can also be
seen. Open Apr to Sep. Mon to Sat 9.30 – 7,
Sun 2 – 7. 15p (ch 7p). *(AM)*
Banff Museum Exhibition of British birds set
out as an aviary. Local history also costumes
on show. Open Jun to end Sep, Wed, Fri, Sat,
Sun 2 – 5. Free. P. *(Tel Peterhead 2554)*

BANNOCKBURN Central *Stirlingshire*
Map 11 NS89
Bannockburn Monument This is the
Borestone Site, by tradition King Robert the
Bruce's command post before the battle
(1314). Bruce is commemorated by a bronze
equestrian statue. Rotunda and site always
open. Visitor centre and historical exposition
in sound and colour, open 4 Apr to 30 Sep,
Mon to Sat 10 – 6 (7, Jul and Aug); also Sun
Jul and Aug 11 – 7. Admission to exhibition
65p (ch 30p). ⚠ 10p. *(Tel 2664)*. (NTS)

BATHGATE Lothian *West Lothian*
Map 11 NS96
*Cairnpapple Hill Sanctuary and Burial
Cairn* 2m N. Monumental temple, in the form
of a stone circle and ditch, of several dates in
the prehistoric period, notably the second
millenium BC. It was recently excavated and
laid out. Open Apr to Sep, weekdays 9.30 – 7.
Sun 2 – 7; closed 1½ days per week. 15p (ch
7p). *(AM)*

BEAULY Highland *Inverness-shire*
Map 14 NH54
Beauly Priory Founded in 1230, one of three
houses of the Valliscaulian Order founded in
Scotland. Only the church remains, a long
narrow building comprising aisleless nave,
transepts and chancel. This is the burial place
of the Mackenzies of Kintail and contains the
fine monument of Sir Kenneth Mackenzie.
Open, see inside front cover. Closed Sat and
Sun. 15p (ch 7p). *(AM)*

BENMORE Strathclyde *Argyll* Map 12 NS18
Benmore Younger Botanic Garden
Woodland and garden on a grand scale,
featuring conifers, rhododendrons, azaleas,
and many other shrubs. ☕ (teas). Open from
Apr to Oct, daily 10 – 6. 10p (ch and pen 5p).
⚠ 5p. Under revision for 1980. *(Tel 036-
985 261)* ♿

BERRIEDALE Highland *Caithness*
Map 15 ND12
Langwell A residence of the Duchess of
Portland, which has fine gardens showing
plant growth in exposed areas. The gardens
only are shown 2 – 7. Dates for 1980 not
available. (Op ch 12 and pen 10p). ⚠ 20p. ☕
(Tel Barrock 275) ♿

BETTYHILL Highland *Caithness*
Map 14 NC76
Strathnaver Museum Fine stone-built, white
harled building, formerly a church, in an area
of outstanding beauty. It contains a
magnificent pitch pine canopied pulpit dated
1774, a fine collection of home-made
furnishings, domestic and farm implements
and Gaelic books. The churchyard contains a
carved stone known as the Farr Stone dating
back to the 10th-C. Open 1st week in Jun to
end Sep, Mon to Sat 2 – 5.30p (ch 10p).
Provisional dates for 1980. P. ♿

BIGGAR Strathclyde *Lanarkshire*
Map 11 NT03
Gladstone Court Museum Entrance by 113
High Street. Interesting museum which
portrays an old-world village street, housed in
century-old coachworks with modern
extension. On display are reconstructed old
shops, complete with fascinating signs and
adverts, a bank, telephone exchange,
photographer's booth, etc. Archive material
on Thomas Blackwood Murray, founder of
Albion Motors. The museum owns an early
Albion Tipper Lorry and organises a
commemorative run for vintage and veteran
vehicles annually in mid Aug. Work has
started on an open-air development which will
include a Gas Works (1839) and other
industrial agricultural buildings. The 17th-C
Covenanter's Farmhouse of Greenhill is
currently being rebuilt at the open-air site.
Museum shop. Open Easter to 31 Oct, daily
(ex Sun morning and local holidays)
10 – 12.30, 2 – 5; other times by appointment.
40p (ch 20p, ch 8 free). P. *(Tel 20005)* ♿

BLAIR ATHOLL Tayside *Perthshire*
Map 14 NN86
Blair Castle Of 13th-C origin, altered in the
18th-C, and later given a castellated exterior.
There are Renaissance-style furnishings,
paintings, Jacobite relics, china, and arms
displayed in 32 rooms. It is the home of the
Duke of Atholl. ☕ Open Easter weekend,
each Sun and Mon in Apr, afterwards daily,
from first Sun in May to second Sun in Oct,
Mon to Sat 10 – 6, Sun 2 – 6; no admission
after 5.30pm. Prices under revision for 1980.
Party. ⚠ *(Tel 355)* ♿

BLAIR DRUMMOND Central *Perthshire*
Map 11 NS79
Scotland's Safari Park Exit 10 off M9, A84
between Doune and Stirling. Features, free in
natural surroundings, wild animals, including
lions, giraffes, buffalo, ankole, eland, zebras,
camels, elephants, monkeys and
chimpanzees, Siberian tiger reserve. Also
pets corner, boat safari, aquatic mammal
show and Astra glide (extra charges).
Amusement and picnic areas. ☕ (Licensed).
Kennels at entrance. Open mid-Mar to end of

Oct, daily from 10am. Prices not available for 1980. ⚠ petrol station *(Tel Doune 456)* ⅃

BLANTYRE Strathclyde *Lanarkshire*
Map 11 NS65
The David Livingstone Centre with 'The Livingstone Memorial'. The birthplace of David Livingstone in 1813 containing personal relics, tableaux and working models. The 'Africa Pavilion' with exhibition describing life in modern Africa and 'Shuttle Row (Social History) Museum'. ⚏ (Apr to Sep). Picnic area. Gardens. Open all year Mon to Sat 10–6, Sun 2–6. 45p (ch and pen 25p). ⚠ *(Tel 823140)* ⅃ B

BOAT OF GARTEN Highland *Inverness-shire* Map 14 NH91
Strathspey Railway The Station. Steam railway covering the five miles from Boat of Garten to Aviemore, a twenty-minute journey. Trains can also be boarded at Aviemore where the station is under construction. Open 17 May to 28 Sep Sat and Sun, also Tue, Wed and Thu 1 Jul to 28 Aug. Family fares, party bookings. Basic return fare £1. ⚠ at Boat of Garten; P 600 yds at Aviemore. *(Tel 692)* ⅃

BO'NESS Central *West Lothian* Map 11 NS98
Kinneil House Situated in a public park, and preserving 16th- and 17th-C wall paintings. Open, see inside front cover. 15p (ch 7p). ⚠ *(AM)*
Kinneil Museum Situated in the 17th-C stable block of Kinneil House, part of a complex of renovated buildings. The ground floor houses regularly changing temporary exhibitions, while the main display on the first floor illustrates the industrial heritage of Bo'ness. Lecture room for educational purposes. Open all year May to Oct, Mon to Sat 10–12 and 1–5. Nov to Apr, Mon, Wed and Fri 10–12 and 1–5. Sat 1–5. Free. ⅃ B

BOTHWELL Strathclyde *Lanarkshire*
Map 11 NS75
Bothwell Castle An impressive, ruined 13th- to 15th-C stronghold. Open Oct to Mar (ex Thu pm and all day Fri); Apr to Sep open all week. Entrance to castle is at Uddington Cross by traffic lights. 15p (ch 7p). ⚠ *(AM)*

BRAEMAR Grampian *Aberdeenshire*
Map 15 NO19
Braemar Castle A picturesque castle, built in 1628; purchased by the Farquharson of Invercauld in 1731. Largely rebuilt in 1748, spiral stone staircase leading to the principle rooms. Situated near the River Dee. *Son et Lumière* late Aug/early Sep. Open May to early Oct, daily 10–6. 60p (ch 13 25p). Provisional for 1980. ⚠ *(Tel 219). (Capt AAC Farquharson of Invercauld)*

BRODIE CASTLE Grampian *Morayshire*
Map 14 NH95
6m E of Nairn, off A96. Largely rebuilt after being burned down in 1645 and with additions of the 18th and 19th centuries. Contents include fine furniture, porcelain and paintings. Opening Jun (provisional date) to 30 Sep, Mon to Sat 11–6, Sun 2–6. 85p (ch 40p). *(To check details Tel Udny 352). (NTS)*

BROUGHTON Borders *Peeblesshire*
Map 11 NT13
Broughton Place Built on the site of a much older house and designed by Sir Basil Spence in 1938, the house is in the style of a 17th-C Scottish tower house. The drawing room and main hall are open to the public and contain paintings by living British artists for sale. The gardens, which are occasionally

open under Scotland's Gardens Scheme, afford fine views of the Tweeddale hills. Open, Easter to end Sep daily (ex Wed) 10.30–6. Free. ⚠ *(Tel 234)* ⅃ B

BRUAR Tayside *Perthshire* Map 14 NN86
Clan Donnachaidh (Robertson) Museum
A newly founded small museum for items of historical interest, documents, books and pictures associated with the Clan Donnachaidh, one of whose early chiefs fought for King Robert the Bruce. There is an interesting craft room. Open Easter to 15 Oct, Mon to Sat 10–5.30, Sun 2–5.30. At other times by arrangement with the curator. Clan gathering 3rd Sat in Jan. Clan items for sale. ⚠ *(Tel Clavine 264, or Curator's residence Clavine 222)* ⅃

BUCKIE Grampian *Banffshire* Map 15 NJ46
Buckie Museum and Peter Anson Gallery
Maritime museum opened in 1973 containing exhibits relating to the fishing industry in the Moray Firth area from mid 19th C to the present day. Mr Peter Anson donated his collection of 400 pictures of fishing vessels, from the earliest times to modern dual purpose craft, to the museum. Open May to Sep, Mon 2–5, Tue to Sat 10–12.30, 2–5. Free. ⚠ *(Tel 31150)* ⅃

BURGHEAD Grampian *Moray* Map 15 NJ16
Burghead Museum 16–18 Grant Street. Illustrates the archaeology of the Laich of Mory from 2500 BC–1300 AD. Open Tues 5.30pm–8.30pm, Thu 2–5, Sat 9.30–12.30. Free. ⚠ *(Tel Forres 73701)*

CAERLAVEROCK Dumfries and Galloway *Dumfriesshire* Map 11 NY06
Caerlaverock Castle A famous medieval stronghold, besieged by Edward I in 1300. Mainly 14th to 15th-C, with a Renaissance wing of 1638. Open, see inside front cover. 25p (ch 12p). ⚠ *(AM)*
Wildfowl Trust Outstanding hide facilities, observation towers, and observatory, providing impressive views of the magnificent flocks of barnacle, and pink-footed geese, and the large number of wigeon, pintail, etc, that spend most of the winter in the refuge. Open 1 Sep to 15 May (ex 24, 25 Dec). Guided tours 11 and 2 daily. 65p (ch 35p, pen 55p). ⚠ Party 20+ *(Tel Glencaple 200)*

CAIRNDOW Strathclyde *Argyll* Map 10 NN11
Strone House Gardens featuring rhododendrons, azaleas, conifers and daffodils. The tallest tree in Britain, measuring 190ft, is located within the gardens. Picnic area. Open 1 Apr to 30 Sep, 9–9. 30p (ch and pen free). ⚠ 20p *(Tel 284) (Rt Hon the Lord Glenkinglas PC).*

CALLANDER Central *Perthshire*
Map 11 NN60
Kilmahog Woollen Mill At one time thriving woollen mill, famous throughout the district for hand-woven blankets and tweed. Part of the old structure can be seen, also an old water wheel which has been preserved and is still in working order. Woollens can be purchased in the store. Open all year Mon to Fri 9–8, Sat and Sun 9–6. ⚠ *(Tel 30268)* ⅃

CARDONESS CASTLE Dumfries and Galloway *Kirkcudbrightshire* Map 11 NX55
A late 15th-C stronghold, overlooking Fleet Bay, once home of the McCullochs of Galloway. Notable fireplaces. Open from Apr to Sep, weekdays 9.30–7 (Sun 2–7); from Oct to Mar 9.30–4 (Sun 2–4). 20p (ch 10p). ⚠ *(AM)*

CARNASSERIE CASTLE Strathclyde *Argyll*
Map 10 NM80
Built in the late 16th C by John Carswell, first
Protestant Bishop of the Isles, who translated
into Gaelic and published Knox's *Liturgy* in
1567. It was taken and partly destroyed in
Argyll's rebellion of 1685, and consists of a
towerhouse, with a courtyard built on to it.
Open, see inside front cover. Free. *(AM)*

CARRADALE Strathclyde *Argyll*
Map 10 NR83
Carradale House Off B879. Overlooks the
lovely Kilbrennen Sound. Beautiful gardens,
with flowering shrubs, mainly rhododendrons,
best visited Apr to Jun. Plants, vegetables
and shrubs for sale. Open from Apr to end of
Sep. 20p (ch 12 free). ⚠ *(Tel 234)* ⓬

CARRBRIDGE Highland *Inverness-shire*
Map 14 NH92
Landmark Europe's first 'visitor' centre, with
an exhibition on the history of Strathspey, a
multi-screen programme in the auditorium
showing in sound and vision the story of The
Highlands from the last Ice Age to the present
day, and evening film shows. Also craft and
bookshop, ⚄, nature trail, with picnic area,
open-air sculpture park. Open summer
9.30 – 10.30, winter 9.30 – 5. Admission to
Exhibition and Auditorium 60p (ch 30p). ⚠ ⓬

CARSLUITH CASTLE Dumfries and
Galloway *Kirkcudbrightshire* Map 11 NX45
A roofless 16th-C tower house on Wigtown
Bay. A previous owner was the last abbot of
Sweetheart Abbey. Entry free on application
to Custodian. Open, see inside front cover.
(AM)

CASTLE DOUGLAS Dumfries and Galloway
Kirkcudbrightshire Map 11 NX76
Threave Castle Follow A75 SW to Bridge of
Dee (3m) then take unclass rd to N. Standing
on an islet in the River Dee, this lonely castle,
erected by Archibald the Grim in the 14th C, is
four storeys in height, with round towers
guarding the outer wall. It was dismantled by
the Covenanters in 1640. Open Apr to Sep,
weekdays 9.30 – 7, Sun 2 – 7 Oct to Mar
weekdays 9.30 – 4, Sun 2 – 4. 20p (incl ferry)
(ch 10p). Access to castle is by rowing boat.
(AM)
Threave Gardens 1½m SW. Fine gardens
noted for daffodils in Apr and May, and
rhododendrons in May and Jun. Walled
garden and glasshouses. Open all year, daily
9 – sunset, walled garden and glasshouses
9 – 5. (The house is NTS School of
Gardening). Visitor centre open 1 Apr to 31
Oct. 75p (ch 35p). *(Tel 2575)*. *(NTS)*

CASTLES GIRNIGOE AND SINCLAIR
Highland *Caithness* Map 15 ND35
Two adjacent ruined castles of the Sinclairs,
in a striking rock setting at Noss Head,
Girnigoe is 15th-C and Sinclair dates from the
early 16th-C. After c1697 both castles were
abandoned. They can be seen at any time.
Free.

CASTLE KENNEDY Dumfries and Galloway
Wigtownshire Map 10 NX15
Castle Kennedy Gardens Situated 3m E of
Stranraer on A75. 17th-C and later gardens,
with a fine collection of rhododendrons,
azaleas, magnolias and other shrubs.
Situated on peninsula between two lochs, the
gardens offer a choice of walks. ⚄. Open 1
Apr to 26 Sep, daily (ex Sat) 10 – 5. 50p (ch 16
20p). Garden centre adjoining gardens. ⚠
(Tel Stranraer 2024) ⓬

CAUSEWAYHEAD Central *Stirlingshire*
Map 11 NS89
Wallace Monument 220ft-high tower erected
in 1869, in which Sir William Wallace's
famous two-handed sword is preserved. No
fewer than seven battlefields are visible from
the summit of the monument, in addition to a
wide panoramic view towards the Highlands.
There is a Hall of Heroes. Audio-visual
system on life of Wm Wallace. ⚄ & souvenirs.
Open all year Nov to Jan 10 – 4, Oct and Feb
10 – 5, Sep and Mar 10 – 6, Apr and Aug 10 – 7,
May to Jul 10 – 8. 15p (ch and pen 10p). Under
revision for 1980. Party. P at foot of Abbey
Craig. *(Tel Stirling 2140)*

CAWDOR Highland *Nairnshire* Map 14 NH84
Cawdor Castle Home of the Thanes of
Cawdor since the early 14th C. Home of the
present Earl of Cawdor, with its drawbridge,
its ancient tower built around a tree, and its
freshwater well inside the house, is a glorious
reminder of Scotland's colourful and often
bloody history. Nature trails, pitch and putt. ⚄
(licensed). Open 1 May to 30 Sep daily
10 – 5.30 (last admission 5 pm). Provisional
prices for 1980, £1.25 (ch 16 and pen 65p)
subject to alteration. Party 20+ £1 (ch 50p). ⚠
(Tel 615) ⓬

CLACKMANNAN Central
Clackmannanshire Map 11 NS99
Clackmannan Tower A fine 14th- and 15th-C
tower house, battlemented and turreted, and
at one time moated. Now under repair and not
open, but can be closely viewed from outside.
(AM)

CLAVA CAIRNS Highland *Inverness-shire*
Map 14 NH74
Situated on the south bank of the River Nairn,
this group of burial cairns has three concentric
rings of great stones. They are of late neolithic
or early Bronze Age. Open regularly. Free.

COLDSTREAM Borders *Berwickshire*
Map 12 NT84
Dundock Wood 1½m W on A697. Magnificent
display of rhododendrons and azaleas (mid
May to end of Jun depending on season). It is
also a large bird sanctuary. The wood and
grounds are open at all times. Estate
interpretation centre in Hirsel House grounds.
Nature walks. Admission by collecting box. ⚠
(Tel 2345 and 2439) ⓬

COLPY Grampian *Aberdeenshire*
Map 15 NJ63
Williamston House Attractive gardens, with
a lochan. Ancient St Michael's Well nearby.
Gardens open Jun to Sep, 10 – 7 daily. 20p
(ch 5p) by collection box at garden entrance.
Garden produce and plants for sale. Teas
available by prior arrangement. ⚠ *(Tel Colpy
227)*. *(Cdr M S L Burnett)*

COMRIE Tayside *Perthshire* Map 11 NN72
Museum of Scottish Tartans Occupies an
18th-C building situated in the centre of town
on the A85. The collection is the most
comprehensive in the world of books,
pictures, prints, maps and manuscripts
relating to the history and development of
Tartans and Highland Dress. Specialised
library, and research collection of over 1,300
specimens of Tartans, and a unique system
(Sindex) which records details of every known
tartan. Open all year, summer Mon to Sat
10 – 1, 2 – 5, Sun 2 – 5; winter weekdays
10.30 – 12.30, 2 – 4 (closed Sun). 35p (ch and
pen 20p). Party. Under revision for 1980. P.
(Tel 779) ⓬

CORGARFF Grampian *Aberdeenshire*
Map 15 NJ20
Corgarff Castle 16th-C tower, which was
besieged in 1571, and is associated with the
Jacobite Risings of 1715 and 1745. Later it
became a military barracks. Open Apr to Sep,
weekdays 9.30 – 7, Sun 2 – 7. 15p (ch 7p). ⚘
(AM)

CORSOCK Dumfries and Galloway
Kirkcudbrightshire Map 11 NX77
Corsock House Gardens Specialising in a
fine show of species rhododendrons,
woodland walks, and a water garden. Also
classical temples and bridge. View of the
valley of the River Urr. Open 2.30 – 5.30, each
Sun in May; other times by appointment. May
to Sep. 30p. ⚘ (small). *(Mr F L Ingall)*

CRAIGIEVAR Grampian *Aberdeenshire*
Map 15 NJ50
Craigievar Castle Unaltered tower house,
built 1610 to 1626, with a notable
Renaissance ceiling. Perhaps the most
characteristic example of the true Scottish
Baronial period. It enjoys a lovely setting
between the valleys of the Dee and the Don.
Castle open 1 May to 30 Sep, 2 – 7 daily (ex
Fri), last visitors 6.15. Grounds open all year,
9.30 – sunset. Castle 80p (ch 40p), school
parties 35p; grounds by donation. *(Tel
Lumphanan 635). (NTS)*

CRATHES Grampian *Kincardineshire*
Map 15 NO79
Crathes Castle and Gardens A picturesque
16th-C structure noted for its magnificent
painted ceilings and famous gardens. Castle
open May to Sep, Mon to Sat 11 – 6, Sun 2 – 6;
(last admission 5.15). Gardens and grounds

open daily all the year from 9.30 to dusk.
Castle only, 75p (ch 35p); gardens only 40p
(ch 20p); grounds and cars 60p, minibuses
£1.50, coaches £5, May to Sep only. *(Tel
525). (NTS)*

CREETOWN Dumfries and Galloway
Kirkcudbrightshire Map 11 NX45
*Creetown Gem Rock Museum and Art
Gallery* Largest private collection in Great
Britain with many of the exhibits collected by
the proprietors on their world travels. Also
extensive collection of walking sticks and
drinking mugs. Lapidary workshops open to
view. Craft shop and lapidary requirements
for sale. Open daily 9.30 – 6. 20p (ch 7 free, ch
7 – 16 5p). ⚘ *(Tel Creetown 357)* ♿

CRICHTON Lothian *Midlothian* Map 11 NT36
Crichton Castle A 14th- to 16th-C castle,
notable for the Earl of Bothwell's Italianate
wing. Open weekdays (ex Fri from Oct to
May), summer 9.30 – 7; winter 9.30 – 4; Sun,
summer 2 – 7; winter 2 – 4. 15p (ch 7p). *(AM)*

CRIEFF Tayside *Perthshire* Map 11 NN82
Innerpeffray Library 4½m SE of B8062. A
late 18th-C building, housing Scotland's
second oldest library founded in 1691 (the
oldest library founded in 1683 is at Kirkwall,
Orkney). Accessible all year weekdays (ex
Thu) 10 – 1 and 2 – 5 (4, Nov to Feb), Sun all
year 2 – 4. 30p (ch 10p). ⚘ *(Tel 2819)*

CROMARTY Highland *Ross and Cromarty*
Map 14 NH76
Hugh Miller's Cottage House c1711
birthplace in 1802 of Hugh Miller, the
geologist. Open 1 May to 30 Sep, Mon to Sat
10 – 12 and 1 – 5; Jun to Sep also Sun 2 – 5.
40p (ch 20p). *(Tel 245). (NTS)*

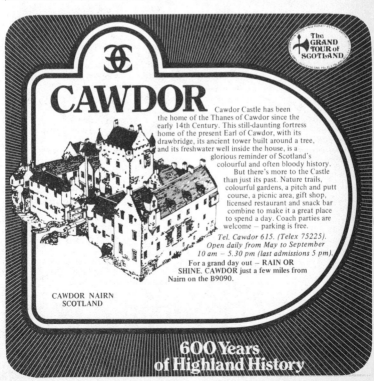

CULLODEN MOOR Highland *Inverness-shire* Map 14 NH74
Culloden Battlefield The Cairn, built in 1881, recalls the famous battle of 1746, when 'Bonnie' Prince Charles Edward Stuart's army was routed by the Duke of Cumberland's forces. Near the Graves of the Clans is the Well of the Dead, and also the Cumberland Stone. The battle fought around Old Leanach Farmhouse, now a museum. Site always open. There is also a Trust Visitor Centre and exhibition open 4 Apr to mid Oct Mon to Sat 9.30–6.30, Sun 2–6.30, except Jun to end Aug Mon to Sat 9.30–9.30, Sun 2–6.30. Admission to Visitor Centre and museum (includes audio-visual exhibition in centre and parking). 65p (ch 30p). Party 20+ 45p (ch 15p). ⚠ *(Tel 607).* (NTS)

CULROSS Fife *Fife* Map 11 NS98
Abbey Cistercian monastery founded by Malcolm, Earl of Fife in 1217. The choir is still used as the parish church and parts of the nave remain. Fine central tower, still complete, bears the arms of abbot Masoun (1498–1513). Open, see inside front cover. Free. *(AM)*

Culross Palace Dated 1597 and 1611, and noted for the painted rooms and walled gardens. Open, see inside front cover. 25p (ch 12p). *(AM)*

Dunimarle Castle Part of this castle is now a museum, with valuable paintings, silver, books, and rare items of furniture, once belonging to Napoleon. Open 1 Apr to 31 Oct, daily 11–6. 40p (ch 14 20p). ⚠ *(Tel Newmills 229)* ♿ B

CULZEAN CASTLE Strathclyde *Ayrshire* Map 10 NS21
18th-C castle, in a fine Firth of Clyde setting of 500 acres. The castle was designed by Robert Adam and contains fine plaster ceilings, a splendid central staircase, and a circular drawing room. There is a collection of portraits of the Kennedys, Earls of Cassillis, and Marquesses of Ailsa. Guest flat presented to the late General Eisenhower. Open 1 Apr to 30 Sep, daily 10–6 (last admission 5.30). Oct daily 10–4. £1 (ch 50p), party 75p per person, schools 50p per person. Jul and Aug £1.20 (ch 60p). No party reduction. *(Tel Kirkoswald 236).* (NTS)

CULZEAN COUNTRY PARK Strathclyde *Ayrshire* Map 10 NS21
565 acres including 1783 walled garden, camellia house, orangery, swan pond, aviary. The home farm buildings by Robert Adam have been converted into a Reception and Interpretation Centre. Park open all year. Centre 1 Apr to end Sep daily 10–6; Oct daily 10–4. Admission charges not yet decided. *(NTS)*

CUPAR Fife *Fife* Map 11 NO31
Hill of Tarvit Mansion House and Garden 2m S off A916. A mansion house remodelled in 1906 by Sir Robert Lorimer, with a notable collection of furniture, tapestries and paintings. Open 4 to 7 Apr, then 1 May to 30 Sep daily (ex Fri) 2–6, last admission 5.30. Gardens and grounds (ex arable land) open all year 10–dusk. House and gardens 85p (ch 40p); gardens only 30p (ch 15p). *(Tel 3127).* (NTS)

DOLLAR Central *Clackmannanshire* Map 11 NS99
Castle Campbell and Dollar Glen 1m N. 15th-C tower with 16th- and 17th-C additions, in a picturesque Ochil Hills setting above the Dollar Glen, providing splendid views. Open, see inside front cover. 20p (ch 10p). ⚠ *(Castle AM and Glen NTS)*

DORNIE Highland *Ross and Cromarty* Map 14 NG82
Eilean Donan Castle Stands at the meeting-point of Lochs Duich, Alsh, and Long. Connected to the mainland by a causeway. This Seaforth fortress, erected originally in 1220, was destroyed in 1719, after being held by Jacobite troops, and was restored in 1912. Beautiful mountain setting. Open Easter to end Sep, daily 10–6. 30p. P. *(Tel 202).* (Mr J D H MacRae)

DOUNE Central *Perthshire* Map 11 NN70
Doune Castle 14th-C stronghold, well restored, with two fine towers and associations with Bonnie Prince Charlie and Scott's *Waverley.* It stands on the banks of the River Teith. Open 1 Apr to 31 Oct, daily 10–6 (ex Thu in Apr and Oct). 40p (ch 20p). Under revision for 1980. ⚠ 5p. *(Tel 203).* (Earl of Moray)

Doune Motor Museum Situated 9m NW of Sterling on A84. Approximately 35 cars on display. Motor Racing Hill Climbs held in Apr, Jun and Sep. Picnic area, tourist shop and garden centre. Open 1 Apr to 31 Oct, daily. Admission prices not available. ⚠ Telephone for information. *(Tel 203)* ♿

DRUMCOLTRAN TOWER Dumfries and Galloway *Kirkcudbrightshire* Map 11 NX86
A 16th-C tower house, three-storeys in height and built to an oblong plan, with a projecting tower or wing. Standard hours, apply to key keeper. Free. *(AM)*

DRUMNADROCHIT Highland *Inverness-shire* Map 14 NH53
Urquhart Castle Historic, mainly 14th-C castle overlooking Loch Ness, destroyed before the 1715 Rising and possibly built originally by the Lords of the Isles. Open, see inside front cover. 25p (ch 12p). *(AM)*

DRYBURGH Borders *Berwickshire*
Map 12 NT53
Dryburgh Abbey One of the famous Border group of monasteries founded by David I. The ruins are of great beauty and occupy a lovely situation in a horseshoe bend of the River Tweed. Within the church are the graves of Sir Walter Scott and Earl Haig. Open, see inside front cover. 25p (ch 12p). ⚠ *(AM)*

DUFFTOWN Grampian *Banffshire*
Map 15 NJ33
Balvenie Castle Mainly 15th- and 16th-C, the ancient home of the Comyns, preserving a remarkable iron 'yett'. Open, see inside front cover. 15p (ch 7p). ⚠ *(AM)*
Dufftown Museum The Tower. Small local history museum. Civic regalia. Mortlach Kirk material. Open Jun to Sep daily 10–5 (7 Jul and Aug). *(Tel 501)*
Glenfiddich Distillery N of town, off A941. Situated by the 'Robbie Dubh' or 'Black Robert' stream, this distillery was founded in 1886 by Major William Grant in the heart of the Speyside country. A visitor's Reception Centre houses a bar and a Scotch whisky museum. Gift shop. Open 8 Jan to 23 Dec. Trained guides give tours Mon to Fri 9–5. Free. ⚠ *(Tel 375)*

DUFFUS Grampian *Moray* Map 15 NJ16
Duffus Castle Off B9012. Motte and bailey castle, with 8-acre bailey surrounding rebuilt 15th-C hall and 14th-C tower, now split into two halves. Open all reasonable times. Free. ⚠ *(AM)*

DUMBARTON Strathclyde *Dunbartonshire*
Map 10 NS37
Dumbarton Castle Atop 240ft high rock, with ancient gateway preserved. Associations with Mary, Queen of Scots. Open, see inside front cover. 20p (ch 10p). *(AM)*

DUMFRIES Dumfries and Galloway *Dumfriesshire* Map 11 NX97
Burns House Robert Burns died in this house in 1796. In the house are displayed memorials and personal relics of the poet. Open all year, 29 Mar to 30 Sep Mon to Sat 10–1, Sun 2–7, 1 Oct to 28 Mar Mon to Sat 10–12 and 2–5. 10p (ch 5p). P. *(Tel 5297)*
Burns Mausoleum St Michael's Churchyard. Situated here is the tomb of the poet, the mausoleum being in the form of a Grecian temple. Here also are buried Jean Armour, Burns' wife, and their five sons. A sculptured group depicts the Muse of Poetry throwing her cloak over Burns at the plough. Opens as Burns House by arrangement with Curator. P. *(Tel 5297)*

Dumfries Museum and Camera Obscura The Observatory, Church Street. Large collection of local history, archaeology, geology, local birds and animals. The Old Bridge House branch museum (on the Old Bridge) contains period rooms portraying the local way of life in the past. Open all year (Old Bridge House 1 Apr to 30 Sep only) Mon to Sat 10–1, 2–5 (ex Tue), Sun 2–5 Apr to Sep only. Museum and Old Bridge House free. Camera Obscura. 15p (ch 5p). P. *(Tel 3374)*
Lincluden College Originally the site of a Benedictine nunnery, founded by Uchtred, Lord of Galloway in 1164. This was suppressed at the end of the 14th C by Archibald the Grim, 3rd Earl of Douglas, who established in its place a college of eight secular canons under a provost. The present remains are that of the collegiate church, dating from the early 15th C and the provost's house, dating from the 16th C. Open, see inside front cover. 15p (ch 7p). *(AM)*

DUNBAR Lothian *East Lothian* Map 12 NT67
Myreton Motor Museum Castle Park. A branch of the museum founded at Aberlady. A collection of historic motor cars from 1896, motorcycles from 1903, cycles from 1863 and commercial vehicles. Many famous and obscure makes. Tractors, farm machinery and horse-drawn vehicles. Open Easter to Oct, daily 10–6. 40p (ch 14 10p), subject to alteration. ⚠ *(municipal). (Tel 62365)* &

DUNBEATH Highland *Caithness*
Map 15 ND12
Laidhay Croft Museum Late 18th- to early 19th-C Caithness-type longhouse with dwelling, byre and stable under one roof and detached winnowing barn. All thatched and furnished in typical croft style. Open Easter to 30 Sep daily 9–6. 30p (ch 14 and pen 15p). ⚠ &

DUNBLANE Central *Perthshire*
Map 11 NN70
Keir 2m S off B824. Beautiful gardens featuring rhododendrons, shrubs, herbaceous borders, and water gardens, which will be open 3 Apr to end of Oct, Tue, Wed, Thu 2–6. 40p. ⚠ *(Tel 822200). (Mrs W J Stirling of Keir)* &

DUNDEE Tayside *Angus* Map 11 NO43
Barrack Street Museum Ward Road. Shipping and industrial exhibits relating especially to local ships built at or associated with Dundee. There are also art and photographic exhibitions. Open from Mon to Sat 10–5.30; closed Sun. P. *(Tel 25492 & 3 ext 17 or 27866 for educational services)*

Broughty Castle and Museum Broughty
Ferry. 4m E. 15th-C castle rebuilt as an
estuary fort in the mid 19th C. Displays
relating to former Burgh of Broughty Ferry,
whaling, natural history of the Tay, arms and
armour, also Ecology Gallery. Open all year,
Mon to Sat (ex Fri) 10–1 and 2–5.30; Sun
(Jun to Sep only) 2–5. Free. ⚠

Museum and Art Gallery Albert Square.
Covers in depth local archaeology, history,
natural history, and geology. There is a
display devoted to the works of Mary Slessor,
the missionary. The Art Gallery portrays the
principal British and European masters. Open
from Mon to Sat 10–5.30; closed Sun. Free.
P. &

Claypotts Broughty Ferry. 4m E.
Claverhouse of Dundee's castle, of unusual
appearance, built between 1569 and 1588,
showing angle towers with crowstepped
gables. Open, see inside front cover (ex to
Apr 1980). 15p (ch 7p). *(AM)*

Mills Observatory Situated in Balgay Park
the observatory, erected in 1935, is equipped
with a 10in Cooke refracting telescope, and
two 4in Terrestrial telescopes. Open Apr to
end of Sep, Mon to Fri 2–7, Sat 2–5; Oct to
Mar, Mon to Fri 2–10, Sat 2–5. Closed Sun
and public hols. 5p (ch 2p). Family Party 8p.
⚠ & B

Orchar Art Gallery Beach Cresent, Broughty
Ferry. 4m E. The gallery displays oil-paintings
and water-colours mostly by Scottish artists of
the 19th C. Among the etchings are 36 by
Whistler. Open Mon to Sat (ex Fri) 10–1 and
2–5; Sun Jun to Sep only 2–5. Free. ⚠ *(Tel
77337)*

St Mary's Tower Kirk Style, Nethergait. A
15th-C bell tower or steeple containing a
magnificent peal of bells also displays
relevant to the Tower. Open Easter to Oct,
daily (ex Fri) 1–5, Sun 2–5. 5p (ch 2p).
Family Party 8p. P. *(Tel 25492/3 ext 16)*

Spalding Golf Museum Camperdown Park.
The museum in Camperdown House portrays
the history of golf through three centuries and
includes an iron club of *c*1680. ⚲ available at
Camberdown House. Open Mon to Thu and
Sat 1–5 (closed Fri), also Sun Easter to Oct
2–5. Free. ⚠ &

DUNDONNELL Highland *Ross and
Cromarty* Map 14 NH18
Dundonnell House 2m SE. An 18th-C
house, noted for its fine gardens, featuring
Chinese, Japanese, and other rare plants and
shrubs. Collection of exotic birds. Teas
available on open days. Times and dates
published by Scotland's Garden scheme and
in the press. ⚠ *(Tel 206)*. *(Messrs Alan, Neil
and Alastair Roger)*

DUNDRENNAN Dumfries and Galloway
Kirkcudbrightshire Map 11 NX74
Dundrennan Abbey The remains of a
Cistercian house founded by David I and
Fergus Lord of Galloway in 1142. Here Mary
Queen of Scotts spent her last night on native
soil before seeking shelter in England. Open,
see inside front cover. 20p (ch 10p). *(AM)*

DUNFERMLINE Fife Map 11 NT08
Andrew Carnegie Birthplace Junction of
Moodie Street and Priory Lane. The cottage in
which the great philanthropist was born in
1835. Personal relics, presentation caskets.
Roll of Honour of Carnegie Hero Fund Trust
displayed in a memorial Hall. Open May to
Aug, Mon to Sat 11–1 and 2–7, Sun 2–6;
Sep to Apr Mon to Sat 11–1 and 2–5, Sun
2–6. Street P. *(Tel 24302 or 23638)* &

Dunfermline Abbey Benedictine house
founded by Queen Margaret and the
foundations of her church remain beneath the
present Norman nave. The site of the choir is
now occupied by a modern parish church, at
the east end of which are remains of St
Margaret's shrine dating from the 13th C. King
Robert Bruce is buried in the choir and his
grave is marked by a modern brass. Guest
house was a Royal palace where Charles I
was born. Situated in Pittencrieff Park. Open,
see inside front cover. Free. *(AM)*

Dunfermline Museum Viewfield Terrace.
Interesting and varied displays of local
history, domestic bygones and damask linen.
Periodic special exhibitions. Open 1 Apr to 30
Sep Mon to Sat (ex Tue) 11–5, Sun 1–5; Oct
to 31 Mar Wed to Sat 11–5, Sun 1–5. Free.
⚠ *(Tel 21814)*

Pittencrieff House Museum Situated in a
rugged glen, with lawns, hothouses, and
gardens, overlooked by the ruined 11th-C
Malcolm Canmore's tower. Fine 17th-C
mansion house, with costume and art
galleries. Views of Forth estuary and
Dunfermline Abbey. Open May to Sep Mon to
Sat (ex Tue) 11–5; Sun 1–5. ⚠ *(Tel 21814)*

DUNKELD Tayside *Perthshire* Map 11 NO04
Loch of Lowes Wild Life Reserve Variety of
wild life. Great crested grebes and other
waterfowl in natural surroundings can be
watched through high powered binoculars
from observation hide. Exhibition and slide
programme in visitor centre. Open Apr to Sep,
daily 10–7 Apr, May and Sep; 10–8.30 Jun to
Aug. Hide open all times. Free. Special
arrangements for parties booked in advance.
⚠ limited. *(Tel 337, Apr to Sep, or Ballinluig
267 Oct to Mar)*

Trust Visitor Centre 'Little Houses' dating
from the rebuilding of village after the Battle of
Dunkeld in 1689. Restoration undertaken by
NTS and Perth County Council who received
a Saltire Society award in 1958. Visitor Centre
open 4 Apr to 30 Sep 10–6, Sun 2–6. Free.
(Tel 460). *(NTS)*

DUNS Borders *Berwickshire* Map 12 NT75
Jim Clark Room This room in Newtown
Street contains motor racing trophies won by
the famous driver Jim Clark, who was killed in
Germany in 1968. Included are the two world
Championship Trophies of 1963 and 1965
and other Grand Prix awards. Clark was the
only Honorary Burgess of Duns and his
parents gifted the trophies to the town. Open
Apr to Sep Mon to Sat 10–1, 2–6, Sun 2–6.
30p (ch 16 15p). Parties during winter by
special arrangement. Jim Clark Memorial
Rally Jul. Under revision for 1980. P.
Manderston 1½m E off A6105. A fine
Edwardian house with magnificent State
Rooms and extensive domestic offices, all
completed in 1905, emphasising a high
standard of workmanship. Stables, marble
dairy, gardens, woodland garden and
lakeside walks. ⚲ Open 18 May to 18 Sep,
Sun and Thu 2–5.30, also Scottish and
English BHs. Charges not available. ⚠ *(Tel
3450)* &

EASDALE Strathclyde *Argyll* Map 10 NM71
An Cala Garden Featuring cherry trees,
azaleas, roses, water and rock gardens. Teas
available in village. Open mid Apr to mid Sep,
Mon and Thu 2–6. 20p (ch 5p). Dogs
admitted if on lead. ⚠ *(Mrs H I Blakeney)* &
main garden.

EAST FORTUNE Lothian *East Lothian*
Map 12 NT57

Museum of Flight East Fortune Airfield. (A Royal Scottish Museum Outstation). The airship base from which the R34 set out in July 1919 to make the first double crossing of the Atlantic, now displays the history of aircraft and rockets. Working exhibits which visitors may operate. Exhibits include Supermarine *Spitfire* Mk 16, De Havilland *Sea Vampire*, and Hawker *Sea Hawk*. Open Jul and Aug daily 10–4, also open days yet to be decided. Free. ⚠ *(Tel 031-225 7534)* ⚠ &

EAST LINTON Lothian *East Lothian* Map 12 NT57
Hailes Castle 1 m SW on unclass rd. An old castle or fortified manor house of the Gourlays and Hepburns, with a 16th-C chapel, dismantled by Cromwell in 1650. Open, see inside front cover. 15p (ch 7p). ⚠ *(AM)*
Preston Mill This is the sole working water-mill to survive on the River Tyne, perhaps the only functioning example in Scotland. Conical roof, projecting wind vane and red pantiles. Open all year, Mon to Sat 10–12.30 and 2–7.30; closes at 4.30 pm Oct to Mar. 40p (ch 20p). Phantassie Doocot, a short walk away, once held 500 birds. *(Tel 426). (NTS)*

ECCLEFECHAN Dumfries and Galloway *Dumfriesshire* Map 11 NY17
Carlyle's Birthplace A characteristic late 18th-C Scottish artisan's house, where Thomas Carlyle was born in 1795. Collection of manuscripts and personal relics. Open 4 Apr to 31 Oct, daily (ex Sun) 10–6. 25p (ch 10p). *(Tel 666). (NTS)*

EDINBURGH Lothian *Midlothian* Map 11 NT27
Acheson House, Scottish Craft Centre A fine 17th-C mansion in the Royal Mile, opposite Canongate Church. Headquarters of the Scottish Craft Centre. Open daily (ex Sun and PH) 10–5. Free. P.
Canongate Tolbooth Dates from 1591 and shows a curious projecting clock. The J Telfar Dunbar Tartan Collection is on show. Special exhibitions throughout the year. Open Jun to Sep, Mon to Sat 10–6, and also Sun 2–5 during Festival; Oct to May 10–5. Free. ⚠ *(Tel 031-556/5813)*
Craigmillar Castle 14th-C stronghold associated with Mary, Queen of Scots, and also the Earl of Mar. Notable 16th- and 17th-C apartments. Open Apr to Sep, weekdays 9.30–7, Sun 2–7; Oct to Mar 9.30–4, Sun 2–4. Closed 1½ days per week Oct to Mar. 20p (ch 10p). ⚠ *(AM)*
Edinburgh Castle An historic stronghold, famous for the Crown Room, Banqueting Hall, Scottish United Services Museum, St Margaret's Chapel (faced by Mons Meg, a 15th-C cannon) and the impressive Scottish National War Memorial. Open Nov to Apr, weekdays 9.30–5.05, Sun 12.30–4.20; May to Oct, weekdays 9.30–6, Sun 11–6 (subject to Tattoo requirements). Last admissions 45 min before closing. Admission May to Oct, 40p (ch 16 20p); Nov to Apr 25p (ch 16 12p); War Memorial and precincts free. ⚠ *(AM)*
Edinburgh Zoo The Scottish National Zoological Park. Set in 80 acres of grounds, this zoo is one of the finest in Europe, containing a superb collection of animals, fish, birds and reptiles. Also magnificent panoramic views of Edinburgh and surrounding countryside. ⚱ (also licensed). Open all year, summer 9–7 (Sun opens 9.30) (5 or dusk winter). £1.20 (ch 15 and pen 60p). Party application to *Bookings Officer,*

Zoological Park, Murrayfield, Edinburgh EH12 6TS. (Tel 031-334 9171) ⚠ &
George Heriot's School Lauriston Place. Dates from 1628 and was founded by George Heriot, the 'Jingling Geordie' of Sir Walter Scott's *Fortunes of Nigel*. Open Mon to Fri (ex BH) 9.30–4.30. Free. & B
The Georgian House 7 Charlotte Square. Lower floors open as typical Georgian House, furnished as it might have been by first owners, showing domestic surroundings and reflecting social conditions of that age. Open 4 Apr to 26 Oct, Mon to Sat 10–5, Sun 2–5. 1 Nov to 31 Jan Sat 10–4.30, Sun 2–4.30. (Closed 20/21 and 27/28 Dec). 75p (ch 35p) (includes audio-visual shows). *(Tel 031-226 5922). (NTS)*
Gladstone's Land 483 Lawnmarket. Built in 1620, contains fine examples of tempera painting on the walls and ceiling and is furnished as a typical 17th-C home. Ground floor includes shop front and goods of the period. Open 4 Apr to 26 Oct, Mon to Sat 10–5, Sun 2–5; 1 Nov to 31 Jan, Sat 10–4.30, Sun 2–4.30. (Closed 20/21 and 27/28 Dec). 50p (ch 25p). *(NTS)*
Holyroodhouse At E end of Canongate. Historic Royal Palace of 16th and 17th C, built by Sir William Bruce, and associated with Mary, Queen of Scots, and also Prince Charles Edward. The picture gallery and the state apartments are outstanding. Ruined 13th-C nave of former Abbey church. Open from Nov to Apr, Mon to Fri 9.30–5.15, Sat 11–4; from May to Oct, weekdays 9.30–6, Sun 11–5.15 (last entry 45 mins before closing time). Closed when occupied by the Royal Family, and also for 10 days, probably in late spring (see Press), during the Lord High Commissioner's visit. Also closed about 2 weeks before and 1 week after visit. 45p (ch and pen 20p) from May to Oct. Nov to Apr 30p (ch and pen 15p). All details subject to review. ⚠ *(AM)*
Huntly House Canongate. Dates from 1570. It is now the interesting City Museum of local history, containing among other things, collections of silver, glass and pottery. Open Jun to Sep, Mon to Sat 10–6; Oct to May 10–5. During Festival period Sun 2–5. Free.
John Knox's House High Street, 15th-C house, preserving old wooden galleries. Built by the goldsmith to Mary Queen of Scots. Open weekdays only 10–5. 25p (ch 15p).
Lady Stair's House Off Lawnmarket. Restored house, dating from 1622. Museum, with literary relics of Robert Burns, Sir Walter Scott and Robert Louis Stevenson. Open Jul to Sep, Mon to Sat 10–6; Oct to May 10–5 (during Festival period, Sun 2–5). Free. ⚠
Museum of Childhood 38 High Street. Children's life in the past. Open Jun to Sep, Mon to Sat 10–6, Oct to May 10–5, also during Edinburgh's Festival period on Sun 2–6. 30p (ch 15 10p). ⚠
National Gallery of Scotland The Mound. One of the most distinguished of the smaller galleries in Europe, containing collections of Old Masters, Impressionists and Scottish paintings including: Raphael's *Bridgewater Madonna*, Constable's *Dedham Vale*, and masterpieces by Titian, Velasquez, Raeburn, Van Gogh and Gauguin. Drawings, water-colours and original prints by Turner, Goya, Blake, etc (shown on request Mon to Fri 10–12.30 and 2–4.30). Postcards and colour slides on sale at the gallery shop. Museum open daily, Mon to Sat 10–5, Sun 2–5 (Mon to Sat 10–6 [Sun 11–6] during Festival). Free. P (meters). *(Tel 031–556 8921)* &

National Museum of Antiquities of Scotland 1 Queen Street. Extensive collections and national treasures from all parts of Scotland covering the prehistoric, Roman and later periods and illustrating everyday life and history. Open Mon to Sat 10 – 5 (6 during Festival) Sun 2 – 5 (11 – 6 during Festival). Free. P (meters). *(Tel 031 – 556 8921 ext 35)*

Outlook Tower Castlehill. This tower contains a fine *camera obscura*, which has operated since 1892. A guide gives a 15-minute tour of the city and its surroundings. Scottish Books and Craft shop. Open all year 9.30 – 6.30; winter 9.30 – 4.30. 50p (ch 30p). Notable view. *(Tel 031 – 226 3709)*

Parliament House East of George IV Bridge. Dates from 1639, but façade was replaced in 1829. Hall has a fine hammer-beam roof. The Scottish Parliament met there before the Union of 1707. ⚑ Open Mon to Fri 10 – 4.

Register House East end of Princes Street. designed by Robert Adam, it was founded in 1774. Headquarters of the Scottish Record Office and the repository for National Archives of Scotland. Summer exhibition Jul to Sep. Open all year (ex certain PH) Mon to Fri 9 – 4.45; Sat 9 – 12.30 (Historical search room only). Free. ⚠ *(Tel 031 – 556 6585)* ♿

Royal Botanic Garden Inverleith Row. Famous garden, noted especially for the rhododendron collection, rock garden, and new exhibition hall. ⚑ (Apr to Sep) The garden is open Feb to Oct, 9 to 1 hr before sunset Mon to Sat, Sun 11 to 1 hr before sunset; Nov to Jan, Mon to Sat 9 – sunset, Sun 11 – sunset; plant houses open 10 – 5 and exhibition hall open 11 – 5 (during Festival period open on Sun from 10am). Free. ⚠ Sorry, no animals. ♿

also Scottish National Gallery of Modern Art Inverleith House, Botanic gardens Temporary home since 1960 of the National Gallery's collection of 20th-C painting, sculpture and graphic art. Among many modern masters represented are Derain, Picasso, Giacometti, Magritte, Henry Moore and Barbara Hepworth. Some sculpture is displayed in the garden immediately surrounding the Gallery. Print room and library also open to the public (closed for lunch). ⚑ Open all year, Mon to Sat 10 – 5, Sun 2 – 5 (10 – 6, Sun 11 – 6 during Festival, closes at sunset during winter). Free. P. *(Tel 031 – 332 3754)*

Royal Scottish Museum Chambers Street. The most comprehensive display in Britain under one roof comprising the decorative arts, natural history, geology (minerals and fossils), and technology. Colliery locomotive of 1813, many scale-model locomotives, models of ships. Aeronautics, space flight, science and Victorian engineering. Lectures, gallery talks and films at advertised times. Special exhibitions. ⚑ (Mon to Sat 10 – 4) Open weekdays 10 – 5, Sun 2 – 5. Free. P (meters). ♿

Scottish National Portrait Gallery Queen Street. Striking red Victorian building containing portraits of men and women who have contributed to Scottish history. The collection includes such popular figures as Mary Queen of Scots, James VI and I, Burns, Sir Walter Scott and Ramsay MacDonald. Many other artists, statesmen, soldiers and scientists are portrayed in all media, including sculpture. Collections also illustrate the development of Highland dress. Open all year, Mon to Sat, 10 – 5, Sun 2 – 5 (10 – 6, Sun

11 – 6 during Festival). Free. P (meters). *(Tel 031 – 556 8921)* ♿

West Register House Charlotte Square. The former St George's church, designed by Robert Reid in the Greco-Roman style in 1811. Auxiliary repository for the Scottish Record Office and houses its museum. Open all year (ex PH) Mon to Fri 9 – 4.45. Free. ⚠ ♿

EDZELL Tayside *Angus* Map 15 NO56
Edzell Castle 16th C, and associated with Mary, Queen of Scots, preserved walled garden from 1604. Open, 9.30 – 4.30 Mon to Fri only. 15p (ch 7p). *(AM)*

ELGIN Grampian *Moray* Map 15 NJ26
Elgin Museum The museum conserves and displays the heritage of Elgin and Moray. It contains a world-famed collection of fossils of the Old Red Sandstone. Open 15 Mar to 15 Oct, Mon to Sat (ex Tue, but open Tue during Jul and Aug) 10 – 12.30 and 2 – 5; 16 Oct to 14 Mar, Wed and Sat 10 – 12. 20p (ch 5p) Under revision for 1980. ⚠

Pluscarden Abbey 6m SW on unclass road. The original monastery was founded by Alexander II in 1230. Restorations and reconstruction took place in the 14th and 19th C, and the Abbey has been re-occupied by the Benedictines since 1948. Open daily 5am – 8.30pm. Free. ⚠ *(Tel Dallas 257)* ♿ B

ELLISLAND FARM Dumfries and Galloway *Dumfriesshire* Map 11 NX98
In this farm on the west bank of the Nith, Robert Burns composed *Tam O'Shanter* and other poems and songs. Material associated with the poet is on display. Burns lived here from 1788 to 1791. No restriction on times of visiting and admission is free. ⚠ (limited). ♿ B

FALKIRK Central *Stirlingshire* Map 11 NS87
Falkirk Museum Temporary exhibitions only until further notice. Open all year Mon to Sat 9 – 5. Free. P. *(Tel 27703)*

Rough Castle One of the most remarkable Roman military sites in Britain, situated on the Antonine, or Roman Wall. It covers one acre, with double ditches and defensive pits. Excavations revealing a bathhouse and other buildings made in 1903. Accessible at any reasonable time. Free. ⚠ *(AM)*

Scottish Railway Preservation Society Wallace Street Depot. Fine collection of restored steam locomotives and vintage rolling stock. Engines in steam on certain weekends. ⚑ Open all year (ex Christmas and New Year) Sat and Sun 11 – 5. 15p (ch 14 and pen 10p), prices increased on 'steam' days. ⚠ *(Tel 20790)* **(79)**

FALKLAND Fife *Fife* Map 11 NO20
Falkland Palace and Gardens Historic former hunting palace of Stuart Kings and Queens, situated below the Lomond Hills. The mid 16th-C buildings include a notable courtyard façade. Chapel Royal and apartments restored. Royal tennis court of 1539, second oldest extant. Visitor Centre. Palace and Gardens open 1 Apr to 31 Oct, Mon to Sat 10 – 6; Sun 2 – 6. Last visitors to Palace 5.15. Admission to Palace and gardens £1 (ch 50p); gardens only 50p (ch 25p). Parties 75p (school parties 35p). ⚠ 10p. *(Tel 397)*. *(NTS)*

FETTERCAIRN Tayside *Kincardineshire* Map 15 NO67
Fasque Home of the Gladstone family since 1829, the large mansion reflects the life of the original owner, Sir John Gladstone, and of subsequent generations and their families. Four times Prime Minister, William Gladstone, lived at Fasque from 1830 to

1851. Also illustrated is the life and work of the many servants who contributed to the running of the household. Collection of agricultural and other local machinery. Extensive parkland with red deer and Soay sheep. Open May to Sep incl, daily (ex Fri) 1.30–5.30 (last entry 5). 75p (ch 40p, pen 60p) subject to review. ⚠ *(Tel 201)* & B

FINTRY Central *Stirlingshire* Map 11 NS68
Culcreuch Castle Castle dates from 1320 to 1460. ☍ Open 1 May to 30 Sep. Sun 12.30 Piper's Cold table lunch. Sun 2.30 to 6 Castle and gardens 60p (ch 30p). Fri 8.30 Ceilidh £1.20. Sat 8.30 Country dance £1.20. ⚠ *(Tel 228). (Hercules Robinson of Culreuch)* & B

FORRES Grampian *Moray* Map 14 NJ05
Falconer Museum Tolbooth Street. Items relating to Hugh Falconer; fossil fish; natural history; ethnography; weaponry and Culbin archaeological finds. Open May to Sep, daily 10–5 (7 Jul and Aug). Free. P. *(Tel 73701)* & B
Nelson Tower Located on Cluny Hill, within Grant Park, overlooking Forres. The Tower was erected in 1806 by the survivors of the battle of Trafalgar and offers magnificent views of Moray Firth, Black Isle and inland mountains. Key available from Forres Tourist Information Centre at Falconer Museum (£1 deposit). Open mid May to end Sep. Daily 10–6. *(Tel 72938)*
Suenos' Stone A notable 20ft high monument, with a sculptured cross on one side and groups of warriors on the reverse. Accessible at all times. Free. *(AM)*

FORT AUGUSTUS Highland *Inverness-shire* Map 14 NH30
Great Glen Exhibition History and traditions of people of the Great Glen, rare maps and prints. Latest information on the search for Loch Ness Monster. Evening audio-visual shows. Four buildings on site. Open Jun to Sep, Mon–Sat 10–6. Sun 2–6. 30p (ch 15 15p). P. &

FORT GEORGE Highland *Inverness-shire* Map 14 NH75
Fort George As 18th-C fort, visited by Dr Johnson and Boswell in 1773. Open Apr to Sep, weekdays 9.30–7, Sun 2–4; Oct to Mar 9.30–4, Sun 2–4. 25p (ch 12p). P. *(AM)*
Also Queen's Own Highlanders Museum Housed in the fort, exhibits include period uniforms, silver and medals. The Georgian garrison church dates from 1768. Open Apr to Sep weekdays 10–6.30, Sun 2–6. Oct to Mar, weekdays 10–4, Sun 2–6.30; closed 1, 2 Jan, 25, 26 Dec and PH. *(Tel Ardersier 2274 ext 47)*

FORT WILLIAM Highland *Inverness-shire* Map 14 NN17
Inverlochy Castle Well-preserved example of a 13th-C and later stronghold, famous for the battle fought nearby in 1645, when Montrose defeated the Campbells. Now under repair and interior not accessible, but may be viewed from the outside. Free. *(AM)*
West Highland Museum A museum of local and particularly Jacobite interest, including an exhibition about the '45 rising with the well-known 'secret portrait' of Prince Charles Edward Stuart. Relics from the former fort, archaeology, wildlife, geology, and folk exhibits. Open mid Jun to mid Sep, 9.30–9; Oct to May 9.30–1, 2.15–5. Closed Sun. 20p (ch 10p)

GAIRLOCH Highland *Ross-shire* Map 14 NG87
Gairloch Heritage Museum Achtercairn. A converted farmstead now houses the museum which relates the way of life in the typical West Highland parish of Gairloch from the earliest times to the 20th century. Open-air display area in front of building. ☍ Open 19 May to 30 Sep daily (ex Sun) 10–1 and 2–4. 20p (ch 10 10p). P 50yds. *(Tel Badachro 243)*

GALASHIELS Borders *Selkirkshire* Map 12 NT43
Bernat Klein Exhibition Waukrigg Mill. This exhibition is intended to show the sequence, the thought process and the stages between the conception of a design idea and its realisation as a finished product. The exhibition consists of approximately 100 paintings, sketches, photographs, patterns and other objects, specially selected from Bernat Klein's work for the purpose. It also shows the relationship between the countryside in which the designer lives and works and the designs which he and those working with him, produce. Open all year daily 10–4. Free. ⚠ *(Tel 2764). (Mrs Jennifer Mellor)* &

GLAMIS Tayside *Angus* Map 15 NO34
Glamis Castle The ancestral seat of the Earl of Strathmore and Kinghorne, family home of Her Majesty Queen Elizabeth, The Queen Mother and birthplace in 1930 of HRH Princess Margaret. Mainly late 17th-C but with an older tower. The drawing room ceiling of 1621 and the painted panels in the chapel are notable. Open 1 May to 1 Oct Mon to Thu and Sun 1–5, also Fri from 1 Jul. £1 (ch 40p, pen 80p). Grounds only, half-price. Prices subject to review for 1980. ⚠ *(Earl of Strathmore and Kinghorne)* & B
Angus Folk Museum Kirkwynd Cottages. Row of restored 17th-C cottages, now housing the Angus Folk Collection of agricultural and domestic equipment and cottage furniture etc. Open 1 May to 30 Sep, daily 1–6 (last admission 5.30) and on request. 45p (ch 20p). *(NTS)*

GLASGOW Strathclyde *Lanarkshire* Map 11 NS56
Bellahouston Park Ibrox. 171 acres of parkland only 3 miles from the city centre. Site of the Empire Exhibition of 1938. Sunken garden and rock garden. Multi-purpose Sports Centre situated at west end of park, with all-weather Athletic Centre adjacent and nursery ski slope. ☍ in Sports Centre. Open daily 7–dusk. Free. ⚠ at ski slope and sports centre. &
Botanic Garden Off Great Western Road. Established in 1817, it contains an outstanding collection of plants. The Kibble Palace open 10–4.45 (4.15 in winter), is a unique glasshouse with, among others, a famous collection of tree ferns. The main glasshouse open Mon to Sat 1–4.45 (4.15 in winter), Sun 12–4.45 (4.15 in winter), contains numerous tropical and exotic plants. The 40 acres of gardens include systematic and herb gardens, and a chronological border. Open daily 7–dusk. Free. ⚠ *(Tel 041–334 2422)* &
Crookston Castle Probably 13th C, with an earlier defensive ditch. Visited by Mary Queen of Scots, and Darnley in 1565. Open, see inside front cover. 15p (ch 7p). *(AM)*
Glasgow Art Gallery and Museum Kelvingrove Park, Italian, Flemish, Dutch, French and British paintings representing the finest civic art collection in Great Britain. Collections of pottery, porcelain, silver, sculpture, arms and armour. Plus archaeology, ethnography, natural history, etc, and selections from the world famous

Visit

Glasgow Museums & Art Galleries

Art Gallery and Museum, Kelvingrove, 041-334 1134

Museum of Transport, Albert Drive, 041-423 8000

Haggs Castle, St. Andrews Drive, 041-427 2725

People's Palace, Glasgow Green, 041-554 0223

Pollok House, Pollokshaws Road, 041-632 0274

St. Enoch's Exhibition Centre, St. Enoch's Square, 041-221 6454

Open daily 10 am — 5 pm, Sundays 2 pm — 5 pm.

Burrell Collection. ♨ Open Mon to Sat 10 – 5, Sun 2 – 5. Closed 25 Dec and 1 Jan. Free. ⚠ *(Tel 041 – 334 1134)* ⅋

Greenbank Clarkston. Off A726 on southern outskirts of the city. Small garden at which has been established a Gardening Advice Centre, particularly suitable for the owners of small gardens. Lectures, demonstrations etc. Garden open all year daily 10 – 5. Advice centre open all year Mon – Fri 10 – 5, also Sat and Sun 1 Apr to 31 Oct, 2.30 – 5. 40p (ch 20p). *(NTS)*

Haggs Castle 100 St Andrew's Drive. Built in 1585, the castle is a museum created for children. The theme is exploration of time – particularly the last 400 years since the castle was built. Activities in the adjacent workshop allow visitors to become practically involved in the past. Open all year (ex 25 Dec and 1 Jan) Mon to Sat 10 – 6.15, Sun 2 – 5. Free. *(Tel 041 – 427 2725)*

Hunterian Museum The University of Glasgow. The museum is named after the 18th-C surgeon, Dr William Hunter, who bequeathed his own collections to the University. The geological, archaeological, ethnographical, numismatic and historical collections are exhibited in the main building of the University. The Hunterian Art Gallery is expected to open in 1980. *(Tel 041 – 339 8855 ext 7431* for information). Open all year Mon to Fri 9 – 5, Sat 9 – 12. Free. ⚠ *(Tel 041 – 339 8855 ext 221)* ⅋ B

Linn Park Cathcart. Southern outskirts of Glasgow. Comprises more than 200 acres of pine, deciduous woodland, and riverside walks. Britain's first public park nature trail (1965) features many varieties of flowers, trees, and insects. Children's zoo. Collection of British ponies and Highland cattle. There is also a ruined 14th-C castle, with a Mary Queen of Scots historical plaque. ♨ at Golf Clubhouse. Open daily 7 – dusk. Free. ⚠ ⅋

People's Palace Glasgow Green. Contains a fascinating visual record of the history and life of the City. In addition to items illustrating prehistoric and medieval Glasgow, there are interesting relics of Mary, Queen of Scots, the Battle of Langside, the Tobacco Lords of the 18th C, and the history of the music hall. Fine examples of Glasgow craftsmanship, particularly pottery, are on view, and there are special displays illustrating the social and domestic life. A wide range of pictures brings to life people and places of note. Open Mon to Sat 10 – 5, Sun 2 – 5. Free. ⚠ *(Tel 041 – 554 0223)*

Pollock Park 361 acres, formerly a private estate containing an extensive collection of flowering shrubs and trees in a natural setting.

Display rose garden, nature trails, jogging track. Open daily 7 – dusk. Demonstration and display garden open daily 10 – 4. Demonstrations held fortnightly, Sat mornings. Free. Also **Pollock House** situated within the grounds, a William Adam building (1752), containing the famous Stirling-Maxwell Collection of Spanish and other paintings, works by William Blake, silver, furniture, etc. ♨ Open all year Mon to Sat 10 – 5, Sun 2 – 5. Free. ⚠ *(Tel 041 – 632 0274, restaurant 041 – 649 7547)*

Provan Hall Auchinlea Road, E4. 15th-C house, once mansion of lands of Provan. Well restored, and considered most perfect example of a simple pre-Reformation house remaining in Scotland. For information on opening hours contact Glasgow District Council, Parks Dept. *(NTS)*

Ross Hall Park Crookson. Beautifully kept gardens with artificial ponds featuring a variety of aquatic plants and stocked with fish. Extensive heather and rock gardens. Garden and woodland nature trails. Open Apr to Sep, daily 1 – 8; Oct to Mar, daily 1 – 4. Free. ⚠ *(Tel 041 – 882 3554)* ⅋

Rouken Glen Park Thornliebank. Fine park with lovely walks through the glen, waterfall at head of the glen is a noted beauty spot. Large walled garden. Boating on picturesque loch. ♨ Open daily 7 – dusk. Free. ⚠ *(Tel 041 – 638 1077)* ⅋

Transport Museum Albert Drive, near Eglinton Toll. A life-size presentation of land transport, showing the development of the bicycle, horse-drawn vehicles, tramcars, Scottish motor cars from vintage to present day and railway locomotives, also the Clyde room with an outstanding collection of ship modes. ♨ Open Mon to Sat 10 – 5, Sun 2 – 5. Free. ⚠ *(Tel 041 – 423 8000)* ⅋

Victoria Park Whiteinch. This park has the best known fossilized tree stumps of the prehistoric Coal Age period, discovered in 1887, and housed in the Fossil Grove building. Open Mon to Sat from 8am (Sun from 10am). The park has extensive carpet bedding depicting centennial events. Open daily 7 – dusk. Free. P. ⅋

GLENAPPS Strathclyde *Ayrshire* Map 10 NX08

Castle Gardens Daffodils, azaleas, rhododendrons, flowering shrubs, terraces, lily ponds, herbaceous borders. Open May to Aug incl, daily (ex Sat). ♨ 30p (ch 12 15p) Party ⚠ *(Rt Hon Earl and Countess of Inchcape)* ⅋

GLENCOE Highland *Argyll* Map 14 NN15

Glencoe and North Lorn Folk Museum Housed in two heather-thatched cottages, one of cruck construction, in main street of Glencoe. Macdonald relics, local domestic and agricultural exhibits, and Jacobite relics costume and embroidery. Open mid May to end Sep, Mon to Sat 10 – 5.30. 15p (ch 10p) Under revision for 1980. P.

Glen Coe Visitor Centre Situated at north end of Glen Coe close to site of 1692 massacre. Ranger-Naturalist service available. Open 4 Apr to mid May and mid Sep to mid Oct daily 10 – 5; mid May to mid Sep, daily 10 – 7. 10p including ⚠. *(NTS)*

GLENELG Highland *Inverness-shire* Map 14 NG81

Glenelg Brochs Reached by way of the steep and winding Marn Rattachen pass, off A87. Situated in Glen Beag, on a byroad. Remains of two brochs, known as Dun Telve and Dun Troddan. Probably of Iron Age date, some 30ft in height, and showing well-preserved walls, galleries, and courts. Picturesque Highland setting. Accessible at all reasonable times. Free. *(AM)*

GLENFINNAN Highland *Inverness-shire* Map 14 NM98

Moument Erected in 1815 to commemorate the Highlanders who followed Prince Charles Edward in 1745. Plaques on retaining wall give a dedication in English, Gaelic, and Latin. The monument stands in a superb setting of mountains at the head of Loch Shiel. Visitor Centre. Open daily 4 Apr to 31 May 9.30 – 6; Jun to Aug 9.30 – 8; Sep to mid Oct 9.30 – 6. 30p (ch 15p) including ⚠ *(Tel Kinlocheil 250)*. *(NTS)*

GLENGOULANDIE DEER PARK Tayside *Perthshire* Map 14 NN75

8m NW of Aberfeldy on B846. A fine herd of red deer, Highland cattle, endangered species and other birds and animals live in the park in surroundings as like their natural environment as possible. Pets must not be allowed out of cars. Picnic area. Shop. Open 1 Apr to 30 Sep daily 9 – two hours before sunset. 20p (ch 10p), cars £1. ⚠ *(Tel Kenmore 306)* ⚠

GLENLIVET Grampian *Banffshire* Map 15 NJ12

Glenlivet Distillery Off B9136 12m SW of Dufftown (via B9009 and B9008). The reception centre contains an exhibition of ancient artefacts used in malting, peat cutting and distilling. Shop. Open May to Sep, Mon to Fri 10 – 4. Free. ⚠ *(Tel 202 or Lhanbryde 251)* **(79)**

GLENLUCE Dumfries and Galloway *Wigtownshire* Map 10 NX15

Glenluce Abbey 2m NW of the village. A Cistercian house founded in 1192 by Roland, Earl of Galloway. The ruins occupy a site of great beauty and are themselves of much architectural interest and distinction. Open, Apr to Sep, see inside front cover. Closed 1½ days per week. Oct to Mar Sat and Sun pm. 15p (ch 7p). ⚠ *(AM)*

GOGAR Lothian *Midlothian* Map 11 NT17

Suntrap Gogarbank. 1½m S off Gogar Moor-Ransfield road. Small garden containing a Gardening Advice Centre, with lecture hall, glass-houses, demonstrations etc, adapted to help owners of small gardens. Garden open all year, daily 9 – dusk. Advice Centre open all year, Mon to Fri 9 – 5 (1 Mar to 31 Oct, also Sat and Sun 2.30 – 5). 30p (ch accompanied by adult 15p). *(Tel 031-339 7283)* ⚠ *(NTS)*

GOLSPIE Highland *Sutherland* Map 14 NH89

Dunrobin Castle 1m NE. The ancient seat of the Earls and Dukes of Sutherland. Much of the interior is open to the public and contains a wide variety of furniture, paintings and exhibits. Museum with many antique exhibits of local and general interest within the grounds. Magnificent formal gardens. ⚲ Open 1 May to 30 Sep daily Mon to Sat 10.30 – 5.30, Sun 1 – 5.30. £1 (ch 50p) subject to alteration. Party. ⚠ *(Tel 377) (Countess of Sutherland)* ⚠ B

GORDON Borders *Berwickshire* Map 12 NT64

Mellerstain House 3m S on unclass road. Adam house with fine plaster ceilings, period furniture and pictures. Terraced gardens and lake. Historic Vehicle display 8 Jun. ⚲ Open 4 – 7 Apr then 1 May to 30 Sep, Mon to Fri and Sun 1.30 – 5.30 (last admission 5). 80p (ch 14 40p, pen 60p). ⚠ Dogs must be on a lead. *(Lord Binning)*

GREENOCK Strathclyde *Renfrewshire* Map 10 NS27

Mclean Museum and Art Gallery 9 Union Street. A museum displaying exhibits relating to local history, ethnography, natural history, geology, and shipping, including river steamers (paddle), cargo vessels. There are also relics of James Watt. Inverclyde art exhibition last week in Feb and Mar; Greenock Art Club exhibition in Sep/Oct. Open all year, Mon to Sat 10 – 5 (closed Sat 1 – 2). Free. P. *(Tel 23741)*

HAMILTON Strathclyde *Lanarks* Map 11 NS75

Hamilton District Museum Muir Street. Collections of local history and crafts, paintings and early photographs, farming, horse and motor transport and period kitchen, all housed in late 17th-C inn with 18th-C Assembly Hall with musicians gallery. Also the Regimental Museum of the Cameronians, Scottish Rifles. Open all year daily (ex Sun) Mon to Fri 10 – 12 and 1 – 5, Sat 10 – 5. Free. ⚠ *(Tel 283981)*

HAWICK Borders *Roxburghshire* Map 12 NT51

Museum and Art Gallery Wilton Lodge. The museum contains exhibits of natural history, local history, hosiery trade, archaeology, geology, coins and medals. The Art Gallery has exhibitions throughout the year. Open all year, Apr to Oct Mon to Sat 10 – 5 (2 – 5 Sun) Nov to Mar Mon to Sat 10 – 4 (closed Sun). 20p (ch 16 10p) under review. P. *(Tel 3457)*

HERMITAGE Borders *Roxburghshire* Map 12 NY59

Hermitage Castle An old Douglas stronghold, mainly 14th-C, well-restored, with Mary, Queen of Scots associations. Open, see inside front cover. 20p (ch 10p). ⚠ *(AM)*

HUNTLY Grampian *Aberdeenshire* Map 15 NJ53

Agricultural Museum 3½m SE. Opened in 1972; this museum contains an interesting collection of about 450 items of farm and farmhouse equipment, including farm implements, horse and cattle equipment, butter- and cheese-making utensils, corn dollies and many hand-tools. Sales dept, selling farm and country antiques. 'Farming Yesteryear' Field Days 26, 27 May with old horse implements, steam powered threshing mill and other items. Open daily at all reasonable times. Collections in aid of Royal Scottish Agricultural Benevolent Institution. ⚠ *(Tel Drumblade 231)*

Huntly Castle Formerly Palace of Strathbogie, dates largely from 1602, with elaborate heraldic embellishments. Open, see inside front cover. 20 (ch 10p). ⚠ *(AM)*

Huntly Museum The Square. Local history and changing special exhibitions every year. Governed by North East of Scotland Library Committee. Open all year (ex Mon) Tue to Sat 10–12, 2–4. Free. *(Tel Peterhead 2554)*

INNERLEITHEN Borders *Peebleshire*
Map 11 NT33

Traquair House 1 m S on B709. Scotland's oldest inhabited, and most romantic house, dating back to the 10th C. Twenty-seven English and Scottish Kings have stayed here. Rich in association with Mary, Queen of Scots, and the Jacobite Risings. Contains a fine collection of historical treasures, many recently discovered. Unique 18th-C brewhouse licensed to sell own beer. Woodland walks, 5 craft workshops. Craft Fair 16/17 Aug (please check dates). Gift shop, Antiques and Bric a Brac. ⚐ Open 5 to 13 Apr, then remaining Sun in Apr; thereafter daily 1 May to 5 Oct, 1.30–5.30. Also Jul and Aug only 10.30–5.30 (last admission 5). ⚠ *(Tel 830323). (Mr P Maxwell Stuart)* ⚿ B

INVERARAY Strathclyde *Argyll*
Map 10 NN00

Inveraray Bell Tower The 126ft tower was planned in 1914, and the ring of ten bells were hung in the great bell chamber in 1931. From the roof of the tower is an excellent view. Exhibition of vestments and campanology and there will be a 'ring-in' daily during Inveraray Week at the end of July. Open Spring BH to 30 Sep, Mon to Sat 10–1, 2–5, Sun 2–5. 25p (ch and pen 10p). ⚠

Inveraray Castle A fine mansion of the late 18th-C by Robert Mylne and Roger Morris. The great hall and armoury, staterooms, tapestries and furniture are of note. The ancestral home of the Dukes of Argyll. Shop. ⚐ Open Apr to 28 Jun daily (ex Fri) 10–12.30 and 2–6; 29 Jun to 30 Sep, weekdays 10–6, Sun 2–6 (last admission 5.30). £1 (ch 15 and pen 50p). Admission prices under revision for 1980. ⚠ *(Tel 2203)*

INVERESK Lothian *Midlothian* Map 11 NT37

Inveresk Lodge Garden New garden featuring numerous varieties of plants for small gardens. Garden only shown all the year, Mon, Wed and Fri 10–4.30, on Sun 2–5 when house is occupied. 30p (ch accompanied by adults 15p). *(NTS)*

INVERNESS Highland *Inverness-shire*
Map 14 NH64

Abertarff House Church Street. The town house of Lord Lovat, built in 1593, it is now the headquarters of An Comunn Gaidhealach. It has a stone turnpike staircase and contains an exhibition of the origins and history of the Gaels, a sales point for Gaelic books and records and English books on the Highlands. Open all year, Mon to Fri 9–5 (9–1 Wed, 9–4.30 on Fri, 10–1 Sat). Free. *(Tel 31226)*

INVERTROSSACHS Central *Perthshire*
Map 11 NH50

Nature reserve in extremely fine setting beside Loch Venachar. Open May to Aug by prior appointment only. 50p (ch 25p). ⚠ *(Tel Callander 30010)* ⚿

INVERURIE Grampian *Aberdeenshire*
Map 15 NJ72

Inverurie Museum Town House, Thematic displays changing 4- or 6-monthly. Permanent local history and archaeology exhibition. Reserve collections may be viewed by appointment. Established in 1884, this museum is now governed by the North East Scotland Library Service Committee. Open all year, Mon to Fri 2–5, Sat 10–12. Free. *(Tel Peterhead 2554)*

IRVINE Strathclyde *Ayrshire* Map 10 NS34

Eglinton Castle and Gardens Irvine Road Kilwinning. Late 18th-C castle, built for 13th Earl of Eglinton. Castle ruin set in a 12-acre garden. Site of the famous Eglinton Tournament of 1839. Always open. Free. ⚠ *(Tel 74166)*

JEDBURGH Borders *Roxburghshire*
Map 12 NT62

Jedburgh Abbey One of the four famous border monasteries founded by Davi I. The remains of the church are mostly Norman or Transitional. Also small museum, containing many carved fragments of medieval work and some important monuments from the Anglian period. Open, see inside front cover Apr to Sep. During Oct to Mar closed 1½ days per week. 25p (ch 12p) ⚠ *(AM)*

The Castle Jail This is the former county prison, dating from 1820–3, on the site of the medieval castle, demolished in 1409. There were three blocks, used for different categories of prisoners. Possibly the last surviving example of its kind. A small museum is also open to visitors. Open Apr to Sep, Mon to Sat 10–12, 1–5, Suns 1–5. 10p (ch 16 5p). P. *(Tel Hawick 3457)*

Mary Queen of Scots House A historic and picturesque bastle house built in the early 16th C. Now a museum with exhibits relating to the Queen and to the earlier story of Jedburgh and district. Open Mar to Oct daily 10–5.30. 20p (ch 16 10p). ⚠

KELLIE CASTLE AND GARDENS Fife *Fife*
Map 12 NO50

Fine example of the domestic architecture of the Scottish lowlands. The mainly 16th- and 17th-C building probably assumed its present dimensions in 1606. Notable plasterwork and panelling painted with 'romantic' landscapes. Audio-visual show. Open 4 Apr to 30 Sep, daily (ex Fri) 2–6; gardens 4 Apr to 30 Sep, daily 10–dusk. Admission to castle and gardens 85p (ch 40p); gardens only 30p (ch accompanied by an adult 15p). Party 20+ (55p each). *(Tel Arncroach 271). (NTS)* ⚿ (gardens)

KELSO Borders *Roxburghshire*
Map 12 NT73

Kelso Abbey Little but the abbey church remains, and that only in imposing fragments, which are almost wholly of Norman and Transitional work. The best preserved portion is the north transept. Open see inside front cover. Free. *(AM)*

KEMNAY Grampian *Aberdeenshire*
Map 15 NJ71

Castle Fraser 2½m SW on unclass rd. This castle is considered by many to be the most spectacular of the Castles of Mar. The massive Z-plan castle, with splendid architectural embellishments was begun about 1575 by the sixth laird, Michael Fraser, and incorporates an earlier castle. It was completed in 1636. An exhibition tells the story of 'The Castles of Mar'. Open 1 May to 30 Sep Mon to Sat 11–6, Sun 2–6 (last admission 5.15). Garden and grounds open all year 9.30–sunset. Castle 80p (ch 40p), school parties 35p; grounds by donation. ⚠ *(NTS)*

KILBARCHAN Strathclyde *Renfrewshire*
Map 10 NS46

Weaver's Cottage An early 18th-C
craftsman's house, formerly used by
weavers. Looms, weaving equipment,
domestic utensils. Open 1 May to 31 Oct, Tue,
Thu, Sat and Sun 2–5. 40p (ch 20p). *(NTS)*

KILCHRENAN Strathclyde *Argyll*
Map 10 NN02
Ardanaiseig 3m NE at end of unclass road.
The gardens have azaleas, rhododendrons,
rare shrubs and trees. Splendid views across
Loch Awe. Open 1 Apr to 31 Oct, daily 10–8.
30p (ch 16 free). ⚠ *(Mr and Mrs J M Brown)*

KILDRUMMY Grampian *Aberdeenshire*
Map 15 NJ41
Kildrummy Castle A splendid, ruined, 13th-
C fortress, with an imposing gatehouse and
notable 15th- to 16th-C additions. Gallantly
defended by Sir Nigel Bruce in 1306. Open,
see inside front cover. 15p (ch 7p). ⚠ *(AM)*
Kildrummy Castle Garden Trust Two of the
Trustees are the Professors of Forestry and
Botany, University of Aberdeen. At foot of the
medieval castle lies the Water garden running
under a copy of the 14th-C Brig O'Balgownie.
Facing south is the shrub bank. The ancient
quarry from which the ruins were built,
contains a variety of alpines and shrubs from
overseas. Festival 8 Jun 1.30–5. Plants for
sale. Open 1 Apr to 31 Oct, daily, 9–5. 25p (ch
5p). ⚠ 10p (inside Hotel gates). (Coaches
50p by appointment). *(Tel 264, 277 and 288)*
&

KILLIECRANKIE Tayside *Perthshire*
Map 14 NN96
Trust Visitor Centre Situated close to site of
1689 battle where Jacobite army, led by
'Bonnie Dundee', routed King William's
troops. Battle display. Open 4 Apr to 30 Sep,
Mon to Sat 10–6; Sun 1–6; 1 Jul to 31 Aug,
Mon to Sat 9.30–6, Sun 1–6. 20p (ch 10p). ⚠
(Tel 233). *(NTS)*

KILMARNOCK Strathclyde *Ayrshire*
Map 10 NS43
Burns Museum Outstanding Burns
memorial, including 1st Kilmarnock edition of
1786, original manuscripts (including *Tam
O'Shanter, Cottar's Saturday Nigh* etc).
Burns' letters and works, and McKie Burns
library. Panoramic views towards Arran from
Tower. Open May to Sep daily 1–5 Oct to Apr
Sat and Sun 1–5. 3p. *(Tel 26401)*
Dean Castle Dean Road. Fortified tower built
1350 with lower keep, Great Hall and Upper
Hall in perfect condition. Exhibitions of
European arms and armour, early keyboard
and other musical instruments. Palace has
Long Gallery, kitchen and tower in equally
good condition. Restoration shows Dean
Castle as it was in 14th-15th C. 42 acres of
gardens and nature trail. Concerts of period
music and other historical performances. ⚐.
Open mid May to mid Sep, Mon to Fri 2–5,
Sat and Sun 10–5 (organised parties
throughout the year by arrangement). Free.
P. *(Tel 26401)*
Dick Institute Elmbank Avenue. The
museum contains exhibits of geology
(including fossils), small arms, shells,
ethnography, numismatics, and
archaeological specimens. The art gallery
(paintings and etchings) and the library
(Ayrshire and Burns printed books, etc) are of
interest. Open My to Sep, Mon, Tue, Thu and
Fri 10–8 (Wed and Sat until 5pm); Oct to Apr
10–5. Free. ⚠ *(Tel 26401)* &

KILMARTIN Strathclyde *Argyll* Map 10 NR89
Dunadd Fort 3m S, A816. A prehistoric hill-
fort incorporating walled enclosures. It was
once the capital of the ancient Scots kingdom
of Dalriada. Accessible at all reasonable
times. Free. *(AM)*

KILMORY Strathclyde *Argyll* Map 10 NR77
Castle Sween 2½m N. Lonely ruin, situated on
the rocky western coast of Knapdale,
probably one of the earliest stone castles in
Scotland dating from the mid 12th C. The
castle was destroyed by Sir Alexander
Macdonald in 1647. Open at all times. Free.
(AM)

KILMUN Strathclyde *Argyll* Map 10 NS18
Kilmun Arboretum and Forest Plots A large
collection of conifer and broadleaved tree
species planted in plots and specimen
groups. Established by the Forestry
Commission in 1930, and now extending to
100 acres on a hillside overlooking the Holy
Loch. Open all year during daylight hours.
Entrance and car park at Forestry
Commission District Office, Kilmun, from
which an illustrated guide book is available.

KILSYTH Strathclyde *Stirlingshire*
Map 11 NS77
Colzium House Partly a museum, with
attractive walled garden, and associated with
Montrose's victory over the Covenanters in
1645. Recreational facilities include pitch and
putt and a football field in grounds. House
open Mon, Tue, Wed, Fri, Sun 2–5 and
7–dusk (ex when booked for private
functions), grounds open at all times. Free. ⚠
(Tel 823110)

KINCRAIG Highland *Inverness-shire*
Map 14 NH80
Highland Wild Life Park Native animals of
Scotland past and present, including wolves,
bears, reindeer, wildcat and European Bison.
Open daily 1 Mar to first Sun in Nov 10–6 (or

1½ hrs before dusk if earlier). ⚏, picnic site, shop, children's park and temporary caravan park. £3 per car (prices subject to review for 1980). Kennels for pets at entrance. ⚠ *(Tel 270)* &

KINGUSSIE Highland *Inverness-shire* Map 14 NH70
Highland Folk Museum Contains an interesting display of Highland crafts and furnishings; a farming museum; reconstructed Hebridean mill, and primitive 'black house' set in 6 acres of garden. Picnic garden. Open all year Apr – Oct, Mon to Sat 10 – 6, Sun 2 – 6; Nov to Mar Mon to Fri 10 – 3. 45p (ch 4 – 13 10p) subject to review for 1980. ⚠ *(Tel 307)* &

KINNESSWOOD Tayside *Kinross-shire* Map 11 NO10
Michael Bruce Cottage and Museum The Loan. The cottage birth-place of Michael Bruce (1746 – 67), the gentle poet of Loch Leven, where his father once operated a loom. Now a Michael Bruce museum displaying family relics. Annual commemoration service 1st Sun in Jul at 6 pm. Open on application to *Mr T Buchan, The Garage, Drummond Place*. Free. ⚠ *(Tel Cowdenbeath 510832)*

KINROSS Tayside *Kinross-shire* Map 11 NO10
Kinross House Gardens Dates from 1685 to 1692, from designs by Sir William Bruce. Gardens only open May to Sep daily 2 – 7. 30p (ch 10p). Admission prices under review for 1980. ⚠ *(Tel 63467)* &
Loch Leven Castle Castle Island. From this historic, ruined, 15th-C and earlier island stronghold in the River Dee, Mary Queen of Scots escaped in 1568, after a year's imprisonment. Scott's novel *The Abbot* describes the event. Erected by Archibald the Grim in the 14th C, it has four storeys in height, with round towers guarding the outer wall. It was dismantled by the Covenanters in 1640. Open Apr to Sep 10 – 6. Sun 2 – 6. Free. Ferry Charge 25p (ch 12p). *(AM)*

KINTORE Grampian *Aberdeenshire* Map 15 NJ71
Balbithan House 2½m NE. A fine 17th-C house, with an interesting garden, situated near the River Don. Contains small museum with collection of Scottish kitchen antiques. Also gallery of original flower and landscape water-colours, all for sale. Nursery garden with plants for sale. Open May to Sep. 50p (ch 16 10p). Admission prices under revision for 1980. ⚠ To view please *Tel 2282 (Mrs McMurtrie)*

KIRKBEAN Dumfries and Galloway *Dumfriesshire* Map 11 NX95
Arbigland Garden 1m SE adjacent to Paul Jones cottage. The gardens and dower house of this mansion have been evolving through three centuries. Paul Jones the US Admiral worked here under his father, who was the gardener in the 1740s. Woodland, water and formal gardens arranged around a sandy bay. ⚏ Shop. Open 1 May to 30 Sep, Tue, Thu and Sun 2 – 6. Charges not available. Parties by prior arrangement. ⚠ *(Tel 213)*

KIRKCALDY Fife *Fife* Map 11 NT29
Industrial Museum Forth House, 100yds from main museum. Collection of horse-drawn vehicles, blacksmith's forge etc. Open May to Sep, Mon to Sat 2 – 5, other times by arrangement. &
John McDouall Stuart Museum Rectory Lane, Dysart. A memorial to the Scottish explorer, John McDouall Stuart

(1815 – 1866), who was the first man to cross Australia from south to north during the years 1861 – 2. Museum of the Year award winner 1978. Open May to Sep daily 2 – 5; other times by arrangement. Opening times and days under revision for 1980. Free. P 100yds. *(Tel 60732)*
Museum and Art Gallery War Memorial Grounds. Next to Kirkcaldy station. General museum concerning the surrounding area, its history, natural history and archaeology. Collection of local pottery, including the famous Wemyss Ware, other decorative arts and a collection of Scottish Art, which includes works by William McTaggart and Peploe. Temporary exhibitions throughout the year. Open all year (ex Local Hols) Mon to Sat 11 – 5, Sun 2 – 5. Free. ⚠ *(Tel 0592 60732)*
Ravenscraig Castle A prominent ruined structure, founded in 1460, and perhaps the first castle designed for defence with firearms. The ashlar masonry is notable. Open, see inside front cover. 15p (ch 7p). *(AM)*

KIRKCUDBRIGHT Dumfries and Galloway *Kirkcudbrightshire* Map 11 NX65
Broughton House An 18th-C house, noted for the collection of pictures by E A Hornel, a library, and an attractive garden. Open Apr to Oct daily 11 – 1 and 2 – 5; Nov to Mar, Sat, Sun and Mon 2 – 4 only. 30p (ch 14 to 18 15p; ch 14 accompanied free).
Maclellan's Castle A notable, ruined structure from 1582. Open, see inside front cover. 20p (ch 10p). ⚠ *(AM)*
Stewarty Museum A museum displaying objects connected with Galloway, including firearms, domestic and agricultural implements, and a good natural history section. Open Easter to mid Oct, Mon to Sat 10 – 1, 2 – 5. 30p (ch 14 10p). P (street). *(Tel 30797)*

KIRKOSWALD Strathclyde *Ayrshire* Map 10 NS20
Souter Johnnie's Cottage A thatched 18th-C cottage, the former home of the village cobbler, John Davidson, the original Souter Johnnie of Burns' 'Tam O'Shanter'. Life-size figures of the Souter and his friends in the garden. Open 4 Apr to 30 Sep. Sat to Thu 12 – 5, other times by appointment. 30p (ch accompanied by adults 15p). *(Tel 243)*. *(NTS)*

KIRRIEMUIR Tayside *Angus* Map 15 NO35
Barrie's Birthplace A small house at 9 Brechin Road containing personal mementoes of Sir James Barrie, who was born here in 1860. Open 1 May to 30 Sep, weekdays 10 – 12.30 and 2 – 6, Sun 2 – 6; or by arrangement. 40p (ch accompanied by adult 20p). *(Tel 2646)*. *(NTS)*

KNOCKANDO Grampian *Moray* Map 15 NJ14
Tamdhu Distillery Visitors are able to see the complete process of whisky being made. Open 1 May to 29 Sep, Mon to Fri 10 – 4. Free. ⚠ *(Tel Carron 221)*. *(The Highland Distilleries Co Ltd)*

LANGBANK Strathclyde *Renfrewshire* Map 10 NS37
Finlaystone Estate 1m W. Gardens, garden centre and woodland walks and jogging trail. Open all year Mon to Sat 9 – 5, Sun 2 – 5. ⚏ May to Aug, Sat and Sun 2 – 5. House with doll and Victorian collections open to parties by arrangement. ⚠ *(Tel 285/235)* & B

LARGS Strathclyde *Ayrshire* Map 10 NS25
Skelmorlie Aisle A splendid example of a Renaissance monument, erected by Sir

Robert Montgomery of Skelmorlie in 1636, stands in an aisle, formerly the north transept of the old church of Largs, and is the only portion now preserved. The monument, which is built in stone, consists of a gallery raised above a partially sunk burial chamber. Open Apr to Sep (see inside front cover), Oct to Mar on application to custodian. 15p (ch 7p). *(AM)*

LAURISTON CASTLE Lothian *Midlothian* Map 11 NT27
On NW outskirts of Edinburgh, 1 m E of Cramond. A late 16th-C mansion, with furniture and antiques, displaying English and French styles. Associated with John Law, the early 18th-C broker. Open Apr to Oct, daily (ex Fri) 11 – 1 and 2 – 5; from Nov to Mar, Sat and Sun only 2 – 4. 45p (ch 15 20p). Grounds 11 – dusk, free. ⚠ *(Tel 031-336 2060)*

LAWERS Tayside *Perthshire* Map 11 NN64
Mountain Visitor Centre On slopes of Perthshire's highest mountain, 3,984ft, noted for variety of Alpine flowers, and species of birds to be seen. Centre includes exhibition and self-guided and guided trails. Open 4 Apr to 25 May, Mon to Sat 11 – 4, Sun 10 – 5.30; 26 May to 30 Sep, daily 10 – 5.30. 30p (ch 10p). ⚠ *(Tel Killin 397). (NTS)*

LINLITHGOW Lothian *West Lothian* Map 11 NS97
Blackness Castle 4½m NE. A 15th-C tower and later stronghold, formerly a Covenanters' prison and at one time used as a powder magazine. Massive 17th-C artillery emplacements. Open, see inside front cover. 20p (ch 10). ⚠ *(AM)*
House of The Binns 4m E off A904. A 15th-C and later house, with 17th-C plaster ceilings. General Tam Dalyell raised the Royal Scots Greys here in 1681. Panoramic viewpoint in grounds. Open 5/6 Apr, then 1 May to 30 Sep daily (ex Fri) 2 – 5.30. Parkland 10 – 7. 75p (ch 35p). Members of Royal Scots Dragoon Guards, successors to Royal Scots Greys admitted free when in uniform. *(NTS)*
Linlithgow Palace A fine, but ruined 15th- and 16th-C structure, associated with Mary, Queen of Scots (born here in 1542), and also with Prince Charles Edward. Chapel, great hall, and quadrangle fountain are notable. Open, see inside front cover. 25p (ch 12p). ⚠ *(AM)*

LOCHAWE Strathclyde *Argyll* Map 10 NN12
Cruachan Power Station 3m W off A85, near Pass of Brander. This important power station of the North of Scotland Hydro-electric Board pumps water from Loch Awe to a spectacular high level reservoir up on Ben Cruachan. The station is open to the public from 9 – 5. 50p (ch 11 – 16 20p; ch 10 accompanied, free) and a minibus service into the underground station is provided for touring motorists during the summer. Under revision for 1980. ⚠
Kilchurn Castle 1½m E on A85. Dates from 1440, with additions of the 16th and 17th C, in a beautiful mountain setting at the north-east extremity of Loch Awe. Closed for repair but can be seen at close quarters. Free. *(AM)*

LOCHCARRON Highland *Ross and Cromarty* Map 14 NG83
Strome Castle 3m SE. A fragmentary ruin of the Macdonalds of Glengarry, blown up by Kenneth Mackenzie of Kintail in 1602. There are wide views across the Inner Sound to Scalpay, Raasay and the Coolins of Skye. Accessible at all reasonable times. *(NTS)*

LOCHTY Fife *Fife* Map 12 NO50
Lochty Private Railway Steam trains run on Sun from Lochty to Knightsward, hauled by the restored War Department Tank Locomotive No. 16. Train includes ex LNER Observation Coach, part of pre-war 'Coronation Express'. There are regular services Jun to Sep, Sun from 2 – 5. Return fare 45p (ch 14 20p). ⚠

LOCHMABEN Dumfries and Galloway *Dumfriesshire* Map 11 NY08
Rammerscales 3m S off B7020. Contains a fine circular staircase, elegant public rooms, and a long library at the top of the house. There are Jacobite relics and links with Flora Macdonald. Also a small collection of works by modern artists. Picnic areas in grounds which have fine views over Annandale. Open 5 Jun to 16 Sep every Tue and Thu and alternate Suns (otherwise by appointment) 2 – 5. 50p (ch 14 25p). ⚠ *(Tel 361)*

LUSS Strathclyde *Dunbartonshire* Map 10 NS39
Rossdhu House 3½m S. Historic home of the Chiefs of Clan Colquhoun on the banks of Loch Lomond. Lochside walks, picnic area and bathing beach. Craft and gift shop ⚑. Open Easter weekend, then May to mid Oct, daily 10.30 – 5 (last admission). Admission to house and grounds 85p (ch 45p); Grounds only 65p (ch and pen 35p) subject to review. ⚠ *(Tel 231)*

MARYPARK Grampian *Banffshire* Map 15 NJ13
Glenfarclas Distillery 1m W. One of the finest Highland Malt whiskies is produced here. There is an exhibition, museum, craft shop and visitor centre. Open all year (ex 25 Dec, 1 and 2 Jan) Mon to Fri 9 – 4.30. Free. ⚠ *(Tel Ballindalloch 257)*

MAUCHLINE Strathclyde *Ayrshire* Map 11 NS42
National Burns Memorial and Cottage Homes The memorial tower of 1896 stands

north of the town on the Kilmarnock road and
has a Burns museum containing many relics
of the poet. ☞ Open most of the year 9–6.
15p (ch 10p). ⚠ *(Tel Ayr 50213)*
MAYBOLE Strathclyde *Ayrshire*
Map 10 NS20
Crossraguel Abbey 2m SW. A cluniac
monastery founded by Duncan, Earl of
Carrick in 1244. The remains of the abbey are
very extensive and of high architectural
distinction. They consist of the church,
claustral buildings, outer court with an
imposing castellated gatehouse and abbot's
house. Open, see inside front cover. 15p (ch
7p). ⚠ *(AM)*
MELROSE Borders *Roxburghshire*
Map 12 NT53
Abbotsford House 2m W off A6091. 19th-C
mansion on the River Tweed. Built by Sir
Walter Scott; this is where he died. Contains
his library and a collection of historical relics.
☞ Open 20 Mar to 31 Oct, Mon to Sat 10–5
Sun 2–5. 70p (ch 16 35p). Party 60p (ch 30p).
(subject to alteration). ⚠ *(Tel Galashiels
2043). (Mrs P Maxwell-Scott)* ⅃
Melrose Abbey Probably the most famous
ruin in Scotland, owing much of its modern
fame to the glamour given to it by Sir Walter
Scott. This was a beautiful Cistercian abbey,
repeatedly wrecked during the wars of
Scottish independence and notably by
Richard II in 1385. Most of the ruins belong to
the 15th-C reconstruction. The heart of
Robert the Bruce was discovered buried here
some 20 years ago, and was reburied in front
of the altar. Open see inside front cover. 25p
(ch 12p). ⚠ Also **Abbey Museum** housed in
15th- to 16th-C former Commendator's
House, containing carved stones, etc, and
situated in the abbey grounds. Details as
above. *(AM)*
Priorwood Gardens Special garden with
flowers for drying. Visitor centre and shop,
picnic area adjacent to Melrose Abbey. Open
4 Apr to mid Oct Mon to Sat 10–5, Sun
1.30–5.30; mid Oct to 24 Dec Mon 2–5.30,
Tue to Sat 10–5.30. Free. *(Tel 2555). (NTS)*
MENSTRIE Central *Clackmannanshire*
Map 11 NS89
Menstrie Castle 16th-C fortress now
restored partly as modern flats. It was the
birthplace in 1657 of Sir William Alexander,
the founder of Nova Scotia. The Nova Scotia
Commemoration Rooms devised and
furnished by the NTS are shown May to Sep,
Wed, Sat, and Sun 2.30–5 and on application
to caretaker in castle. Free. *(NTS and
Clackmannan District Council)*
METHLICK Grampian *Aberdeenshire*
Map 15 NJ83

Haddo House 2m SE. Designed by William
Adam in 1731 and replaces a previous
building called the Place of Kellie. Much of the
interior is 'Adam Revival' of about 1880, and
the contents of this stately yet homely house
are unique in their variety and appeal. Open 1
May to 30 Sep, Mon to Sat 11–6, Sun 2–6
(last visitors 5.15). 85p (ch 40p). House
closed 10/11 May. *(NTS)*
MEY Highland *Caithness* Map 15 ND27
Castle of Mey Gardens Dates from 1606 and
is now a home of Her Majesty Queen
Elizabeth, the Queen Mother. Fine views
across the Pentland Firth towards the
Orkneys. ☞ Gardens only shown. Opening
dates for 1980 not available. 20p (ch 12 and
pen 10p). ⚠ 20p. *(Tel Barrock 275)* ⅃
MILNATHORT Tayside *Kinross-shire*
Map 11 NO10
Burleigh Castle A 16th-C tower house, with a
courtyard enclosure and roofed angle tower,
dating from 1582. Open, see inside front
cover. Key with keeper at farm opposite. Free.
(AM)
MINARD Strathclyde *Argyll* Map 10 NR99
Crarae Gardens Woodland garden, with
rhododendrons, eucalyptus, rare trees, and
shrubs, in a Highland glen. Open 1 Mar to end
of Oct, daily from 8 am. 50p (ch 16 free) by
collecting box. ⚠ *(Tel Furnace 284). (Sir Ilay
Campbell of Succoth Bt)*
MOFFAT Dumfries and Galloway
Dumfriesshire Map 11 NT00
Ladyknowe Mill Small weaving unit,
skirtmaking department where garments can
be seen in process. Showroom for sale of
woollens, tweeds and tartans. Scottish gifts
and souvenirs. ☞ Open all year, mid Mar to
end Oct daily 9–5, Nov to mid Mar Mon to Fri
9–5. Free. ⚠ *(Tel 20134)* ⅃
MONIAIVE Dumfries and Galloway
Dumfriesshire Map 11 NX79
Maxwelton House Stronghold of Earls of
Glencairn until 1611, and later birthplace of
Annie Laurie. Fascinating house, recently
restored, covering 500 years of architectural
whims. Own chapel, and museum of ancient
domestic appliances. Annie Laurie's boudoir
and other rooms in the house open May to
Sep Wed and Thu afternoon 2–5, also 4th
Sun in month. 60p (ch 10 20p). No dogs. ⚠
(Tel 384). (Maxwelton House Trust)
MUCHALLS Grampian *Kincardineshire*
Map 15 NO89
Muchalls Castle 17th-C castle, with fine
fireplaces and plaster ceilings. Open May to
Sep, Tue and Sun 3–5. 30p (ch 10p, babies
free). No dogs. ⚠ *(Tel Newtonhill 30217). (Mr
and Mrs M A Simpson)*

MUSSELBURGH Lothian *Midlothian*
Map 11 NT37
Pinkie House A fine Jacobean building of
1613 and later, incorporating a tower of 1390.
Fine painted ceiling in the long gallery. The
house now forms part of the well-known
Loretto School. Open every Tue 2–4. Party.
⚠ *(Tel 031-665 2825)*

MUTHILL Tayside *Perthshire* Map 11 NN81
Drummond Castle Gardens 1m N. Beautiful
formal gardens. Open (gardens only) 1 Apr to
30 Sep, Wed and Sun 2–6. 40p (ch 20p).
Under revision for 1980. ⚠ *(Tel 257). (The
Grimsthorpe and Drummond Castle Trust
Ltd)*

NEW ABBEY Dumfries and Galloway
Kirkcudbrightshire Map 11 NX96
Sweetheart Abbey One of the most beautiful
monastic ruins in Scotland, built for the Lady
Devorgilla of Galloway, in memory of her
husband John Balliol, in 1273. In 1289 the
Lady was buried in front of the high altar with
the 'sweet heart' of her husband resting on
her bosom. Open, see inside front cover. 20p
(ch 10p). ⚠ *(AM)*

NEWTONMORE Highland *Inverness-shire*
Map 14 NN79
Clan Macpherson House and Museum A
museum containing interesting relics of the
'forty-five', including the 'black chanter' of the
Clan Chattan (1395), the Green Banner and
the Charmed Sword, etc. Open May to Sep,
Mon to Sat 10–12 and 2–6. Free (donation).
⚠ *(Tel 332)* ⅊

NORTH BERWICK Lothian *East Lothian*
Map 12 NT58
North Berwick Museum School Road. Small
museum in former Burgh school with sections
on local history, archaeology, shipping, and
natural history (especially birds). Open Jun
and Sep weekends only; Jul and Aug daily,
Mon to Sat 10–1, 2–5, Sun 2–5 (subject to
review). Free. ⚠ *(Tel 3470)*
Tantallon Castle 2m E on A198. A famous
14th-C stronghold of the Douglases facing
towards the lonely Bass Rock from the rocky
Firth of Forth shore. Nearby earthworks of
16th- and 17th-C date. Open, see inside front
cover. 25p (ch 12p). *(AM)*

OBAN Strathclyde *Argyll* Map 10 NM83
Dunstaffnage Castle 3m N on Peninsular. A
ruined four-sided 13th-C Campbell
stronghold, showing a gatehouse, two round
towers, and walls 10ft thick. Once the prison
of Flora MacDonald. Open, see inside front
cover. Free. ⚠ *(AM)*
Macdonald's Mill ½m S of centre of Oban, on
A816. Exhibition of the Story of Spinning and

Weaving, and demonstrations of this ancient
Scottish industry. Also showroom containing
modern products. Vending machines. Open
Mar to Oct Mon to Fri 9–7.30, Sat 9–5;
demonstrations Mon to Fri only. Free. ⚠ ⅊

OLD DAILLY Strathclyde *Ayrshire*
Map 10 NX29
Bargany Gardens 4m NE on B734 from
Girvan. Woodland walks; snowdrops,
bluebells and daffodils in profusion. Fine
display of azaleas and rhododendrons round
lily pond in May and Jun. Autumn colours.
Many fine ornamental trees. Plants for sale.
Picnic area. Gardens open 1 Feb to 31 Oct
daily 10–7 (4 in winter). Contribution box. ⚠
(buses by arrangement). *(Tel 227)* ⅊

OLD DEER Grampian *Aberdeenshire*
Map 15 NJ94
Deer Abbey The remains of the Cistercian
Abbey, founded in 1219, include the southern
claustral range, the Abbot's House and the
infirmary. The famous Book of Deer, compiled
in the former Celtic monastery on a different
site, is now in the University Library at
Cambridge. The ruins are accessible Apr to
Sep, weekdays 9.30–7, Sun 2–7. 15p (ch
7p). ⚠ *(AM)*

OLDMELDRUM Grampian *Aberdeenshire*
Map 15 NJ82
Glengarioch Distillery Distillery Road.
Distillation of Scotch Whisky and horticultural
unit using waste heat from the distillery. Open
all year ex Jul and Aug. Telephone for times.
Free. ⚠ *(Tel 2706)*

PAISLEY Strathclyde *Renfrewshire*
Map 11 NS46
Paisley Museum and Art Galleries High
Street. Contains collections illustrating local
industrial and natural history of Paisley and
district. World-famous collection of Paisley
shawls. Art collection with emphasis on 19th-
C Scottish artists. Open all year (ex Sun and
PH) Mon, Wed, Thu and Fri 10–5, Tue 10–8,
Sat 10–6. Free. ⚠ *(Tel 041-889 3151)*

PALNACKIE Dumfries and Galloway
Kirkcudbrightshire Map 11 NX85
Orchardton Tower A rare example of a
circular late 15th-C tower, built originally by
John Cairns. Open, see inside front cover, on
application to the Custodian. Free. *(AM)*

PATHHEAD Lothian *Midlothian* Map 11 NT36
Prestonhall A late 18th-C mansion designed
by Robert Mitchell. Set in parkland with
beautiful old trees. Open all year by
appointment only. 75p house, garden and
park. ⚠ *(Tel Ford [Midlothian] 320309).
(Major J D Callander MC)*

BARGANY

Bargany, Girvan, Ayrshire
Captain N Dalrymple-Hamilton R.N.

Route B734 from Girvan 3 miles

Visitors welcomed to this private garden, open daily from 10am-7pm,
February 1 to October 31. Free-will contribution box by the car park.
Picnic areas. Paths through fine woodlands, shrub gardens, rock garden
and walled garden. May/June azaleas, rhododendrons, spectacular
sight round lily pond. Spring display of snowdrops, wild hyacinth,
daffodils, cherry blossom. Bus parties by arrangement with owner.
Tel: Old Dailly 227.

PEEBLES Borders *Peebleshire*
Map 11 NT23
Kailzie 2½m SE on B7062. Extensive grounds with fine old trees, Burnside walk with bulbs, rhododendrons and azaleas. Walled garden with herbaceous and shrub rose borders. High class pottery. Waterfowl pond, Art gallery. ☟ 2.30 – 5 Jun to Sep. Open Easter to end of Oct daily 10 – 6.30. 35p. ⚠ *(Tel 20007)* 🚹

Neidpath Castle On the river Tweed. The earliest known owners of the lands of Neidpath were the Frasers. The land passed to the Hays of Yester, ancestors of the Earls and Marquises of Tweeddale, about 1310 when Mary, daughter of Sir Symon Fraser married Sir Gilbert de Haya. Construction of the Castle apparently began during the 14th C. After the battle of Dunbar in 1650, Lord Yester garrisoned the castle against Cromwellian forces, surrendering in December 1650. Purchased by the first Duke of Queensbury in 1686. Has passed through several heirs to the present Lord Wemyss' Trust. Open 12 Apr to 14 Oct, Mon to Sat 10 – 1 and 2 – 6, Sun 1 – 6, subject to availability of staff. 30p (ch 5 – 14 10p). Dogs on leads only. ⚠

PENCAITLAND Lothian *East Lothian*
Map 12 NT46
Winton House Dates from 1620, with 19th-C additions, a fine example of Scottish Renaissance architecture, with beautiful plaster ceilings, pictures, furnishings, and unique carved stone chimneys. Associations with King Charles I and Sir Walter Scott. Terraced garden. Open to parties by prior written or telephone appointment from *Sir David Ogilvy Bt (Tel 349222)*. Admission to house and gardens 700p (provisional price for 1980) reduction for children. ⚠

PERTH Tayside *Perthshire* Map 11 NO12
Branklyn Garden on Dundee Road, A85. Has been described as the finest garden of its size in all Britain. Little more than two acres, it is noted for its collection of rhododendrons, shrubs and alpine plants. Open 1 Mar to 31 Oct, daily 10 – sunset or by arrangement. 50p (ch 25p). ⚠ 5p. *(Tel 25535). (NTS)*
The Black Watch Regimental Museum Balhousie Castle, Hay Street. Treasures of the 42nd/73rd Highland Regiment from 1725 – 1979 including painting, silver, colours and uniforms. Open May to Oct Mon to Fri 10 – 12 and 2 – 4.30 (Nov to Apr 3.30). Free. ⚠ *(Tel 26287 ext 3)*
Elcho Castle 5m SE on S bank of River Tay. A well-preserved 16th-C stronghold, with wrought-iron window grilles. Open from Apr to Sep, weekends 9.30 – 7, Sun 2 – 7; from Oct to Mar. weekdays 9.30 – 4, Sun 2 – 4. 15p (ch 7). ⚠ *(AM)*
Fair Maid's House North Port. Situated near the historic North Inch where the battle of the Clans was fought in 1396. It was built near the former Dominican monastery and in the 14th C became the home of Simon Glover, a glovemaker, whose daughter Catherine was the heroine of Sir Walter Scott's *Fair Maid of Perth*. The house was a guildhall for over 150 years. It was renovated in the 19th C and is now a centre for Scottish Crafts and Antiques. A recently uncovered wall is said to be the oldest visible wall in Perth. Open all year Mon to Sat 10 – 5. P. *(Tel 25976)*
Huntingtower Formerly known as Ruthven Castle. A castellated 15th- and 16th-C structure, with a painted ceiling. Famous as the scene of the so-called 'Ruthven Raid' of 1582. Open, see inside front cover. 15p (ch 7p). *(AM)*
Perth Museum and Art Gallery George Street. Purpose-built in 1935 to house collections of fine and applied art, social & local history, natural history, archaeology etc. Special events monthly, holiday activities for schoolchildren. Open all year, Mon to Sat 10 – 1 and 2 – 5, Sun 2 – 4. Free, ⚠ *(Tel Perth 32488)* 🚹

PETERCULTER Grampian *Aberdeenshire*
Map 15 NJ80
Drum Castle 3m W. The oldest part, the great square tower – one of the three oldest tower houses in Scotland – dates from the late 13th C. A charming mansion was added in 1619, with characteristic features of the period, enclosing a quadrangle. In 1323 King Robert the Bruce gave a charter of the Royal Forest of Drum to William de Irwin. This family connection remained unbroken until the death in 1975 of Mr H Q Forbes Irvine, who bequeathed the castle and over 400 acres of land to the Trust. Open 1 May to 30 Sep Mon to Sat 11 – 6, Sun 2 – 6; (last visitors 5.15). 75p (ch 35p). Grounds open all year 9.30 – sunset (by donation). ⚠ 10p. *(Tel Drumoak 204)*. *(NTS)*

PETERHEAD Grampian *Aberdeenshire*
Map 15 NK14
Arbuthnot Museum and Art Gallery A museum specialising in local exhibits, particularly those relating to the fishing industry; includes also Arctic and whaling specimens. British coin collection. Open Mon to Fri 10 – 12 and 2 – 5 (4.30 Fri), Sat 2 – 5. Free. *(Tel 2554)*

PITCAPLE Grampian *Aberdeenshire*
Map 15 NJ72
Pitcaple Castle Built in the 15th C, a castle
owned by the Leslies and Lumsdens. Many
historical associations and family relics. Still
lived in as a home. Visitors welcomed Apr to
Sep during reasonable hours if convenient.
Large parties at other times by prior
appointment. 50p (ch 16 25p). ⚠ *(Tel 204)*.
(Capt and Mrs Burges-Lumsden of Pitcaple)

PITLOCHRY Tayside *Perthshire*
Map 14 NN95
Faskally Wayside Centre 2m NW.
Incorporates woodland/lochside parking,
picnic facilities, children's play area and
nature trail. Open May to Sep daily 8 – 7.50. ⚠
20p per vehicle. *(Tel Killiecrankie 223)*
*Pitlochry Power Station Dam and Fish
Pass* There is a permanent definitive
exhibition of hydro electricity at Pitlochry
Power Station, with audio-visual
presentation. The Power Station is not open,
but there is a viewing gallery in exhibition
area. Fish Pass observation chamber open
during daylight hours. ⬛ Exhibition open
Easter to Oct daily 10 – 6 (8.30 Jul an Aug, ex
Mon). 15p (ch 5p, free if accompanied). Under
revision for 1980. ⚠ (limited).

PITMEDDEN Grampian *Aberdeenshire*
Map 15 NJ82
Pitmedden A fine late 17th-C garden, now
re-created. Sundials, pavilions, and
fountains. Elaborate floral desings. Gardens
only open all year, daily 9.30 – dusk. 40p
(20p). Grounds by donation. *(Tel Udny 445)*.
(NTS) ⬤
Tolquhon Castle 2m NE off B999. A late
16th-C quadrangular mansion, now roofless.
and enclosing an early 15th-C tower. Fine
gatehouse and courtyard. Open, see inside
front cover. 15p (ch 7p). ⚠ *(AM)*

POLMONT Central *Stirlingshire*
Map 11 NS97
Westquarter Dovecot This notable example
of a Scottish dovecot is dated 1647 and
carries the arms of Sir William Livingstone.
The exterior can be seen regularly. *(AM)*

POOLEWE Highland *Ross and Cromarty*
Map 14 NG88
Inverewe Remarkable gardens, full of
interest and beauty from Mar to Oct (at their
best May to early Jun), and containing rare
and sub-tropical plants. They were
commenced in 1862 by Osgood Mackenzie.
Magnificent mountain background, Loch
Maree lies to south. ⬛ (open Apr to Sep).
Open daily (incl Sun), all the year, 9 – 9 (or
dusk if earlier). Visitor centre, 1 Apr to mid Oct
10 – 6.30 or dusk if earlier, Sun 1 – 6.30 or
dusk if earlier. 95p (ch 45p), adult parties 55p
per person. ⚠ 10p. *(Tel 229)*. *(NTS)* ⬤

PORT GLASGOW Strathclyde *Renfrewshire*
Map 10 NS37
Newark Castle Dates from the 16th and 17th
C, preserving a courtyard and hall; the hall
carries an inscription of 1596. Fine turrets and
remains of painted ceilings. Once a home of
the Maxwells. Open, see inside front cover.
15p (ch 7p). ⚠ *(AM)*

PORT LOGAN Dumfries and Galloway
Wigtownshire Map 10 NX04
Logan Botanic Garden An annexe of the
Royal Botanic Garden in Edinburgh. Notable
garden containing a wide range of plants from
the warm temperate regions of the world. ⬛
Open Apr to 30 Sep, daily 10 – 5. ⚠ Car and
passengers 30p. No animals. Under revision
for 1980. *(Tel 077 – 686 231)* ⬤

PORT OF MENTEITH Central *Perthshire*
Map 11 NN50
Inchmahome Priory The 13th-C ruins of the
church and cloisters of an Augustinian house,
founded by Walter Comyn in 1238. Famous
as the retreat of the infant Mary, Queen of
Scots, in 1543. The ruins are situated on an
island in the Lake of Menteith and are open
Apr to mid-Nov, weekdays 9.30 – 7, Sun 2 – 7.
Ferry subject to cancellation in adverse
weather conditions. Advisable to check 25p
(ch 12p) *(Tel Stirling 62421)*. ⚠ At ferry. *(AM)*

QUEENSFERRY (South) Lothian *West
Lothian* Map 11 NT17
Hopetoun House 2m W on unclass road.
residence of the Marquess of Linlithgow MC.
Scotland's greatest Adam mansion.
Magnificent reception rooms, pictures,
furnishings, and spacious grounds. Red and
fallow deer and St Kilda sheep. Nature trail.
Views of Forth Road Bridge. Open 27 Apr to 22 Sep, daily 11 – 5.40. £1 (ch
and pen 50p) Subject to review for 1980. ⚠ ⬤
B
William Sanderson and Son 27 The Loan.
Blending and bottling plant where VAT 69 and
The Antiquary de Luxe Whiskies are prepared
for United Kingdom and all export markets.
Open all year (ex for Edinburgh statutory
holidays, first two weeks in Jul and Christmas
week), for conducted tours. Mon to Fri at 10
and 2. No tour Fri afternoons. Visits by prior
appointment only. Free. ⚠ (limited). P. *(Tel
031-331 1500)*

QUEEN'S VIEW Tayside *Perthshire*
Map 14 NN85
Tummel Forest Centre Exhibits show
changes in Tummel Valley since Queen
Victoria's visit in 1866. Included are a
diorama, a model of a Highland Clachan in the
forest, which has recently been excavated
and partly restored. Slides and sound show.
Information desk. Forest walks. Picnic areas.
Regular access. Open Easter to Sep 9 – 6.
Free. ⚠ ⬤ B

REAY Highland *Caithness* Map 14 NC96
*Dounreay United Kingdom Atomic Energy
Authority Exhibition* 2m NE. Scale models,
charts, and panels, relating to the fast reactor
and nuclear energy generally housed in a
former airfield control overlooking the plant,
conspicuous for its 135ft sphere and the
Prototype fast reactor. Limited number of
afternoon tours to the reactor. Tickets from
Thurso Tourist Information Centre. Open May
to Sep, daily 9 – 4. Free. ⚠ *(Tel Thurso 2121
ext 656)*

RHU Strathclyde *Dunbartonshire*
Map 10 NS28
Glenarn A woodland garden with a
remarkable collection of rhododendron
species and hybrids, also Chilean and
Australasian shrubs and trees. Open 1 Apr to
30 Jun, daily, dawn to dusk. 40p (ch 15p). P
(roadside). ⬤

RHYNIE Grampian *Aberdeenshire*
Map 15 NJ42
Druminnor Castle 1½m SE. This 15th-C
castle was a former home of the Forbes
family, and incorporates a small museum of
local household, garden and ancient utensils.
The building has been restored and
preserves a hall fireplace of 1660. Open May
to Sep Wed 2.30 – 5.30. 50p (ch 30p). ⚠ *(Tel
248)*. *(Andrew Forbes)* **(79)**
Leith Hall and Garden 3½m NE on B9002. A
house built round a courtyard, with Jacobite

relics and a fine rock garden. The earliest part dates from 1650. Open 1 May to 30 Sep, Mon to Sat 11–6, Sun 2–6 (last visitors 5.15). Gardens and grounds open all year 9.30–sunset. House 75p (ch 35p), school parties 25p per person. Gardens and grounds by donation. *(Tel Kennethmont 216). (NTS)* & B

ROTHES Grampian *Moray* Map 15 NJ24
Glen Grant Distillery Established 1840. Thr whisky produced here is regarded as one of the best, and is used in many first-class blends as well as being sold as a single Glen Grant Malt in bottle. Traditional malt whisky methods of distillation are used together with the most modern equipment. Reception, Shop and Hospitality Bar. Open Easter to mid Oct 10–4. Free. & *(Tel 243 or 327)*

RUTHWELL Dumfries and Galloway *Dumfriesshire* Map 11 NY16
Ruthwell Cross Off B724. One of Europe's most famous carved crosses resting in the Parish Church in an apse built specially for it. The date is probably 8th-C and the 18ft-high cross is richly carved with Runic characters showing the earliest form of English in Northumbrian dialect. Free. Key of church obtainable from the *Key Keeper, Kirkyett Cottage, Ruthwell. (AM)*
Henry Duncan Museum First Savings Bank founded here in 1810. Interior set in period furnishings around a peat fire and contains many early savings bank documents, four lock security kist, collection of home savings banks from Great Britain and abroad, International Money Corner etc. Personal pencil drawings. Open daily. Free. & *(Tel Clarencefield 640)* &

ST ANDREWS Fife *Fife* Map 12 NO51
Castle Ruined 14th-C stronghold where Cardinal Beaton was murdered in 1546. Captured by the French fleet in the following year. Open, see inside front cover. 25p (ch 12p). *(AM)*

ST VIGEANS Tayside *Angus* Map 12 NO64
St Vigeans Museum A notable collection of more than 40 sculptured stones dating from early Christian and medieval periods, including the well-known inscribed Drosten Stone. They are housed in a cottage museum. Open Apr to Sep, Fri to Mon only 9.30–7; Oct to Mar, 9.30–4. 15p (ch 7p). *(AM)*.

SALTCOATS Strathclyde *Ayrshire* Map 10 NS24
North Ayrshire Museum A museum located in the ancient former Parish Church, with interesting old churchyard gravestones. Exhibits portray local historical items, and early 19th-C interiors. Open mid Apr to Oct Mon to Sat (ex Wed) 10–4. & *(Tel 64174)* &

SCONE Tayside *Perthshire* Map 11 NO02
Scone Palace Home of Earl of Mansfield in town famous in Scottish history as the 'Royal City of Scone'. A seat of government in Pictish times, the home of the Stone of Destiny until 1296 when Edward I removed it to Westminster Abbey; Scottish kings were crowned at Scone until 1651. A religious centre for more than 1,000 years. Present palace, largely rebuilt in 1803, incorporates part of the earlier 1580 palace. Fine collection of French furniture, china, 16th-C needlework, including bed hangings worked by Mary, Queen of Scots, ivories and *objets d'art*. The Pinetum has one of the finest collections of rare conifers in the country, and the woodland garden displays rhododendrons and azaleas. ℘ (licensed). Open end Apr to 1st week Oct, Mon to Sat 10–6, Sun 2–6. No admission after 5.30 pm. Admission to house, grounds and pinetum. Opening times and prices under revision. & *(Rt Hon the Earl of Mansfield)*

SELKIRK Borders *Selkirkshire* Map 12 NT42
Bowhill 2½m off A708. For many generations the Border home of the Scots of Buccleuch. The house contains an outstanding collection of pictures, porcelain and furniture, Monmouth's saddlery and relics, Sir Walter Scott's proofs and portraits. Special Wilkie exhibition. Adventure woodland play area and pony trekking. ℘ (afternoon teas). Open 5, 6 and 7 Apr; May, Jun and Sep, Sat, Sun, Wed and Thu; Jul and Aug daily (ex Fri) 2–6 (last entry 5.15). Admission prices not yet decided. P. *(Tel 20732)* &
Halliwells House Private museum of old ironmongery housed in a close of mid 17th-C cottages and stables. Open May to Sep, weekdays 9.30–11, 2–4. P. **(79)**
Selkirk Museum Ettrick Terrace. Occupies first floor of former Town Jail, built in 1803, and includes items of local history, craft tools, flags, photographs, Common-Riding items, mementoes of local celebrities including Sir Walter Scott, Mungo Park and Andrew Lang. Open Jun to late Sep, Mon–Fri 2–5. Free. P 30yds. *(Tel Selkirk 20096)*

STIRLING Central *Stirlingshire* Map 11 NS79
Cambuskenneth Abbey Founded in 1147 by David I, this abbey was the scene of Bruce's important parliament of 1326. It is also the burial place of James III and his wife. Open Apr to Sep weekdays 9.30–7, Sun 2–7. 15p (ch 7p). *(AM)*
Stirling Castle Upper Castle Hill. A historic 13th-C and earlier structure. The Renaissance additions of the 16th C are notable. Queen Victoria's lookout and the Ladies' Rock are viewpoints. Open Apr, May and Sep 9.30–6.15, Sun 11–6; Jun, Jul and Aug 9.30–8, Sun 11–7; Oct, Mar 9.30–4, Sun 1–4. 1 Apr to 30 Sep 30p (ch 15p); 10 Oct to 31 Mar 25p (ch 12p). & *(AM)*
Landmark Scotland's second Landmark Centre, with exhibition and shop in restored old building overlooking River Forth near castle. Multi-screen presentation of the history of Stirling Castle. ℘ Open all year, daily summer 9–8, winter 9–5. Theatre and exhibition 60p (ch 30p). P. *(Tel 62517)* &
Mar's Wark Broad Street. A partly ruined Renaissance mansion, with a gatehouse enriched by sculptures. Built by the Regent Mar in 1570. Open at all times. Free. *(AM)*
The Museum of the Argyll and Sutherland Highlanders Situated in King James V Palace of Stirling Castle and contains fine collection of regimental silver and plate, colours, pipe banners, painting and items of uniform. Also collection of medals, covering period from Waterloo to present day, including a number of Victorian crosses. Open 1 Apr to 31 Oct, Mon to Sat 10–6, Sun 12–6 (closes at 4 in Oct). Free. &

STOBO Borders *Peeblesshire* Map 11 NT13
Dawyck Arboretum 2m SW. 8m SW Peebles. Impressive gardens, noted for collections of trees and shrubs. House not shown. Arboretum open daily from Easter to end Sep, 10–5. & &

STONEHAVEN Grampian *Kincardineshire*
Map 15 NO88
Dunnottar Castle 1½m S off A92. On a
headland facing North Sea, dates from late
14th to 16th C. Besieged by Montrose in
1645. The Scottish regalia were kept here for
safety in the 17th C. Open all year (ex Sats in
Winter) Mon to Sat 9–6, Sun 2–5. 30p (ch 15
10p). ⚿ *(Tel 62173)*
Stonehaven Tolbooth Once a 16th-C
storehouse of the Earls Marischal, later used
as a prison. Restored and re-opened in 1963
by the Queen Mother; fishing and local history
museum. Open from Jun to Sep, daily (ex
Tue) 2–5 Sat 10–12. Free. ⚲ ⚿ *(Tel
Peterhead 2554)* &

TARBOLTON Strathclyde *Ayrshire*
Map 10 NS42
Bachelors' Club A 17th-C house, taking its
name from the society which Robert Burns
and his friends founded there in 1780. Period
furnishings. Contains a small museum. Open
1 Apr to 30 Sep daily 10–6, other times by
appointment. 30p (ch 15p). *(Tel 424). (NTS)*

THORNHILL Dumfries and Galloway
Dumfriesshire Map 11 NX89
Drumlanrig Castle 3½m NW. 17th-C castle in
pink stone with 15 lead cupola turrets.
Celebrated collection of paintings, Louis XIV
furniture, silver and Bonnie Prince Charlie
relics. Woodland walks and picnic spots.
Open 5, 6 and 7 Apr, then Sat, Sun, Wed and
Thu in May and Jun and BH Mon 12.30–5
(last entry 4.30). Daily Jul and Aug 11–5 (last
entry 4.30), ground incl adventure woodland
open till 6pm. Party. Admission prices not yet
decided. ⚿ *(Tel 30248)* &

TARFSIDE Tayside *Angus* Map 15 NO57
The Retreat 1m E. Former shooting lodge,
with museum of local country life and
handicrafts. Shop. ⚲ Beautiful glen setting.
Open from Easter to 1 Jun, Sun only, 2–6;
from Jun to end of Sep, daily 2–6. 30p (ch 12
15p) subject to alteration. ⚿

TOMINTOUL Grampian *Banffshire*
Map 15 NJ11
Tomintoul Museum The Square.
Reconstructed farm kitchen. Cobbler's and
harness displays. Jun to Sep 10–6 (7 Jul and
Aug). Free. ⚿ *(Tel 285)*

TONGLAND Dumfries and Galloway
Kirkcudbrightshire Map 11 NX65
Tongland Tour Visitors can be part of the
SSEB Galloway hydro-electricity scheme. It
includes a visit to the dam and power station
at Tongland. A fish ladder is an attraction to
the tour. Also small exhibition at the
Portakabin reception area. Open Jul to Sep.
Mon to Sat 9–5 by appointment only. Free. ⚿
people wishing to make the tour are picked up
by bus in Kirkcudbright, and later returned.
(Tel Kirkcudbright 30144)

TORPHICHEN Lothian *West Lothian*
Map 11 NS97
Torphichen Preceptory This was the
principal seat of the knights of St John. The
central tower and trancepts of their church still
remain. The west tower is of Romanesque
date; and the nave, now the parish church,
was rebuilt in the 18th C. Open, see inside
front cover, ex Wed and alternate Fri when
closed all day. 15p (ch 7p). *(AM)*

TORRIDON Highland *Ross and Cromarty*
Map 14 NG85
Trust Visitor Centre Situated at junction of
A896 and Diabeg road amid some of
Scotland's finest scenery. Audio-visual

presentations on wild life and static display at
nearby Mains of the life of the red deer, also
collection of live animals; both open 1 Jun to
30 Sep, Mon to Sat 10–6, Sun 1–6.
Programme of walks available on request.
Admission to Deer Museum 20p (ch 10p),
audio-visual display 20p (ch 10p). *(NTS)*

TRANENT Lothian *East Lothian*
Map 12 NT47
*Prestongrange Historical Site and Mining
Museum* Site with around 800 years of coal
mining history, the centre piece of which is a
Cornish beam pumping engine – the only one
left in Scotland. Its five-storey building is
scheduled as an industrial Monument and
contains plans and documents. The former
power house is now an exhibition hall. Mining
artefacts on show. Outside are two colliery
shunting locomotives, one of which can be
seen working on first Sun in month, and a
100-year-old steam navvy. Around the site
the foundations of many old engines have
been exposed. Open Mon to Fri 9–4.30, Sat
by arrangement, Sun Apr to Oct incl
(volunteers at work). ⚿ Enquiries to *David
Spence, Hon Curator, 24 Woodlands Grove,
Edinburgh EH15 3PD (Tel 031–661 2718)* or
*Mr G B Duncan, Director, Physical Planning,
East Lothian District Council, Haddington.*

TURRIFF Grampian *Aberdeenshire*
Map 15 NJ75
Craigston Castle 4m NE off B9105. Early
17th-C, and little altered since its construction
by John Urquhart. Remarkable wood
carvings. Viewable by written permission
from *Bruce Urquhart, Turriff. (Tel King
Edward 228)*
Delgatie Castle 2m E off unclass rd. The
12th- to 16th-C, with turnpike stair of 97 steps,
groined and painted ceilings, arms, armour,
pictures and furnishings. Oldest archery
meeting in Scotland dating back to 1584, held
1st Sat in Jul. Open by previous arrangement
at any date or time. 50p. ⚿ 25p. *(Capt Hay of
Hayfield).*

UDDINGSTON Strathclyde *Lanarkshire*
Map 11 NS66
Calderpark Zoo Birds, mammals, and
reptiles housed in spacious new enclosures
and buildings. Other attractions include
ample picnic sites, souvenir shop, and
children's shows. ⚲ Open all year, daily 9–5
(or 7, depending on season). 85p (ch and pen
40p, ch 3 free). Party. ⚿ *(Tel 041–771 1185)*

WALKERBURN Borders *Peeblesshire*
Map 11 NT33
Scottish Museum of Wool Textiles
Tweedvale Mill. Museum contains a variety of
objects connected with the Scottish woollen
industry. Also demonstrations of hand
spinning and hand weaving. Open all year
Mon to Fri 10–5; weekends by arrangement.
Demonstrations Easter to Oct. 20p (ch 16 and
pen 10p). ⚿ *(Tel 281)* &

WANLOCKHEAD Dumfries and Galloway
Dumfriesshire Map 11 NS81
Museum of Scottish Lead Mining On B797
at N end of Mennock Pass. Conserves,
displays and interprets the physical and
documentary history of lead mining in
Scotland. Indoor museum and library. 1½-mile
Visitor Walkway links a variety of mining and
social structures including mine-head,
pumping, ore preparation and smelting sites,
lades, tramways and old cottages. Open
Easter to end Sep daily 11–5. 25p (ch 10p).
⚿ *(Tel Leadhills 387)*

WEST KILBRIDE Strathclyde *Ayrshire*
Map 10 NS24
Hunterston Castle 2½m NW on unclass road
near coast. 15th-C Peel Tower with five
rooms furnished on show to the public. Walled
garden. Opening dates and times not yet
decided. 40p (ch 16 10p). ⚠ *(Tel West
Kilbride 823–151)*

WHITHORN Dumfries and Galloway
Wigtownshire Map 10 NX44
Whithorn Priory First Christian church in
Scotland, founded by Fergus, Lord of
Galloway in the 12th C. The ruins are scanty,
and their chief feature of interest is the fine
Norman doorway of the nave. The museum
preserves a notable group of early Christian
monuments, including the Latinus stone
dating from the 5th C. Open, see inside front
cover. 15p. (ch 7p). *(AM)*

WICK Highland *Caithness* Map 15 ND34
Castle of Old Wick A four-storeyed, ruined
square tower, known also as Castle Oliphant,
probably of 12th-C date. Besieged in 1569 by
the Master of Caithness. Accessible except
when adjoining rifle range is in use. Free.
(AM)

SCOTTISH ISLANDS

ARRAN, ISLE OF Strathclyde *Bute*
Map 10 NS03
BRODICK CASTLE Part dates from the 13th
C, with extensions of 1652 and 1844. The
former stronghold of the Dukes of Hamilton
contains a wonderful art collection.
Outstanding gardens. Open 4 to 30 Apr, Mon,
Wed and Sat 1–5,; 1 May to 30 Sep Mon to
Sat 1–5 Sun 2–5. Gardens open daily all
year 10–5. Castle and gardens 85p (ch 40p).
Gardens only 50p (ch 25p). Party rates, castle
and gardens 70p (ch 35p). ♨ May to Sep,
Mon to Sat 10–5, Sun 1–5 (no lunches on
Sun). ⚠ 10p. *(Tel Brodick 2202). (NTS)*

BRODICK
Rosaburn Heritage Museum Set in part of a
former croft farm, the museum illustrates the
changing way of life of the island's
inhabitants. Features include a working
blacksmith's shop, a cottage furnished in
early 1920's style, a stable block with six
horses and several coaches and an open air
display of old farm equipment. Open Easter to
Sep daily (ex Sat). 25p (ch 15p). ⚠ *(Tel
Brodick 2140/2401)*

BUTE ISLE OF Strathclyde *Bute*
Map 10 NS06

ROTHESAY
Rothesay Castle 13th-C moated castle, with
lofty curtain walls, defended by drum towers
enclosing a circular courtyard. Open, see
inside front cover, Sun 2–4. 20p (ch 10p).
(AM)
The Bute Museum Contents are all from the
county of Bute. Natural history room contains
exhibits of birds, mammals and items from the
seashore. History room has varied collections
of recent bygones including models of Clyde
steamers. There is a collection of early
Christian crosses. Prehistoric section
contains flints and pots from two recently
excavated neolithic burial cairns. Details of
nature trails on the island are on sale. Open all
year, Apr to Sep 10.30–12.30, 2.30–4.30,
Oct to Mar 2.30–4.30. Sun Jun to Sep
2.30–4.30. 20p (ch and pen 10p). P (street).

GIGHA, ISLE OF Strathclyde *Argyll*
Map 10 NR64
ARDMINISH
Achamore Unique garden of azaleas and
rhododendrons, created by the late Sir James
Horlick Bt. Open all year 10–sunset. 40p (ch
and pen 20p). P. *(Tel Gigha 254). (D W N
Landale)*

GREAT CUMBRAE ISLAND
Strathclyde *Bute* Map 10 NS15
MILLPORT
Museum of the Cumbraes Garrison House.
The museum tells the story of life on and
around the Cumbraes and features many old
photographs and objects. Also photographs
of some of the steamers which achieved fame
on the Millport run. Open during summer
months Tue to Sat 10–4.30 or at other times
by appointment. Free. P 150yd. *(Tel 741)*

MULL, ISLE OF Strathclyde *Argyll*
Map 10 NM73
CRAIGNURE
Duart Castle The restored ancestral home of
the Macleans which dates from 1250 is in a
splendid setting by Duart Point, overlooking
the Sound of Mull and Firth of Lorne. ♨ (teas).
Open May to Sep, Mon to Fri 10.30–6; in
addition Jul and Aug Sat and Sun. 40p (ch
20p). P. 5p *(The Rt Hon the Lord Maclean KT
GCVO KBE)* frequent motor launch service
from Oban direct to Castle pier and steamer to
Craignure.
Torosay Castle and Gardens 19th-C house
containing family portraits, wildlife pictures, a
superb collection of Stags' 'Heads' (antlers)
and the huge head of a prehistoric Irish elk,
dug out of a bog in Co Monaghan. Victorian
library and archive rooms with family

scrapbooks and photographs covering the last 100 years. 11 acres of Italian gardens and grounds with Venetian statues and a plantation of Australian gum trees and many other Gulf Stream shrubs. ⚓ (teas). Open 15 May to early Oct daily 11−5 (last entry). £1 (ch, students and pen 40p, accompanied small ch free). Gardens only (when house not open) half price in 'Honesty Box'. Dogs in garden only. ⚠ *(Tel 421)*

DERVAIG Map 13 NM45
The Old Byre Visitor Centre Torra Chlachainn. 1m S off B8073. Converted with skill and imagination the centre provides a vivid reconstruction of the past life of the crofters at the time of the clearances. Authentic cottage interiors with life-size figures and animals. 1978 winner of special Certificate of Commendation in BTA 'Come to Britain Trophy' competition. 1979 awarded 1st prize in 'Museum of the year award for Scotland'. Audio-visual presentations every half-hour. Gift stall. ⚓. Open 1 May to 30 Sep Mon to Fri 10.30−5, Sun 2−5 (exhibition closes at 5.30 daily). 50p (ch 12 25p). Under revision for 1980. ⚠ *(Tel 229)*

ORKNEY ISLANDS Map 16 HY22
DOUNBY
The Brough of Birsay 6m NW. Ruined Romanesque church consisting of nave chancel and semicircular apse, with claustral buildings on north side. Adjacent to the ruins are remains of Viking dwellings which have been unearthed and are not conserved. Open, see inside front cover. (Closed on Mon in winter). Crossing by foot except at high water (no boat). 15p (ch 7p). *(AM)*
Click Mill NW of town, off B9057. Example of one of the rare old Orcadian horizontal water-mills, in working condition. Open at all times. Free. *(AM)*
Skara Brae 4m SW. A notable collection of well-preserved Stone Age dwellings, engulfed in drift sand, including stone furniture and fireplace. The most remarkable survival of its kind in Britain, much of it was first discovered in 1850 after a layer of sand was disturbed by a gale. Open, see inside front cover. 20p (ch 10p). *(AM)*

FINSTOWN HY31
Maeshowe Chambered Cairn Britain's finest megalithic tomb, of Neolithic date (*c* 1800 BC). Masonry in a remarkable state of preservation, showing Viking carvings and runes. Open, see inside front cover. Apply to key-keeper at nearby farmhouse. 20p (ch 10p). *(AM)*

Standing Stones 3m SW on A965. Remains of stone circle, second millenium BC. Nearby is the Ring of Brogar, of *c* 1600 BC, consisting of a splendid circle of upright stones with a surrounding ditch. Open at any reasonable time. Free. *(AM)*

KIRKWALL HY41
Bishop's Palace A ruined palace dating originally from the 12th C. Round tower built by Bishop Reid with addition of *c* 1600 by Patrick Stewart, Earl of Orkney. Open, see inside front cover. Apply custodian of Earl Patrick's Palace. 15p (ch 7p). *(AM)*
Earl Patrick's Palace Built *c* 1607 by Patrick Stewart, Earl of Orkney, and considered one of the finest Renaissance buildings in Scotland. Although roofless, much still remains. The oriel windows are notable. Accessible, see inside front cover ex Oct to Mar Mon to Sat 9.30−dusk, Sun 2−dusk. 15p (ch 7p) (incl Bishop's Palace). *(AM)*
Tankerness House Broad Street. Dating from the 16th C, this is one of the finest vernacular town houses in Scotland. It is now a museum of Orkney history with growing archaeological and folk life collections. Special exhibitions. Open all year, Mon to Sat 10.30−1, 2−5. Free. P. *(Tel 3191)*

STROMNESS HY20
Stromness Museum Alfred Street. The museum occupies the former Town Hall and was founded by the Orkney Natural History Society in 1837. Deals mainly with Orkney maritime and natural history, notably in bird and shell collections. There is also a New Stone Age collection. Special exhibition of Orkney interest each summer. Open 11−12.30 and 1.30−5 (from 10.30am in Jul and Aug). Closed Sun, Thu afternoon and local holidays also 3 weeks Feb−Mar. 10p (ch 3p). ⚠ *(Tel 850025)*
Stromness Art Centre The Pier Arts Centre. Collection housed in warehouse building on its own stone pier. Also galleries for visiting exhibitions and children's work. Arts library and reading room in adjacent house. Open all year 11−12.30 and 1.30−5, Thu 11−1, Sun 2−5. Free. P 50yds. *(Tel Stromness 850209)*

WESTRAY HY44
Noltland Castle Near Westray. Situated on an island in the north-west of the group, this early 15th-C ruined castle suffered several sieges and was finally destroyed in 1746. The fine hall, vaulted kitchen, and notable winding staircase are the main features of interest. Open at all reasonable times on application to custodian. Free. *(AM)*

SHETLAND ISLANDS Map 16 HU

MOUSA ISLAND HU42
Mousa Broch Best preserved Pictish drystone tower in Scotland. Rises to a height of 40ft and is exceptionally complete. Reached by boat from Leebotton, on Mousa Sound. Open, see inside front cover. Apply keeper. Free. *(AM)*

SCALLOWAY HU33
Scalloway Castle Erected by Patrick Stewart, Earl of Orkney, *c* 1600, and designed on the 'two-stepped' plan. Open, see inside front cover, on application to the Custodian. Free. *(AM)*

SUMBURGH HU30
Jarlshof Prehistoric Site Remarkable Bronze Age, Iron Age, Viking, and Medieval settlements. The 17th-C Laird's House is the 'Jarlshof' of Scott's novel *The Pirate*. The remains are accessible, see inside front cover. 20p (ch 10p). *(AM)*

SKYE, ISLE OF Highland *Inverness-shire* Map 13 NG

ARMADALE NG60
Clan Donald Centre Situated ½m N of pier in the recently-restored north wing of Armadale Castle, the Seat of the Macdonalds, a building dating from the early 18th C, although main part, now derelict, was built in 1815. Flora Macdonald was married from Armadale in 1750. Also famous arboretum, over 300 years old, and sheltered woodland gardens overlooking the Sound of Sleat. ☕ Museum and shop. Centre open Easter end Oct, 10–5.30; gardens always open. 30p (ch 10p). Party. P. *(Tel Ardvasar 227)* &

COLBOST NG24
The Skye Black House Folk Museum On B884. Typical 19th-C house of the area containing implements and furniture of bygone days, with peat fire burning throughout the day. A replica of an illicit whisky still can be seen behind the museum. Open Easter to 31 Oct daily 10–7. 35p (ch 10–16 10p). ⚠ *(Tel Glendale 291)*

DUNVEGAN NG24
Dunvegan Castle 13th-C and later. Historic and romantic home of the Chief of Macleod since the 13th C. Pit dungeon and famous 'fairy' flag. ☕ Shop. Open Easter to mid Oct, Mon to Sat 2–5; late May to Sep 10.30–5.

80p (ch 14 40p, pen 50p) under revision for 1980. P. 10p. *(John Macleod of Macleod).* *(Tel 206)*

GLENDALE NG15
Skye Watermill On the shores of Loch Pooltiel, a 200-year-old grain mill and kiln, recently restored to full working order. ☕. Open Easter to 31 Oct, Mon to Sat 10–7. 30p (ch 10p, ch 6 free, pen 15p). ⚠ *(Tel 223)*

KILMUIR NG24
Skye Cottage Museum The museum consists of three 100-year-old thatched cottages giving excellent coverage to the croft house of that period. It shows a fine selection of implements, tools, etc used by the men and women of the Highlands and a very interesting collection of old letters, papers and pictures are on display. Open 15 May to 30 Sep Mon to Sat 9–6. 30p (ch 15p). ⚠ *(Tel Duntulm 270)* & **(79)**

WESTERN ISLES

BARRA, ISLE OF Outer Hebrides
Western Isles *Inverness-shire* Map 13 NL

CASTLEBAY NL69
Kisimul Castle Facing Castlebay, an early 15th-C island stronghold, the historic home of the MacNeils of Barra. Open May to end Sep, Sat and Wed. Free. Accessible by boat from Castlebay, ferry charge 50p (ch 25p). *(The MacNeil of Barra XLV)*

LEWIS, ISLE OF Outer Hebrides
Western Isles *Ross and Cromarty* Map 13 NB

ARNOL NB34
Black House Museum Good example of traditional Hebridean dwelling. Retains many of its original furnishings. Open Apr to Sep, weekdays 9.30–7; Oct to Mar, weekdays 9.30–4. 15p (ch 7p). ⚠ *(AM)* &

CALLANISH NB23
Callanish Standing Stones Unique collection of megaliths comprising an avenue 27ft in width, with 19 standing stones, terminating in a 37ft-wide circle containing 13 additional stones. Other stones, burial cairns, and circles in the near vicinity. Accessible at all times. Free. ⚠ *(AM)*

CARLOWAY NB24
Dun Carloway Broch Well-preserved broch, or Pictish tower, about 30ft in height, one of the finest in the Western Isles. Accessible at all times. Free. ⚠ *(AM)*

P.K.F.

Grant-aided Properties

The following buildings have been given a grant by the Historic Buildings Council for England and are either open by appointment or for a total of 30 days a year. We suggest you contact places direct for further information. The majority of these establishments will be found within the guide.

AVON
Bath – Guildhall; Pump Room
Bristol – Kings Weston House;
　　Manor House, Bishopsworth;
　　Theatre Royal
Dodington House
Twickenham Court

BEDFORDSHIRE
Elstow – Whitbread Cottages
Old Warden – Swiss Garden,
　　Old Warden Park;
　　Warden Abbey
Ridgmont – Old Saints Church

BERKSHIRE
Bray – Monkey Island Hotel
Burchetts Green – Bee House, Hall Place
Uffington – Tom Brown's School
Windsor – Canon Cloisters; 2 The Cloisters
Wraysbury – King John's Hunting Lodge

BUCKINGHAMSHIRE
Brill – Boarstall Tower
Hartwell House (Grecian Temple)
High Wycombe – 1/3 Church St,
　　2 White Hart St
Stowe – Garden, Buildings; School
West Wycombe Park – Garden, Buildings

CAMBRIDGESHIRE
Brampton – Samuel Pepys' House
Buckden Palace
Burghley House
Ely – The Almondry
Kimbolton Castle
Peterborough – Thorpe Hall
Soham – Downfields; Windmill
Wimpole Hall
Wisbech – Peckover House

CHESHIRE
Adlington Hall
Combermere Abbey
Handorth Hall
Haslington Hall
Little Morton Hall
Lyme Park
Styal – Quarrybank Mill
Tatton Park – Old Hall

CORNWALL
Cotehele House
Lanhydrock House
Poundstock – Guildhouse

CUMBRIA
Appleby – Red House
Carlisle – Deanery Tower
Drumburgh Castle
Grasmere – Dove Cottage
Kirkoswald – The College
Levens Hall
Preston – Patrick Hall

DERBYSHIRE
Bridlingcote Hall
Hardwick Hall
Melbourne Hall
Sudbury Hall
Whitwell Hall

DEVON
Bishop's Nympton – South Yarde
Castle Drogo
Compton Castle
Gidleigh – West Chapple
Lawrence Castle
Saltram House
Tiverton Castle
Torquay – Torre Abbey Chapel

DORSET
Bloxworth House
Sherborne – School; The Slype

DURHAM
Bishop Auckland Castle
Bowes Museum – The Lodges
Durham – Church of St Mary le Bow

ESSEX
Brightlingsea – Jacobes Hall
Clovile Hall
Dunmow Great – The Clock House
Finchingfield – Spains Hall
Laindon – All Saints Church
Layer Marney Tower
Little Coggeshall – Abbey Mill
St Osyth's Priory
Steeple Bumpstead – Moat Hall

GLOUCESTERSHIRE
Berkeley – Temple of Vaccina, The Chantry
Cheltenham – Pittville Pump Room
Dyrham Park
Elmore Court
Minchinhampton – Old Market House
Painswick Post Office
Tetbury – Chavenage House
Uley – Stout's Hill
Westonbirt School – Italian Garden

HAMPSHIRE
Basing – Tithe Barn
Beaulieu – Palace House
Breamore House
Charford Manor
Ringwood – Greyfriars
Stockbridge – Marsh Court

HEREFORD & WORCESTER
Abberley Hall
Besford Court
Clodock – Ty Mawr Farm
Eastnor Castle
Eye Manor
Hereford – The Old House
Lower Maescoed – Old Court Farm
Middle Littleton – Tithe Barn
Moccas Hall
Staunton – Red House, Pillows Green
Upton Bishop – Tedgewood Farm
Weobley – Corner Hall
Worcester – Guildhall

HERTFORDSHIRE
Ashridge College
Berden Hall
Berkhamsted – Court House
Knebworth House
Ware – Place House

HUMBERSIDE
Beverley – The Friary
Burton Constable Hall
Hull – Old Grammar School
Ulceby – Wootton Hall

ISLE OF WIGHT
Haseley Manor, Arreton

KENT
Betteshanger House
Canterbury – Poor Priests' Hospital
Cobham Hall
Cowden – Bassetts Farm
Gravesend – New Tavern Court
Hadlow Castle (tower)
Herne Windmill
Knole House
Lenham – Honeywood House
Maidstone – Douglas Lodge, Old College;
      Stonewall Hunton
Rolvenden – Great Maythem

LANCASHIRE
Borwick Hall
Hoghton Tower
Longridge – Dun Cow Rib Farm
Stoneyhurst College – The Pavilions

LEICESTERSHIRE
Leicester – Belgrave Hall
Medbourne Manor
Shenton Hall
Stanford Hall
Wymondham Windmill

LINCOLNSHIRE
Alford Windmill
Aubourn Hall
Boston – Rochford Tower
Culverthorpe Hall
Harlaxton Manor
Harrington Hall
Somerton Tower

LONDON (GREATER)
Camden – Keat's House, Hampstead
      Perceval House, Hampstead
Enfield – Tudor Grammar School
Hammersmith – Fulham Palace
      Kelmscott House, Upper Mall
Hovering – Oretons, Rainham Road
      Hornchurch
Hounslow – Beaufort House
      Great Conservatory, Syon Park
Islington – Hoxton Hall, Hoxton St, N1
      St George's Elizabethan Theatre N7
Merton – Eagle House, London Rd, Mitcham
Richmond upon Thames – Garrick's Temple,
      Hampton
      Sir Richard Burton's Tomb, Mortlake
      White Lodge, Richmond Park
Sutton – Little Holland House, Carshalton
Tower Hamlets – Whitechapel Art Gallery
Waltham Forest – Water House, Forest Rd,
      Walthamstow
Westminster – 100 Bayswater Rd, W2
      Deans Yard, SW1
      84 Margaret St, W1

MANCHESTER (GREATER)
Bramall Hall

MERSEYSIDE
Liverpool – Oriel Chambers, Water St
Speke Hall

NORFOLK
Felbrigg Court
Heydon Hall

King's Lynn – King's Staithe Mews; Lattice
      House; Town Hall
Langley Hall (Chedgrave Lodges)
Norwich – Bacon House
Oxburgh Hall
Sutton – Wort's Mill

NORTHAMPTONSHIRE
Apelthorpe Hall
Geddington – The Old Forge
Kettering – Carey Mission House
Little Oakley Church
Newton – Church of St Faith
Northampton – Halsilrigg Manor
Oakley Hall
Southwick Hall
Upton Hall

NORTHUMBERLAND
Bamburgh Castle
Beaufort Castle
Cragside Hall
Lindisfarne Castle
Woodburn – Church of St Mary the Virgin

NOTTINGHAMSHIRE
Clumber Park
Holme Pierrepont Hall
Keyworth – The Barn
Worksop – Manor Lodge

OXFORDSHIRE
Aynhoe Park
Blenheim Palace
Cottisford – Old Manor House
Cuddesdon
Fawley Court
Mapledurham – Chagey Court
      Old Manor House; Mill
Oxford – Great Tower, Magdalen College;
      51 Holywell St; Keble College;
      St Paul's; Bell Tower, Christchurch
Wheatley – Shotover House, The Temple
Woodstock – The Manor

SALOP
Adcote School
Attingham Park
Bentham Hall
Condover Hall
Ellesmere – Adcote School
Market Drayton – The Old House;
      41 Shropshire St
Pitchford Hall

SOMERSET
Croscombe – Old Baptist Chapel
Dunster Castle
East Coker – Hymorford House
Forde Abbey
Frome – Blue House Almhouses
Tintinhull House
West Compton House

STAFFORDSHIRE
Alton Towers
Barlaston Hall
Blithfield Hall
Broughton Hall
Brund Mill
Chillington Hall
Oakley Hall
Pillaton Old Hall
Stafford – Ancient High House
Stoke-on-Trent – The Roundhouse, Etruria
Tixall Park – Gatehouse

SUFFOLK
Bentley Hall
Bury St Edmunds – Unitarian Chapel
Friston Mill
Hadleigh – The Deanery Tower
Ickworth House
Ixworth Abbey
Melford Hall
Pakenham – Newe House; Watermill

SURREY
Farnham – Castle, New Place
Thames Ditton – Newlands

SUSSEX (EAST)
Forest Row – Kidbrooke Park
Hove – Goldstone Pumping Station
Northiam – Brickwall
St Leonards – Clock House

SUSSEX (WEST)
Arundel Castle
Chichester – See House, Chapel, The Palace
Petworth House

TYNE AND WEAR
Newcastle upon Tyne – Blackfriars; Old
    Assembly Room
South Shields – Old Town Hall

WARWICKSHIRE
Baddesley Clinton
Compton Wynyates – The Windmill
Coombe Abbey
Honington Hall
Stoneleigh Abbey

WARWICK – Elizabethan House;
    Lord Leycester Hospital;
    Northgate House

WEST MIDLANDS
Birmingham – St Mary's Convent
Moseley Old Hall

WILTSHIRE
Bradford-on-Avon – Barton Farm;
    St Olave's;
    Silver St House
Constable Burton Hall
Corsham – Warden's House, Hungerford
    Almhouses
Devizes – Brownston House
Malmesbury – Abbey House
Marlborough – Saints Peter and Paul
Swindon – Railway Accident Hospital

YORKSHIRE (NORTH)
Arncliffe Hall
Beningsbrough Hall
Carlton Towers
Castle Howard
Duncombe Park
Kiplin Hall
Old Scriven, Home Farmhouse
Richmond – Old Station Buildings
Rievaulx Abbey
Skipton – High Corn Mill
York – Treasurer's House

YORKSHIRE (SOUTH)
Hickleton Hall
Sheffield – Oakes Park

Follow the Country Code and preserve your heritage

Guard against all risk of fire

Leave all gates as you find them (which usually means fastening them)

Keep dogs under proper control

Keep to the paths across farm land

Avoid damaging fences, hedges and walls

Leave no litter

Safeguard water supplies

Protect and do not disturb wild life

Protect wild plants and trees (do not take specimens)

Go carefully on country roads

Respect the life of the countryside

INDEX

This is not a fully comprehensive index. Establishments with the same name as the town or village will not be found in the index but in their alphabetical order in the Country concerned.

Stately Homes, Museums, Castles and Gardens in Britain

Your suggestions

In an effort to make this Guide as varied and interesting as possible, we have given this page to you. Please fill in this form if you know of any building or place of interest that does not appear in this book and which you feel merits our attention.

BLOCK LETTERS PLEASE

Name of building or place of interest:.................................

....

Address: ....

....

Reason for your suggestion: ....

....

....

....

....

....

....

....

Your name:...

Your address: ....

....

Membership No: ....

Please send to:
**The Automobile Association
Publications Research Unit
Fanum House, Basingstoke,
Hants RG21 2EA**

Your views

Please take this opportunity to tell us what you think of our Guide.

Send your completed form to:
> **The Automobile Association**
> **Publications Research Unit**
> **Fanum House, Basingstoke,**
> **Hants RG21 2EA**

BLOCK LETTERS PLEASE

Name ....

Address ....

....

Membership No. ....

Comments ....

....

....

....

....

....

....

....

....

....

....

....

....

....

....

....

We will take your suggestions and views into consideration but are unable to enter into any correspondence.